Encyclopedia
of
MASSACHUSETTS
INDIANS

Encyclopedia
of
MASSACHUSETTS
INDIANS

Tribes, Nations and People of the
Woodlands Areas

VOLUME TWO
TREATIES

Somerset Publishers, Inc,
P.O. Box 160
St. Clair Shores, Michigan 48080

Editor and Publisher
FRANK H. GILLE

Associate Publisher
GAIL HAMLIN-WILSON

Managing Editor
DONALD B. RICKY

Editorial Contributions

James Clifton, R.O. Clymer, David H. Corocoran, Adolph L. Dial
Jacques Dorais, Edith M. Dorian, Ernest C. Downs, Eula E. Doonkee
Phil Baer, Charkes A. Bishop, Bradley A. Blake, Donald N. Brown,
Linda Ellans, Emmett M. Essin, Albert B. Elasser, Mark S. Fleisher
Mary E. Fleming, John G. Fought, Ken Harper, Arthur E. Hippler
Jean Jackson, Thelma Kimmel, Harriet E. M. Klein, Eleanor Leacock
Frank J. Lipp, Marvin K. Mayers, Mildred Mayhall, Roy W. Meyer
Jerald T. Milanch, Karen Mohr, Robert V. Morey, Kathleen A. Mooney
Jan Onofrio-Grimm, J.V. Powell, Peter G. Ramsden, Carol L. Riley
Norman D. Thomas, Janelle B. Walker

Printed in the United States of America

ISBN 0-403-09330-9

INTRODUCTION

In 1995, the Native American Rights Fund, a Colorado-based advocacy group distributed a treatise titled *A Brief U. S. Government Guide to the Use of Laws to Suppress Indians*. They indicated that such a guide was never actually published but based on the Government's two hundred years of experience with Indians it certainly could have been and it would have read something like this:

> To suppress Indian cultures and absorb Indian people into white society in a manner according to the law, it is vital to create a body of law that supports this intention. Therefore, the government must move quickly on these five fronts to pass laws and carry out policies that:
>
> 1. Destroy Native Economies.
> The best way to control Indians, better even than a well-armed cavalry, is to destroy the economies on which their lives depend. Act immediately to impose an economic monopoly on Indians. Pass laws that prohibit tribes from selling their land to any party except the government. Enforce restrictions that require Indians to engage in commerce exclusively with government agents. By excluding Indians from free market competition, they will, by necessity, become dependent on the government for their survival.

INTRODUCTION

2. Take Away Indian Land.

At the same time, take away lands that are at the base of both tribal economies and cultures. Many of these lands may be obtained with ease by the signing of treaties between presidents and tribal chiefs, who are naively trusting and consistently uphold their agreements.

Should future disputes arise over the rightful ownership of land, these treaties can be easily ignored, as Indians possess no knowledge of our laws, only their own primitive customs. If tribes refuse to vacate lands that are desirable for the nation's growth and progress, pass laws to force their removal, creating "reservations" for Indians on western lands undesirable for civilized society. This new reservation system will provide the double advantage of further undermining Indian economies while making Indians easier for government agents to control.

3. Dismantle Indian Families and Cultures.

Education is the most powerful tool for dismantling Indian cultures and assimilating Indians into civilized society. However, because adult Indians are generally resistant to civilizing influences, government programs must focus on the children.

Create federal policy that authorizes and funds a system of government boarding schools where Indian children can be isolated from their families. Require uninterrupted attendance for four to eight years. Use the harshest discipline to stamp out Indian languages and culture, whipping or depriving of food recalcitrant children who continue to speak their Indian language. As resistance to this systematic breakup of the family may be strong, and parents may try to withhold their children from boarding schools, authorize the US cavalry to enter reservations each fall and round up the children.

4. Stamp Out Indian Religions.

Because religion is the foundation that holds Indian communities and cultures together, the suppression of Indian religions is vital to domination. Pass laws that prohibit the practice on reservations of religions, dances, and other cultural events of tribal importance. At Indian boarding schools, severely punish children who attempt to continue to attend Indian religious ceremonies. Accompany these actions with passive support of the prevalent belief among white citizens that Indians are culturally and spiritually inferior.

Make no move to protect Indian "worship" sites, which are usually nothing more than forests, waterfalls, and other such natural sites, from development and destruction. Offer no protection to Indian dead. Rather, encourage anthropologists and treasure hunters to dig up Indian graves and sell remains and burial items to private collectors and museums. Constant devaluation of Native religions and desecration of sacred sites will cause Indians, in the word of President Andrew Jackson, "to cast off their savage habits and become an interesting, civilized, and Christian community."

5. Eradicate Tribal Powers of Self-Government and Self-Determination.

The notion that each tribe is a sovereign, self-governing nation is dangerous, but unfortunately confirmed in the earliest federal law of the nation. Rather

INTRODUCTION

than try to overturn the law, ignore it. Tacitly allow states to pass their own laws that illegally extend their rule over tribes. Make no move to stop the states from destroying tribal and personal rights, from subjecting Indians to endless harassment and invasion of their lands by white settlers, or from taxing tribes for their resources.

Ignore the authority of tribal courts to settle disputes on reservations and force Indians to travel hundreds of miles to bring their grievances to white courts where their ignorance of the system and lack of facility with the English language will put them at a serious disadvantage.

By using laws in these five crucial areas to undermine Indian culture and economy, it can be expected that within a relatively short time, Indians living on this land will be assimilated into white society or sufficiently suppressed as to pose no serious threat to the advancement and development of the United States of America.

The presentation of treaties that follows in this volume gives vivid testimony to these views with the words and names of the participants.

The Publisher

INDIAN TREATIES
of the American woodlands nations

TREATY WITH THE DELAWARES {1778, Sept. 17}

Articles of agreement and confederation, made and entered into by Andrew and Thomas Lewis, Esquires, Commissioners for, and in Behalf of the United States of North-America of the one Part, and Capt. White Eyes, Capt. John Kill Buck, Junior, and Capt. Pipe, Deputies and Chief Men of the Delaware Nation of the other Part.

ARTICLE 1. That all offences or acts of hostilities by one, or either of the contracting parties against the other, be mutually forgiven, and buried in the depth of oblivion, never more to be had in remembrance.

ARTICLE 2. That a perpetual peace and friendship shall from henceforth take place, and subsist between the contracting parties aforesaid, through all succeeding generations: and if either of the parties are engaged in a just and necessary war with any other nation or nations, that then each shall assist the other in due proportion to their abilities, till their enemies are brought to reasonable terms of accommodation: and that if either of them shall discover any hostile designs forming against the other, they shall give the earliest notice thereof that timeous measures may be taken to prevent their ill effect.

ARTICLE 3. And whereas the United States are engaged in a just and necessary war, in defence and support of life, liberty and independence, against the King of England and his adherents, and as said King is yet possessed of several posts and forts on the lakes and other places, the reduction of which is of great importance to the peace and security of the contracting parties, and as the most practicable way for the troops of the United States to some of the posts and forts is by passing through the country of the Delaware nation, the aforesaid deputies, on behalf of themselves and their nation, do hereby stipulate and agree to give a free passage through their country to the troops aforesaid, and the same to conduct by the nearest and best ways to the posts, forts or towns of the enemies of the United States, affording to said troops such supplies of corn, meat, horses, or whatever may be in their power for the accommodation of such troops, on the commanding officer's, &c. paying, or engaging to pay, the full value of whatever they can supply them with.

And the said deputies, on the behalf of their nation, engage to join the troops of the United States aforesaid, with such a number of their best and most expert warriors as they can spare, consistent with their own safety, and act in concert with them; and for the better security of the old men, women and children of the aforesaid nation, whilst their warriors are engaged against the common enemy.

It is agreed on the part of the United States, that a fort of sufficient strength and capacity be built at the expense of the said States, with such assistance as it may be in the power of the said Delaware Nation to give, in the most convenient place, and advantageous situation, as shall be agreed on by the commanding officer of the troops aforesaid, with the advice and concurrence of the deputies of the aforesaid Delaware Nation, which fort shall be garrisoned by such a number of the troops of the United States, as the commanding officer can spare for the present, and hereafter by such numbers, as the wise men of the United States in council, shall think most conducive to the common good.

For the better security of the peace and friendship now entered into by the contracting parties, against all infractions of the same by the citizens of either party, to the prejudice of the other, neither party shall proceed to the infliction of punishments on the citizens of the other, otherwise than by securing the offender or offenders by imprisonment, or any other competent means, till a fair and impartial trial can be had by judges or juries of both parties, as near as can be to the laws, customs and usages of the contracting parties and natural justice: The mode of such trials to be hereafter fixed by the wise men of the United States in Congress assembled, with the assistance of such deputies of the Delaware nation, as may be appointed to act in concert with them in adjusting this matter to their mutual liking. And it is further agreed between the parties aforesaid, that neither shall entertain or give countenance to the enemies of the other, or protect in their respective states, criminal fugitives, servants or slaves, but the same to apprehend, and secure and deliver to the State or States, to which such enemies, criminals, servants or slaves respectively belong.

ARTICLE 5. Whereas the confederation entered into by the Delaware nation and the United States, renders the first dependent on the latter for all the articles of clothing, utensils and implements of war, and it is judged not only reasonable, but indispensably necessary, that the aforesaid Nation be supplied with such articles from time to time, as far as the United States may have it in their power, by a well-regulated trade, under the conduct of an intelligent, candid agent, with an adequate salary, one more influenced by the love of his country, and a constant attention to the duties of his department by promoting the common interest, than the sinister purposes of converting and binding all the duties of his office to his private emolument: Convinced of the necessity of such measures, the Commissioners of the United States, at the earnest solicitation of the deputies aforesaid, have engaged in behalf of the United States, that such a trade shall be afforded said nation, conducted on such principles of mutual interest as the wisdom of the United States in Congress assembled shall think most conducive to adopt for their mutual convenience.

ARTICLE 6. Whereas the enemies of the United States have endeavored, by every artifice in their power, to possess the Indians in general with an opinion, that it is the design of the States aforesaid, to extirpate the Indians and take possession of their country: to obviate such false suggestion, the United States do engage to guarantee to the aforesaid nation of Delawares, and their heirs, all their territorial rights in the fullest and most ample manner, as it hath been bounded by former treaties, as long as they the said Delaware nation shall abide by, and hold fast the chain of friendship now entered into. And it is further agreed on between the contracting parties should it for the future be found conducive for the mutual interest of both parties to invite any other tribes who have been friends to the interest of the United States, to join the present confederation, and to form a state whereof the Delaware nation shall be the head, and have a representation in Congress: Provided, nothing contained in this article to be considered as conclusive until it meets with the approbation of Congress. And it is also the intent and meaning of this article, that no protection or countenance shall be afforded to any who are at present our enemies, by which they might escape the punishment they deserve.

In witness whereof, the parties have hereunto interchangeably set their hands and seals, at Fort Pitt, September seventeenth, anno Domini one thousand seven hundred and seventy-eight.

Andrew Lewis, Thomas Lewis, White Eyes, his x mark, The Pipe, his x mark, John Kill Buck, his x mark

In presence of: Lach'n McIntosh, brigadier-general, commander the Western Department, Daniel Brodhead, colonel Eighth Pennsylvania Regiment, W. Crawford, colonel, J ohn Campbell, John Stephenson, John Gibson, colonel Thirteenth Virginia Regiment, A. Graham, brigade major, Lach. McIntosh, jr., major brigade, Benjamin Mills, Joseph L. Finley, captain Eighth Pennsylvania Regiment, John Finley, captain Eighth Pennsylvania Regiment.

TREATY WITH THE WYANDOT, ETC. {1785, Jan. 21}

Articles of a treaty concluded at Fort M'Intosh, the twenty-first day of January, one thousand seven hundred and eighty-five, between the Commissioners Plenipotentiary of the United States of America, of the one Part, and the Sachems and Warriors of the Wiandot, ware, Chippawa and Ottawa Nations of the other.

The Commissioners Plenipotentiary of the United States in Congress assembled, give peace to the Wiandot, Delaware, Chippewa, and Ottawa nations of Indians, on the following conditions:

ARTICLE 1. Three chiefs, one from among the Wiandot, and two from among the Delaware nations, shall be delivered up to the Commissioners of [7] the United States, to be by the retained till all the prisoners, white and black, taken by the said nations, or any of them, shall be restored.

ARTICLE 2. The said Indian nations do acknowledge themselves and all their tribes to be under the protection of the United States and of no other sovereign whatsoever.

ARTICLE 3. The boundary line between the United States and the Wiandot and Delaware nations, shall begin at the mouth of the river Cayahoga, and run thence up the said river to the portage between that and the Tus-carawas branch of Meskingum; then down the said branch to the forks at the crossing place above Fort Lawrence; then westerly to the portage of the Big Miami, which runs into the Ohio, at the mouth of which branch the fort stood which was taken by the French in one thousand seven hundred and fifty-two; then along the said portage to the Great Miami or Ome river, and down the south-east side of the same to its mouth; thence along the south shore of lake Erie, to the mouth of Cayahoga where it began.

ARTICLE 4. The United States allot all the lands contained within the said lines to the Wiandot and Delaware nations, to live and to hunt on, and to such of the Ottawa nation as now live thereon; saving and reserving for the establishment of trading posts, six miles square at the mouth of Miami or Ome river, and the same at the portage on that branch of the Big Miami which runs into the Ohio, and the same on the lake of Sanduske where the fort formerly stood, and also two miles square on each side of the lower rapids of Sanduske river, which posts and the lands annexed to them, shall be to the use and under the government of the United States.

ARTICLE 5. If any citizen of the United States, or other person not being an Indian, shall attempt to settle on any of the lands allotted to the Wiandot and Delaware nations in this treaty, except on the lands reserved to the United States in the preceding article, such person shall forfeit the protection of the United States, and the Indians may punish him as they please.

ARTICLE 6. The Indians who sign this treaty, as well in behalf of all their tribes as of themselves, do acknowledge the lands east, south and west of the lines described in the third article, so far as the said Indians formerly claimed the same, to belong to the United States; and none of their tribes shall presume to settle upon the same, or any part of it.

ARTICLE 7. The post of Detroit, with a district beginning at the mouth of the river Rosine, on the west end of lake Erie, and running west six miles up the southern bank of the said river, thence northerly and always six miles west of the strait, till it strikes the lake St. Clair, shall be also reserved to the sole use of the United States.

ARTICLE 8. In the same manner the post of Michillimachenac with its dependencies, and twelve miles square about the same, shall be reserved to the use of the United States.

ARTICLE 9. If any Indian or Indians shall commit a robbery or murder on any citizen of the United States, the tribe to which such offenders may belong, shall be bound to deliver them up at the nearest post, to be punished according to the ordinances of the United States.

ARTICLE 10. The Commissioners of the United States, in pursuance of the humane and liberal views of Congress, upon this treaty's being signed, will direct goods to be distributed among the different tribes for their use and comfort.

SEPARATE ARTICLE. It is agreed that the Delaware chiefs, Kelelamand or lieutenant-colonel Henry, Hengue Pushees or the Big Cat, Wicocalind or Captain White Eyes, who took up the hatchet for the United States, and their families, shall be received into the Delaware nation, in the same situation and rank as before the war, and enjoy their due portions of the lands given to the Wiandot and Delaware nations in this treaty, as fully as if they had not taken part with America, or as any other person or persons in the said nations.

Go. Clark, Richard Butler, Arthur Lee, Daunghquat, his x mark, Abraham Kuhn, his x mark, Ottawerreri, his x mark, Hobocan, his x mark, Walendightun, his x mark, Tatapoxic, his x mark, Wingenmn, his x mark, Packelant, his x mark, Gingewanno, his x mark, Waanoos, his x mark, Konalawassee, his x mark, Shawnaqum, his x mark, Quecookkia, his x mark

Witness: Sam'l J. Atlee, Fras. Johnston, Pennsylvania Commissioners. I. Bradford, George Slaughter, Van wearingen, Alex. Campbell, John Boggs, Jos. Harmar, lieutenant-colonel commandant. G. Evans, Alex. owrey, D. Luckett, Joseph Nicholas, interpreter.

TREATY WITH THE CHOCTAW {1786, Jan. 3}

Articles of a treaty concluded at Hopewell, on the Keowée, near Seneca Old Town, between Benjamin Hawkins, Andrew Pickens and Joseph Martin, Commissioners Plenipotentiary of the United States of America of the one part; and Yockonahoma, great Medal Chief of Soonacoha Yockehoopoie leading Chief of Bugtooholoo; Mingo-hoopoie, leading Chief of Hashooqua; Tobocoh, great Medal Chief of Congetoo; Pooshemastubie, Gorget Captain of Senayazo; and thirteen small Medal Chiefs of the first Class, twelve Medal and Gorget

Captains, Commissioners Plenipotentiary of all the Choctaw Nation, of the other part.

THE Commissioners Plenipotentiary of the United States of America give peace to all the Choctaw nation, and receive them into the favor and protection of the United States of America, on the following conditions:

ARTICLE 1. The Commissioners Plenipotentiary of all the Choctaw nation, shall restore all the prisoners, citizens of the United States, or subjects of their allies, to their entire liberty, if any there be in the Choctaw nation. They shall also restore all the negroes, and all other property taken during the late war, from the citizens, to such person, and at such time and place as the Commissioners of the United States of America shall appoint, if any there be in the Choctaw nation.

ARTICLE 2. The Commissioners Plenipotentiary of all the Choctaw nation, do hereby acknowledge the tribes and towns of the said nation, and the lands within the boundary allotted to the said Indians to live and hunt on, as mentioned in the third article, to be under the protection of the United States of America, and of no other sovereign whosoever.

ARTICLE 3. The boundary of the lands hereby allotted to the Choctaw nation to live and hunt on, within the limits of the United States of America, is and shall be the following, viz: Beginning at a point on the thirty-first degree of north latitude, where the Eastern boundary of the Natches district shall touch the same; thence east along the said thirty-first degree of north latitude, being the southern boundary of the United States of America, until it shah strike the eastern boundary of the lands on which the Indians of the said nation did live and hunt on the twenty-ninth of November, one thousand seven hundred and eighty-two, while they were under the protection of the King of Great-Britain; thence northerly along the said eastern boundary, until it shall meet the northern boundary of the said lands; thence westerly along the said northern boundary, until it shall meet the western boundary thereof; thence southerly along the same to the beginning: saving and reserving for the establishment of trading posts, three tracts or parcels of land of six miles square each, at such places as the United (States) in Congress assembled shall think proper; which posts, and the lands annexed to them, shall be to the use and under the government of the United States of America.

ARTICLE 4. If any citizen of the United States, or other person not being an Indian, shall attempt to settle on any of the lands hereby allotted to the Indians to live and hunt on, such person shall forfeit the protection of the United States of America, and the Indians may punish him or not as they please.

ARTICLE 5. If any Indian or Indians, or persons, residing among them, or who shall take refuge in their nation, shall commit a robbery or murder or other capital crime on any citizen of the United States of America, or person under their protection, the tribe to which such offender may belong, or the nation, shall be bound to deliver him or them up to be punished according to the ordinances of the United States in Congress assembled: Provided, that the punishment shall not be greater than if the robbery or murder, or other capital crime, had been committed by a citizen on a citizen.

ARTICLE 6. If any citizen of the United States of America, or person under their protection, shall commit a robbery or murder, or other capital crime, on any Indian, such offender or offenders shall be punished in the same manner as if the robbery or murder, or other capital crime, had been committed on a citizen of the United States of America; and the punishment shall be in presence of some of the Choctaws, if any will attend at the time and place; and that they may have an opportunity so to do, due notice, if practicable, of the time of such intended punishment, shall be sent to some one of the tribes.

ARTICLE 7. It is understood that the punishment of the innocent, under the idea of retaliation, is unjust and shall not be practiced on either side, except where there is a manifest violation of this treaty; and then it shall be preceded, first by a demand of justice, and if refused, then by a declaration of hostilities.

ARTICLE 8. For the benefit and comfort of the Indians, and for the prevention of injuries, or oppressions on the part of the citizens or Indians, the United States in Congress assembled, shall have the sole and exclusive right of regulating the trade with the Indians, and managing all their affairs in such manner as they think proper.

ARTICLE 9. Until the pleasure of Congress be known, respecting the eighth article, all traders, citizens of the United States of America, shall have liberty to go to any of the tribes or towns of the Choctaws, to trade with them, and they shall be protected in their persons and property, and kindly treated.

ARTICLE 10. The said Indians shall give notice to the citizens of the United States of America, of any designs which they may know or suspect to be formed in any neighboring tribe, or by any person whosoever, against the peace, trade or interest of the United States of America.

ARTICLE 11. The hatchet shall be forever buried, and the peace given by the United States of America, and friendship re-established between the said states on the one part, and all the Choctaw nation on the other part, shall be universal; and the contracting parties shall use their utmost endeavors to maintain the peace given as aforesaid, and friendship re-established.

In witness of all and every thing herein determined, between the United States of America and all the Choctaws, we, their underwritten commissioners, by virtue of our full powers, have signed this definitive treaty, and have caused our seals to be hereunto affixed.

Done at Hopewell, on the Keowee, this third day of January, in the year of our Lord one thousand seven hundred and eighty-six.

Benjamin Hawkins, Andrew Pickens, Jos. Martin, Yockenahoma, his x mark, Yockehoopoie, his x mark, Mingohoopoie, his x mark, Tobocoh, his x mark, Pooshemastuby, his x mark, Pooshahooma, his x mark, Tuscoonoohoopoie, his x mark, Shinshemastuby, his x mark, Yoopahooma, his x mark,
Stoonokoohoopoie, his x mark, Tehakuhbay, his x mark, Pooshemastuby, his x mark, Tuskkahoomoih, his x mark,Tushkahoomock, his x mark, Yoostenochla, his x mark, Tootehooma, his x mark, Toobenohoomoch, his x mark, Cshecoopoohoomoch, his x mark, Stonakoohoopoie, his x mark, Tushkoheegohta, his x mark, Teshuhenochloch, his x mark, Pooshonaltla, his x mark, Okanconnooba, his x ark, Autoonachuba, his x mark, Pangehooloch, his x mark, Steabee, his x mark, Tenetchenna, his x mark, Tushkementahock, his x mark, Tushtallay, his x mark, Cshnaangchabba, his x mark, Cunnopoie, his x mark

Witness: Wm. Blount, John Woods, Saml. Taylor, Robert Anderson, Benj. Lawrence. John Pitchlynn, James Cole, Interpreters.

TREATY WITH THE CHICKASAW {1786, Jan. 10}

Articles of a treaty, concluded at Hopewell, on the Keowe'e, near Seneca Old Town, between Benjamin Hawkins, Andrew Pickens, and Joseph Martin, Commissioners Plenipotentiary of the United States of America, of the one Part; and Piomingo, Head Warrior and First Minister of the Chickasaw Nation; Mingatushka, one of the leading Chiefs; and Latopoia, first beloved Man of the said Nation, Commissioners Plenipotentiary of all the Chickasaws, of the other Part.

THE Commissioners Plenipotentiary of the United States of America give peace to the Chickasaw Nation, and receive them into the favor and protection of the said States, on the following conditions:

ARTICLE 1. The Commissioners Plenipotentiary of the Chickasaw nation, shall restore all the prisoners, citizens of the United States, to their entire liberty, if any there be in the Chickasaw nation. They shall also restore all the negroes, and all other property taken during the late war, from the citizens, if any there be in the Chickasaw nation, to such person, and at such time and place, as the Commissioners of the United States of America shall appoint.

ARTICLE 2. The Commissioners Plenipotentiary of the Chickasaws, do hereby acknowledge the tribes and the towns of the Chickasaw nation, to be under the protection of the United States of America, and of no other sovereign whosoever.

ARTICLE 3. The boundary of the lands hereby allotted to the Chickasaw nation to live and hunt on, within the limits of the United States of America, is, and shall be the following, viz: Beginning on the ridge that divides the waters running into the Cumberland, from those running into the Tennessee, at a point in a line to be run north-east, which shall strike the Tennessee at the mouth of Duck river; thence running westerly along the said ridge, till it shall strike the Ohio; thence down the southern banks thereof to the Mississippi; thence down the same, to the Choctaw line or Natches district; thence along the said line, or the line of the district eastwardly as far as the Chickasaws claimed, and lived and hunted on, the twenty-ninth of November, one thousand seven hundred and eighty-two. Thence the said boundary, east-wardly, shall be the lands allotted to the Choctaws and Cherokees to live and hunt on, and the lands at present in the possession of the Creeks; saving and reserving for the establishment of a trading post, a tract or parcel of land to be laid out at the lower port of the Muscle shoals, at the mouth of Ocochappo, in a circle, the diameter of which shall be five miles on the (a) river, which post, and the lands annexed thereto, shall be to the use and under the government of the United States of America.

ARTICLE 4. If any citizen of the United States, or other person not being an Indian, shall attempt to settle on any of the lands hereby allotted to the Chickasaws to live and hunt on, such person shall forfeit the protection of the United States of America, and the Chickasaws may punish him or not as they please.

ARTICLE 5. If any Indian or Indians, or persons residing among them, or who shall take refuge in their nation, shall commit a robbery or murder, or other capital crime, on any citizen of the United States, or person under their protection, the tribe to which such offender or offenders may belong, or the nation, shall be bound to deliver him or them up to be punished according to the ordinances of the United States in Congress assembled: Provided, that the punishment shall not be greater, than if the robbery or murder, or other capital crime, had been committed by a citizen on a citizen.

ARTICLE 6. If any citizen of the United States of America, or person under their protection, shall commit a robbery or murder, or other capital crime, on any Indian, such offender or offenders shall be punished in the same manner as if the robbery or murder or other capital crime had been committed on a citizen of the United States of America; and the punishment shall be in presence of some of the Chickasaws, if any will attend at the time and place, and that they may have an opportunity so to do, due notice, if practicable, of such intended punishment, shall be sent to some one of the tribes.

ARTICLE 7.   It is understood that the punishment of the innocent under the idea of retaliation is unjust, and shall not be practiced on either side, except where there is a manifest violation of this treaty; and then it shall be preceded, first by a demand of justice, and if refused, then by a declaration of hostilities.

ARTICLE 8.   For the benefit and comfort of the Indians, and for the prevention of injuries or oppressions on the part of the citizens or Indians, the [16] United States in Congress assembled shall have the sole and exclusive right of regulating the trade with the Indians, and managing all their affairs in such manner as they think proper.

ARTICLE 9.   Until the pleasure of Congress be known respecting the eighth article, all traders, citizens of the United States, shall have liberty to go to any of the tribes or towns of the Chickasaws to trade with them, and they shall be protected in their persons and property, and kindly treated.

ARTICLE 10.   The said Indians shall give notice to the citizens of the United States of America, of any designs which they may know or suspect to be formed in any neighboring tribe, or by any person whosoever, against the peace: trade or interests of the United States of America.

ARTICLE 11.   The hatchet shall be forever buried, and the peace given by the United States of America, and friendship re-established between the said States on the one part, and the Chickasaw nation on the other part, shall be universal, and the contracting parties shall use their utmost endeavors to maintain the peace given as aforesaid, and friendship re-established.

In witness of all and every thing herein contained, between the said States and Chickasaws, we, their underwritten commissioners, by virtue of our full powers, have signed this definitive treaty, and have caused our seals to be hereunto affixed.

Done at Hopewell, on the Keowee, this tenth day of January, in the year of our Lord one thousand seven hundred and eighty-six.

Benjamin Hawkins, And'w. Pickens, Jos. Martin, Piomingo, his x mark, Mingatushka, his x mark, Latopoia, his x mark

Witness: Wm. Blount, Wm. Hazard, Sam. Taylor, James Cole, Sworn Interpreter.

TREATY WITH THE SHAWNEE {1786, Jan. 31}

Articles of a Treaty concluded at the Mouth of the Great Miami, on the Northwestern Bank of the Ohio, the thirty-first day of January, one thousand seven hundred and eighty-six, between the Commissioners Plenipotentiary of the United States of America, of the one Part, and the Chiefs and Warriors of the Shawanoe Nation, of the other Part.

ARTICLE 1. Three hostages shall be immediately delivered to the Commissioners, to remain in the possession of the United States until all the prisoners, white and black, taken in the late war from among the citizens of the United States, by the Shawanoe nation, or by any other Indian or Indians residing in their towns, shall be restored.

ARTICLE 2. The Shawanoe nation do acknowledge the United States to be the sole and absolute sovereigns of all the territory ceded to them by a treaty of peace, made between them and the King of Great Britain, the fourteenth day of January, one thousand seven hundred and eighty-four.

ARTICLE 2. If any Indian or Indians of the Shawanoe nation, or any other Indian or Indians residing in their towns, shall commit murder or robbery on, or do any injury to the citizens of the United States, or any of them, that nation shall deliver such offender or offenders to the officer commanding the nearest post of the United States, to be punished according to the ordinances of Congress; and in-like manner, any citizen of the United States, who shall do an injury to any Indian of the Shawa-noe nation, or to any other Indian or Indians residing in their towns, and under their protection, shall be punished according to the laws of the United States.

The Shawanoe nation having knowledge of the intention of any nation or body of Indians to make war on the citizens of the United States, or of their counselling together for that purpose, and neglecting to give information thereof to the commanding officer of the nearest post of the United States, shall be considered as parties in such war, and be punished accordingly: and the United States shall in like manner inform the Shawanoes of any injury designed against them.

ARTICLE 5. The United States do grant peace to the Shawanoe nation, and do receive them into their friendship and protection.

ARTICLE 6. The United States do allot to the Shawanoe nation, lands within their territory to live and hunt upon, beginning at the south line of the lands allotted to the Wiandots and Delaware nations, at the place where the main brnch of the Great Miami, which falls into the Ohio, intersects said line; then down the river Miami, to the fork of that river, next below the old fort which was taken by the French in one thousand seven hundred and fifty-two; thence due

11

west to the river de la Panse; then down that river to the river Wabash, beyond which lines none of the citizens of the United States shall settle, nor disturb the Shawanoes in their settlement and possessions; and the Shawanoes do relinquish to the United States, all title, or pretense of title, they ever had to the lands east, west and south, of the east, west and south lines before described.

ARTICLE 7. If any citizen or citizens of the United States, shall presume to settle upon the lands allotted to the Shawanoes by this treaty, he or they shall be put out of the protection of the United States.
In testimony whereof, the parties hereunto have affixed their hands and seals, the day and year first above mentioned.

G. Clark, Musquaconocah, his x mark, Richard Butler, Meanymsecah, his x mark, Samuel H. Parsons, Waupaucowela, his x mark, Aweecony, his x mark, Nihipeewa, his x mark, Kakawipilathy, his x mark, Nihinessicoe, his x mark, Malunthy, his x mark

Attest: Alexander Campbell, Secretary Commissioners.

Witnesses: W. Finney, Maj. B. B., Thos. Doyle, Capt. B. B. Nathan McDowell, Ensign John Saffenger, Henry Govy, Kagy Galloway, his x mark, John Boggs, Samuel Montgomery, Daniel Elliott, James Ranker, Nathaniel Smith, Joseph Suffrein, his x mark, or Kemepemo Shawno, Isaac Zane, (Wyandot) his x mark, The Half King of the Wyandots, his x mark, The Crane of the Wyandots, his x mark, Capt. Pipe, of the Delawares, his x mark, Capt. Bohongehelas, his x mark, Tetebockshicka, his x mark, The Big Cat of the Delawares, his x mark, Pierre Droullar.

TREATY WITH THE WYANDOT, ETC. {1789, Jan. 9}
Proclamation, Sept. 27, 1789.

Articles of a Treaty Made at Fort Harmar, between Arthur St. Clair, Governor of the Territory of the United States North-West of the River Ohio, and Commissioner Plenipotentiary of the United States of America, for removing all Causes of Controversy, regulating trade, and settling Boundaries, with the Indian Nations in the Northern Department, of the one Part; and the Sachems and Warriors of the Wiandot, Delaware, Ottawa, Chippewa, Pattawatima and Sac Nations, on the other Part.

ARTICLE 1. WHEREAS the United States in Congress assembled, did, by their Commissioners George Rogers Clark, Richard Butler, and Arthur Lee, Esquires, duly appointed for that purpose, at a treaty holder with the Wyandot, Delaware, Ottawa, and Chippewa nations, at Fort M'Intosh on the twenty-first day of January, in the year of our Lord one thousand seven hundred and eighty-five, conclude a peace with the Wyandots, Delawares, Ottawas and Chippewas, and take them into their friendship and protection: And whereas at the said treaty it was stipulated that all prisoners that had been made by those nations, or either of them, should be delivered up to the United States. And whereas the said nations have now agreed to and with the aforesaid Arthur St. Clair, to renew and confirm all the engagements they had made with the United States of America, at the before mentioned treaty, except so far as are altered by these presents. And there are now in the possession of some individuals of these nations, certain prisoners, who have been taken by others not in peace with the said United States, or in violation of the treaties subsisting between the United States and them; the said nations agree to deliver up all the prisoners now in their hands (by what means soever they may have come into their possession) to the said Governor St. Clair, at Fort Harmar, or in his absence, to the officer commanding there, as soon as conveniently may be; and for the true performance of this agreement, they do now agree to deliver into his hands, two persons of the Wyandot Nation, to be retained in the hands of the United States as hostages, until the said prisoners are restored; after which they shall be sent back to their nation.

ARTICLE 2. And whereas at the before mentioned treaty it was agreed between the United States and said nations, that a boundary line should be fixed between the lands of those nations and the territory of the [19] United States; which boundary is as follows, viz:Beginning at the mouth of Cayahoga river, and running thence up the said river to the portage between that and the Tuscarawa branch of Muskingum, then down the said branch to the forks at the crossing-place above fort Lawrence, thence westerly to the portage on that branch of the Big Miami river which runs into the Ohio, at the mouth of which branch the fort stood which was taken by the French in the year of our Lord one thousand seven hundred and fifty-two, then along the said portage to the Great Miami or Omie river, and down the south-east side of the same to its mouth; thence along the southern shore of Lake Erie to the mouth of Cayahoga, where it began.

And the said Wyandot, Delaware, Ottawa and Chippewa Nations, for and in consideration of the peace then granted to them by the said United States, and the presents they then received, as well as of a quantity of goods to the value of six thousand dollars, now delivered to them by the said Arthur St. Clair, the receipt whereof they do hereby acknowledge, do by these presents renew and confirm the said boundary line; to the end that the same may remain as a division line between the lands of the United States of America, and the lands of said nations, forever.

And the undersigned Indians do hereby in their own names, and the names of their respective nations and tribes, their heirs and descendants, for the consideration above-mentioned, release, quit claim, relinquish and cede to the said

United States, all the land east, south and west of the lines above described, so far as the said Indians formerly claimed the same; for them the said United States to have and to hold the same in true and absolute propriety forever.

ARTICLE 3. The United States of America do by these presents relinquish and quit claim to the said nations respectively, all the lands lying between the limits above described, for them the said Indians to live and hunt upon, and otherwise to occupy as they shall see fit:. But the said nations, or either of them, shall not be at liberty to sell or dispose of the same, or any part thereof, to any sovereign power, except the United States; nor to the subjects or citizens of any other sovereign power, nor to the subjects or citizens of the United States.

ARTICLE 4. It is agreed between the said United States and the said nations, that the individuals of said nations shah be at liberty to hunt within the territory ceded to the United States, without hindrance or molestation, so long as they demean themselves peaceably, and offer no injury or annoyance to any of the subjects or citizens of the said United States.

ARTICLE 5. It is agreed that if any Indian or Indians of the nations before mentioned, shall commit a murder or robbery on any of the citizens of the United States, the nation or tribe to which the offender belongs, on complaint being made, shall deliver up the person or persons complained of, at the nearest post of the United States; to the end that he or they may be tried, and if found guilty, punished according to the laws established in the territory of the United States north-west of the river Ohio, for the punishment of such offences, if the same shall have been committed within the said territory; or according to the laws of the State where the offence may have been committed, if the same has happened in any of the United States. In like manner, if any subject or citizen of the United States shall commit murder or robbery on any Indian or Indians of the said nations, upon complaint being made thereof, he or they shall be arrested, tried and punished agreeable to the laws of the state or of the territory wherein the offence was committed; that nothing may interrupt the peace and harmony now established between the United States and said nations.

ARTICLE 6. And whereas the practice of stealing horses has prevailed very much, to the great disquiet of the citizens of the United States, and if persisted in, cannot fail to involve both the United States of America and the Indians in endless animosity, it is agreed that it shall be put an entire stop to on both sides; nevertheless, should some individuals, in defiance of this agreement, and of the laws provided against such offences, continue to make depredations of that nature, the person convicted thereof shall be punished with the utmost severity the laws of the respective states, or territory of the United States north-west of the Ohio, where the offence may have been committed, will admit of: And all horses so stolen, either by the Indians from the citizens or subjects of the United States, or by the citizens or subjects of the United States from any of the

Indian nations, may be reclaimed, into whose possession soever they may have passed, and, upon due proof, shall be restored; any sales in market overt, notwithstanding. And the civil magistrates in the United States respectively, and in the territory of the United States north-west of the Ohio, shall give all necessary aid and protection to Indians claiming such stolen horses.

ARTICLE 7. Trade shall be opened with the said nations, and they do hereby respectively engage to afford protection to the persons and property of such as may be duly licensed to reside among them for the purposes of trade, and to their agents, factors and servants; but no person shall be permitted to reside at their towns, or at their hunting camps, as a trader, who is not furnished with a license for that purpose, under the hand and seal of the Governor of the territory of the United States north-west of the Ohio, for the time being, or tinder the hand and seal of one of his deputies for the management of Indian affairs; to the end that they may not be imposed upon in their traffic. And if any person or persons shall intrude themselves without such licence, they promise to apprehend him or them, and to bring them to the said Governor, or one of his deputies, for the purpose before mentioned, to be dealt with according to law: And that they may be defended against persons who might attempt to forage such licenses, they further engage to give information to the said Governor, or one of his deputies, of the names of all traders residing among them from time to time, and at least once in every year.

ARTICLE 8. Should any nation of Indians meditate a war against the United States, or either of them, and the same shall come to the knowledge of the before mentioned nations, or either of them, they do hereby engage to give immediate notice thereof to the Governor, or in his absence to the officer commanding the troops of the United States at the nearest post. And should any nation with hostile intentions against the United States, or either of them, attempt to pass through their country, they will endeavor to prevent the same, and in like manner give information of such attempt to the said Governor or commanding officer, as soon as possible, that all causes of mistrust and suspicion may be avoided between them and the United States: In like manner the United States shall give notice to the said Indian nations, of any harm that may be meditated against them, or either of them, that shall come to their knowledge; and do all in their power to hinder and prevent the same, that the friendship between them may be uninterrupted.

ARTICLE 9. If any person or persons, citizens or subjects of the United States, or any other person not being an Indian, shall presume to settle upon the lands confirmed to the said nations, he and they shall be out of the protection of the United States; and the said nations may punish him or them in such manner as they see fit.

ARTICLE 10. The United States renew the reservations heretofore made in the before mentioned treaty at Fort M'Intosh, for the establishment of trading posts, in manner and form following; that is to say: Six miles square at the mouth of the Miami or Omie river; six miles square at the portage upon that branch of the Miami which runs into the Ohio; six miles square upon the lake Sandusky where the fort formerly stood; and two miles square upon each side the Lower Rapids on Sandusky river, which posts, and the lands annexed to them, shall be for the use and under the government of the United States.

ARTICLE 11. The post at Detroit, with a district of land beginning at the mouth of the river Rosine, at the west end of lake Erie, and running up the southern bank of said river six miles; thence northerly, and always six miles west of the strait, until it strikes the lake St. Clair, shall be reserved for the use of the United States.

ARTICLE 12. In like manner the post at Michilimackinac, with its dependencies, and twelve miles square about the same, shall be reserved to the sole use of the United States.

ARTICLE 13. The United States of America do hereby renew and confirm the peace and friendship entered into with the said nations, at the treaty before mentioned, held at Fort M'Intosh; and the said nations again acknowledge themselves, and all their tribes, to be under the protection of the said United States, and no other power whatever.

ARTICLE 14. The United States of America do also receive into their friendship and protection, the nations of the Pattiwatimas and Sacs; and do hereby establish a league of peace and amity between them respectively; and all the articles of this treaty, so far as they apply to these nations, are to be considered as made and concluded in all, and every part, expressly with them and each of them.

ARTICLE 15. And whereas in describing the boundary before mentioned, the words, if strictly constructed, would carry it from the portage on that branch of the Miami, which runs into the Ohio, over to the river Au Glaize; which was neither the intention of the Indians, nor of the Commissioners; it is hereby declared, that the line shall run from the said portage directly to the first fork of the Miami river, which is to the southward and eastward of the Miami village, thence down the main branch of the Miami river to the said village, and thence down that river to Lake Erie, and along the margin of the lake to the place of beginning.

Done at Fort Harmar, on the Muskingum, this ninth day of January, in the year of Our Lord one thousand seven hundred and eighty-nine.

In witness whereof, the parties have hereunto interchangeably set their hands and seals.

Arthur St. Clair

Delawares: Peoutewatamie, his x mark, Captain Pipe, his x mark, Konatikina, his x mark, Wmgenond, his x mark.

Sacs: Pekelan, his x mark, Tepakee, his x mark, Teamway, his x mark, Kesheyiva, his x mark.

Chippewas: Nanamakeak, his x mark, Wetenasa, his x mark, Mesass, his x mark, Soskene, his x mark, Paushquash, his x mark, Pewanakum, his x mark, Pawasicko, his x mark.

Ottawas: Teyandatontec, his x mark, Wewiskia, his x mark, Cheyawe, his x mark, Neagey, his x mark, Doueyenteat, his x mark, Tarhe, his x mark.

Pattawatimas: Terhataw, his x mark, Windigo, his x mark, Datasay, his x mark, Wapaskea, his x mark, Maudoronk, his x mark, Nequea, his x mark, Skahomat, his x mark,

In presence of : Jos. Harmar, lieutenant-colonel, commandant, First U. S. Regiment, and brigadier-general by brevet, Richard Butler, Jno. Gibson, Will. McCurdey, captain, E. Denny, ensign, First U. S. Regiment, A. Hartshorn, ensign, Robt. Thompson, ensign, First U.S. Regiment, Frans. Muse, ensign, J. Williams, jr., Wm. Wilson, Joseph Nicholas, James Rinkin.

Be it remembered, That the Wyandots have laid claim to the lands that were granted to the Shawanese, at the treaty held at the Miami, and have declared, that as the Shawanese have been so restless, and caused so much trouble, both to them and to the United States, if they will not now be at peace, they will dispossess them, and take the country into their own hands; for that the country is theirs of right, and the Shawanese are only living upon it by their permission. They further lay claim to all the country west of the Miami boundary, from the village to the lake Erie, and declare that it is now under their management and direction.

SEPARATE ARTICLE.

Whereas the Wyandots have represented, that within the reservation from the river Rosine along the Strait, they have two villages from which they cannot with any convenience remove; it is agreed, that they shall remain in possession of the same, and shall not be in any manner disturbed therein.

SEPARATE ARTICLE.

Should a robbery or murder be committed by an Indian or Indians of the said nations upon the citizens or subjects of the United States or any of them, or by the citizens or subjects of the United States or any of them, upon any Indian or Indians of the said nations, the parties accused of the same shall be tried, and, if found guilty, be punished according to the laws of the state, or of the territory of the United States, as the case may be, where the same was committed; and should any horses be stolen, either by the Indians of the said nations from the citizens or subjects of the United States or any of them, or by any of the said citizens and subjects from any of the said Indians, they may be reclaimed, into whose possession soever they may have come; and, upon due proof, shall be restored, any sales in open market notwithstanding. And the parties convicted shall be punished with the utmost severity the laws will admit; and the said nations engage to deliver the parties that may be accused of their nations of either of the before-mentioned crimes, at the nearest post of the United States, if the crime was committed within the territory of the United States, or to the civil authority of the States, if it shall have happened within any of the United States.

TREATY WITH THE SIX NATIONS {1789, Jan. 9}

Articles of a treaty made at Fort Harmar, the ninth day of January, in the year of our Lord one thousand seven hundred and eighty-nine, between Arthur St. Clair, esquire, governor of the territory of the United States of America, northwest of the river Ohio, and commissioner plenipotentiary of the said United States, for removing all causes of controversy, regulating trade, and settling boundaries, between the Indian nations in the northern department and the said United States, of the one part, and the sachems and warriors of the Six Nations, of the other part:

ARTICLE 1. WHEREAS the United States, in congress assembled, did, by their commissioners, Oliver Wolcott, Richard Butler, and Arthur Lee, esquires, duly appointed for that purpose, at a treaty held with the said Six Nations, viz: with the Mohawks, Oneidas, Onondagas, Tus-caroras, Cayugas, and Senekas, at fort Stanwix, on the twenty-second day of October, one thousand seven hundred and eighty-four, give peace to the said nations, and receive them into their friendship and protection: And whereas the said nations have now agreed to and with the said Arthur St. Clair, to renew and confirm all the engagements and stipulations entered into at the beforementioned treaty at fort Stanwix: and whereas it was then and there agreed, between the United States of America and the said Six Nations, that a boundary line should be fixed between the lands of the said Six Nations and the territory of the said United States, which boundary line is as follows, viz: Beginning at the mouth of a creek, about four miles east of Niagara, called Ononwayea, or Johnston's Landing Place, upon the lake named by the Indians Cawego, and by us Ontario; from thence southerly, in a direction always four miles east of the carrying place, between lake Erie and lake Ontario, to the mouth of Tehoseroton, or Buffalo creek, upon lake Erie; thence south, to the northern boundary of the state of Pennsylvania; thence west, to the end of the said north boundary; thence south, along the west boundary of the said state to the river Ohio.

The said line, from the mouth of Ononwayea to the Ohio, shall be the western boundary of the lands of the Six Nations, so that the Six Nations shall and do yield to the United States, all claim to the country west of the said boundary; and then they shall be secured in the possession of the lands they inhabit east, north, and south of the same, reserving only six miles square, round the fort of Oswego, for the support of the same. The said Six Nations, except the Mohawks, none of whom have attended at this time, for and in consideration of the peace then granted to them, the presents they then received, as well as in consideration of a quantity of goods, to the value of three thousand dollars, now delivered to them by the said Arthur St. Clair, the receipt whereof they do hereby acknowledge, do hereby renew and confirm the said boundary line in the words beforementioned, to the end that it may be and remain as a division line between the lands of the said Six Nations and the territory of the United States, forever.

And the undersigned Indians, as well in their own names as in the name of their respective tribes and nations, their heirs and descendants, for the considerations beforementioned, do release, quit claim, relinquish, and cede, to the United States of America, all the lands west of the said boundary or division line, and between the said line and the strait, from the mouth of Ononwayea and Buffalo Creek, for them, the said United States of America, to have and to hold the same, in true and absolute propriety, forever.

ARTICLE 2. The United States of America confirm to the Six Nations, all the lands which they inhabit, lying east and north of the beforementioned boundary line, and relinquish and quit claim to the same and every part thereof, excepting only six miles square round the fort of Oswego, which six miles square round said fort is again reserved to the United States by these presents.

ARTICLE 3. The Oneida and Tuscarora nations, are also again secured and confirmed in the possession of their respective lands.

ARTICLE 4. The United States of America renew and confirm the peace and friendship entered into with the Six Nations, (except the Mohawks), at the treaty beforementioned, held at fort Stanwix, declaring the same to be perpetual. And if the Mohawks shall, within six months, declare their assent to the same, they shall be considered as included.

Done at Fort Harmar, on the Muskingum, the day and year first above written.

In witness whereof, the parties have hereunto, interchangeably, set their hands and seals.

Ar. St. Clair, Cageaga, or Dogs Round the Fire, Sawedowa, or The Blast, Kiondushowa, or Swimming Fish, Oncahye, or Dancing Feather, Sohaeas, or Falling Mountain, Otachsaka, or Broken Tomahawk, his x mark, Tekahias, or Long Tree, his x mark, Onecnsetee, or Loaded Man, his x mark, Kiahtulaho, or Snake, Aqueia, or Bandy Legs, Kiandogewa, or Big Tree, his x mark,

Owenewa, or Thrown in the Water, his x mark, Gyantwaia, or Cornplanter, his x mark, Gyasota, or Big Cross, his x mark, Kannassee, or New Arrow, Achiout, or tlalf Town, Anachout, or The Wasp, his x mark, Chishckoa, or Wood Bug, his x mark, Sessewa, or Big Bale of a Kettle, Sciahowa, or Council Keeper, Tewanias, or Broken Twig, Sonachshowa, or Full Moon, Cachunwasse, or Twenty Canoes, Hickonquash, or Tearing Asunder.

In presence of: Jos. Harntar, lieutenant-colonel commanding First U. S. Regiment and brigadier-general by brevet, Richard Butler, Jno. Gibson, Will. M'Curdy, captain, Ed. Denny, ensign First U. S. Regiment, A. Hartshorn, ensign, Robt. Thompson, ensign, First U. S. Regiment, Fran. Leile, ensign, Joseph Nicholas.

SEPARATE ARTICLE. Should a robbery or murder be committed by an Indian or Indians of the Six Nations, upon the citizens or subjects of the United States, or by the citizens or subjects of the United States, or any of them, upon any of the Indians of the said nations, the parties accused of the same shall be tried, and if found guilty, be punished according to the laws of the state, or of the territory of the United States, as the case may be, where the same was committed. And should any horses be stolen, either by the Indians of the said nations, from the citizens or subjects of the United States, or any of them, or by any of the said citizens or subjects from any of the said Indians, they may be reclaimed into whose possession soever they may have come; and, upon due proof, shall be restored, any sale in open market notwithstanding; and the persons convicted shall be punished with the utmost severity the laws will admit. And the said nations engage to deliver the persons that may be accused, of their nations, of either of the beforementioned crimes, at the nearest post of the United States, if the crime was committed within the territory of the United States; or to the civil authority of the state, if it shall have happened within any of the United States.

TREATY WITH THE CHEROKEE {1791, July 2}
Proclamation Feb. 7, 1792.

A Treaty of Peace and Friendship made and concluded between the President of the United States of America, on the Part and Behalf of the said States, and the undersigned Chiefs and Warriors of the Cherokee Nation of Indians, on the Part and Behalf of the said Nation.

The parties being desirous of establishing permanent peace and friendship between the United States and the said Cherokee Nation, and the citizens and members thereof, and to remove the causes of war, by ascertaining their limits and making other necessary, just and friendly arrangements: The President of the United States, by William Blount, Governor cf the territory of the United

States of America, south of the river Ohio, and Superintendent of Indian affairs for the southern district, who is vested with full powers for these purposes, by and with the advice and consent of the Senate of the United States: And the Cherokee Nation, by the undersigned Chiefs and Warriors representing the said nation, have agreed to the following articles, namely:

ARTICLE 1. There shall be perpetual peace and friendship between all the citizens of the United States of America, and all the individuals composing the whole Cherokee nation of Indians.

ARTICLE 2. The undersigned Chiefs and Warriors, for themselves and all parts of the Cherokee nation, do acknowledge themselves and the said Cherokee nation, to be under the protection of the said United States of America, and of no other sovereign whosoever; and they also stipulate that the said Cherokee nation will not hold any treaty with any foreign power, individual state, or with individuals of any state.

ARTICLE 3. The Cherokee nation shall deliver to the Governor of the territory of the United States of America, south of the river Ohio, on or before the first day of April next, at this place, all persons who are now prisoners, captured by them from any part of the United States: And the United States shall on or before the same day, and at the same place, restore to the Cherokees, all the prisoners now in captivity, which the citizens of the United States have captured from them.

ARTICLE 4. The boundary between the citizens of the United States and the Cherokee nation, is and shall be as follows: Beginning at the top of the [30] Currahee mountain, where the Creek line passes it; thence a direct line to Tugelo river; thence northeast to the Occunna mountain, and over the same along the South-Carolina Indian boundary to the North-Carolina boundary; thence north to a point from which a line is to be extended to the river Clinch, that shah pass the Holston at the ridge which divides the waters running into Little River from those running into the Tennessee; thence up the river Clinch to Campbell's line, and along the same to the top of Cumberland mountain; thence a direct line to the Cumberland river where the Kentucky road crosses it; thence down the Cumberland river to a point from which a south west line will strike the ridge which divides the waters of Cumberland from those of Duck river, forty miles above Nashville; thence down the said ridge to a point from whence a south west line will strike the mouth of Duck river.

And in order to preclude forever all disputes relative to the said boundary, the same shall be ascertained, and marked plainly by three persons appointed on the part of the United States, and three Cherokees on the part of their nation.
And in order to extinguish forever all claims of the Cherokee nation, or any part thereof, to any of the land lying to the right of the line above described,

21

beginning as aforesaid at the Currahee mountain, it is hereby agreed, that in addition to the consideration heretofore made for the said land, the United States will cause certain valuable goods, to be immediately delivered to the undersigned Chiefs and Warriors, for the use of their nation; and the said United States will also cause the sum of one thousand dollars to be paid annually to the said Cherokee nation. And the undersigned Chiefs and Warriors, do hereby for themselves and the whole Cherokee nation, their heirs and descendants, for the considerations above-mentioned, release, quit-claim, relinquish and cede, all the land to the right of the line described, and beginning as aforesaid.

ARTICLE 5. It is stipulated and agreed, that the citizens and inhabitants of the United States, shall have a free and unmolested use of a road from Washington district to Mero district, and of the navigation of the Tennessee river.

ARTICLE 6. It is agreed on the part of the Cherokees, that the United States shall have the sole and exclusive right of regulating their trade.

ARTICLE 7. The United States solemnly guarantee to the Cherokee nation, all their lands not hereby ceded.

ARTICLE 8. If any citizen of the United States, or other person not being an Indian, shall settle on any of the Cherokees' lands, such person shall forfeit the protection of the United States, and the Cherokees may punish him or not, as they please.

ARTICLE 9. No citizen or inhabitant of the United States, shall attempt to hunt or destroy the game on the lands of the Cherokees; nor shall any citizen or inhabitant go into the Cherokee country, without a passport first obtained from the Governor of some one of the United States, or territorial districts, or such other person as the President of the United States may from time to time authorize to grant the same.

ARTICLE 10. If any Cherokee Indian or Indians, or person residing among them, or who shall take refuge in their nation, shall steal a horse from, or commit a robbery or murder, or other capital crime, on any citizens or inhabitants of the United States, the Cherokee nation shall be bound to deliver him or them up, to be punished according to the laws of the United States.

ARTICLE 11. If any citizen or inhabitant of the United States, or of either of the territorial districts of the United States, shall go into any town, settlement or territory belonging to the Cherokees, and shall there commit any crime upon, or trespass against the person or property of any peaceable and friendly Indian or Indians, which if committed within the jurisdiction of any state, or within the jurisdiction of either of the said districts, against a citizen or white inhabitant thereof, would be punishable by the laws of such state or district, such offender or offenders, shall be subject to the same punishment, and shall be proceeded against in the same manner as if the offence had been committed within the jurisdiction of the state or district to which he or they may belong, against a citizen or white inhabitant thereof.

ARTICLE 12. In case of violence on the persons or property of the individuals of either party, neither retaliation or reprisal shall be committed by the other, until satisfaction shall have been demanded of the party of which the aggressor is, and shall have been refused.

ARTICLE 13. The Cherokees shall give notice to the citizens of the United States, of any designs which they may know, or suspect to be formed in any neighboring tribe, or by any person whatever, against the peace and interest of the United States.

ARTICLE 14. That the Cherokee nation may be led to a greater degree of civilization, and to become herdsmen and cultivators, instead of remaining in a state of hunters, the United States will from time to time furnish gratuitously the said nation with useful implements of husbandry, and further to assist the said nation in so desirable a pursuit, and at the same time to establish a certain mode of communication, the United States will send such, and so many persons to reside in said nation as they may judge proper, not exceeding four in number, who shall qualify themselves to act as interpreters. These persons shall have lands assigned by the Cherokees for cultivation for themselves and their successors in office; but they shall be precluded exercising any kind of traffic.

ARTICLE 15. All animosities for past grievances shall henceforth cease, and the contracting parties will carry the foregoing treaty into full execution with all good faith and sincerity.

ARTICLE 16. This treaty shall take effect and be obligatory on the contracting parties, as soon as the same shall have been ratified by the President of the United States, with the advice and consent of the Senate of the United States.

In witness of all and every thing herein determined between the United States of America and the whole Cherokee nation, the parties have hereunto set their hands and seals, at the treaty ground on the bank of the Holston, near the mouth of the French Broad, within the United States, this second day of July, in the year of our Lord one thousand seven hundred and ninety-one.

William Blount, governor in and over the territory of the United States of America south of the river Ohio, and superintendent of Indian Affairs for the southern district, Chuleoah, or the Boots, his x mark, Squollecuttah, or Hanging Maw, his x mark, Occunna, or the Badger, his x mark, Enoleh, or Black Fox, his x mark, Nontuaka, or the Northward, his x mark, Tekakiska, his x

mark, Chutloh, or King Fisher, his x mark, Tuckaseh, or Terrapin, his x mark, Kateh, his x mark, Kunnochatutloh, or the Crane, his x mark, Cauquillehanah, or the Thigh, his x mark, Chesquotteleneh, or Yellow Bird, his x mark, Chicka-sawtehe, or Chickasaw Killer, his x mark, Tuskegatehe, Tuskega Killer, his x mark, Kulsatehe, his x mark, Tinkshalene, his x mark, Sawutteh, or Slave Catcher, his x mark, Aukuah, his x mark, Oosenaleh, his x mark, Kenotetah, or Rising Fawn, his x mark, Kanetetoka, or Standing Turkey, his x mark, Yone-watleh, or Bear at Home, his x mark, Long Will, his x mark, Kunoskeskie, or John Watts, his x mark, Nenetooyah, or Bloody Fellow, his x mark, Chuqui-latague, or-Double Head, his x mark, Koolaquah, or Big Acorn, his x mark, Toowayelloh, or Bold Hunter, his x mark, Jahleoonoyehka, or Middle Striker, his x mark, Kinnesah, or Cabin, his x mark, Tullotehe, or Two Killer, his x mark, Kaalouske, or Stopt Still, his x mark, Kulsatche, his x mark, Auquotague, the Little Turkey's Son, his x mark, Talohteske, or Upsetter, his x mark,
Cheakoneske, or Otter Lifter, his x mark, Keshukaune, or She Reigns, his x mark, Toonaunailoh, his x mark, Teesteke, or Common Disturber, his x mark, Robin McClemore, Skyuka, John Thompson, Interpreter, James Cery, Inter-preter.

Done in presence of: Dan'l Smith, Secretary Territory United States south of the river Ohio
Fauche, of Georgia, Titus Ogden, North Carolina, Thomas Kennedy, of Ken-tucky, Jno. Chisolm, Washington District, Jas. Robertson, of Mero District, Robert King, Claiborne Watkins, of Virginia, Thomas Gegg, Jno. McWhitney, of Georgia.

Feb. 17, 1792.
Proclamation, Feb. 17, 1792.

Additional Article To the Treaty made between the United States and the Cherokees on the second day of July, one thousand seven hundred and ninety-one.
It is hereby mutually agreed between Henry Knox, Secretary of War, duly authorized thereto in behalf of the United States, on the one part, and the under-signed chiefs and warriors, in behalf of themselves and the Cherokee nation, on the other part, that the following article shall be added to and considered as part of the treaty made between the United States and the said Cherokee nation on the second day of July, one thousand seven hundred and ninety-one; to wit:

The sum to be paid annually by the United States to the Cherokee nation of In-dians, in consideration of the relinquishment of land, as stated in the treaty made with them on the second day of July, one thousand seven hundred and ninety-one, shall be one thousand five hundred dollars instead of one thousand dollars, mentioned in the said treaty.

In testimony whereof, the said Henry Knox, Secretary of War, and the said chiefs and warriors of the Cherokee nation, have hereunto set their hands and seals, in the city of Philadelphia, this seventeenth day of February, in the year of our Lord, one thousand seven hundred and ninety-two.

H. Knox, Secretary of War, Iskagua, or Clear Sky, his x mark (formerly Nene-tooyah, or Bloody Fellow), Nontuaka, or the Northward, his x mark, Chutloh, or King Fisher, his x mark, Katigoslah, or the Prince, his x mark, Teesteke, or Common Disturber, his x mark, Suaka, or George Miller, his x mark,

In presence of: Thomas Grooter, Jno. Stagg, jr, Leonard D. Shaw, James Cery, sworn intrepreter to the Cherokee Nation.

TREATY WITH THE SEVEN NATIONS
OF CANADA {1796, May 31}
Proclamation, Jan. 1, 1797.

At a treaty held at the city of New York, with the Nations or Tribes of Indians, denominating themselves the Seven Nations of Canada; Abraham Ogaen, Commissioner, appointed under the authority of the United States, to hold the Treaty; Ohaweio, alias Goodstream, Teharaywanege, alias Thomas Williams, two Chiefs of the Caghna-wayas; Atiatoharongwan, alias Colonel Lewis Cook, a Chief the St. Regis Indians, and William Gray, Deputies, authorized to repre-sent these Seven Nations or Tribes of Indians at the Treaty, and Mr. Gray, serving also as Interpreter; Egbert Benson, Richard Vrick and James Watson, Agents for the State of New York; William Constable and Daniel M'Cormick, purchasers under Alexander Macomb:

THE agents for the state, having, in the presence, and with the approbation of the commissioner, proposed to the deputies for the Indians, the compensation hereinafter mentioned, for the extinguishment of their claim to all lands within the state, and the said deputies being willing to accept the same, it is thereupon granted, agreed and concluded between the said deputies and the said agents,-as follows: The said deputies do, for and in the name of the said Seven Nations or tribes of Indians, cede, release and quit claim to the people of the state of New-York forever, all the claim, right, or title of them, the said Seven Nations or tribes of Indians, to lands within the said state: Provided nevertheless, That the tract equal to six miles square, reserved in the sale made by the commissioners of the land-office of the said state, to Alexander Macomb, to be applied to the use of the Indians of the village of St. Regis, shall still remain so reserved.

The said agents do, for, and in the name of the people of the state of New-York, grant to the said Seven Nations or tribes of Indians, that the people of the state of New-York shall pay to them, at the mouth of the river Chazy, on Lake

25

Champlain, on the third Monday in August next, the sum of one thousand two hundred and thirty-three pounds, six shillings and eight-pence, and the further sum of two hundred and thirteen pounds six shillings and eight-pence, lawful money of the said state, and on the third Monday in August, yearly, forever thereafter, the like sum of two hundred and thirteen pounds six shillings and eight-pence: Provided nevertheless, That the people of the state of New-York shall not be held to pay the said sums, unless in respect to the two sums to be paid on the third Monday in August next, at least twenty, and in respect to the said yearly sum to be paid thereafter, at least five of the principal men of the said Seven Nations or tribes of Indians, shall attend as deputies to receive and to give receipts for the same.

The said deputies having suggested, that the Indians of the village of St. Regis have built a mill on Salmon river, and another on Grass river, and that the meadows on Grass river are necessary to them for hay.

In order, therefore, to secure to the Indians of the said village, the use of the said mills and meadows, in case they should hereafter appear not to be included within the above tract so to remain reserved; it is, therefore, also agreed and concluded between the said deputies, the said agents, and the said William Constable and Daniel M'Cormick, for themselves and their associates, purchasers under the said Alexander Macomb, of the adjacent lands, that there shall be reserved, to be applied to the use of the Indians of the said village of St. Regis, in like manner as the said tract is to remain reserved, a tract of one mile square, at each of the said mills, and the meadows on both sides of the said Grass river from the said mill thereon, to its confluence with the river St. Lawrence.

In testimony whereof, the said commissioner, the said deputies, the said agents, and the said William Constable and Daniel McCormick, have hereunto, and to two other acts of the same tenor and date, one to remain with the United States, another to remain with the State of New York, and another to remain with the said Seven Nations or tribes of Indians, set their hands and seals, in the city of New York, the thirty-first day of May, in the twentieth year of the independence of the United States, one thousand seven hundred and ninety-six.

Abraham Ogden, Egbert Benson, Richard Varick, James Watson, William Constable, Daniel McCormick, Ohaweio, alias Goodstream, his x mark, Otiatokarongwan, alias Col. Lewis Cook, his x mark, William Gray, Teharagwanegen, alias Thos. Willlams, his x mark,.

Signed, sealed, and delivered, in the presence of: Samuel Jones, recorder of the city of New York, John Tayler, recorder of the city of Albany, Joseph Ogden Hoffman, attorney general of the State of New York.

TREATY WITH THE CHEROKEE {1794, June 26}

WHEREAS the treaty made and concluded on Holston river, on the second day of July, one thousand seven hundred and ninety-one, between the United States of America and the Cherokee nation of Indians, has not been fully carried into execution by reason of some misunderstandings which have arisen:

ARTICLE 1. And whereas the undersigned Henry Knox, Secretary for the department of War being authorized thereto by the President of the United States, in behalf of the said United States, and the undersigned Chiefs and Warriors, in their own names, and in behalf of the whole Cherokee nation, are desirous of re-establishing peace and friendship between the said parties in a permanent manner, Do hereby declare, that the said treaty of Holston is, to all intents and purposes, in full force and binding upon the said parties, as well in respect to the boundaries therein mentioned as in all other respects whatever.

ARTICLE 2. It is hereby stipulated that the boundaries mentioned in the fourth article of the said treaty, shall be actually ascertained and marked in the manner prescribed by the said article, whenever the Cherokee nation shall have ninety days notice of the time and place at which the commissioners of the United States intend to commence their operation. [34]

ARTICLE 3. The United States, to evince their justice by amply compensating the said Cherokee nation of Indians for all relinquishments of land made either by the treaty of Hopewell upon the Keowee river, concluded on the twenty-eighth of November, one thousand seven hundred and eighty-five, or the aforesaid treaty made upon Holston river, on the second of July, one thousand seven hundred and ninety-one, do hereby stipulate, in lieu of all former sums to be paid annually to furnish the Cherokee Indians with goods suitable for their use, to the amount of five thousand dollars yearly.

ARTICLE 4. And the said Cherokee nation, in order to evince the sincerity of their intentions in future, to prevent the practice of stealing horses, attended with the most pernicious consequences to the lives and peace of both parties, do hereby agree, that for every horse which shall be stolen from the white inhabitants by any Cherokee Indians, and not returned within three months, that the sum of fifty dollars shall be deducted from the said annuity of five thousand dollars.

ARTICLE 5. The articles now stipulated will be considered as permanent additions to the treaty of Holston, as soon as they shall have been ratified by the President of the United States and the Senate of the United States.

In witness of all and every thing herein determined between the United States of America and the whole Cherokee nation, the parties have hereunto set their hands and seals in the city of Philadelphia, within the United States, this twenty-sixth day of June, in the year of our Lord one thousand seven hundred and ninety-four.

H. Knox, Secretary of War, Tekakisskee, or Taken out of the Water, his x mark, Nontuaka, or the Northward, his x mark, Cinasaw, or the Cabin, his x mark, Skyuka, his x mark, Chuquilatague, or Double Head, his x mark, John McCleemore, his x mark, Walahue, or the Humming Bird, Chuleowee, his x mark, Ustanaqua, his x mark, Kullusathee, his x mark, Siteaha, his x mark, Keenaguna, or the Lying Fawn, his x mark, Chatakaelesa, or the Fowl Carrier,

Done in presence of: John Thompson, Arthur Coodey, Interpreters, William Wofford, of the State of Georgia, W. McCaleb, of South Carolina, Cantwell Jones, of Delaware, Samuel Lewis, of Philadelphia.

TREATY WITH THE SIX NATIONS {1794, Nov. 11}

A Treaty between the United States of America, and the Tribes of Indians called the Six Nations.

The President of the United States having determined to hold a conference with the Six Nations of Indians, for the purpose of removing from their minds all causes of complaint, and establishing a firm and permanent friendship with them; and Timothy Pickering being appointed sole agent for that purpose; and the agent having met and conferred with the Sachems, Chiefs and Warriors of the Six Nations, in a general council: Now, in order to accomplish the good design of this conference, the parties have agreed on the following articles; which, when ratified by the President, with the advice and consent of the Senate of the United States, shall be binding on them and the Six Nations.

ARTICLE 1. Peace and friendship are hereby firmly established, and shall be perpetual, between the United States and the Six Nations.

ARTICLE 2. The United States acknowledge the lands reserved to the Oneida, Onondaga and Cayuga Nations, in their respective treaties with the state of New-York, and called their reservations, to be their property; and the United States will never claim the same, nor disturb them or either of the Six Nations, nor their Indian friends residing thereon and united with them, in the free use and enjoyment thereof: but the said reservations shall remain theirs, until they choose to sell the same to the people of the United States, who have the right to purchase.

ARTICLE 3. The land of the Seneka nation is bounded as follows: Beginning on Lake Ontario, at the north-west corner of the land they sold to Oliver Phelps, the line runs westerly along the lake, as far as O-yong-wong-yeh Creek, at Johnson's Landing-place, about four miles eastward from the fort of Niagara; then southerly up that creek to its main fork, then straight to the main fork of Stedman's creek, which empties into the river Niagara, above fort Schlosser, and then onward, from that fork, continuing the same straight course, to that river; (this line, from the mouth of O-y(o)ng-wong-yeh Creek to the river Niagara, above fort Schlosser, being the eastern boundary of a strip of land, extending from the same line to Niagara river, which the Seneka nation ceded to the King of Great-Britain, at a treaty held about thirty years ago, with Sir William Johnson;) then the line runs along the river Niagara to Lake Erie; then along Lake Erie to the north-east corner of a triangular piece of land which the United States conveyed to the state of Pennsylvania, as by the President's patent, dated the third day of March, 1792; then due south to the northern boundary of that state; then due east to the south-west corner of the land sold by the Seneka nation to Oliver Phelps; and then north and northerly, along Phelps's line, to the place of beginning on Lake Ontario. Now, the United States acknowledge all the land within the aforementioned boundaries, to be the property of the Seneka nation; and the United States will never claim the same, nor disturb the Seneka nation, nor any of the Six Nations, or of their Indian friends residing thereon and united with them, in the free use and enjoyment thereof: but it shall remain theirs, until they choose to sell the same to the people of the United States, who have the right to purchase.

ARTICLE 4. The United States having thus described and acknowledged what lands belong to the Oneidas, Onondagas, Cayugas and Senekas, and engaged never to claim the same, nor to disturb them, or any of the Six Nations, or their Indian friends residing thereon and united with them, in the free use and enjoyment thereof: Now, the Six Nations, and each of them, hereby engage that they will never claim any other lands within the boundaries of the United States; nor ever disturb the people of the United States in the free use and enjoyment thereof.

ARTICLE 5. The Seneka nation, all others of the Six Nations concurring, cede to the United States the right of making a wagon road from Fort Schlosser to Lake Erie, as far south as Buffaloe Creek; and the people of the United States shall have the free and undisturbed use of this road, for the purposes of travelling and transportation. And the Six Nations, and each of them, will forever allow to the people of the United States, a free passage through their lands, and the free use of the harbors and rivers adjoining and within their respective tracts of land, for the passing and securing of vessels and boats, and liberty to land their cargoes where necessary for their safety.

ARTICLE 6. In consideration of the peace and friendship hereby established, and of the engagements entered into by the Six Nations; and because the United States desire, with humanity and kindness, to contribute to their comfortable support; and to render the peace and friendship hereby established, strong and perpetual; the United States now deliver to the Six Nations, and the Indians of the other nations residing among and united with them, a quantity of goods of the value of ten thousand dollars. And for the same considerations, and with a view to promote the future welfare of the Six Nations, and of their Indian friends aforesaid, the United States will add the sum of three thousand dollars to the one thousand five hundred dollars, heretofore allowed them by an article ratified by the President, on the twenty-third day of April, 1792; (a) making in the whole, four thousand five hundred dollars; which shall be expended yearly forever, in purchasing clothing, domestic animals, implements of husbandry, and other utensils suited to their circumstances, and in compensating useful artificers, who shall reside with or near them, and be employed for their benefit. The immediate application of the whole annual allowance now stipulated, to be made by the superintendent appointed by the President for the affairs of the Six Nations, and their Indian friends aforesaid.

ARTICLE 7. Lest the firm peace and friendship now established should be interrupted by the misconduct of individuals, the United States and Six Nations agree, that for injuries done by individuals on either side, no private revenge or retaliation shall take place; but, instead thereof, complaint shall be made by the party injured, to the other: By the Six Nations or any of them, to the President of the United States, or the Superintendent by him appointed: and by the Superintendent, or other person appointed by the President, to the principal chiefs of the Six Nations, or of the nation to which the offender belongs: and such prudent measures shall then be pursued as shall be necessary to preserve our peace and friendship unbroken; until the legislature (or great council) of the United States shall make other equitable provision for the purpose.

NOTE. It is clearly understood by the parties to this treaty, that the annuity stipulated in the sixth article, is to be applied to the benefit of such of the Six Nations and of their Indian friends united with them as aforesaid, as do or shall reside within the boundaries of the United States: For the United States do not interfere with nations, tribes or families, of Indians elsewhere resident.
In witness whereof, the said Timothy Pickering, and the sachems and war chiefs of the said Six Nations, have hereto set their hands and seals.

Done at Konondaigua, in the State of New York, the eleventh day of November, in the year one thousand seven hundred and ninety-four.

Timothy Pickering, Onoyeahnee, his x mark, Konneatorteeoooh, his x mark, or Handsome Lake, Tokenhyouhau, his x mark, alias Captain Key, Oneshauee, his x mark, Hendrick Aupaumut, David Neesoonhuk, his x mark, Kanatsoyh, alias Nicholas Kusik, Sohhonteoquent, his x mark, Ooduhtsait, his x mark, Konoohqung, his x mark, Tossonggaulolus, his x mark, John Skenendoa, his x mark, Oneatorleeooh, his x mark, Kussauwatau, his x mark,

Eyootenyootauook, his x mark, Kohnycaugong, his x mark, alias Jake Stroud, Shaguiesa, his x mark, Teeroos, his x mark, alias Captain Prantup, Soosha-oowau, his x mark, Henry Young Brant, his x mark, Sonhyoowauna, his x mark, or Big Sky, Onaahhah, his x mark, Hotoshahenh, his x mark, Kaukon-danaiya, his x mark, Nondiyauka, his x mark, Kossishtowau, his x mark, Oo-jaugenta, his x mark, or Fish Carrier, Toheonggo, his x mark, Ootaguasso, his x mark, Joonondauwaonch, his x mark, Kiyauhaonh, his x mark, Ootaujeaugenh, his x mark, or Broken Axe,

Tauhoondos, his x mark, or Open the Way, Twaukewasha, his x mark, Sequi-dongquee, his x mark, alias Little Beard, Kodjeote, his x mark, or Half Town, Kenjauaugus, his x mark, or Stinking Fish, Soonohquaukau, his x mark, Twen-niyana, his x mark, Jishkaaga, his x mark, or Green Grasshopper, alias Little Billy, Tuggehshotta, his x mark, Tehongyagauna, his x mark, Tehongyoowush, his x mark, Konneyoowesot, his x mark, Tioohquottakauna, his x mark, or Woods on Fire, Taoundaudeesh, his x mark,

Honayawus, his x mark, alias Farmer's Brother, Soggooyawauthau, his x mark, alias Red Jacket, Konyootiayoo, his x mark, Sauhtakaongyees, his x mark, or Two Skies of a length, Ounnashattakau, his x mark, Kaungyanehquee, his x mark, Sooayoowau, his x mark, Kaujeagaonh, his x mark, or Heap of Dogs, Soonoohshoowau, his x mark, Soonongjoowau, his x mark, Kiantwhauka, his x mark, alias Cornplanter, Kaunehshonggoo, his x mark,

Witnesses: Israel Chapin, Israel Chapin, jr, William Shepard, jr, Horatio Jones, James Smedley, Joseph Smith, John Wickham, Jasper Parish, Augustus Porter., Interpreters, James K. Garnsey, Henry Abeele, William Ewing.

TREATY WITH THE ONEIDA, ETC. {1794, Dec. 2}

Proclamation, Jan. 21, 1795.

A treaty between the United States and the Oneida, Tuscorora and Stockbridge Indians, dwelling in the Country of the Oneidas.

WHEREAS, in the late war between Great-Britain and the United States of America, a body of the Oneida and Tuscorora and the Stockbridge Indians, ad-hered faithfully to the United States, and assisted them with their warriors; and in consequence of this adherence and assistance, the Oneidas and Tuscororas, at an unfortunate period of the war, were driven from their homes, and their houses were burnt and their property destroyed: And as the United States in the time of their distress, acknowledged their obligations to these faithful friends, [38] and promised to reward them: and the United States being now in a condi-tion to fulfil the promises then made: the following articles are stipulated by the respective parties for that purpose; to be in force when ratified by the President and Senate.

ARTICLE 1. The United States will pay the sum of five thousand dollars, to be distributed among individuals of the Oneida and Tuscorora nations, as a compensation for their individual losses and services during the late war between Great-Britain and the United States. The only man of the Kaughnawaugas now remaining in the Oneida country, as well as some few very meritorious persons of the Stockbridge Indians, will be considered in the distribution.

ARTICLE 2. For the general accommodation of these Indian nations, residing in the country of the Oneidas, the United States will cause to be erected a complete grist-mill and saw-mill, in a situation to serve the present principal settlements of these nations. Or if such one convenient situation cannot be found, then the United States will cause to be erected two such grist-mills and saw-mills, in places where it is now known the proposed accommodation may be effected. Of this the United States will judge.

ARTICLE 3. The United States will provide, during three years after the mills shall be completed, for the expense of employing one or two suitable persons to manage the mills, to keep them in repair, to instruct some young men of the three nations in the arts of the miller and sawyer, and to provide teams and utensils for carrying on the work of the mills.

ARTICLE 4. The United States will pay one thousand dollars, to be applied in building a convenient church at Oneida, in the place of the one which was there burnt by the enemy, in the late war.

ARTICLE 5. In consideration of the above stipulations to be performed on the part of the United States, the Oneida, Tuscorora and Stockbridge Indians aforementioned, now acknowledge themselves satisfied, and relinquish all other claims of compensation and rewards for their losses and services in the late war. Excepting only the unsatisfied claims of such men of the said nations as bore commissions under the United States, for any arrears which may be due to them as officers.

In witness whereof, the chiefs of those nations, residing in the country of the Oneidas, and Timothy Pickering, agent for the United States, have hereto set their hands and seals, at Oneida, the second day of December, in the year one thousand seven hundred and ninety-four.

Timothy Pickering,
Wolf Tribe: Odotsaihte, his x mark, Konnoquenyau, his x mark, Head sachems of the Oneidas.
John Skenendo, eldest war chief, his x mark,
Bear Tribe: Lodowik Kohsauwetau,his x mark, Cornelius Kauhiktoton, his x mark, Thos. Osauhataugaunlot, his x mark,

Turtle Tribe: Shonohleyo, warchief, his x mark, PeterKonnauterlook, sachem, his x mark, Daniel Teouneslees, son of Sken-endo, war chief, his x mark, Tuscaroras: Thaulondauwaugon, sachem, his x mark, Kanatjogh, or Nicholas Cusick, war chief, his x mark,

Witnesses to the signing and sealing of the agent of the United States, and of the chiefs of the Oneida and Tuscarora nations: S. Kirkland, James Dean, Interpreter.

Witnesses to the signing and sealing of the four chiefs of the Stockbridge Indians, whose names are below:
Saml. Kirkland, John Sergeant.
Stockbridge Indians: Hendrick Aupaumut, Joseph Quonney,

TREATY WITH THE WYANDOT, ETC. {1795, Aug. 3}
Proclamation, Dec. 2, 1795.

A treaty peace between the United States of America and the Tribes of Indians, called the Wyandots Delawares Shawanoes Ottawas, Chipewas, Putawatimes, Miamis, Eel-river, Wea's, Kickapoos, Piankashaws, and Kaskaskias.

To put an end to a destructive war, to settle all controversies, and to restore harmony and a friendly intercourse between the said United States, and Indian tribes; Anthony Wayne, major-general, commanding the army of the United States, and sole commissioner for the good purposes above-mentioned, and the said tribes of Indians, by their Sachems, chiefs, and warriors, met together at Greeneville, the head quarters of the said army, have agreed on the following articles, which, when ratified by the President, with the advice and consent of the Senate of the United States, shall be binding on them and the said Indian tribes.

ARTICLE 1. Henceforth all hostilities shall cease; peace is hereby established, and shall be perpetual; and a friendly intercourse shall take place, between the said United States and Indian tribes.

ARTICLE 2. All prisoners shall on both sides be restored. The Indians, prisoners to the United States, shall be immediately set at liberty. The people of the United States, still remaining prisoners among the Indians, shall be delivered up in ninety days from the date hereof, to the general or commanding officer at Greeneville, Fort Wayne or Fort Defiance; and ten chiefs of the said tribes shall remain at Greeneville as hostages, until the delivery of the prisoners shall be effected.

ARTICLE 3. The general boundary line between the lands of the United States, and the lands of the said Indian tribes, shall begin at the mouth of Cayahoga river, and run thence up the same to the portage between that and the Tuscarawas branch of the Muskingum; thence down that branch to the crossing place above Fort Lawrence; thence westerly to a fork of that branch of the great Miami river running into the Ohio, at or near which fork stood Loromie's store, and where commences the portage between the Miami of the Ohio, and St. Mary's river, which is a branch of the Miami, which runs into Lake Erie; thence a westerly course to Fort Recovery, which stands on a branch of the Wabash; then south-westerly in a direct line to the Ohio, so as to intersect that river opposite the mouth of Kentucke or Cuttawa river. And in consideration of the peace now established; of the goods formerly received from the United States; of those now to be delivered, and of the yearly delivery of goods now stipulated to be made hereafter, and to indemnify the United States for the injuries and expenses they have sustained during the war; the said Indians tribes do hereby cede and relinquish forever, all their claims to the lands lying eastwardly and southwardly of the general boundary line now described; and these lands, or any part of them, shall never hereafter be made a cause or pretence, on the part of the said tribes or any of them, of war or injury to the United States, or any of the people thereof.

And for the same considerations, and as an evidence of the returning friendship of the said Indian tribes, of their confidence in the United States, and desire to provide for their accommodation, and for that convenient intercourse which will be beneficial to both parties, the said Indian tribes do also cede to the United States the following pieces of land; to-wit. (1.) One piece of land six miles square at or near Loromie's store before mentioned. (2.) One piece two miles square at the head of the navigable water or landing on the St. Mary's river, near Girty's town. (3.) One piece six miles square at the head of the navigable water of the Au-Glaize river.

(4.) One piece six miles square at the continence of the Au-Glaize and Miami rivers, where Fort Defiance now stands. (5.) One piece six miles square at or near the confluence of the rivers St. Mary's and St. Joseph's, where Fort Wayne now stands, or near it. (6.) One piece two miles square on the Wabash river at the end of the portage from the Miami of the lake, and about eight miles westward from Fort Wayne. (7.) One piece six miles square at the Ouatanon or old Weea towns on the Wabash river. (8.) One piece twelve miles square at the British fort on the Miami of the lake at the foot of the rapids. (9.) One piece six miles square at the mouth of the said river where it empties into the Lake. (10.) One piece six miles square upon Sandusky lake, where a fort formerly stood. (11.) One piece two miles square at the lower rapids of Sandusky river.

(12.) The post of Detroit and all the land to the north, the west and the south of it, of which the Indian title has been extinguished by gifts or grants to the

French or English governments; and so much more land to be annexed to the district of Detroit as shall be comprehended between the river Rosine on the south, lake St. Clair on the north, and a line, the general course whereof shall be six miles distant from the west end of lake Erie, and Detroit river. (13.) The post of Michillimackinac, and all the land on the island, on which that post stands, and the main land adjacent, of which the Indian title has been extinguished by gifts or grants to the French or English governments; and a piece of land on the main to the north of the island, to measure six miles on lake Huron, or the strait between lakes Huron and Michigan, and to extend three miles back from the water of the lake or strait, and also the island De Bois Blanc, being an extra and voluntary gift of the Chipewa nation.

(14.) One piece of land six miles square at the mouth of Chikago river, emptying into the south-west end of Lake Michigan, where a fort formerly stood. (15.) One piece twelve miles square at or near the mouth of the Illinois river, emptying into the Mississippi. (16.) One [41] piece six miles square at the old Piorias fort and village, near the south end of the Illinois lake on said Illinois river: And whenever the United States shall think proper to survey and mark the boundaries of the lands hereby ceded to them, they shall give timely notice thereof to the said tribes of Indians, that they may appoint some of their wise chiefs to attend and see that the lines are run according to the terms of this treaty.

And the said Indian tribes will allow to the people of the United States a free passage by land and by water, as one and the other shall be found convenient, through their country, along the chain of posts herein before mentioned; that is to say, from the commencement of the portage aforesaid at or near Loromie's store, thence along said portage to the St. Mary's, and down the same to Fort Wayne, and then down the Miami to lake Erie: again from the commencement of the portage at or near Loromie's store along the portage from thence to the river Au-Glaize, and down the same to its junction with the Miami at Fort Defiance: again from the commencement of the portage aforesaid, to Sandusky river, and down the same to Sandusky bay and lake Erie, and from Sandusky to the post which shall be taken at or near the foot of the rapids of the Miami of the lake: and from thence to Detroit. Again from the mouth of Chikago, to the commencement of the portage, between that river and the Illinois, and down the Illinois river to the Mississippi, also from Fort Wayne along the portage aforesaid which leads to the Wabash, and then down the Wabash to the Ohio. And the said Indian tribes will also allow to the people of the United States the free use of the harbors and mouths of rivers along the lakes adjoining the Indian lands, for sheltering vessels and boats, and liberty to land their cargoes where necessary for their safety.

ARTICLE 4. In consideration of the peace now established and of the cessions and relinquishments of lands made in the preceding article by the said tribes of

Indians, and to manifest the liberality of the United States, as the great means of rendering this peace strong and perpetual; the United States relinquish their claims to all other Indian lands northward of the river Ohio, eastward of the Mississippi, and westward and southward of the Great Lakes and the waters uniting them, according to the boundary line agreed on by the United States and the king of Great-Britain, in the treaty of peace made between them in the year 1783. But from this relinquishment by the United States, the following tracts of land, are explicitly excepted. 1st. The tract Of one hundred and fifty thousand acres near the rapids of the river Ohio, which has been assigned to General Clark, for the use of himself and his warriors. 2d. The post of St. Vincennes on the river Wabash, and the lands adjacent, of which the Indian title has been extinguished. 3d. The lands at all other places in possession of the French people and other white settlers among them, of which the Indian title has been extinguished as mentioned in the 3d article; and 4th. The post of fort Massac towards the mouth of the Ohio. To which several parcels of land so excepted, the said tribes relinquish all the title and claim which they or any of them may have.

And for the same considerations and with the same views as above mentioned, the United States now deliver to the said Indian tribes a quantity of goods to the value of twenty thousand dollars, the receipt whereof they do hereby acknowledge; and henceforward every year forever the United States will deliver at some convenient place northward of the river Ohio, like useful goods, suited to the circumstances of the Indians, of the value of nine thousand five hundred dollars; reckoning that value at the first cost of the goods in the city or place [42] m the United States, where they shall be procured. The tribes to which those goods are to be annually delivered, and the proportions in which they are to be delivered, are the following.

1st. To the Wyandots, the amount of one thousand dollars. 2nd. To the Delawares, the amount of one thousand dollars. 3d. To the Shawanese, the amount of one thousand dollars. 4th. To the Miamis, the amount of one thousand dollars. 5th. To the Ottawas, the amount of one thousand dollars. 6th. To the Chippewas, the amount of one thousand dollars. 7th. To the Putawatimes, the amount of one thousand dollars. 8th. And to the Kickapoo, Weea, Eel-river, Piankashaw and Kaskaskias tribes, the amount of five hundred dollars each.

Provided, That if either of the said tribes shall hereafter at an annual delivery of their share of the goods aforesaid, desire that a part of their annuity should be furnished in domestic animals, implements of husbandry, and other utensils convenient for them, and in compensation to useful artificers who may reside with or near them, and be employed for their benefit, the same shall at the subsequent annual deliveries be furnished accordingly.

ARTICLE 5. To prevent any misunderstanding about the Indian lands relinquished by the United States in the fourth article, it is now explicitly declared, that the meaning of that relinquishment is this: The Indian tribes who have a right to those lands, are quietly to enjoy them, hunting, planting, and dwelling thereon so long as they please, without any molestation from the United States; but when those tribes, or any of them, shall be disposed to sell their lands, or any part of them, they are to be sold only to the United States; and until such sale, the United States will protect all the said Indian tribes in the quiet enjoyment of their lands against all citizens of the United States, and against all other white persons who intrude upon the same. And the said Indian tribes again acknowledge themselves to be under the protection of the said United States and no other power whatever.

ARTICLE 6. If any citizen of the United States, or any other white person or persons, shall presume to settle upon the lands now relinquished by the United States, such citizen or other person shall be out of the protection of the United States; and the Indian tribe, on whose land the settlement shall be made, may drive off the settler, or punish him in such manner as they shall think fit; and because such settlements made without the consent of the United States, will be injurious to them as well as to the Indians, the United States shall be at liberty to break them up, and remove and punish the-settlers as they shall think proper, and so effect that protection of the Indian lands herein before stipulated.

ARTICLE 7. The said tribes of Indians, parties to this treaty, shall be at liberty to hunt within the territory and lands which they have now ceded to the United States, without hindrance or molestation, so long as they demean themselves peaceably, and offer no injury to the people of the United States.

ARTICLE 8. Trade shall be opened with the said Indian tribes; and they do hereby respectively engage to afford protection to such persons, with their property, as shall be duly licensed to reside among them for the purpose of trade, and to their agents and servants; but no person shall be permitted to reside at any of their towns or hunting camps as a trader, who is not furnished with a license for that purpose, under the hand and seal of the superintendent of the department north-west of the Ohio, or such other person as the President of the United States shall authorize to grant such licenses; to the end, that the said Indians may not be imposed on in their trade. And if any licensed trader shall abuse his privilege by unfair dealing, upon complaint and proof thereof, his license shall be taken from him, and he shall be further punished according to the laws of the United States. And if any person shall intrude himself as a trader, without such license, the said Indians shall take and bring him before the superintendent or his deputy, to be dealt with according to law. And to prevent impositions by forged licenses, the said Indians shall at least once a year give information to the superintendant or his deputies, of the names of the traders residing among them.

ARTICLE 9. Lest the firm peace and friendship now established should be interrupted by the misconduct of individuals, the United States, and the said Indian tribes agree, that for injuries done by individuals on either side, no private revenge or retaliation shall take place; but instead thereof, complaint shall be made by the party injured, to the other: By the said Indian tribes, or any of them, to the President of the United States, or the superintendent by him appointed; and by the superintendent or other person appointed by the President, to the principal chiefs of the said Indian tribes, or of the tribe to which the offender belongs; and such prudent measures shall then be pursued as shall be necessary to preserve the said peace and friendship unbroken, until the Legislature (or Great Council) of the United States, shall make other equitable provision in the case, to the satisfaction of both parties.

Should any Indian tribes meditate a war against the United States or either of them, and the same shall come to the knowledge of the before-mentioned tribes, or either of them, they do hereby engage to give immediate notice thereof to the general or officer commanding the troops of the United States, at the nearest post. And should any tribe, with hostile intentions against the United States, or either of them, attempt to pass through their country, they will endeavor to prevent the same, and in like manner give information of such attempt, to the general or officer commanding, as soon as possible, that all causes of mistrust and suspicion may be avoided between them and the United States. In like manner the United States shall give notice to the said Indian tribes of any harm that may be meditated against them, or either of them, that shall come to their knowledge; and do all in their power to hinder and prevent the same, that the friendship between them may be uninterrupted.

ARTICLE 10. All other treaties heretofore made between the United States and the said Indian tribes, or any of them, since the treaty of 1783, between v the United States and Great Britain, that come within the purview of this treaty, shall henceforth cease and become void.

In testimony whereof, the said Anthony Wayne, and the sachems and war chiefs of the beforementioned nations and tribes of Indians, have hereunto set their hands and affixed their seals.

Done at Greenville, in the territory of the United States northwest [44] of the river Ohio, on the third day of August, one thousand seven hundred and ninety-five.

Anthony Wayne,
Wyandots: Tarhe, or Crane, his x mark, J. Williams, jun. his x mark, Teyyaghtaw, his x mark, Haroenyou, or half king's son, his x mark, Tehaawtorens, his x mark, Awmeyeeray, his x mark, Stayetah, his x mark,

Shateyyaronyah, or Leather Lips, his x mark, Daughshuttayah, his x mark, Shaawrunthe, his x mark,

Delawares: Tetabokshke, or Grand Glaize King, his x mark, Lemantanquis, or Black King, his x mark, Wabatthoe, his x mark, Maghpiway, or Red Feather, his x mark, Kikthawenund, or Anderson, his x mark, Bukongehelas, his x mark, Peekeelund, his x mark, Wellebawkeelund, his x mark, Peekeetelemund, or Thomas Adares, his x mark, Kishkopekund, or Captain Buffalo, his x mark, Amenahehan, or Captain Crow, his x mark, Queshawksey, or George Washington, his x mark, Weywinquis, or Billy Siscomb, his x mark, Moses, his x mark.

Shawanees: Misquacoonacaw, or Red Pole, his x mark, Cutthewekasaw, or Black Hoof, his x mark, Kaysewaesekah, his x mark, Weythapamattha, his x mark, Nianymseka, his x mark, Waytheah, or Long Shanks, his x mark, Weyapiersenwaw, or Blue Jacket, his x mark, Nequetaughaw, his x mark, Hahgooseekaw, or Captain Reed, his x mark,

Ottawas: Augooshaway, his x mark, Keenoshameek, his x mark, La Malice, his x mark, Machiwetah, his x mark, Thowonawa, his x mark, Secaw, his x mark,

Chippewas: Mashipinashiwish, or Bad Bird, his x mark, Nahshogashe, (from Lake Superior) his x mark, Kathawasung, his x mark, Masass, his x mark, Nemekass, or Little Thunder, his x mark, Peshawkay, or Young Ox, his x mark, Nanguey, his x mark, Meenedohgeesogh, his x mark, Peewanshemenogh, his x mark, Weymegwas, his x mark, Gobmaatick, his x mark,

Ottawa: Chegonickska, (an Ottawa from Sandusky) his x mark,

Pattawatimas of the river St.Joseph: Thupenebu, his x mark, Nawac, (for himself and brother Etsimethe) his x mark, Nenanseka, his x mark, Keesass, or Run, his x mark, Kabamasaw, (for himself and brother Chisaugan) his x mark, Sugganunk, his x mark, Wapmeme, or White Pigeon, his x mark, Wacheness, (for himself and brother Pedagoshok) his x mark, Wabshicawnaw, his x mark, La Chasse, his x mark, Meshegethenogh, (for himself and brother Wawasek) his x mark, Hingoswash, his x mark, Anewasaw, his x mark, Nawbudgh, his x mark, Missenogomaw, his x mark, Waweegshe, his x mark, Thawme, or Le Blanc, his x mark, Geeque, (for himself and brother Shewinse) his x mark,

Pattawatimas of Huron: Okia, his x mark, Chamung, his x mark, Segagewan, his x mark, Nanawme, (for himself and brother A. Gin) his x mark, Marchand, his x mark, Wenameac, his x mark,

Miamis: Nagohquangogh, or Le Gris, his x mark, Meshekunnoghquoh, or Little Turtle, his x mark,

Miamis and Eel Rivers: Peejeewa, or Richard Ville, his x mark, Cochkepoghtogh, his x mark,

Eel River Tribe: Shamekunnesa, or Soldier, his x mark,
Miamis: Wapamangwa, or the White Loon, his x mark,

Weas, for themselves and the Piankeshaws: Amacunsa, or Little Beaver, his x mark, Acoolatha, or Little Fox, his x mark, Francis, his x mark,
Kickapoos and Kaskaskias: Keeawhah, his x mark, Nemighka, or Josey Renard, his x mark, Paikeekanogh, his x mark,
Delawares of Sandusky: Hawkinpumiska, his x mark, Peyamawksey, his x mark, Reyntueco, (of the Six Nations, living at Sandusky) his x mark,

In presence of (the word "goods" in the sixth line of the third article; the word "before" in the twenty-sixth line of the third article: the words "five hundred" in the tenth line of the fourth article, and the word "Piankeshaw" in the fourteenth line of the fourth article, being first interlined)

H. De Butts, first aid de camp and secretary to Major General Wayne.
Wm. H. Harrison, aid de camp to Major General Wayne.
T. Lewis, aid de camp to Major General Wayne.
James O' Hara, quartermaster general.
John Mills, major of infantry and adjutant general , Caleb Swan, P.M. T. U. S., Geo. Demter, lieutenant artillery, Vigo, P. Frs. La Fontaine, Ant. Lasselle, H. Lasselle, Jn. Beau Bien, David Jones, chaplain U. S., S. Lewis Beaufait, R. Lachambre, Jas. Pepen. Baties Coutien, P. Navarre.

Sworn interpreters: Wm. Wells, Jacques Lassella, M. Morins, Bt. Sans Crainte, Christopher Miller, Robert Wilson, Abraham Willlares, his x mark, Isaac Zane, his x mark, John Konkapot, Jacob Konkapot.

TREATY WITH THE CREEKS {1796, June 29}
Proclamation, Mar. 18, 1797.

A treaty of peace and friendship made and concluded between the President of the United States of America, on the one Part, and Behalf of the said States, and the undersigned Kings, Chiefs and Warriors of the Creek Nation of Indians, on the Part of the said Nation. (a) The parties being desirous of establishing permanent peace and friendship between the United States and the said Creek nation, and the citizens and members thereof; and to remove the causes of war, by ascertaining their limits, and making other necessary, just and friendly arrangements; the President of the United States, by Benjamin Hawkins, George Clymer, and Andrew Pickens, Commissioners whom he hath constituted with powers for these purposes, by and with the advice and consent of the Senate; and the Creek Nation of Indians, by the undersigned Kings, Chiefs and Warriors, representing the whole Creek Nation, have agreed to the following articles:

ARTICLE 1. The Treaty entered into, at New-York, between the parties on the 7th day of August, 1790, is, and shall remain obligatory on the contracting parties, according to the terms of it, except as herein provided for.

ARTICLE 2. The boundary line from the Currahee mountain, to the head, or source of the main south branch of the Oconeé river, called, by the white people, Appalatchee, and by the Indians, Tulapocka, and down the middle of the same, shall be clearly ascertained, and marked, at such time, and in such manner, as the President shall direct. And the Indians will, on being informed of the determination of the President, send as many of their old chiefs, as he may require, to see the line ascertained and marked.

ARTICLE 3. (b) The President of the United States of America shall have full powers, whenever he may deem it advisable, to establish a trading or military post on the south side of the Alatamaha, on the bluff, about one mile above Beard's bluff; or any where from thence down the said river on the lands of the Indians, to garrison the same with any part of the military force of the United States, to protect the posts, and to prevent the violation of any of the provisions or regulations subsisting between the parties: And the Indians do hereby annex to the post aforesaid, a tract of land of five miles square, bordering one side on the river; which post and the lands annexed thereto, are hereby ceded to, and shall be to the use, and under the government of the United States of America.

ARTICLE 4. (c) As soon as the President of the United States has determined on the time and manner of running the line from the Currahee mountain, to the head or source of the main south branch of the Oconee, and notified the chiefs of the Creek land of the same, a suitable number of persons on their part shall attend to see the same completed: And if the President should deem it proper, then to fix on any place or places adjoining the river, and on the Indian lands for military or trading posts; the Creeks who attend there, will concur in fixing the same, according to the wishes of the President. And to each post the Indians shall annex a tract of land of five miles square, bordering one side on the river. And the said lands shall be to the use and under the government of the United States of America. Provided always, that whenever any of the trading or military posts mentioned in this treaty, shall, in the opinion of the President of the United States of America, be no longer necessary for the purposes intended by this cession, the same shall revert to, and become a part of the Indian lands.

ARTICLE 5. Whenever the President of the United States of America, and the king of Spain, may deem it advisable to mark the boundaries which separate their territories, the President shall give notice thereof to the Creek chiefs, who will furnish two principal chiefs, and twenty hunters to accompany the persons employed on this business, as hunters and guides from the Chocktaw country, to the head of St. Mary's. The chiefs shall receive each half a dollar per day, and the hunters one quarter of a dollar each per day, and ammunition, and a reasonable value for the meat delivered by them for the rise of the persons on this service.

ARTICLE 6. The Treaties of Hopewell, between the United States and the Chock-taws and Chickasaws, and at Holston between the Cherokees and the United States, mark the boundaries of those tribes of Indians. And the Creek nation do hereby relinquish all claims to any part of the territory inhabited or claimed by the citizens of the United States, in conformity with the said treaties.

ARTICLE 7. The Creek nation shall deliver, as soon as practicable, to the superintendent of Indian affairs, at such place as he may direct, all citizens of the United States; white inhabitants and negroes who are now prisoners in any part of the said nation, agreeably to the treaty at New-York, and also all citizens, white inhabitants, negroes and property taken since the signing of that treaty. And if any such prisoners, negroes or property should not be delivered, on or before the first day of January next, the governor of Georgia may empower three persons to repair to the said nation, in order to claim and receive such prisoners, negroes and property, under the direction of the President of the United States.

ARTICLE 8. In consideration of the friendly disposition of the Creek nation towards the government of the United States, evidenced by the stipulations in the present treaty, and particularly the leaving it in the discretion of the President to establish trading or military posts on their lands; the commissioners of the United States, on behalf of the said states, give to the said nation, goods to the value of six thousand dollars, and stipulate to send to the Indian nation, two blacksmiths, with strikers, to be employed for the upper and lower Creeks with the necessary tools.

ARTICLE 9. All animosities for past grievances shall henceforth cease, and the contracting parties will carry the foregoing treaty into full execution with all good faith and sincerity. Provided nevertheless, That persons now under arrest, in the state of Georgia, for a violation of the treaty at New-York, are not to be included in this amnesty, but are to abide the decision of law.

ARTICLE 10. This treaty shall take effect and be obligatory on the contracting parties, as soon as the same shall have been ratified by the President of the United. States, by and with the advise and consent of the senate.

Done at Colerain, the 29th of June, one thousand seven hundred and ninety-six.

Benjamin Hawkins, George Clymer, Andrew Pickens,
Cowetas: Chruchateneah, his x mark, Tusikia Mico, his x mark, Inclenis Mico, his x mark, Tuskenah, his x mark, OokfuskeeTustuneka, his x mark, Clewalee Tustuneka, his x mark,
Cussitas: Tusikia Mico, his x mark, Cussita Mieo, his x mark, Fusateehee Mico, his x mark, Opoey Mico, his x mark,

Broken Arrows: Tustuneka Mico, his x mark, Othley Opoey, his x mark, Opoey Tustuneka, his x mark, Oboethly Tustuneka, his x mark,
Euchees: Euchee Mieo, his x mark,
Usuehees: Osaw Enehah, his x mark, Ephah Tuskenah, his x mark, Tusikia Mico, his x mark,
Chehaws: Chehaw Mico, his x mark,

Talehanas: Othley Poey Mieo, his x mark, Othley Poey Tustimiha, his x mark,
Oakmulgees: Opoey Thloeco, his x mark, Paraehuekley, his x mark, Tuskenah, his x mark,
Euphales: Pahose Mieo, his x mark, Tustunika Chopeo, his x mark,
Ottassees: Fusatchee Hulloo Mieo, his x mark, Tusikia Mieo, his x mark, Mico Opoey, his x mark,
Tallessees: Tallessee Mico, his x mark, Othley Poey Mico, his x mark,
Little Oakjoys: Meeke Matla, his x mark,
Hicory Ground: Opoey Mico, his x mark,
Kuyalegees: Kelese Hatkie, his x mark,
Weakis: Neneh omotca Opoey, his x mark, Tusikia Mico, his x mark,
Cleewallees: Opoey-e-Matla, his x mark,
Coosis: Hosonupe Hodjo, his x mark,
Tuckabathees: Holahto Mieo, his x mark, Tustunika Thloeeo, his x mark,
Oakfuskees: Pashphalaha, his x mark,
Abaeouehees: Spani Hodjo, his x mark, Tustonika, his x mark,
Upper Euphaules: Opoey, his x mark,
Natehees: Ahinibe, his x mark,
Upper Cheehaws: Spokoi Hodjo, his x mark, Tustunika, his x mark,
Maekasookos: Tuskeehenehaw, his x mark,
Oconees: Knapematha Thloeco, his x mark,
Cusetahs: Cusa Mieo, his x mark, Tusekia Mieo Athee, his x mark, Halartee Matla, his x mark, Talahoua

Mico, his x mark, Neathlocto, his x mark, Nuckfamico, his x mark, Estechaco Mico, his x mark, Tuskegee Tuskinagee, his x mark, Cochus Mico, his x mark, Opio Hajo, his x mark, Oneas Tustenagee, his x mark, Alak Ajo, his x mark, Stilcpeck Chatee, his x mark, Tuchesee Mico, his x mark,
Kealeegees: Cheea Hajo, his x mark,
Hitchetaws: Talmasee Matla, his x mark,
Tuckabatchees: Tustincke Hajo, his x mark, Okolissa, his x mark, Coweta Matla, his x mark, Coosa Mico, his x mark, Fusatchee Mico, his x mark, Pio Hatkee, his x mark, Foosatchee Mico, his x mark, Neathlaco, his x mark, Tuchabatchee Howla, his x mark, Spoko Hajo, his x mark,
Coosis: Tuskegee Tustinagee, his x mark, Talmasa Watalica, his x mark,
Euphalees:
Totkes Hago, his x mark,

43

Otasees: Opio Tustinagee, his x mark, Yafkee Mall Hajo, his x mark, OboyethleeTustinagee, his x mark, Tustinagee Hajo, his x mark, Hillibee Tustinagee Hajo, his x mark, Effa Tuskeena, his x mark, Emathlee Loco, his x mark, Tustanagee Mico, his x mark, Yaha Tustinagee, his x mark, Cunctastee Tustanagee, his x mark,

Ottasees: Coosa Tustinagee, his x mark, Neamatle Matla, his x mark,
Kialeegees: Chuckchack Nincha, his x mark, Opoyo Matla, his x mark, Lachlee Matla, his x mark,
Big Tallasees: Chowostia Hajo, his x mark, Neathloco Opyo, his x mark, Neathloco, his x mark, Chowlactley Mico, his x mark, Tocoso Hajo, his x mark, Hoochee Matla, his x mark, Howlacta, his x mark, Tustinica Mico, his x mark, Opoy Fraico, his x mark,
Big Talassee: Houlacta, his x mark, Etcatee Hajo, his x mark, Chosolop Hajo, his x mark, Coosa Hajo, his x mark,
Tuchabatchees: Chohajo, his x mark,
Weeokees: Tusticnika Hajo, his x mark,
Tuchabathees: Neamatoochee, his x mark,
Cussitas: Telewa Othleopoya, his x mark, Talmasse Matla, his x mark, Niah Weathla, his x mark,

Emathlee-laco, his x mark, Ottesee Matla, his x mark, Muclassee Matla, his x mark, Eufallee Matla, his x mark,
Tuckabatchees: Cunipee Howla, his x mark,
Cowetas: Hospotak Tustinagee, his x mark,
Natchez: Spoko Hodjo, his x mark,
Uchees: Tustinagee Chatee, his x mark,
Usuchees: Spokoca Tustinagee, his x mark, Othley-poey-Tustinagee, his x mark, Tuskeeneah, his x mark,

Witness: J. Seagrove, superintendent Indian affairs, C. N.Henry Gaither, lieutenant-colonel commandant, Const. Freeman, A. W. D., major artillery and engineers, Samuel Tinsley, captain, Third sub-legion, Samuel Allison, ensign, Second sub-legion, John W. Thompson, ensign, First U. S. legion, Geo. Gillasspy, surgeon, L. U. S, Tim. Barnard, D. A. and sworn interpreter, James Burges, D. A. and sworn interpreter, James Jordan. Richard Thomas. Alexander Cornels, William Eaton, captain, Fourth U. S. sub-legion, Commandant at Colerain, and secretary to the commission.

(a) This treaty was ratified on condition that the third and fourth articles should be modified as follows:
The Senate of the United States, two-thirds of the Senators present concurring, did, by their resolution of the second day of March instant, "consent to, and advise the President of the United States, to ratify the Treaty of Peace and Friendship, made and concluded at Coleraine, in the state of Georgia, on the

29th June, 1796, between the President of the United States of America, on the part and behalf of the said States, and the Kings, Chiefs and Warriors of the Creek nation of Indians, on the part of the said nation: Provided, and on condition, that nothing in the third and fourth articles of the said treaty, expressed in the words following, Article 3d, The President of the United States of America shall have full powers, whenever he may deem it advisable, to establish a trading or military post on the south side of the Altamaha, on the bluff, about one mile above Beard's bluff; or any where from thence down the said river on the lands of the Indians, to garrison the same with any part of the military force of the United States, to protect the post, and to prevent the violation of any of the provisions or regulations subsisting between the parties: And the Indians do hereby annex to the post aforesaid, a tract of land of five miles square, bordering one side on the river, which post and the lands annexed thereto, are hereby ceded to, and shall be to the use, and under the government of the United States of America.

"'Art. 4th, as soon as the President of the United States has determined on the time and manner of running the line from the Currahee mountain, to the head or source of the main south branch of the Oconnee, and notified the Chiefs of the Creek land of the same, a suitable number of persons on their part shall attend, to see the same completed: And if the President should deem it proper, then to fix on any place or places adjoining the river, and on the Indian lands for military or trading posts: the Creeks who attend there, will concur in fixing the same, according to the wishes of the President.

And to each post, the Indians shall annex a tract of land of five miles square, bordering one side on the river.

And the said lands shall be to the use and under the government of the United States of America. Provided always, that whenever any of the trading or military posts mentioned in this treaty, shall, in the opinion of the President of the United States of America, be no longer necessary for the purposes intended by this cession, the same shall revert to, and become a part of the Indian lands,' shall be construed to affect any claim of the state of Georgia, to the right of preemption in the land therein set apart for military or trading posts; or to give to the United States without the consent of the said state, any right to the soil, or to the exclusive legislation over the same, or any other right than that of establishing, maintaining, and exclusively governing military and trading posts within the Indian territory mentioned in the said articles, as long as the frontier of Georgia may require these establishments."

(b) See note at the beginning of the treaty.
(c) See note at the beginning of the treaty.

AGREEMENT WITH THE SENECA {1797, Sept. 15}

Contract entered into, under the sanction of the United States of America, between Robert Morris and the Seneca nation of Indians.

This indenture, made the fifteenth day of September, in the year of our Lord one thousand seven hundred and ninety-seven, between the sachems, chiefs, and warriors of the Seneca nation of Indians, of the first part, and Robert Morris, of the city of Philadelphia, Esquire, of the second part:

Whereas the Commonwealth of Massachusetts have granted, bargained, and sold unto the said Robert Morris, his heirs and assigns forever, the pre-emptive right, and all other the right, title and interest which the said Commonwealth had to all the tract of land hereinafter particularly mentioned, being part of a tract of land lying within the State of New York, the right of pre-emption of the soil whereof, from the native Indians, was ceded and granted by the said State of New York, to the said Commonwealth: and whereas, at a treaty held under the authority of the United States, with the said Seneca nation of Indians, at Genesee, in the county of Ontario, and State of New York, on the day of the date of these presents, and on sundry days immediately prior thereto, by the Honorable Jeremiah Wadsworth, Esquire, a commissioner appointed by the President of the United States, to hold the same in pursuance of the constitution, and of the act of the Congress of the United States, in such case made and provided, it was agreed, in the presence and with the approbation of the said commissioner, by the sachems, chiefs and warriors of the said nations of Indians, for themselves and in behalf of their nation, to sell to the said Robert Morris, and to his heirs and assigns forever, all their right to all that tract of land above recited, and hereinafter particularly specified, for the sum of one hundred thousand dollars, to be by the said Robert Morris vested in the stock of the bank of the United States, and held in the name of the President of the United States, for the use and behoof of the said nation of Indians, the said agreement and sale being also made in the presence, and with the approbation of the honorable William Shepard, Esquire, the superintendent appointed for such purpose, in pursuance of a resolve of the General Court of the Commonwealth of Massachusetts, passed the eleventh day of March, in the year of our Lord one thousand seven hundred and ninety-one; now this indenture witnesseth, that the said parties, of the first part, for and in consideration of the premises above recited, and for divers other good and valuable considerations them thereunto moving, have granted, bargained, sold, aliened, released, enfeoffed, and confirmed; and by these presents do grant, bargain, sell, alien, release, enfeoff, and confirm, unto the said party of the second part, his heirs and assigns forever, all that certain tract of land, except as is hereinafter excepted, lying within the county of Ontario and State of New York, being part of a tract of land, the right of pre-emption whereof was ceded by the state of New York to the Commonwealth of Massachusetts, by deed of cession executed at Hartford, on the sixteenth day of December, in the year of our Lord one thousand seven hundred and eighty-six, being all such part thereof as is not included in the Indian purchase made by Oliver Phelps and Nathaniel Gorham, and bounded as follows, to wit: easterly, by the land confirmed to Oliver Phelps and Nathaniel Gorham by the legislature of the Commonwealth of Massachusetts, by and act passed the twenty-first day of November, in the year of our Lord one thousand seven hundred and eighty-eight.

From there southerly, by the north boundary line of the State of Pennsylvania; westerly, partly by a tract of land, part of the land ceded by the State of Massachusetts to the United States, and by them sold to Pennsylvania, being a right angled triangle, whose hypothenuse is in or along the shore of Lake Erie; partly by Lake Erie, from the northern point of that triangle to the Southern bounds of a tract of land a mile in width, lying on and along the east side of the strait of Niagara, and partly by the said tract to lake Ontario; and on the north, by the boundary line between the United States and the King of Great Britain; excepting, nevertheless, and reserving always out of this grant and conveyance, all such pieces or parcels of the aforesaid tract, and such privileges thereunto belonging as are next hereinafter mentioned, which said pieces or parcels of land so excepted are, by the parties to these presents, clearly and fully understood to remain the property of the said parties of the first part, in as full and ample manner as if these presents had not been executed; that is to say, excepting and reserving to them, the said parties of the first part, and their nation, one piece or parcel of the aforesaid tract, at Canawaugas, of two square miles, to be laid out in such manner as to include the village extending in breadth one mile along the river; one other piece or parcel at Big Tree, of two square miles, to be laid out in such manner as to include the village, extending in breadth along the river one mile,

One other piece or parcel of two square miles at Little Beard's town, extending one mile along the river, to be laid off in such manner as to include the village; one other tract of two square miles at Squawky Hill, to be laid off as follows, to wit: one square mile to be laid off along the river, in such manner as to include the village, the other directly west thereof and contiguo's thereto; one other piece or parcel at Gar-dean, beginning at the mouth of Steep Hill creek, thence due east until it strikes the old path, thence south until a due west line will intersect with certain steep rocks on the west side of Genesee river, then extending due west, due north and due east, until it strikes the first mentiones bound, enclosing as much land on the west side as on the east side of the river. One other piece or parcel at Kaounadeau extending in length eight miles along the river and two miles in breadth. One other piece or parcel at Cataraugos, beginning at the mouth of the Eighteen mile or Koghquaugu creek, thence a line or line to be drawn parallel to lake Erie, at the distance of one mile from there, to the mouth of Cataraugos creek, thence a line or lines extending 12 miles up the north side of said creek at the distance of one mile therefrom, thence a direct line to the said creek, thence down the said creek to lake Erie, thence along the lake to the first mentioned creek, and thence to the place of beginning. Also one other piece at Cataraugos, beginning at the shore of lake Erie, on the south side of Cataraugos creek, at the distance of one mile from the mouth thereof, thence running one mile from the lake, thence on a line parallel thereto, to a point within one mile from the Connondau-weyea creek, thence up the said creek one mile, on a line parallel thereto, thence on a direct line to the said creek, thence down the same to lake Erie, thence along the lake to the place of beginning.

Also one other piece or parcel of forty-two square miles, at or near the Allegenny river. Also, two hundred square miles, to be laid off partly at the Buffalo and partly at the Tonnawanta creeks. Also, excepting and reserving to them, the said parties of the first part and their heirs, the privilege of fishing and hunting on the said tract of land hereby intended to be conveyed. And it is hereby understood by and between the parties to these presents, that all such pieces or parcels of land as are hereby reserved and are not particularly described as to the manner in which the same are to be laid off, shall be laid off in such manner as shall be determined by the sachems, chiefs, residing at or near the respective villages where such reservations are made, a particular note whereof to be indorsed on the back of this deed, and recorded therewith, together with all and singular the rights, privileges, hereditaments, and appurtenances thereunto belonging, or in anywise appertaining. And all the estate, right, title, and interest, whatsoever, of them the said parties of the first part and their nation, of, in, and to the said tract of land above described, except as is above excepted, to gave and to hold all and singular the said granted premises, with the appurtenances to the said party of the second part, his heirs and assigns, to his and their proper use, benefit and behoof forever.

In witness whereof, the parties to these presents have hereunto interchangeably set their hands and seals, the day and year first above written.

Robert Morris, by his attorney, Thomas Morris, Koyengquahtah, alias Young King, his x mark, Soonookshewan, his x mark, Konutaico, alias Handsome Lake, his x mark, Sattakanguyase, alias Two Skies of a length, his x mark, Onayawos, or Farmer's Brother, his x mark, Soogooyawautau, alias Red Jacket, his x mark, Gishkaka, alias Little Billy, his x mark, Kaoundoowana, alias Pollard, his x mark, Ouneashataikau, or Tall Chief, by his agent, Stevenson, his x mark, Teahdowainggua, alias Thos. Jemison, his x mark, Onnonggaiheko, alias Infant, his x mark, Tekonnondee, his x mark, Oneghtaugooau, his x mark, Connawaudeau, his x mark, Taosstaiefi, his x mark, Koeentwahka, or Corn Planter, his x mark, Oosaukaunendauki, alias to Destroy a Town, his x mark, Sooeoowa, alias Parrot Nose, his x mark, Toonahookahwa, his x mark, Howwennounew, his x mark, Kounahkaetoue, his x mark, Taouyaukauna, his x mark, Woudougoohkta, his x mark, Sonauhquaukau, his x mark, Twaunauiyana, his x mark,

Takaunoudea, his x mark, Shequinedaughque, or Little Beard, his x mark, Jowaa, his x mark, Saunajee, his x mark, Tauoiyuquatakausea, his x mark, Taoundaudish, his x mark, Tooauquinda, his x mark, Ahtaou, his x mark, Taukooshoondakoo, his x mark, Kauneskanggo, his x mark, Soononjuwau, his x mark, Tonowauiya, or Captain Bullet, his x mark, Jaahkaaeyas, his x mark, Taugihshauta, his x mark, Sukkenjoonau, his x mark, Ahquatieya, or Hot Bread, his x mark, Suggonundau, his x mark, Taunowaintooh, his x mark, Konnonjoowauna, his x mark, Soogooeyandestak, his x mark, Hautwanauekkau, by Young King, his x mark, Sauwejuwan, his x mark, Kaunoohshauwen, his x mark, Taukonondaugekta, his x mark, Kaouyanoughque, or John Jemison, his x mark, Holegush, his x mark, Taknaahquau, his x mark.

Sealed and delivered in presence of: Nat. W. Howell, Joseph Ellicott, Israel Chapin, James Rees, Henry, aron Hills, Henry Abeel, Jaspar Parrish, Horatio Jones, Interpreters.

Done at a full and general treaty of the Seneka nation of Indians, held at Genesee, in the county of Ontario, and State of New York, on the fifteenth day of September, in the year of our Lord one thousand seven hundred and ninety-seven, under the authority of the United States.

In testimony whereof, I have hereunto set my hand and seal, the day and year aforesaid.

Jere. Wadsworth,

Pursuant to a resolution of the legislature of the Commonwealth of Massachusetts, passed the eleventh day of March, in the year of our Lord one thousand seven hundred and ninety-one, I have attended a full and general treaty of the Seneka nation of Indians, at Genesee, in the county of Ontario, when the within instrument was duty executed in my presence by the sachems, chiefs, and warriors of the said nation, being fairly and properly understood and transacted by all the parties of Indians concerned, and declared to be done to their universal satisfaction: I therefore certify and approve of the same.

William Shepard.

TREATY WITH THE MOHAWK {1797, Mar. 29}
Proclamation, Apr. 27, 1798.

Relinquishment to New York, by the Mohawk nation of Indians, under the sanction of the United States of America, of all claim to lands in that state.

At a treaty held under the authority of the United States, with the Mohawk nation of Indians, residing in the province of Upper Canada, within the dominions of the king of Great Britain, present, the honorable Isaac Smith, commissioner appointed by the United States to [51] hold this treaty; Abraham Ten Broeck, Egbert Benson, and Ezra L'Hommedieu, agents for the state of New York; captain Joseph Brandt, and captain John Deserontyon, two of the said Indians and deputies, to represent the said nation at this treaty.

The said agents having, in the presence, and with the approbation of the said commissioner, proposed to and adjusted with the said deputies, the compensation as hereinafter mentioned to be made to the said nation, for their claim, to be extinguished by this treaty, to all lands within the said state: it is thereupon finally agreed and done, between the said agents, and the said deputies, as follows, that is to say: the said agents do agree to pay to the said deputies, the sum of one thousand dollars, for the use of the said nation, to be by the said deputies paid over to, and distributed among, the persons and families of the said nation, according to their usages.

The sum of five hundred dollars, for the expenses of the said deputies, during the time they have attended this treaty: and the sum of one hundred dollars, for their expenses in returning, and for conveying the said sum of one thousand dollars, to where the said nation resides. And the said agents do accordingly, for and in the name of the people of the state of New York, pay the said three several sums to the said deputies, in the presence of the said commissioner. And the said deputies do agree to cede and release, and these presents witness, that they accordingly do, for and in the name of the said nation, in consideration of the said compensation, cede and release to the people of the state of New York, forever, all the right or title of the said nation to lands within the said state: and the claim of the said nation to lands within the said state, is hereby wholly and finally extinguished.

In testimony whereof, the said commissioner, the said agents, and the said deputies, have hereunto, and to two other acts of the same tenor and date, one to remain with the United States, one to remain with the said State, and one delivered to the said deputies, to remain with the said nation, set their hands and seals, at the city of Albany, in the said State, the twenty-ninth day of March, in the year one thousand seven hundred and ninety-seven.

Isaac Smith, Abm. Ten Broeck, Egbt. Benson, Ezra L'Hommedieu, Jos. Brandt, John Deserontyon,

Witnesses: Robert Yates, John Tayler, Chas. Williamson, Thomas Morris, The mark of x John Abeel, alias the Cornplanter, a chief of the Senekas.
Subscribed in presence of Nat. W. Howell.

TREATY WITH THE CHEROKEE {1798, Oct. 2}

Articles of a Treaty between the United States of America, and the Cherokee Indians.

WHEREAS, the treaty made and concluded on Holston River, on the second day of July, in the year one thousand seven hundred and ninety-one, between the United States of America, and the Cherokee nation of Indians, had not been carried into execution, for some time thereafter, by reason of some misunderstandings which had arisen: And whereas, in order to remove such misunderstandings, and to provide for carrying the said treaty into effect, and for reestablishing more fully the peace and friendship between the parties, another treaty was held, made and concluded by and between them, at Philadelphia, the twenty-sixth day of June, in the year one thousand seven hundred and ninety-four: In which, among other things, it was stipulated, that the boundaries mentioned in the fourth article of the said treaty of Holston, should be actually ascertained and marked, in the manner prescribed by the said article, whenever the Cherokee nation should have ninety days' notice of the time and place at which the commissioners of the United States intended to commence their operation:

And whereas further delays in carrying the said fourth article into complete effect did take place, so that the boundaries mentioned and described therein, were not regularly ascertained and marked, until the latter part of the year, one thousand seven hundred and ninety-seven: before which time, and for want of knowing the direct course of the said boundary, divers settlements were made, by divers citizens of the United States, upon the Indian lands over and beyond the boundaries so mentioned and described in the said article, and contrary to the intention of the said treaties: but which settlers were removed from the said Indian lands, by authority of the United States, as soon after the boundaries had been so lawfully ascertained and marked as the nature of the case had admitted: And whereas, for the purpose of doing justice to the Cherokee nation of Indians, and remedying inconveniences arising to citizens of the United States from the adjustment of the boundary line between the lands of the Cherokees and those of the United States, or the citizens thereof, or from any other cause in relation to the Cherokees; and in order to promote the interests and safety of the said states, and the citizens thereof, the President of the United States, by and with the advice and consent of the Senate thereof, hath appointed George Walton, of Georgia.

And the President of the United States hath also appointed Lieutenant-Colonel Thomas Butler, commanding the troops of the United States, in the state of Tennessee, to be commissioners for the purpose aforesaid: And who, on the part of the United States, and the Cherokee nation, by the undersigned chiefs

51

and warriors, representing the said nation, have agreed to the following articles, namely:

ARTICLE 1. The peace and friendship subsisting between the United States and the Cherokee people, are hereby renewed, continued, and declared perpetual.

ARTICLE 2. The treaties subsisting between the present contracting parties, are acknowledged to be of full and operating force; together with the construction and usage under their respective articles, and so to continue.

ARTICLE 3. The limits and boundaries of the Cherokee nation, as stipulated and marked by the existing treaties between the parties, shall be and remain the same, where not altered by the present treaty.

ARTICLE 4. in acknowledgement for the protection of the United States, and for the considerations hereinafter expressed and contained, the Cherokee nation agree, and do hereby relinquish and cede to the United States, all the lands within the following points and lines, viz: From a point on the Tennessee river, below Tellico block-house, called the Wild-cat Rock, in a direct line to the Militia spring, near the Maryville road leading from Tellico. From the said spring to the Chill-bowie mountain, by a line so to be run, as will leave all the farms on Nine-mile Creek to the Northward and eastward of it; and to be continued along Chill-bowie mountain, until it strikes Hawkins's line. Thence along the said line to the great Iron mountain; and from the top of which a line to be continued in a southeastwardly course to where the most southwardly branch of Little river crosses the divisional line to Tugga-loe river: From the place of beginning, the Wild-cat Rock, down the northeast margin of the Tennessee river (not including islands)to a point or place one mile above the junction of that river with the Clinch, and from thence by a line to be drawn in a right angle, until it intersects Hawkins's line leading from Clinch. Thence down the said line to the river Clinch; thence up the said river to its junction with Emmery's river; and thence up Emmery's river to the foot of Cumberland mountain. From thence a line to be drawn, northeastwardly, along the foot of the mountain, until it intersects with Campbell's line.

ARTICLE 5. To prevent all future misunderstanding about the line described in the foregoing article, two commissioners shall be appointed to superintend the running and marking the same, where not ascertained by the rivers, immediately after signing this treaty; one to be appointed by the commissioners of the United States, and the other by the Cherokee nation; and who shall cause three maps or charts thereof to be made out; one whereof shall be transmitted and deposited in the war office of the United States; another with the executive of the state of Tennessee, and the third with the Cherokee nation, which said line shall form a part of the boundary between the United States and the Cherokee nation.

ARTICLE 6. In consideration of the relinquishment and cession hereby made, the United States upon signing the present treaty, shall cause to be delivered to the Cherokees, goods, wares and merchandise, to the amount of five thousand dollars, and shall cause to be delivered, annually, other goods, to the amount of one thousand dollars, in addition to the annuity already provided for; and will continue the guarantee of the remainder of their country for ever, as made and contained in former treaties.

ARTICLE 7. The Cherokee nation agree, that the Kentucky road, running between the Cumberland mountain and the Cumberland river, where the same shall pass through the Indian land, shall be an open and free road for the use of the citizens of the United States in like manner as the road from Southwest point to Cumberland river. In consideration of which it is hereby agreed on the part of the United States, that until settlements shall make it improper, the Cherokee hunters shall be at liberty to hunt and take game upon the lands relinquished and ceded by this treaty.

ARTICLE 8. Due notice shall be given to the principal towns of the Cherokees, of the time proposed for delivering the annual stipends; and sufficient supplies of provisions shall be furnished, by and at the expense of the United States, to subsist such reasonable number that may be sent, or shall attend to receive them during a reasonable time.

ARTICLE 9. It is mutually agreed between the parties, that horses stolen and not returned within ninety days, shall be paid for at the rate of sixty dollars each; if stolen by a white man, citizen of the United States, the Indian proprietor shall be paid in cash; and if stolen by an Indian from a citizen, to be deducted as expressed in the fourth article of the treaty-of Philadelphia. This article shall have retrospect to the commencement of the first conferences at this place in the present year, and no further. And all animosities, aggressions, thefts and plunderings, prior to that day shall cease, and be no longer remembered or demanded on either side.

ARTICLE 10. The Cherokee nation agree, that the agent who shall be appointed to reside among them from time to time, shall have a sufficient piece of ground allotted for his temporary use.

And lastly, This treaty, and the several articles it contains, shall be considered as additional to, and forming a part of, treaties already subsisting between the United States and the Cherokee nation, and shall be carried into effect on both sides, with all good faith as soon as the same shall be approved and ratified by the President of the United States, and the Senate thereof.

In witness of all and every thing herein determined between the United States of America, and the whole Cherokee nation, the parties hereunto set their hands and seals in the council house, near Tellico, on Cherokee ground, and within the United States, this second day of October, in the year one thousand seven hundred and ninety-eight, and in the twenty-third year of the independence and sovereignty of the United States.

Thos. Butler, Geo. Walton, Nenetuah, or Bloody Fellow, his x mark, Ostaiah, his x mark, Jaunne, or John, his x mark, Oortlokecteh, his x mark, Chockonnistaller, or Stallion, his x mark, Noothoietah, his x mark, Kunnateelah, or Rising Fawn, his x mark, Utturah, or Skin Worm, his x mark, Weelee, or Will, his x mark, Oolasoteh, his x mark, Tlorene, his x mark, Jonnurteekee, or Little John, Oonatakoteekee, his x mark, Kanowsurhee, or Broom, his x mark, Yonah Oolah, Bear at Home, his x mark, Tunksalenee, or Thick Legs, his x mark, Oorkullaukee, his x mark, Kumamah, or Butterfly, his x mark, Chattakuteehee, his x mark,

Witnesses: Elisha I. Hall, secretary of the commission, Silas Dinsmoor, Indian agent to the Cherokees, Kanitta, or Little Turkey, his x mark, Kettegiskie, his x mark, Tauquotihee, or the Glass, his x mark, Chuquilatague, his x mark, Salleekookoolah, his x mark, Tallotuskee, his x mark, Chellokee, his x mark, Tuskeegatee, or Long Fellow, his x mark, Neekaanneah, or Woman Holder, his x mark, Kulsateehee, his x mark, Keetakeuskah, or Prince, his x mark, Charley, his x mark, Akooh, his x mark, Sawanookeh, his x mark, Yonahequah, or Big Bear, his x mark, Keenahkunnah, his x mark, Kaweesoolaskee, his x mark, Teekakalohenah, his x mark, Ookouseteeh, or John Taylor, his x mark.

TREATY WITH THE CHICKASAW {1801, Oct. 24}
Ratified, May 1, 1802.
Proclaimed, May 4, 1802.

A treaty, of reciprocal advantages and mutual convenience between the United States of America and the Chickasaws.

THE President of the United States of America, by James Wilkinson brigadier general in the service of the United States, Benjamin Hawkins of North Carolina, and Andrew Pickens of South Carolina, commissioners of the United States, who are vested with full powers, and the Mingco, principal men and warriors of the Chickasaw nation, representing the said nation, have agreed to the following articles.

ARTICLE 1. The Mingco, principal men and warriors of the Chickasaw nation of Indians, give leave and permission to the President of the United States of America, to lay out, open and make a convenient wagon road through their land between the settlements of Mero District in the state of Tennessee, and those of Natchez in the Mississippi Territory, in such way and manner as he may deem proper; and the same shall be a high way for the citizens of the United States, and the Chickasaws. The Chickasaws shall appoint two discreet men to serve as assistants, guides or pilots, during the time of laying out and opening the road, under the direction of the officer charged with that duty, who shall have a reasonable compensation for their service: Provided always, that the necessary ferries over the water courses crossed by the said road shall be held and deemed to be the property of the Chickasaw nation.

ARTICLE 2. The commissioners of the United States give to the Mingco of the Chickasaws, and the deputation of that nation, goods to the value of seven hundred dollars, to compensate him and them and their attendants for the expense and inconvenience they may have sustained by their respectful and friendly attention to the President of the United States of America, and to the request made to them in his name to permit the opening of the road. And as the persons, towns, villages, lands, hunting grounds, and other rights and property of the Chickasaws, as set forth in the treaties or stipulations heretofore entered into between the contracting parties, more especially in and by a certificate of the President of the United Sates of America, under their seal of the first of July 1794, are in the peace and under the protection of the United States, the commissioners of the United States do hereby further agree, that the President of the United States of America, shall take such measures from time to time, as he may deem proper, to assist the Chickasaws to preserve entire all their rights against the encroachments of unjust neighbors, of which he shall be the judge, and also to preserve and perpetuate friendship and brotherhood between the white people and the Chickasaws.

ARTICLE 3. The commissioners of the United States may, if they deem it advisable, proceed immediately to carry the first article into operation; and the treaty shall take effect and be obligatory on the contracting parties, as soon as the same shall have been ratified by the President of the United States of America, by and with the advice and consent of the Senate of the United States.

In testimony whereof, we, the plenipotentiaries, have hereunto subscribed our names and affixed our seals, at Chickasaw Bluffs, the twenty-fourth of October, 1801.

James Wilkinson, Brigadier General, Benjamin Hawkins, Andw. Pickens, Chimnimbe Mingo, his x mark, Immuttauhaw, his x mark, Chumaube, his x mark, George Colbert, his x mark, William McGillivray, his x mark, Opiehoomuh, his x mark, Olohtohopoie, his x mark, Minkemattauhau, his x mark, Tuskkoopoie, his x mark, William Glover, his x mark, Thomas Brown, his x mark, William Colbert, W.C. Mooklushopoie, his x mark, Opoieolauhtau, his x mark, Teschoolauhtau, his x mark, Teschoolauptau, his x mark, James Underwood, his x mark, Samuel Mitchell, agent to the Chickasaws, Malcolm McGee, his x signature, interpreter to the Chickasaws, William R. Bootes, captain Third Regiment and aid de camp, J. B. Wallach, lieutenant and aid de camp, Jn. Wilson, lieutenant Third Regiment, Chochuchee, his x mark, John W. Hooker, United States factor, Edw. Butler, captain commanding at Tellleo, Robert Purdy, lieutenant Fourth U. S. Regiment, Ludwell Grymes, Jno. McDonald, Daniel Ross, Mattw. Wallace, esquire.

TREATY WITH THE CHOCTAW {1801, Dec. 17}
Ratified April 30, 1802.
Proclaimed May 4, 1802.

A treaty of friendship, limits and accommodation between the United States of America and the Chactaw nation of Indians.

THOMAS JEFFERSON, President of the United States of America, by James Wilkinson, of the state of Maryland, Brigadier-General in the army of the United States, Benjamin Hawkins, of North Carolina, and Andrew Pickens, of South Carolina, commissioners plenipotentiary of the United States on the one part, and the Mingos, principal men and warriors of the Chactaw nation, representing the said nation in council assembled, on the other part, have entered into the following articles and conditions, viz:

ARTICLE 1. Whereas the United States in Congress assembled, did by their commissioners Plenipotentiary, Benjamin Hawkins, Andrew Pickens, and Joseph Martin, at a treaty held with the chiefs and head men of the Chactaw nation at Hopewell, on the Keowe, the third day of January, in the year of our Lord, one thousand seven hundred and eighty-six, give peace to the said nation, and receive it into the favor and protection of the United States of America; it is agreed by the parties to these presents respectively, that the Chactaw nation, or such part of it as may reside within the limits of the United States, shall be and continue under the care and protection of the said States; and that the mutual confidence and friendship which are hereby acknowledged to subsist between the contracting parties shall be maintained and perpetuated.

ARTICLE 2. The Mingos principal men and warriors of the Chactaw nation of Indians, do hereby give their free consent, that a convenient and durable wagon way may be explored, marked, opened and made under the orders and instructions of the President of the United States, through their lands to commence at the northern extremity of the settlements of the Mississippi Territory, and to be extended from thence, by such route as may be selected and surveyed under the authority of the President of the United States, until it shall strike the lands claimed by the Chickasaw nation; and the same shall be and continue for ever, a high-way for the citizens of the United States and the Chactaws; and the said

Chactaws shall nominate two discreet men from their nation, who may be employed as assistants, guides or pilots, during the time of laying out and opening the said high-way, or so long as may be deemed expedient, under the direction of the officer charged with this duty, who shall receive a reasonable compensation for their services.

ARTICLE 3. The two contracting parties covenant and agree that the old line of demarkation heretofore established by and between the officers of his Britannic Majesty and the Chactaw nation, which runs in a parallel direction with the Mississippi river and eastward thereof, shall be retraced and plainly marked, in such way and manner as the President may direct, in the presence of two persons to be appointed by the said nation; and that the said line shall be the boundary between the settlements of the Mississippi Territory and the Chactaw nation. And the said nation does by these presents relinquish to the United States and quit claim for ever, all their right, title and pretension to the land lying between the said line and the Mississippi river, bounded south by the thirty-first degree of north latitude, and north by the Yazoo river, where the said line shall strike the same; and on the part of the commissioners it is agreed, that all persons who may be settled beyond this line, shall be removed within it, on the side towards the Mississippi, together with their slaves, household furniture, tools, materials and stock, and that the cabins or houses erected by such persons shall be demolished.

ARTICLE 4. The President of the United States may, at his discretion, proceed to execute the second article of this treaty; and the third article shall be carried into effect as soon as may be convenient to the government of the United States, and without unnecessary delay on the one part or the other, of which the President shall be the judge; the Chactaws to be seasonably advised, by order of the President of the United States, of the time when, and the place where, the re-survey and re-marking of the old line referred to in the preceding article, will be commenced.

ARTICLE 5. The commissioners of the United States, for and in consideration of the foregoing concessions on the part of the Chactaw nation, and in full satisfaction for the same, do give and deliver to the Mingos, chiefs and warriors of the said nation, at the signing of these presents, the value of two thousand dollars in goods and merchandise, net cost of Philadelphia, the receipt whereof is hereby acknowledged; and they further engage to give three sets of blacksmith's tools to the said nation.

ARTICLE 6. This treaty shall take effect and be obligatory on the contracting parties, so soon as the same shall be ratified by the President of the United States of America, by and with the advice and consent of the Senate thereof.
In testimony whereof, the commissioners plenipotentiary of the United States, and the Mingos, principal men, and warriors, of the Choctaw nation, have

hereto subscribed their names and affixed their seals, at Fort Adams, on the Mississippi, this seventeenth day of December, in the year of our Lord one thousand eight hundred and one, and of the independence of the United States the twenty-sixth.

James Wilkinson, Benjamin Hawkins, Andrew Pickens, Tuskona Hopoia, his x mark, Toota Homo, his x mark, Mingo Hom Massatubby, his x mark, Oak Shumme, his x mark, Mingo Pooscoos, his x mark, Buckshun Nubby, his x mark, Shappa Homo, his x mark, Hiupa Homo, his x mark, Illatalla Homo, his x mark, Hoehe Homo, his x mark, Tuspena Chaabe, his x mark, Muclusha Hopoia, his x mark, Capputanne Thlueco, his x mark, Robert McClure, his x mark, Poosha Homo, his x mark,
Baka Lubbe, his x mark,

Witnesses present: Alexander Macomb, jun. secretary to the commission, John McKee, deputy Superintendent, and agent to the Choctaws, Henry Gaither, lieutenant colonel, commandant, John H. Brull, major, Second Regiment Infantry, Bw. Shaumburgh, captain, Second Regiment Infantry, Frans. Jones, Assistant Quartermaster General Benjamin Wilkinson, lieutenant and paymaster, Third United States Regiment, J.B. Walbach, aid-de-camp to the commanding general, J. Wilson, lieutenant, Third Regiment Infantry, Samuel Jeton, lieutenant, Second Regiment of Artillery and Engineers, John F. Carmichael, surgeon, Third Regiment United States Army, Saml. Hanly, Michael McKinsey, Chas. Hicks, interpreter, James Cazey, interpreter, John Thompson,

TREATY WITH THE SENECA {1802, June 30}
Ratified Jan. 12,1803:
Proclaimed Jan.12 1803.

This Indenture, made the thirtieth day of June, in the year of our Lord one thousand eight hundred and two, between the Sachems, Chief, and Warriors of the Seneca nation of indians, of the first part, and Wi/hem Wi//ink, Pieter Van Eeghen, Hendrik Vol/enhoven, W Wi//ink the younger, I Wi/link the younger (son of Jan) Jan Gabriel Van Staphorst, Roe/of Van Staphorst, the younger, Come/is Vollen-hoven, and Hendrik Seye, a/I of the city ofAmsterdam, and repubik ofBatavia, by Joseph El/icott, esquire, their agent and attorney, of the second part

WHEREAS at a treaty held under the authority of the United States with the said Seneca nation of Indians, at Buffalo creek, in the county of Ontario, and state of New-York, on the day of the date of these presents, by the honorable John Taylor, esquire, a commissioner appointed by the President of the United States to hold the same, in pursuance of the constitution, and of the act of the Congress of the United States, in such case made and provided, a con-

58

vention was entered into in the presence and with the approbation of the said commissioner, between the said Seneca nation of Indians and the said Wilhelm Willink, Pieter Van Eeghen, Hendrik Vollenhoven, W. Willink the younger, I. Willink the younger (son of Jan) Jan Gabriel Van Staphorst, Roelof Van Staphorst the younger, Cornelis Vollenhoven, and Hendrik Seye, by the said Joseph Ellicott, their agent and attorney, lawifilly constituted and appointed for that purpose.

NOW THIS INDENTURE WITNESSETH, That the said parties of the first part, for and in consideration of the lands hereinafter described, do hereby exchange, cede, and forever quit claim to the said parties of the second part, their heirs and assigns, ALL those lands situate, lying and being in the county of Ontario and state ofNew-York, being part of the lands described and reserved by the said parties of the first part, in a treaty or convention held by the honoraNe Jeremiah Wadsworth, esquire, under the authority of the United States on the Genesee river the 15th day of September, one thousand seven hundred and ninety-seven, in words following, viz:

"BEGINNJNG at the mouth of the eighteen mile or Kogh-quaw-gu creek, thence a line or lines to be drawn parallel to lake Erie, at the distance of one mile from the lake, to the mouth of Cataraugos creek, thence a line or lines extending twelve miles up the north side of said creek, at the distance of one mile therefrom, thence a direct line to the said creek, thence down the said creek to lake Erie, thence along the lake, to the first mentioned creek, and thence to the place of beginmng. Also one other piece at Cataraugos, beginning at the shore of lake Erie, on the south side of Cataraugos creek, at the distance of one mile from the mouth thereof; thence running one mile from the lake, thence on a line parallel thereto, to a point within one mile from the Con-non-dau-we-gea creek, thence up the said creek one mile on a line parallel thereto, thence on a direct line to the said creek, thence down the same to lake Erie, thence along the.lake to the place of beginning;" reference being thereunto had will fully appear. TOGETHER with all and singular the rights, privileges, hereditaments and appurtenances thereunto belonging, or in any wise appertaining. AND all the estate, right, title, and interest whatsoever, of them, the said parties of the first part, and their nation, of; in and to the said tracts of land, above described, TO HAVE AND TO HOLD all and singular the said granted premises, with the appurtenances, to the said parties of the second part, their heirs and assigns, to their only proper use, benefit and behoof forever.

AND in consideration of the said lands described and ceded as aforesaid, the said parties of the second part, by Joseph Ellicott, their agent and attorney as aforesaid, do hereby exchange, cede, release, and quit claim to the said parties of the first part, and their nation (the said parties of the second part, reserving to themselves the right of preemption) all that certain tract or parcel of land situate as aforesaid. BEGINNING at a post marked No.0. standing on the bank of lake Erie, at the mouth of Cataraugos creek, and on the north bank thereof; thence along the shore of said lake N. 110 E. 21 chains; N. thirteen degrees east 45 chains; N. 9O E. 14 chains 65 links to a post; thence east 119 chains to a post; thence south 4 chains 27 links to a post; thence east 640 chains to a post standing in the meridian between the 8th and 9th ranges; thence along said meridian south 617 chains 75 links, to a post standing on the south bank of Cataraugos creek; thence west 160 chains to a post; thence north 290 chains 25 links to a post; thence west 482 chains 31 links to a post; thence north 219 chains 50 links to a post standing on the north bank of Cataraugos creek; thence down the same and along the several meanders thereof, to the place of beginning. To HOLD to the said parties of the first part in the same manner and by the same tenure as the lands reserved by the said parties of the first part in and by the said treaty or convention entered into on Genesee river, the 15th day of September, one thousand seven hundred and ninety-seven, as aforesaid, were intended to be held.

In testimony whereof, the parties to these presents have hereunto, and to two other indentures of the same tenor and date, one to remain with the United States, one to remain with the said parties of the first part, and one other to remain with the said parties of the second part, interchangeably set their hands and seals the day and year first above written. Conneatiu, his x mark, Koeentwahka, or Corn Planter, his x mark, Wondongoohka, his x mark, Tekonnondu, his x mark, Tekiaindau, his x mark, Sagooyes, his x mark, Towyocauna, or Blue Sky, his x mark, Koyingquautah or Young King, his x mark, Kaoundoowand, or Pollard, his x mark, Connawaudeau, his x mark, Soonoyou, his x mark, Auwennausa, his x mark, Soogooyawautau, or Red Jacket, his x mark, Coshkoutough, his x mark, Teyokaihossa, his x mark, Onayawos, or Farmer's Brother, his x mark, Sonaugoies, his x mark, Oishkaka, or Little Billy, his x mark, Sussaoowau, his mark, Wuhem Willink, Pieter Van Beghen, Hendflk Vollenhoven, W. Willink, the younger, I. Willink, the younger, (son of Jan), Jan Gabriel Van Staphorst, Roelof Van Staphorst, the younger, Cornelia Vollenhoven, and Hendrik Seye, by their attorney, Joseph Ellicott.

Sealed and delivered in the presence of John Thomson, Israel Chapin, James W. Stevens, Horatio Jones, Jasper Parfish, Interpreters.

Done at a full and general treaty of the Seneka nation of Indians, held at Buffalo creek, in the county of Ontario, and State of New York, on the thirteenth day of June, in the year of our Lord one thousand eight hundred and two, under the authority of the United States.

In testimony whereof, I have hereunto set my hand and seal, the day and year aforesaid.

John Tayler.

TREATY WITH THE SENECA {1802, June 30}
Ratified Feb. 7,1803.
Proclaimed, Feb. 7,1803.

At a treaty he/d under the authority of the United States, at Buffa/o Creek in the county of Ontario, and state ofNew- York between the Sachems, Chief and Warriors of the Seneca Nation of Indians, on behaTfofsaid nation, and Oliver Pheips, Esq. of the county of Ontario, Isaac Bronson, Esq. of the city ofNew-York and Horatio Jones, of the said county of On tano, in the presence of John Tay/er, President of the United States Esq. Commissioner appointed by the for ho/ding said treaty.

KNOW ALL MEN by these presents, that the said Sachems, Chiefs and Warriors, for and in consideration of the sum of twelve hundred dollars, lawful money of the United States, unto them in hand paid by the said Oliver Phelps, Isaac Bronson and Horatio Jones, at or immediately before the sealing and delivery hereof; the receipt whereof is hereby acknowledged, HAVE and by those presents DO grant, remise, release and forever quit claim and confirm unto the said Oliver Isaac Bronson and Horatio Jones, and to their heirs and assigns, ALL that tract of land commonly called and known by the name of Little Beard's Reservation, situate, lying and being in the said county of Ontario, BOUNDED on the East by the Genesee river and Little Beard's Creek, on the south and west by other lands of the said parties of the second part, and on the north by Big Tree Reservationcontaining two square miles, or twelve hundred and eighty acres, together with all and singular, the hereditaments and appurtenances whatsoever thereunto belonging, or in any wise appertaining, to hold to them the said Oliver Phelps, Isaac Bronson and Horatio Jones, their heirs and assigns, to the only proper use and behoof of them the said Oliver Phelps, Isaac Bronson and Horatio Jones their heirs and assigns forever In terimony, the and commissioner have hereunto, and to two other instruments of the same tenor and date, one to remain with the United States, one to remain with the Seneka nation of Indians, and one to remain with the said Oliver Pheips, Isaac Bronson, and Horatio Jones, interchangeably set their hands and seals. Dated the 30th day of June, in the year of our Lord one thousand eight hundred and two.

Conneatiu, his x mark, Koeentwahka, or Corn Planter, his x mark, Wondongoohkta, his x mark, Tekonnondu, his x mark, Jekiaindau, his x mark, Sagooyes, his x mark, Touyocauna, or Blue Sky, his x mark, Koyingquautah, or Young King, his x mark, Soogooyawautau, or Red Jacket, his x mark, Onayawos, or Farmer's Brother, his x mark, Kaoundoowand, or Pollard, his x mark, Auwermausa, his x mark.

Sealed and delivered in the presence of
John Thomson, James W. Stevens, Israel Chapin, Jasper Parrish, interpreter.

TREATY WITH THE CHOCTAW {1802, Oct. 17}
Ratified June 20, 1803.
Proclaimed Jan. 20, 1803.

A provisional convention entered into and made by brigadier general James Wilkinson, of the state of Maryland, commissioner for holding conferences with the Indians south of the Ohio River, in behalf of the United States, on the one part, and the whole Choctaw nation, by their chiefs, head men, and principal warriors, on the other part.

Preamble. For the mutual accommodation of the parties, and to perpetuate that concord and friendship, which so happily subsists between them, they do hereby freely, voluntarily, and without constraint, covenant and agree,

ARTICLE 1. That the President of the United States may, at his discretion, by a commissioner or commissioners, to be appointed by him, by and with the advice and consent of the Senate of the United States, retrace, connect, and plainly remark the old line of limits, established by and between his Britannic majesty and the said Choctaw nation, which begins on the left bank of the Chickasawhay river and runs thence in an easterly direction to the right bank of the Tombigby river, terminating on the same, at a bluff well known by the name of Hach-a-Tig-geby, but it is to be clearly understood, that two commissioners, to be appointed by the said nation, from their own body, are to attend the commissioner or commissioners of the United States, who may be appointed to perform this service, for which purpose the said Choctaw nation shall be seasonably advised by the President of the United States, of the particular period at which the operation may be commenced, and the said Choctaw commissioners shall be subsisted by the United States, so long as they may be engaged on this business, and paid for their services, during the said term, at the rate of one dollar per day.

ARTICLE 2. The said line, when thus remarked and re-established, shall form the boundary between the United States and the said Choctaw nation in that quarter, and the said Choctaw nation, for, and in consideration of one dollar, to them in hand paid by the said United States, the receipt whereof is hereby acknowledged, do hereby release to the said United States, and quit claim for ever, to all that tract of land which is included by the beforenamed line on the north, by the Chickasawhay river on the west, by the Tombigby and the Mobile rivers on the east, and by the boundary of the United States on the south.

ARTICLE 3. The chiefs, head men, and warriors, of the said Choctaw nation, do hereby constitute, authorise and appoint, the chiefs and head men of the upper towns of the said nation, to make such alteration in the old boundary line near the mouth of the Yazou river, as may be found convenient, and may be done without injury to the said nation.

ARTICLE 4. This convention shall take effect and become obligatory on the contracting parties as soon as the President of the United States, by and with the advice and consent of the Senate, shall have ratified the same.

In testimony whereof, the parties have hereunto set their hands and affixed their seals, at Fort Confederation, on the Tombigbee, in the Choctaw country, this 17th day of October, in the year of our Lord, one thousand eight hundred and two, and of the independence of the United Sates the twenty-seventh.

James Wilkinson,

In behalf of the lower towns and Chicasawhay: Tuskona Hoopoio, his x mark, Mingo Pooskoos, his x mark, Mingo Pooskoos, 2d, his x mark, Poosha Matta-haw, his x mark.

In behalf of the upper towns: Oak Chummy, his x mark, Tuskee Maiaby, his x mark,

TREATY WITH THE DELAWARES, ETC. {1803, June 7}
Proclamation Dec. 26, 1803.

Articles of a treaty between the United States of America, and the Delawares, Shawanoes, Putawatimies, Miamies, Eel River, Weeas, Kickapoos, Pianka-shaws, and Kaskaskias nations of Indians.

ARTICLES of a treaty made at Fort Wayne on the Miami of the Lake, between William Henry Harrison, governor of the Indiana territory, superintendent of Indian affairs and commissioner plenipotentiary of the United States for con-cluding any treaty or treaties which may be found necessary with any of the Indian tribes north west of the Ohio, of the one part, and the tribes of Indians called the Delawares, Shawa-noes, Putawatimies, Miamies and Kickapoos, by their chiefs and head warriors, and those of the Eel river, Weeas, Piankashaws and Kaskaskias by their agents and representatives Tuthinipee, Winnemac., Richerville and Little Turtle (who are properly authorized by the said tribes) of the other part.

ARTICLE 1. Whereas it is declared by the fourth article of the treaty of Greenville, that the United States reserve for their use the post of St. Vincennes and all the lands adjacent to which the Indian titles had been extinguished: And whereas, it has been found difficult to determine the precise limits of the said tract as held by the French and British governments: it is hereby agreed, that the boundaries of the said tract shall be as follow: Beginning at Point Coupee on the Wabash, and running thence by a line north seventy-eight degrees, west twelve miles, thence by a line parallel to the general course of the Wabash, until it shall be intersected by a line at right angles to the same, passing through the mouth of White river, thence by the last mentioned line across the Wabash and towards the Ohio seventy-two miles, thence by a line north twelve degrees west, until it shall be intersected by a line at right angles to the same, passing through Point Coupee, and by the last mentioned line to the place of beginning.

ARTICLE 2. The United States hereby relinquish all claim which they may have had to any lands adjoining to or in the neighborhood of the tract above described.

ARTICLE 3. As a mark of their regard and attachment to the United States, whom they acknowledge for their only friends and protectors, and for the consideration herein after mentioned, the said tribes do hereby relinquish and cede to the United States the great salt spring upon the Saline creek which falls into the Ohio below the mouth of the Wabash, with a quantity of land surrounding it, not exceeding four miles square, and which may be laid off in a square or oblong as the one or the other may be found most convenient to the United States: And the said United States being desirous that the Indian tribes should participate in the benefits to be derived from the said spring, hereby engage to deliver yearly and every year for the use of the said Indians, a quantity of salt not exceeding one hundred and fifty bushels, and which shall be divided among the several tribes in such manner as the general council of the chiefs may determine.

ARTICLE 4. For the considerations before mentioned and for the convenience which the said tribes will themselves derive from such establishments it is hereby agreed that as soon as the tribes called the Kickapoos, Eel Rivet', Weeas, Piankashaws and Kaskaskias shall give their consent to the measure, the United States shall have the right of locating three tracts of lands (of such size as may be agreed upon with the last mentioned tribes) on the main road between Vincennes and Kaskaskias, and one other between Vincennes and Clarksville for the purpose of erecting houses of entertainment for the accommodation of travellers. But it is expressly understood that if the said locations are made on any of the rivers, which cross the said road, and ferries should be established on the same, that in times of high water any Indian or Indians belonging to either of the tribes who are parties to this treaty shall have the privilege of crossing such ferry toll free.

ARTICLE 5. Whereas there is reason to believe that if the boundary lines of the tract described in the first article should be run in the manner therein directed, that some of the settlements and locations of land made by the citizens of the United States will fall in the Indian countryIt is hereby agreed that such alterations shall be made in the direction of these lines as will include them; and a quantity of land equal in quantity to what may be thus taken shall be given to the said tribes either at the east or the west end of the tract.

In testimony whereof, the commissioner of the United States, and the chiefs and warriors of the Delawares, Shawanees, Pattawatimas, Miamis, and Kickapoos, and those of the Eel Rivers, Weas, Piankeshaws, and Kaskaskias, by their agents and representatives Tuthinipee, Winnemac, Richewille, and the Little Turtle, who are properly authorized, by the said tribes, have hereunto subscribed their names and affixed their seals, at fort Wayne, this seventh day of June, in the year of our Lord one thousand eight hundred and three, and of the independence of the United States the twenty-seventh.

William Henry Harrison

Miamis: Richewille, his x mark, Meseekunnoghquoh, or Little Turtle, his x mark,
On behalf of themselves: Eel Rivers, Weas, Piankeshaws and Kaskaskias, whom they represent.
Kickapoos: Nehmehtohah, or standing, his x mark, Pashsheweha, or cat, his x mark,
Shawanees: Neahmemsieeh, his x mark, Pattawatimas:Tuthinipee, his x mark, Winnemac, his x mark,
On behalf of the Pattawatimas, and Eel Rivers, Weas, Piankeshaws, and Kaskaskias, whom they represent:
Wannangsea, or five medals, his x mark, Keesas, or sun, his x mark,
 Delawares: Teta Buxike, his x mark, Bukongehelas, his x mark, Hockingpomskenn, his x mark, Kechkawhanund, his x mark,
 Shawanees: Cuthewekasaw, or Black Hoof, his x mark, Methawnasice, his x mark,

Signed, sealed, and delivered in the presence of: J. R. Jones, secretary to commission, John Gibson, Secretary Indian Territory, Tho. Pasteur, captain, First Regiment Infantry, William Wells, interpreter, John Johnson, United States factor, H. Aupaumut, chief of Muhhecon, Thomas Freeman.

The proceedings at the within treaty were faithfully interpreted by us, John Gibson and William Wells; that is, for the Delawares, John Gibson, and for the rest of the tribes, William Wells. Latalahomah, his x mark, Mooklahoosoopoieh, his x mark, Mingo Horn Astubby, his x mark, Tuskahomah, his x mark,

Witnesses present: Silas Dinsmoor, Agent to the Choctaws, John Pitchlynn, Turner Brashears, Peter H. Naisalis, John Long, Interpreters.

TREATY WITH THE DELAWARES {1804, Aug. 18}
Ratified Jan. 21, 1805.
Proclaimed Feb. 14, 1805.

A treaty between the United States of America and the Delaware tribe of Indians.

THE Delaware tribe of Indians finding that the annuity which they receive from the United States, is not sufficient to supply them with the articles which are necessary for their comfort and convenience, and afford the means of introducing amongst them the arts of civilized life, and being convinced that the extensiveness of the country they possess, by giving an opportunity to their hunting parties to ramble to a great distance from their towns, is the principal means of retarding this desirable event; and the United States being desirous to connect their settlements on the Wabash with the state of Kentucky: therefore the said United States, by William Henry Harrison, governor of the Indiana territory, superintendent of Indian affairs, and their commissioner plenipotentiary for treating with the Indian tribes northwest of the Ohio river; and the said tribe of Indians, by their sachems, chiefs, and head warriors, have agreed to the following articles, which when ratified by the President of the United States, by and with the advice and consent of the Senate, shall be binding on the said parties.

ARTICLE 1. The said Delaware tribe, for the considerations hereinafter mentioned, relinquishes to the United States forever, all their right and title to the tract of country which lies between the Ohio and Wabash rivers, and below the tract ceded by the treaty of Fort Wayne, and the road leading from Vincennes to the falls of Ohio.

ARTICLE 2. The said tribe shall receive from the United States for ten years, an additional annuity of three hundred dollars, which is to be exclusively appropriated to the purpose of ameliorating their condition and promoting their civilization. Suitable persons shall be employed at the expense of the United States to teach them to make fences, cultivate the earth, and such of the domestic arts as are adapted to their situation; and a further sum of three hundred dollars shall be appropriated annually for five years to this object. The United States will cause to be delivered to them in the course of the next spring, horses fit for draft, cattle, hogs and implements of husbandry to the amount of four hundred dollars, The preceding stipulations together with goods to the amount of eight hundred dollars which is now delivered to the said tribe, (a part of which is to be appropriated to the satisfying certain officials of the said tribe, whose horses have been taken by white people) is to be considered as full compensation for the relinquishment made in the first article.

ARTICLE 3. As there is great reason to believe that there are now in the possession of the said tribe, several horses which have been stolen from citizens of the United States, the chiefs who represent the said tribe are to use their utmost endeavors to have the said horses forthwith delivered to the superintendent of Indian affairs or such persons as he may appoint to receive them. And as the United States can place the utmost reliance on the honor and integrity of those chiefs who have manifested a punctilious regard to the engagements entered into at the treaty of Grenville, it is agreed that in relation to such of the horses stolen as aforesaid, but which have died or been removed beyond the reach of the chiefs, the United States will compensate the owners for the loss of them without deducting from the annuity of the said tribe the amount of what may be paid in this way. But it is expressly understood that this provision is not to extend to any horses which have been stolen within the course of twelve months preceding the date hereof.

ARTICLE 4. The said tribe having exhibited to the above-named commissioner of the United States sufficient proof of their right to all the country which lies between the Ohio and White river, and the Miami tribe who were the original proprietors of the upper part of that country having explicitly acknowledged the title of the Delawares at the general council held at Fort Wayne in the month of June, 1803, the said United States will in future consider the Delawares as the rightful owners of all the country which is bounded by the white river on the north, the Ohio on the south, the general boundary line running from the mouth of the Kentucky river on the east, and the tract ceded by this treaty, and that ceded by the treaty of Fort Wayne, on the west and south west.

ARTICLE 5. As the Piankishaw tribe have hitherto obstinately persisted in refusing to recognize the title of the Delawares to the tract of country ceded by this treaty, the United States will negotiate with them and will endeavor to settle the matter, in an amicable way; but should they reject the propositions that may be made to them on this subject, and should the United States not think proper to take possession of the said country without their consent; the stipulations and promises herein made on behalf of the United States, shall be null and void.

ARTICLE 6. AS the road from Vincennes to Clark's grant will form a very inconvenient boundary, and as it is the intention of the parties to these presents that the whole of the said road shall be within the tract ceded to the United States, it is agreed that the boundary in that quarter shall be a straight line to be drawn parallel to the course of the said road from the eastern boundary of the tracts ceded by the treaty of Fort Wayne to Clark's grant; but the said line is not to pass at a greater distance than half a mile from the most northerly bend of said load.

In witness whereof, the commissioner plenipotentiary of the United States, and the chiefs and head men of the said tribe, have hereunto set their hands and affixed their seals.

Done at Vincennes, the eighteenth day of August, in the year of our Lord one thousand eight hundred and four; and of the independence of the United States the twenty-ninth.

William Henry Harrison, Jeta Buxika, his x mark, Bokongehelas, his x mark, Alimee, or Geo. White Eyes, his x mark, Hocking Pomskann, his x mark, Tomaguee, or the beaver, his x mark.

Signed, sealed, and delivered in the presence of: John Gibson, secretary to commission, Henry Vanderburg, judge of Indiana Territory, Vigo, colonel of Knox County, I. T. Militia, B. Parker, attorney-general of the Indiana Territory, John Rice Jones, of Indiana Territory, Robert Buntin, prothonotary of Knox County, Indiana Territory, Geo. Wallace, jr., of Indiana Territory, Antoine Marchal, of I. T, Joseph Barron, interpreter, Edward Hempstead, attorney at law.

I do certify, that each and every article of the foregoing treaty was carefully explained, and precisely interpreted, by me, to the Delaware chiefs who have signed the same.

John Gibson.

TREATY WITH THE WYANDOT, ETC. {1805, July 4}
Proclamation, Apt. 24, 1806.

A treaty between the United States of America, and the sachems, chiefs, and warriors of the Wyandot, Ottawa, Chipawa, Munsee and Delaware, Shawanee, and Pottawatima nations, holden at Fort Industry, on the Miami of the lake, on the fourth day of July, Anno Domini, one thousand eight hundred and five.

ARTICLE 1. The said Indian nations do again acknowledge themselves and all their tribes, to be in friendship with, and under the protection of the United States.

ARTICLE 2. The boundary line between the United States, and the nations aforesaid, shall in future be a meridian line drawn north and south, through a boundary to be erected on the south shore of lake Erie, one hundred and twenty miles due west of the west boundary line of the state of Pennsylvania, extending north until it intersects the boundary line of the United States, and extending south it intersects a line heretofore established by the treaty of Grenville.

ARTICLE 3. The Indian nations aforesaid, for the consideration of friendship to the United States, and the sums of money hereinafter mentioned, to be paid annually to the Wyandot, Shawnee, Munsee and Delaware nations, have ceded and do hereby cede and relinquish to said United States for ever, all the lands belonging to said United States, lying east of the aforesaid line, bounded southerly and easterly by the line established by said treaty of Grenville, and northerly by the northernmost part of the forty first degree of north latitude.

ARTICLE 4. The United States, to preserve harmony, manifest their liberality, and in consideration of the cession made in the preceding article, will, every year forever hereafter, at Detroit, or some other convenient place, pay and deliver to the Wyandot, Munsee, and Delaware nations, and those of the Shawanee and Seneca nations who reside with the Wyandots, the sum of eight hundred and twenty five dollars, current money of the United States, and the further sum of one hundred and seventy five dollars, making in the whole an annuity of one thousand dollars; which last sum of one hundred and seventy five dollars, has been secured to the President, in trust for said nations, by the Connecticut land company, and by the company incorporated by the name of "the proprietors of the half million acres of land lying south of lake Erie, called Sufferer's Land," payable annually as aforesaid, and to be divided between said nations, from time to time, in such proportions as said nations, with the approbation of the President, shall agree.

ARTICLE 5. To prevent all misunderstanding hereafter, it is to be expressly remembered, that the Ottawa and Chipawa nations, and such of the Pottawatima nation as reside on the river Huron of lake Erie, and in the neighborhood thereof, have received from the Connecticut land company, and the company incorporated by the name of "the proprietors of the half million acres of land lying south of Lake Erie, called Sufferer's Land," the sum of four thousand dollars in hand, and have secured to the President of the United States, in trust for them, the further sum of twelve thousand dollars, payable in six annual instalments of two thousand each; which several sums is the full amount of their proportion of the purchases effected by this treaty, and also by a treaty with said companies bearing even date herewith; which proportions were agreed on and concluded by the whole of said nations in their general council; which several sums, together with two thousand nine hundred and sixteen dollars and sixty seven cents, secured to the President, to raise said sum of one hundred and seventy five dollars annuity as aforesaid, is the amount of the consideration paid by the agents of the Connecticut Reserve, for the cession of their lands.

ARTICLE 6. The said Indian nations, parties to this treaty, shall be at liberty to fish and hunt within the territory and lands which they have now ceded to the United States, so long as they shall demean themselves peaceably.

In witness whereof, Charles Jouett, esquire, a commissioner on the part of the United States, and the sachems, chiefs, and warriors, of the Indian nations aforesaid, have hereto set their hands and seals.

Charles Jouett,

Ottawa: Nekeik, or Little Otter, his x mark, Kawachewan, or Eddy, his x mark, Mechimenduch, or Big Bowl, his x mark, Aubaway, his x mark, Ogonse, his x mark, Sawgamaw, his x mark, Tusquagan, or McCarty, his x mark, Tondaw-ganie, or the Dog, his x mark, Ashawet, his x mark,

Chippewa: Macquettoquet, or Little Bear, hisx mark, Quitehonequit, or Big Cloud, his x mark, Queoonequetwabaw, his x mark, Oseaquassanu, or Young Boy, his x mark, Monimaek, or Cat Fish, his x mark, Tonquish, his x mark,

Pattawatima: Noname, his x mark, Mogawh, his x mark,

Wyandot: Tarhee, or the Crane, his x mark, Miere, or Walk in Water, his x mark, Thateyyanayoh, or Leather Lips, his x mark, Harrowenyou, or Cherokee Boy, his x mark, Tschauendah, his x mark, Tahunehawettee, or Adam Brown, his x mark, Shawrunthie, his x mark,

Munsee and Delaware: Puckconsittonal, his x mark, Paahmehelot, his x mark, Pamoxet, or Armstrong, his x mark, Pappellelond, or Beaver Hat, his x mark,

Shawanee: Weyapurseawaw, or Blue Jacket, his x mark, Cutheaweasaw, or Black Hoff, his x mark, Auonasechla, or Civil Man, his x mark, Isaac Peters, his x mark,

In presence of: Wm. Dean, C. F. L. C, J. B. Mower, Jasper Parrish, Whitmore Knaggs, William Walker, Interpreters, Israel Ruland, E. Brush.

TREATY WITH THE CHICKASAW {1805, July 23}
Ratified May 22, 1807.
Proclaimed May 23, 1807.

Articles of arrangement made and concluded in the Chickasaw country, between James Robertson and Silas Dinsmoor, commissioners of the United States of the one part, and the Mingo chiefs and warriors of the Chickasaw nation of Indians on the other part.

ARTICLE 1. WHEREAS the Chickasaw nation of Indians have been for some time embarrassed by heavy debts due to their merchants and traders, and being destitute of funds to effect important improvements in their country, they have agreed and do hereby agree to cede to the United States, and forever quit claim to the tract of country included within the following bounds, to wit: beginning on the left bank of Ohio, at the point where the present Indian boundary adjoins the same, thence down the left bank of Ohio to the Tennessee river, thence up the main channel of the Tennessee river to the mouth of Duck river; thence up the left bank of Duck river to the Columbian highway or road leading from Nashville to Natchez, thence along the said road to the ridge dividing the waters running into Duck river from those running into Buffaloe river, thence easterly along the said ridge to the great ridge dividing the waters running into the main Tennessee river from those running into Buffaloe river near the main source of Buffaloe river, thence in a direct line to the Great Tennessee river near the Chickasaw old fields or eastern point of the Chickasaw claim on that river; thence northwardly to the great ridge dividing the waters running into the Tennessee from those running into Cumberland river, so as to include all the waters running into Elk river, thence along the top of the said great ridge to the place of beginning: reserving a tract of one mile square adjoining to, and below the mouth of Duck river on the Tennessee, for the use of the chief O'Koy or Tishumastubbee.

ARTICLE 2. The United States on their part, and in consideration of the above cession, agree to make the following payments, to wit: Twenty thousand dollars for the use of the nation at large, and for the payment of the debts due to their merchants and traders; and to George Colbert and O'Koy two thousand dollars, that is, to each one thousand dollars. This sum is granted to them at the request of the national council for services rendered their nation, and is to be subject to their individual order, witnessed by the resident agent; also to Chinubbee Mingo, the king of the nation, an annuity of one hundred dollars, during his natural life, granted as a testimony of his personal worth and friendly disposition. All the above payments are to be made in specie.

ARTICLE 3. In order to preclude for ever all disputes relative to the boundary mentioned in the first section, it is hereby stipulated, that the same shall be ascertained and marked by a commissioner or commissioners on the part of the United States, accompanied by such person as the Chickasaws may choose, so soon as the Chickasaws shall have thirty days' notice of the time and place, at which the operation is to commence: and the United States will pay the person appointed on the part of the Chickasaws two dollars per day during his actual attendance on that service.

ARTICLE 4. It is hereby agreed on the part of the United States, that from and after the ratification of these articles, no settlement shall be made by any citizen, or permitted by the government of the United States, on that part of the present cession included between the present Indian boundary and the Tennessee, and between the Ohio and a line drawn due north from the mouth of Buffaloe to the ridge dividing the waters of Cumberland from those of the Tennessee river, to the term of three years.

ARTICLE 5. The articles now stipulated will be considered as permanent additions to the treaties now in force between the contracting parties, as soon as they shall have been ratified by the President of the United States of America, by and with the advice and consent of the Senate of the said United States.

In witness of all and every thing herein determined, the parties have hereunto interchangeably set their hands and seals, in the Chickasaw country, this twenty-third day of July, in the year of our Lord one thousand eight hundred and five, and of the independence of the United States of America the thirtieth.

Commissioners: James Robertson, Silas Dinsmoor

Chiefs and warriors: Chenubbee Mingo, the king, his x mark, George Colbert, his x mark, O Koy, his x mark, Tiphu Mashtubbee, his x mark, Choomubbee, his x mark, Mingo Mattaha, his x mark, E. Mattaha Meko, his x mark, Wm. MeGillivry, his x mark, Tisshoo Hooluhta, his x mark, Levi Colbert; his x mark,

Signed, sealed, and interchanged, in presence of: Thomas Augustine Claiborne, secretary to the commissioners, W.P. Anderson, of Tennessee, Malcolm McGee, his x mark, Samuel Mitchell, United States agent to the Chickasaw nation, John Pitchlynn, Christopher Olney, John McKee, Wm. Tyrrell, R. Chamberlin, second lieutenant Second Regiment Infantry, Sworn interpreters.

TREATY WITH THE DELAWARES, ETC. {1805, Aug. 21}
Proclamation, Apr. 24, 1806.

A treaty between the United States of America, and the tribes of Indians called the Delawares, Pottawatimies, Miames, Eel River, and Weas.

ARTICLES of a treaty made and entered into, at Grouseland, near Vincennes, in the Indiana territory, by and between William Henry Harrison, governor of said territory, superintendent of Indian affairs, and commissioner plenipotentiary of the United States, for treating with the north western tribes of Indians, of the one part, and the tribes of Indians called the Delaware's, Putawatimis, Miamis, Eel River, and Weas, jointly and severally by their chiefs and head men, of the other part.

ARTICLE 1. Whereas, by the fourth article of a treaty made between the United States and the Delaware tribe, on the eighteenth day of August, eighteen hundred and four, the said United States engaged to consider the said Delaware's as the proprietors of all that tract of country which is bounded by the White river on the north, the Ohio and Clark's grant on the south, the general boundary line running from the mouth of Kentucky river on the east, and the tract ceded by the treaty of fort Wayne, and the road leading to Clark's grant on the west and south west. And whereas, the Miami tribes, from whom the Delawares derived their claim, contend that in their cession of said tract to the Delaware's, it was never their intention to convey to them the right of the soil,

72

but to suffer them to occupy it as long as they thought proper, the said Delaware's have, for the sake of peace and good neighborhood, determined to relinquish their claim to the said tract, and-do by these presents release the United States from the guarantee made in the before-mentioned article of the treaty of August, eighteen hundred and four.

ARTICLE 2. The said Miami, Eel River, and Wea tribes, cede and relinquish to the United States forever, all that tract of country which lies to the south of a line to be drawn from the north east corner of the tract ceded by the treaty of fort Wayne, so as to strike the general boundary line, running from a point opposite to the mouth of the Kentucky river, to fort Recovery, at the distance of fifty miles from its commencement on the Ohio river.

ARTICLE 3. In consideration of the cession made in the preceding article, the United States will give an additional permanent annuity to said Miamis, Eel River, and Wea tribes, in the following proportions, viz: to the Miamis, six hundred dollars; to the Eel River tribe, two hundred and fifty dollars; to the Weas, two hundred and fifty dollars; and also to the Putawatemies, an additional annuity of five hundred dollars, for ten years, and no longer; which, together with the sum of four thousand dollars which is now delivered, the receipt whereof they do hereby acknowledge, is to be considered as a full compensation for the land now ceded.

ARTICLE 4. As the tribes which are now called the Miamis, Eel River, and Weas, were formerly and still consider themselves as one nation, and as they have determined that neither of these tribes shall dispose of any part of the country which they hold in common; in order to quiet their minds on that head, the United States do hereby engage to consider them as joint owners of all the country on the Wabash and its waters, above the Vincennes tract, and which has not been ceded to the United States, by this or any former treaty; and they do farther engage that they will not purchase any part of the said country without the consent of each of the said tribes. Provided always, That nothing in this section contained, shall in any manner weaken or destroy any claim which the Kickapoos, who are not represented at this treaty, may have to the country they now occupy on the Vermillion river.

ARTICLE 5. The Putawatimies, Miami, Eel River, and Wea tribes, explicitly acknowledge the right of the Delawares to sell the tract of land conveyed to the United States by the treaty of the eighteenth day of August, eighteen hundred and four, which tract was given by the Piankashaws to the Delawares, about thirty-seven years ago.

ARTICLE 6. The annuities herein stipulated to be paid by the United States, shall be delivered in the same manner, and under the same conditions as those which the said tribes have heretofore received.

ARTICLE 7. This treaty shall be in force and obligatory on the contracting parties as soon as the same shall have been ratified by the President, by, and with the advice and consent of the Senate of the United States.
In testimony whereof, the said commissioner plenipotentiary of the United States, and the sachems, chiefs, and head men of the said tribes, have hereunto set their hands and affixed their seals.

Done at Grouseland, near Vincennes, on the twenty-first day of August, in the year eighteen hundred and five, and of the independence of the United States the thirtieth.

William Henry Harrison,

Delawares: Hocking Pomskan, his x mark, Kecklawhenund, orWilliam Anderson, his x mark, Allime, or White Eyes, his x mark, Tomague, or Beaver, his x mark,
Pattawatimas: Topanepee, his x mark, Lishahecon, his x mark, Wenamech, his x mark,
Miamis: Kakonweconner, or Long Legs, his x mark, Missingguimeschan, or Owl, his x mark, Wabsier, or White Skin, his x mark, Mashekanochquah, or Little Turtle, his x mark, RiChardville, his x mark,
Eel Rivers: Wanonecana, or Night Stander, his x mark, Metausauner, or Sam, his x mark, Archekatauh, or Earth, his x mark.
Weas: Assonnonquah, or Labossiere, his x mark, Misquaconaqua, or Painted Pole, his x mark, Ohequanah, or Little Eyes, his x mark,
Delawares: Missenewand, or Captain Bullet, his x mark.

Done in the presence of: B. Parke, secretary to the commissioner, John Gibson, secretary Indiana Territory, John Griffin, a judge of the Indiana Territory, B. Chambers, president of the council, Jesse B. Thomas, Speaker of the House of Representatives, John Rice Jones, Samuel Gwathmey, Pierre Menard, Members legislative council Indiana Territory, Davis Floyd, Shadrach Bond, William Biggs, John Johnson, Members house of representatives Indiana Territory, W. Wells, agent of Indian affairs, Vigo, colonel of Knox County Militia, John Conner, Joseph Barron, Sworn interpreters.

ADDITIONAL ARTICLE. It is the intention of the contracting parties, that the boundary line herein directed to be run from the north east corner of the Vincennes tract to the boundary line running from the mouth of the Kentucky river, shall not cross the Embarras or Drift Wood fork of White river, but if it should strike the said fork, such an alteration in the direction of the said line is to be made, as will leave the whole of the said fork in the Indian territory.

TREATY WITH THE CHEROKEE {1805, Oct. 2}
Proclamation, Apr. 24, 1806.

Articles of a treaty agreed upon between the United States of America, by their commissioners Return J. Meigs and Daniel Smith, appointed to hold conferences with the Cherokee Indians, for the purpose of arranging certain interesting matters with the said Cherokees, of the one part, and the undersigned chiefs and head men of the said nation, of the other part.

ARTICLE 1. All former treaties, which provide for the maintenance of peace and preventing of crimes, are on this occasion recognized and continued in force.

ARTICLE 2. The Cherokees quit claim and cede to the United States, all the land which they have heretofore claimed, lying to the north of the following boundary line: beginning at the mouth of Duck river, running thence up the main stream of the same to the junction of the fork, at the head of which fort Nash stood, with the main south fork; thence a direct course to a point on the Tennessee river bank opposite the mouth of Hiwassa river.

If the line from Hiwassa should leave out Field's Settlement, it is to be marked round his improvement, and then continued the straight course; thence up the middle of the Tennessee river, (but leaving all the islands to the Cherokees) to the mouth of Clinch river; thence up the Clinch river to the former boundary line agreed upon with the said Cherokees, reserving at the same time to the use of the Cherokees a small tract lying at and below the mouth of Clinch river; from the mouth extending thence down the Tennessee river, from the mouth of Clinch to a notable rock on the north bank of the Tennessee, in view from South West Point; thence a course at right angles with the river, to the Cumberland road; thence eastwardly along the same, to the bank of Clinch river, so as to secure the ferry landing to the Cherokees up to the first hill, and down the same to the mouth thereof, together with two other sections of one square mile each, one of which is at the foot of Cumberland mountain, at and near the place where the turnpike gate now stands; the other on the north bank of the Tennessee river, where the Cherokee Talootiske now lives.

And whereas, from the present cession made by the Cherokees, and other circumstances, the site of the garrisons at South West Point and Tellico are become not the most convenient and suitable places for the accommodation of the said Indians, it may become expedient to [83] remove the said garrisons and factory to some more suitable place; three other square miles are reserved for the particular disposal of the United States on the north bank of the Tennessee, opposite to and below the mouth of Hiwassa.

ARTICLE 3. In consideration of the above cession and relinquishment, the United States agree to pay immediately three thousand dollars in valuable merchandise, and eleven thousand dollars within ninety days after the ratification of this treaty, and also an annuity of three thousand dollars, the commencement of which is this day. But so much of the said eleven thousand dollars, as the said Cherokee may agree to accept in useful articles of, and machines for, agriculture and manufactures, shall be paid in those articles, at their option.

ARTICLE 4. The citizens of the United States shall have the free and unmolested use and enjoyment of the two following described roads, in addition to those which are at present established through their country; one to proceed from some convenient place near the head of Stone's river, and fall into the Georgia road at a suitable place towards the southern frontier of the Cherokees. The other to proceed from the neighborhood of Franklin, on Big Harpath, and crossing the Tennessee at or near the Muscle Shoals, to pursue the nearest and best way to the settlements on the Tombigbee. These roads shall be viewed and marked out by men appointed on each side for that purpose, in order that they may be directed the nearest and best ways, and the time of doing the business the Cherokees shall be duly notified.

ARTICLE 5. This treaty shall take effect and be obligatory on the contracting parties, as soon as it is ratified by the President of the United States, by and with the advice and consent of the Senate of the same.
In testimony whereof, the said commissioners, and the undersigned chiefs and head men of the Cherokees, have hereto set their hands and seals.
Done at Tellico, the twenty-fifth day of October, one thousand eight hundred and five.

Return J. Meigs, Daniel Smith.
Fox, or Ennollee, his x mark, Path Killer, or Nenohuttahe, his x mark, Glass, or Tauquatehee, his x mark, Double head, or Dhuqualutauge, his x mark, Dick Justice, his x mark, Tounhull, or Toonayeh, his x mark, Turtle at Home, or Sullidooahwolu, his x mark, Chenawee, his x mark, Slave Boy, or Oosaunabee, his x mark, Tallotiskee, his x mark, Broom, or Cunnaweesoskec, his x mark, John Greenwood, or Sour Mush, his x mark, Chulioah, his x mark, Katigiskee, his x mark, William Shawry, or Eskaculiskee, his x mark, Taochalar, his x mark, James Davis, or Coowusaliskee, his x mark, John Jolly, or Eulatakee, his x mark, Bark, or Eulloolka, his x mark, John McLemore, or John Euskulacau, his x mark, Big Bear, or Yohanaqua, his x mark, Dreadfulwater, or Aumaudoskee, his x mark, Challaugittihee, his x mark, Calliliskee, or Knife Sheath, his x mark, Closenee, his x mark, Challow, or Kingfisher, his x mark, John Watts, jr., his x mark,
Sharp Arrow, or Costarauh, his x mark, John Dougherty, or Long John, his x mark, Tuckasee, or Terrapin, his x mark, Tuskegittihee, or Long Fellow, his x mark, Tochuwor, or Red Bird, his x mark, Catihee, or Badgerson, his x mark.

Witnesses: Rob. Purdy, secretary to the commissioner, W. Yates, Lieutenant Artillerists, Wm. L. Lovely, assistant agent, Nicholas Byers, United States factor, Go. W. Campbell, Will. Polk, James Blair, Jno. Smith, T. Thomas, N. Clark, Chas. Hicks, interpreter.

TREATY WITH THE CHEROKEE {1805, Oct. 27}
Proclamation, June 10, 1806.

Articles of a treaty between the United States of America, by their commissioners, Return J Meigs and Daniel Smith, who are appointed to hold conferences with the Cherokee for the purpose of arranging certain interesting matters with the said Indians, of the one part, and the undersigned chiefs and head men of the Cherokees, of the other part, concluded at Tellico.

ARTICLE 1. Whereas it has been represented by the one party to the other that the section of land on which the garrison of South West Point stands, and which extends to Kingston, is likely to be a desirable place for the assembly of the state of Tennessee to convene at (a committee from that body now in session having viewed the situation) now the Cherokees being possessed of a spirit of conciliation, and seeing that this tract is desired for public purposes, and not for individual advantages, (reserving the ferries to themselves) quit claim and cede to the United States the said section of land, understanding at the same time, that the buildings erected by the public are to belong to the public, as well as the occupation of the same, during the pleasure of the government; we also cede to the United States the first island in the Tennessee, above the mouth of Clinch.

ARTICLE 2. And whereas the mail of the United States is ordered to be carried from Knoxville to New-Orleans, through the Cherokee, Creek and Choctaw countries; the Cherokees agree that the citizens of the United States shall have, so far as it goes through their country, the free and unmolested use of a road leading from Tellico to Tombigbe, to be laid out by viewers appointed on both sides, who shall direct it the nearest and best way; and the time of doing the business the Cherokees shall be notified of.

ARTICLE 3. In consideration of the above cession and relinquishment, the United States agree to pay to the said Cherokee Indians sixteen hundred dollars in money, or useful merchandise at their option, within ninety days after the ratification of this treaty.

ARTICLE 4. This treaty shall be obligatory between the contracting parties as soon as it is ratified by the President, by and with the advice and consent of the Senate of the United States.

In testimony whereof, the said commissioners, and the undersigned chiefs and head men of the Cherokees, have hereto set their hands and seals.

Done at Tellico, this twenty-seventh day of October, in the year of our Lord one thousand eight hundred and five.

Return J. Meigs, Danl. Smith.
Black Fox, or Ennone, his x mark, The Glass, or Tunnquetihee, his x mark, Kutigeskee, his x mark, Toochalar, his x mark, Turtle at Home, or Sullicookiewalar, his x mark, Dick Justice, his x mark, John Greenwood, or Eakosettas, his x mark, Chuleah, or Gentleman Tom, his x mark, Broom, or Cannarwesoske, his x mark, Bald Hunter, or Toowayullau, His x mark, John Melamere, or Euquellooka, his x mark, Closehie, or Creeping, his x mark, Double Head, or Chuquacuttague, his x mark, Chickasawtihee, or Chickasawtihee Killer, his x mark,.

Witness: Robert Purdy, secretary to the commissioners, William Yates, B. Com'g, Nicholas Byers, United, tates factor, Wm. Lovely, assistant agent, B. M'Ghee, Saml. Love, James Blair, Hopkins Lacey, Chs. Hicks, interpreter.

TREATY WITH THE CREEKS {1805, Nov. 14}
Proclamation, June 2, 1806.

A convention between the United States and the Creek Nation of Indians, concluded at the City of Washington, on the fourteenth day November, in the year of our Lord one thousand eight hundred and five.

Articles of a Convention made between Henry Dearborn, secretary of war, being specially authorized therefor by the President of the United States, and Oche Haujo, William M'Intosh, Tuskenehau Chapee, Tuskenehau, Enehau Thlucco, Checopehcke, Emantlau, chiefs and head men of the Creek nation of Indians, duly authorized and empowered by said nation.

ARTICLE 1. The aforesaid chiefs and head men do hereby agree, in consideration of certain sums of money and goods to be paid to the said Creek nation by the government of the United States as hereafter stipulated, to cede and forever quit claim, and do, in behalf of their nation, hereby cede, relinquish, and forever quit claim unto the United States all right, title, and interest, which the said nation have or claim, in or unto a certain tract of land, situate between the rivers Oconee and Ocmulgee (except as hereinafter excepted) and bounded as follows, viz:

Beginning at the high shoals of Apalacha, where the line of the treaty of fort Wilkinson touches the same, thence running in a straight line, to the mouth of

Ulcofauhatche, it being the first large branch or fork of the Ocmulgee, above the Seven Islands: Provided, however, That if the said line should strike the Ulcofauhatche, at any place above its mouth, that it shall continue round with that stream so as to leave the whole of it on the Indian side; then the boundary to continue from the mouth of the Ulcofauhatche, by the water's edge of the Ocmulgee river, down to its junction with the Oconee; thence up the Oconee to the present boundary at Tauloohatche creek; thence up said creek and following the present boundary line to the first-mentioned bounds, at the high shoals of Apalacha, excepting and reserving to the Creek nation, the title and possession of a tract of land, five miles in length and three in breadth, and bounded as follows, viz: Beginning on the eastern shore of the Ocmulgee river, at a point three miles on a straight line above the mouth of a creek called Oakehoncoolgau, which empties into the Ocmulgee, near the lower part of what is called the old Ocmulgee fieldsthence running three miles eastwardly, on a course at right angles with the general course of the river for five miles below the point of beginning;thence, from the end of the three miles, to run five miles parallel with the said course of the river; thence westwardly, at right angles with the last-mentioned line to the river; thence by the river to the first-mentioned bounds.

And it is hereby agreed, that the President of the United States, for the time being, shall have a right to establish and continue a military post, and a factory or trading house on said reserved tract; and to make such other use of the said tract as may be found convenient for the United States, as long as the government thereof shall think proper to continue the said military post or trading house. And it is also agreed on the part of the Creek nation, that the navigation and fishery of the Ocmulgee, from its junction with the Oconee to the mouth of the Ulcofauhatchee, shall be free to the white people; provided they use no traps for taking fish; but nets and seines may be used, which shall be drawn to the eastern shore only.

ARTICLE 2. It is hereby stipulated and agreed, on the part of the Creek nation that the government of the United States shall forever hereafter have a right to a horse path, through the Creek country, from the Ocmulgee to the Mobile, in such direction as shall, by the President [86] of the United States, be considered most convenient, and to clear out the same, and lay logs over the creeks: And the citizens of said States, shall at all times have a right to pass peaceably on said path, under such regulations and restrictions, as the government of the United States shall from time to time direct; and the Creek chiefs will have boats kept at the several rivers for the conveyance of men and horses, and houses of entertainment established at suitable places on said path for the accommodation of travellers; and the respective ferriages and prices of entertainment for men and horses, shall be regulated by the present agent, Col. Hawkins, or by his successor in office, or as is usual among white people.

ARTICLE 3. It is hereby stipulated and agreed, on the part of the United States, as a full consideration for the land ceded by the Creek nation in the first article, as well as by permission granted for a horse path through their country, and the occupancy of the reserved tract, at the old Ocmulgee fields, that there shall be paid annually to the Creek nation, by the United States for the term of eight years, twelve thousand dollars in money or goods, and implements of husbandry, at the option of the Creek nation, seasonably signified from time to time, through the agent of the United States, residing with said nation, to the department of war; and eleven thousand dollars shall be paid in like manner, annually, for the term of the ten succeeding years, making in the whole, eighteen payments in the course of eighteen years, without interest: The first payment is to be made as soon as practicable after the ratification of this convention by the government of the United States, and each payment shall be made at the reserved tract, on the old Ocmulgee fields.

ARTICLE 4. And it is hereby further agreed, on the part of the United States, that in lieu of all former stipulations relating to blacksmiths, they will furnish the Creek nation for eight years, with two blacksmiths and two strikers.

ARTICLE 5. The President of the United States may cause the line to be run from the high shoals of Apalacha, to the mouth of Ulcofauhatche, at such time, and in such manner, as he may deem proper, and this convention shall be obligatory on the contracting parties as soon as the same shall have been ratified by the government of the United States.

Done at the place, and on the day and year above written.

H. Dearborn, Oche Haujo, his x mark, William McIntosh, his x mark, Tuskenehau Chapco, his x mark, Tuskenehau. his x mark, Enehau Thlucco, his x mark, Chekopeheke Emanthau, his x mark,

Signed and sealed in presence of: James Madison, Rt. Smith, Benjamin Hawkins, Timothy Barnard, Jno. Smith, Andrew McClary.

TREATY WITH THE CHOCTAW {1805, Nov. 16}
Proclamation, Feb. 25, 1808.

A Treaty of Limits between the United States of America and the Chaktaw Nation of Indians.

THOMAS JEFFERSON, President of the United States of America, by James Robertson, of Tennessee, and Silas Dinsmoor, of New Hampshire, agent of the United States to the Chaktaws, commissioners plenipotentiary of the United States, on the one part, and the Mingoes, Chiefs and warriors of the Chaktaw nation of Indians, in council assembled, on the other part, have entered into the following agreement, viz:

ARTICLE 1. The Mingoes, chiefs, and warriors of the Chaktaw nation of Indians in behalf of themselves, and the said nation, do by these presents cede to the United States of America, all the lands to which they now have or ever had claim, lying to the right of the following lines, to say. Beginning at a branch of the Humacheeto where the same is intersected by the present Chaktaw boundary, and also by the path leading from Natchez to the county of Washington, usually called M'Clarey's path, thence eastwardly along M'Clarey's path, to the east or left bank of Pearl river, thence on such a direct line as would touch the lower end of a bluff on the left bank of Chickasawhay river the first above the Hiyoowannee towns, called Broken Bluff, to a point within four miles of the Broken Bluff, thence in a direct line nearly parallel with the river to a point whence an east line of four mines in length will intersect the river below the lowest settlement at present occupied and improved in the Hiyoowannee town, thence still east four miles, thence in a direct line nearly parallel with the river to a point on a line to be run from the lower end of the Broken Bluff to Faluktabunnee on the Tombigbee river four miles from the Broken Bluff, thence along the said line to Faluktabunnee, thence east to the boundary between the Creeks and Chaktaws on the ridge dividing the waters running into the Alabama from those running into Tombigbee, thence southwardly along the said ridge and boundary to the southern point of the Chaktaw claim.

Reserving a tract of two miles square run on meridians and parallels so as to include the houses and improvements in the town of Fuketcheepoonta, and reserving also a tract of five thousand one hundred and twenty acres, beginning at a post on the left bank of Tombigbee river opposite the lower end of Hatchatigbee Bluff, thence ascending the river four miles front and two back one half, for the use of Alzira, the other half for the use of Sophia, daughters of Samuel Mitchell, by Molly, a Chaktaw woman. The latter reserve to be subject to the same laws and regulations as may be established in the circumjacent country; and the said Mingoes of the Chaktaws, request that the government of the United States may confirm the title of this reserve m the said Alzira and Sophia.

ARTICLE 2. For and in consideration of the foregoing cession on the part of the Chaktaw nation, and in full satisfaction for the same, the commissioners of the United States, do hereby covenant, and agree with the said nation in behalf of the United States, that the said States shall pay to the said nation fifty thousand five hundred dollars, for the following purposes, to wit:

Forty eight thousand dollars to enable the Mingoes to discharge the debt due to their merchants and traders; and also to pay for the depredations committed on stock, and other property by evil disposed persons of the said Chaktaw nation;

two thousand five hundred dollars to be paid to John Pitchlynn, to compensate him for certain losses sustained in the Chaktaw country, and as a grateful testimonial of the nation's esteem. And the said States shall also pay annually to the said Chaktaws, for the use of the nation, three thousand dollars in such goods (at neat cost of Philadelphia) as the Mingoes may choose, they giving at least one year's notice of such choice.

ARTICLE 3. The commissioners of the United States, on the part of the said States, engage to give to each of the three great Medal Mingoes, Pukshunubbee-Mingo, Hoomastubbee, and Pooshamattaha, five hundred dollars in consideration of past services in their nation, and also to pay to each of them an annuity of one hundred and fifty dollars during their continuance in office. It is perfectly understood, that neither of those great Medal Mingoes is to share any part of the general annuity of the nation.

ARTICLE 4. The Mingoes, chiefs, and warriors of the Chaktaws, certify that a tract of land not exceeding fifteen hundred acres, situated between the Tombigbee river and Jackson's creek, the front or river line extending down the river from a blazed white oak standing on the left bank of the Tombigbee near the head of the shoal, next above Hobukentoopa, and claimed by John M'Grew was in fact granted to the said M'Grew by Opiomingo Hesnitta, and others, many years ago, and they respectfully request the government of the United States to establish the claim of the said M'Grew to the said fifteen hundred acres.

ARTICLE 5. The two contracting parties covenant and agree that the boundary as described in the second (first) article shall be ascertained and plainly marked, in such way and manner as the President of the United States may direct, in the presence of three persons to be appointed by the said nation; one from each of the great medal districts, each of whom shall receive for this service two dollars per day during his actual attendance, and the Chaktaws shall have due and seasonable notice of the place where, and time when, the operation shall commence.

ARTICLE 6. The lease granted for establishments on the roads leading through the Chaktaw country, is hereby confirmed in all its conditions, and, except in the alteration of boundary, nothing in this instrument shall affect or change any of the pre-existing obligations of the contracting parties.

ARTICLE 7. This treaty shall take effect and become reciprocally obligatory so soon as the same shall have been ratified by the President of the United States of America, by and with the advice and consent of the Senate of the United States.

Done on Mount Dexter, in Pooshapukanuk, in the Choctaw country, this sixteenth day of November, in the year of our Lord one thousand eight hundred arid five, and of the independence of the United States of America the thirtieth.

Commissioners: James Robertson, Silas Dinsmoor.
Great Medal Mingos: Pukshunnubbee, his x mark, Mingo Hoomastubbee, his x mark, Pooshamattaha, his x mark.
Chiefs and warriors: Ookchummee, his x mark, Tuskamiubbee, his x mark, James Perry, his x mark, Levi Perry, his x mark, Isaac Perry, his x mark, William Turnbull,

Witnesses present at signing and sealing: Thomas Augustine Claiborn, secretary to the commissioners, John M' Kee, Samuel Mitchell, United States agent to the Chickasaws, William Colbert, of the Chickasaws, his x mark, Lewis Ward, Charles Juzan, John Carnes, his x mark, Tooteehooma, his x mark, Hoosheehooma, his x mark, Tootuhooma, 2d. his x mark, George James, his x mark, Robert McClure, his x mark, Tuskeamingo, his x mark, Hattukubbeehooluhta, his x mark, Fishoommastubbee, his x mark, Anoguaiah, his x mark, Lewis Lucas, his x mark, James Pitchlvnn, his x mark, Panshee Eenanhla, his x mark, Pansheehoomubbu, his x mark, Garrud E. Nelson, David Chore, Nathaniel Tolsom,.

TREATY WITH THE CHEROKEE {1806, Jan. 7}
Ratified May 22, 1807.
Proclaimed May 23, 1807.

A convention between the United States and the Cherokee nation of Indians, concluded at the city of Washington, on the seventh day of January, in the year one thousand eight hundred and six.

Articles of a Convention made between Henry Dearborn, secretary of war, being specially authorized thereto by the President of the United States, and the undersigned chiefs and head men of the Cherokee nation of Indians, duly authorized and empowered by said nation.

ARTICLE 1. The undersigned chiefs and head men of the Cherokee nation of Indians, for themselves and in behalf of their nation, relinquish to the United States all right, title, interest and claim, which they or their nation have or ever had to all that tract of country which lies to the northward of the river Tennessee and westward of a line to be run from the upper part of the Chickasaw Old Fields, at the upper point of an island, called Chickasaw island, on said river, to the most easterly head waters of that branch of said Tennessee river called Duck river, excepting the two following described tracts, viz: one tract bounded southerly on the said Tennessee river, at a place called the Muscle Shoals, westerly by a creek called Te Kee, ta, no-eh or Cyprus creek, and easterly by Chu, wa, lee, or Elk river or creek, and northerly by a line to be drawn from a point on said Elk river ten miles on a direct line from its mouth or junction with Tennessee river, to a point on the said Cyprus Creek, ten miles on a direct line from its junction with the Tennessee river.

The other tract is to be two miles in width on the north side of Tennessee river, and to extend northerly from that river three miles, and bounded as follows, viz: beginning at the mouth of Spring Creek, and running up said creek three miles on a straight line, thence westerly two miles at right angles with the general course of said creek, thence southerly on a line parallel with the general course of said creek to the Tennessee river, thence up said river by its waters to the beginning: which first reserved tract is to be considered the common property of the Cherokees who now live on the same; including John D. Chesholm, An, tow, we and Cheh Chub, and the other reserved tract on which Moses Melton now lives, is to be considered the property of said Melton and of Charles Hicks, in equal shares.

And the said chiefs and head men also agree to relinquish to the United States all right or claim which they or their nation have to what is called the Long Island in Holston river.

ARTICLE 2. The said Henry Dearborn on the part of the United States hereby stipulates and agrees that in consideration of the relinquishment of title by the Cherokees, as stated in the preceding article, the United States will pay to the Cherokee nation two thousand dollars in money as soon [91] as this convention shall be duly ratified by the government of the United States; and two thousand dollars in each of the four succeeding years, amounting in the whole to ten thousand dollars; and that a grist mill shall within one year from the date hereof, be built in the Cherokee country, for the use of the nation, at such place as shall be considered most convenient; that the said Cherokees shall be furnished with a machine for cleaning cotton; and also, that the old Cherokee chief, called the Black Fox, shall be paid annually one hundred dollars by the United States during his life.

ARTICLE 3. It is also agreed on the part of the United States, that the government thereof will use its influence and best endeavors to prevail on the Chickasaw nation of Indians to agree to the following boundary between that nation and the Cherokees to the southward of the Tennessee river, viz: beginning at the mouth of Caney Creek near the lower part of the Muscle Shoals, and to run up said creek to its head, and in a direct line from thence to the Flat Stone or Rock, the old corner boundary.

But it is understood by the contracting parties that the United States do not engage to have the aforesaid line or boundary established, but only to endeavor to prevail on the Chickasaw nation to consent to such a line as the boundary between the two nations.

ARTICLE 4. It is further agreed on the part of the United States that the claims which the Chickasaws may have to the two tracts reserved by the first article of this convention on the north side of the Tennessee river, shall be settled by the United States in such manner as will be equitable, and will secure to the Cherokees the title to the said reservations.

Done at the place, and on the day and year first above written.

Henry Dearborn, Double Head, his x mark, James Vanu, his x mark, Tallotiskee, his x mark, Chulioa, his x mark, Sour Mush, his x mark, Turtle at home, his x mark, Katihu, his x mark, John McLemore, his x mark, Broom, his x mark, John Jolly, his x mark, John Lowry, his x mark, Red Bird, his x mark, John Walker, his x mark, Young Wolf, his x mark, Skeuha, his x mark, Sequechu, his x mark, Wm. Showry, his x mark,

In presence of: Return J. Meigs, Benjamin Hawkins, Daniel Smith, John Smith, Andrew McClary, John McClarey.

I certify the foregoing convention has been faithfully interpreted.

Charles Hicks, Interpreter.

Elucidation of a convention with the Cherokee Nation.

Sept. 11, 1897.
Proclamation, Apr. 22, 1808.

WHEREAS, by the first article of a convention between the United States and the Cherokee nation, entered into at the city of Washington, on the seventh day of January, one thousand eight hundred and six, it was intended on the part of the Cherokee nation, and so understood by the Secretary of War, the commissioner on the part of the United States, to cede to the United States all the right, title and [92] interest which the said Cherokee nation ever had to a tract of country contained between the Tennessee river and the Tennessee ridge (so called); which tract of country had since the year one thousand seven hundred and ninety four, been claimed by the Cherokees and Chickasaws: the eastern boundary whereof is limited by a line so to be run from the upper part of the Chickasaw Old Fields, as to include all the waters of Elk river, any thing expressed in said convention to the contrary notwithstanding. It is therefore now declared by James Robertson and Return J. Meigs, acting under the authority of the executive of the United States, and by a delegation of Cherokee chiefs, of whom Eunolee or Black Fox, the king or head chief of said Cherokee nation, acting on the part of, and in behalf of said nation, is one, that the eastern limits of said ceded tract shall be bounded by a line so to be run from the upper end of the Chickasaw Old Fields, a little above the upper point of an island, called Chickasaw Island, as will most directly intersect the first waters of Elk river, thence carried to the Great Cumberland mountain, in which the waters of Elk river have their source, then along the margin of said mountain until it shall intersect lands heretofore ceded to the United States, at the said Tennessee ridge. And in consideration of the readiness shown by the Cherokees to explain, and to place the limits of the land ceded by the said convention out of all doubt. And in consideration of their expenses in attending council, the executive of the United States will direct that the Cherokee nation shall receive the sum of two thousand dollars, to be paid to them by their agent, at such time as the said executive shall direct, and that the Cherokee hunters, as hath been the custom in such cases, may hunt on said ceded tract, until by the fullness of settlers it shall become improper. And it is hereby declared by the parties, that this explanation ought to be considered as a just elucidation of the cession made by the first article of said convention.

Done at the point of departure of the line at the upper end of the island opposite to the upper part of the said Chickasaw Oil Fields, the eleventh day of September, in the year one thousand eight hundred and seven.

James Robertson, Return J. Meigs, Eunolee, or Black Fox, his x mark, Fauquitee, or Glass, his x mark, Fulaquokoko, or Turtle at home, his x mark, Richard Brown, his x mark, Sowolotoh, king's brother, his x mark.

Witnesses present: Thomas Freeman, Thomas Orme, Mdl. Mackey, Lewis Lefto, John Pitchlynn, United States interpreter, Will. Tyrrell, assistant interpreter.

The foregoing articles have been faithfully interpreted.

Timothy Barnard, interpreter.

TREATY WITH THE OTTAWA, ETC. {1807, Nov. 17}
Proclamation, Jan. 27, 1808.

Articles of a treaty made at Detroit, this seventeenth day of November, in the year of our Lord, one thousand eight hundred and seven, by William Hull, governor of the territory of Michigan, and superintendent of Indian affairs, and sole commissioner of the United States, to conclude and sign a treaty or treaties, with the several nations of Indians, North west of the river Ohio, on the one part, and the sachems, chiefs, and warriors of the Ottoway, Chippeway, Wyandotte, and Pottawatamie nations of Indians, on the other part. To confirm and perpetuate the friendship, which happily subsists between the United States and the nations aforesaid to manifest the sincerity of that friendship, and to settle arrangements mutually beneficial to the [93] parties; after a full explanation and perfect understanding, the following articles are agreed to, which, when ratified by the President, by and with the advice and consent of the Senate of the United States, shall be binding on them, and the respective nations of Indians.

ARTICLE 1. The sachems, chiefs, and warriors of the nations aforesaid, in consideration of money and goods, to be paid to the said nations, by the government of the United States as hereafter stipulated; do hereby agree to cede and forever quit claim, and do in behalf of their nations hereby cede, relinquish, and forever quit claim, unto the said United States, all right, title, and interest, which the said nations now have, or claim, or ever had, or claimed, in, or unto, the lands comprehended within the following described lines and boundaries: Beginning at the mouth of the Miami river of the lakes, and running thence up the middle thereof, to the mouth of the great Au Glaize river, thence running due north, until it intersects a parallel of latitude, to be drawn from the outlet of lake Huron, which forms the river Sinclair; thence running north east the course, that may be found, will lead in a direct line, to White Rock, in lake Huron, thence due east, until it intersects the boundary line between the United States and Upper Canada, in said lake, thence southwardly, following the said boundary line, down said lake, through river Sinclair, lake St. Clair, and the river Detroit, into lake Erie, to a point due east of the aforesaid Miami river, thence west to the place of beginning.

ARTICLE 2. It is hereby stipulated and agreed on the part of the United States, as a consideration for the lands, ceded by the nations aforesaid, in the preceding article, that there shall be paid to the said nations, at Detroit, ten thousand dollars, in money, goods, implements of husbandry, or domestic animals, (at the option of the said nations, season-ably signified, through the superintendent of Indian affairs, residing with the said nations, to the department of war) as soon as practicable, after the ratification of the treaty, by the President, with the advice and consent of the Senate of the United States.

Of this sum, three thousand three hundred and thirty three dollars thirty three cents and four mills, shall be paid to the Ottoway nation, three thousand three hundred and thirty three dollars thirty three cents and four mills, to the Chippeway nation, one thousand six hundred sixty six dollars sixty six cents and six mills, to the Wyandotte nation, one thousand six hundred sixty six dollars sixty six cents and six mills, to the Pottawatamie nation, and likewise an annuity forever, of two thousand four hundred dollars, to be paid at Detroit, in manner as aforesaid: the first payment to be made on the first day of September next, and to be paid to the different nations, in the following proportions: eight hundred dollars to the Ottoways, eight hundred dollars to the Chippeways, four hundred dollars to the Wyandottes, and four hundred dollars to such of the Pottawatamies, as now reside on the river Huron of lake Erie, the river Raisin, and in the vicinity of the said rivers.

ARTICLE 3. It is further stipulated and agreed, if at any time hereafter, the said nations should be of the opinion, that it would be more for their interest, that the annuity aforesaid should be paid by instalments, the United States will agree to a reasonable commutation for the annuity, and pay it accordingly.

ARTICLE 4. The United States, to manifest their liberality, and disposition to encourage the said Indians, in agriculture, further stipulate, to furnish the said Indians with two blacksmiths, one to reside with the Chippeways, at Saguina, and the other to reside with the Ottaways, at the Miami, during the term of ten years; said blacksmiths are to do such work for the said nations as shall be most useful to them.

ARTICLE 5. It is further agreed and stipulated, that the said Indian nations shall enjoy the privilege of hunting and fishing on the lands [94] ceded as aforesaid, as long as they remain the property of the United States.

ARTICLE 6. It is distinctly to be understood, for the accommodation of the said Indians, that the following tracts of land within the cession aforesaid, shall be, and hereby are reserved to the said Indian nations, one tract of land six miles square, on the Miami of lake Erie, above Roche dè Boeuf, to include the village, where Tondaganie, (or the Dog) now lives. Also, three miles square on the said river, (above the twelve miles square ceded to the United States by the treaty of Greenville) including what is called Presque Isle; also four miles square on the Miami bay, including the villages where Meshkemau and Waugau now live. Also, three miles square on the river Raisin, at a place called Macon, and where the river Macon falls into the river Raizin, which place is about fourteen miles from the mouth of said river Raizin; also, two sections of one mile square each, on the river Rouge, at Seginsiwin's village; also two sections of one mile square each, at Tonquish's village, near the river Rouge; also three miles square on lake St. Clair, above the river Huron, to include Machonce's village.

Also, six sections, each section containing one mile square, within the cession aforesaid, in such situations as the said Indians shall elect, subject, however, to the approbation of the President of the United States, as to the places of location. It is further understood and agreed, that whenever the reservations cannot conveniently be laid out in squares, they shall be laid out in paralelograms, or other figures, as found most practicable and convenient, so as to contain the area specified in miles, and in all cases they are to be located in such manner, and in such situations, as not to interfere with any improvements of the French or other white people, or any former cessions.

ARTICLE 7. The said nations of Indians acknowledge themselves to be under the protection of the United States, and no other power, and will prove by their conduct that that are worthy of so great a blessing.

In testimony whereof, the said William Hull, and the sachems and war chiefs representing the said nations, have hereunto set their hands and seals.

Done at Detroit, in the territory of Michigan, the day and year first above written.

William Hull,

Chippewas: Peewanshemenogh, his x mark, Mamaushegauta, or Bad Legs, his x mark

Pooquigauboawie, his x mark,Aubauway, his x mark, Kiosk, his x mark, Kawaehewan, his x mark, Poquaquet, or the Ball, his x mark, Segangewan, his x mark, Quitehonequit, or Big Cloud, his x mark, Quiconquish, his x mark, Puckenese, or the Spark of Fire, his x mark, Negig, or the Otter, his x mark, Measita, his x mark, Macquettequet, or Little Bear, his x mark, Nemekas, or Little Thunder, his x mark, Sawanabenase, or Pechegabua, or Iyonayotha, his x mark, Tonquish, his x mark, Miott, his x mark, Meuetugesheck, or the Little Cedar, his x mark,

Ottawas: Aubauway, his x mark, Kawachewan, his x mark, Sawgamaw, his x mark, Ogouse, his x mark, Wasagashick, his x mark,

Pattawatimas: Toquish, his x mark, Noname, his x mark, Nawme, his x mark, Ninnewa, his x mark, Skush, his x mark,

Wyandots: Skahomet, his x mark, Miere, or Walk in the Water, his x mark, Grand Blanc, his x mark,

TREATY WITH THE DELAWARES, ETC. {1809, Sept. 30}
Proclamation, Jan. 16, 1810.

A treaty between the United States of America, ande tribes of Indians called the Delawares, Putawatimies, Miamis and Eel River Miamies.

JAMES MADISON, President of the United States, by William Henry Harrison, governor and commander-in-chief of the Indiana territory, superintendent of Indian affairs, and commissioner plenipotentiary of the United States for treating with the said Indian tribes, and the Sachems, Head men and Warriors of the Delaware, Putawatame, Miami and Eel River tribes of Indians, have agreed and concluded upon the following treaty; which, when ratified by the said President, with the advice and consent of the Senate of the United States, shall be binding on said Parties.

ARTICLE 1. The Miami and Eel River tribes, and the Delawares and Puta-watimies, as their allies, agree to cede to the United States all that tract of country which shall be included between the boundary line established by the treaty of Fort Wayne, the Wabash, and a line to be drawn from the mouth of a creek called Racoon Creek, emptying into the Wabash, on the south-east side, about twelve miles below the mouth of the Vermilion river, so as to strike the boundary line established by the treaty of Grouseland, at such a distance from its commencement at the north-east corner of the Vincennes tract, as will leave the tract now ceded thirty miles wide at the narrowest place.

And also all that tract which shall be included between the following bounda-ries, viz: beginning at Fort Recovery, thence southwardly along the general boundary line, established by the treaty of Greenville, to its intersection with the boundary line established by the treaty of Grouseland; thence along said line to a point from which a line drawn parallel to the first mentioned line will be twelve miles distant from the same, and along the said parallel line to its in-tersection with a line to be drawn from Fort Recovery, parallel to the line es-tablished by the said treaty of Grouseland.

ARTICLE 2. The Miamies explicitly acknowledge the equal right of the De-lawares with themselves to the country watered by the White river. But it is also to be clearly understood that neither party shall have the right of disposing of the same without the consent of the other: and any improvements which shall be made on the said land by the Delawares, or their friends the Moche-cans, shall be theirs forever.

ARTICLE 3. The compensation to be given for the cession made in the first article shall be as follows, viz: to the Delawares a permanent annuity of five hundred dollars; to the Miamies a like annuity of five hundred dollars; to the Eel river tribe a like annuity of two hundred and fifty dollars; and to the Puta-watimies a like annuity of five hundred dollars.

ARTICLE 4. All the stipulations made in the treaty of Greenville, relatively to the manner of paying the annuities, and the right of the Indians to hunt upon the land, shall apply to the annuities granted and the land ceded by the present treaty.

ARTICLE 5. The consent of the Wea tribe shall be necessary to complete the title to the first tract of land here ceded; a separate convention shall be entered into between them and the United States, and a reasonable allowance of goods given them in hand, and a permanent annuity, which shall not be less than three hundred dollars, settled upon them.

ARTICLE 6. The annuities promised by the third article, and the goods now delivered to the amount of five thousand two hundred dollars, shall be considered as a full compensation for the cession made in the first article.

ARTICLE 7. The tribes who are party to this treaty being desirous of putting an end to the depredations which are committed by abandoned individuals of their own color, upon the cattle, horses, &c. of the more industrious and careful, agree to adopt the following regulations, viz: when any theft or other depredation shall be committed by any individual or individuals of one of the tribes above mentioned, upon the property of any individual or individuals of another tribe, the chiefs of the party injured shall make application to the agent of the United States, who is charged with the delivery of the annuities of the tribe to which the offending party belongs, whose duty it shall be to hear the proofs and allegations on either side, and determine between them: and the amount of his award shall be immediately deducted from the annuity of the tribe to which the offending party belongs, and given to the person injured, or to the chief of his village for his use.

ARTICLE 8. The United States agree to relinquish their right to the reservation, at the old Ouroctenon towns, made by the treaty of Greenville, so far at least as to make no further use of it than for the establishment of a military post.

ARTICLE 9. The tribes who are party to this treaty, being desirous to show their attachment to their brothers the Kickapoos, agree to cede to the United States the lands on the north-west side of the Wabash, from the Vincennes tract to a northwardly extention of the line running from the mouth of the aforesaid Raccoon creek, and fifteen miles in width from the Wabash, on condition that the United States shall allow them an annuity of four hundred dollars. But this article is to have no effect unless the Kickapoos will agree to it.

In testimony whereof, the said William Henry Harrison, and the sachems and war chiefs of the before mentioned tribes, have hereunto set their hands and affixed their seals, at Fort Wayne, this thirtieth of September, eighteen hundred and nine.

William Henry Harrison

Delawares: Anderson, for Hockingpomskon, who is absent, his x mark, Anderson, his x mark, Petchekekapon, his x mark, The Beaver, his x mark, Captian Killbuck, his x mark,
Pattawatimas: Winnemac, his x mark, Five Medals, by his son, his x mark, Mogawgo, his x mark, Shissahecon, for himself and his brother Tuthinipee, his x mark, Ossmeet, brother to Five Medals, his x mark, Nanousekah, Penamo's

son, his x mark, Mosser, his x mark, Chequinimo, his x mark, Sackanackshut, his x mark, Cohengee, his x mark,
Miamis: Pucan, his x mark, The Owl, his x mark, Meshekenoghqua, or the Little Turtle, his x mark, Wapemangua, or the Loon, his x mark, Silver Heels, his x mark, Shawapenomo, his x mark,
Eel Rivers: Charley, his x mark, Sheshangomequah, or Swallow, his x mark, The young Wyandot, a Miami of Elk Hart, his x mark,.

In presence of Peter Jones, secretary to the Commissioner, John Johnson, Indian agent, A. Heald, Capt. U. S. Army, A. Edwards, surgeon's mate, Ph. Ostrander, Lieut. U. S. Army, John Shaw, Stephen Johnston, J. Hamilton, sheriff of Dearborn County, Hendrick Aupaum, ut. William Wells, John Conner, Joseph Barron, Abraham Ash, Sworn Intepreters, George McDougall, chief judge court D. H. and D, C. Rush, attorney general, Jacob Visger, associate judge of the D. court, Jos. Watson, secretary to the legislature of Michigan, Abijah Hull, surveyor for Michigan Territory, Harris H. Hickman, counsellor at law, Abraham Fuller Hull,, ounsellor at law and secretary to the Commission, Whitmore Knaggs, William Walker, Sworn Interpreters.

TREATY WITH THE WYANDOT, ETC. {1814, July 22}
Ratified, Dec. 13, 1814.
Proclaimed Dec. 21 1814.

At treaty of Peace and friendship between the United States of America, and the tribes of Indians called thee Wyandots, Delawares, Shawanoese, Senecas, and Miamies.

THE said United States of America, by William Henry Harrison, late a major general in the army of the United States, and Lewis Cass, governor of the Michigan territory, duly authorized and appointed commissioners for the purpose, and the said tribes, by their head men, chiefs, and warriors, assembled at Greenville, in the state of Ohio, have agreed to the following articles, which, when ratified by the president of the United States, by and with the advice and consent of the Senate thereof, shall be binding upon them and the said tribes.

ARTICLE 1. The United States and the Wyandots, Delaware's, Shawanoese, and Senecas, give peace to the Miamie nation of Indians, formerly designated as the Miamie Eel River and Weea tribes; they extend this indulgence also to the bands of the Putawatimies, which adhere to the Grand Sachem Tobinipee, and to the chief Onoxa, to the Ottawas of Blanchard's creek, who have attached themselves to the Shawanoese tribe, and to such of the said tribe as adhere to the chief called the Wing, in the neighborhood of Detroit, and to the Kickapoos, under the direction of their chiefs who sign this treaty.

ARTICLE 2. The tribes and bands abovementioned, engage to give their aid to the United States in prosecuting the war against Great-Britain, and such of the Indian tribes as still continue hostile; and to make no peace with either without the consent of the United States. The assistance herein stipulated for, is to consist of such a number of their warriors from each tribe, as the president of the United States, or any officer having his authority therefor, may require.

ARTICLE 3. The Wyandot tribe, and the Senecas of Sandusky and Stony Creek, the Delaware and Shawanoes tribes, who have preserved their fidelity to the United States throughout the war, again acknowledge themselves under the protection of the said states, and of no other power whatever; and agree to aid the United States, in the manner stipulated for in the former article, and to make no peace but with the consent of the said states.

ARTICLE 4. In the event of a faithful performance of the conditions of this treaty, the United States will confirm and establish all the boundaries between their lands and those of the Wyandots, Delawares, Shawanoese and Miamies, as they existed previously to the commencement of the war.

In testimony whereof, the said commissioners, and the said head men, chiefs, and warriors, of the beforementioned tribes of Indians, have hereunto set their hands and affixed their seals.

Done at Greenville, in the State of Ohio, this twenty-second day of July, in the year of our Lord one thousand eight hundred and fourteen, and of the independence of the United States the thirty-ninth.

William Henry Harrison, Lewis Cass,
Wyandots: Tarhe, or Crane, his x mark, Harroneyough, or Cherokee Boy, his x mark, Tearroneauou, or between the Legs, his x mark, Menoucou, his x mark, Rusharra, or Stookey, his x mark, Senoshus, his x mark, Zashuona, or Big Arm, his x mark, Teanduttasooh, or Punch, his x mark, Tapuksough, or John Hicks, his x mark, Ronoinness, or Sky come down, his x mark, Teendoo, his x mark, Ronaiis, his x mark, Omaintsiarnah, or Bowyers, his x mark,
Delawares: Taiunshrah, or Charles, his x mark, Tiundraka, or John Bolesle, his x mark, Eroneniarah, or Shroneseh; his x mark, Kicktohenina, or Captain Anderson, his x mark, Lemottenuckques, or James Nanticoke, his x mark, Laoponnichle, or Baube, his x mark, Joon Queake, or John Queake, his x mark, Kill Buck, his x mark, Neachcomingd, his x mark, Montgomery Montawe, his x mark, Capt. Buck, his x mark, Hooque, or Mole, his x mark, Captain White Eyes, his x mark,

Captain Pipe, his x mark, McDaniel, his x mark, Captain Snap, his x mark, Shawanees: Cutewecusa, or Black Hoof, his x mark, Tamenetha, or Butter, his x mark, Piaseka, or Wolf, his x mark, Pomtha, or Walker, his x mark,

Shammonetho, or Snake, his x mark, Pemthata, or Turkey flying by, his x mark, Wethawakasika, or Yellow Water, his x mark, Quetawah, Sinking, his x mark, Sokutchemah, or Frozen, his x mark, Wynepuechsika, or Corn Stalk, his x mark, Chiachska, or captain Tom, his x mark, Quitawepeh, or captain Lewis, his x mark, Teawascoota, or Blue Jacket, his x mark,

Tacomtequah, or Cross the water, his x mark,

Ottawas: Watashnewa, or Bear's Legs, his x mark, Wapachek, or White Fisher, his x mark, Tootagen, or Bell, his x mark, Aughquanahquose, or Stumptail Bear, his x mark, Mcokenuh, or Bear King, his x mark,

Senekas: Coontindnau, or Coffee Houn, his x mark, Togwon, his x mark, Endosquierunt, or John Harris, his x mark, Cantareteroo, his x mark, Cuntahtentuhwa, or Big Turtle, his x mark, Renonnesa, or Wiping Stick, his x mark, Corachcoonke, or Reflection, or Civil John, his x mark, Coonautanahtoo, his x mark, Seeistahe, Black, his x mark, Tooteeandee, Thomas Brand, his x mark, Haneusewa, his x mark, Uttawuntus, his x mark, Lutauqueson, his x mark,

Miamis: Pecon, his x mark, Lapassine, or Ashenonquah, his x mark, Osage, his x mark, Natoweesa, his x mark, Meshekeleata, or the Big man, his x mark, Sanamahhonga, or Stone Eater, his x mark, Neshepehtah, or Double Tooth, his x mark, Metoosania, or Indian, his x mark, Chequia, or Poor Racoon, his x mark, Wapepecheka, his x mark, his x mark, Chingomega Eboo, or Owl, his x mark, Kewesekong, or Circular Travelling, his x mark, Wapasabanah, or White Racoon, his x mark,

Chekemetine, or Turtle's Brother, his x mark, Pocondoqua, or Crooked, his x mark, Chequeah, or Poor Racoon, a Wea, or Little Eyes, his x mark, Showilingeshua, or Open Hand, his x mark, Okawea, or Porcupine, his x mark, Shawanoe, his x mark, Mawansa, or Young Wolf, his x mark, Meshwawa, or Wounded, his x mark, Sangwecomya, or Buffaloe, his x mark, Pequia, or George, his x mark, Keelswa, or Sun, his x mark, Wabsea, or White Skin, his x mark, Wansepea, or Sunrise, his x mark,

Angatoka, or Pile of Wood, his x mark,

Pattawatimas: Toopinnepe, his x mark, Onoxa, or Five Medals, his x mark, Metea, his x mark, Conge, or Bear's foot, his x mark, Nanownseca, his x mark, Chagobbe, or One who sees all over, his x mark, Meshon, his x mark, Penosh, his x mark, Checanoe, his x mark, Neshcootawa, his x mark, Tonguish, his x mark, Nebaughkua, his x mark, Wesnanesa, his x mark, Chechock, or Crane, his x mark, Kepoota, his x mark, Mackoota, or Crow, his x mark, Papeketcha, or Flat Belly, his x mark,

Kickapoos: Ketoote, or Otter, his x mark, Makotanecote, or Black Tree, his x mark, Sheshepa, or Duck, his x mark, Wapekonnia, or White Blanket, his x mark, Acooche, or the Man Hun, his x mark, Chekaskagalon, his x mark,

In presence of (the words "and the Wyandots, Delawares, Shawanees, and Senekas," interlined in the first article before signing): James Dill, secretary to the commissioners, Jno. Johnston, Indian agent, B. F. Stickney, Indian agent,

James J. Nisbet, associate judge of court of common pleas, Preble County, Thos. G. Gibson, Antoine Boindi, Wm. Walker, William Connor, J. Bts. Chandonnai, Stephen Ruddeed, James Pelteir, Joseph Bertrand, sworn interpreters, Thos. Ramsey, captain First Rifle Regiment, John Conner, John Riddle, colonel First Regiment Ohio Militia.

TREATY WITH THE PIANKASHAW {1815, July 18}
Ratified, Dec. 26, 1815.

A treaty of peace and friendship, made and concluded at Portage des Sioux between William Clark, Miami Edwards, and Auguste Chouteau, Commissioners Plenipotentiary of the United States of America, on the part and behalf of the said States, of the one part; and the undersigned Chiefs and Warriors of the Piankishaw Tribe or Nation, on the part and behalf of the said Tribe or Nation, of the other part.

THE parties being anxious of re-establishing peace and friendship between the United States and the said tribe or nation, and of being placed in all things, and in every respect, on the same footing upon which they stood before the war, have agreed to the following articles:

ARTICLE 1. Every injury or act of hostility by one or either of the contracting parties against the other, shall be mutually forgiven and forgot.

ARTICLE 2. There shall be perpetual peace and friendship between all the citizens of the United States of America and all the individuals composing the Piankishaw tribe or nation.

ARTICLE 3. The contracting parties, in the sincerity of mutual friendship, recognize, re-establish, and confirm, all and every treaty, contract, or agreement, heretofore concluded between the United States and the said Piankishaw tribe or nation.
In witness of all and every thing herein determined between the United States of America, and the said Piankeshaw tribe or nation: we, their underwritten commissioners, and chiefs aforesaid, by virtue of our full powers, have signed this definitive treaty, and have caused our seals to be hereunto affixed. [112]

Done at Portage des Sioux, this eighteenth day of July, in the year of our Lord, one thousand eight hundred and fifteen, and of the independence of the United States of America the fortieth.

William Clark, Ninian Edwards, Auguste Choteau, La-ma-noan, or the Axe, his x mark, La-mee-pris-jeau, or Sea-wolf, his x mark, Mon-sai-raa, or Rusty, his x mark, Wa-pan-gia, or Swan, his x mark, Na-maing-sa, or the Fish, his x mark.

Done at Portage des Sioux, in the presence of:

R. Wash, secretary to the commissioners, Thomas Forsyth, Indian agent, N. Boilvin, agent, T. Paul, C. C. M, Maurice Blondeaux, John Hay, John Miller, colonel Third Infantry, Richard Chitwood, major mounted, Wm. Irvine Adair, captain Third Regiment U. S. Infantry, Cyrus Edwards, Saml. Solomon, Jacques Mette, Louis Decouagne, John A. Cameron, sworn interpr't'rs, F. Duchouquet, United States interpreter, W. Louis Bufait, Indian interpreter, J. Bts. Chandonnai, interpreter, W. Knaggs, Antoine Bondi, Jean Bt. Massac, his x mark.

TREATY WITH THE WYANDOT, ETC. {1815, Sept. 8}
Ratified Dec. 26, 1815.

A Treaty between the United States of America and the Wyandot, Delaware, Seneca, Shawanoe, Miami, Chippewa, Ottawa, and Potawatimie, Tribes of Indians, residing within the limits of the State of Ohio, and the Territories of Indiana and Michigan.

WHEREAS the Chippewa, Ottawa, and Potawatimie, tribes of Indians, together with certain bands of the Wyandot, Delaware, Seneca, Shawanoe, and Miami tribes, were associated with Great Britain in the late war between the United States and that power, and have manifested a disposition to be restored to the relations of peace and amity with the said States; and the President of the United States having appointed William Henry Harrison, late a Major General in the service of the United States, Duncan M'Arthur, late a Brigadier in the service of the United States, and John Graham, Esquire, as Commissioners to treat with the said tribes; the said Commissioners and the Sachems, Headmen, and Warriors, of said tribes having met in Council at the Spring Wells, near the city of Detroit, have agreed to the following Articles, which, when ratified by the President, by and with the advice and consent of the Senate of the United States, shall be binding on them and the said tribes:

ARTICLE 1. The United States give peace to the Chippewa, Ottawa, and Potawatimie, tribes.

ARTICLE 2. They also agree to restore to the said Chippewa, Ottawa, and Potawatimie tribes all the possessions, rights, and privileges, which they enjoyed, or were entitled to, in the year one thousand eight hundred and eleven, prior to the commencement of the late war with Great Britain; and the said tribes, upon their part, agree again to place themselves under the protection of the United States, and of no other power whatsoever.

ARTICLE 3. In consideration of the fidelity to the United States which has been manifested by the Wyandot, Delaware, Seneca, and Shawanoe, tribes, throughout the late war, and of the repentance of the Miami tribe, as manifested by placing themselves under the protection of the United States, by the treaty of Greenville, in eighteen hundred and fourteen, the said States agree to pardon such of the chiefs and warriors of said tribes as may have continued hostilities against them until the close of the war with Great Britain, and to permit the chiefs of their respective tribes to restore them to the stations and property which they held previously to the war.

ARTICLE 4. The United States and the beforementioned tribes or nations of Indians, that is to say, the Wyandot, Delaware, Seneca, Shawanoe, Miami, Chippewa, Ottawa, and Potawatimies, agree to renew and confirm the treaty of Greenville, made in the year one thousand seven hundred and ninety-five, and all subsequent treaties to which they were, respectively, parties, and the same are hereby again ratified and confirmed in as full a manner as if they were inserted in this treaty.

Done at Spring Wells, the eighth day of September, in the year of our Lord one thousand eight hundred and fifteen, and of the independence of the United States, the fortieth.
In testimony whereof, they, the said commissioners, and the sachems, head men and warriors of the different tribes, have hereunto set their hands, and affixed their seals.

William Henry Harrison, Duncan McArthur, John Graham,
Wyandot chiefs: Tarhee, or the crane, his x mark, Harrouyeou, or Cherokee boy, his x mark, Sanohskee, or long house, his x mark, Outoctutimoh, or cub, his x mark, Myecruh, or walk in the water, his x mark, Tyanumka, his x mark, Mymehamkee, or Barnett, his x mark, Shawanoe chiefs: Cutaweskeshah, or black hoof, his x mark, Nutsheway, or wolf's brother, his x mark, Tamenatha, or butler, his x mark, Shemenetoo, or big snake, his x mark, Outhowwa-heshegath, or yellow plume, his x mark, Quatawwepay, or capt. Lewis, his x mark, Mishquathree, or capt. Reid, his x mark, Tecumtequah, his x mark,

Ottawa chiefs: Tontegenah, orthedog, his x mark, Tashcuygon, or McArtlmr, his x mark, Okemas, or little chief, his x mark, Nashkemah, his x mark, Watashnewah, his x mark, Onqunogesh, or ugly fellow, his x mark, Menitugawboway, or the devil standing, his x mark, Kelystum, or first actor, his x mark, Ottawas from Mackinack: Kemenechagon, or the bastard, his x mark, Karbenequane, or the one who went in front, his x mark,
Ottawa from Grand River: Mechequez, his x mark,

A Winnebago from Mackinack: Wassachum, or first to start the whites, his x mark, Chippewa chiefs: Papnescha, or turn round about, his x mark, Nowgeschick, or twelve o' clock, his x mark, Shamanetoo, or God Almighty, his x mark, Wissenesoh, his x mark, Cacheonquet, or big cloud, his x mark, Pasheskiskaquashcum, Menactome, or the little fly, his x mark, Enewame, or crow, his x mark, Nauaquaoto, his x mark, Paanassee, or the bird, his mark,

Delaware chiefs: Toctowayning, or Anderson, his x mark, Lamahtanoquez, his x mark, Matahoopan, his x mark, Aaheppan, or the buck, his x mark, Jim Killbuck, his x mark, Captain Beaver, his x mark, McDonald, his x mark,
Seneca chiefs: Tahummindoyeh, or between words, his x mark, Yonundankykueurent, or John Harris, his x mark, Masomea, orCivilJohn, his x mark, Saccorawahtah, OT wiping stick, his x mark,

Potawatimie chiefs: Topeeneebee, his x mark, Nonngeesai, or five medals, his x mark, Naynauawsekaw, his x mark, Joeeonce, his x mark, Cocneg, his x mark, Ohshawkeebee, his x mark, Waineamaygoas, his x mark, Meeksawbay, his x mark, Mongaw, his x mark, Nawnawmee, his x mark, Chay Chauk, or the crane, his x mark, Wanaunaiskee, his x mark, Pashapow, his x mark, Honkemani, or the chief, his x mark, Neesscatimeneemay, his x mark, Ponngeasais, his x mark, Nounnawkeskawaw, his x mark,

Chickawno, his x mark, Mitteeay, his x mark, Messeecawee, his x mark, Neepoashe, his x mark, Kaitchaynee, his x mark, Waymeego, or W. H. Harrison, his x mark, Louison, his x mark, Osheouskeebee, his x mark,

Miami chiefs: Pacan, his x mark, Singomesha, or the owl, his x mark, Totanag, or the butterfly, his x mark, Osage, or the neutral, his x mark, Wabsioung, or the white skin, his x mark, Wapaassabina, or white racoon, his x mark, Otteutaqua, or a blower of his breath, his x mark, Makatasabina, or black racoon, his x mark,

Wapeshesa, or white appearance in the water, his x mark, Motosamea, or Indian, his x mark, Shacanbe, his x mark, Shequar, or the poor racoon, his x mark, Cartanquar, or the sky, his x mark, Okemabenaseh, or the king bird, his x mark, Wapenaseme, or the collector of birds, his x mark, Mecinabee, or the setting stone, his x mark, Annawba, his x mark, Mashepesheewingqua, or tiger's face, his x mark,

Signed in the presence of: A. L. Langhan, secretary to the commission, Lewis Cass, James Miller, brig. general U. S. Army, Willoughby Morgan, major U. S. Army, A. B. Woodward, Hy. B. Brevoort, late Major Forty-fifth Infantry, John Bidder, Captain U. S. Corps Artillery, James May, J. P., Peter Audrain, Reg. L. O. D., Jn. K. Walker, Wyandot interpreter, Francis Jansen, James Riley, interpreter, William Kingg, Francois Mouton, John Kenzie, interpreter, F. Duchouquet, United States interpreter,

TREATY WITH THE CHEROKEE {1816, Mar. 22}
Ratified Apr. 8, 1816

Articles of a treaty made and concluded at the City of Washington, on the twenty-second day of March, one thousand eight hundred and sixteen, between George Graham, being ,specially authorized by the President of the United States thereto, and the undersigned Chiefs and Headmen of the Cherokee Nation, duly authorized and empowered by the said Nation.

ARTICLE 1. Whereas the Executive of the State of South Carolina has made an application to the President of the United States to extinguish the claim of the Cherokee nation to that part of their lands which lie within the boundaries of the said State, as lately established and agreed upon between that State and the State of North Carolina; and as the Cherokee nation is disposed to comply with the wishes of their brothers of South Carolina, they have agreed and do hereby agree to cede to the State of South Carolina, and forever quit claim to, the tract of country contained within the following bounds, viz:: beginning on the east bank of the Chattuga river, where the boundary line of the Cherokee nation crosses the same, running thence, with the said boundary line, to a rock on the Blue Ridge, where the boundary line crosses the same, and which rock has been lately established as a corner to the States of North and South Carolina; running thence, south, sixty-eight and a quarter degrees west, twenty miles and thirty-two chains, to a rock on the Chattuga river at the thirty-fifth degree of north latitude, another corner of the boundaries agreed upon by the State of North and South Carolina; thence, down and with the Chattuga, to the beginning.

ARTICLE 2. For and in consideration of the above cession, the United States promise and engage that the State of South Carolina shall pay to the Cherokee nation, or its accredited agent, the sum of five thousand dollars, within ninety days after the President and Senate shall have ratified this treaty: Provided, That the Cherokee nation shall have sanctioned the same in Council: And provided also, That the Executive of the State of South Carolina shall approve of the stipulations contained in this article.

In testimony whereof, the said commissioner, and the undersigned chiefs and head men of the Cherokee nation, have hereto set their hands and seals.

George Graham, Colonel John Lowry, his x mark, Major John Walker, his x mark, Major Ridge, his x mark, Richard Taylor, John Ross, Cheucunsene, his x mark,

Witnesses present at signing and sealing: Return J. Meigs, Jacob Laub, Gid. Davis, W., Louis Bufait, Indian interpreter, J. Bts. Chandonnai, interpreter, W. Knaggs, Antoine Bondi, Jean Bt. Massac, his x mark.

TREATY WITH THE WEA AND KICKAPOO {1816, June 4}
Proclamation, Dec. 30, 1816.

Articles of a treaty made and entered into at Fort Harrison, in the Indiana Territory between Benjamin Parke, specially authorized thereto by the president of the United States, of the one part, and the tribes of Indians called the Weas and Kickapoos, by their chiefs and head men of the other part.

ARTICLE 1. The Weas and Kickapoos again acknowledge themselves in peace and friendship with the United States.

ARTICLE 2. The said tribes acknowledge the validity of, and declare their determination to adhere to, the treaty of Greenville, made in the year seventeen hundred and ninety-five, and all subsequent treaties which they have respectively made with the United States.

ARTICLE 3. The boundary line, surveyed and marked by the United States, of the land on the Wabash and White rivers, ceded in the year eighteen hundred and nine, the said tribes do hereby explicitly recognize and confirm, as having been executed conformably to the several treaties they have made with the United States.

ARTICLE 4. The chiefs and warriors of the said tribe of the Kickapoos acknowledge that they have ceded to the United States all that tract of country which lies between the aforesaid boundary line on the north west slate of the Wabashthe Wabash, the Vermillion river, and a line to be drawn from the north west corner of the said boundary line, so as to strike the Vermillion river twenty miles in a direct line from its mouth, according to the terms and conditions of the treaty they made with the United States on the ninth day of December, in the year eighteen hundred and nine.

In testimony whereof, the said Benjamin Parke, and the chiefs and head men of the said tribes, have hereunto set their hands and affixed their seals, at fort Harrison, in the Indiana territory, the fourth day of June, in the year of our Lord, one thousand eight hundred and sixteen.

B. Parke.
Weas: Mesaupeekaunga, or Gamlan, his x mark, Jacco, his x mark, Kesanguekamya, or Buffalo, his x mark, Chequiha, or Little Eyes, his x mark, Mahquakouonga, or Negro Legs, his x mark, Pequaih, or George, his x mark,

Kenokosetah, or Long Body, his x mark, OWl, (a Miami) his x mark, MahChekeleatah, or Big Man, (a Miami) his x mark,
Kickapoos: Sheshepah, or Little Duck, his x mark, Kaanehkaka, or Drunkard's Son, his x mark, Shekonah, or Stone, his x mark, Mahquah, or Bear, his x mark, Penashee, or Little Turkey, his x mark, Mehtahkokeah, or Big Tree, his x mark, Mauquasconiah, or Big Tree, his x mark, Kcetahtey, or Little Otter, his x mark, Nepiseeah, or Blackberry, his x mark, Pehsquonatah, or Blackberry Flower, his x mark, Tecumthena, or Track in Prairie, his x mark.

Done in the presence of: John L. McCollough, secretary to the commission, John T. Chunn, major, commanding Fort Harrison, Gab. I. Floyd, lieutenant U. S. Army, Th. McCall, of Vincennes, Henry Gilham, of Vincennes, N. B. Baily, of Vincennes, G. C. Copp, Michael Brouillet, interpreter, at Fort Harrison, Joseph Barron, sworn interpreter.

TREATY WITH THE OTTAWA, ETC. {1816, Aug. 24}
Proclamation, Dec. 30, 1816.

A treaty of Peace, Friendship, and Limits, made and concluded between Ninian Edwards, William Clark, and Auguste Chouteau, commissioners plenipotentiary of the United States of America, on the part and behalf of said states, of the one part, and the chiefs and warriors of the united tribes of Ottawas, Chippewas, and Pottowotomees, residing on the Illinois and Melwakee rivers, and their waters, and on the southwestern parts Lake Michigan, of the other part.

WHEREAS a serious dispute has for some time past existed between the contracting parties relative to the right to a part of the lands ceded to the United States by the tribes of Sacs and Foxes, on the third day of November, one thousand eight hundred and four, and both parties being desirous of preserving a harmonious and friendly intercourse, and of establishing permanent peace and friendship, have, for the purpose of removing all difficulties, agreed to the following terms:

ARTICLE 1. The said chiefs and warriors, for themselves and the tribes they represent, agree to relinquish, and hereby do relinquish, to the United States, all their right, claim, and title, to all the land contained in the before-mentioned cession of the Sacs and Foxes, which lies south of a due west line from the southern extremity of Lake Michigan to the Mississippi river, And they moreover cede to the United States all the land contained within the following bounds, to wit: beginning on the left bank of the Fox river of Illinois, ten miles above the mouth of said Fox river; thence running so as to cross Sandy creek, ten miles above its mouth; thence, in a direct line, to a point ten miles north of the west end of the Portage, between Chicago creek, which empties into Lake Michigan, and the river Depleines, a fork of the Illinois; thence, in a direct line, to a point on Lake Michigan, ten miles northward of the mouth of Chicago creek; thence, along the lake, to a point ten miles southward of the mouth of the said Chicago creek; thence, in a direct line, to a point on the Kankakee, ten miles above its mouth; thence, with the said Kankakee and the Illinois river, to the mouth of Fox river, and thence to the beginning: Provided, nevertheless, That the said tribes shall be permitted to hunt and fish within the limits of the land hereby relinquished and ceded, so long as it may continue to be the property of the United States.

ARTICLE 2. In consideration of the aforesaid relinquishment and cession, the United States have this day delivered to said tribes a considerable quantity of merchandise, and do agree to pay them, annually, for the term of twelve years, goods to the value of one thousand dollars, reckoning that value at the first cost of the goods in the city or place in which they shall be purchased, without any charge for transportation; which said goods shall be delivered to the said tribes at some place on the Illinois river, not lower down than Peoria. And the said United States do moreover agree to relinquish to the said tribes all the land contained in the aforesaid cession of the Sacs and Foxes, which lies north of a due west line, from the southern extremity of Lake Michigan to the Mississippi river, except three leagues square at the mouth of the Ouisconsing river, including both banks, and such other tracts, [133] on or near to the Ouisconsing and Mississippi rivers, as the president of the United States may think proper to reserve:-Provided, That such other tracts shall not in the whole exceed the quantity that would be contained in five leagues square.

ARTICLE 3. The contracting parties, that peace and friendship may be permanent, promise that in all things whatever, they will act with justice and correctness towards each other, and that they will, with perfect good faith, fulfill all the obligations imposed upon them by former treaties.
In witness whereof, the said Ninian Edwards, William Clark, and Auguste Chouteau, commissioners aforesaid, and the chiefs and warriors of the aforesaid tribes, have hereunto subscribed their names and affixed their seals, this twenty-fourth day of August, one thousand eight hundred and sixteen, and of the independence of the United States the forty-first.

Ninian Edwards, William Clark, Auguste Chouteau,
Mucketeypokee, or Black Partridge, his x mark, Sinnowchewone, by his brother Ignatius, his x mark, Mucketepennese,or Black Bird, his x mark, Bendegakewa, his x mark, Pemasaw, or Walker, his x mark, Ontawa, Nangesay, alias Stout, his x mark, Chamblee, his x mark, Cacake, his x mark, Shawanoe, his x mark, Wapunsy, his x mark, Cunnepepy, his x mark, Wonesee, his x mark, Richeikeming, or Lake, his x mark, Cabenaw, his x mark, Opaho, his x mark, Cowwesaut, his x mark, Chekinaka, his x mark, Macheweskeaway, his x mark, Spanquissee, his x mark, Ignatius, his x mark, Takaonenee, his x mark, Ottawonce, his x mark, Tawwaning, orTrader, his x mark, Cashshakee, his x

mark, Nigigwash, his x mark, Shesheburigge, Mowais, or Little Wolf, his x mark,

Done at St. Louis, in the presence of: R. Wash, secretary to the commission, R. Graham, Indian agent for the Territory of Illinois, Thomas Forsyth, Indian agent, J. Maul, lieutenant Eighth Regiment of Infantry,

TREATY WITH THE CHEROKEE {1816, Sept. 14}
Proclamation, Dec. 30, 1816.

To perpetuate peace and friendship between the United States and Cherokee tribe, or nation, of Indians, and to remove all future causes of dissension which may arise from indefinite territorial boundaries, the president of the United States of America, by major general Andrew Jackson, general David Meriwether, and Jesse Franklin, esquire, commissioners plenipotentiary on the one part, and the Cherokee delegates on the other, covenant and agree to the following articles and conditions, which, when approved by the Cherokee nation, and constitutionally ratified by the government of the United States, shall be binding on all parties:

ARTICLE 1. Peace and friendship are hereby firmly established between the United States and Cherokee nation or tribe of Indians.

ARTICLE 2. The Cherokee nation acknowledge the following as their western boundary: South of the Tennessee river, commencing at Camp Coffee, on the south side of the Tennessee river, which is opposite the Chickasaw Island, running from thence a due south course to the top of the dividing ridge between the waters of the Tennessee and Tombigby rivers, thence eastwardly along said ridge, leaving the head waters of the Black Warrior to the right hand, until opposed by the west branch of Well's Creek, down the east bank of said creek to the Coosa river, and down said river. [134]

ARTICLE 3. The Cherokee nation relinquish to the United States all claim, and cede all title to lands laying south and west of the line, as described in the second article; and, in consideration of said relinquishment and cession, the commissioners agree to allow the Cherokee nation an annuity of six thousand dollars, to continue for ten successive years, and five thousand dollars, to be paid in sixty days after the ratification of the treaty, as a compensation for any improvements which the said nation may have had on the lands surrendered.

ARTICLE 4. The two contracting parties covenant, and agree, that the line, as described in the second article, shall be ascertained and marked by commissioners, to be appointed by the president of the United States; that the marks shall be bold; trees to be blazed on both sides of the line, and the fore and aft trees to be marked with the letters U. S.; that the commissioners shall be accompanied by two persons, to be appointed by the Cherokee nation, and that said nation, shall have due and seasonable notice when said operation is to be commenced.

ARTICLE 5. It is stipulated that the Cherokee nation will meet general Andrew Jackson, general David Meriwether, and Jesse Franklin, esquire, in council, at Turkey's Town, Coosa river, on the 28th of September, (instant) there and then to express their approbation, or not, of the articles of this treaty; and if they do not assemble at the time and place specified, it is understood that the said commissioners may report the same as a tacit ratification, on the part of the Cherokee nation, of this treaty.

In testimony whereof, the said commissioners and undersigned chiefs and delegates of the Cherokee nation, have hereto set their hands and seals.

Done at the Chickasaw council house, this fourteenth day of September, in the year of our Lord one thousand eight hundred and sixteen.

Andrew Jackson, D. Meriwether, J. Franklin, Toochalar, Oohulookee, Wososey, Gousa, Spring Frog, Oowatata, John Beuge, John Bawldridge, Sallocooke Fields, George Guess, Bark, Campbell, Spirit, Young Wolf, Oolitiskee.

Witness: James Gadsden, secretary to the commissioners, Arthur P. Hayne, inspector general, division of the South, James C. Bronaugh, hospital surgeon, U.S. Army, John Gordon, John Rhea, Thomas Wilson, interpreter for the Cherokees, A. McCoy, interpreter for the Cherokees.

Ratified at Turkey Town, by the whole Cherokee nation in council assembled. In testimony whereof, the subscribing commissioners of the United States, and the undersigned chiefs and warriors of the Cherokee nation, have hereto set their hands and seals, this fourth day of October, in the year of our Lord one thousand eight hundred and sixteen.

Andrew Jackson, D. Meriwether,

Path Killer, his x mark, The Glass, his x mark, Sour Mush, his x mark, Chulioa, his x mark,

Witness: James Gadsden, secretary, Return J. Meigs, Richard Taylor, interpreter, A. McCoy, interpreter.
Dick Justice, his x mark, Richard Brown, his x mark, Bark, his x mark, The Boot, his x mark, Chickasawlua, his x mark.

TREATY WITH THE CHICKASAW {1816, Sept. 20}
Proclamation, Dec. 30, 1816.

To settle all territorial controversies, and to perpetuate that peace and harmony which has long happily subsisted between the United States and Chickasaw nation, the president of the United States of America, by major general Andrew Jackson, general David Meriwether, and Jesse Franklin, esq. on the one part, and the whole Chickasaw nation, in council assembled, on the other, have agreed on the following articles, which when ratified by the president, with the advice and consent of the senate of the United States, shall be binding on all parties:

ARTICLE 1. Peace and friendship are hereby firmly established, and perpetuated, between the United States of America and Chickasaw nation.

ARTICLE 2. The Chickasaw nation cede to the United States (with the exception of such reservations as shall hereafter be specified) all right or title to lands on the north side of the Tennessee river, and relinquish all claim to territory on the south side of said river, and east of a line commencing at the mouth of Caney creek, running up said creek to its source, thence a due south course to the ridge path, or commonly called Gaines's road, along said road south westwardly to a point on the Tombigby river, well known by the name of the Cotton Gin port, and down the west bank of the Tombigby to the Chocktaw boundary.

ARTICLE 3. In consideration of the relinquishment of claim, and cession of lands, made in the preceding article, the commissioners agree to allow the Chickasaw nation twelve thousand dollars per annum for ten successive years, and four thousand five hundred dollars to be paid in sixty days after the ratification of this treaty into the hands of Levi Colbert, as a compensation for any improvements which individuals of the Chickasaw nation may have had on the lands surrendered; that is to say, two thousand dollars for improvements on the east side of the Tombigby, and two thousand five hundred dollars for improvements on the north side of the Tennessee river.

ARTICLE 4. The commissioners agree that the following tracts of land shall be reserved to the Chickasaw nation:
First. One tract of land for the use of Col. George Colbert and heirs, and which is thus described by said Colbert: "Beginning on the north bank of the Tennessee river, at a point that, running north four miles, will include a big spring, about half way between his ferry and the mouth of Cypress, it being a spring that a large cow-path crosses its branch near where a cypress tree is cut down; thence westwardly to a point, four miles from the Tennessee river, and standing due north of a point on the north bank of the river, three (four) miles below his ferry on the Tennessee river, and up the meanders of said river to the beginning point."

105

Second. A tract of land two miles square on the north bank of the Tennessee river, and at its junction with Beach creek, for the use of Appassan Tubby and heirs.

Third. A tract of land one mile square, on the north side of the Tennessee river, for the use of John M'Cleish and heirs, the said tract to be so run as to include the said M'Cleish's settlement and improvements on the north side of Buffalo creek.

Fourth. Two tracts of land, containing forty acres each, on the south side of Tennessee river, and about two and a half miles below the Cotton Gin port, on the Tombigby river, which tracts of land will be pointed out by Major Levi Colbert, and for the use of said Colbert and heirs.

It is stipulated that the above reservations shall appertain to the Chickasaw nation only so long as they shall be occupied, cultivated, or used, by the present proprietors or heirs, and in the event of all or either of said tracts of land, so reserved, being abandoned by the present proprietors or heirs, each tract or tracts of land, so abandoned, [136] shall revert to the United States as a portion of that territory ceded by the second article of this treaty.

ARTICLE 5. The two contracting parties covenant and agree that the line on the south side of the Tennessee river, as described in the second article of this treaty, shall be ascertained and marked by commissioners to be appointed by the president of the United States; that the marks shall be bold; trees to be blazed on both sides of the line, and the fore and aft trees to be marked with the letters U.S. That the commissioners shall be attended by two persons to be designated by the Chickasaw nation, and that the said nation shall have due and seasonable notice when said operation is to be commenced.

ARTICLE 6. In consideration of the conciliatory disposition evinced, during the negotiation of this treaty, by the Chickasaw chiefs and warriors, but more particularly as a manifestation of the friendship and liberality of the president of the United States, the commissioners agree to give, on the ratification of this treaty, to Chinnubby, king of the Chickasaws, to Tishshominco, William M'Gilvery, Arpasarshtubby, Samuel Scely, James Brown, Levi Colbert, Ickaryoucullaha, George Pettygrove, Immartarharmicko, Chickasaw chiefs, and to Malcolm M'Gee interpreter one hundred and fifty dollars each, in goods or cash, as may be preferred, and to major William Glover, colonel George Colbert, Capt. Rabbitt, Hoparyeahoummar, Immoukelourshsharhoparyea, Hoparyea, Houllartir, Tushkerhopoyyea, Hoparyeahoummar, jun. Immoukelusharhopoyyea, James Colbert, Coweamarthlar, and Iilna-chouwarhopoyyea, military leaders, one hundred dollars each; and, as a particular mark of distinction and favor for his long services and faithful adherence to the United States government, the commissioners agree to allow to general William Colbert an annuity of one hundred dollars for and during his life.

ARTICLE 7. "Whereas the chiefs and warriors of the Chickasaw nation have found, from experience, that the crowd of pedlars, who are constantly traversing their nation from one end to the other, is of a serious disadvantage to the nation; that serious misunderstandings and disputes frequently take place, as well as frauds, which are often practised on the ignorant and uninformed of the nation, therefore it is agreed by the commissioners on the part of the government, and the chiefs of the nation, that no more licenses shall be granted by the agent of the Chickasaws to entitle any person or persons to trade or traffic merchandise in said nation; and that any person or persons, whomsoever, of the white people, who shall bring goods and sell them in the nation, contrary to this article, shall forfeit the whole of his or their goods, one half to the nation and the other half to the government of the United States; in all cases where this article is violated, and the goods are taken or seized, they shall be delivered up to the agent, who shall hear the testimony and judge accordingly."

This article was presented to the commissioners by the chiefs and warriors of the Chickasaw nation, and by their particular solicitation embraced in this treaty.

In testimony whereof, the said commissioners and undersigned chiefs and warriors have set their hands and seals.

Done at the Chickasaw council house, this twentieth day of September, in the year of our Lord one thousand eight hundred and sixteen.

Andrew Jackson, D. Meriwether, J. Franklin,

Chinnubby, King, his x mark, Tishshomingo, his x mark, William McGilvery, his x mark, Arpasarhtubby, his x mark, Samuel Seeley, his x mark, James Brown, his x mark, Levi Colbert, his x mark, Ickaryoucuttaha, his x mark,

George Pettygrove, his x mark, Immartarharmicco, his x mark, Maj. Gen. Wm. Colbert, his x mark, Major William Glover, his x mark, Major George Colbert, his x mark, Captain Rabbit, his x mark, Horoyeahoummar, his x mark, Immouklusharhopoyea, his x mark,

Hopoyeahoullarter, his x mark, Tushkarhopoyea, his x mark, Hopoyeahoummar, jr., his x mark, Immouklusharhopyea, his x mark, James Colbert, his x mark, Coweamarthtar, his x mark, Illachouwarhopoyea, his x mark,.

Witness: James Gadsden, secretary, William Cocke.

TREATY WITH THE CHOCTAW {1816, Oct. 24}
Proclamation, Dec. 30, 1816.

A treaty of cession between the United States of America and the Choctaw nation of Indians.

JAMES MADISON, president of the United States of America, by general John Coffee, John Rhea, and John M'Kee, esquires, commissioners on the part of the United States, duly authorized for that purpose, on the one part, and the mingoes, leaders, captains, and warriors, of the Chactaw nation, in general council assembled, in behalf of themselves and the whole nation, on the other part, have entered into the following articles, which, when ratified by the president of the United States, with the advice and consent of the senate, shall be obligatory on both parties:

ARTICLE 1. The Chactaw nation, for the consideration hereafter mentioned, cede to the United States all their title and claim to lands lying east of the following boundary, beginning at the mouth of Ooktibbuha, the Chickasaw boundary, and running from thence down the Tombigby river, until it intersects the northern boundary of a cession made to the United States by the Chactaws, at Mount Dexter, on the 16th November, 1805.

ARTICLE 2. In consideration of the foregoing cession, the United States engage to pay to the Chactaw nation the sum of six thousand dollars annually, for twenty years; they also agree to pay them in merchandise, to be delivered immediately on signing the present treaty, the sum of ten thousand dollars.

Done and executed in full and open council, at the Choctaw trading house, this twenty-fourth day of October, in the year of our Lord one thousand eight hundred and sixteen, and of the independence of the United States the forty-first.

John Coffee, John Rhea, John McKee,

Mushoolatubee, his x mark, Pooshamallaha, his x mark, Pukshunnubbu, his x mark, General Terror, his x mark, Choctaw Eestannokee, his x mark, General Humming Bird, his x mark, Talking warrior, his x mark, David Folsom, Bob Cole, his x mark, Oofuppa, his x mark, Hoopoieeskitteenee, his x mark, Hoopoieemiko, his x mark, Hoopoieethoma, his x mark,

Witness: Tho. H. Williams, secretary to the commission, John Pitchlynn, interpreter, Turner Broshear, interpreter, M. Mackey, interpreter, Silas Dinsmoor, R. Chamberlin, John Rhea, Malcum McGee, James Colbert, interpreter.

TREATY WITH THE CHEROKEE {1817, July 8}
Proclamation, Dec. 26, 1817.

Articles of a treaty concluded, at the Cherokee Agency, within the Cherokee
nation, between major general Andrew Jackson, Joseph M'Minn, governor of
the state of Tennessee, and general David Meriwether, commissioners plenipotentiary of the United States of America, of the one part, and the chiefs, head
men, and warriors, of the Cherokee nation, east of the Mississippi river, and the
chiefs, head men, and warriors, of the Cherokees on the Arkansas river, and
their deputies, John D. Chisholm and James Rogers, duly authorized by the
chiefs of the Cherokees on the Arkansas river, in open council, by written
power of attorney, duly signed and executed, in presence of Joseph Sevier and
William Ware.

WHEREAS in the autumn of the year one thousand eight hundred and eight, a
deputation from the Upper and Lower Cherokee towns, duly authorized by their
nation, went on to the city of Washington, the first named to declare to the
President of the United States their anxious desire to engage in the pursuits of
agriculture and civilized life, in the country they then occupied, and to make
known to the President of the United States the impracticability of inducing the
nation at large to do this, and to request the establishment of a division line
between the upper and lower towns, so as to include all the waters of the Hi-
wassee river to the upper town, that, by thus contracting their society within
narrow limits, they proposed to begin the establishment of fixed laws and a
regular government:

The deputies from the lower towns to make known their desire to continue the
hunter life, and also the scarcity of game where they then lived, and, under
those circumstances, their wish to remove across the Mississippi river, on some
vacant lands of the United States. And whereas the President of the United
States, after maturely considering the petitions of both parties, on the ninth day
of January, A. D. one thousand eight hundred and nine, including other subjects, answered those petitions as follows: "The United States, my children, are
the friends of both parties, and, as far as can be reasonably asked, they are
willing to satisfy the wishes of both. Those who remain may be assured of our
patronage, our aid, and good neighborhood. Those who wish to remove, are
permitted to send an exploring party to reconnoitre the country on the waters of
the Arkansas and White rivers, and the higher up the better, as they will be the
longer unapproached by our settlements, which will begin at the mouths of
those rivers. The regular districts of the government of St. Louis are already
laid off to the St. Francis.

"When this party shall have found a tract of country suiting the emigrants, and
not claimed by other Indians, we will arrange with them and you the exchange
of that for a just portion of the country they leave, and to a part of which, pro-

portioned to their numbers, they have a right. Every aid towards their removal, and what will be necessary for them there, will then be freely administered to them; and when established in their new settlements, we shall still consider them as our children, give them the benefit of exchanging their peltries for what they will want at our factories, and always hold them firmly by the hand."

And whereas the Cherokees, relying on the promises of the President of the United States, as above recited, did explore the country on the west side of the Mississippi, and made choice of the country on the Arkansas and White rivers, and settled themselves down upon United States lands, to which no other tribe of Indians have any just claim, and have duly notified the President of the United States thereof, and of their anxious desire for the full and complete ratification of his promise, and, to that end, as notified by the President of the United States, have sent on their agents, with full powers to execute a treaty, relinquishing to the United States all the right, title, and interest, to all lands of right to them belonging, as part of the Cherokee nation, which they have left, and which they are about to leave, proportioned to their numbers, including, with those now on the Arkansas, those who are about to remove thither, and to a portion of which they have an equal right agreeably to their numbers.

Now, know ye, that the contracting parties, to carry into full effect the before recited promises with good faith, and to promote a continuation of friendship with their brothers on the Arkansas river, and for that purpose to make an equal distribution of the annuities secured to be paid by the United States to the whole Cherokee nation, have agreed and concluded on the following articles, viz:

ARTICLE 1. The chiefs, head men, and warriors, of the whole Cherokee nation, cede to the United States all the lands lying north and east of the following boundaries, viz: Beginning at the high shoals of the Appalachy river, and running thence, along the boundary line between the Creek and Cherokee nations, westwardly to the Chatahouchy river; [142] thence, up the Chatahouchy river, to the mouth of Souque creek; thence, continuing with the general course of the river until it reaches the Indian boundary line, and, should it strike the Turrurar river, thence, with its meanders, down said river to its mouth, in part of the proportion of land in the Cherokee nation east of the Mississippi, to which those now on the Arkansas and those about to remove there are justly entitled.

ARTICLE 2. The chiefs, head men, and warriors, of the whole Cherokee nation, do also cede to the United States all the lands lying north and west of the following boundary lines, viz: Beginning at the Indian boundry line that runs from the north bank of the Tennessee river, opposite to the mouth of Hywassee river, at a point on the top of Walden's ridge, where it divides the waters of the Tennessee river from those of the Sequatchie river; thence, along the said ridge, southwardly, to the bank of the Tennessee river, at a point near to a place called the Negro Sugar Camp, opposite to the upper end of the first island above Running Water Town; thence, westwardly, a straight line to the mouth of Little Sequatchie river; thence, up said river, to its main fork; thence, up its northernmost fork, to its source; and thence, due west, to the Indian boundary line.

ARTICLE 3. It is also stipulated by the contracting parties, that a census shall be taken of the whole Cherokee nation, during the month of June, in the year of our Lord one thousand eight hundred and eighteen, in the following manner, viz: That the census of those on the east side of the Mississippi river, who declare their intention of remaining, shall be taken by a commissioner appointed by the President of the United States, and a commissioner appointed by the Cherokees on the Arkansas river; and the census of the Cherokees on the Arkansas river, and those removing there, and who, at that time, declare their intention of removing there, shall be taken by a commissioner appointed by the President of the United States, and one appointed by the Cherokees east of the Mississippi river.

ARTICLE 4. The contracting parties do also stipulate that the annuity due from the United States to the whole Cherokee nation for the year one thousand eight hundred and eighteen, is to be divided between the two parts of the nation in proportion to their numbers, agreeably to the stipulations contained in the third article of this treaty; and to be continued to be divided thereafter in proportion to their numbers; and the lands to be apportioned and surrendered to the United States agreeably to the aforesaid enumeration, as the proportionate part, agreeably to their numbers, to which those who have removed, and who declare their intention to remove, have a just right, including these with the lands ceded in the first and second articles of this treaty.

ARTICLE 5. The United States bind themselves, in exchange for the lands ceded in the first and second articles hereof, to give to that part of the Cherokee nation on the Arkansas as much land on said river and White river as they have or may hereafter receive from the Cherokee nation east of the Mississippi, acre for acre, as the just proportion due that part of the nation on the Arkansas agreeably to their numbers; which is to commence on the north side of the Arkansas river, at the mouth of Point Remove or Budwell's Old Place; thence, by a straight line, northwardly, to strike Chataunga mountain, or the hill first above Shield's Ferry on White river, running up and between said rivers for complement, the banks of which rivers to be the lines; and to have the above line, from the point of beginning to the point on White river, run and marked, which shall be done soon after the ratification of this treaty; and all citizens of the United States, except Mrs. P. Lovely, who is to remain where she lives during life, removed from within the bounds as above named. And it is further stipulated, that the treaties heretofore between the Cherokee nation and the United States are to continue in full force with both parts of the nation, and both parts thereof entitled to all the immunities and privilege which the old nation enjoyed under the aforesaid treaties; the United States reserving the right of establishing factories, a military post, and roads, within the boundaries above defined.

ARTICLE 6. The United States do also bind themselves to give to all the poor warriors who may remove to the western side of the Mississippi river, one rifle gun and ammunition, one blanket, and one brass kettle, or, in lieu of the brass kettle, a beaver trap, which is to be considered as a full compensation for the improvements which they may leave; which articles are to be delivered at such point as the President of the United States may direct: and to aid in the removal of the emigrants, they further agree to furnish fiat bottomed boats and provisions sufficient for that purpose: and to those emigrants whose improvements add real value to their lands, the United States agree to pay a full valuation for the same, which is to be ascertained by a commissioner appointed by the President of the United States for that purpose, and paid for as soon after the ratification of this treaty as practicable. The boats and provisions promised to the emigrants are to be furnished by the agent on the Tennessee river, at such time and place as the emigrants may notify him of; and it shall be his duty to furnish the same.

ARTICLE 7. And for all improvements which add real value to the lands lying within the boundaries ceded to the United States, by the first and second articles of this treaty, the United States do agree to pay for at the time, and to be valued in the same manner, as stipulated in the sixth article of this treaty; or, in lieu thereof, to give in exchange improvements of equal value which the emigrants may leave, and for which they are to receive pay. And it is further stipulated, that all these improvements, left by the emigrants within the bounds of the Cherokee nation east of the Mississippi river, which add real value to the lands, and for which the United States shall give a consideration, and not so exchanged, shall be rented to the Indians by the agent, year after year, for the benefit of the poor and decrepid of that part of the nation east of the Mississippi river, until surrendered by the nation, or to the nation. And it is further agreed, that the said Cherokee nation shall not be called upon for any part of the consideration paid for said improvements at any future period.

ARTICLE 8. And to each and every head of any Indian family residing on the east side of the Mississippi river, on the lands that are now, or ,nay hereafter be, surrendered to the United States, who may wish to become citizens of the United States, the United States do agree to give a reservation of six hundred and forty acres of land, in a square, to include their improvements, which are to be as near the centre thereof as practicable, in which they will have a life estate, with a reversion in fee simple to their children, reserving to the widow her dower, the register of whose names is to be filed in the office of the Cherokee agent, which shall be kept open until the census is taken as stipulated in the third article of this treaty. Provided, That if any of the heads of families, for whom reservations may be made, should remove therefrom, then, in that case, the right to revert to the United States. And provided further, That the land which may be reserved under this article, be deducted from the amount which has been ceded under the first and second articles of this treaty.

ARTICLE 9. It is also provided by the contracting parties, that nothing in the foregoing articles shall be construed so as to prevent any of the parties so contracting from the free navigation of all the waters mentioned therein.

ARTICLE 10. The whole of the Cherokee nation do hereby cede to the United States all right, title, and claim, to all reservations made to Doublehead and others, which were reserved to them by a treaty made and entered into at the city of Washington, bearing date the seventh of January, one thousand eight hundred and six.

ARTICLE 11. If. It is further agreed that the boundary lines of the lands ceded to the United States by the first and second articles of this treaty, and the boundary line of the lands ceded by the United States in the fifth article of this treaty, is to be run and marked by a commissioner or commissioners appointed by the President of the United States, who shall be accompanied by such commissioners as the Cherokees may appoint; due notice thereof to be given to the nation.

ARTICLE 12. The United States do also bind themselves to prevent the intrusion of any of its citizens within the lands ceded by the first and second articles of this treaty, until the same shall be ratified by the President and Senate of the United States, and duly promulgated.

ARTICLE 13. The contracting parties do also stipulate that this treaty shall take effect and be obligatory on the contracting parties so soon as the same shall be ratified by the President of the United States, by and with the advice and consent of the Senate of the United States.

In witness of all and every thing herein determined, by and between the before recited contracting parties, we have, in full and open council, at the Cherokee Agency, this eighth day of July, A. D. one thousand eight hundred and seventeen, set our hands and seals.

Andrew Jackson, Joseph McMinn, D. Meriwether, United States Commis'rs.

Richard Brown, his x mark, Cabbin Smith, his x mark, Sleeping Rabbit, his x mark, George Saunders, his x mark, Roman Nose, his x mark, Currobe Dick, his x mark, John Walker, his x mark, George Lowry, Richard Taylor, Walter Adair, James Brown, Kelachule, his x mark, Sour Mush, his x mark, Chulioa, his x mark, Chickasautchee, his x mark, The Bark of Chota, his x mark, The

Bark of Hightower, his x mark, Big Half Breed, his x mark, Going Snake, his x mark, Leyestisky, his x mark, Ch. Hicks, Young Davis, his x mark, Souanooka, his x mark, The Locust, his x mark, Beaver Carrier, his x mark, Dreadful Water, his x mark, Chyula, his x mark, Ja. Martin, John McIntosh, his x mark, Katchee of Cowee, his x mark, White Man Killer, his x mark,
Arkansas chiefs: Toochalar, his x mark, The Glass, his x mark, Wassosee, his x mark, John Jolly, his x mark, The Gourd, his x mark, Spring Frog, his x mark, John D. Chisholm, James Rogers, Wawhatchy, his x mark, Attalona, his x mark, Kulsuttchee, his x mark, Tuskekeetchee, his x mark, Chillawgatchee, his x mark, John Smith, his x mark, Toosawallata, his x mark,

In presence of: J. M. Glassel, secretary to the commission, Thomas Wilson, clerk to the commissioners, Walter Adair, John Speirs, interpreter, his x mark, A. McCoy, interpreter, James C. Bronaugh, hospital surgeon, U.S. Army, Isham Randolph, captain First Redoubtables, Wm. Meriwether, Return J. Meigs, agent Cherokee Nation.

TREATY WITH THE WYANDOT, ETC. {1817, Sept. 29}
Proclamation, Jan. 4, 1819.
Supplementary treaty, post, p. 162.

Articles of a treaty made and concluded, at the foot of the Rapids of the Miami of Lake Erie, between Lewis Cass and Duncan McArthur, commissioners of the United States, with full power and authority to hold conferences, and conclude and sign a treaty or treaties with all or any of the tribes or nations of Indians within the boundaries of the state of Ohio, of and concerning all matters interesting to the United States and the said nations of Indians on the one part; and the sachems, chiefs, and warriors, of the Wyandot, Seneca, Delaware, Shawanese, Potawatomees, Ottawas, and Chippeway, tribes of Indians.

ARTICLE 1. The Wyandot tribe of Indians, in consideration of the stipulations herein made on the part of the United States, do hereby forever cede to the United States the lands comprehended within the following lines and boundaries: Beginning at a point on the southern shore of lake Erie, where the present Indian boundary line intersects the same, between the mouth of Sandusky bay and the mouth of Portage river; thence, running south with said line, to the line established in the year one thousand seven hundred and ninety-five, by the treaty of Greenville, which runs from the crossing place above fort Lawrence to Loramie's store; thence, westerly, with the last mentioned line, to the eastern line of the reserve at Loramie's store; thence, with the lines of said reserve, north and west, to the northwestern corner thereof; thence to the northwestern corner of the reserve on the river St. Mary's, at the head of the navigable waters thereof; thence, east, to the western bank of the St. Mary's river aforesaid.

Thence, down on the western bank of the said river, to the reserve at fort Wayne; thence, with the lines of the last mentioned reserve, easterly and northerly, to the north bank of the river Miami of lake Erie; thence, down on the north bank of the said river, to the western line of the land ceded to the United States by the treaty of Detroit, in the year ,one thousand eight hundred and seven; thence, with the said line, south, to the middle of said Miami river, opposite the mouth of the Great Auglaize river; thence, down the middle of said Miami river, and easterly with the lines of the tract ceded to the United States by the treaty of Detroit aforesaid, so far that a south line will strike the place of beginning.

ARTICLE 2. The Potawatomy, Ottawas, and Chippeway, tribes of Indians, in consideration of the stipulations herein made on the part of the United States, do hereby forever cede to the United States the land comprehended within the following lines and boundaries: Beginning where the western line of the state of Ohio crosses the river Miami of lake Erie, which is about twenty-one miles above the mouth of the Great Auglaize river; thence, down the middle of the said Miami river, to a point north of the mouth of the Great Auglaize river; thence, with the western line of the land ceded to the United States by the treaty of Detroit, in one thousand eight hundred and seven, north forty-five miles; then, west, so far that a line south will strike the place of beginning; thence, south, to the place of beginning.

ARTICLE 3. The Wyandot, Seneca, Delaware, Shawnese, Potawatomy, Ottawas, and Chippeway, tribes of Indians accede to the cessions mentioned ill the two preceding articles.

ARTICLE 4. In consideration of the cessions and recognitions stipulated in the three preceding articles, the United States agree to pay to the Wyandot tribe, annually, forever, the sum of four thousand dollars, in specie, at Upper Sandusky: To the Seneca tribe, annually, forever, [146] the sum of five hundred dollars, in specie, at Lower Sandusky: To the Shawnese tribe, annually, forever, the sum of two thousand dollars, in specie, at Wapaghkonetta: To the Potawatomy tribe, annually, for the term of fifteen years, the sum of one thousand three hundred dollars, in specie, at Detroit: To the Ottawas tribe, annually, for the term of fifteen years, the sum of one thousand dollars, in specie, at Detroit: To the Chippewa tribe, annually, for the term of fifteen years, the sum of one thousand dollars, in specie, at Detroit: To the Delaware tribe, in the course of the year one thousand eight hundred and eighteen, the sum of five hundred dollars, in specie, at Wapaghkonetta, but no annuity: And the United States also agree, that all annuities due by any former treaty to the Wyandot, Shawnese, and Delaware tribes, and the annuity due by the treaty of Greenville, to the Ottawas and Chippewas tribes, shall be paid to the said tribes, respectively, in specie.

ARTICLE 5. The schedule hereunto annexed, is to be taken and considered as part of this treaty; and the tracts herein stipulated to be granted to the Wyandot, Seneca, and Shawnese, tribes of Indians, are to be granted for the use of the persons mentioned in the said schedule, agreeably to the descriptions, provisions, and limitations, therein contained.

ARTICLE 6. The United States agree to grant, by patent, in fee simple, to Doanquod, Howoner, Rontondee, Tauyau, Rontayau, Dawatont, Manocue, Tauyaudautauson, and Haudaunwaugh, chiefs of the Wyandot tribe, and their successors in office, chiefs of the said tribe, for the use of the persons and for the purposes mentioned in the annexed schedule, a tract of land twelve miles square, at Upper Sandusky, the centre of which shall be the place where fort Ferree stands; and also a tract of one mile square, to be located where the chiefs direct, on a cranberry swamp, on Broken Sword creek, and to be held for the use of the tribe.

The United States also agree to grant, by patent, in fee simple, to Tahawmadoyaw, captain Harris, Isahownusay, Joseph Tawgyou, captain Smith, Coffeehouse, Running About, and Wiping stick, chiefs of the Seneca tribe of Indians, and their successors in office, chiefs of the said tribe, for the use of the persons mentioned in the annexed schedule, a tract of land to contain thirty thousand acres, beginning on the Sandusky river, at the lower corner of the section hereinafter granted to William Spicer; thence, down the said river, on the east side, with the meanders thereof at high water mark, to a point east of the mouth of Wolf creek; thence, and from the beginning, east, so far that a north line will include the quantity of thirty thousand acres aforesaid.

The United States also agree to grant, by patent, in fee simple, to Catewekesa or Black Hoof, Byaseka or Wolf, Pore the or Walker, Shemenetoo or Big Snake, Othawakeseka or Yellow Feather, Chakalowah or the Tail's End, Pemthala or John Perry, Wabepee or White Colour, chiefs of the Shawnese tribe, residing at Wapaghkonetta, and their successors in office, chiefs of the said tribe, residing there, for the use of the persons mentioned in the annexed schedule, a tract of land ten miles square, the centre of which shall be the councilhouse at Wapaghkonetta.

The United States also agree to grant, by patent, in fee simple, to Peeththa or Falling Tree, and to Onowaskemo or the Resolute Man, chiefs of the Shawnese tribes, residing on Hog Creek, and their successors in office, chiefs of the said tribe, residing there, for the use of the persons mentioned in the annexed schedule, a tract of land containing twenty-five square miles, which is to join the tract granted at Wapaghkonetta, and to include the Shawnese settlement on Hog creek and to be laid off as near as possible in a square form.

The United States also agree to grant, by patent, in fee simple, to Quatawape or Captain Lewis, Shekaghkela or Turtle, Skilowa or Robin, chiefs of the Shawnese tribe of Indians residing at Lewistown, and to Mesomea or Civil John, Wakawuxsheno or the White Man, Oquasheno or Joe, and Willaquasheno or When you are tired sit down, chiefs of the Seneca tribe of Indians residing at Lewistown, and to their successors in office, chiefs of the said Shawnese and Seneca tribes, for the use of the persons mentioned in the annexed schedule, a tract of land t9 contain forty-eight square miles, to begin at the intersection of the line run by Charles Roberts, in the year one thousand eight hundred and twelve, from the source of the Little Miami river to the source of the Sciota river, in pursuance of instructions from the commissioners appointed on the part of the United States, to establish the western boundary of the Virginia Military Reservation, with the Indian boundary line established by the treaty of Greenville, in one thousand seven hundred and ninety-five, from the crossings above fort Lawrence to Loramie's store, and to run from such intersection, northerly, with the first mentioned line, and westerly, with the second mentioned line, so as to include the quantity as nearly in a square form as practicable, after excluding the section of land hereinafter granted to Nancy Stewart.

There shall also be reserved for the use of the Ottawas Indians, but not granted to them, a tract of land on Blanchard's fork of the Great Auglaize river, to contain five miles square, the centre of which tract is to be where the old trace crosses the said fork, and one other tract to contain three miles square, on the Little Auglaize river, to include Oquanoxa's village.

ARTICLE 7. And the said chiefs or their successors may, at any time they may think proper, convey to either of the persons mentioned in the said schedule, or his heirs, the quantity secured thereby to him, or may refuse so to do. But the use of the said land shall be in the said person; and after the share of any person is conveyed by the chiefs to him, he may convey the same to any person whatever. And any one entitled by the said schedule to a portion of the said land, may, at any time, convey the same to any person, by obtaining the approbation of the President of the United States, or of the person appointed by him to give such approbation. And the agent of the United States shall make an equitable partition of the said share when conveyed.

ARTICLE 8. At the special request of the said Indians, the United States agree to grant, by patent, in fee simple, to the persons hereinafter mentioned, all of whom are connected with the said Indians, by blood or adoption, the tracts of land herein described:

To Elizabeth Whitaker, who was taken prisoner by the Wyandots, and has ever since lived among them, twelve hundred and eighty acres of land, on the west side of the Sandusky river, below Croghansville, to be laid off in a square form, as nearly as the meanders of the said river will admit, and to run an equal distance above and below the house in which the said Elizabeth Whitaker now lives.

To Robert Armstrong, who was taken prisoner by the Indians, and has ever since lived among them, and has married a Wyandot woman, one section, to contain six hundred and forty acres of land, on the west side of the Sandusky river, to begin at the place called Camp Ball, and to run up the river, with the meanders thereof, one hundred and sixty poles, and, from the beginning, down the river, with the meanders thereof, one hundred and sixty poles, and from the extremity of these lines west for quantity.

To the children of the late William M'Collock, who was killed in August, one thousand eight hundred and twelve, near Maugaugon, and who are quarter-blood Wyandot Indians, one section, to contain six hundred and forty acres of land, on the west side of the Sandusky river, adjoining the lower line of the tract hereby granted to Robert Armstrong, and extending in the same manner with and from the said river.

To John Vanmeter, who was taken prisoner by the Wyandots, and who has ever since lived among them, and has married a Seneca woman, and to his wife's three brothers, Senecas, who now reside on Honey creek, one thousand acres of land, to begin north, forty-five degrees west, one hundred and forty poles from the house in which the said John Vanmeter now lives, and to run thence, south, three hundred and twenty poles, thence, and from the beginning, east for quantity.

To Sarah Williams, Joseph Williams, and Rachel Nugent, late, Rachel Williams, the said Sarah having been taken prisoner by the Indians, and ever since lived among them, and being the widow, and the said Joseph and Rachel being the children, of the late Isaac Williams, a half-blood Wyandot, one quarter section of land, to contain one hundred and sixty acres, on the east side of the Sandusky river, below Croghansville, and to include their improvements at a place called Negro Point.

To Catharine Walker, a Wyandot woman, and to John R. Walker, her son, who was wounded in the service of the United States, at the battle of Mauguagon, in one thousand eight hundred and twelve, a section of six hundred and forty acres of land each, to begin at the northwestern corner of the tract hereby granted to John Vanmeter and his wife's brothers, and to run with the line thereof, south, three hundred and twenty poles, thence, and from the beginning, west for quantity.

To William Spicer, who was taken prisoner by the Indians, and has ever since lived among them, and has married a Seneca woman, a section of land, to contain six hundred and forty acres, beginning on the east bank of the Sandusky river, forty poles below the lower corner of said Spicer's cornfield, thence, up the river on the east side, with the meanders thereof, one mile, thence, and from the beginning, east for quantity.

To Nancy Stewart, daughter of the late Shawnese chief Blue Jacket, one section of land, to contain six hundred and forty acres, on the Great Miami river below Lewistown, to include her present improvements, three quarters of the said section to be on the southeast side of the river, and one quarter on the northwest side thereof.

To the children of the late Shawnese chief captain Logan, or Spamagelabe, who fell in the service of the United States during the late war, one section of land, to contain six hundred and forty acres, on the east side of the Great Auglaize river, adjoining the lower line of the grant of ten miles at Wapaghkonetta and the said river.

To Anthony Shane, a half blood Ottawas Indian, one section of land, to contain six hundred and forty acres, on the east side of the river St. Mary's, and to begin opposite the house in which said Shane now lives, thence, up the river, with the meanders thereof, one hundred and sixty poles, and from the beginning down the river, with the meanders thereof, one hundred and sixty poles, and from the extremity of the said lines east for quantity.

To James M'Pherson, who was taken prisoner by the Indians, and has ever since lived among them, one section of land, to contain six hundred and forty acres, in a square form, adjoining the northern or western line of the grant of forty-eight miles at Lewistown, at such place as he may think proper to locate the same.

To Horonu, or the Cherokee Boy, a Wyandot chief, a section of land, to contain six hundred and forty acres, on the Sandusky river, to be laid off in a square form, and to include his improvements.

To Alexander D. Godfroy and Richard Godfroy, adopted children of the Potawatomy tribe, and at their special request, one section of land, to contain six hundred and forty acres, in the tract of country herein ceded to the United States by the Potawatomy, Ottawas, and Chippewas, tribes, to be located by them, the said Alexander and Richard, after the said tract shall have been surveyed.

To Sawendebans, or the Yellow Hair, or Peter Minor, an adopted son of Tondaganie, or the Dog, and at the special request of the Ottawas, out of the tract reserved by the treaty of Detroit, in one thousand eight hundred and seven, above Roche de Boeuf, at the village of the said Dog, a section of land, to contain six hundred and forty acres, to be located in a square form, on the north side of the Miami, at the Wolf Rapid.

119

ARTICLE 9. The United States engage to appoint an agent, to reside among or near the Wyandots, to aid them in the protection of their persons and property, to manage their intercourse with the government and citizens of the United States, and to discharge the duties which commonly appertain to the office of Indian agent; and the same agent is to execute the same duties for the Senecas and Delawares on the Sandusky river. And an agent for similar purposes, and vested with similar powers, shall be appointed, to reside among or near the Shawnese, whose agency shall include the reservations at Wapaghkonetta, at Lewistown, at Hog creek, and at Blanchard's creek. And one mile square shall be reserved at Malake for the use of the agent for the Shawnese.

And the agent for the Wyandots and Senecas shall occupy such land in the grant at Upper Sandusky, as may be necessary for him and the persons attached to the agency.

ARTICLE 10. The United States engage to erect a saw-mill and a gristmill, upon some proper part of the Wyandot reservation, for their use, and to provide and maintain a blacksmith, for the use of the Wyandots and Senecas, upon the reservation of the Wyandots, and another blacksmith, for the use of the Indians at Wapaghkonetta, Hog creek, and Lewistown.

ARTICLE 11. The stipulations contained in the treaty of Greenville, relative to the right of the Indians to hunt upon the land hereby ceded, while it continues the property of the United States, shall apply to this treaty; and the Indians shall, for the same term, enjoy the privilege of making sugar upon the same land, committing no unnecessary waste upon the trees.

ARTICLE 12. The United States engage to pay, in the course of the year one thousand eight hundred and eighteen, the amount of the damages which were assessed by the authority of the secretary of war, in favor of several tribes and individuals of the Indians, who adhered to the cause of the United States during the late war with great Britain, and whose property was, in consequence of such adherence, injured or destroyed. And it is agreed, that the sums thus assessed shall be paid in specie, at the places, and to the tribes or individuals, hereinafter mentioned, being in conformity with the said assessment; that is to say:

To the Wyandots, at Upper Sandusky, four thousand three hundred and nineteen dollars and thirty-nine cents.
To the Senecas, at Lower Sandusky, three thousand nine hundred and eighty-nine dollars and twenty-four cents.
To the Indians at Lewis and Scoutashs towns, twelve hundred and twenty-seven dollars and fifty cents.

To the Delawares, for the use of the Indians who suffered losses at Greentown and at Jerome's town, three thousand nine hundred and fifty-six dollars and fifty cents, to be paid at Wapaghkonetta.

To the representatives of Hembis, a Delaware Indian, three hundred and forty-eight dollars and fifty cents, to be paid at Wapaghkonetta.

To the Shawnese, an additional sum of four hundred and twenty dollars, to be paid at Wapaghkonetta.

To the Senecas, an additional sum of two hundred and nineteen dollars, to be paid at Wapaghkonetta.

ARTICLE 13. And whereas the sum of two thousand five hundred dollars has been paid by the United States to the Shawnese, being one half of five years annuities due by the treaty of Fort Industry, and whereas the Wyandots contend that the whole of the annuity secured by that treaty is to be paid to them, and a few persons of the Shawnese and Senecas tribes; now, therefore, the commissioners of the United States, believing that the construction given by the Wyandots to the said treaty is correct, engage that the United States shall pay to the said Wyandot tribe in specie, in the course of the year one thousand eight hundred and eighteen, the said sum of two thousand five hundred dollars.

ARTICLE 14. The United States reserve to the proper authority, the right to make roads through any part of the land granted or reserved by this treaty; and also to the different agents, the right of establishing taverns and ferries for the accommodation of travellers, should the same be found necessary.

ARTICLE 15. The tracts of land herein granted to the chiefs, for the use of the Wyandot, Shawnese, Seneca, and Delaware Indians, and the reserve for the Ottawa Indians, shall not be liable to taxes of any kind so long as such land continues the property of the said Indians.

ARTICLE 16. Some of the Ottawa, Chippewa, and Potawatomy tribes, being attached to the Catholic religion, and believing they may wish some of their children hereafter educated, do grant to the rector of the Catholic church of St. Anne of Detroit, for the use of the said church, and to the corporation of the college at Detroit, for the use of the said college, to be retained or sold, as the said rector and corporation may judge expedient, each, one half of three sections of land, to contain six hundred and forty acres, on the river Raisin, at a place called Macon; and three sections of land not yet located, which tracts were reserved, for the use of the said Indians, by the treaty of Detroit, in one thousand eight hundred and seven; and the superintendent of Indian affairs, in the territory of Michigan, is authorized, on the part of the said Indians, to select the said tracts of land.

ARTICLE 17. The United States engage to pay to any of the Indians, the value of any improvements which they may be obliged to abandon in consequence of the lines established by this treaty.

ARTICLE 18. The Delaware tribe of Indians, in consideration of the stipulations herein made on the part of the United States, do hereby forever cede to the United States all the claim which they have to the thirteen sections of land reserved for the use of certain persons of their tribe, by the second section of the act of congress, passed March the third, one thousand eight hundred and seven, providing for the disposal of the lands of the United States between the United States Military Tract and the Connecticut Reserve, and the lands of the United States between the Cincinnati and Vincennes districts.

ARTICLE 19. The United States agree to grant, by patent, in fee simple, to Jeeshawau, or James Armstrong, and to Sanondoyourayquaw, or Silas Armstrong, chiefs of the Delaware Indians, living on the Sandusky waters, and their successors in office, chiefs of the said tribe, for the use of the persons mentioned in the annexed schedule, in the same manner, and subject to the same conditions, provisions, and limitations, as is hereinbefore provided for the lands granted to the Wyandot, Seneca, and Shawnese, Indians, a tract of land, to contain nine square miles, to join the tract granted to the Wyandots of twelve miles square, to be laid off as nearly in a square form as practicable, and to include Captain Pipe's village.

ARTICLE 20. The United States also agree to grant, by patent, to the chiefs of the Ottawas tribe of Indians, for the use of the said tribe, a tract of land, to contain thirty-four square miles, to be laid out as nearly in a square form as practicable, not interfering with the lines of the tracts reserved by the treaty of Greenville on the south side of the Miami river of Lake Erie, and to include Tushquegan, or M'Carty's village; which tracts, thus granted, shall be held by the said tribe, upon the usual conditions of Indian reservations, as though no patent were issued.

ARTICLE 21. This treaty shall take effect, and be obligatory on the contracting parties, as soon as the same shall have been ratified by the President of the United States, by and with the advice and consent of the Senate thereof.

In testimony whereof, the said Lewis Cass and Duncan McArthur, commissioners as aforesaid, and the sachems, chiefs, and warriors, of the Wyandot, Seneca, Shawanee, Delaware, Pattawatima, Ottawa, and Chippewa tribes of Indians, have hereunto set their hands, at the foot of the Rapids of the Miami of lake Erie, this twenty-ninth day of September, in the year of our Lord one thousand eight hundred and seventeen.

In presence of: Wm. Turner, secretary to the commissioners, W. Knaggs, Indian agent, G. Godfroy, Indian ageht, John Johnson, Indian agent, R.A. Forsyth, jr., secretary Indian department.
B. F. Stickney, Indian agent, Sworn Interpreters, Peter Ryley, William Conner, Henry I. Hunt, H. W. Walker, Jos. Vance, John R. Walker, Jonathan Leslie, James McPherson, Alvan Coe, F. Duchouquet, John Gunn, A. Shane, C.L. Cass, lieutenant U. S. Army, J. B. Beaugrand.
Chippewas: Wasonnezo, his x mark, Okemance, or the Young Chief, his x mark, Shinguax, or Cedar, his x mark, Kinobee, his x mark, Chinguagin, his x mark, Sheganack, or Black Bird, his x mark, Mintougaboit, or the Devil Standing, his x mark, Wastuau, his x mark, Penquam, his x mark, Chemokcomon, or American his x mark, Papeeumegat, his x mark, Matwaash, or Heard Fell Down, his x mark, Potaquam, his x mark, Pensweguesic, the Jay Bird, his x mark, Weabskewen, or t. he White Man, his x mark,
Waynoce, his x mark

Pattawatimas: Metea, his x mark, Wynemac, his x mark, Wynemakons, or the Front, his x mark, Ocheackabee, his x mark, Conge, his x mark, Wankeway, his x mark, Perish, his x mark, Tonguish, his x mark, Papekitcha, or Flat Belly, his x mark, Medomin, or Corn, his x mark, Saguemai, or Musketo, his x mark, Waweacee, or Full Moon, his x mark, Ninwichemon, his x mark, Misscnonsai, his x mark, Waysagua, his x mark, Nannanmee, his x mark, Nannanseku, his x mark, Meanqueah, his x mark, Wawenoke, his x mark, Ashenekazo, his x mark, Nanemucskuck, his x mark, Ashkebee, his x mark, Makotai, his x mark, Wabinsheway, White Elk, his x mark, Gabriel, or Gabiniai, his x mark, Waishit, his x mark, Naonquay, his x mark, Meshawgonay, his x mark, Nitchetash, his x mark, Skewbicack, his x mark, Chechalk, or Crane, his x mark

Wyandots: Dunquad, or Half King, his x mark, Runtunda, or War Pole, his x mark, Aronuc, or Cherokee Boy, his x mark, T. Aruntue, or Between the legs, his x mark, D. Wottondt, or John Hicks, his x mark, T. Undetaso, or Geo. Punch, his x mark, Menonkue, or Thomas, his x mark, Undauwau, or Matthews, his x mark,
Delawares: Kithtuwheland, or Anderson, his x mark, Punchhuck, or Capt. Beaver, his x mark, Tahunqeecoppi, or Capt. Pipe, his x mark, Clamatonockis, his x mark, Aweallesa, or Whirlwind, his x mark,
Shawanees: Cateweekesa, or Black Hoof, his x mark, Biaseka, or Wolf, his x mark, Porethe, or Walker, his x mark, Shemenetu, or Big Snake, his x mark, Chacalowa, or Tail's End, his x mark, Pemthata, or Perry, his x mark, Othawakeska; or Yellow Feather, his x mark, Wawathethaka, or Capt. Reed, his x mark, Tecumtequa, his x mark, Quitewe, War Chief, his x mark, Cheacksca, or Captain Tom, his x mark, Quitawepea, or Captain Lewis, his x mark,

Senecas: Methomea, or Civil John, his x mark, Sacourewceghta, or Whiping Stick, his x mark, Shekoghkell, or Big Turtle, his x mark, Aquasheno, or Joe, his x mark, Wakenuceno, White Man, his x mark, Samendue, or Captain Sigore, his x mark, Skillcway, or Robbin, his x mark, Dasquoerunt, his x mark, Ottawas: Tontagimi, or the Dog, his x mark, Misquegin, McCarty, his x mark, Pontiac, his x mark, Oquenoxas, his x mark, Tashmwa, his x mark, Nowkesick, his x mark, Wahekeighke, his x mark, Kinewaba, his x mark, Twaatum, his x mark, Supay, his x mark, Nashkema, his x mark, Kuwashewon, his x mark, Kusha, his x mark,

Schedule referred to in the foregoing treaty, and to be taken and considered as part thereof.

Three sections, to contain six hundred and forty acres each, are to be reserved out of the tract of twelve miles square to be granted to the Wyandots. One of the said sections is to be appropriated to the use of a missionary, one for the support of schools, and one for the support of mechanics, and to be under the direction of the chiefs. Two sections, of six hundred and forty acres each, are to be granted to each of the following persons, being the chief of the Wyandot tribe, and his six counsellors, namely: Doouquod, or half king; Routoudu, or Warpole; Tauyaurontoyou, or Between the logs; Dawatout, or John Hicks; Manocue, or Thomas; Sauyoudautausaw, or George Ruuh; and Hawdowuwaugh, or Matthews.

And, after deducting the fifteen sections thus to be disposed of, the residue of the said tract of twelve miles square is to be equally divided among the following persons, namely: Hoocue, Roudootouk, Mahoma, Naatoua, Mautanawto, Maurunquaws, Naynuhanky, Abrm. Williams, sen. Squautaugh, Tauyouranuta, Tahawquevouws, Dasharows, Tray-hetou, Hawtooyou, Maydounaytove, Neudooslau, Deecalrautousay, Houtooyemaugh, Datoowawna, Matsave-aanyourie, James Ranken, Sentumass, Tahautoshowweda, Madudara, Shaudauave, Shamadeesay, Sommodowot, Moautaau, Nawsottomaugh, Maurawskinquaws, Tawtoo-lowme, Shawdouycayourou, Showwcno, Dashotto, Sennewdorow, Toayttooraw, Mawskattaugh, Tahawshodeuyea, I-taunaraw reudee, Shau-romou, Tawyaurontoreyea, Roumelay, Nadocays, Carryumanduetaugh, Bigarms, Madonrawcays. Haurauoot, Syhrundash, Tahorowtsemdee, Roosayn, Dautoresay, Nashawtoomous, Skawduutoutee, Sanorowsha, Nautennee, Youansha, Aumatonrow, Ohoutautoon, Tawyougaustayou, Sootonteeree, Dootooau, Hawreewaucudee, Yourahatsa,Towntoreshaw, Syuwewataugh, Cauyou, Omitztseshaw, Gausawaugh, Skashoways-squaw, Mawdovdoo, Narowayshaus, Nawcatay, Isuhowhayeato, Mya-tousha, Tauoodowma, Youhreo, George Williams, Oharvatoy, Saharossor, [153] Isaac Williams, Squindatee, Mayeatohot, Lewis Coon, isatouque or John Coon, Tawaumanocay or E. Wright, Owawtatuu, Isontraudee, Tomatsahoss, Sarrahoss, Tauyoureehoryeow, Saudotoss, Towrordu or Big Ears, Tauomatsarau, Taho

TREATY WITH THE CREEKS {1818, Jan. 22}
Proclamation, Mar. 28, 1818.

A treaty of limits between the United States and the Creek nation of Indians, made and concluded at the Creek Agency, on Flint river, the twenty-second day of January, in the year of our Lord, one thousand eight hundred and eighteen.

JAMES MONROE, President of the United States of America, by David Brydie Mitchell, of the state of Georgia, agent of Indian affairs for the Creek nation, and sole commissioner, specially appointed for that purpose, on the one part, and the undersigned kings, chiefs, head men, and warriors, of the Creek nation, in council assembled, on behalf of the said nation, of the other part, have entered into the following articles and conditions, viz:

ARTICLE 1. The said kings, chiefs, head men, and warriors, do hereby agree, in consideration of certain sums of money to be paid to the said Creek nation, by the government of the United States, as hereinafter stipulated, to cede and forever quit claim, (and do, in behalf of their said nation, hereby cede, relinquish, and forever quit claim,) unto the United States, all right, title, and interest, which the said nation have, or claim, in or unto, the two following tracts of land, situate, lying, and being, within the following bounds; that is to say: 1st. Beginning at the mouth of Goose Creek, on the Alatamahau river, thence, along the line leading to the Mounts, at the head of St. Mary's river, to the point where it is intersected by the line run by the commissioners of the United States under the treaty of Fort Jackson, thence, along the said last-mentioned line, to a point where a line, leaving the same, shall run the nearest and a direct course, by the head of a creek called by the Indians Alcasalckie, to the Ocmulgee river; thence, down the said Ocmulgee river, to its junction with the Oconee, the two rivers there forming the Alatamahau; thence, down the Alatamahau, to the first-mentioned bounds, at the mouth of Goose creek.
2d. Beginning at the high shoals of the Appalachee river, and from thence, along the line designated by the treaty made at the city of Washington, on the fourteenth day of November, one thousand eight hundred and five (fifteen), to the Ulcofouhatchie, it being the first large branch, or fork, of the Ocmulgee, above the Seven Islands; thence, up the eastern bank of the Ulcofouhatchie, by the water's edge, to where the path, leading from the high shoals of the Appalachie to the shallow ford on the Chatalo-chic, crosses the same; and, from thence, along the said path, to the shallow ford on the Chatahochie river; thence, up the Chatahochie river, by the water's edge, on the eastern side, to Suwannee old town; thence, by a direct line, to the head of Appalachie; and thence, down the same, to the first-mentioned bounds at the high shoals of Appalachie.

ARTICLE 2. It is hereby stipulated and agreed, on the part of the United States, as a full consideration for the two tracts of land ceded by the Creek nation in the preceding article, that there shall be paid to the Creek nation by the United States, within the present year, the sum of twenty thousand dollars, and ten thousand dollars shall be paid annually for the term of ten succeeding years, without interest; making, in the whole, eleven payments in the course of eleven years, the present year inclusive; and the whole sum to be paid, one hundred and twenty thousand dollars.

ARTICLE 3. And it is hereby further agreed, on the part of the United States, that, in lieu of all former stipulations relating to blacksmiths, they will furnish the Creek nation for three years with two blacksmiths and strikers.

ARTICLE 4. The President may cause any line to be run which may be necessary to designate the boundary of any part of both, or either, of the tracts of land ceded by this treaty, at such time, and in such manner, as he may deem proper. And this treaty shall be obligatory on the contracting parties as soon as the same shall be ratified by the government of the United States.

Done at the place, and on the day before written.

D. B. Mitchell.

Tustunnugee Thlucco, his x mark, Tustunnugee Hopoie, his x mark, William McIntosh, Tuskeenchaw, his x mark, Hopoie Haujo, his x mark, Cotchau Haujo, his x mark, Inthlansis Haujo, his x mark, Cowetau Micco, his x mark, Cusselau Micco, his x mark, Eufaulu Micco, his x mark, Hopoethlc Hauja, his x mark, Hopoie Hatkee, his x mark, Yoholo Micco, his x mark,.

TREATY WITH THE WYANDOT, ETC. {1818, Sept. 17}
Proclamation, Jan. 4, 1819.

Articles of a treaty made and concluded, at St. Mary's, in the state of Ohio, between Lewis Cass and Duncan McArthur, commissioners of the United States, with full power and authority to hold conferences, and conclude and sign a treaty or treaties, with all or any of the tribes or nations of Indians within the boundaries of the state of Ohio, of and concerning all matters interesting to the United States and the said nations of Indians, and the sachems, chiefs, and warriors, of the Wyandot, Seneca, Shawnese, and Ottawas, tribes of Indians; being supplementary to the treaty made and concluded with the said tribes, and the Delaware, Potawatamie, and Chippewa, tribes of Indians, at the foot of the Rapids of the Miami of Lake Erie, on the twenty-ninth day of September, in the year of our Lord one thousand eight hundred and seventeen.

ARTICLE 1. It is agreed, between the United States and the parties hereunto, that the several tracts of land, described in the treaty to which this is supplementary, and agreed thereby to be granted by the United States to the chiefs of the respective tribes named therein, for the use of the individuals of the said tribes, and also the tract described in the twentieth article of the said treaty, shall not be thus granted, but shall be excepted from the cession made by the said tribes to the United States, reserved for the use of the said Indians, and held by them in the same manner as Indian reservations have been heretofore held. But (it) is further agreed, that the tracts thus reserved shall be reserved for the use of the Indians named in the schedule to the said treaty, and held by them and their heirs forever, unless ceded to the United States.

ARTICLE 2. It is also agreed that there shall be reserved for the use of the Wyandots, in addition to the reservations before made, fifty-five thousand six hundred and eighty acres of land, to be laid off in two tracts, the first to adjoin the south line of the section of six hundred and forty acres of land heretofore reserved for the Wyandot chief, the Cherokee Boy, and to extend south to the north line of the reserve of twelve miles square, at Upper Sandusky, and the other to adjoin the east line of the reserve of twelve miles square, at Upper Sandusky, and to extend east for quantity.

There shall also be reserved, for the use of the Wyandots residing at Solomon's town, and on Blanchard's fork, in addition to the reservations before made, sixteen thousand acres of land, to be laid off in a square form, on the head of Blanchard's fork, the centre of which shall be at the Big Spring, on the trace leading from Upper Sandusky to fort Findlay; and one hundred and sixty acres of land, for the use of the Wyandots, on the west side of the Sandusky river, adjoining the said rivet', and the lower line of two sections of land, agreed, by the treaty to which this is supplementary, to be granted to Elizabeth Whitaker.

There shall also be reserved, for the use of the Shawnese, in addition to the reservations before made, twelve thousand eight hundred acres of land, to be laid off adjoining the east line of their reserve of ten miles square, at Wapaughkonetta; and for the use of the Shawnese and Senecas, eight thousand nine hundred and sixty acres of land, to be laid off adjoining the west line of the reserve of forty-eight square miles at Lewistown. And the last reserve hereby made, and the former reserve at the same place, shall be equally divided by an east and west line, to be drawn through the same. And the north half of the said tract shall be reserved for the use of the Senecas who reside there, and the south half for the use of the Shawnese who reside there.

There shall also be reserved for the use of the Senecas, in addition to the reservations before made, ten thousand acres of land, to be laid off on the east side of the Sandusky river, adjoining the south line of their reservation of thirty thousand acres of land, which begins on the Sandusky river, at the lower corner of William Spicer's section, and excluding therefrom the said William Spicer's section.

127

ARTICLE 3. It is hereby agreed that the tracts of land, which, by the eighth article of the treaty to which this is supplementary, are to be granted by the United States to the persons therein mentioned, shall never be conveyed, by them or their heirs, without the permission of the President of the United States.

ARTICLE 4. The United States agree to pay to the Wyandots an additional annuity of five hundred dollars, forever; to the Shawnese, and to the Senecas of Lewistown, an additional annuity of one thousand dollars, forever; and to the Senecas an additional annuity of five hundred dollars, forever; and to the Otta-was an additional annuity of one thousand five hundred dollars, forever. And these annuities shall be paid at the places, and in the manner, prescribed by the treaty to which this is supplementary.

ARTICLE 5. This treaty shall take effect, and be obligatory on the contracting parties, as soon as the same shall be ratified by the President of the United States, by and with the advice and consent of the Senate thereof.

In testimony whereof, the said Lewis Cass and Duncan McArthur, commis-sioners as aforesaid, and the sachems, chiefs, and warriors, of the Wyandot, Seneca, Shawanee, and Ottawa tribes of Indians, have hereunto set their hands, at St. Mary's, in the state of Ohio, this seventeenth day of September, in the year of our Lord one thousand eight hundred and eighteen.

Lewis Cass, Duncan McArthur
Ottawas: Keueaghbon, or Bald Eagle, his x mark, Peshekata, or Marked Legs, his x mark, Shwanabe, or Muskrat, his x mark, Toutogana, or The Dog, his x mark, Tushquagon, or McCarty, his x mark, Mushkema, his x mark,
Shawanees: Cuttewekasa, or Black Hoof, his x mark, Shemenetu, or Big Snake, his x mark, Biaseka, or Wolf, his x mark, Pomthe, or Walker, his x mark, Chacalawa, or Long Tail, his x mark, Pemthata, or Perry, his x mark, Red Man, or Capt. Reed, his x mark, Chiakeska, or Captain Tom, his x mark, Tecuntequa, or Elk in the Water, his x mark, Quitawepa, or Colonel Lewis, his x mark, Captain Pipe, his x mark, James Armstrong, his x mark,
Ottowas: Metesheneiwa, or Bear'sMan, his x mark, Oquenoxe, his x mark, Pe-neshaw, or Eagle, his x mark,
Wyandots: Douquad, or Half King, his x mark, Rontondu, or War Pole, his x mark, Tuayaurontoyou, or Between the Logs, his x mark, Dauatout, or John Hicks his x mark, Horonu or Cherokee Boy, his x mark, Teoudetosso, or George Punch, his x mark, Hawdoro, or Matthews, his x mark, Skoutous, his x mark, Quouqua, his x mark,
Senecas: Methomea, or Civil John, his x mark, Skekoghkell, or Big Turtle, his x mark, Waghkonoxie, or White Bone, his x mark, Tochequia, or Yellow Bone, His x mark, Captain Togone, his x mark, Cunneshohant, or Harris, his x mark, Tousonecta, or his Blanket. Down, his x mark, Wiping Stick, his x mark.

In presence of: Wm. Turner, secretary, John Johnston, Indian agent, B. F. Stickney, Indian agent, B. Parke, district judge of Indiana, Jonathan Jennings, governor of Indiana, Wm. P. Rathbone, army contractor, Alexander Wolcott, jr., Indian agent, Detroit, John Conner, J. T. Chmm, major of Third Infantry, R. A. Forsyth, jr., secretary Indian Department, G. M. Grosvenor, captain Eighth Infantry.

Sworn interpreters: Henry I. Hunt, John Kenzer, subagent, F. Duchouquet, W. Knaggs,

A. Shane, John B. Walker, L. Jouett, Indian agent, Tustunnugec, his x mark, Fatuske Hcnehau, his x mark, Yauhau Haujo, his x mark, Tuskeegee Emautla, his x mark, Tustunnugee Hoithleloeo, his x mark,

Present: D. Brearly, colonel Seventh Infantry, Wm. S. Mitchell, assistant agent, I. A. C. N, M. Johnson, lieutenant corps of artillery, S1. Hawkins, George (G. L.) Lovet, Interpreters.

TREATY WITH THE DELAWARES {1818, Oct. 3}
Proclamation, Jan. 15, 1819.

Articles of a treaty made and concluded at St. Mary's, in the state of Ohio, between Jonathan Jennings, Lewis Cass, and Benjamin Parke, commissioners of the United States, and the Delaware nation of Indians.

ARTICLE 1. The Delaware nation of Indians cede to the United States all their claim to land in the state of Indiana.

ARTICLE 2. In consideration of the aforesaid cession, the United States agree to provide for the Delawares a country to reside in, upon the west side of the Mississippi, and to guaranty to them the peaceable possession of the same.

ARTICLE 3. The United States also agree to pay the Delawares the full value of their improvements in the country hereby ceded: which valuation shall be made by persons to be appointed for that purpose by the President of the United States; and to furnish the Delawares with one hundred and twenty horses, not to exceed in value forty dollars each, and a sufficient number of perogues, to aid in transporting them to the west side of the Mississippi; and a quantity of provisions, proportioned to their numbers, and the extent of their journey.

ARTICLE 4. The Delawares shall be allowed the use and occupation of their improvements, for the term of three years from the date of this treaty if they so long require it.

ARTICLE 5. The United States agree to pay to the Delawares a perpetual annuity of four thousand dollars; which, together with all annuities which the United States, by any former treaty, engaged to pay to them, shall be paid in silver, at any place to which the Delawares may remove.

ARTICLE 6. The United States agree to provide and support a blacksmith for the Delawares, after their removal to the west side of the Mississippi.

ARTICLE 7. One half section of land shall be granted to each of the following persons, namely; Isaac Wobby, Samuel Cassman, Elizabeth Petchaka, and Jacob Dick; and one quarter of a section of land shall be granted to each of the following persons, namely; Solomon Tindell, and Benoni Tindell; all of whom are Delawares; which tracts of land shall be located, after the country is surveyed, at the first creek above the old fort on White river, and running up the river; and shall be held by the persons herein named, respectively, and their heirs; but shall never be conveyed or transferred without the approbation of the President of the United States.

ARTICLE 8. A sum, not exceeding thirteen thousand three hundred and twelve dollars and twenty-five cents, shall be paid by the United States, to satisfy certain claims against the Delaware nation; and shall be expended by the Indian agent at Piqua and Fort Wayne, agreeably to a schedule this day examined and approved by the commissioners of the United States.

ARTICLE 9. This treaty, after the same shall be ratified by the President and Senate of the United States, shall be binding on the contracting parties.

In testimony whereof, the said Jonathan Jennings, Lewis Cass, and Benjamin Parke, commissioners as aforesaid, and the chiefs and warriors of the Delaware nation of Indians, have hereunto set their hands, at St. Mary's, in the State of Ohio, this third day of October, in the year of our Lord one thousand eight hundred and eighteen.

Jonathan Jennings, Lew. Cass, B. Parke,
Kithteeleland, or Anderson, his x mark, Lapahnihe, or Big Bear, his x mark, James Nanticoke, his x mark, Apacahund, or White Eyes, his x mark, Captain Killbuck, his x mark, The Beaver, his x mark, Netahopuna, his x mark, Captain Tunis, his x mark, Captain Ketchum, his x mark, The Cat, his x mark
Ben Beaver, his x mark, The War Mallet, his x mark, Captain Caghkoo, his x mark, The Buck, his x mark, Petchenanalas, his x mark, John Quake, his x mark, Quenaghtoothmait, his x mark, Little Jack, his x mark.

In the presence of: James Dill, secretary to the commissioners, William Turner, secretary, Jno. Johnston, Indian agent, B. F. Stickhey, S. I. A, John Conner, William Conner, interpreter, John Kinzie, sub-agent, G. Godfroy, sub-agent, John T. Chunn, major, Third U. S. Infantry, J. Hackley, captain, Third Infantry, William Oliver, Hilary Brunot, lieutenant, Third Infantry, David Oliver, R. A. Forsyth, jr., secretary Indian Department.

TREATY WITH THE CHICKASAW {1818, Oct. 19}
Proclamation, Jan. 7, 1819.

Treaty with the Chickasaws, to settle all territorial controversies, and to remove all ground of complaint or dissatisfaction, that might arise to interrupt the peace and harmony which have so long and so happily existed between the United States of America and the Chickesaw nation of Indians, James Monroe, President of the said United States, Isaac Shelby and Andrew Jackson, of the one part, and the whole Chickasaw nation, by their chiefs, head men, and warriors, in full council assembled, of the other part, have agreed on the following articles; which, when ratified by the President and Senate of the United States of America, shall form, a treaty binding on all parties.

ARTICLE 1. Peace and friendship are hereby firmly established and made perpetual, between the United States of America and the Chickesaw nation of Indians.

ARTICLE 2. To obtain the object of the foregoing article, the Chickesaw nation of Indians cede to the United States of America, (with the exception of such reservation as shall be hereafter mentioned) all claim or title which the said nation has to the land lying north of the south boundary of the state of Tennessee, which is bounded south by the thirty-fifth degree of north latitude, and which lands, hereby ceded, lies within the following boundary, viz: Beginning on the Tennessee river, about thirty-five miles, by water, below colonel George Colbert's ferry, where the thirty-fifth degree of north latitude strikes the same; [175] thence, due west, with said degree of north latitude, to where it cuts the Mississippi river at or near the Chickasaw Bluffs; thence, up the said Mississippi river, to the mouth of the Ohio; thence, up the Ohio river, to the mouth of Tennessee river; thence, up the Tennessee river, to the place of beginning.

ARTICLE 3. In consideration of the relinquishment of claim and cession of lands in the preceding article, and to perpetuate the happiness of the Chickasaw nation of Indians, the commissioners of the United States, before named, agree to allow the said nation the sum of twenty thousand dollars per annum, for fifteen successive years, to be paid annually; and, as a farther consideration for the objects aforesaid, and at the request of the chiefs of the said nation, the commissioners agree to pay captain John Gordon, of Tennessee, the sum of one thousand one hundred and fifteen dollars, it being a debt due by general William Colbert, of said nation, to the aforesaid Gordon; and the further sum of two thousand dollars, due by said nation of Indians, to captain David Smith, now of Kentucky, for that sum by him expended, in supplying himself and forty-five soldiers from Tennessee, in the year one thousand seven hundred and ninety-five, when assisting them (at their request and invitation) in defending their towns against the invasion of the Creek Indians; both which sums, (on the application of the said nation) is to be paid, within sixty days after the ratification of this treaty, to the aforesaid Gordon and Smith.

ARTICLE 4. The commissioners agree, on the further and particular application of the chiefs, and for the benefit of the poor and warriors of the said nation, that a tract of land, containing four miles square, to include a salt lick or springs, on or near the river Sandy, a branch of the Tennessee river, and within the land hereby ceded, be reserved, and to be laid off in a square or oblong, so as to include the best timber, at the option of their beloved chief Levi Colbert, and major James Brown, or either of them; who are hereby made agents and trustees for the nation, to lease the said salt lick or springs, on the following express conditions, viz: For the benefit of this reservation, as before recited, the trustees or agents are bound to lease the said reservation to some citizen or citizens of the United States, for a reasonable quantity of salt, to be paid annually to the said nation, for the use thereof; and that, from and after two years after the ratification of this treaty, no salt, made at the works to be erected on this reservation, shall be sold within the limits of the same for a higher price than one dollar per bushel of fifty pounds weight; on failure of which the lease shall be forfeited, and the reservation revert to the United States.

ARTICLE 5. The commissioners agree, that there shall be paid to Oppassantubby, a principal chief of the Chickesaw nation, within sixty days after the ratification of this treaty, the sum of five hundred dollars, as a full compensation for the reservation of two miles square, on the north side of Tennessee river, secured to him and his heirs by the treaty held, with the said Chickesaw nation, on the twentieth day of September, 1816; and the further sum of twenty-five dollars to John Lewis, a half breed, for a saddle he host while in the service of the United States; and, to shew the regard the President of the United States has for the said Chickesaw nation, at the request of the chiefs of the said nation, the commissioners agree that the sum of one thousand and eighty-nine dollars shall be paid to Maj. James Colbert, interpreter, within the period stated in the first part of this article, it being the amount of a sum of money taken from his pocket, in the month of June, 1816, at the theatre in Baltimore: And the said commissioners, as a further regard for said nation, do agree that the reservations made to George Colbert and Levi Colbert, in the treaty held at the council house of said nation, on the twenty-sixth (twentieth) day of September, 1816, the first to Col. George Colbert, on the north side of Tennessee river, and those to Maj. Levi Colbert, on the east side of the Tombigby river, shall enure to the sole use of the said Col. George Colbert, and Maj. Levi Colbert, their heirs and assigns, forever, with their butts and bounds, as defined by said treaty, and agreeable to the marks and boundaries as laid off and marked by the surveyor of the United States.

Where that is the case, and where the reservations has not been laid off and marked by a surveyor of the United States, the same shall be so done as soon after the ratification of this treaty as practicable, on the application of the reservees, or their legally appointed agent under them, and agreeably to the definition in the before recited treaty. This agreement is made on the following express conditions: that the said land, and those living on it, shall be subject to the laws of the United States, and all legal taxation that may be imposed on the land or citizens of the United States inhabiting the territory where said land is situate. The commissioners further agree, that the reservation secured to John McCleish, on the north side of Tennessee river, by the before recited treaty, in consequence of his having been raised in the state of Tennessee, and marrying a white woman, shall enure to the sole use of the said John McCleish, his heirs and assigns, forever, on the same conditions attached to the lands of Col. George Colbert and Maj. Levi Colbert, in this article.

ARTICLE 6. The two contracting parties covenant and agree, that the line of the south boundary of the state of Tennessee, as described in the second article of this treaty, shall be ascertained and marked by commissioners appointed by the President of the United States; that the marks shall be bold; the trees to be blazed on both sides of the line, and the fore and aft trees marked U. S.; and that the commissioners shall be attended by two persons, to be designated by the Chickasaw nation; and the said nation shall have due and seasonable notice when said operation is to be commenced. It is further agreed by the commissioners, that all improvements actually made by individuals of the Chickesaw nation, which shall be found within the lands ceded by this treaty, that a fair and reasonable compensation shall be paid therefor, to the respective individuals having made or owned the same.

ARTICLE 7. In consideration of the friendly and conciliatory disposition evinced during the negotiation of this treaty, by the Chickasaw chiefs and warriors, but more particularly, as a manifestation of the friendship and liberality of the President of the United States, the commissioners agree to give, on the ratification of this treaty, to Chinnubby, King of the Chickesaws nation, to Teshuamingo, William M'Gilvery, Anpassantubby, Samuel Seely, James Brown, Levi Colbert, Ickaryoucuttaha, George Pettygrove, Immartarharmicco, Chickasaw chiefs, and to Mal-cum M'Gee, interpreter to this treaty, each, one hundred and fifty dollars, in cash; and to Major William Glover, Col. George Colbert, Hopoyeahaummar, Immauklusharhopoyea, Tushkarhopoye, Hopoyeahaummar, jun. Immauklusharhopyea, James Colbert, Coweamarthlar, Illachouwarhopoyea, military leaders, one hundred dollars each; and do further agree, that any annuity heretofore secured to the Chickasaw nation of Indians, by treaty, to be paid in goods, shall hereafter be paid in cash.

In testimony whereof the said commissioners, and undersigned chiefs and warriors, have set their hands and seals. Done at the treaty ground east of Old Town, this nineteenth day of October, in the year of our Lord one thousand eight hundred and eighteen.

Isaac Shelby, Andrew Jackson.

Levi Colbert, his x mark, Samuel Seely, his x mark, Chinnubby, King, his x mark, Teshuamingo, his x mark, William McGilvery, his x mark, Arpasheush-tubby, his x mark, James Brown, his x mark, Ickaryaucuttaha, his x mark, Georgo Pettygrove; his x mark, Immartaharmico, his x mark, Major General William Colbert, his x mark, Major William Glover, his x mark, Hopaya-haummar, his x mark, Immouklusharhopoyea, his x mark, Tuskaehopoyea, his x mark, Hopoyahaummar, jun. his x mark, Immaaklusharhopoyea, his x mark, James Cotbert, Cowemarthlar, his x mark, Illackhanwarhopoyes, his x mark, Col. George Colbert, his x mark.

In the presence of: Robert Butler, adjutant-general and secretary, Th. J. Sherburne, agent for the Chickasaw nation of Indians, Maleulm McGee, interpreter, his x mark,.

TREATY WITH THE CHEROKEE {1819, Feb. 27}
Proclamation, Mar. 10, 1819.

Articles of a congregation made between John C. Calhoun, Secretary of War, being specially authorized therefor by the President of the United States, and the undersigned Chiefs and Head Men of the Cherokee nation of Indians, duly authorized and empowered by said nation, at the City of Washington, on the twenty-seventh day of February, in the year of our Lord one thousand eight hundred and nineteen.

WHEREAS a greater part of the Cherokee nation have expressed an earnest desire to remain on this side of the Mississippi, and being desirous, in order to commence those measures which they deem necessary to the civilization and preservation of their nation, that the treaty between the United States and them, signed the eighth of July, eighteen hundred and seventeen, might, without further delay, or the trouble or expense of taking the census, as stipulated in the said treaty, be finally adjusted, have offered to cede to the United States a tract of country at least as extensive as that which they probably are entitled to under its provisions, the contracting parties have agreed to and concluded the following articles.

ARTICLE 1. The Cherokee nation cedes to the United States all of their lands lying north and east of the following line, viz: Beginning on the Tennessee river, at the point where the Cherokee boundary with Madison county, in the Alabama territory, joins the same; thence, along the main channel of said river, to the mouth of the Highwassee; thence, along its main channel, to the first hill which closes in on said river, about two miles above Highwassee Old Town; thence, along the ridge which divides the waters of the Highwassee and Little Tellleo, to the Tennessee river, at Tallassee; thence, along the main channel, to the junction of the Cowee and Nanteyalee; thence, along the ridge in the fork of said river, to the top of the Blue Ridge.

Thence, along the Blue Ridge to the Unicoy Turnpike Road; thence, by a straight line, to the nearest main source of the Chestatee; thence, along its main channel, to the Chatahouchee; and thence to the Creek boundary; it being understood that all the islands in the Chestatee, and the parts of the Tennessee and Highwassee, (with the exception of Jolly's Island, in the Tennessee, near the mouth of the Highwassee) which constitute a portion of the present boundary, belong to the Cherokee nation; and it is also understood, that the reservations contained in the second article of the treaty of Tellleo, signed the twenty-fifth October, eighteen hundred and five, and a tract equal to twelve miles square, to be located by commencing at the point formed by the intersection of the boundary line of Madison county, already mentioned, and the north bank of the Tennessee river; thence, along the said line, and up the said river twelve miles, are ceded to the United States, in trust for the Cherokee nation as a school fund.

It is to be sold by the United States, and the proceeds vested as is hereafter provided in the fourth article of this treaty; and, also, that the rights vested in the Unicoy Turn-hike Company by the Cherokee nation according to certified copies of the instruments securing the rights, and herewith annexed, are not to be affected by this treaty; and it is further understood and agreed by the said parties, that the lands hereby ceded by the Cherokee nation, are in full satisfaction of all claims which the United States have on them, on account of the cession to a part of their nation who have or may hereafter emigrate to the Arkansaw; and this treaty is a final adjustment of that of the eighth of July, eighteen hundred and seventeen.

ARTICLE 2. The United States agree to pay, according to the stipulations contained in the treaty of the eighth of July, eighteen hundred and seventeen, for all improvements on land lying within the country ceded by the Cherokees, which add real value to the land, and do agree to allow a reservation of six hundred and forty acres to each head of any Indian family residing within the ceded territory, those enrolled for the Arkansaw excepted, who choose to become citizens of the United States, in the manner stipulated in said treaty.

ARTICLE 3. It is also understood and agreed by the contracting parties, that a reservation, in fee simple, of six hundred and forty acres square, with the exception of Major Walker's, which is to be located as is hereafter provided, to include their improvements, and which are to be as near the centre thereof as possible, shall be made to each of the persons whose names are inscribed on the certified list annexed to this treaty, all of whom are believed to be persons of industry, and capable of managing their property with discretion, and have, with few exceptions, made considerable improvements on the tracts reserved. The reservations are made on the condition, that those for whom they are intended shall notify, in writing, to the agent for the Cherokee nation, within six months after the ratification of this treaty, that it is their intention to continue to reside permanently on the land reserved.

The reservation for Lewis Ross, so to be laid off as to include his house, and out-buildings, and ferry adjoining the Cherokee agency, reserving to the United States all the public property there, and the continuance of the said agency where it now is, during the pleasure of the government; and Major Walker's, so as to include his dwelling house and ferry: for Major Walker an additional reservation is made of six hundred and forty acres square, to include his grist and saw mill; the land is poor, and principally valuable for its timber. In addition to the above reservations, the following are made, in fee simple; the persons for whom they are intended not residing on the same: To Cabbin Smith, six hundred and forty acres, to be laid off in equal parts, on both sides of his ferry on Tellico, commonly called Blair's ferry.

To John Ross, six hundred and forty acres, to be laid off so as to include the Big Island in Tennessee river, being the first below Tellico which tracts of land were given many years since, by the Cherokee nation, to them; to Mrs. Eliza Ross, step daughter of Major Walker, six hundred and forty acres square, to be located on the river below and adjoining Major Walker's; to Margaret Morgan, six hundred and forty acres square, to be located on the west of, and adjoining, James Riley's reservation; to George Harlin, six hundred and forty acres square, to be located west of, and adjoining, the reservation of Margaret Morgan; to James Lowry, six hundred and forty acres square, to be located at Crow Mocker's old place, at the foot of Cumberland mountain; to Susannah Lowry, six hundred and forty acres, to be located at the Toll Bridge on Battle Creek; to Nicholas Byers, six hundred and forty acres, including the Toqua Island, to be located on the north bank of the Tennessee, opposite to said Island.

ARTICLE 4. The United States stipulate that the reservations, and the tract reserved for a school fund, in the first article of this treaty, shall be surveyed and sold in the same manner, and on the same terms, with the public lands of the United States, and the proceeds vested, under the direction of the President of the United States, in the stock of the United States, or such other stock as he may deem most advantageous to the Cherokee nation. The interest or dividend on said stock, shall be applied, under his direction, in the manner which he shall judge best calculated to diffuse the benefits of education among the Cherokee nation on this side of the Mississippi.

ARTICLE 5. It is agreed that such boundary lines as may be necessary to designate the lands ceded by the first article of this treaty, may be run by a commissioner or commissioners to be appointed by the President of the United States, who shall be accompanied by such commissioners as the Cherokees may appoint, due notice thereof to be given to the nation; and that the leases which have been made under the treaty of the eighth of July, eighteen hundred and seventeen, of land lying within the portion of country reserved to the Cherokees, to be void; and that all white people who have intruded, or may hereafter intrude, on the lands reserved for the Cherokees, shall be removed by the United States, and proceeded against according to the provisions of the act passed thirtieth March, eighteen hundred and two, entitled "An act to regulate trade and intercourse with the Indian tribes, and to preserve peace on the frontiers."

ARTICLE 6. The contracting parties agree that the annuity to the Cherokee nation shall be paid, two-thirds to the Cherokees east of the Mississippi, and one-third to the Cherokees west of that river, as it is estimated that those who have emigrated, and who have enrolled for emigration, constitute one-third of the whole nation; but if the Cherokees west of the Mississippi object to this distribution, of which due notice shall be given them, before the expiration of one year after the ratification of this treaty, then the census, solely for distributing the annuity, shall be taken at such times, and in such manner, as the President of the United States may designate.

ARTICLE 7. The United States, in order to afford the Cherokees who reside on the lands ceded by this treaty, time to cultivate their crop next summer, and for those who do not choose to take reservations, to remove, bind themselves to prevent the intrusion of their citizens on the ceded land before the first of January next.

ARTICLE 8. This treaty to be binding on the contracting parties so soon as it is ratified by the President of the United States, by and with the advice and consent of the Senate.

Done at the place, and on the day and year, above written.

J. C. Calhoun.

Ch. Hicks, Jno. Ross, Lewis Ross, John Martin, James Brown, Geo. Lowry, Gideon Morgan, jr.

Cabbin Smith, his x mark, Sleeping Rabbit, his x mark, Small Wood, his X mark, John Walker, his x mark, Currohee Dick, his x mark,.

Witnesses: Return J. Meigs, C. Vandeventer, Elias Earle, John Lowry.

List of persons referred to in the 3d article of the annexed Treaty.
Within the chartered limits of North Carolina: Richard Walker, Yonah, alias Big Bear.
Georgia: John Martin, Peter Linch, Daniel Davis, George Parris, Walter S. Adair,
Alab. Ter.: Thos. Wilson, Richard Riley, James Riley, Edward Gunter,
Tennessee: Robert MeLemore, John Baldridge, Lewis Ross, Fox Taylor, Rd Timberlake, David Fields, (to include his mill), James Brown, (to include his field by the long pond), William Brown, John Brown, Elizabeth Lowry, George Lowry, John Benge, Mrs. Eliz. Peck, John Walker, Sr.
John Walker, Jr. (unmarried), Richard Taylor, John McIntosh, James Starr, Samuel Parks, The Old Bark, (of Chota)

No. of reservees within the limits of
North Carolina, 2
Georgia, 5
Alabama Terr. 4
Tennessee, 20

Total No. of reserves, 31

I hereby certify, that I am, either personally, or by information on which I can rely, acquainted with the persons before named, all of whom I believe to be persons of industry, and capable of managing their property with discretion; and who have, with few exceptions, long resided on the tracts reserved, and made considerable improvements thereon.

Return J. Meigs, Agent in the Cherokee nation.

(COPY.) Cherokee Agency, Highwassee Garrison.
Mar. 8, 1813.

We, the undersigned Chiefs and Councillors of the Cherokees in full council assembled, do hereby give, grant, and make over unto Nicholas Byer's and David Russell, who are agents in behalf of the states of Tennessee and Georgia, full power and authority to establish a Turnpike Company, to be composed of them, the said Nicholas and David, Arthur Henly, John Lowry, Atto and one other person, by them to be hereafter named, in behalf of the state of Georgia; and the above named persons are authorized to nominate five proper and fit persons, natives of the Cherokees, who, together with the white men aforesaid,

138

are to constitute the company; which said company, when thus established, are hereby fully authorized by us, to lay out and open a road from the most suitable point on the Tennessee River, to be directed the nearest and best way to the highest point of navigation on the Tugelo River; which said road, when opened and established, shall continue and remain a free and public highway, unmolested by us, to the interest and benefit of the said company, and their successors, for the full term of twenty years, yet to come, after the same may be open and complete; after which time, said road, with all its advantages, shall be surrendered up and reverted in, the said Cherokee nation.

And the said company shall have leave, and are hereby authorized, to erect their public stands, or houses of entertainment, on said road, that is to say: one at each end, and one in the middle, or as nearly so as a good situation will permit: with leave also to cultivate one hundred acres of land at each end of the road, and fifty acres at the middle stand, with a privilege of a sufficiency of timber for the use and consumption of said stands. And the said Turnpike Company do hereby agree to pay the sum of one hundred and sixty dollars yearly to the Cherokee nation, for the aforesaid privilege, to commence after said road is opened and in complete operation. The said company are to have the benefit of one ferry on Tennessee river, and such other ferry or ferries as are necessary on said road; and, likewise, said company shall have the exclusive privilege of trading on said road during the aforesaid term of time.

In testimony of our full consent to all and singular the above named privileges and advantages, we have hereunto set our hands and affixed our seals, this eighth day of March, eighteen hundred and thirteen.

Outahelce, his x mark, Naire, above, his x mark, Theelagathahee, his x mark, The Raven, his x mark, Two Killers, his x mark, Teeistiskee, his x mark, John Boggs, his mark, Quotiquaskee, his mark, Currihee, Dick, his mark, Ooseekee, his mark, Toochalee, Chulio, Dick Justice, Wausaway, Big Cabbin, The Bark, Nettle Carrier, Seekeekee, John Walker, Dick Brown, Charles Hick,

Witnesses present:
Wm. L. Lovely, assistant agent, William Smith, George Colville, James Carey, Richard Taylor, Interpreters.

The foregoing agreement and grant was amicably negotiated and concluded in my presence.
Return J. Meigs.

I certify I believe the within to be a correct copy of the original.

Charles Hicks.
WASHINGTON CITY, March 1, 1819.

CHEROKEE AGENCY,
January 6, 1817.

We, the undersigned Chiefs of the Cherokee nation, do hereby grant unto Nicholas Byers, Arthur H. Henly, and David Russell, proprietors of the Unicoy road to Georgia, the liberty of cultivating all the ground contained in the bend on the north side of Tennessee river, opposite and below Chota Old Town, together with the liberty to erect a grist mill on Four Mile creek, for the use and benefit of said road, and the Cherokees in the neighbourhood thereof; for them, the said Byers, Henly, and Russell, to have and to hold the above privileges during the term of lease of the Unicoy road, also obtained from the Cherokees, and sanctioned by the President of the United States.

In witness whereof, we hereunto affix our hands and seals, in presence of: John

McIntosh, Charles Hicks,
Path Killer, Tuchalar, The Gloss, John Walker, Path Killer, jr, Going Snake.

Witness: Return J. Meigs, United States agent.

The above instrument was executed in open Cherokee council, in my office, in January, 1817.

Return J. Meigs.

CHEROKEE AGENCY,
8th July, 1817.

The use of the Unicoy road, so called, was for twenty years.
Return J. Meigs.

I certify I believe the within to be a correct copy of the original.

Ch. Hicks.

WASHINGTON CITY, March 1, 1819.

Martin Colbert, J. C. Bronaugh, assistant inspector general S. D., Thos. H. Shelby, of Kentucky, R. K. Call, Captain U. S. Army, Benjamin Smith, of Kentucky, Richard I. Easter, A. D. Q. M. General.
Ms. B. Winchester, W. B. Lewis.

TREATY WITH THE OTTAWA AND CHIPPEWA {1820, July 6}
Proclamation, Mar. 8, 1821.

Articles of a treaty, made and concluded at L'Arbre Croche and Michilimackinac, in the territory of Michigan, between the United States of America, by their Commissioner Lewis Cass, and the Ottawa and Chippewa nation of Indians.

ARTICLE 1. The Ottawa and Chippewa nations of Indians cede to the United States the Saint Martin Islands in Lake Huron, containing plaster of Paris, and to be located under the direction of the United States.

ARTICLE 2. The Ottawa and Chippewa nations of Indians acknowledge to have this day received a quantity of goods in full satisfaction of the above cession.

ARTICLE 3. This treaty shall be obligatory on the contracting parties after the same shall be ratified by the President of the United States, by and with the advice and consent of the Senate thereof.

In testimony whereof, the said Lewis Cass, commissioner as aforesaid, and the chiefs and warriors of the Ottawa and Chippewa nations of Indians, have hereunto set their hands, at Michilimackinac and L'Arbre Croche, in the territory of Michigan, this 6th day of July, in the year of our Lord one thousand eight hundred and twenty.

Lewis Cass.

Ottawa chiefs: Chemogueman, or Big Knife, his x mark, Skahjenini, his x mark,Misesonguay, his x mark, Pahquesegun, or Smoking Weed, his x mark, Papametaby, his x mark, Ceitawa, his x mark [189]

Shawanoe, his x mark, Oninjuega, or Wing, Ottawa chief, his x mark, Cuddimalmese, or Black Hawk, Ottawa chief, his mark, Dionesau, his x mark, Kojenoikoose, or Long, his x mark,

Chippewa chiefs: Kenojekum, or Pike, his x mark, Cachetokee, his x mark, Gimoewon, or Rain, his x mark, Chiboisquisegun, or Big Gun, his x mark, Skubinesse, or Red Bird, his x mark, Weashe, his x mark, Nebaguam, his x mark. Ainse, his x mark, Shaganash, or Englishman, his x mark,

Witnesses present: Jed. Morse, D. D, Gilbert Knapp, Richard C. Morse, H. G. Gravenant, sworn interpreter, George Boyd, Indian agent.

TREATY WITH THE CHOCTAW {1820, Oct. 18}
Proclamation, Jan. 8, 1821.

A treaty of friendship, limits, and accommodation, between the United States of America and the Choctaw nation of Indians, begun and concluded at the Treaty Ground, in said nation, near Doak's Stand, on the Natchez Road.

PREAMBLE. WHEREAS it is an important object with the President of the United States, to promote the civilization of the Choctaw Indians, by the establishment of schools amongst them; and to perpetuate them as a nation, by exchanging, for a small part of their land here, a country beyond the Mississippi River, where all, who live by hunting and will not work, may be collected and settled together.And whereas it is desirable to the state of Mississippi, to obtain a small part of the land belonging to said nation; for the mutual accommodation of the parties, and for securing the happiness and protection of the whole Choctaw nation, as well as preserving that harmony and friendship which so happily subsists between them and the United States, James Monroe, President of the United States of America, by Andrew Jackson, of the State of Tennessee, Major General in the Army of the United States, and General Thomas Hinds, of the State of Mississippi, Commissioners Plenipotentiary of the United States, on the one part, and the Mingoes, Head Men, and Warriors, of the Choctaw nation, in full Council assembled, on the other part, have freely and voluntarily entered into the following articles, viz:

ARTICLE 1. To enable the President of the United States to carry into effect the above grand and humane objects, the Mingoes, Head Men, and Warriors, of the Choctaw nation, in full council assembled, in behalf of themselves and the said nation, do, by these presents, cede to the United States of America, all the land lying and being within the boundaries following, to wit:Beginning on the Choctaw boundary, East of Pearl River, at a point due South of the White Oak spring, on the old Indian path; thence north to said spring; thence northwardly to a black oak, standing on the Natchez road, about forty poles eastwardly from Doake's fence, marked A. J and blazed, with two large pines and a black oak standing near thereto, and marked as pointers; thence a straight line to the head of Black Creek, or Bouge Loosa; thence down Black Creek or Bouge Loosa to a small Lake; thence a direct course, so as to strike the Mississippi one mile below the mouth of the Arkansas River; thence down the Mississippi to our boundary; thence around and along the same to the beginning.

ARTICLE 2. For and in consideration of the foregoing cession, on the part of the Choctaw nation, and in part satisfaction for the same, the Commissioners of the United States, in behalf of said States, do hereby cede to said nation, a tract of country west of the Mississippi River, situate between the Arkansas and Red River, and bounded as follows:-Beginning on the Arkansas River, where the lower boundary line of the Cherokees strikes the same; thence up the Arkansas to the Canadian Fork, and up the same to its source; thence due South to the Red River; thence down Red River, three miles below the mouth of Little River, which empties itself into Red River on the north side; thence a direct line to the beginning.

ARTICLE 3. To prevent any dispute upon the subject of the boundaries mentioned in the 1st and 2d articles, it is hereby stipulated between the parties, that the same shall be ascertained and distinctly marked by a Commissioner, or Commissioners, to be appointed by the United States, accompanied by such person as the Choctaw nation may select; said nation having thirty days previous notice of the time and place at which the operation will commence. The person so chosen by the Choctaws, shall act as a pilot or guide, for which the United States will pay him two dollars per day, whilst actually engaged in the performance of that duty.

ARTICLE 4. The boundaries hereby established between the Choctaw Indians and the United States, on this side of the Mississippi river, shall remain without alteration until the period at which said nation shall become so civilized and enlightened as to be made citizens of the United States, and Congress shall lay off a limited parcel of land for the benefit of each family or individual in the nation.

ARTICLE 5. For the purpose of aiding and assisting the poor Indians, who wish to remove to the country hereby ceded on the part of the United States, and to enable them to do well and support their families, the Commissioners of the United States engage, in behalf of said States, to give to each warrior a blanket, kettle, rifle gun, bullet moulds and nippers, and ammunition sufficient for hunting and defence, for one year. Said warrior shall also be supplied with corn to support him and his family, for the same period, and whilst traveling to the country above ceded to the Choctaw nation.

ARTICLE 6. The Commissioners of the United States further covenant and agree, on the part of said States, that an agent shall be appointed, in due time, for the benefit of the Choctaw Indians who may be permanently settled in the country ceded to them beyond the Mississippi river, and, at a convenient period, a factor shall be sent there with goods, to supply their wants. A Blacksmith shall also be settled amongst them, at a point most convenient to the population; and a faithful person appointed, whose duty it shall be to use every reasonable [193] exertion to collect all the wandering Indians belonging to the Choctaw nation, upon the land hereby provided for their permanent settlement.

ARTICLE 7. Out of the lands ceded by the Choctaw nation to the United States, the Commissioners aforesaid, in behalf of said States, further covenant and agree, that fifty-four sections of one mile square shall be laid out in good land, by the President of the United States, and sold, for the purpose of raising a fund, to be applied to the support of the Choctaw schools, on both sides of the Mississippi river. Three-fourths of said fund shall be appropriated for the benefit of the schools here; and the remaining fourth for the establishment of one or more beyond the Mississippi; the whole to be placed in the hands of the President of the United States, and to be applied by him, expressly and exclusively, to this valuable object.

ARTICLE 8. To remove any discontent which may have arisen in the Choctaw Nation, in consequence of six thousand dollars of their annuity having been appropriated annually, for sixteen years, by some of the chiefs, for the support of their schools, the Commissioners of the United States oblige themselves, on the part of said States, to set apart an additional tract of good land, for raising a fund equal to that given by the said chiefs, so that the whole of the annuity may remain in the nation, and be divided amongst them. And in order that exact justice may be done to the poor and distressed of said nation, it shall be the duty of the agent to see that the wants of every deaf, dumb, blind, and distressed, Indian, shall be first supplied out of said annuity, and the balance equally distributed amongst every individual of said nation.

ARTICLE 9. All those who have separate settlements, and fall within the limits of the land ceded by the Choctaw nation to the United States, and who desire to remain where they now reside, shall be secured in a tract or parcel of land one mile square, to include their improvements. Any one who prefers removing, if he does so within one year from the date of this treaty, shall be paid their full value, to be ascertained by two persons, to be appointed by the President of the United States.

ARTICLE 10. As there are some who have valuable buildings on the roads and elsewhere upon the lands hereby ceded, should they remove, it is further agreed by the aforesaid Commissioners, in behalf of the United States, that the inconvenience of doing so shall be considered, and such allowance made as will amount to an equivalent. For this purpose, there shall be paid to the Mingo, Puckshenubbee, five hundred dollars; to Harrison, two hundred dollars; to Captain Cobb, two hundred dollars; to William Hays, two hundred dollars; to O'Gleno, two hundred dollars; and to all others who have comfortable houses, a compensation in the same proportion.

ARTICLE 11. It is also provided by the Commissioners of the United States, and they agree in behalf of said states, that those Choctaw Chiefs and Warriors, who have not received compensation for their services during the campaign to Pensacola, in the late war, shall be paid whatever is due them over and above the value of the blanket, shirt, flap, and leggins, which have been delivered to them.

ARTICLE 12. In order to promote industry and sobriety amongst all classes of the Red people, in this nation, but particularly the poor, it is further provided by the parties, that the agent appointed to reside here, shall be, and he is hereby, vested with full power to seize and confiscate all the whiskey which may be introduced into said nation, except that used at public stands, or brought in by the permit of the agent, or the principal Chiefs of the three Districts.

ARTICLE 13. To enable the Mingoes, Chiefs, and Head Men of the Choctaw nation, to raise and organize a corps of Light-Horse, consisting of ten in each District, so that good order, may be maintained, and that all men, both white and red, may be compelled to pay their just debts, it is stipulated and agreed, that the sum of two hundred dollars shall be appropriated by the United States, for each district, annually, and placed in the hands of the agent, to pay the expenses incurred in raising and establishing said corps; which is to act as executive officers, in maintaining good order, and compelling bad men to remove from the nation, who are not authorized to live in it by a regular permit from the agent.

ARTICLE 14. Whereas the father of the beloved Chief Mushulatubbee, of the Lower Towns, for and during his life, did receive from the United States the sum of one hundred and fifty dollars, annually; it is hereby stipulated, that his son and successor Mushulatubbee, shall annually be paid the same amount during his natural life, to commence from the ratification of this Treaty.

ARTICLE 15. The peace and harmony subsisting between the Choctaw Nation of Indians and the United States, are hereby renewed, continued, and declared to be perpetual.

ARTICLE 16. These articles shall take effect, and become obligatory on the contracting parties, so soon as the same shall be ratified by the President, by and with the advice and consent of the Senate of the United States.

In testimony whereof, the commissioners plenipotentiary of the United States and the Mingoes, head men, and warriors, of the Choctaw nation, have hereunto subscribed their names and affixed their seals, at the place above written, this eighteenth day of October, in the year of our Lord one thousand eight hundred and twenty, and of the independence of the United States the forty-fifth.

Andrew Jackson, Thomas Hinds, Commissioners,
Medal Mingoes: Puckshenubbee, his x mark, Pooshawattaha, his x mark, Mushulatubbee, his x mark,
Chiefs and warriors: General Humming Bird, his x mark, James Hanizon, his x mark, Talking Warrior, his x mark, Little Leader, his x mark, Captain Bob Cole, his x mark, Red Fort, or Oolatahooma, his x mark, Choctawistonocka, his x mark, Oglano, his x mark, Chuleta, his x mark, John Frazier, his x mark,

Oakchunhmia, his x mark., Nockestona, his x mark, Chapahooma, his x mark, Onanchahabee, his x mark, Copatanathoco, his x mark, Atahobia, his x mark, Opehoola, his x mark, Chetantanchahubbee, his x mark,

Captain Lapala, his x mark, Panchahabbee, his x mark, Chuckahicka, his x mark, Tallahomia, his x mark, Totapia, his x mark, Hocktanlubbee, his x mark, Tapawanchahubbee, his x mark, Capt. Red Bird, his x mark, Capt. Jerry Carhey, his x mark, Chapanchahabbee, his x mark, Tunnupnuia, his x mark, Ponhoopia, his x mark,

Ticbehacubbee, his x mark, Suttacanchihubbee, his x mark, Capt. William Beams, his x mark, Captain James Pitchlynn, Capt. James Garland, his x mark, Tapanahomia, his x mark, Thlahomia, his x mark, Tishotata, his x mark, Inoquia, his x mark, Ultetoncubbee, his x mark, Palochubbee, his x mark, Jopannu, his x mark, Captain Joel H. Vail, Tapanastonahamia, his x mark, Hoopihomia, his x mark, Chelutahomia, his x mark, Tuskiamingo, his x mark, Young Captain, his x mark, Chiefs and warriors:

Hakatubbee, his x mark, Tishoo, his x mark, Capt. Bobb, his x mark, Hopeanchahabee, his x mark, Capt. Bradley, his x mark, Capt. Daniel M'Curtain, his x mark, Mucklisahopia, his x mark, Nuckpullachubbee, his x mark, George Turnbull, Captain Thomas M'Curtain, his x mark, Oakehonahooma, his x mark, Capt. John Cairns, his x mark, Topenastonahooma, his x mark, Holatohamia, his x mark, Col. Boyer, his x mark, Holantachanshahubbee, his x mark, Chuckahabbee, his x mark, Washaschahopia, his x mark, [195]

Chatamakaha, his x mark, Hapeahomia, his x mark, William Hay, his x mark, Captain Samuel Cobb, his x mark, Lewis Brashears, his x mark, Muckelehamia, his x mark, Capt. Sam. Magee, his x mark, Ticbehamia, his x mark, Doctor Red Bird, his x mark,

Oontoola, his x mark, Pooshoushabbee, his x mark, Casania, his x mark, Joseph Nelson, his x mark, Unahubbee, his x mark, Red Duck, his x mark, Muttahubbee, his x mark, Capt. Ihokahatubbee, his x mark, Alex. Hamilton, Capt. Red Knife, his x mark, Shapahroma, his x mark, Capt. Tonnanpoocha, his x mark, Mechamiabbee, his x mark, Tuskanohamia, his x mark, Tookatubbetusea, his x mark, William Frye, his x mark, Greenwood Leftore, his x mark, Archibald MaGee, his x mark, Capt. Ben Burris, his x mark, Tusconohicca, his x mark, Capt. Lewis Perry, his x mark, Henekachubbee, his x mark, Tussashamia, his x mark, Capt. Charles Durant, his x mark, Plate Durant, his x mark

Witnesses present at sealing and signing: Saml. R. Overton, secretary to the commission, Eden Brashears, J. C. Bronaugh, assistant surgeon-general, S. D., U. S. Army, H. D. Downs, Wm. F. Cangent, Wm. M. Graham, first lieutenat, Corps of Artillery, Andrew J. Donelson, brevet second lieutenant Corps of Engineers and aid-de-camp to General Jackson, P. A. Vandorn, John H. Esty, John Pitchlynn, United States interpreter, M. Mackey, United States interpreter, Edmund Falsome, interpreter, X, James Hughes, Geo. Fisher, Jas. Jackson, jr.

TREATY WITH THE CREEKS {1821, Jan. 8}
Proclamation, Mar. 2, 1821.

Articles of a treaty entered into at the Indian Spring, in the Creek Nation, by Daniel M. Forney, of the State of North Carolina, and David Meriwether, of the State of Georgia, specially appointed for that purpose, on the part of the United States; and the Chiefs, Head Men, and Warriors, of the Creek Nation, in council assembled.

ARTICLE 1. The Chiefs, Head Men, and Warriors, of the Creek Nation, in behalf of the said nation, do, by these presents, cede to the United States all that tract or parcel of land, situate, lying, and being, east of the following bounds and limits, viz: Beginning on the east bank of Flint river, where Jackson's line crosses, running thence, up the eastern bank of the same, along the water's edge, to the head of the principal western branch; from thence, the nearest and a direct line, to the Chatahooche river, up the eastern bank of the said river, along the water's edge, to the shallow Ford, where the present boundary line between the state of Georgia and the Creek nation touches the said river: Provided, however, That, if the said line should strike the Chatahooche river, below the Creek village Buzzard-Roost, there shall be a set-off made, so as to leave the said village one mile within the Creek nation; excepting and reserving to the Creek nation the title and possession, in the manner and form specified, to all the land hereafter excepted, viz: one thousand acres, to be laid off in a square, so as to include the Indian Spring in the centre thereof; as, also, six hundred and forty acres on the western bank of the Oakmulgee river, So as to include the improvements at present in the possession of the Indian Chief General M'Intosh.

ARTICLE 2. It is hereby stipulated, by the contracting parties, that the title and possession of the following tracts of land shall continue in the Creek nation so long as the present occupants shall remain in the personal possession thereof, viz: one mile square, each, to include, as [196] near as may be, in the centre thereof, the improvements of Michey Barnard, James Barnard, Buckey Barnard, Cussena Barnard, and Efauemathlaw, on the east side of Flint river; which reservations shall constitute a part of the cession made by the first article, so soon as they shall be abandoned by the present occupants.

ARTICLE 3. It is hereby stipulated, by the contracting parties, that, so long as the United States continue the Creek agency at its present situation on Flint river, the land included within the following boundary, viz: beginning on the east bank of Flint river, at the mouth of the Boggy Branch, and running out, at right angles, from the river, one mile and a half; thence up, and parallel with, the river, three miles: thence, parallel with the first line, to the river; and thence, down the river, to the place of beginning; shall be reserved to the Creek nation for the use of the United States agency, and shall constitute a part of the cession made by the first article, whenever the agency shall be removed.

ARTICLE 4. It is hereby stipulated and agreed, on the part of the United States, as a consideration for the land ceded by the Creek nation by the first article, that there shall be paid to the Creek nation, by the United States, ten thousand dollars in hand, the receipt whereof is hereby acknowledged; forty thousand dollars as soon as practicable after the ratification of this convention; five thousand dollars, annually, for two years thereafter; sixteen thousand dollars, annually, for five years thereafter; and ten thousand dollars, annually, for six years thereafter; making, in the whole, fourteen payments in fourteen successive years, without interest, in money or goods and implements of husbandry., at the option of the Creek nation, seasonably signified, from time to time, through the agent of the United States residing with said nation, to the Department of War. And, as a further consideration for said cession, the United States do hereby agree to pay to the state of Georgia whatever balance may be found due by the Creek nation to the citizens of said state, whenever the same shall be ascertained, in conformity with the reference made by the commissioners of Georgia, and the chiefs, head men, and warriors, of the Creek nation, to be paid in five annual instalments without interest, provided the same shall not exceed the sum of two hundred and fifty thousand dollars; the commissioners of Georgia executing to the Creek nation a full and final relinquishment of all the claims of the citizens of Georgia against the Creek nation, for property taken or destroyed prior to the act of Congress of one thousand eight hundred and two, regulating the intercourse with the Indian tribes.

ARTICLE 5. The President of the United States shall cause the line to be run from the head of Flint river to the Chatahooche river, and the reservations made to the Creek nation to be laid off, in the manner specified in the first, second, and third, articles of this treaty, at such time and in such manner as he may deem proper, giving timely notice to the Creek nation; and this Convention shall be obligatory on the contracting parties, as soon as the same shall have been ratified by the government of the United States.

Done at the Indian Spring, this eighth day of January, A. D.

D. M. Forney, D. Meriwether, Wm. McIntosh,
Tustunnugee Hopoie, his x mark, Efau Emauthlau, his x mark, Holoughlan, or Col. Blue, his x mark, Cussetau Micco, his x mark, Soletan Haujo, his x mark, Etomme Tustunmuggee, his x mark, Taskagee Emauthlau, his x mark, Tuckle Luslee, his x mark, Tuckte Lustee Haujo, his x mark, Cunepee Emauthlau, his x mark, Hethlepoie, his x mark, Tuskeenaheocki, his x mark, Chaughle Micco, his x mark, Isfaune Tustunnuggee Haujo, his x mark, Thlucco Haujo, his x mark, Itchu Haujo, his x mark, labamaTustunnuggee,his x mark, Holoughlan Tustunnuggee, his x mark, Auhauluck Yohola, his x mark, Oseachee Tustunnuggee, his x mark, Houpauthlee Tustunnuggee, his x mark, Nenehaumaughto-

ochie, hisx mark, Henelau Tixico, his x mark, Tusekeagh Haujo, his x mark, Joseph Marshall,

In presence of I. McIntosh, David Adams, Daniel Newman, Commissioners of Georgia.
D. B. Mitchell, Agent for I. A. William Meriwether, secretary U. S.C.
William Cook, secretary C. G.
William Hambly, S. Hawkins, George Levett, interpreters.

TREATY WITH THE OTTAWA, ETC. {1821, Aug. 29}
Proclamation, Mar. 25, 1822.

Articles of a treaty made and concluded at Chicago, in the State of Illinois, between Lewis Cass and Solomon Sibley, Commissioners of the United States, and the Ottawa, Chippewa, and Pottawatamie, Nations of Indians.

ARTICLE 1. The Ottawa, Chippewa, and Pottawatamie, Nations of Indians cede to the United States all the Land comprehended within the following boundaries: Beginning at a point on the south bank of the river St. Joseph of Lake Michigan, near the Parc aux Vaches, due north from Rum's Village, and running thence south to a line drawn due east from the southern extreme of Lake Michigan, thence with the said line east to the Tract ceded by the Pottawatamies to the United States by the Treaty of Fort Meigs in 1817, if the said line should strike the said Tract, but if the said line should pass north of the said Tract, then such line shall be continued until it strikes the western boundary of the Tract ceded to the United States by the Treaty of Detroit in 1807, and from the termination of the said line, following the boundaries of former cessions, to the main branch of the Grand River of Lake Michigan, should any of the said lines cross the said River, but if none of the said lines should cross the said River, then to a point due east of the source of the said main branch of the said river, and from such point due west to the source of the said principal branch, and from the crossing of the said River, or from the source thereof, as the case may be, down the said River, on the north bank thereof to the mouth; thence following the shore of Lake Michigan to the south bank of the said river St. Joseph, at the mouth thereof, and thence with the said south bank to the place of beginning.

ARTICLE 2. From the cession aforesaid, there shall be reserved, for the use of the Indians, the following Tracts:
One tract at Mang-ach-qua Village, on the river Peble, of six miles square.
One tract at Mick-ke-saw-be, of six miles square.
One tract at the village of Na-to-wa-se-pe, of four miles square. One tract at the village of Prairie Ronde, of three miles square.

One tract at the village of Match-e-be narh-she-wish, at the head of the Keka-lamazoo river.

ARTICLE 3. There shall be granted by the United States to each of the following persons, being all Indians by descent, and to their heirs, the following Tracts of Land:

To John Burnet, two sections of land.
To James Burnet, Abraham Burnet, Rebecca Burnet, and Nancy Burner, each one section of land; which said John, James, Abraham, Rebecca, and Nancy, are children of Kaw-kee-me, sister of Top-ni-be, principal chief of the Potwa-tamie nation.
The land granted to the persons immediately preceding, shall begin on the north bank of the river St. Joseph, about two miles from the mouth, and shall extend up and back from the said river for quantity.
To John B. La Lime, son of Noke-no-qua, one-half of a section of land, adjoining the tract before granted, and on the upper side thereof.
To Jean B. Chandonai son of Chip-pe-wa-qua, two sections of land, on the river St. Joseph, above and adjoining the tract granted to J. B. La Lime.
To Joseph Dazé, son of Chip-pe-wa-qua, one section of land above and adjoining the tract granted to Jean B. Chandonai.
To Monguago, one-half of a section of land, at Mish-she-wa-ko-kink.
To Pierre Moran or Peeresh, a Potawatamie Chief, one section of land, and to his children two sections of land, at the mouth of the Elkheart river.
To Pierre Le Clerc, son of Moi-qua, one section of land on the Elkheart river, above and adjoining the tract granted to Moran and his children.
The section of land granted by the Treaty of St. Mary's, in 1818, to Peercab or Perig, shall be granted to Jean B. Cicot, son of Pe-say-quot, sister of the said Peeresh, it having been so intended at the execution of the said Treaty.
To O-she-ak-ke-be or Benac, one-half of a section of land on the north side of the Elk-heart river, where the road from Chicago to Fort Wayne first crosses the said river.
To Me-naw-che, a Potawatamie woman, one-half of a section of land on the eastern bank of the St. Joseph, where the road from Detroit to Chicago first crosses the said river.
To Theresa Chandler or To-e-ak-qui, a Potawatamie woman, and to her daughter Betsey Fisher, one section of land on the south side of the Grand River, opposite to the Spruce Swamp.
To Charles Beaubien and Medart Beaubien, sons of Man-na-ben-a- each one-half of a section of land near the village of Ke-wi-go-eem, on the Washtenaw river.

To Antoine Roland, son of I-gat-pat-a-wat-a-mie-qua, one-half of a section of land adjoining and below the tract granted to Pierre Moran. To William Knaggs or Was-es-kuk-son, son of Ches-qua, one-half of a section of land adjoining and below the tract granted to Antoine Roland.

To Madeline Bertrand, wife of Joseph Bertrand, a Potawatamie woman, one section of land at the Parc aux Vaches, on the north side of the river St. Joseph.

To Joseph Bertrand, junior, Benjamin Bertrand, Laurent Bertrand. Theresa Bertrand, and Amable Bertrand, children of the said Made-line Bertrand, each one half of a section of land at the portage of the Kankakee river.

To John Riley, son of Me-naw-cum-a-go-quoi, one section of land, at the mouth of the river Au Foin, on the Grand River, and extending up the said River.

To Peter Riley, the son of Me-naw-cum-e-go-qua, one section of land, at the mouth of the river Au Foin, on the Grand River, and extending down the said river.

To Jean B. Le Clerc, son of Moi-qua, one half of a section of land, above and adjoining the tract granted to Pierre Le Clerc.

To Joseph La Framboise, son of Shaw-we-no-qua, one section of land upon the south side of the river St. Joseph, and adjoining on the upper side the land ceded to the United States, which said section is also ceded to the United States.

The Tracts of Land herein stipulated to be granted, shall never be leased or conveyed by the grantees or their heirs to any persons whatever, without the permission of the President of the-United States. And such tracts shall be located after the said cession is surveyed, and in conformity with such surveys as near as may be, and in such manner as the President may direct.

ARTICLE 4. In consideration of the cession aforesaid, the United States engage to pay to the Ottawa nation, one thousand dollars in specie annually forever, and also to appropriate annually, for the term of ten years, the sum of fifteen hundred dollars, to be expended as the President may direct, in the support of a Blacksmith, of a Teacher, and of a person to instruct the Ottawas in agriculture and in the purchase of cattle and farming utensils. And the United States also engage to pay to the Potawatamie nation five thousand dollars in specie, annually, for the term of twenty years, and also to appropriate annually, for the term of fifteen years, the sum of one thousand dollars, to be expended as the President may direct, in the support of a Blacksmith and a Teacher. And one mile square shall be selected, under the direction of the President, on the north side of the Grand River, and one mile square on the south side of the St. Joseph, and within the Indian lands not ceded, upon which the blacksmiths and teachers employed for the said tribes, respectively, shall reside.

ARTICLE 5. The stipulation contained in the treaty of Greenville, relative to the right of the Indians to hunt upon the land ceded while it continues the property of the United States, shall apply to this treaty.

ARTICLE 6. The United States shall have the privilege of making and using a road through the Indian country, from Detroit and Fort Wayne, respectively, to Chicago.

ARTICLE 7. This Treaty shall take effect and be obligatory on the contracting parties, so soon as the same shall be ratified by the President of the United States, by and with the advice and consent of the Senate thereof.

In testimony whereof, the said Lewis Cass and Solomon Sibley, commissioners as aforesaid, and the chiefs and warriors of the said Ottawa, Chippewa, and Pattiwatima nations, have hereunto set their hands, at Chicago aforesaid, this 29th day of August, in the year of our Lord one thousand eight hundred and twenty-one.

Lewis Cass, Solomon Sibley.
Ottawas: Kewagoushcum, his x mark, Nokawjegaun, his x mark, Kee-o-to-aw-be, his x mark, Ket-che-me-chi-na-waw, his x mark, Ep-pe-san-se, his x mark, Kay-nee-wee, his x mark, Mo-a-put-to, his x mark, Mat-che-pee-na-che-wish, his x mark,
Chippewas: Met-tay-waw, his x mark, Mich-cl, his x mark,

Pattiwatimas: To-pen-Re-bee, his x mark, Mee-te-ay, his x mark, Chee-banse, his x mark, Loui-son, his x mark, Wee-saw, his x mark, Kee-po-taw, his x mark, Shay-auk-ke-bee, his x mark, Sho-mang, his x mark, Waw-we-uck-ke-meck, his x mark, Nay-ou-chee-mon, his x mark, Kon-gee, his x mark, Shee-shaw-gan, his x mark, Aysh-cam, his x mark, Meek-say-mank, his x mark, May-ten-way, his x mark, Shaw-wen-Re-me-lay, his x mark, Franeois, his x mark, Mauk-see, his x mark, Way-me-go, his x mark, Man-daw-min, his x mark, Quay-guee, his x mark, Aa-pen-naw-bee, his x mark, Mat-cha-wee-yaas, his x mark, Mat-cha-pag-gish, his x mark, Mongaw, his x mark, Pug-gay-gaus, his x mark, Ses-cobe-mesh, his x mark, Chee-gwa-mack-gwa-go, his x mark,

Waw-seb-baw, his x mark, Pee-chee-co, his x mark, Quoi-quoi-taw, his x mark, Pe-an-nish, his x mark, Wy-ne-naig, his x mark, Onuck-ke-meck, his x mark, Ka-way-sin, his x mark, A-meck-kose, his x mark, Os-see-meet, his x mark, Shaw-ko-to, his x mark, No-shay-we-quat, his x mark, Mee-gwun, his x mark, Mes-she-ke-ten-now, his x mark, Kee-no-to-go, his x mark, Wa-baw-nee-she, his x mark, Shaw-waw-nay-see, his x mark, Atch-wee-muck-quee, his x mark, Pish-she-baw-gay, his x mark, Waw-ba-saye, his x mark, Meg-ges-seese, his x mark, Say-gaw-koo-nuck, his x mark, Shaw-way-no, his x mark, Shee-shaw-gun, his x mark, To-to-race, his x mark, Ash-kee-wee, his x mark, Shay-auk-ke-bee, his x mark, Aw-be-tone, his x mark.

In presence of: Alex. Wolcott, jr. Indian agent, Jno. R. Williams, Adjutant-General, M.
Ma. G. Godfroy, Indian agent, W. Knaggs, Indian agent, Jacob Viaget, Henry I. Hunt, A. Phillips, paymaster, U. S. Army, R. Montgomery, Jacob B. Varnum, United States factor, John B. Beaubie, R. Conrad, Ten Eyck, J. Whipley, George Miles, jun, Henry Connor, James Barnerd, John Kenzie, subagent.

The tract reserved at the village of Match-e-be-nash-she-wish, at the head of the Ke-kal-i-ma-zoo river, was by agreement to be three miles square. The extent of the reservation was accidentally omitted.
The tract at Match-ebenashshewish to be 3 miles square.

Lewis Cass, Solomon Sibley.

AGREEMENT WITH THE SENECA {1823, Sept. 3}
Unratified.

At a treaty held under the authority of the United States at Moscow, in the county of Livingston, in the State of New York, between the sachems, chiefs, and warriors of the Seneka nation of Indians in behalf of said nation, and John Greig and Henery B. Gibson of Canandaigua in the county of Ontario, in the presence of Charles Carroll, esquire, commissioner appointed by the United States for holding said treaty, and of Nathaniel Gorham, esquire, superintendent, in behalf of the State of Massachusetts.

Know all men by these presents, that the said sachems, chiefs, and warriors, for and in consideration of the sum of four thousand two hundred and eighty-six dollars, lawful money of the United States, to them in hand paid by the said John Greig and Henry B. Gibson, at or immediately before the ensealing and delivery of these presents, the receipt whereof is hereby acknowledged, have granted, bargained, sold, aliened, released, quit claimed and confirmed unto the said John Greig and Henry B. Gibson, and by these presents do grant, bargain, sell, alien, release, quit claim, and confirm, unto the said John Greig and Henry B. Gibson, their heirs and assigns, forever, all that tract, piece or parcel of land commonly called and known by the name of the Gordeau reservation, situate, lying and being in the counties of Livingston and Genesee, in the State of New York, bounded as follows, that is to say: Beginning at the mouth of Steep Hill creek, thence due east, until it strikes the Old Path, thence south until a due west line will intersect with certain steep rocks on the west side of Genesee river, thence extending due west, due north, and due east, until it strikes the first mentioned bound, enclosing as much land on the west side as on the east side of the river, and containing according to the survey and measurement made of the same by Augustus Porter, surveyor, seventeen thousand nine hundred and twenty-seven 137-160 acres, be the same more or less: excepting nevertheless, and always reserving out of this grant and conveyance, twelve hundred and eighty acres of land, bounded as follows.

That is to say; on the east by Genesee river, on the south by a line running due west from the centre of the Big Slide so called, on the north by a line parallel to the south line and two miles distant therefrom, and on the west by a line running due north and south, and at such a distance from the river as to include the said quantity of twelve hundred and eighty acres and no more; which said twelve hundred and eighty acres are fully and clearly understood, to remain the property of the said parties of the first part, and their nation, in as full and ample a manner, as if these presents had not been executed: together with all and singular the rights, privileges, hereditaments, and appurtenances, to the said hereby granted premises belonging or in anywise appertaining, and all the estate, right, title, and interest, whatsoever, of them the said parties of the first part, and of their nation, of, in, and to, the said tract of land above described, except as is above excepted. To have and to hold all and singular the above granted premises with the appurtenances, unto the said John Greig and Henry B. Gibson, their heirs and assigns, to the sole and only proper use, benefit, and behoof, of the said John Greig and Henry B. Gibson, their heirs and assigns forever.

In testimony whereof, the parties to these presents have hereunto, and to three other instruments of the same tenor and date, one to remain with the United States, one to remain with the State of Massachusetts, one to remain with the Senaka nation of Indians, and one to remain with the said John Greig and Henry B. Gibson, interchangeably [1034] set their hands and seals, the third day of September, in the year of our Lord one thousand eight hundred and twenty three.

Saquiungarluchta, or Young King, his x mark, Karlundawana, or Pollard, his x mark, Sagouata, or Red Jacket, his x mark, Tishkaaga, or Little Billy, his x mark, Tywaneash, or Black Snake, his x mark, Kahalsta, or Strong, his x mark,

Chequinduchque, or Little Beard, his x mark, Tuyongo, or Seneka White, his x mark, Onondaki, or Destroy Town, his x mark, Lunuchshewa, or War Chief, his x mark, Genuchsckada, or Stevenson, his x mark, Mary Jamieson, her x mark, Talwinaha, or Little Johnson, his x mark, Atachsagu, or John Big Tree, his x mark, Teskaiy, or John Pierce, his x mark, Teaslaegee, or Charles Cornplanter, his x mark, Teoneukaweh, or Bob Stevens, his x mark, Checanadughtwo, or Little Beard, His x mark, Canada, his x mark.

Sealed and delivered in the presence of: Nat. W. Howell, Ch. Carroll, Jasper Parfish, Horatio Jones.

Done at a treaty held with the sachems, chiefs, and warriors of the Seneka nation of Indians at Moscow, in the county of Livingston and State of New York, on the third day of September, one thousand eight hundred and twenty-three, under the authority of the United States.

In testimony whereof, I have hereunto set my hand and seal, the day and year aforesaid, by virtue of a commission issued under the seal of the common-wealth of Massachusetts, bearing date the 31st day of August, A. D. 1815, pursuant to a resolution of the legislature of the said commonwealth, passed the eleventh day of March, one thousand seven hundred and ninety-one.

N. Gorham, Superintendent.

I have attended a treaty of the Seneka nation of Indians held at Moscow in the county of Livingston and State of New York, on the third day of September, in the year of our Lord one thousand eight hundred and twenty-three, when the within instrument was duly executed in my presence, by the sachems, chiefs, and warriors of the said nation, being fairly and properly understood and trans-acted by all the parties of Indians concerned, and declared to be done to their full satisfaction. I do therefore certify and approve the same.

Ch. Carroll, Commissioner.

TREATY WITH THE FLORIDA TRIBES OF INDIANS {1823, Sept. 18}
Proclamation. Jan. 2, 1824.

ARTICLE 1. THE undersigned chiefs and warriors, for themselves and their tribes, have appealed to the humanity, and thrown themselves on, and have promised to continue under, the protection of the United States, and of no other nation, power, or sovereign; and, in consideration of the promises and stipula-tions hereinafter made, do cede and relinquish all claim or title which they may have to the whole territory of Florida, with the exception of such district of country as shall herein be allotted to them.

ARTICLE 2. The Florida tribes of Indians will hereafter be concentrated and confined to the following metes and boundaries: commencing five miles north of Okehumke, running in a direct line to a point five miles west of Setarky's settlement, on the waters of Amazura, (or Withla-huchie river) leaving said settlement two miles south of the line; from thence, in a direct line, to the south end of the Big Hammock, to include Chickuchate; continuing, in the same di-rection, for five miles beyond the said Hammockprovided said point does not approach nearer than fifteen miles the sea coast of the Gulf of Mexico; if it does, the said line will terminate at that distance from the sea coast; thence, south, twelve miles.; thence in a southeast direction, until the same shall strike within five miles of the main branch of Charlotte river; thence, in a due east direction, to within twenty miles of the Atlantic coast; thence, north, fifteen west, for fifty miles and from this last, to the beginning point.

ARTICLE 3.   The United States will take the Florida Indians under their care and patronage, and will afford them protection against all persons whatsoever; provided they conform to the laws of the United States, and refrain from making war, or giving any insult to any foreign nation, without having first obtained the permission and consent of the United States: And, in consideration of the appeal and cession made in the first article of this treaty, by the aforesaid chiefs and warriors, the United States promise to distribute among the tribes, as soon as concentrated, under the direction of their agent, implements of husbandry, and stock of cattle and hogs, to the amount of six thousand dollars, and an annual sum of five thousand dollars a year, for twenty successive years, to be distributed as the President of the United States shall direct, through the Secretary of War, or his Superintendents and Agent of Indian Affairs.

ARTICLE 4.   The United States promise to guaranty to the said tribes the peaceable possession of the district of country herein assigned them, reserving the right of opening through it such roads, as may, from time to time, be deemed necessary; and to restrain and prevent all white persons from hunting, settling, or otherwise intruding upon it. But any citizen of the United States, being lawfully [204] authorized for that purpose, shall be permitted to pass and repass through the said district, and to navigate the waters thereof, without any hindrance, toll, or exaction, from said tribes.

ARTICLE 5.   For the purpose of facilitating the removal of the said tribes to the, district of country allotted them, and, as a compensation for the losses sustained, or the inconveniences to which they may be exposed by said removal, the United States will furnish them with rations of corn, meat, and salt, for twelve months, commencing on the first day of February next; and they further agree to compensate those individuals who have been compelled to abandon improvements on lands, not embraced within the limits allotted, to the amount of four thousand five hundred dollars, to be distributed among the sufferers, in a ratio to each, proportional to the value of the improvements abandoned. The United States further agree to furnish a sum, not exceeding two thousand dollars, to be expended by their agent, to facilitate the transportation of the different tribes to the point of concentration designated.

ARTICLE 6.   An agent, sub-agent, and interpreter, shall be appointed, to reside within the Indian boundary aforesaid, to watch over the interests of said tribes; and the United States further stipulate, as an evidence of their humane policy towards said tribes, who have appealed to their liberality, to allow for the establishment of a school at the agency, one thousand dollars per year for twenty successive years; and one thousand dollars per year, for the same period, for the support of a gun and blacksmith, with the expenses incidental to his shop.

ARTICLE 7. The chiefs and warriors aforesaid, for themselves and tribes, stipulate to be active and vigilant in the preventing the retreating to, or passing through, of the district of country assigned them, of any absconding slaves, or fugitives from justice; and further agree, to use all necessary exertions to apprehend and deliver the same to the agent, who shall receive orders to compensate them agreeably to the trouble and expenses incurred.

ARTICLE 8. A commissioner, or commissioners, with a surveyor, shall be appointed, by the President of the United States, to run and mark, (blazing fore and aft the trees) the line as defined in the second article of this treaty, who shall be attended by a chief or warrior, to be designated by a council of their own tribes, and who shall receive, while so employed, a daily compensation of three dollars.

ARTICLE 9. The undersigned chiefs and warriors, for themselves and tribes, having objected to their concentration within the limits described in the second article of this treaty, under the impression that the said limits did not contain a sufficient quantity of good land to subsist them, and for no other reason: it is, therefore, expressly understood, between the United States and the aforesaid chiefs and warriors, that, should the country embraced in the said limits, upon examination by the Indian agent and the commissioner, or commissioners, to be appointed under the 8th article of this treaty, be by them considered insufficient for the support of the said Indian tribes; then the north line, as defined in the 2d article of this treaty, shall be removed so far north as to embrace a sufficient quantity of good tillable land.

ARTICLE 10. The undersigned chiefs and warriors, for themselves and tribes, have expressed to the commissioners their unlimited confidence in their agent, Col. Gad Humphreys, and their interpreter, Stephen Richards, and, as an evidence of their gratitude for their services and humane treatment, and brotherly attentions to their wants, request that one mile square, embracing the improvements of Enehe Mathla, at Tallahassee (said improvements to be considered as the centre) be conveyed, in fee simple, as a present to Col. Gad Humphreys.And they further request, that one mile square, at the Ochesee Bluffs, embracing Stephen Richard's field on said Bluffs, be conveyed in fee simple, as a present to said Stephen Richards. The commissioners accord in sentiment with the undersigned chiefs and warriors, and recommend a compliance with their wishes to the President and Senate of the United States; but the disapproval, on the part of the said authorities, of this article, shall, in no wise, affect the Other articles and stipulations concluded on in this treaty.

In testimony whereof, the commissioners, William P. Duval, James Gadsden, and Bernard Segui, and the undersigned chiefs and warriors, have hereunto subscribed their names and affixed their seals. Done at camp on Moultrie creek,

157

in the territory of Florida, this eighteenth day of September, one thousand eight hundred and twenty-three, and of the independence of the United States the forty-eighth.

William P. Duval, James Gadsden, Bernard Segui, Nea Mathla, his x mark, To-kose Mathla, his x mark, Ninnee Homata Tustenuky, his x mark, Miconope, his x mark, Nocosee Ahola, his x mark, John Blunt, his x mark, Otlemata, his x mark, Tuskeencha, his x mark, Tuski Hajo, His x mark, Econchatimico, his x mark, Emoteley, his x mark, Mulatto King, his x mark, Chocholohano, his xmark, Ematlochee, his x mark, Wokse Holata, his x mark, Amathla Ho, his x mark, Holatefiscico, His x mark, Chefiscico Hajo, his x mark, Lathloa Mathla, his x mark, Senufky, his x mark, Alak Hajo, his x mark, Fahelustee Hajo, his x mark, Octahamico, his x mark, Tusteneck Hajo, his x mark, Okoskee Amathla, his x mark, Ocheeny Tustenuky, his x mark, Phillip, his x mark, Charley Amathla, his x mark, John Hoponey, his x mark, Rat Head, his x mark, Holatta Amathla, his x mark, Foshatchimico, his x mark.

Signed, sealed, and delivered, in the presence of: George Murray, secretary to the commission, G. Humphreys, Indian agent, Stephen Richards, interpreter, Isaac N. Cox, J. Erving, captain, Yourth Artillery, Harvey Brown, lieutenant, Fourth Artillery, C. D'Espinville, lieutenant, Fourth Artillery, Jno. B. Scott, lieutenant, Fourth Artillery, William Travers, Horatio S. Dexter.

ADDITIONAL ARTICLE. Whereas Neo Matlila, John Blunt, Tuski Hajo, Mulatto King, Emath-lochee, and Econchatimico, six of the principal Chiefs of the Florida Indians, and parties to the treaty to which this article has been an-nexed, have warmly appealed to the Commissioners for permission to remain in the district of country now inhabited by them; and, in consideration of their friendly disposition, and past services to the United States, it is, therefore, stipulated, between the United States and the aforesaid Chiefs, that the follow-ing reservations shall be surveyed, and marked by the Commissioner, or Com-missioners, to be appointed under the 8th article of this Treaty: For the use of Nea Mathla and his connections, two miles square, embracing the Tuphulga village, on the waters of Rocky Comfort Creek. For Blunt and Tuski Hajo, a reservation, commencing on the Apalachicola, one mile below Tuski Hajo's improvements, running up said river four miles; thence, west, two miles; thence, southerly, to a point two miles due west of the beginning; thence, east, to the beginning point.

For Mulatto King and Emathlochee, a reservation, commencing on the Apala-chicola, at a point to include Yellow Hair's improvements; thence, up said river, for four miles; thence, west, one mile; thence, southerly, to a point one mile west of the beginning; and thence, east, to the beginning point. For Econchati-mico, a reservation, commencing on the Chatahoochie, one mile below Econ-chatimico's house; thence, up said river, for four miles; thence, one mile, west;

thence, southerly, to a point one mile west of the beginning; thence, east, to the beginning point.

The United States promise to guaranty the peaceable possession of the said reservations, as defined, to the aforesaid chiefs and their descendents only, so long as they shall continue to occupy, improve, or cultivate, the same; but in the event of the abandonment of all, or either of the reservations, by the chief or chiefs, to whom they have been allotted, the reservation, or reservations, so abandoned, shall revert to the United States, as included in the cession made in the first article of this treaty. It is further understood, that the names of the individuals remaining on the reservations aforesaid, shall be furnished, by the chiefs in whose favor the reservations have been made, to the Superintendent or agent of Indian Affairs, in the territory of Florida; and that no other individuals shall be received or permitted to remain within said reservations, without the previous consent of the Superintendent or Agent aforesaid; And, as the aforesaid Chiefs are authorized to select the individuals remaining with them.

So they shall each be separately held responsible for the peaceable conduct of their towns, or the individuals residing on the reservations allotted them. It is further understood, between the parties, that this agreement is not intended to prohibit the voluntary removal, at any future period, of all or either of the aforesaid Chiefs and their connections, to the district of country south, allotted to the Florida Indians, by the second article of this Treaty, whenever either, or all may think proper to make such an election; the United States reserving the right of ordering, for any outrage or misconduct, the aforesaid Chiefs, or either of them, with their connections, within the district of country south, aforesaid.

It is further stipulated, by the United States that, of the six thousand dollars, appropriated for implements of husbandry, stock, &c. in the third article of this Treaty, eight hundred dollars shall be distributed, in the same manner, among the aforesaid chiefs and their towns; and it is understood, that, of the annual sum of five thousand dollars, to be distributed by the President of the United States, they will receive their proportion. It is further stipulated, that, of the four thousand five hundred dollars, and two thousand dollars, provided for by the 5th article of this Treaty, for the payment for improvements and transportation, five hundred dollars shall be awarded to Neo Mathla, as a compensation for the improvements abandoned by him, as well as to meet the expenses he will unavoidably be exposed to, by his own removal, and that of his connections.

In testimony whereof, the commissioners, William P. Duval, James Gadsden, and Bernard Segui, and the undersigned chiefs and warriors, have hereunto subscribed their names and affixed their seals. Done at camp, on Moultrie creek, in the territory of Florida, this eighteenth day of September, one thousand eight hundred and twenty-three, and of the independence of the United States the forty-eighth.

Wm. P. Duval, his x mark, James Gadsden, Bernard Segui, Nea Mathla, his x mark, John Blunt, his x mark, Tuski Hajo, his x mark, Mulatto King, his x mark, Emathlochee, his x mark, Econchatimico, his x mark.

Signed, sealed, delivered, in presence of: George Murray, secretary to the commission, Ja. W. Ripley, G. Humphreys, Indian agent, Stephen Richards, interpreter.

The following statement shows the number of men retained by the Chiefs, who have reservations made them, at their respective villages:

	Number of Men.	
Blount	43	
Cochran	45	
Mulatto King		30
Emathlochee		28
Econchatimico		38
Neo Mathia		30
Total	214	

TREATY WITH THE CHOCTAW {1825, Jan. 20}
Proclamation, Feb. 19, 1825.

Articles of a convention made between John C. Calhoun, Secretary of War, being specially authorized therefor by the President of the United States, and the undersigned Chiefs and Head Men of the Choctaw Nation of Indians, duly authorized and empowered by said Nation, at the City of Washington, on the twentieth day of January, in the year of our Lord one thousand eight hundred and twenty-five.

WHEREAS a Treaty of friendship, and limits, and accommodation, having been entered into at Doake's Stand, on the eighteenth of October, in the year one thousand eight hundred and twenty, between Andrew Jackson and Thomas Hinds, Commissioners on the part of the United States, and the Chiefs and Warriors of the Choctaw Nation of Indians; and whereas the second article of the Treaty aforesaid provides for a cession of lands, west of the Mississippi, to the Choctaw Nation, in part satisfaction for lands ceded by said Nation to the United States, according to the first article of said treaty: And whereas it being ascertained that the cession aforesaid embraces a large number of settlers, citizens of the United States; and it being the desire of the President of the United States to obviate all difficulties resulting therefrom, and also, to adjust other matters in which both the United States and the Choctaw Nation are interested:

the following articles have been agreed upon, and concluded, between John C. Calhoun, Secretary of War, specially authorized therefor by the President of the United States, on the one part, and the undersigned Delegates of the Choctaw Nation, on the other part:

ARTICLE 1. The Choctaw Nation do hereby cede to the United States all that portion of the land ceded to them by the second article of the Treaty of Doak Stand, as aforesaid, lying east of a line beginning on the Arkansas, one hundred paces east of Fort Smith, and running thence, due south, to Red river: it being understood that this line shall constitute, and remain, the permanent boundary between the United States and the Choctaws; and the United States agreeing to remove such citizens as may be settled on the west side, to the east side of said line, and prevent future settlements from being made on the west thereof.

ARTICLE 2. In consideration of the cession aforesaid, the United States do hereby agree to pay the said Choctaw Nation the sum of six thousand dollars, annually, forever; it being agreed that the said sum of six thousand dollars shall be annually applied, for the term of twenty years, under the direction of the President of the United States, to the support of schools in said nation, and extending to it the benefits of instruction in the mechanic and ordinary arts of life; when, at the expiration of twenty years, it is agreed that the said annuity may be vested in stocks, or otherwise disposed of, or continued, at the option of the Choctaw nation.

ARTICLE 3. The eighth article of the treaty aforesaid having provided that an appropriation of lands shall be made for the purpose of raising six thousand dollars a year for sixteen years, for the use of the Choctaw Nation; and it being desirable to avoid the delay and expense attending the survey and sale of said land; the United States do hereby agree to pay the Choctaw Nation, in lieu thereof, the sum of six thousand dollars, annually, for sixteen years, to commence with the present year. And the United States further stipulate and agree to take immediate measures to survey and bring into market, and sell, the fifty-four sections of land set apart by the seventh article of the treaty aforesaid, and apply the proceeds in the manner provided by the said article.

ARTICLE 4. It is provided by the ninth section of the treaty aforesaid, that all those of the Choctaw Nation who have separate settlements, and fall within the limits of the land ceded by said Nation to the United States, and desire to remain where they now reside, shall be secured in a tract or parcel of land, one mile square, to include their improvements. It is, therefore, hereby agreed, that all who have reservations in conformity to said stipulation, shall have power, with the consent of the President of the United States, to sell and convey the same in fee simple. It is further agreed, on the part of the United States, that those Choctaws, not exceeding four in number, who applied for reservations, and received the recommendation of the Commissioners, as per annexed copy of said recommendation, shall have the privilege, and the right is hereby given to them, to select, each of them, a portion of land, not exceeding a mile square, any where within the limits of the cession of 1820, when the land is not occupied or disposed of by the United States; and the right to sell and convey the same, with the consent of the President, in fee simple, is hereby granted.

ARTICLE 5. There being a debt due by individuals of the Choctaw Nation to the late United States trading house on the Tombigby, the United States hereby agree to relinquish the same; the Delegation, on the part of their nation, agreeing to relinquish their claim upon the United States, to send a factor with goods to supply the wants of the Choctaws west of the Mississippi, as provided for by the 6th article of the treaty aforesaid.

ARTICLE 6. The Choctaw nation having a claim upon the United States, for services rendered in the Pensacola Campaign, and for which it is stipulated, in the 11th article of the treaty aforesaid, that payment shall be made, but which has been delayed for want of the proper vouchers, which it has been found, as yet, impossible to obtain; the United States, to obviate the inconvenience of further delay, and to render justice to the Choctaw Warriors for their services in that campaign, do hereby agree upon an equitable settlement of the same, and fix the sum at fourteen thousand nine hundred and seventy-two dollars fifty cents; which, from the muster rolls, and other evidence in the possession of the Third Auditor, appears to be about the probable amount due, for the services aforesaid, and which sum shall be immediately paid to the Delegation, to be distributed by them to the Chiefs and Warriors of their nation, who served in the campaign aforesaid, as may appear to them to be just.

ARTICLE 7. It is further agreed, that the fourth article of the treaty aforesaid, shall be so modified, as that the Congress of the United States shall not exercise the power of apportioning the lands, for the benefit of each family, or individual, of the Choctaw Nation, and of bringing them under the laws of the United States, but with the consent of the Choctaw Nation.

ARTICLE 8. It appearing that the Choctaws have various claims against citizens of the United States, for spoliations of various kinds, but which they have not been able to support by the testimony of white men, as they were led to believe was necessary, the United States, in order to a final settlement of all such claims, do hereby agree to pay to the Choctaw Delegation, the sum of two thousand dollars, to be distributed by them in such way, among the claimants, as they may deem equitable. It being understood that this provision is not to affect such claims as may be properly authenticated, according to the provision of the act of 1802.

ARTICLE 9. It is further agreed that, immediately upon the Ratification of this Treaty, or as soon thereafter as may be, an agent shall be appointed for the

Choctaws West of the Mississippi, and a Blacksmith be settled among them, in conformity with the stipulation contained in the 6th Article of the Treaty of 1820.

ARTICLE 10. The Chief Puck-she-nubbee, one of the members of the Delegation, having died on his journey to see the President, and Robert Cole being recommended by the Delegation as his successor, it is hereby agreed, that the said Robert Cole shall reserve the medal which appertains to the office of Chief, and, also, an annuity from the United States, of one hundred and fifty dollars a year, during his natural life, as was received by his predecessor.

ARTICLE 11. The friendship heretofore existing between the United States and the Choctaw Nation, is hereby renewed and perpetuated.

ARTICLE 12. These articles shall take effect, and become obligatory on the contracting parties, so soon as the same shall be ratified by the President, by and with the advice and consent of the Senate of the United States.
In testimony whereof, the said John C, Calhoun, and the said delegates [214] of the Choctaw nation, have hereunto set their hands, at the city of Washington, the twentieth day of January, one thousand eight hundred and twenty-five.

J. C. Calhoun,
Mooshulatubbee, his x mark, Robert Cole, his x mark, Daniel McCurtain, his x mark, Talking Warrior, his x mark, Red Fort, his x mark, Nittuckachee, his x mark, David Folsom, his x mark, J. L. McDonald.

In presence of: Thos. L. McKenney, Hezekiah Miller, John Pitchlynn, United States interpreter.

TREATY WITH THE CREEKS {1825, Feb. 12}
Proclamation, Mar. 7, 1825.

Articles of a convention, entered into and concluded at the Indian Springs, between Duncan. G. Campbell, and James Meriwether, Commissioners on the part of the United States of America, duly authorised, and the Chiefs of the Creek Nation, in Council assembled.

WHEREAS the said Commissioners, on the part of the United States, have represented to the said Creek Nation that it is the policy and earnest wish of the General Government, that the several Indian tribes within the limits of any of the states of the Union should remove to territory to be designated on the west side of the Mississippi river, as well for the better protection and security of said tribes, and their improvement in civilization, as for the purpose of enabling the United States, in this instance, to comply with the compact entered into with the State of Georgia, on the twenty-fourth day of April, in the year one thousand eight hundred and two: And the said Commissioners having laid the late Message of the President of the United States, upon this subject, before a General Council of said Creek Nation, to the end that their removal might be effected upon terms advantageous to both parties:

And whereas the Chiefs of the Creek Towns have assented to the reasonableness of said proposition, and expressed a willingness to emigrate beyond the Mississippi, those of Tokaubatchee excepted:
These presents therefore witness, that the contracting parties have this day entered into the following Convention:

ARTICLE 1.   The Creek nation cede to the United States all the lands lying within the boundaries of the State of Georgia, as defined by the compact hereinbefore cited, now occupied by said Nation, or to which said Nation have title or claim; and also, all other lands which they now occupy, or to which they have title or claim, lying north and west of a line to be run from the first principal falls upon the Chatauhoochie river, above Cowetau town, to Ocfuskee Old Town, upon the Tallapoosa, thence to the falls of the Coosaw river, at or near a place called the Hickory Ground.

ARTICLE 2.   It is farther agreed between the contracting parties, that the United States will give, in exchange for the lands hereby acquired, the like quantity, acre for acre, westward of the Mississippi, on the Arkansas river, commencing at the mouth of the Canadian Fork thereof, and running westward between said rivers Arkansas and Canadian Fork, for quantity. But whereas said Creek Nation have considerable improvements within the limits of the territory hereby ceded, and will moreover have to incur expenses in their removal, it is further stipulated, that, for the purpose of rendering a fair equivalent for the losses and inconveniences which said Nation will sustain by removal, and to enable them to obtain supplies in their new settlement, the United States agree to pay to the Nation emigrating from the lands herein ceded, the sum of four hundred thousand dollars, of which amount there shall be paid to said party of the second part, as soon as practicable after the ratification of this treaty, the sum of two hundred thousand dollars. And as soon as the said party of the second part shall notify the Government of the United States of their readiness to commence their removal, there shall be paid the further sum of one hundred thousand dollars. And the first year after said emigrating party shall have settled in their new country, they shall receive of the amount first above named, the further sum of twenty-five thousand dollars. And the second year, the sum of twenty-five thousand dollars. And annually, thereafter, the sum of five thousand dollars, until the whole is paid.

ARTICLE 3.   And whereas the Creek Nation are now entitled to annuities of thirty thousand dollars each, in consideration of cessions of territory heretofore made, it is further stipulated that said last mentioned annuities are to be hereafter divided in a just proportion between the party emigrating and those that may remain.

ARTICLE 4. It is further stipulated that a deputation from the said parties of the second part, may be sent out to explore the territory herein offered them in exchange; and if the same be not acceptable to them, then they may select any other territory, west of the Mississippi, on Red, Canadian, Arkansas, or Missouri Riversthe territory occupied by the Cherokees and Choctaws excepted; and if the territory so to be selected shall be in the occupancy of other Indian tribes, then the United States will extinguish the title of such occupants for the benefit of said emigrants.

ARTICLE 5. It is further stipulated, at the particular request of the said parties of the second part, that the payment and disbursement of the first sum herein provided for, shall be made by the present Commissioners negotiating this treaty.

ARTICLE 6. it is further stipulated, that the payments appointed to be made, the first and second years, after settlement in the West, shall be either in money, merchandise, or provisions, at the option of the emigrating party.

ARTICLE 7. The United States agree to provide and support a blacksmith and wheelwright for the said party of the second part, and give them instruction in agriculture, as long, and in such manner, as the President may think proper.

ARTICLE 8. Whereas the said emigrating party cannot prepare for immediate removal, the United States stipulate, for their protection against the incroachments, hostilities, and impositions, of the whites, and of all others; but the period of removal shall not extend beyond the first day of September, in the year eighteen hundred and twenty-six.

ARTICLE 9. This treaty shall be obligatory on the contracting parties, so soon as the same shall be ratified by the President of the United States, by and with the consent of the Senate thereof.
In testimony whereof, the commissioners aforesaid, and the chiefs and head men of the Creek nation, have hereunto set their hands and seals this twelfth day of February, in the year of our Lord one thousand eight hundred and twenty-five.

Duncan G. Campbell
James Meriwether, Commissioners on the part of the United States.

William McIntosh, head chief of Cowetaus, Etommee Tustunnuggee, of
Cowetan, his x mark, Holahtau, or Col. Blue, his x mark, Cowetau Tustunnug-
gee, his x mark, Artus Mico, or Roby McIntosh, his x mark,
Chilly McIntosh, Cohausee Ematla, of New Yauco, Joseph Marshall, his x
mark, Athlan Hajo, his x mark, Nineomau Tochee, of New Yauco, Tuskenahah,
his x mark, Benjamin Marshall, Konope Emautla, Sand Town, his x mark,
Coccus Hajo, his x mark, Forshatepu Mico, his x mark, Chawaeala Mieo, Sand
Town, his x mark, Oethlamata Tustunnuggee, his x mark, Foetalustee Emaulta,
Sand Town, his x mark
Tallasee Hajo, his x mark,his x mark, Tuskegee Tustunnuggee, his x mark,
Josiah Gray, from Hitchatee, his x mark, Foshajee Tustunnuggee, his x mark,
William Kannard, from Hitchatee, his x mark, Emau Chuccolocana, his x mark,
Abeco Tustunnuggee, his x mark, Neha Thlucto Hatkee, from Hitch-Hijo Hajo,
his x mark, Thla Tho Hajo, his x mark,
Halathla Fixico, from Big Shoal, his x mark, Tomleo Holueto, his x mark, Yah
Te Ko Hajo, his x mark, Alex. Lasley, from Talledega, his x mark, No cosee
Emautla, his x mark, Col. Wm. Miller, Thleeatchca, his x mark, Espokoke
Hajo, from Talledega, his x mark, Abeco Tustunnuggee, his x mark, Emauthla
Hajo, from Talledega, his x mark, Hoethlepoga Tustunnuggee, his x mark, Nin-
comatachee, from Talledega, his x mark, Hepocokee Emautla, his x mark,his x
mark, Samuel Miller, his x mark, Chuhah Hajo, from Talledega, his x mark,
Tomoc Mico, his x mark, Charles Miller, his x mark, Erie Ematla, from Talle-
dega, his x mark, Tallasee Hoja,. or John Carr, his x mark, Atausee Hopoie,
from Talledega, his x mark, Otulga Emautla, his x mark, Ahalaco Yoholo of
Cusetau, his x mark
James Fife, from Tallodega, his x mark, Walueeo Hajo, of New Yaueo, his x
mark.

Executed on the day as above written, in presence of: John Crowell, agent for
Indian affairs, Wm. F. Hay, secretary, Wm. Meriwether, Wm. Hambly, United
States interpreter.

July 25, 1825. Whereas, by a stipulation in the Treaty of the Indian Springs, in
1821, there was a reserve of land made to include the said Indian Springs for
the use of General William M'Intosh, be it therefore known to all whom it may
concern, that we, the undersigned chiefs and head men of the Creek nation, do
hereby agree to relinquish all the right, title, and control of the Creek nation to
the said reserve, unto him the said William M'Intosh and his heirs, forever, in
as full and ample a manner as we are authorized to do.

July 25, 1825. Big B. W. Warrior, Yoholo Micco, his x mark, Little Prince, his
x mark, Hopoie Hadjo, his x mark, Tuskehenahau, his x mark, Oakefuska Yohola, his x mark, John Crowell, agent for Indian affairs,

Feb. 14, 1825. Whereas the foregoing articles of convention have been concluded Additional article between the parties thereto: And, whereas, the Indian Chief, General William McIntosh, claims title to the Indian Spring Reservation (upon which there are very extensive buildings and improvements) by virtue of a relinquishment to said McIntosh, signed in full council of the nation: And, whereas the said General William McIntosh hath claim to another reservation of land on the Ocmulgee river, and by his lessee and tenant, is in possession thereof:

Now these presents further witness, that the said General William McIntosh, and also the Chiefs of the Creek Nation, in council assembled, do quit claim, convey, and cede to the United States, the reservations aforesaid, for, and in consideration of, the sum of twenty-five thousand dollars, to be paid at the time and in the manner as stipulated, for the first instalment provided for in the preceding treaty. Upon the ratification of these articles, the possession of said reservations shall be considered as passing to the United States, and the accruing rents of the present year shall pass also.

In testimony whereof, the said commissioners, on the part of the United States, and the said William McIntosh, and the chiefs of the Creek nation, have hereunto set their hands and seals, at the Indian Springs, this fourteenth day of February, in the year of our Lord one thousand eight hundred and twenty-five.

Duncan G. Campbell, James Meriwether, United States commissioners.
William McIntosh, Eetommee Tustunnuggee, his x mark, Tuskegoh Tustunnuggee, his x mark, Cowstau Tustunnuggee, his x mark, Col. Wm. Miller, his x mark, Josiah Gray, his x mark, Nehathlucco Hatches, his x mark, Alexander Lasley, his x mark, William Canard, his x mark.

Witnesses at execution: Wm. F. Hay, secretary, Wm. Hambly, United States interpreter.

TREATY WITH THE CREEKS {1826, Jan. 24}
Proclamation, Apr. 22, 1826.

Articles of a treaty made at the City of Washington, this twenty-fourth day of January, one thousand eight hundred and twenty-six, between James Barbour, Secretary of War, thereto specially authorized by the President of the United States, and the undersigned, Chiefs and Head Men of the Creek Nation of Indians, who have received full power from the said Nation to conclude and arrange all the matters herein provided for.

WHEREAS a treaty was concluded at the Indian Springs, on the twelfth day of February last, between Commissioners on the part of the United States, and a portion of the Creek Nation, by which an extensive district of country was ceded to the United States.

And whereas a great majority of the Chiefs and Warriors of the said Nation have protested against the execution of the said Treaty, and have represented that the same was signed on their part by persons having no sufficient authority to form treaties, or to make cessions, and that the stipulations in the said Treaty are, therefore, wholly void.

And whereas the United States are unwilling that difficulties should exist in the said Nation, which may eventually lead to an intestine war, and are still more unwilling that any cessions of land should be made to them, unless with the fair understanding and full assent of the Tribe making such cession, and for a just and adequate consideration, it being the policy of the United States, in all their intercourse with the Indians, to treat them justly and liberally, as becomes the relative situation of the parties.

Now, therefore, in order to remove the difficulties which have thus arisen, to satisfy the great body of the Creek Nation, and to reconcile the contending parties into which it is unhappily divided, the following articles have been agreed upon and concluded, between James Barbour, Secretary of War, specially authorized as aforesaid, and the said Chiefs and Head Men representing the Creek Nation of Indians:

ARTICLE 1. The Treaty concluded at the Indian Springs, on the twelfth day of February, one thousand eight hundred and twenty-five, between Commissioners on the part of the United States and the said Creek Nation of Indians, and ratified by the United States on the seventh day of March, one thousand eight hundred and twenty-five, is hereby declared to be null and void, to every intent and purpose whatsoever; and every right and claim arising from the same is hereby cancelled and surrendered.

ARTICLE 2. The Creek Nation of Indians cede to the United States all the land belonging to the said Nation in the State of Georgia, and lying on the east side of the middle of the Chatahoochie river. And, also, another tract of land lying within the said State, and bounded as follows: Beginning at a point on the western bank of the said river, forty-seven miles below the point where the boundary line between the Creeks and Cherokees strikes the Chatahoochie river, near the Buzzard's Roost, measuring the said distance in a direct line, and not following the meanders of the said river; and from the point of beginning, running in a direct line to a point in the boundary line, between the said Creeks and the Cherokees., thirty miles west of the said Buzzard's Roost; thence to the Buzzard's Roost, and thence with the middle of the said river to the place of beginning.

ARTICLE 3. Immediately after the ratification of this Treaty, the United States agree to pay to the Chiefs of the said Nation the sum of two hundred and seventeen thousand six hundred dollars to be divided among the Chiefs and Warriors of the said Nation.

ARTICLE 4. The United States agree to pay to the said Nation an additional perpetual annuity of twenty thousand dollars.

ARTICLE 5. The difficulties which have arisen in the said nation, in consequence of the Treaty of the Indian Springs, shall be amicably adjusted, and that portion of the Creek Nation who signed that treaty shall be admitted to all their privileges, as members of the Creek Nation, it being the earnest wish of the United States, without undertaking to decide upon the complaints of the respective parties, that all causes of dissatisfaction should be removed.

ARTICLE 6. That portion of the Creek Nation, known as the friends and followers of the late General William McIntosh, having intimated to the government of the United States their wish to remove west of the Mississippi, it is hereby agreed, with their assent, that a deputation of five persons shall be sent by them, at the expense of the United States, immediately after the ratification of this treaty, to examine the Indian country west of the Mississippi, not within either of the States or Territories, and not possessed by the Choctaws or Cherokees. And the United States agree to purchase for them, if the same can be conveniently done upon reasonable terms, wherever they may select, a country, whose extent shall, in the opinion of the President, be proportioned to their numbers. And if such purchase cannot be thus made, it is then agreed that the selection shall be made where the President may think proper, just reference being had to the wishes of the emigrating party.

ARTICLE 7. The emigrating party shall remove within twenty-four months, and the expense of their removal shall be defrayed by the United States. And such subsistence shall also be furnished them, for a term not exceeding twelve months after their arrival at their new residence, as, in the opinion of the President, their numbers and circumstances may require.

ARTICLE 8. An agent, or sub-agent and Interpreter, shall be appointed to accompany and reside with them. And a blacksmith and wheelwright shall be furnished by the United States. Such assistance shall also be rendered to them in their agricultural operations, as the President may think proper.

ARTICLE 9. In consideration of the exertions used by the friends and followers of General McIntosh to procure a cession at the Indian Springs, and of their past difficulties and contemplated removal, the United States agree to present to the Chiefs of the party, to be divided among the Chiefs and Warriors, the sum of one hundred thousand dollars, if such party shall amount to three thousand persons, and in that proportion for any smaller number. Fifteen thousand dollars of this sum to be paid immediately after the ratification of this treaty, and the residue upon their arrival in the country west of the Mississippi.

ARTICLE 10. It is agreed by the Creek Nation, that an agent shall be appointed by the President, to ascertain the damages sustained by the friends and followers of the late General McIntosh, in consequence of the difficulties growing out of the Treaty of the Indian Springs, as set forth in an agreement entered into with General Gains, at the Broken Arrow,(a) and which have been done contrary to the laws of the Creek Nation; and such damages shall be repaired by the said Nation, or the amount paid out of the annuity due to them.

ARTICLE 11. All the improvements which add real value to any part of the land herein ceded shall be appraised by Commissioners, to be appointed by the President; and the amount thus ascertained shall be paid to the parties owning such improvements.

ARTICLE 12. Possession of the country herein ceded shall be yielded by the Creeks on or before the first day of January next.

ARTICLE 13. The United States agree to guarantee to the Creeks all the country, not herein ceded, to which they have a just claim, and to make good to them any losses they may incur in consequence of the illegal conduct of any citizen of the United States within the Creek country.

ARTICLE 14. The President of the United States shall have authority to select, in some part of the Creek country, a tract of land, not exceeding two sections, where the necessary public buildings may be erected, and the persons attached to the agency may reside.

ARTICLE 15. Wherever any stream, over which it may be necessary to establish ferries, forms the boundary of the Creek country, the Creek Indians shall have the right of ferriage from their own land, and the citizens of the United States from the land to which the Indian title is extinguished.

ARTICLE 16. The Creek Chiefs may appoint three Commissioners from their own people, who shall be allowed to attend the running of the lines west of the Chatahoochy river, and whose expenses, while engaged in this duty, shall be defrayed by the United States.

ARTICLE 17. This treaty, after the same has been ratified by the President and Senate, shall be obligatory on the United States and on the Creek Nation.
In testimony whereof, the said James Barbour, Secretary of War, authorized as aforesaid, and the chiefs of the said Creek nation of Indians, have hereunto set their hands, at the City of Washington, the day and year aforesaid.

James Barbour,
O-poth-le Yoholo, his x mark, John Stidham, his x mark, Mad Wolf, his x
mark, Menawee, his x mark, Tuskeekee Tustunnuggee, his x mark, Charles
Cornells, his x mark, Timpoochy Barnard, his x mark, Apauly Tustunnuggee,
his x mark, Coosa Tustunnuggee, his x mark, Nahetluc Hopie, his x mark,
Selocta, his x mark, Ledagi, his x mark, Yoholo Micco, his x mark.

In presence of: Thomas L. McKenney, Lewis Cass, John Crowell, agent for
Indian Affairs, Hezekiah Miller, John Ridge, secretary Creek delegation, David
Vann.

SUPPLEMENTARY ARTICLE TO THE CREEK TREATY OF THE
TWENTY-FOURTH JANUARY, 1826.
Mar. 31, 1826.

WHEREAS a stipulation in the second article of the Treaty of the twenty-fourth
day of January, 1826, between the undersigned, parties to said Treaty, provides
forhe running of a line "beginning at a point on the western bank of the Chatahoochee river, forty-seven miles below the point where the boundary line between the Creeks and Cherokees strikes the said river, near the Buzzard's
Roost, measuring the said distance in a direct line, and not following the meanders of the said river, and from the point of beginning, running in a direct line
to a point in the boundary line between the said Creeks and the Cherokees
thirty miles west of the said Buzzard's Roost, thence to the Buzzard's Roost,
and thence with the middle of said river to the place of beginning."

And whereas it having been represented to the party to the said Treaty in behalf
of the Creek Nation, that a certain extension of said lines might embrace in the
cession all the lands which will be found to lie within the chartered limits of
Georgia, and which are owned by the Creeks, the undersigned do hereby agree
to the following extension of said lines, viz: In the place of "forty-seven miles,"
as stipulated in the second article of the Treaty aforesaid, as the point of beginning,-the undersigned agree that it shall be fifty miles, in a direct line below the
point designated in the second article of said Treaty.

Thence running in a direct line to a point in the boundary line between the
Creeks and Cherokees, forty-five miles west of said Buzzard's Roost, in the
place of "thirty miles," as stipulated in said Treaty; thence to the Buzzard's
Roost, and thence to the place of beginningit being understood that these lines
are to stop at their intersection with the boundary line between Georgia and
Alabama, wherever that may be, if that line shall cross them in the direction of
the Buzzard's Roost, at a shorter distance than it is provided they shall run; and
provided, also, that if the said dividing line between Georgia and Alabama shall

not be reached by the extension of the two lines aforesaid, the one three, and the other fifteen miles, they are to run and terminate as defined in this supplemental article to the Treaty aforesaid.

It is hereby agreed, in consideration of the extension of said lines, on the part of the other party to the Treaty aforesaid, in behalf of the United States, to pay to the Creek Nation, immediately upon the ratification of said Treaty, the sum of thirty thousand dollars.

In witness whereof, the parties aforesaid have hereunto set their hands and seals, this thirty-first day of March, in the year of our Lord one thousand eight hundred twenty-six.

James Barbour, Charles Cornells, his x mark, Opothle Yoholo, his x mark, Apauly Tustunnuggee, his x mark, John Stidham, his x mark, Coosa Tustunnuggee, his x mark, Mad Wolf, his x mark, Nahetlue Hopie, his x mark, Tuskeekee Tustunnuggee, his x mark, Selocta, his x mark, Timpooehy Barnard, his x mark, Yoholo Mieeo, his x mark, Ledagi, his x mark, Menawee, his x mark,

In presence of: Thomas L. McKenney, John Crowell, agent for Indian affairs, John Ridge, secretary, David Vann, Wm. Hambly.

(a) This agreement, which is unratified, is set forth in the Appendix, post, p. 1034. The original can not be found, but a copy is among the files of the Indian Office, General Files, Creek, 1825-1826. E. P.Gaines

TREATY WITH THE CHIPPEWA {1826, Aug. 5}
Proclamation, Feb. 7, 1827.

Articles of a treaty made and concluded at the Font du Lac of Lake Superior, this fifth day of August, in the year of our Lord one thousand eight hundred and twenty-six, between Lewis Cass and Thomas L McKenney, Commissioners on the part of the United States, and the Chippewa Tribe of Indians.

WHEREAS a Treaty was concluded at Prairie du Chien in August last, by which the war, which has been so long carried on, to their mutual distress, between the Chippewas and Sioux, was happily terminated by the intervention of the United States; and whereas, owing to the remote and dispersed situation of the Chippewas, full deputations of their different bands did not attend at Prairie du Chien, which circumstance, from the loose nature of the Indian government, would render the Treaty of doubtful obligation, with respect to the bands not represented; and whereas, at the request of the Chippewa Chiefs, a stipulation was inserted in the Treaty of Prairie du Chien, by which the United States agreed to assemble the Chippewa Tribe upon Lake Superior during the present year, in order to give full effect to the said Treaty, to explain its stipulations and to call upon the whole Chippewa tribe, assembled at their general council fire, to give their formal assent thereto, that the peace which has been concluded may be rendered permanent, therefore

ARTICLE 1. The Chiefs and Warriors of the Chippewa Tribe of Indians hereby fully assent to the Treaty concluded in August last at Prairie du Chien, and engage to observe and fulfil the stipulations thereof.

ARTICLE 2. A deputation shall be sent by the Chippewas to the Treaty to be held in 1827, at Green Bay, with full power to arrange and fix the boundary line between the Chippewas and the Winnebagoes and Menomonees, which was left incomplete by the treaty of Prairie du Chien, in consequence of the non-attendance of some of the principal Menomonee Chiefs.

ARTICLE 3. The Chippewa tribe grant to the government of the United States the right to search for, and carry away, any metals or minerals from any part of their country. But this grant is not to affect the title of the land, nor the existing jurisdiction over it.

ARTICLE 4. It being deemed important that the half-breeds, scattered through this extensive country, should be stimulated to exertion and improvement by the possession of permanent property and fixed residences, the Chippewa tribe, in consideration of the affection they bear to these persons, and of the interest which they feel in their welfare, grant to each of the persons described in the schedule hereunto annexed, being half-breeds and Chippewas by descent, and it being understood that the schedule includes all of this description who are at-tached to the Government of the United States, six hundred and forty acres of land, to be located, under the direction of the President of the United States, upon the islands and shore of the St. Mary's river, wherever good land enough for this purpose can be found; and as soon as such locations are made, the ju-risdiction and soil thereof are hereby ceded.

It is the intention of the parties, that, where circumstances will permit, the grants be surveyed in the ancient French manner, bounding not less than six arpens, nor more than ten, upon the river, and running back for quantity; and that where this cannot be done, such grants be surveyed in any manner the President may direct. The locations for Oshauguscodaywayqua and her descen-dents shall be adjoining the lower part of the military reservation, and upon the head of Sugar Island. The persons to whom grants are made shall not have the privilege of conveying the same, without the permission of the President.

ARTICLE 5. In consideration of the poverty of the Chippewas, and of the sterile nature of the country they inhabit, unfit for cultivation, and almost destitute of game, and as a proof of regard on the part of the United States, it is agreed that an annuity of two thousand dollars, in money or goods, as the President may direct, shall be paid to the tribe, at the Sault St. Marie. But this annuity shall continue only during the pleasure of the Congress of the United States.

ARTICLE 6. With a view to the improvement of the Indian youths, it is also agreed, that an annual sum of one thousand dollars shall be appropriated to the support of an establishment for their education, to be located upon some part of one St. Mary's river, and the money to be expended under the direction of the President; and for the accommodation of such school, a section of land is hereby granted. But the payment of the one thousand dollars stipulated for in this article, is subject to the same limitation described in the preceding article.

ARTICLE 7. The necessity for the stipulations in the fourth, fifth and sixth articles of this treaty could be fully apparent, only from personal observation of the condition, prospects, and wishes of the Chippewas, and the Commissioners were therefore not specifically instructed upon the subjects therein referred to; but seeing the extreme poverty of these wretched people, finding them almost naked and starving, and ascertaining that many perished during the last winter, from hunger and cold, they were induced to insert these articles. But it is expressly understood and agreed, that the fourth, fifth and sixth articles, or either of them, may be rejected by the President and Senate, without affecting the validity of the other articles of the treaty.

ARTICLE 8. The Chippewa tribe of Indians fully acknowledge the authority and jurisdiction of the United States, and disclaim all connection with any foreign power, solemnly promising to reject any messages, speeches, or councils, incompatible with the interest of the United States, and to communicate information thereof to the proper agent, should any such be delivered or sent to them.

ARTICLE 9. This treaty, after the same shall be ratified by the President and Senate of the United States, shall be obligatory on the contracting parties. Done at the Fond du Lac of lake Superior, in the territory of Michigan, the day and year above written, and of the independence of the United States the fifty-first.

Lewis Cass, Thos. L. McKenney,
St. Marys: Shingauba Wassin, his x mark, Shewaubeketoan, his x mark, Wayishkee, his x mark, Sheegud,. his x mark.
River St. Croix: Peezhickee, his x mark, Noden, his x mark, Nagwunabee, his x mark, Kaubemappa, his x mark, Chaucopee, his x mark, Jaubeance, his x mark, Ultauwau, his x mark, Myeengunsheens, his x mark, Moasomonee, his x mark, Muckuday peenaas, his x mark, Sheeweetaugun, his x mark.

La Pointe: Peexhickee, his x mark, Keemeewun, his x mark, Kaubuzoway, his x mark, Wyauweenind, his x mark, Peekwaukwotoansekay, his x mark.
Ottoway L: Paybaumikoway, his X mark.
Lac de Flambeau: Gitshee Waubeeshaans, his x mark, Moazonee, his x mark, Gitshee Migeezee, his x mark, Mizhauquot, his x mark.

Ontonagon: Keeshkeetowug, his x mark, Peenaysee, his x mark, Mautaugumee, his x mark, Kweeweezaisish, his x mark.
Vermilion Lake: Attickoans, his x mark, Gyutsheeininee, his x mark, Jaukway, his x mark, Madwagkunageezhigwaab, his x mark, Jaukogeezhigwaishkun, his x mark, Neezboday, his x mark, Nundoeheeais, his x mark, Ogeemaugeegid, his x mark, Anneemeekees, his x mark.
Ontonagon: Kauwaishkung, his x mark, Mautaugumee, his x mark.
Snake River: Waymittegoash, his x mark, Iskquagwunaabee, his x mark, Meegwunaus, his x mark.
Lae de Flambeau: Pamoossay, his x mark, Maytaukooseegay, his x mark.
Rainy Lake: Aanubkumigishkunk, his x mark.
Sandy Lake: Osaumemikee, his x mark, Gitshee Waymirteegoost, his x mark, Paashuninleel, his x mark, Wauzhuskokok, his x mark, Nitmnogaubowee, his x mark, Wattap, his x mark.

Fond du Lac: Shingoop, his x mark, Monetogeezisoans, his x mark, Mongazid, his x mark, Manetogeezhig, his x mark, Ojauneemauson, his x mark, Miskwautais, his x mark, Naubunaygerzhig, his x mark, Unnauwaubundaun, his x mark, Pautaubay, his x mark, Migeesee, his x mark.
Ontonagon: Waubishkeepeenaas, his x mark, Tweeshtweeshkeeway, his x mark, Kundekund, his x mark, Oguhbayaunuhquotwaybee, his x mark, Paybamnausing, his x mark, Keeshkeemun, his x mark.
River de Corbeau: Maugugaubowie, his x mark, Pudud, his x mark, Naugdunosh, his x mark, Ozhuskuckoen, his x mark, Waubogee, his x mark, Sawbanosh, his x mark, Keewayden, his x mark, Gitsheemeewininee, his x mark, Wynunee, his x mark, Obumaugeezhig, his x mark, Payboumidgeewung, his x mark, Mangeegaubou, his x mark, Paybaumogeezhig, his x mark, Kaubemappa, his x mark, Waymittegoazhu, his x mark, Oujupenaas, his x mark, Madwayossin, his x mark.

In presence of: A. Edwards, secretary to the commission; E. Boardman, captain commanding detachment, Henry R. Schoolcraft, United States Indian agent, Z. Pitcher, assistant surgeon, J. B. Kingsbury, lieutenant, Second Infantry, E. A. Brush, Daniel Dingley, A. Morrison, B. Champman, Henry Connor, W. A. Levake, J. O. Lewis.

SUPPLEMENTARY ARTICLE. As the Chippewas who committed the murder upon four American citizens, in June, 1824, upon the shores of Lake Pepin, are not present at this council, but are far in the interior of the country, so that they cannot be apprehended and delivered to the proper authority before the commencement of the next Summer; and, as the Commissioners have been specially instructed to demand the surrender of these persons, and to state to the Chippewa tribe the consequence of suffering such a flagitious outrage to go unpunished, it is agreed, that the persons guilty of the beforementioned murder shall be brought in, either to the Sault St. Marie, or Green Bay, as early next summer as practicable, and surrendered to the proper authority; and that, in the mean time, all further measures on the part of the United States, in relation to this subject, shall be suspended.

Lewis Cass, Thomas L. McKenney.

Representing the bands to whom the persons guilty of the murder belong, for themselves and the Chippewa tribe: Gitshee Meegeesee, his x mark, Metau-koosegay, his x mark, Ouskunzheema, his x mark, Keenesteno, his x mark.

Witnesses: A. Edwards, secretary to the commission, E. Boardman, captain commanding detachment, Henry R. Schoolcraft, United States Indian agent. Henry Connor, interpreter.

Schedule referred to in the preceding:
To Oshauguscodaywagqua, wife of John Johnston, Esq., to each of her children, and to each of her grand children, one section.
To Saugemauqua, widow of the late John Baptiste Cadotte, and to her children, Louison, Sophia, Archangel, Edward, and Polly, one section each.
To Keneesequa, wife of Samuel Ashman, and to each of her children, one section.
To Teegaushau, wife of Charles H. Oakes, and to each of her children, one section.
To Thomas Shaw, son of Obimetunoqua, and to his wife Mary, being also of Indian descent, each one section.

To Fanny Levake, daughter of Meeshwauqua, and to each of her children, one section.
To Obayshaunoquotoqua, wife of Francis Geolay, Jr. one section.
To Omuckackeence, wife of John Holiday, and to each of her children, one section.
To Obimegeezhigoqua, wife of Joseph Due Chene, Jr, and to each of her children, one section.
To Monedoqua, wife of Charles Cloutier, one section.
To Susan Yarns, daughter of Odanbitogeezhigoqua, one section.
To Henry Sayer and John Sayer, sons of Obemau unoqua, each one section.
To each of the children of John Tanner, being of Chippewa descent, one section.

To Wassidjeewunoqua, and to each of her children, by George Johnston, one section.

To Michael Cadotte, senior, son of Equawaice, one section.

To Equaysayway, wife of Michael Cadotte, senior, and to each of her children living within the United States, one section.

To each of the children of Charlotte Warren, widow of the late Truman A. Warren, ,one section.

To Mary Chapman, daughter of Equameeg, and wife of Bela Chapman, and to each of her children, one section.

To Saganoshequa, wife of John H. Fairbanks, and to each of her children, one section.

To Shaughunomonee, wife of William Morrison, and to each of her children, one section.

To each of the children of the late Ingwaysuh, wife of Joseph Coté, one section.

To each of the children of Angelique Coté, late wife of Pierre Coté, one section.

To Pazhikwutoqua, wife of William Airken, and to each of her children, one section.

To Susan Davenport, grand daughter of Misquabunoqua, and wife of Ambrose Davenport, and to each of her children, one section.

To Waubunequa, wife of Augustin Belanger, and to each of her children, one section.

To Charlotte Louisa Morrison, wife of Allan Morrison, and daughter of Manitowidjewung, and to each of her children, one section.

To each of the children of Eustace Roussain, by Shauwunaubunoqua, Wauwaussumoqua, and Payshaubunoqua, one section.

To Isabella Dingley, wife of Daniel Dingley and daughter of Pima geezhigoqua, and to each of her children, one section.

To George Birkhrad, being a Chippewa by descent, one section.

To Susan Conner, wife of Thomas Conner, and daughter of Pimegeezhigoqua, and to each of her children, one section.

To the children of George Ermatinger, being of Shawnee extraction, two sections collectively.

To Ossinahjeenuoqua, wife of Michael Cadotte, Jr, and each of her children, one section.

To Minedemoeyah, wife of Pierre Duvernay, one section. To Ogeemaugeezhigoqua, wife of Basil Boileau, one section. To Wauneaussequa, wife of Paul Boileau, one section.

To Kaukaubesheequa, wife of John Baptiste Corbeau, one section. To John Baptiste Du Chene, son of Pimegeizhigoqua, one section.

To each of the children of Ugwudaushee, by the late Truman A. Warren, one section.

To William Warren, son of Lyman M. Warren, and Mary Cadotte, one section.
To Antoine, Joseph, Louis, Chalot, and Margaret Charette, children of Equameeg, one section.
To the children of Francois Boutchar, by Waussequa, each one section.
To Angelique Brabent, daughter of Waussegundum, and wife of Alexis Brabent, one section.
To Odishqua, of Sault St. Marie, a Chippewa, of unmixed blood, one section.
To Pamidjeewung, of Sault St. Marie, a Chippewa, of unmixed blood, one section.
To Waybossinoqua, and John J. Wayishkee, children of Wayishkee, each one section.
Lewis Cass, Thos. L. McKenney.

TREATY WITH THE CREEKS {1827, Nov. 15}
Proclamation, Mar. 4, 1828.

Articles of agreement made and concluded at the Creek Agency, on the fifteenth day of November, one thousand eight hundred and twenty-seven, between Thomas L. McKenney, and John Crowell, in behalf of the United States, of the one part, and Little Prince and Chiefs and Head Men of the Creek Nation, of the other part.

WHEREAS a Treaty of Cession was concluded at Washington City in the District of Columbia, by JAMES BARBOUR, Secretary of War, of the one part, and OPOTHLEOHOLO, JOHN STIDHAM, and OTHERS, of the other part, and which Treaty bears date the twenty-fourth day of January, one thousand eight hundred and twenty-six; and whereas, the object of said Treaty being to embrace a cession by the Creek Nation, of all the lands owned by them within the chartered limits of Georgia, and it having been the opinion of the parties, at the time when said Treaty was concluded, that all, or nearly all, of said lands were embraced in said cession, and by the lines as defined in said Treaty, and the supplemental article thereto: and whereas it having been since ascertained that the said lines in said Treaty, and the supplement thereto, do not embrace all the lands owned by the Creek Nation within the chartered limits of Georgia, and the President of the United States having urged the Creek Nation further to extend the limits as defined in the Treaty aforesaid, and the Chiefs and head men of the Creek Nation being desirous of complying with the wish of the President of the United States, therefore, they, the Chiefs and head men aforesaid, agree to cede, and they do hereby cede to the United States, all the remaining lands now owned or claimed by the Creek Nation, not heretofore ceded, and which, on actual survey, may be found to lie within the chartered limits of the State of Georgia

In consideration whereof, and in full compensation for the above cession, the undersigned, THOMAS L. MCKENNEY, and JOHN CROWELL, in behalf of the United States, do hereby agree to pay to the Chiefs and head men of the Creek Nation aforesaid, and as soon as may be after the approval and ratification of this agreement, in the usual forms, by the President and Senate of the United States, and its sanction by a council of the Creek Nation, to be immediately convened for the purpose, or by the subscription of such names, in addition to those subscribed to this instrument, of Chiefs and head men of the nation, as shall constitute it the act of the Creek Nationthe sum of twenty-seven thousand four hundred and ninety-one dollars.

It is further agreed by the parties hereto, in behalf of the United States, to allow, on account of the cession herein made, the additional sum of fifteen thousand dollars, it being the understanding of both the parties, that five thousand dollars of this sum shall be applied, under the direction of the President of the United States, towards the education and support of Creek children at the school in Kentucky, known by the title of the "Chocktaw Academy," and under the existing regulations; also, one thousand dollars towards the support of the Withington, and one thousand dollars towards the support of the Asbury stations, so called, both being schools in the Creek Nation, and under regulations of the Department of War; two thousand dollars for the erection of four horse mills, to be suitably located under the direction of the President of the United States; one thousand dollars to be applied to the purchase of cards and wheels, for the use of the Creeks, and the remaining five thousand dollars, it is agreed, shall be paid in blankets and other necessary and useful goods, immediately after the signing and delivery of these presents.

In witness whereof, the parties have hereunto set their hands and seals, this fifteenth day of November, one thousand eight hundred and twenty-seven.

Thomas L. McKenney, John Crowell, Little Prince, his x mark, Epau-emathla, his x mark, Timpouchoe Burnard, his x mark, Hathlan Haujo, his x mark, Okejuoke Yau-holo, his x mark, Cassetaw Micco, his x mark,

In presence of: Luther Blake, secretary, Andrew Hamill, Whitman C. Hill, Thomas Crowell.

Whereas, the above articles of agreement and cession were entered into at the Creek agency on the day and date therein mentioned, between the Little Prince, the head man of the nation, and five other chiefs, and Thomas L. McKenney and John Crowell, commissioners on the part of the United States, for the cession of all the lands owned or claimed by the Creek nation, and not heretofore ceded, and which, on actual survey, may be found to lie within the chartered limits of the State of Georgia, and which said agreement was made subject to the approval and ratification by the President and Senate of the United States, and the approval and sanction of the Creek nation, in general council of the said nation.

Now, these presents witnesseth, that we, the undersigned, chiefs and head men of the Creek nation in general council convened, at Wetumph, the third day of January, one thousand eight hundred and twenty-eight, have agreed and stipulated with John Crowell, commissioner on the part of the United States, for and in consideration of the additional sum of five thousand dollars, to be paid to us in blankets, and other necessary articles of clothing, immediately after the signing and sealing of these presents, to sanction, and by these presents do hereby approve, sanction, and ratify, the above mentioned and foregoing articles of agreement and session.

In witness whereof, the parties have hereunto set their hands and seals, the day and date above mentioned.

John Crowell, Arthlau Hayre, his x mark.
Broken Arrow Town: Little Prince, his x mark, Tuskugu, his x mark, Cotche Hayre, his x mark,
Cusetau Town: Tukchenaw, his x mark, Epi Emartla, his x mark, Oakpushu Yoholo, his x mark,
Cowetau Town: Neah Thleuco, his x mark,
Tomasa Town: Colitcnu Ementla, his x mark,

In presence of: Luther Blake, secretary, Andrew Hamill, Enoch Johnson, Thomas Crowell.
Benjamin Marshall, Paddy Carr, interpreters, Joseph Marshall, John Winslett, Cowetaw Micco, his x mark,
Oswichu Town: Halatta Tustinuggu, his x mark, Octiatchu Emartla, his x mark, Charles Emartla, his x mark
Uchee Town: Timpoeche Barned, his x mark, Chawaccola
Hatchu Town: Coe E. Hayo, his x mark, Powas Yoholo, his x mark, Ema Hayre, his x mark,

TREATY WITH THE WESTERN CHEROKEE {1828, May 6}
Proclamation, May 28, 1828

Articles of a Convention, concluded at the City of Washington this sixth day of May, in the year of our Lord one thousand eight hundred and twenty-eight, between James Barbour, Secretary of War, being especially authorized therefor by the President of the United States, and the undersigned, Chiefs and Head Men of the Cherokee Nation of Indians, West of the Mississippi, they being duly authorized and empowered by their Nation.

WHEREAS, it being the anxious desire of the Government of the United States to secure to the Cherokee nation of Indians, as well those now living within the limits of the Territory of Arkansas, as those of their friends and brothers who reside in States East of the Mississippi, and who may wish to join their brothers of the West, a permanent home, and which shall, under the most solemn guarantee of the United States, be, and remain, theirs forever a home that shall never, in all future time, be embarrassed by having extended around it the lines, or placed over it the jurisdiction of a Territory or State, nor be pressed upon by the extension, in any way, of any of the limits of any existing Territory or State; and, Whereas, the present location of the Cherokees in Arkansas being unfavorable to their present repose, and tending, as the past demonstrates, to their future degradation and misery; and the Cherokees being anxious to avoid such consequences, and yet not questioning their right to their lands in Arkansas, as secured to them by Treaty, and resting also upon the pledges given them by the President of the United States, and the Secretary of War, of March, 1818, and 8th October, 1821, in regard to the outlet to the West, and as may be seen on referring to the records of the War Department, still being anxious to secure a permanent home, and to free themselves, and their posterity, from an embarrassing connexion with the Territory of Arkansas, arid guard themselves from such connexions in future.

Whereas, it being important, not to the Cherokees only, but also to the Choctaws, and in regard also to the question which may be agitated in the future respecting the location of the latter, as well as the former, within the limits of the Territory or State of Arkansas, as the case may be, and their removal therefrom; and to avoid the cost which may attend negotiations to rid the Territory or State of Arkansas whenever it may become a State, of either, or both of those Tribes, the parties hereto do hereby conclude the following Articles, viz:

ARTICLE 1. The Western boundary of Arkansas shall be, and the same is, hereby defined, viz: A line shall be run, commencing on Red River, at the point where the Eastern Choctaw line strikes said River, and run due North with said line to the River Arkansas, thence in a direct line to the South West corner of Missouri.

ARTICLE 2. The United States agree to possess the Cherokees, and to guarantee it to them forever, and that guarantee is hereby solemnly pledged, of seven millions of acres of land, to be bounded as follows, viz: Commencing at that point on Arkansas River where the Eastern Choctaw boundary line strikes said River, and running thence with the Western line of Arkansas, as defined in the foregoing article, to the South-West corner of Missouri, and thence with the Western boundary line of Missouri till it crosses the waters of Neasho, generally called Grand River, thence due West to a point from which a due South course will strike the present North West corner of Arkansas Territory, thence continuing due South, on and with the present Western boundary line of the

181

Territory to the main branch of Arkansas River, thence down said River to its junction with the Canadian River, and thence up and between the said Rivers Arkansas and Canadian, to a point at which a line running North and South from River to River, will give the aforesaid seven millions of acres. In addition to the seven millions of acres thus provided for, and bounded, the United States further guarantee to the Cherokee Nation a perpetual outlet, West, and a free and unmolested use of all the Country lying West of the Western boundary of the above described limits, and as far West as the sovereignty of the United States, and their right of soil extend.

ARTICLE 3. The United States agree to have the lines of the above cession run without delay, say not later than the first of October next, and to remove, immediately after the running of the Eastern line from the Arkansas River to the South-West corner of Missouri, all white persons from the West to the East of said line, and also all others, should there be any there, who may be unacceptable to the Cherokees, so that no obstacles arising out of the presence of a white population, or a population of any other sort, shall exist to annoy the Cherokeesand also to keep all such from the West of said line in future.

ARTICLE 4. The United States moreover agree to appoint suitable persons whose duty it shall be, in conjunction with the Agent, to value all such improvements as the Cherokees may abandon in their removal from their present homes to the District of Country as ceded in the second Article of this agreement, and to pay for the same immediately after the assessment is made, and the amount ascertained. It is further agreed, that the property and improvements connected with the agency, shall be sold under the direction of the Agent, and the proceeds of the same applied to aid in the erection, in the country to which the Cherokees are going, of a Grist, and Saw Mill, for their use. The aforesaid property and improvements are thus defined: Commence at the Arkansas River opposite William Stinnetts, and run due North one mile, thence due East to a point from which a due South line to the Arkansas River would include the Chalybeate, or Mineral Spring, attached to or near the present residence of the Agent, and thence up said River (Arkansas) to the place of beginning.

ARTICLE 5. It is further agreed, that the United States, in consideration of the inconvenience and trouble attending the removal, and on account of the reduced value of a great portion of the lands herein ceded to the Cherokees, as compared with that of those in Arkansas which were made theirs by the Treaty of 1817, and the Convention of 1819, will pay to the Cherokees, immediately after their removal which shall be within fourteen months of the date of this agreement, the sum of fifty thousand dollars; also an annuity, for three years, of two thousand dollars, towards defraying the cost and trouble which may attend upon going after and recovering their stock which may stray into the Territory in quest of the pastures from which they may be drivenalso, eight thousand seven hundred and sixty dollars, for spoliations committed on them, (the

Cherokees) which sum will be in full of all demands of the kind up to this date, as well as those against the Osages, as those against citizens of the United States.

This being the amount of the claims for said spoliations, as rendered by the Cherokees, and which are believed to be correctly and fairly stated. Also, one thousand two hundred dollars for the use of Thomas Graves, a Cherokee Chief, for losses sustained in his property, and for personal suffering endured by him when confined as a prisoner, on a criminal, but false accusation; also, five hundred dollars for the use of George Guess, another Cherokee, for the great benefits he has conferred upon the Cherokee people, in the beneficial results which they are now experiencing from the use of the Alphabet discovered by him, to whom also, in consideration of his relinquishing a valuable saline, the privilege is hereby given to locate and occupy another saline on Lee's Creek.

It is further agreed by the United States, to pay two thousand dollars annually, to the Cherokees, for ten years, to be expended under the direction of the President of the United States in the education of their children, in their own country, in letters and the mechanic arts; also, one thousand dollars towards the purchase of a Printing Press and Types to aid the Cherokees in the progress of education, and to benefit and enlighten them as a people, in their own, and our language. It is agreed further that the expense incurred other than that paid by the United States in the erection of the buildings and improvements, so far as that may have been paid by the benevolent society who have been, and yet are, engaged most instructing the Cherokee children, shall be paid to the society, it being the understanding that the amount shall be expended in the erection of other buildings and improvements, for like purposes, in the country herein ceded to the Cherokees, The United States relinquish their claim due by the Cherokees to the late United States Factory, provided the same does not exceed three thousand five hundred dollars.

ARTICLE 6. It is moreover agreed, by the United States, whenever the Cherokees may desire it, to give them a set of plain laws, suited to their condition- also, when they may wish to lay off their lands, and own them individually, a surveyor shall be sent to make the surveys at the cost of the United States.

ARTICLE 7. The Chiefs and Head Men of the Cherokee Nation, aforesaid, for and in consideration of the foregoing stipulations and provisions, do hereby agree, in the name and behalf of their Nation, to give up, and they do hereby surrender, to the United States, and agree to leave the same within fourteen months, as herein before stipulated, all the lands to which they are entitled in Arkansas, and which were secured to them by the Treaty of 8th January, 1817, and the Convention of the 27th February, 1819.

ARTICLE 8. The Cherokee Nation, West of the Mississippi having, by this agreement, freed themselves from the harassing and ruinous effects consequent upon a location amidst a white population, and secured to themselves and their posterity, under the solemn sanction of the guarantee of the United States, as contained in this agreement, a large extent of unembarrassed country; and that their Brothers yet remaining in the States may be induced to join them and enjoy the repose and blessings of such a State in the future, it is further agreed, on the part of the United States, that to each Head of a Cherokee family now residing within the chartered limits of Georgia, or of either of the States, East of the Mississippi, who may desire to remove West, shall be given, on enrolling himself for emigration, a good Rifle, a Blanket, and Kettle, and five pounds of Tobacco: (and to each member of his family one Blanket)

Also, a just compensation for the property he may abandon, to be assessed by persons to be appointed by the President of the United States. The cost of the emigration of all such shall also be borne by the United States, and good and suitable ways opened, and provisions procured for their comfort, accommodation, and support, by the way, and provisions for twelve months after their arrival at the Agency; and to each person, or head of a family, if he take along with him four persons, shall be paid immediately on his arriving at the Agency and reporting himself and his family or followers, as emigrants and permanent settlers, in addition to the above, provided he and they shall have emigrated from within the Chartered limits of the State of Georgia, the sum of fifty dollars, and this sum in proportion to any greater or less number that may accompany him from within the aforesaid Chartered limits of the State of Georgia.

ARTICLE 9. It is understood and agreed by the parties to this Convention, that a Tract of Land, two miles wide and six miles long, shall be, and the same is hereby, reserved for the use and benefit of the United States, for the accommodation of the military force which is now, or which may hereafter be, stationed at Fort Gibson, on the Neasho, or Grand River, to commence on said River half a mile below the aforesaid Fort, and to run thence due East two miles, thence Northwardly six miles, to a point which shall be two mile distant from the River aforesaid, thence due West to the said River, and down it to the place of beginning. And the Cherokees agree that the United States shall have and possess the right of establishing a road through their country for the purpose of having a free and unmolested way to and from said Fort.

ARTICLE 10. It is agreed that Captain James Rogers, in consideration of his having lost a horse in the service of the United States, and for services rendered by him to the United States, shall be paid, in full for the above, and all other claims for losses and services, the sum of Five Hundred Dollars.

ARTICLE 11. This Treaty to be binding on the contracting parties so soon as it is ratified by the President of the United States, by and with the advice and consent of the Senate.

Done at the place, and on the date and year above written.

James Barbour.

Black Fox, his x mark, Thomas Graves, his x mark, George Guess, (a) Thomas Maw, (a)George Marvis, (a) John Looney, (a) John Rogers, J. W. Flawey, counsellor of Del., Chiefs of the delegation.

Witnesses: Thos. L. McKenney, James Rogers, interpreter, D. Kurtz, H. Miller, Thomas Murray, D. Brown, secretary Cherokee delegation, Pierye Pierya, E. W. Duval, United States agent, etc.

Ratified with the following proviso:
"Provided, nevertheless, that the said convention shall not be so construed as to extend the northern boundary of the perpetual outlet west,' provided for and guaranteed in the second article of said convention, north of the thirty-sixth degree of north latitude, or so as to interfere with the lands assigned, or to be assigned, west of the Mississippi river, to the Creek Indians who have emigrated, or may emigrate, from the States of Georgia and Alabama, under the provisions of any treaty or treaties heretofore concluded between the United States and the Creek tribe of Indians; and provided further,. That nothing in the said convention shall be construed to cede or assign to the Cherokees any lands heretofore ceded or assigned to any tribe or tribes of Indians, by any treaty now existing and in force, with any such tribe or tribes." [292]

DEPARTMENT OF WAR, 31st May, 1828.
To the Hon. HENRY CLAY, Secretary of State:
SIR: I have the honor to transmit, herewith, the acceptance of the terms, by the Cherokees, upon which the recent convention with them was ratified. You will have the goodness to cause the sane to be attached to the treaty, and published with it.
I have the honor to be; very respectfully, your obedient servant,
Sam'l. L. Southard.

COUNCIL ROOM, WILLIAMSON'S HOTEL, Washington, May 31st, 1828.
To the SECRETARY OF WAR, Washington City:

SIR: The undersigned, chiefs of the Cherokee nation, west of the Mississippi, for and in behalf of said nation, hereby agree to, and accept of, the terms upon which the Senate of the United States ratified the convention, concluded at Washington on the sixth day of May, 1828, between the United States and said nation.
In testimony whereof, they hereunto subscribe their names and affix their seals.

Thomas Graves, his x mark, George Maw, his x mark, George Guess, his x mark, Thomas Maryis, his x mark, John Rogers.

Signed and sealed in the presence of: E. W. Duval, United States agent, etc, Thomas Murray, James Rogers, interpreter.

(a) Written by the signers in their language, and in the characters now in use among them, as discovered by George Guess.

TREATY WITH THE DELAWARES {1829, Aug. 3}
Proclamation, Jan. 2, 1830.

Articles of agreement made between John M'Elain, thereto specially authorized by the President of the United States, and the band of Delaware Indians, upon the Sandusky River, in the State of Ohio, for the cession of a certain reservation of land in the said State.

ARTICLE 1. The said band of Delaware Indians cede to the United States the tract of three miles square, adjoining the Wyandot reservation upon the San-dusky river, reserved for their use by the treaty of the Rapids of the Maumee, concluded between the United States and the Wyandots, Seneca, Delaware, Shawnees, Potawatamies, Ottawas, and Chippiwa tribes of Indians, on the twenty-ninth day of September, in the year of our Lord one thousand eight hundred and seventeen, and the said tribe of Delawares engage to remove to and join their nation on the west side of the Mississippi, on the land allotted to them, on or before the first day of January next, at which time peaceable pos-session of said reservation is to be given to the United States.

ARTICLE 2. In consideration of the stipulations aforesaid, it is agreed, that the United States shall pay to the said band the sum of three thousand dollars: two thousand dollars in hand, the receipt of which is hereby acknowledged by the undersigned Chiefs of said tribe, and the remaining balance of one thousand dollars to be appropriated to the purchase of horses, clothing, provisions, and other useful articles, to aid them on their journey so soon as they are prepared to remove.

In witness whereof, the said John McElvain, and the chiefs of the said band, have hereunto set their hands and seals at Little Sandusky, [304] in the State of Ohio, this third day of August, in the year of our Lord one thousand eight hun-dred and twenty-nine.

John McElvain,
Captain Pipe, his x mark, William Matacur, his x mark, Captain Wolf, his x mark, Eli Pipe, his x mark,.

Solomon Joneycake, his x mark, Joseph Armstrong, his x mark, George Wil- liams, his x mark,

In presence of: Nathaniel McLean, Cornelius Wilson, H. Barrett.

TREATY WITH THE DELAWARES {1829, Sept. 24}
Proclamation, Mar. 24, 1831.

Supplementary article to the Delaware Treaty, concluded at St. Mary's n the State of Ohio, on the 3d of October, 1818.

WHEREAS the foregoing Treaty stipulates that the United States hall provide for the Delaware Nation, a country to reside in, West of the Mississippi, as the permanent residence of their Nation; and whereas the said Delaware Nation, are now willing to remove, on the following conditions, from the country on James' fork of White river in the State of Missouri, to the Country selected in the fork of the Kansas and Missouri River, as recommended by the government, for the permanent residence of the whole Delaware Nation; it is hereby agreed upon by the parties, that the country in the fork of the Kansas and Missouri Rivers, ex- tending up the Kansas River, to the Kansas Line, and up the Missouri River to Camp Leavenworth, and thence by a line drawn Westwardly, leaving a space ten miles wide, north of the Kansas boundary line, for an outlet; shall be con- veyed and forever secured by the United States, to the said Delaware Nation, as their permanent residence: And the United States hereby pledges the faith of the government to guarantee to the said Delaware Nation forever, the quiet and peaceable possession and undisturbed enjoyment of the same, against the claims and assaults of all and every other people whatever.

And the United States hereby agrees to furnish the Delaware Nation with forty horses, to be given to their poor and destitute people, and the use of six wagons and ox-teams, to assist the nation in removing their heavy articles to their per- manent home; and to supply them with all necessary farming utensils and tools necessary for building houses, &c: and to supply them with provisions on their journey, and with one year's provisions after they get to their permanent resi- dence; and to have a grist and saw mill erected for their use, within two years after their complete removal.

And it is hereby expressly stipulated and agreed upon by the parties, that for and in consideration of the full and entire relinquishment by the Delaware Na- tion of all claim whatever to the country now occupied by them in the State of Missouri, the United States shall pay to the said Delaware Nation, an additional permanent annuity of one thousand dollars.
And it is further stipulated that thirty-six sections of the best land within the limits hereby relinquished, shall be selected under the direction of the President

of the United States, and sold for the purpose of raising a fund, to be applied under the direction of the President, to the support of schools for the education of Delaware children.

It is agreed upon by the parties that this supplementary article shall be concluded in part only, at this time, and that a deputation of a Chief, or Warrior, from each town with their Interpretor shall proceed with the Agent to explore the country more fully, and if they approve of said country, to sign their names under ours, which shall be considered as finally concluded on our part; and after the same shall be ratified by the President and Senate of the United States, shall be binding on the contracting parties.

In testimony whereof the United States Indian agent, and the chiefs and warriors of the Delaware nation of Indians, have hereunto set their hands at Council camp, on James's fork of White river, in the State of Missouri, this 24th day of September, in the year of our Lord one thousand eight hundred and twenty-nine.

Geo. Vashon, United States Indian agent,
Wm. Anderson, principal chief, his x mark, Capt. Paterson, head chief, his x mark, Pooshies, or the cat, his x mark, Capt. Suwaunock, whiteman, his x mark, Jonny Quick, his x mark, John Gray, his x mark, George Guirty, his x mark, Capt. Beaver, his x mark, Naunotetauxien, his x mark, Little Jack, his x mark, Capt. Pipe, his x mark, Big Island, his x mark.

Signed in presence of: James Connor, Delaware interpreter, Anth'y Shane, Shawanee interpreter.

These last six chiefs and warriors having been deputed to examine the country, have approved of it, and signed their names at Council camp in the fork of the Kansas and Missouri river, on the 19th October, 1829.

Nauochecaupauc, his x mark, Nungailautone, his x mark, James Gray, his x mark, Sam Street, his x mark, Aupaneek, his x mark, Outhteekawshaweat, his x mark.

TREATY WITH THE CHOCTAW {1830, Sept. 27}
Proclamation, Feb. 24, 1831.

A treaty of perpetual friendship, cession and limits, entered into by John H. Eaton and John Coffee, for and in behalf of the Government of the United States, and the Mingoes, Chiefs, Captains and Warriors of the Choctaw Nation, begun and held at Dancing Rabbit Creek, on the fifteenth of September, in the year eighteen hundred and thirty.

WHEREAS the General Assembly of the State of Mississippi has extended the laws of said State to persons and property within the chartered limits of the same, and the President of the United States has said that he cannot protect the Choctaw people from the operation of these laws; Now therefore that the Choctaw may live under their own laws in peace with the United States and the State of Mississippi they have determined to sell their lands east of the Mississippi and have accordingly agreed to the following articles of treaty: (This paragraph was not ratified.)

ARTICLE 1.   Perpetual peace and friendship is pledged and agreed upon by and between the United States and the Mingoes, Chiefs, and Warriors of the Choctaw Nation of Red People; and that this may be considered the Treaty existing between the parties all other Treaties heretofore existing and inconsistent with the provisions of this are hereby declared null and void.

ARTICLE 2.   The United States under a grant specially to be made by the President of the U. S. shall cause to be conveyed to the Choctaw Nation a tract of country west of the Mississippi River, in fee simple to them and their descendants, to inure to them while they shall exist as a nation and live on it, beginning near Fort Smith where the Arkansas boundary crosses the Arkansas River, running thence to the source of the Canadian fork; if in the limits of the United States, or to those limits; thence due south to Red River, and down Red River to the west boundary of the Territory of Arkansas; thence north along that line to the beginning. The boundary of the same to be agreeably to the Treaty made and concluded at Washington City in the year 1825. The grant to be executed so soon as the present Treaty shall be ratified.

ARTICLE 3. In consideration of the provisions contained in the several articles of this Treaty, the Choctaw nation of Indians consent and hereby cede to the United States, the entire country they own and possess, east of the Mississippi River; and they agree to move beyond the Mississippi River, early as practicable, and will so arrange their removal, that as many as possible of their people not exceeding one half of the whole number, shall depart during the falls of 1831 and 1832; the residue to follow during the succeeding fall of 1833; a better opportunity in this manner will be afforded the Government, to extend to them the facilities and comforts which it is desirable should be extended in conveying them to their new homes.

ARTICLE 4. The Government and people of the United States are hereby obliged to secure to the said Choctaw Nation of Red People the jurisdiction and government of all the persons and property that may be within their limits west, so that no Territory or State shall ever have a right to pass laws for the government of the Choctaw Nation of Red People and their descendants; and that no part of the land granted them shall ever be embraced in any Territory or State;

but the U. S. shall forever secure said Choctaw Nation from, and against, all laws except such as from time to time may be enacted in their own National Councils, not inconsistent with the Constitution, Treaties, and Laws of the United States; and except such as may, and which have been enacted by Congress, to the extent that Congress under the Constitution are required to exercise a legislation over Indian Affairs. But the Choctaws, should this treaty be ratified, express a wish that Congress may grant to the Choctaws the right of punishing by their own laws, any white man who shall come into their nation, and infringe any of their national regulations.

ARTICLE 5. The United States are obliged to protect the Choctaws from domestic strife and front foreign enemies on the same principles that the citizens of the United States are protected, so that whatever would be a legal demand upon the U. S. for defence or for wrongs committed by an enemy, on a citizen of the U. S. shall be equally binding in favor of the Choctaws, and in all cases where the Choctaws shall be called upon by a legally authorized officer of the U. S. to fight an enemy, such Choctaw shall receive the pay and other emoluments, which citizens of the U. S. receive in such cases, provided, no war shall be undertaken or prosecuted by said Choctaw Nation but by declaration made in full Council, and to be approved by the U. S. unless it be in self defence against an open rebellion or against an enemy marching into their country, in which cases they shall defend, until the U. S. are advised thereof.

ARTICLE 6. Should a Choctaw or any party of Choctaws commit acts of violence upon the person or property of a citizen of the U. S. or join any war party against any neighbouring tribe of Indians, without the authority in the preceding article; and except to oppose an actual or threatened invasion or rebellion, such person so offending shall be delivered up to an officer of the U. S. if in the power-of the Choctaw Nation, that such offender may be punished as may be provided in such cases, by the laws of the U. S.; but if such offender is not within the control of the Choctaw Nation, then said Choctaw Nation shall not be held responsible for the injury done by said offender.

ARTICLE 7. All acts of violence committed upon persons and property of the people of the Choctaw Nation either by citizens of the U. S. or neighbouring Tribes of Red People, shall be referred to some authorized Agent by him to be referred to the President of the U. S. who shall examine into such cases and see that every possible degree of justice is done to said Indian party of the Choctaw Nation.

ARTICLE 8. Offenders against the laws of the U. S. or any individual State shall be apprehended and delivered to any duly authorized person where such offender may be found in the Choctaw country, having fled from any part of U. S. but in all such eases application must be made to the Agent or Chiefs and the expense of his apprehension and delivery provided for and paid by the U. States.

ARTICLE 9. Any citizen of the U. S. who may be ordered from the Nation by the Agent and constituted authorities of the Nation and refusing to obey or return into the Nation without the consent of the aforesaid persons, shall be subject to such pains and penalties as may be provided by the laws of the U. S. in such eases. Citizens of the U.S. travelling peaceably under the authority of the laws of the U. S. shall be under the care and protection of the nation.

ARTICLE 10. No person shall expose goods or other article for sale as a trader, without a written permit from the constituted authorities of the Nation, or authority of the laws of the Congress of the U. S. under penalty of forfeiting the Articles, and the constituted authorities of the Nation shall grant no license except to such persons as reside in the Nation and are answerable to the laws of the Nation. The U. S. shall be particularly obliged to assist to prevent ardent spirits from being introduced into the Nation.

ARTICLE 11. Navigable streams shall be free to the Choctaws who shall pay no higher toll or duty than citizens of the U.S. It is agreed further that the U. S. shall establish one or more Post Offices in said Nation, and may establish such military post roads, and posts, as they may consider necessary.

ARTICLE 12. All intruders shall be removed from the Choctaw Nation and kept without it. Private property to be always respected and on no occasion taken for public purposes without just compensation being made therefor to the rightful owner. If an Indian unlawfully take or steal any property from a white man a citizen of the U. S. the offender shall be punished. And if a white man unlawfully take or steal any thing from an Indian, the property shall be restored and the offender punished. It is further agreed that when a Choctaw shall be given up to be tried for any offence against the laws of the U. S. if unable to employ counsel to defend him, the U. S. will do it, that his trial may be fair and impartial.

ARTICLE 13. It is consented that a qualified Agent shall be appointed for the Choctaws every four years, unless sooner removed by the President; and he shall be removed on petition of the constituted authorities of the Nation, the President being satisfied there is sufficient cause shown. The Agent shall fix his residence convenient to the great body of the people; and in the selection of an Agent immediately after the ratification of this Treaty, the wishes of the Choctaw Nation on the subject shall be entitled to great respect.

ARTICLE 14. Each Choctaw head of a family being desirous to remain and become a citizen of the States, shall be permitted to do so, by signifying his intention to the Agent within six months from the ratification of this Treaty, and he or she shall thereupon be entitled to a reservation of one section of six hundred and forty acres of land, to be bounded by sectional lines of survey; in like manner shall be entitled to one half that quantity for each unmarried child which is living with him over ten years of age; and a quarter section to such child as may be under 10 years of age, to adjoin the location of the parent. If they reside upon said lands intending to become citizens of the States for five years after the ratification of this Treaty, in that case a grant in fee simple shall issue; said reservation shall include the present improvement of the head of the family, or a portion of it. Persons who claim under this article shall not lose the privilege of a Choctaw citizen, but if they ever remove are not to be entitled to any portion of the Choctaw annuity.

ARTICLE 15. To each of the Chiefs in the Choctaw Nation (to wit:) Greenwood Laflore, Nutackachie, and Mushulatubbe there is granted a reservation of four sections of land, two of which shall include and adjoin their present improvement, and the other two located where they please but on unoccupied unimproved lands, such sections shall be bounded by sectional lines, and with the consent of the President they may sell the same. Also to the three principal Chiefs and to their successors in office there shall be paid two hundred and fifty dollars annually while they shall continue in their respective offices, except to Mushulatubbe, who as he has an annuity of one hundred and fifty dollars for life under a former treaty, shall receive only the additional sum of one hundred dollars, while he shall continue in office as Chief; and if in addition to this the Nation shall think proper to elect an additional principal Chief of the whole to superintend and govern upon republican principles he shall receive annually for his services five hundred dollars, which allowance to the Chiefs and their successors in office, shall continue for twenty years.

At any time when in military service, and while in service by authority of the U. S. the district Chiefs under and by selection of the President shall be entitled to the pay of Majors; the other Chief under the same circumstances shall have the pay of a Lieutenant Colonel. The Speakers of the three districts, shall receive twenty-five dollars a year for four years each; and the three secretaries one to each of the Chiefs, fifty dollars each for four years. Each Captain of the Nation, the number not to exceed ninety-nine, thirty-three from each district, shall be furnished upon removing to the West, with each a good suit of clothes and a broad sword as an outfit, and for four years commencing with the first of their removal, shall each receive fifty dollars a year, for the trouble of keeping their people at order in settling; and whenever they shall be in military service by authority of the U. S. shall receive the pay of a captain.

ARTICLE 16. In wagons; and with steam boats as may be found necessarythe U. S. agree to remove the Indians to their new homes at their expense and under the care of discreet and careful persons, who will be kind and brotherly to

them. They agree to furnish them with ample corn and beef, or pork for themselves and families for twelve months after reaching their new homes.
It is agreed further that the U. S. will take all their cattle, at the valuation of
some discreet person to be appointed by the President, and the same shall be
paid for in money after their arrival at their new homes; or other cattle such as
may be desired shall be furnished them, notice being given through their Agent
of their wishes upon this subject before their removal that time to supply the
demand may be afforded.

ARTICLE 17. The several annuities and sums secured under former Treaties to
the Choctaw nation and people shall continue as though this Treaty had never
been made. And it is further agreed that the U. S. in addition will pay the sum
of twenty thousand dollars for twenty years, commencing after their removal to
the west, of which, in the first year after their removal, ten thousand dollars
shall be divided and arranged to such as may not receive reservations under this
Treaty.

ARTICLE 18. The U. S. shall cause the lands hereby ceded to be surveyed; and
surveyors may enter the Choctaw Country for that purpose, conducting themselves properly and disturbing or interrupting none of the Choctaw people. But
no person is to be permitted to settle within the nation, or the lands to be sold
before the Choctaws shall remove. And for the payment of the several amounts
secured in this Treaty, the lands hereby ceded are to remain a fund pledged to
that purpose, until the debt shall be provided for and arranged. And further it is
agreed, that in the construction of this Treaty wherever well founded doubt
shall arise, it shall be construed most favorably towards the Choctaws.

ARTICLE 19. The following reservations of land are hereby admitted. To
Colonel David Fulsom-four sections of which two shall include his present improvement, and two may be located elsewhere, on unoccupied, unimproved
land. To I. Garland, Colonel Robert Cole, Tuppanahomer, John Pytchlynn,
Charles Juzan, Johokebetubbe, Eaychahobia, Ofehoma, two sections, each to
include their improvements, and to be bounded by sectional lines, and the same
may be disposed of and sold with the consent of the President. And that others
not provided for, may be provided for, there shall be reserved as follows:

First. One section to each head of a family not exceeding Forty in number, who
during the present year, may have had in actual cultivation, with a dwelling
house thereon fifty acres or more. Secondly, three quarter sections after the
manner aforesaid to each head of a family not exceeding four hundred and
sixty, as shall have cultivated thirty acres and less than fifty, to be bounded by
quarter section lines of survey, and to be contiguous and adjoining. Third; One
half section as aforesaid to those who shall have cultivated from twenty to
thirty acres the number not to exceed four hundred. Fourth; a quarter section as
aforesaid to such as shall have cultivated from twelve to twenty acres, the num-

ber not to exceed three hundred and fifty, and one half that quantity to such as shall have cultivated from two to twelve acres, the number also not to exceed three hundred and fifty persons. Each of said class of cases shall be subject to the limitations contained in the first class, and shall be so located as to include that part of the improvement which contains the dwelling house. If a greater number shall be found to be entitled to reservations under the several classes of this article, than is stipulated for under the limitation prescribed, then and in that case the Chiefs separately or together shall determine the persons who shall be excluded in the respective districts.

Fifth; Any Captain the number not exceeding ninety persons, who under the provisions of this article shall receive less than a section, he shall be entitled, to an additional quantity of half a section adjoining to his other reservation. The several reservations secured under this article, may be sold with the consent of the President of the U. S. but should any prefer it, or omit to take a reservation for the quantity [315] he may be entitled to, the U. S. will on his removing pay fifty cents an acre, after reaching their new homes, provided that before the first of January next they shall adduce to the Agent, or some other authorized person to be appointed, proof of his claim and the quantity of it. Sixth; likewise children of the Choctaw Nation residing in the Nation, who have neither father nor mother a list of which, with satisfactory proof of Parentage and orphanage being filed with Agent in six months to be forwarded to the War Department, shall be entitled to a quarter section of Land, to be located under the direction of the President, and with his consent the same may be sold and the proceeds applied to some beneficial purpose for the benefit of said orphans.

ARTICLE 20. The U. S. agree and stipulate as follows, that for the benefit and advantage of the Choctaw people, and to improve their condition, their shall be educated under the direction of the President and at the expense of the U. S. forty Choctaw youths for twenty years. This number shall be kept at school, and as they finish their education others, to supply their places shall be received for the period stated. The U. S. agree also to erect a Council House for the Nation at some convenient central point, after their people shall be settled; and a House for each Chief, also a Church for each of the three Districts, to be used also as school houses, until the Nation may conclude to build others; and for these purposes ten thousand dollars shall be appropriated; also fifty thousand dollars (viz:) twenty-five hundred dollars annually shall be given for the support of three teachers of schools for twenty years. Likewise there shall be furnished to the Nation, three Blacksmiths one for each district for sixteen years, and a qualified Mill Wright for five years; Also there shall be furnished the following articles, twenty-one hundred blankets, to each warrior who emigrates a rifle, moulds, wipers and ammunition. One thousand axes, ploughs, hoes, wheels and cards each; and four hundred looms. There shall also be furnished, one ton of iron and two hundred weight of steel annually to each District for sixteen years.

ARTICLE 21. A few Choctaw Warriors yet survive who marched and fought in the army with General Wayne, the whole number stated not to exceed twenty. These it is agreed shall hereafter, while they live, receive twenty-five dollars a year; a list of them to be early as practicable, and within six months, made out, and presented to the Agent, to be forwarded to the War Department.

ARTICLE 22. The Chiefs of the Choctaws who have suggested that their people are in a state of rapid advancement in education and refinement, and have expressed a solicitude that they might have the privilege of a Delegate on the floor of the House of Representatives extended to them. The Commissioners do not feel that they can under a treaty stipulation accede to the request, but at their desire, present it in the Treaty, that Congress may consider of, and decide the application.

Done, and signed, and executed by the commissioners of the United States, and the chiefs, captains, and head men of the Choctaw nation, at Dancing Rabbit creek, this 27th day of September, eighteen hundred and thirty.

Jno. H. Eaton, Jno. Coffee, Greenwood Leflore,
Musholatubbee, his x mark, Nittucachee, his x mark, Holarterhoomah, his x mark, Hopiaunchahubbee. his x mark, Zishomingo, his x mark, Captainthalke, his x mark, James Shield, his x mark, Pistiyubbee, his x mark, Yobalaruneha-hubbee, his x mark, Holubbee, his x mark, Robert Cole, his x mark, Mokelare-harhopin, his x mark, Lewis Perry, his x mark, Artonamarstubbe, his x mark, Hopeatubbee, his x mark, Coshahoomah, his x mark, Chuallahoomah, his x mark, Joseph Kincaide, his x mark, Eyarhocuttubbee, his x mark, Iyacherhopia, his x mark, Offahoomah, his x mark, Archalater, his x mark, Onnahubbee, his x mark, Pisinhocuttubbee, his x mark, Tullarhacher, his x mark, Little leader, his x mark, Maanhutter, his x mark, Cowehoomah, his x mark, Tillamoer, his x mark, Imnullacha, his x mark, Artopilachubbee, his x mark, Shupherunchahub-bee, his x mark, Nitterhoomah, his x mark, Oaklaryubbee, his x mark, Pu-kumna, his x mark, Arpalar, his x mark, Holber, his x mark, Hoparmingo, his x mark, Isparhoomah, his x mark, Tieberhoomah, his x mark, Tishoholarter, his x mark, Mahayarchubbee, his x mark, Artooklubbetushpar, his x mark, Metub-bee, his x mark, Arsarkatubbee, his x mark, Issaterhoomah, his x mark, Cho-htahmatahah, his x mark, Tunnuppashubbee, his x mark, Okocharyer, his x mark, Hoshhopia, his x mark, Warsharshahopia, his x mark, Maarshunchahub-bee, his x mark, Misharyubbee, his x mark, Daniel McCurtain, his x mark, Tushkerharcho, his x mark, Hoktoontubbce, his x mark, Nuknacrahookmarhee, his x mark, Mingo hoomah, his x mark, James Karnes, his x mark, Tishoha-kubbee, his x mark, Narlanalar, his x mark, Pennasha, his x mark, Inharyarker, his x mark, Mottubbee, his x mark, Narharyubbee, his x mark, Ishmaryubbee, his x mark, James McKing, Lewis Wilson, his x mark, Istonarkerharcho, his x mark, Hohinshamartarher, his x mark, Kinsulachubbee, his x mark, Emarhin-

stubbee, his x mark, Gysalndalra, bin, his x mark, Thomas Wall, Sam. S. Worcester, Arlartar, his x mark, Nittahubbee, his x mark, Tishonouan, his x mark, Warsharchahoomah, his x mark, Isaac James, his x mark, ttopiaintushker, his x mark, Aryoshkermer, his x mark, Shemotar, his x mark, Hopiaisketina, his x mark, Thomas Leftore, his x mark, Arnokeehatubbee, his x mark, Shokoperlukna, his x mark, Posherhoomah, his x mark, Robert Folsom, his x mark, Arharyotubbee, his x mark, Kushonolarter, his x mark, James Vaughan, his x mark, Phiplip, his x mark, Meshameye, his x mark, Ishteheka, his x mark, Hcshohomme, his x mark, John McKolbery, his x mark, Benjm. James, his x mark, Tikbachahambe, his x mark, Aholiktube, his x mark, Walking Wolf, his x mark, John Waide, his x mark, Big Axe, his x mark, Bob, his x mark,Tushkochaubbee, his x mark, Ittabe, his x mark, Tishowakayo, his x mark, Folehommo, his x mark, John Garland, his x mark, Koshona, his x mark, Ishleyohamube, his x mark, Jacob Folsom, William Foster, Ontioerharcho, his x mark, Hugh A. Foster, Pierre Juzan, Jno. Pitchlynn, jr., David Folsom, Sholohommastube, his x mark, Tesho, his x mark, Lauwechubee, his x mark, Hoshehammo, his x mark, Ofenowo, his x mark, Ahekoche, his x mark, Kaloshoube, his x mark, Atoko, his x mark, Ishtemeleche, his x mark, Emthtohabe, his x mark, Silas D. Fisher, his x mark, isaac Folsom, his x mark, Hekatube, his x mark, Hakseche, his x mark, Jerry Carhey, his x mark, John Washington. his x mark, Panshastubbee, his x mark, P. P. Pitchlynn, his x mark, Joel 1t. Nail, his x mark, Hopia Stonakey, his x mark, Kocohomma, his x mark, William Wade, his x mark, Panshstickubbee, his x mark, Holittankchahubbee, his x mark, Oklanowa, his x mark, Neto, his x mark, James Fletcher, his x mark, Silas D. Pitchlynn, William Trahorn, his x mark, Toshkahemmitto, his x mark, Tethetayo, his x mark, Emokloshahopie, his x mark, Tishoimita, his x mark, Thomas W. Foster, his x mark, Zadoc Brashears, his x mark, Levi Perkins, his x mark, Isaac Perry, his x mark, Ishlonocka Hoomah, his x mark, Hiram King, his x mark, Ogla Enlah, his x mark, Nultlahtubbee, his x mark, Tuska Hollattuh, his x mark, Kothoantchatmbbee, his x mark, Eyarpulubbee, his x mark, Okentahubbe, his x mark, Living War Club, his x mark, John Jones, his x mark, Charles Jones, his x mark, Isaac'Jones, his x mark, Hocklucha, his x mark, Muscogee, his x mark, Eden Nelson, his x mark.

In presence of: E. Breathitt, secretary to the Commission, William Ward, agent for Choctaws, John Pitchlyn, United States interpreter, M. Mackey, United States interpreter, Geo. S. Gaines, of Alabama, R. P. Currin, Luke Howard, Sam. S. Worcester, Jno. N. Byrn, John Bell, Jno. Bond.

SUPPLEMENTARY ARTICLES TO THE PRECEDING TREATY.
Sept. 28,1830

Various Choctaw persons have been presented by the Chiefs of the nation, with a desire that they might be provided for. Being particularly deserving, an earnestness has been manifested that provision might be made for them. It is therefore by the undersigned commissioners here assented to, with the understanding that they are to have no interest in the reservations which are directed and provided for under the general Treaty to which this is a supplement.

As evidence of the liberal and kind feelings of the President and Government of the United States the Commissioners agree to the request as follows, (to wit) Pierre Juzan, Peter Pitchlynn, G. W. Harkins, Jack Pitchlynn, Israel Fulsom, Louis Laflore, Benjamin James, Joel H. Nail, Hopoynjahubbee, Onorkubbee, Benjamin Laflore, Michael Laflore and Allen Yates and wife shall be entitled to a reservation of two sections of land each to include their improvement where they at present reside, with the exception of the three first named persons and Benjamin Laflore, who are authorized to locate one of their sections on any other unimproved and unoccupied land, within their respective districts.

ARTICLE 2. And to each of the following persons there is allowed a reservation of a section and a half of land, (to wit) James L. McDonald, Robert Jones, Noah Wall, James Campbell, G. Nelson, Vaughn Brashears, R. Harris, Little Leader, S, Foster, J. Vaughn, L. Durans, Samuel Long, T. Magagha, Thos. Everge, Giles Thompson, Tomas Garland, John Bond, William Laflore, and Turner Brashears, the two first named persons, may locate one section each, and one section jointly on any unimproved and unoccupied land, these not residing in the Nation; The others are to include their present residence and improvement.

Also one section is allowed to the following persons (to wit) Middle-ton Mackey, Wesley Train, Choclehomo, Moses Foster, D. W. Wall, Charles Scott, Molly Nail, Susan Colbert, who was formerly Susan James, Samuel Garland, Silas Fisher, D. McCurtain, Oaklahoma, and Polly Fillecuthey, to be located in entire sections to include their present residence and improvement, with the exception of Molly. Nail and Susan Colbert, who are authorized to locate theirs, on any unimproved unoccupied land.

John Pitchlynn has long and faithfully served the nation in character of U. States Interpreter, he has acted as such for forty years, in consideration it is agreed, in addition to what has been done for him there shall be granted to two of his children, (to wit) Silas Pitchlynn, and Thomas Pitchlynn one section of land each, to adjoin the location of their father; likewise to James Madison and Peter sons of Mushulatubbee one section of land each to include the old house and improve-meat where their father formerly lived on the old military road adjoining a large Prerarie.

And to Henry Groves son of the Chief Natticache there is one section of land given to adjoin his father's land.

And to each of the following persons half a section of land is granted on any unoccupied and unimproved lands in the Districts where they respectively live (to wit) Willis Harkins, James D. Hamilton, William [318] Juzan, Tobias Laflore, Jo Doke, Jacob Fulsom; P. Hays, Samuel Worcester; George Hunter, William Train, Robert Nail and Alexander McKee.

And there is given a quarter section of land each to Delila and her five fatherless children, she being a Choctaw woman residing out of the nation; also the same quantity to Peggy Trihan, another Indian woman residing out of the nation and her two fatherless children; and to the widows of Pushmilaha, and Pucktshenubbee, who were formerly distinguished Chiefs of the nation and for their children four quarter sections of land, each in trust for themselves and their children.

All of said last mentioned reservations are to be located under and by direction of the President of the U. States.

ARTICLE 3. The Choctaw people now that they have ceded their lands are solicitous to get to their new homes early as possible and accordingly they wish that a party may be permitted to proceed this fall to ascertain whereabouts will be most advantageous for their people to be located.

It is therefore agreed that three or four persons (from each of the three districts) under the guidance of some discreet and well qualified person or persons may proceed during this fall to the West upon an examination of the country.

For their time and expenses the U. States agree to allow the said twelve persons two dollars a day each, not to exceed one hundred days, which is deemed to be ample time to make an examination. If necessary, pilots acquainted with the country will be furnished when they arrive in the West.

ARTICLE 4. John Donly of Alabama who has several Choctaw grand children, and who for twenty years has carried the mail through the Choctaw Nation, a desire by the Chiefs is expressed that he may have a section of land, it is accordingly granted, to be located in one entire section, on any unimproved and unoccupied land.

Anth'y Shane, interpreter, James Conner, interpreter, Baptiste Peoria, interpreter.

I hereby certify the above to be a true copy from the original in my possession, Geo. Vashon, United States Indian agent, Indian agency, near Kansas river, 24th October, 1829.

TREATY WITH THE CHICKASAW {1830, Aug. 31}
Unratified.
Indian Office, box 1, treaties, 1802-1853.

Articles of a treaty, entered into at Franklin, Tennessee, this 31st day of August, 1830, by John H. Eaton, Secretary of War, and General John Coffee, commissioners appointed by the President, on the part of the United States, and the chiefs and head men of the Chickasaw Nation of Indians, duly authorized, by the whole nation, to conclude a treaty.

ARTICLE 1. The Chickasaw Nation hereby cede to the United States all the lands owned and possessed by them, on the East side of the Mississippi River, where they at present reside, and which lie north of the following boundary, viz: beginning at the mouth of the Oacktibbyhaw (or Tibbee) creek; thence, up the same, to a point, being a marked tree, on the old Natchez road, about one mile Southwardly from Wall's old place; thence, with the Choctaw boundary, and along it, Westwardly, through the Tunicha old fields, to a point on the Mississippe river, about twenty-eight miles, by water, below where the St. Francis river enters said stream, on the West side. All the lands North, and North-East of said boundary, to latitude thirty-five North the South boundary of the State of Tennessee, being owned by the Chickasaws, are hereby ceded to the United States.

ARTICLE 2. In consideration of said cession, the United States agree to furnish to the Chickasaw Nation of Indians, a country, West of the territory of Arkansaw, to lie South of latitude thirty-six degrees and a half, and of equal extent with the one ceded; and in all respects as to timber, water and soil, it shall be suited to the wants and condition of said Chickasaw people. It is agreed further, that the United States will send one or more commissioners to examine and select a country of the description stated, who shall be accompanied by an interpreter and not more than twelve persons of the Chickasaws, to be chosen by the nation, to examine said country; and who, for their expenses and services, shall be allowed two dollars a day each, while so engaged. If, after proper examination, a country suitable to their wants and condition can not be found; then, it is stipulated and agreed, that this treaty, and all its provisions, shall be considered null and void. But, if a country shall be found and approved, the President of the United States shall cause a grant in fee simple to be made out, to be signed by him as other grants are usually signed, conveying the country to the Chickasaw people, and to their children, so long as they shall continue to exist as a nation, and shall reside upon the same.

ARTICLE 3. The Chickasaws being a weak tribe, it is stipulated that the United States will, at all times, extend to them their protection and care against enemies of every description, but it is, at the same time, agreed, that they shall act peacably, and never make war, nor resort to arms, except with the consent and approval of the President, unless in cases where they may be invaded by some hostile power or tribe.

ARTICLE 4. As further consideration, the United States agree, that each warrior and widow having a family, and each white man, having an Indian family, shall be entitled to a half section of land, and if they have no family, to half that quantity. The delegation present, having full knowledge of the population of their country, stipulate, that the first class of cases (those with families), shall not exceed five hundred, and that the other class shall not exceed one hundred persons. The reservations secured under this article, shall be granted in fee simple, to those who choose to remain, and become subject to the laws of the whites; and who, having recorded such intention with the agent, before the time of the first removal, shall continue to reside upon, and cultivate the same, for five years; at the expiration of which time, a grant shall be issued. But should they prefer to remove, and actually remove, then the United States, in lieu of such reservations, will pay for the same, at the rate of one dollar and a half per acre; the same to be paid in ten equal, annual instalments, to commence after the period of the ratification of this treaty, if, at that time, they shall have removed.

ARTICLE 5. It is agreed, that the United States, as further consideration, will pay to said Nation of Indians, fifteen thousand dollars annually, for twenty years; the first payment to be made after their removal shall take place, and they be settled at their new homes, West of the Mississippi.

ARTICLE 6. Whereas Levi Clolbert, George Colbert, Tessemingo, William McGilvery and Saml. Seeley Senr., have been long known, as faithful and steady friends of the United States, and regardless of the interest of their own people; to afford them an earnest of our good feeling, now that they are about to seek a new home; the commissioners, of their own accord, and without any thing of solicitation or request, on the part of said persons, have proposed, and do agree, that they have reservations of four sections each, to include their present improvements, as nearly as may be; or, if they have improvements at any other place than one, then, equally to divide said reservations, so that two sections may be laid off at one place of improvement, and two at another; or, the whole at one place, as the party entitled may choose. They shall be entitled to the same in fee simple, to be resided upon; or, if they prefer it, they may, with the consent of the President, sell and convey the same, in fee. And it is further agreed, that upon the same terms and conditions, a reservation of two sections, to be surveyed together, and to include the improvements of the party entitled, shall and the same is hereby declared to be, secured to Capt. James Brown, James Colbert, John McLish & Isaac Alberson.

ARTICLE 7. The delegation having selected the following persons, as worthy their regard and confidence, to wit;Ish to yo to pe, To pul ka, Ish te ke yo ka tubbe, Ish te ke cha, E le paum be, Piste la tubbe, Ish tim mo lat ka, Pis ta tubbe, Im mo hoal te tubbe, Ba ka tubbe, Ish to ye tubbe, Ah to ko wa, Pak la na ya ubbe, In hie yo che tubbe, Thomas Seally, Tum ma sheck ah, Im mo la subbe, Am le mi ya tubbe; Benjamin Love and Malcomb McGee;it is consented that each of said persons shall be entitled to a reservation of one section of land, to be located in a body, to include their present improvement, and upon which, intending to become resident citizens of the country, they may continue, and at the end of five years, shall receive a grant for the same; or, should they prefer to remove, they shall be entitled, in lieu thereof, to receive from the United States, one dollar and twenty-five cents per acre for the same, to be paid in two equal, annual instalments, to commence after the ratification of this treaty, and after the nation shall have removed.

ARTICLE 8. No person receiving a special reservation, shall be entitled to claim any further reservation, under the provisions of the fourth article of this treaty.

ARTICLE 9. At the request of the delegation, it is agreed that Levi Colbert shall have an additional section of land, to that granted him in the 6th article, to be located where he may prefer, and subject to the conditions contained in said sixth article.

ARTICLE 10. All the reservations made by this treaty, shall be in sections, half sections, or quarter sections, agreeably to the legal surveys made, and shall include the present houses and improvements of the reservees, as nearly as may be.

ARTICLE 11. It is agreed that the Chickasaw people, in removing to their new homes, shall go there at the expense of the United States; and that when they shall have arrived at their new homes, the United States will furnish to each one, for the space of one year, meat and corn rations, for himself and his family; that thereby, time may be afforded to clear the ground, and prepare a crop. And the better to effect this object, it is agreed that one-half the nation shall remove in the fall of 1831, and the other half the following fall. The supplies to be furnished by the United States, are to be delivered at one or two places in the nation, which shall be as convenient to the body of the people as may be practicable; having regard to the position or places, where the supplies may be had or deposited, with the greatest convenience, and least expense to the United States.

ARTICLE 12. The United States, at the time of the removal of each portion of the nation, at the valuation of some respectable person, to be appointed by the President, agree to purchase all the stock they may desire to part with, (except horses), and to pay them therefor, at their new homes, as early as practicable after the ratification of this treaty. Also, to receive their agricultural and farming utencils, and to furnish them, at the West, with axes, hoes and ploughs, suited to their wants respectively. Also, to furnish each family with a spinning wheel and cards, and a loom to every six families.

ARTICLE 13. A council house, and two houses of public worship, which may be used for the purposes of schools, shall be built by the United States; and the sum of four thousand dollars shall be appropriated for that purpose. Also, one blacksmith, and no more, shall be employed at the expense of the government, for twenty years, for the use of the Indians; and a mill-wright for five years, to aid them in erecting their saw and grist-mills.

ARTICLE 14. The sum of two thousand dollars a year, shall be paid for ten years, for the purpose of employing suitable teachers of the Christian religion, and superintending common schools in the nation. And it is further consented, that twenty Chickasaw boys of promise, from time to time, for the period of twenty years, shall be selected from the nation by the chiefs, to be educated within the States at the expense of the United States, under the direction of the Secretary of War.

ARTICLE 15. A desire having been expressed by Levi Colbert, that two of his younger sons, Abijah Jackson Colbert, and Andrew Morgan Colbert, aged seven and five years, might be educated under the direction and care of the President of the United States;and George Colbert having also expressed a wish that his grand-son, Andrew. Frazier, aged about twelve years, might have a similar attention: It is consented, that at a proper age, as far as they may be found to have capacity, they shall receive a liberal education, at the expense of the United States, under the direction and control of the President.

ARTICLE 16. The United States shall have authority, after the ratification of this treaty by the Senate, to survey and prepare the country for sale; but no sale shall take place before the fall of 1832, or until they shall remove. And that every clause and article herein contained may be strictfully fulfilled;   it is stipulated and agreed, that the lands herein ceded shall be, and the same are hereby pledged, for the payment of the several sums which are secured and directed to be paid, under the several provisions of this treaty.

ARTICLE 17. The United States, and the Chickasaw nation of Indians herein stipulate, that perpetual peace, and unaltered and lasting friendship, shall be maintained between them. It is agreed, that the President of the United States will use his good offices, and kind mediation, and make a request of the governor and legislature of the State of Mississippi, not to extend their laws over the Chickasaws; or to suspend their operation, until they shall have time to remove, as limited in this treaty.

In witness of all and every thing herein determined, between the United States, and the delegation representing the whole Chickasaw nation, the parties have hereunto set their hands and seals, at Franklin, Tennessee, within the United States, this thirty-first day of August, one thousand, eight hundred and thirty.

Jn H Eaton, Secr. of War, Jno. Coffee.

Levi Colbert, his x mark, George Colbert, his x mark, James Colbert, his x mark, Wm. McGilvery, his x mark, James Brown, his x mark, Isaac Alberson, his x mark, To pul ka, his x mark, Ish te ke yo ka tubbe, his x mark, Ish te ke cha, his x mark, Im me houl te tubbe, his x mark, In ha yo chet tubbe, his x mark, Ish te ya tubbe, his x mark, Ah to ko wa, his x mark, Ook la na ya ubbc, his x mark, Im mo la subbe, his x mark, Hush tata be, his x mark, In no wake che, his x mark, Oh he cubbe, his x mark, Kin hi the, his x mark, J. W. Lish.

Signed in presence of us: Preston Hay, Secretary, Benj. Reynolds, U. S. agent, Benjamin Love, interpreter, R. M. Gavock, R. P. Currin, Lemuel Smith, Leml. Donelson, Jos. H. Fry, James H. Wilson, J.R. Davis.

Articles, supplementary to a treaty this day entered into, between John H. Eaton and John Coffee, on the part of the United States, and the Chiefs of the Chickasaw nation.

1. It is agreed that the United States will furnish the Chickasaw nation, to be distributed by the agent, under the direction of the chiefs, at or before the time of their removal West of the Mississippi river, three hundred rifles, with moulds and wipers; also, three hundred pounds of good powder, and twelve hundred pounds of lead. They will also furnish as aforesaid, three hundred copper or brass kettles, and six hundred blankets. Likewise three thousand weight of leaf tobacco.

2. Colbert's Island, in the Tennessee river, just below the mouth of Caney Creek, supposed to contain five hundred acres, has always been in the use and occupancy of George Colbert, and has been admitted by the nation, to be his individual property. It is agreed now, that he shall be recognized, as having a title to the same, and that he shall receive from the United States, in consideration of it, one thousand dollars, to be paid in one year after the Chickasaws shall remove to their new homes.

3. James Colbert has represented, that he has a claim of thirteen hundred dollars, of money due from a citizen of the United States;-that he has become insolvent, and is unable to pay it. It is further represented, that by the rule of the Chickasaw people, where an Indian cannot pay a debt due to a white man, the nation assumes it. Also, Levi Colbert shews, that some time since, he purchased of a white citizen, a horse which was stolen, and proven and taken out of his

possession, as stolen property, for which he has not, and cannot, obtain remuneration. Being now about to leave their ancient homes, for a new one, too distant to attend to their business here;it is agreed that a section of land may be located and reserved, to be bound by sectional lines; which land, with the consent of the President, they may sell.

4. The Chickasaw delegation request, that a reservation of land may be made in favor of their excellent agent, Col. Benjamin Reynolds, who, since he has been among them, has acted uprightly and faithfully, and of their sub-agent, Major John L. Allen, who also, has been of much service :The commissioners accordingly consent thereto; and it is stipulated that Col. Reynolds shall have a reservation of five quarter sections of land, to be bounded by sectional lines, or quarter sectional lines, and to lie together, in a body; and in further consideration, it is stipulated, with the consent of said Reynolds, that his pension of two hundred and forty dollars a year, granted to him by the United States, shall thereafter cease and determine. The application in favor of the sub-agent, Maj. Allen, is also recognized, and a reservation of a quarter section is admitted to his wife, to whom and for whose benefit a grant shall issue. But said reservations shall not be located, so as to interfere with other claims to reservations, secured under this treaty, nor shall this treaty be affected if this article is not ratified.

5. The 4th article of the treaty of 19th October 1818, which reserves a salt lick, and authorizes Levi Colbert and James Brown to lease the same for a reasonable quantity of salt, is hereby changed;And with [1040] the consent of the commissioners present, the following agreement, made by Robert P. Currin, for himself and William B. Lewis, is entered as part of this treaty, to wit;
Whereas a lease of land, of four miles square, was secured under the fourth article of a treaty, concluded on the 19th day of October 1818, between the United States and the Chickasaw nation of Indians; and Levi Colbert and James Brown, under the same treaty, were appointed agents and trustees by the Chickasaw nation to make said lease. And whereas William B. Lewis, a citizen of the United States afterwards procured from said trustees, Colbert and Brown, a lease for the same, on condition of his paying annually, a certain amount of salt to said nation, provided he should succeed in finding salt water. And whereas the said William B. Lewis and Robert P. Currin, who subsequently became interested with him, have, as is shown, expended about the sum of three thousand dollars, in endeavoring to find salt water, but without success. And the Indians, who are about to leave their ancient country, being desirous to have this land and lease placed in such a condition, as that some benefit may result to their nation, They do hereby agree with said Robert P. Currin, a citizen of the United States, for himself, and as the agent and attorney in fact of the said William B. Lewis (John H. Eaton and John Coffee, the United States commissioners, to treat with said Chickasaw nation being present and assenting thereto); that the lease heretofore made, be so changed, that the rent therein

agreed to be paid is entirely released and discharged, from the date of said lease, together with all claim arising on account of the same.

And it is now agreed, that said lease shall remain, as heretofore made, with this alteration: that two thousand dollars shall be paid to said Colbert and Brown, trustees as aforesaid, for the Chickasaw nation: to wit: five hundred dollars now in hand; five hundred dollars on the first day of October one thousand-eight hundred and thirty-one; and one thousand dollars on the first day of October one thousand eight hundred and thirty-two. And it is further agreed, in consideration of said alteration of said original contract and lease, herein made and agreed upon; and the said Robert P. Currin, for himself and the said William B. Lewis, for each and for both, he having full authority to act in-the premises, will annually pay to said trustees, four bushels of salt, or the value thereof, as they and the nation may agree to and direct.

In testimony whereof, and in the presence of the commissioners, appointed to treat with the Chickasaw nation of people, on the part of the United States, the parties respectively have hereto set their hands and affixed their seals, this first day of September, one thousand eight hundred and thirty.

Jn. H. Eaton, Secty. of War.
Jno. Coffee.

Levi Colbert, his x mark, George Colbert, his x mark, James Colbert, his x mark, Wm. McGilvery, his x mark, Isaac Alberson, his x mark, James Bown, his x mark, To pul ka, his x mark, Ish te ki yo ka tubbe, his x mark, Ish te he cha, his x mark, Im me houl te tubbe, his x mark, In hei yo chit tubbe, his x mark, Ish te ya tubbe, his x mark, Ah to ko wa, his x mark, Ook la na ya ubbe, his x mark, Im mo la tubbe, his x mark, Hush tata be, his x mark, In no wake che, his x mark, Oh he cubbe, his x mark, Kin hu che, his x mark, J.W. Lish.

Signed in presence of us: Preston Hay, secretary, Benj. Reynolds, U. S. agent, Benjamin Love, as interpreter.

TREATY WITH THE SENECA {1831, Feb. 28}
Proclamation, Mar 24, 1831.

Articles of agreement and conventions, made and concluded at the City of Washington, on the twenty-eighth day of February, in the year of our Lord, one thousand eight hundred and thirty-one, by and between James B. Gardiner, specially appointed Commissioner on the part of the United States, of the one part, and the undersigned, principal Chiefs and Warriors of the Seneca tribe of Indians, residing on the Sandusky river in the State of Ohio, on the part of said tribe, of the other part; for the cession the lands now owned and occupied by the said tribe of Indians, lying on the waters of the Sandusky river, and situate within the territorial limits of the organized counties of Seneca and Sandusky, in said State of Ohio.

WHEREAS the tribe of Seneca Indians, residing on Sandusky River, in the State of Ohio, have earnestly solicited the President of the United States to negotiate with them, for an exchange of the lands, now owned and occupied by them, for lands of the United States, west of the river Mississippi, and for the removal and permanent settlement of said tribe: Therefore, in order to carry into effect the aforesaid objects, the following articles have been agreed upon:

ARTICLE 1. The Seneca tribe of Indians, in consideration of the stipulations herein made on the part of the United States, do forever cede., release and quit claim to the United States, the lands granted to them, by patent, in fee simple, by the sixth section of the Treaty, made at the foot of the Rapids of the Miami River of Lake Erie, on the twenty-ninth day of September, in the year 1817, containing thirty thousand acres, and described as follows: "beginning on the Sandusky river at the lower corner of the section granted to William Spicer; thence down the river on the east side, with the meanders thereof at high water mark, to a point east of the mouth of Wolf Creek; thence, and from the beginning, east, so far that a north line will include the quantity of thirty thousand acres."

And said tribe also cede, as aforesaid, one other tract of land, reserved for the use of the said Senecas, by the second article of the treaty, made at St. Mary's, in the State of Ohio, on the seventeenth day of September, in the year 1818, which tract is described in said treaty as follows: "Ten thousand acres of land, to be laid off on the east side of the Sandusky river, adjoining the south side of their reservation of thirty thousand acres, which begins on the Sandusky river, at the lower corner of William Spicer's section, and excluding therefrom the said William Spicer's section:" making, in the whole of this cession, forty thousand acres.

ARTICLE 2. In consideration of the cessions stipulated in the foregoing article; the United States agree to cause the said tribe of Senecas, consisting of about four hundred souls, to be removed in a convenient and suitable manner, to the western side of the Mississippi river; and will grant them, by patent, in fee simple, as long as they shall exist as a nation and remain on the same, a tract of land, situate on, and adjacent to the northern boundary of the lands heretofore granted to the Cherokee nation of Indians, and adjoining the boundary of the State of Missouri; which tract shall extend fifteen miles from east to west, and seven miles from north to south, containing about sixty-seven thousand acres, be the same more or less; for which the President of the United States shall cause letters patent to be issued, in due form of law, agreeably to the Act of the last session of Congress.

ARTICLE 3. The United States will defray the expenses of the removal of the said Senecas, and will moreover supply them with a sufficiency of wholesome provisions, to support them for one year, after their arrival at their new residence.

ARTICLE 4. Out of the first sales, to be made of the lands herein ceded by the Senecas, the United States will cause a grist mill, a saw mill, and a blacksmith shop to be erected on the lands herein granted to the Senecas, with all necessary tools, to be supported and kept in operation, at the expense of the United States, for the sole benefit of the said Senecas; and for these purposes, the United States will employ a miller and a blacksmith, for such term as the President of the United States, in his discretion, may think proper.

ARTICLE 5. As the Seneca Indians, on their removal, will stand in need of funds to make farms and erect houses; it is agreed that the United States will advance them six thousand dollars, in lieu of the improvements which they have made on the lands herein ceded to the United States; which sum shall be reimbursed from the sales of the lands ceded. An equitable distribution of this sum shall be made by the Chiefs, with the consent of the tribe, in general council assembled, to such individuals of the tribe, as, having left improvements, may be properly entitled to receive the same.

ARTICLE 6. The live stock, farming utensils, and other chattel property which the Senecas now own, and may not be able to take with them, shall be sold by some agent, to be appointed by the President; and the proceeds paid to the owners of such property, respectively.

ARTICLE 7. The expenses of the Chiefs, in coming to and remaining at Washington, and returning to Ohio, as well as the expenses and per diem pay of the native Interpreter accompanying them, shall be paid by the United States.

ARTICLE 8. The United States will expose to public sale, to the highest bidders, at such time and in such manner as the President may direct, the tracts of land herein ceded by the Seneca Indians: And, after deducting from the proceeds of such sale, the minimum price of the public lands; the cost of building the saw and grist mills and blacksmith shop for the Senecas; the cost of surveying the lands; and the sum of six thousand dollars, to be advanced in lieu of their present improvements: it is agreed that any balance which may remain, of the avails of the lands after sale as aforesaid, shall constitute a fund for the future exigencies of the tribe, on which the Government of the United States consent and agree to pay to the Chiefs of the nation, for the use and general benefit of the nation, annually, five per cent on said balance, as an annuity: And if, at any time hereafter, the Seneca Chiefs, by and with the advice and consent of their tribe in General Council assembled, shall make known to the President, their desire that the fund, thus to be created, should be dissolved and given to the tribe; the President shall cause the same to be paid over to them, in such manner as he may direct; provided he shall become satisfied of the propriety of so doing.

ARTICLE 9. It is agreed that any annuity, accruing to the Senecas, by former treaties, shall be paid to them at their intended residence, west of the Mississippi, under the direction of the President.

ARTICLE 10. The United States hereby agree to give to the Senecas, as presents, one hundred rifles, as soon as practicable, and four hundred blankets, for the use of the tribe, to be delivered to them at such time and place as may be directed by the Secretary of War. Also fifty ploughs, fifty hoes and fifty axes, will be given to the tribe, as aforesaid, to assist them in commencing farming.

ARTICLE 11. The Chiefs of the Senecas, being impressed with gratitude towards Henry C. Brish, their sub-agent, for his private advances of money and provisions, and numerous other acts of kindness towards them, as well as his extra services in coming with them to Washington; and having expressed a wish that a quarter section of a hundred and sixty acres of the lands ceded by them, should be granted to him in consideration thereof: the same is hereby granted to him and his heirs to be located under the direction of the President the United States.

ARTICLE 12. The lands granted by this Agreement and Convention to the Seneca tribe of Indians shall not be sold or ceded by them, except to the United States.

ARTICLE 13. It is communicated by the Chiefs here, that, in Council, before they left home, it was agreed by the tribe, that, for their services in coming to the City of Washington, each should receive one hundred dollars, to be paid by said tribe: At the request of said Chiefs, it is agreed that the United States will advance the amount, to wit: five hundred dollars, to be hereafter reimbursed from the sale of their lands in Ohio.

In testimony whereof, the parties respectively have this twenty-eighth of February signed the same and affixed their seals.

James B. Gardiner, Cornstick, his x mark, Small Cloud Spicer, his x mark, Seneca Steel, his x mark, Hard Hickory, his x mark, Capt. Good Hunter, his x mark.

Signed in presence of: Henry C. Brish, Sub-agent, George Herron, Interpreter

TREATY WITH THE SENECA, ETC. {1831, July 20}
Proclamation, Apr. 6, 1832.

Articles of agreement and convention, made and concluded at Lewistown, in the county of Logan, and State of Ohio, on the twentieth day of July, in the year of our Lord one thousand eight hundred and thirty-one, by and between James B. Gardiner, specially appointed commissioner on the part of the United States, and John McElvain, Indian agent for the Wyandots, Senecas and Shawnees, on the one part, and the undersigned principal chiefs and warriors of the mixed band of Senecas and Shawnee Indians residing at and around the said Lewistown, of the other part, for the cession of the lands now owned and occupied by said band, lying on the waters of the Great Miami river, and within the territorial limits of the organized county of Logan, in said State of Ohio.

WHEREAS the President of the United States, under the authority of the Act of Congress, approved May 28th, 1830, has appointed a special commissioner to confer with the different Indian tribes residing within the constitutional limits of the State of Ohio, and to offer for their acceptance the provisions contained in the before recited act. And whereas the mixed band or tribes of Seneca and Shawnee Indians residing at and around Lewistown in said State have expressed their perfect assent to the conditions of said act, and their willingness and anxiety to remove west of the Mississippi river, in order to obtain a more permanent and advantageous home for themselves and their posterity: Therefore, in order to carry into effect the aforesaid objects, the following articles have been agreed upon by the aforesaid contracting parties; which, when approved by the President and ratified by the Senate of the United States, shall be mutually binding upon the United States and the said Seneca and Shawnee Indians.

ARTICLE 1. The Seneca and Shawnee Indians, residing at and around Lewistown in the State of Ohio, in consideration of the stipulations herein made on the part of the United States, do for ever cede, release and quit claim to the United States, the lands granted to them by patent in fee simple by the sixth article of the treaty made at the foot of the rapids of the Miami river of Lake Erie, on the twenty-ninth day of September, in the year 1817, containing forty-eight square miles, and described in said treaty as follows:" Beginning at the intersection of the line run by Charles Roberts in the year one thousand eight hundred and twelve, from the source of the Little Miami river, to the source of the Scioto river, in pursuance of instructions from the commissioners appointed on the part of the United States, to establish the western boundary of the Virginia military reservation, with the Indian boundary line established by the treaty of Greenville in one thousand seven hundred and ninety-five from the crossings above Fort Lawrence to Loramie's store, and to run from such intersection, northerly, with the first mentioned line, so as to include the quantity as

209

nearly in a square form as practicable, after excluding the section of land granted to Nancy Stewart."

And the said Senecas and Shawnees also cede to the United States, in manner aforesaid, one other tract of land, reserved for them by the second article of the treaty made at St. Mary's, in Ohio, on the seventeenth of September, in the year 1818, which tract is described in said treaty as follows: "Eight thousand nine hundred and sixty acres, to be laid off adjoining the west line of the reserve of forty-eight square miles at Lewistown."

ARTICLE 2. In consideration of the cessions stipulated in the foregoing article, the United States agree to cause the said band of Senecas and Shawnees, consisting of about three hundred souls, to be removed in a convenient and suitable manner to the western side of the Mississippi river, and will grant by patent, in fee simple to them and their heirs forever, as long as they shall exist as a nation and remain on the same, a tract of land to contain sixty thousand acres, to be located under the direction of the President of the United States, contiguous to the lands granted to the Senecas of Sandusky by the treaty made with them at the City of Washington, on the 28th of February 1831, and the Cherokee settlementsthe east line of said tract shall be within two miles of the west line of the lands granted to the Senecas of Sandusky, and the south line shall be within two miles of the north line of the lands held by the Cherokees and said two miles between the aforesaid lines, shall serve as a common passway between the before mentioned tribes to prevent them from intruding upon the lands of each other.

ARTICLE 3. The United States will defray the expense of the removal of the said Senecas and Shawnees, and will moreover supply them with a sufficiency of good and wholesome provisions to support them for one year after their arrival at their new residence.

ARTICLE 4. Out of the first sales to be made of the lands herein ceded by the said Senecas and Shawnees, the United States will cause a saw-mill and a blacksmith shop to be erected on the lands granted to the said Indians west of the Mississippi, with all necessary machinery and tools, to be supported and kept in operation at the expense of the [329] United States, for the mutual and sole benefit of the said Senecas and Shawnees, and the United States will employ a blacksmith to execute the necessary work for the said Indians for such time as the President of the United States, in his discretion may think proper.

ARTICLE 5. In lieu of the improvements which have been made on the lands herein ceded; it is agreed that the United States shall advance to the said Senecas and Shawnees the sum of six thousand dollars, to be reimbursed from the sales of the lands herein ceded by them to the United States. A fair and equitable distribution of this sum shall be made by the Chiefs of the said Senecas and

Shawnees, with the consent of their tribes in general council assembled, to such individuals of the tribes as, having left improvements, may be properly entitled to the same.

ARTICLE 6. The live stock, farming utensils, and other chattel property, which the said Senecas and Shawnees now own, and may not be able to carry with them, shall be sold under the superintendence of some suitable person appointed by the Secretary of War, and the proceeds paid over to owners of such property respectively.

ARTICLE 7. The said Senecas and Shawnees shall be removed to their new residence under the care and protection of some competent and proper person, friendly to them and acquainted with their habits, manners and customs; and the chiefs of the said tribes shall have the privilege of nominating such person to the President, who, if approved of by him, shall have charge of their conveyance.

ARTICLE 8. The United States will expose to public sale to the highest bidders, in the manner of selling the public lands, the tracts of land herein ceded by the Senecas and Shawnees; and after deducting from the proceeds of such sale the sum of seventy cents per acre, exclusive of the cost of surveying the lands, the cost of the saw mill and blacksmith shop, and the sum of six thousand dollars to be advanced in lieu of the improvements on the ceded lands; it is agreed that any balance which may remain of the lands after sale as aforesaid, shall constitute a fund for the future necessities of said tribes, on which the Government of the United States agree and consent to pay to the chiefs for the use and general benefit of the said tribes annually, five per cent. on the amount of the said balance as an annuity. Said fund to be continued during the pleasure of Congress, unless the chiefs of the said tribes, by and with the consent of the whole of their people in general council assembled, should desire that the fund thus to be created, should be dissolved and paid over to them, in which case the President shall cause the same to be paid over, if in his discretion he shall think the happiness and prosperity of said tribes would be promoted thereby.

ARTICLE 9. It is agreed that any annuities accruing to the said Senecas and Shawnees by former treaties shall be paid to them at their intended residence west of the Mississippi under the direction of the President.

ARTICLE 10. In consideration of the former good conduct and friendly disposition of the aforesaid band of Senecas and Shawnees towards the American Government, and as an earnest of the kind feelings, and good wishes of their great father for the future welfare and happiness of themselves and their posterity, it is agreed that the United States will give them as presents, the following articles, to wit: one hundred blankets, twenty ploughs, one hundred hoes,

211

fifty axes, ten rifles, twenty sets of horse gears, and Russia sheeting sufficient to make forty tents; the whole to be delivered to them as soon as practicable after their arrival at their new residence, except the blankets and the Russia sheeting for the tents, which shall be given at the time of their setting out on their journey; all of said articles to be distributed by the chiefs according to the just claims and necessities of their people.

ARTICLE 11. The lands granted by this agreement and convention to the said band of Senecas and Shawnees, shall not be sold or ceded by them except to the United States. And the United States guarantee that said lands shall never be within the bounds of any State or Territory, nor subject to the laws thereof; and further that the President of the United States will cause said tribe to be protected at their new residence against all interruption or disturbance from any other tribe or nation of Indians, or from any other person or persons whatever; and he shall have the same care and superintendence over them in the country to which they design to remove, that he has heretofore had over them at their present place of residence.

ARTICLE 12. At the request of the chiefs of the Senecas and Shawnees, there is granted to James McPherson, one half section of land to contain three hundred and twenty acres, to be laid off in such part of the lands here ceded as he may select, so that the said half section shall adjoin the land heretofore donated to him near the southeast corner of that part of the lands herein ceded which was assigned to the Shawnees by the second article of the treaty made at St. Mary's, on the 17th of September, 1818. And this grant is made in consideration of the sincere attachment of the said chiefs and their people for the said James McPherson, who has lived among them and near them for forty years, and from whom they have received numerous and valuable services and benefits; and also in consideration of the able and candid manner in which he has explained to the Indians the policy of the United States in regard to the future welfare and permanent settlement of the Indian tribes.

ARTICLE 13. At the request of the aforesaid chiefs, there is hereby granted to Henry H. McPherson, an adopted son of their nation, a half section of land, to contain three hundred and twenty acres, to be added to a half section of land granted to him by the said chiefs on the 20th day of March 1821, and approved by the President of the United States, which is to be so laid off as to enlarge the last mentioned grant to a square section.

ARTICLE 14. At the special request of the aforesaid chiefs, one quarter section of land, to contain one hundred and sixty acres, is hereby granted to Martin Lane their interpreter, who married a quarter blood Indian woman, and has lived a long time among the Senecas. The said quarter section is to be located under the direction of the President of the United States.

ARTICLE 15. It is understood and agreed by the present contracting parties that the words, "the lands heretofore donated to him" in the twelfth article of this treaty, have direct and sole reference to a verbal donation heretofore made by the said Senecas and Shawnees to the said McPherson, and that the intention is that this treaty should confirm the former as well as the latter grant, so that the said McPherson is entitled to one whole section to be located in the southeast corner of the Shawnee part of the lands herein ceded as aforesaid.

In testimony hereof, the present contracting parties respectively have signed their hands, and affixed their seals, the day and year aforesaid, at Pleasant Plains, near Lewistown, in the State of Ohio.

James B. Gardiner, John McElvain,
Methomea, or Civil John, his x mark, Skilleway, or Robbin, his x mark, Totala Chief, or John Young, his x mark, Pewyache, his x mark, Mingo Carpenter, his x mark, John Jackson, his x mark, Quashacaugh, or Little Lewis, his x mark, James McDonnell, his x mark, Honede, or Civil John's Son, his x mark, Run Fast, his x mark, Yankee Bill, his x mark, Cold Water, his x mark, John Sky, his x mark,

Signed, sealed, and delivered in presence of: David Robb, Sub-Agent, James McPherson, United States Interpreter, H. E. Spencer, Wm. Rianhard, John Shelby, Alexander Thomson, H. B. Strother, Benj. S. Brown, Joseph Parks, his x mark, United States Interpreter, N. Z. McCulloch, D. M. Workman, R. Patterson, A. O. Spencer, Jas. Stewart, Stephen Giffin.

I do hereby certify that each and every article of the foregoing convention and agreement, was carefully explained and fully interpreted by me to the chiefs, head men and warriors who have signed the same.

Martin Lane, United States Interpreter, W. B. Lewis, Henry Toland, P. G. Randolph, R. M. Gavock, Leml., onelson, Leml. Smith, R.P. Currin, Jos. H. Fry, James H. Wilson, J.R. Davis.

TREATY WITH THE OTTAWA {1831, Aug. 30}
Proclamation, April 6, 1832.

Articles of agreement and convention made and concluded this thirtieth day of August, in the year of our Lord one thousand eight hundred and thirty-one, by and between James B. Gardiner, specially appointed commissioner on the part of the United States, on the one part, and the chiefs, head men and warriors of the band of Ottoway Indians residing within the State of Ohio on the other part, for a cession of the several tracts of land now held and occupied by said Indians within said State, by reservations made under the treaty concluded at Detroit on the 17th day of November, 1807, and the treaty made at the foot of the rapids of the Miami river of Lake Erie, on the 29th of September, 1817.

WHEREAS the President of the United States, under the authority of the act of Congress, approved May 28, 1830, has appointed a special commissioner to confer with the different Indian tribes residing within the constitutional limits of the State of Ohio, and to offer for their acceptance the provisions of the before mentioned act: And whereas the band of Ottoways residing on Blanchard's fork of the Great Auglaize river, and on the Little Auglaize river at Oquanoxie's village, have expressed their consent to the conditions of said act, and their willingness to remove west of the Mississippi, in order to obtain a more permanent and advantageous home for themselves and their posterity:

Therefore, in order to carry into effect the aforesaid objects, the following articles of convention have been agreed upon, by the aforesaid contracting parties, which, when ratified by the President of the United States, by and with the consent of the Senate thereof, shall be mutually binding upon the United States and the aforesaid band of Ottoway Indians.

ARTICLE 1. The band of Ottoway Indians, residing on Blanchard's fork of the great Auglaize river, and at Oquanoxa's village on the Little Auglaize river, in consideration of the stipulations herein made on the part of the United States, do forever cede, release and quit claim to the United States, the lands reserved to them by the last clause of the sixth article of the treaty made at the foot of the Rapids of the Miami of the Lake on the 29th of September, 1817; which clause is in the following words: "There shall be reserved for the use of the Ottoway Indians, but not granted to them, a tract of land on Blanchard's fork of the Great Auglaize river, to contain five miles square, the center of which tract is to be where the old trace crosses the said fork; and one other tract, to contain three miles square on the Little Auglaize river, to include Oquanoxa's village," making in said cession twenty-one thousand seven hundred and sixty acres.

ARTICLE 2. The chiefs, head men and warriors of the band of Ottoway Indians, residing at and near the places called Roche de Boeuf and Wolf rapids, on the Miami river of Lake Erie, and within the State of Ohio, wishing to become parties to this convention, and not being willing, at this time, to stipulate for their removal west of the Mississippi; do hereby agree, in consideration of the stipulations herein made for them on the part of the United States, to cede, release and forever quit claim to the United States the following tracts of land, reserved to them by the treaty made at Detroit on the 17th day of November, 1807, to wit, the tract of six miles square above Roche de Boeuf, to include the village where Tondagonie (or Dog) formerly lived; and also three miles square at the Wolf rapids aforesaid, which was substituted for the three miles square granted by the said treaty of Detroit to the said Ottoways to include Presque Isle," but which could not be granted as stipulated in said treaty of Detroit, in consequence of its collision with the grant of twelve miles square to the United States by the treaty of Greenville; making in the whole cession made by this article twenty-eight thousand one hundred and fifty-seven acres, which is exclusive of a grant made to Yellow Hair (or Peter Minor) by the 8th article of the treaty at the foot of the Rapids of Miami, on the 29th of September, 1817, and for which said Minor holds a patent from the General Land Office for 643 acres.

ARTICLE 3. In consideration of the cessions made in the first article of this convention, the United States agree to cause the band of Ottoways residing on Blanchard's fork, and at Oquanoxa's village, as aforesaid, consisting of about two hundred souls., to be removed, in a convenient and suitable manner, to the western side of the Mississippi river; and will grant, by patent in fee simple, to then, and their heirs for ever, as long as they shall exist as a nation, and remain upon the same, a tract of land to contain thirty-four thousand acres, to be located adjoining the south or west line of the reservation equal to fifty miles square, granted to the Shawnees of Missouri and Ohio on the Kanzas river and its branches, by the treaty made at St. Louis, November 7th, 1825.

ARTICLE 4. The United States will defray the expense of the removal of the said band of Ottoways, and will moreover supply them with a sufficiency of good and wholesome provisions to support them for one year after their arrival at their new residence.

ARTICLE 5. In lieu of the improvements which have been made on the lands ceded by the first article of this convention, it is agreed that the United States shall advance to the Ottoways of Blanchard's fork and Oquanoxa's village, the sum of two thousand dollars, to be reimbursed from the sales of the lands ceded by the said first article. And it is expressly understood that this sun, is not to be paid until the said Ottoways arrive at their new residence, and that it is for the purpose of enabling them to erect houses and open farms for their accommodation and subsistence in their new country. A fair and equitable distribution of this sum shall be made by the chiefs of the said Ottoways, with the consent of their people, in general council assembled, to such individuals of their band as may have made improvements on the lands ceded by the first article of this convention, and may be properly entitled to the same.

ARTICLE 6. The farming utensils, live stock and other chattel property, which the said Ottoways of Blanchard's fork and Oquanoxa's village now own, shall be sold, under the superintendence of some suitable person appointed by the Secretary of War; and the proceeds paid to the owners of such property respectively.

ARTICLE 7. The United States will expose to sale to the highest bidder, in the manner of selling the public lands, the tracts ceded by the first article of this convention, and after deducting from the proceeds of such sales the sum of seventy cents per acre, exclusive of the cost of surveying, and the sum of two thousand dollars advanced in lieu of improvements; it is agreed that the balance, or so much thereof as may be necessary, shall be hereby guaranteed for the payment of the debts, which the said Ottoways of Blanchard's fork, and Oquanoxa's village may owe in the State of Ohio and the Territory of Michigan, and agree to be due by them, as provided in the sixteenth article of this convention; and any surplus of the proceeds of said lands, which may still remain, shall be vested by the President in Government stock, and five per cent. thereon shall be paid to the said Ottoways of Blanchard's fork and Oquanoxa's village, as an annuity during the pleasure of Congress.

ARTICLE 8. It is agreed that the said band of Ottoways of Blanchard's fork and Oquanoxa's village, shall receive, at their new residence, a fair proportion of the annuities due to their nation by former treaties, which shall be apportioned under the direction of the Secretary of War, according to their actual numbers.

ARTICLE 9. The lands granted by this agreement and convention to the said band of Ottoways residing at Blanchard's fork and Oquanoxa's village shall not be sold nor ceded by them, except to the United States. And the United States guarantee that said lands shall never be within the bounds of any State or territory, nor subject to the laws thereof, and further, that the President of the United States will cause said band to be protected at their new residence, against all interruption or disturbance from any other tribe or nation of Indians and from any other person or persons whatever: and he shall have the same care and superintendence over them in the country to which they design to remove, that he now has at their present residence.

ARTICLE 10. As an evidence of the good will and kind feeling of the people of the United States towards the said band of Ottoways of Blanchard's fork and Oquanoxa's village; it is agreed that the following articles shall be given them, as presents, to wit: eighty blankets, twenty-five rifle guns, thirty-five axes, twelve ploughs, twenty sets of horse gears, and Russian sheeting sufficient for tents for their whole band; the whole to be delivered according to the discretion of the Secretary of War.

ARTICLE 11. In consideration of the cessions made in the second article of this convention by the chiefs, head men and warriors of the band of Ottoways residing at Roche de Boeuf and Wolf rapids, it is agreed that the United States will grant to said band by patent in fee simple, forty thousand acres of land, west of the Mississippi, adjoining the lands assigned to the Ottoways of Blanchard's fork and Oquanoxa's village, or in such other situation as they may select, on the unappropriated lands in the district of country designed for the emigrating Indians of the United States. And whenever the said band may think proper to accept of the above grant, and remove west of the Mississippi, the

United States agree that they shall be removed and subsisted by the Government in the same manner as is provided in this convention for their brethren of Blanchard's fork and Oquanoxa's village, and they shall receive like presents, in proportion to their actual numbers, under the direction of the Secretary of War. It is also understood and agreed that the said band, when they shall agree to remove west of the Mississippi, shall receive their proportion of the annuities due their nation by former treaties, and be entitled in every respect to the same privileges, advantages and protection, which are herein extended to their brethren and the other emigrating Indians of the State of Ohio.

ARTICLE 12. The lands ceded by the second article of this convention shall be sold by the United States to the highest bidder, in the manner of selling the public lands, and after deducting from the avails thereof seventy cents per acre, exclusive of the cost of surveying, the balance is hereby guaranteed to discharge such debts of the Ottoways residing on the river and bay of the Miami of Lake Erie, as they may herein acknowledge to be due, and wish to be paid. And whatever overplus may remain of the avails of said lands, after discharging their debts as aforesaid, shall be paid to them in money, provided they shall refuse to remove west of the Mississippi, and wish to seek some other home among their brethren in the Territory of Michigan. But should the said band agree to remove west of the Mississippi, then any over-plus which may remain to them, after paying their debts, shall be invested by the President, and five per centum paid to them as an annuity, as is provided for their brethren by this convention.

ARTICLE 13. At the request of the chiefs residing at Roche Boeuf and Wolf rapids, it is agreed that there shall be reserved for the use of Watt be ga kake (one of the chiefs) for three years only, from the signing of this convention, a section of land below and adjoining the section granted to and occupied by Yellow Hair or Peter Minor; and also there is reserved in like manner and for the term of three years, and no longer, for the use of Muck-qui-on-a, or Bearskin, one section and a half, below Wolf rapids, and to include his present residence and improvements. And it is also agreed that the said Bearskin shall have the occupancy of a certain small island in the Maumee river, opposite his residence, where he now raises corn, which island belongs to the United States, and is now unsold; but the term of this occupancy is not guaranteed for three years; but only so long as the President shall think proper to reserve the same from sale. And it is further understood, that any of the temporary reservations made by this article, may be surveyed and sold by the United States, subject to the occupancy of three years, hereby granted to the aforesaid Indians.

ARTICLE 14. At the request of the chiefs of Roche de Boeuf and Wolf rapids, there is hereby granted to Hiram Thebeault (a half blooded Ottoway) a quarter section of land, to contain one hundred and sixty acres and to include his present improvements at the Bear rapids of the Miami of the Lake. Also, one quarter section of land, to contain like quantity, to William McNabb, (a half blooded Ottoway) to adjoin the quarter section granted to Hiram Thebeault. In surveying the above reservations no greater front is to be given on the river, than would properly belong to said quarter sections, in the common manner of surveying the public lands.

ARTICLE 15. At the request of the chiefs of Roche de Boeuf and Wolf rapids, there is granted to the children of Yellow Hair, (or Peter Minor) one half section of land, to contain three hundred and twenty acres, to adjoin the north line of the section of land now held by said Peter. Minor, under patent from the President of the United States, bearing date the 24th of November, 1827, and the lines are not to approach nearer than one mile to the Miami river of the Lake.

ARTICLE 16. It is agreed by the chiefs of Blanchard's fork and Oquanoxa's village, and the chiefs of Roche de Boeuf and Wolf rapids, jointly, that they are to pay out of the surplus proceeds of the several tracts herein ceded by them, equal proportions of the claims against them by John E. Hunt, John Hollister, Robert A. Forsythe, Payne C. Parker, Peter Minor, Theodore E. Phelps, Collister Haskins and S. and P. Carlan. The chiefs aforesaid acknowledge the claim of John E. Hunt to the amount of five thousand six hundred dollars; the claim of John Hollister to the amount of five thousand six hundred dollars; the claim of Robert A. Forsythe to the amount of seven thousand five hundred and twenty-roar dollars, in which is included the claims assigned to said Forsythe by Isaac Hull, Samuel Vance, A. Peltier, Oscar White and Antoine Lepoint.
They also allow the claim of Payne C. Parker to the amount of five hundred dollars; the claim of Peter Minor to the amount of one thousand dollars; the claim of Theodore E. Phelps to the amount of three hundred dollars; the claim of Collister Haskins to the amount of fifty dollars, but the said Haskins claims fifty dollars more as his proper demand: and the claim of S. and P. Carlan to the amount of three hundred and ninety-eight dollars and twenty-five cents. The aforesaid chiefs also allow the claim of Joseph Laronger to the amount of two hundred dollars, and the claim of Daniel Lakin to the amount of seventy dollars. Notwithstanding the above acknowledgments and allowances, it is expressly understood and agreed by the respective parties to this compact, that the several claims in this article, and the items which compose the same, shall be submitted to the strictest scrutiny and examination of the Secretary of War, and the accounting officers of the Treasury Department, and such amount only shall be allowed as may be found just and true.

ARTICLE 17. On the ratification of this convention, the privileges of every description, granted to the Ottoway nation within the State of Ohio, by the treaties under which they hold the reservations of land herein ceded, shall forever cease and determine.

ARTICLE 18. Whenever the deficiency of five hundred and eighty dollars, which accrued in the annuities of the Ottoways for 1830, shall be paid, the parties to this convention, residing on Blanchard's fork and Oquanoxa's village, shall receive their fair and equitable portion of the same, either at their present or intended residence.

ARTICLE 19. The chiefs signing this convention, also agree, in addition to the claims allowed in the sixteenth article thereof, that they owe John Anderson two hundred dollars; and Francis Lavoy two hundred dollars.

ARTICLE 20. It is agreed that there shall be allowed to Nau-on-quai-quc-zhick, one hundred dollars, out of the surplus fund accruing from the sales of the lands herein ceded, in consequence of his not owing any debts, and having his land sold, to pay the debts of his brethren.

In testimony whereof, the aforesaid parties to this convention, have hereunto set their hands and seals at the Indian reserve on the Miami bay of lake Erie, the day and year above written.

James B. Gardiner,

Ar-pm-nai-wau, his x mark, O-quai naas-a, his x mark, Os-cha-no, or Charlo, his x mark, Quacint, his x mark, Waw-ba-ga-cake, his x mark, Che-cauk, his x mark, Peton-o-quet, his x mark, Oshaw-wa-non, his x mark, Pe-nais-we, his x mark, Nau-qua-ga-sheek, his x mark, Pe-nais-won-quet, his x mark, Pe-she-keinee, his x mark, Cum-chaw, (Blanchard's fork) his x mark, Cum-chaw, (Wolf rapids) his x mark, Sus-sain, his x mark, Ca-ba-yaw, his x mark, O-sho-quene, his x mark, Muc-co-tai-pee-nai-see, his x mark, O-sage, his x mark, Pan-tee, his x mark, Me-sau-kee, his x mark, O-mus-se-nau, his x mark, Non-dai-wau, his x mark, E-au-vainee, his x mark,

Signed and sealed in presence of:

Wm. Walker, Secretary to Commissioner, R. A. Forsyth, Sub. Agent of Indian Affairs, Levi S. Humphrey, James H. Forsyth, William Wilson, Henry Conner, Sub-Agent, John Anderson, John McDouell, Dan. B. Miller, Lambert Cauchois, Geo. B. Knaggs, J. J. Godfroy.

I do hereby certify that each article of the foregoing convention was fairly interpreted and fully explained by me to the chiefs, head men, and warriors, who have signed the same.

Henry Conner, Interpreter.

TREATY WITH THE WYANDOT {1832, Jan. 19}
Proclamation, Apr. 6, 1832.

Articles of agreement and convention made and concluded at McCutch-
eonsville, Crawford county, Ohio, on the nineteenth day of January, 1832, by
and between James B. Gardiner, specially appointed commissioner on the part
of the United States, and the Chiefs Headmen and Warriors of the band of
Wyandots, residing at the Big Spring in said county of Crawford, and owning a
reservation of 16,000 acres at that place.

WHEREAS the said band of Wyandots have become fully convinced that,
whilst they remain in their present situation in the State of Ohio, in the vicinity
of a white population, which is continually increasing and crowding around
them, they cannot prosper and be happy, and the morals of many of their people
will be daily becoming more and more vitiatedAnd understanding that the
Government of the United States is willing to purchase the reservation of land
on which they reside, and-for that purpose have deputed the said James B. Gardiner as special commissioner to treat for a cession for the same.

Therefore, to effect the aforesaid objects, the said Chiefs, Headmen and Warriors, and the said James B. Gardiner, have this day entered into and agreed upon
the following articles of convention.

ARTICLE 1.   The band of Wyandots residing at the Big Spring in the county
of Crawford, and State of Ohio, do hereby forever cede and relinquish to the
United States the reservation of sixteen thousand acres of land, granted to them
by the second article of the treaty made at St. Mary's, on the seventeenth day of
September, eighteen hundred and eighteen, which grant is in the following
words, to wit: "There shall be reserved for the use of the Wyandots residing at
Solomon's town and on Blanchard's fork sixteen thousand acres of land, to be
laid off in a square form, on the head of Blanchard's fork, the centre of which
shall he at the Big spring, on the road leading from Upper Sandusky to Fort
Findlay."

ARTICLE 2.   The United States stipulate with the said band of Wyandots that,
as soon as practicable after the ratification of this treaty, the aforesaid tract of
sixteen thousand acres shall be surveyed into sections and put into market and
sold in the ordinary manner of selling the public lands of the United States; and
when the same shall be sold, or as soon as any part thereof shall be disposed of,
(be the price received therefore more or less) there shall be paid to the chiefs,
headmen and warriors, signing this treaty, for the benefit of all the said band of
Wyandots, the sum of one dollar and twenty-five cents per acre for each and
every acre so sold or for sale. The said price shall be paid in silver, and in the
current coin of the United States.

ARTICLE 3. For the improvements now made upon said reservation the United States agree to pay a fair valuation in money, according to the appraisement of Joseph McCutcheon, Esq. (or such person as the Secretary of War may depute for that purpose) and an appraiser to be chosen by the said band of Wyandots. And in case the said appraisers shall not be able to agree upon any of their valuations, they shall call to their assistance some competent citizen of the county of Crawford.

ARTICLE 4. There shall (be) reserved for Roe-nu-nas, one of the oldest chiefs of said band, one half section, to contain three hundred and twenty acres, and to include the improvements where he now lives.

ARTICLE 5. It is expressly understood between the present contracting parties, that the said band of Wyandots may, as they think proper, remove to Canada, or to the river Huron in Michigan, where they own a reservation of land, or to any place they may obtain a right or privilege from others Indians to go.

ARTICLE 6. (Rejected.)

ARTICLE 7. Inasmuch as the band of Wyandots, herein treating, have separated themselves from the Wyandots at Upper Sandusky and on the Sandusky plains, they ask of the General Government that there may be a special sub-agent and protector appointed for them whilst they remain in the State of Ohio, and they respectfully recommend Joseph McCutcheon, Esq. of the county of Crawford, as a fit and proper person to act in such capacity; and that he may have the power to employ such interpreter as he may think proper in his intercourse with said band.

The aforesaid articles of agreement shall be mutually binding upon the present contracting parties, when ratified by the President of the United States, by and with the consent of the Senate thereof.

J. B. Gardiner,
Roe-nu-nas, his x mark, Bear-skin, his x mark, Shi-a-wa, or John Solomon, his x mark, John McLean, his x mark, Matthew Grey Eyes, his x mark, Isaac Driver, his x mark, John D. Brown, Alex. Clarke. [341]

Done in presence of: C. Clarke, Secretary to the Commissioner, Joseph McCutcheon, justice of the peace in the county of Crawford, Ohio, John C. Dewit, Richard Reynolds, G. W. Sampson.

EXPLANATION. In the first draft of this treaty, provision was made for the removal of the band west of the Mississippi, but they refused to accept of a grant of land, or to remove there, and the articles having relation thereto were

accordingly omitted. It was therefore necessary to omit the 6th article; and circumstances did not admit of time to remodel and copy the whole treaty.
J. B. GARDINER, Special Commissioner, &c.

TREATY WITH THE CREEKS {1832, Mar. 24}
Proclamation, Apr. 4, 1832.

Articles of a treaty made at the City of Washington between Lewis Cass, thereto specially authorized by the President of the United States, and the Creek tribe of Indians.

ARTICLE 1.   The Creek tribe of Indians cede to the United States all their land, East of the Mississippi river.

ARTICLE 2.   The United States engage to survey the said land as soon as the same can be conveniently done, after the ratification of this treaty, and when the same is surveyed to allow ninety principal Chiefs of the Creek tribe to select one section each, and every other head of a Creek family to select one half section each, which tracts shall be reserved from sale for their use for the term of five years, unless sooner disposed of by them. A census of these persons shall be taken under the direction of the President and the selections shall be made so as to include the improvements of each person within his selection, if the same can be so made, and if not, then all the persons belonging to the same town, entitled to selections, and who cannot make the same, so as to include their improvements, shall take them in one body in a proper form. And twenty sections shall be selected, under the direction of the President for the orphan children of the Creeks, and divided and retained or sold for their benefit as the President may direct. Provided however that no selections or locations under this treaty shall be so made as to include the agency reserve.

ARTICLE 3. These tracts may be conveyed by the persons selecting the same, to any other persons for a fair consideration, in such manner as the President may direct. The contract shall be certified by some person appointed for that purpose by the President, but shall not be valid till the President approves the same. A title shall be given by the United States on the completion of the payment.

ARTICLE 4. At the end of five years, all the Creeks entitled to these selections, and desirous of remaining, shall receive patents therefor in fee simple, from the United States.

ARTICLE 5. All intruders upon the country hereby ceded shall be removed therefrom in the same manner as intruders may be removed by law from other public land until the country is surveyed, and the selections made; excepting however from this provision those white persons who have made their own improvements, and not expelled the Creeks from theirs. Such persons may remain till their crops are gathered. After the country is surveyed and the selections made, this article shall not operate upon that part of it not included in such selections. But [342] intruders shall, in the manner before described, be removed from these selections for the term of five years from the ratification of this treaty, or until the same are conveyed to white persons.

ARTICLE 6. Twenty-nine sections in addition to the foregoing may be located, and patents for the same shall then issue to those persons, being Creeks, to whom the same may be assigned by the Creek tribe. But whenever the grantees of these tracts possess improvements, such tracts shall be so located as to include the improvements, and as near as may be in the centre. And there shall also be granted by patent to Benjamin Marshall, one section of land, to include his improvements on the Chatahoochee river, to be bounded for one mile in a direct line along the said river, and to run back for quantity. There shall also be granted to Joseph Bruner a colored man, one half section of land, for his services as an interpreter.

ARTICLE 7. All the locations authorized by this treaty, with the exception of that of Benjamin Marshall shall be made in conformity with the lines of the surveys; and the Creeks relinquish all claim for improvements.

ARTICLE 8. An additional annuity of twelve thousand dollars shall be paid to the Creeks for the term of five years, and thereafter the said annuity shall be reduced to ten thousand dollars, and shall be paid for the term of fifteen years. All the annuities due to the Creeks shall be paid in such manner as the tribe may direct.

ARTICLE 9. For the purpose of paying certain debts due by the Creeks and to relieve them in their present distressed condition the sum of one hundred thousand dollars, shall be paid to the Creek tribe, as soon as may be after the ratification hereof, to be applied to the payment of their just debts, and then to their own relief, and to be distributed as they may direct, and which shall be in full consideration of all improvements.

ARTICLE 10. The sum of sixteen thousand dollars shall be allowed as a compensation to the delegation sent to this place, and for the payment of their expenses, and of the claims against them.

ARTICLE 11. The following claims shall be paid by the United States.
For ferries, bridges and causeways, three thousand dollars, provided that the same shall become the property of the United States.
For the payment of certain judgments obtained against the chiefs eight thousand five hundred and seventy dollars.

For losses for which they suppose the United States responsible, seven thousand seven hundred and ten dollars.
For the payment of improvements under the treaty of 1826 one thousand dollars.

The three following annuities shall be paid for life. To Tuske-hew-haw-Cusetaw two hundred dollars. To the Blind Uchu King one hundred dollars. To Neah Mico one hundred dollars.
There shall be paid the sum of fifteen dollars, for each person who has emigrated without expense to the United States, but the whole sum allowed under this provision shall not exceed fourteen hundred dollars.
There shall be divided among the persons, who suffered in consequence of being prevented from emigrating, three thousand dollars.

The land hereby ceded shall remain as a fund from which all the foregoing payments except those in the ninth and tenth articles shall be paid.

ARTICLE 12. The United States are desirous that the Creeks should remove to the country west of the Mississippi, and join their countrymen there; and for this purpose it is agreed, that as fast as the Creeks are prepared to emigrate, they shall be removed at the expense of the [343] United States, and shall receive subsistence while upon the journey, and for one year after their arrival at their new homesProvided however, that this article shall not be construed so as to compel any Creek Indian to emigrate, but they shall be free to go or stay, as they please.

ARTICLE 13. There shall also be given to each emigrating warrior a rifle, moulds, wiper and ammunition and to each family one blanket. Three thousand dollars, to be expended as the President may direct, shall be allowed for the term of twenty years for teaching their children. As soon as half their people emigrate, one blacksmith shall be allowed them, and another when two-thirds emigrate, together with one ton of iron and two hundred weight of steel annually for each blacksmith.-These blacksmiths shall be supported for twenty years.

ARTICLE 14. The Creek country west of the Mississippi shall be solemnly guarantied to the Creek Indians, not shall any State or Territory ever have a right to pass laws for the government of such Indians, but they shall be allowed to govern themselves, so far as may be compatible with the general jurisdiction which Congress may think proper to exercise over them. And the United States will also defend them from the unjust hostilities of other Indians, and will also as soon as the boundaries of the Creek country West of the Mississippi are ascertained, cause a patent or grant to be executed to the Creek tribe; agreeably to the 3d section of the act of Congress of May 2d, (28,) 1830, entitled "An act to provide for an exchange of lands with the Indians residing in any of the States, or Territories, and for their removal West of the Mississippi."

ARTICLE 15. This treaty shall be obligatory on the contracting parties, as soon as the same shall be ratified by the United States.
In testimony whereof, the said Lewis Cass, and the undersigned chiefs of the said tribe, have hereunto set their hands at the city of Washington, this 24th day of March, A. D. 1832.

Lewis Cass,
Opothleholo, his x mark, Tuchebatcheehadgo, his x mark, Eftcroatia, his x mark, Tuchebatche Micco, his x mark, Tomack Micco, his x mark, William McGilvery, his x mark, Benjamin Marshall.

In the presence of: Samuel Bell, William R. King, John Tipton, William Wilkins, C. C. Clay, J. Speight, Samuel W. Mardis, J. C. Isacks, John Crowell, I. A. Benjamin Marshall, Thomas Carr, John H. Brodnax, Interpreters.

TREATY WITH THE SEMINOLE {1832, May 9}
Proclamation, April 12, 1834.

The Seminole Indians, regarding with just respect, the solicitude manifested by the President of the United States for the improvement of their condition, by recommending a removal to a country more suitable to their habits and wants than the one they at present occupy in the Territory of Florida, are willing that their confidential chiefs, Jumper, Fuck-a-lus-ti-had-io, Charley Emartla, Coi-had-jo, Holati-Emartla, Ya-hadjo, Sans Jones, accompanied by their agent Major Phagan, and their faithful interpreter Abraham, should be sent at the expense of the United States as early as convenient to examine the country assigned to the Creeks west of the Mississippi river, and should they be satisfied with the character of that country, and of the favorable disposition of the Creeks to reunite with the Seminoles as one people; the articles of the compact and agreement, herein stipulated at Payne's landing on the Ocklewaha river, this ninth day of May, one thousand eight hundred and thirty-two, between James Gadsden, for and in behalf of the Government of the United States, and the undersigned chiefs and head-men for and in behalf of the Seminole Indians, shall be binding on the respective parties.

ARTICLE 1. The Seminole Indians relinquish to the United. States, all claim to the lands they at present occupy in the Territory of Florida, and agree to emigrate to the country assigned to the Creeks, west of the Mississippi river; it being understood that an additional extent of territory, proportioned to their numbers, will be added to the Creek country, and that the Seminoles will be received as a constituent part of the Creek nation, and be re-admitted to all the privileges as members of the same.

ARTICLE 2. For and in consideration of the relinquishment of claim in the first article of this agreement, and in full compensation for all the improvements, which may have been made on the lands thereby ceded; the United States stipulate to pay to the Seminole Indians, fifteen thousand, four hundred (15,400) dollars, to be divided among the chiefs and warriors of the several towns, in a ratio proportioned to their population, the respective proportions of each to be paid on their arrival in the country they consent to remove to; it being understood that their faithful interpreters Abraham and Cudjo shall receive two hundred dollars each of the above sum, in full remuneration for the improvements to be abandoned on the lands now cultivated by them.

ARTICLE 3. The United States agree to distribute as they arrive at their new homes in the Creek Territory, west of the Mississippi river, a blanket and a homespun frock, to each of the warriors, women and children of the Seminole tribe of Indians.

ARTICLE 4. The United States agree to extend the annuity for the support of a blacksmith, provided for in the sixth article of the treaty at Camp Moultrie for ten (10) years beyond the period therein stipulated, and in addition to the other annuities secured under that treaty; the United States agree to pay the sum of three thousand (3,000) dollars a year for fifteen (15) years, commencing after the removal of the whole tribe; these sums to be added to the Creek annuities and the whole amount to be so divided, that the chiefs and warriors of the Seminole Indians may receive their equitable proportion of the same as members of the Creek confederation

ARTICLE 5. The United States will take the cattle belonging to the Seminoles at the valuation of some discreet person to be appointed by the President, and the same shall be paid for in money to the respective owners, after their arrival at their new homes; or other cattle such as may be desired will be furnished them, notice being given through their agent of their wishes upon this subject, before their removal, that time may be afforded to supply the demand. [345]

ARTICLE 6. The Seminoles being anxious to be relieved from repeated vexatious demands for slaves and other property, alleged to have been stolen and destroyed by them, so that they may remove unembarrassed to their new homes; the United States stipulate to have the same property investigated, and to liquidate such as may be satisfactorily established, provided the amount does not exceed seven thousand (7,000) dollars.

ARTICLE 7. The Seminole Indians will remove within three (3) years after the ratification of this agreement, and the expenses of their removal shall be defrayed by the United States, and such subsistence shall also be furnished them for a term not exceeding twelve (12) months, after their arrival at their new residence; as in the opinion of the President, their numbers and circumstances may require, the emigration to commence as early as practicable in the year eighteen hundred and thirty-three (1833), and with those Indians at present occupying the Big Swamp, and other parts of the country beyond the limits as defined in the second article of the treaty concluded at Camp Moultrie creek, so that the whole of that proportion of the Seminoles may be removed within the year aforesaid, and the remainder of the tribe, in about equal proportions, during the subsequent years of eighteen hundred and thirty-four and five, (1834 and 1835.)

In testimony whereof, the commissioner, James Gadsden, and the undersigned chiefs and head men of the Seminole Indians, have hereunto subscribed their names and affixed their seals. Done at camp at Payne's landing, on the Ocklawaha river in the territory of Florida, on this ninth day of May, one thousand eight hundred and thirty-two, and of the independence of the United States of America the fifty-sixth.

James Gadsden,
Holati Emartla, his x mark, Jumper, his x mark, Fuch-ta-lus-ta-Hadjo, his x mark, Charley Emartla, his x mark, Coa Hadjo, his x mark, Ar-pi-uck-i, or Sam Jones, his x mark, Ya-ha Hadjo, his x mark, Mico-Noha, his x mark, Tokose-Emartla, or Jno. Hicks, his x mark, Cat-sha-Tusta-nuck-i, his x mark, Hola-at-a-Mico, his x mark, Hitch-it-i-Mico, his x mark, E-ne-hah, his x mark, Ya-ha-emartla Chup-ko, his x mark, Moke-his-she-lar-ni, his x mark,

Witnesses: Douglas Vass, Secretary to Commissioner, John Phagan, Agent, Stephen Richards, Interpreter, Abraham, Interpreter, his x mark, Cudjo, Interpreter, his x mark, Erastus Rogers, B. Joscan.

TREATY WITH THE APPALACHICOLA BAND {1832, Oct. 11}
Proclamation, Feb. 13, 1833.

THE undersigned chiefs, for and in behalf of themselves and warriors, surrender to the United States, all their right, title and interest to a reservation of land made for their benefit, in the additional article of the treaty, concluded at Camp Moultrie, in the Territory of Florida, on the 18th of September, eighteen hundred and twenty-three, and which is described in said article, "as commencing on the Appalachicola, one mile below Tuski Hajo's improvements, running up said river four miles, thence west two miles, thence southerly to a point due west of the beginning, thence east to the beginning point," and agree to remove with their warriors and families, now occupying said reservation, and amounting in all to (256) two hundred and fifty-six souls, to the west of the Mississippi river, beyond the limits of the States and Territories of the United States of America.

ARTICLE 2. For, and in consideration of said surrender, and to meet the Charges of a party to explore immediately the country west in search of a home more suitable to their habits, than the one at present occupied, and in full compensation for all the expenses of emigration, and subsistence for themselves and party: The United States agree to pay to the undersigned chiefs, and their warriors, thirteen thousand dollars; three thousand dollars in cash, the receipt of which is herewith acknowledged, and ten thousand dollars whenever they have completed their arrangements, and have commenced the removal of their whole party.

ARTICLE 3. The undersigned chiefs, with their warriors and families, will evacuate the reservation of land surrendered by the first article of this agreement, on or before the first of November, eighteen hundred and thirty-three; but should unavoidable circumstances prevent the conclusion of the necessary preparatory arrangements by that time, it is expected that the indulgence of the government of the United States will be reasonably extended for a term, not to exceed however another year.

ARTICLE 4. The United States further stipulate to continue to Blunt and Davy (formerly Tuski Hajo deceased) the Chiefs of the towns now consenting to emigrate, their proportion of the annuity of five thousand dollars which they at present draw, and to which they are entitled under the treaty of Camp Moultrie, so long as they remain in the Territory of Florida, and to advance their proportional amount of the said annuity for the balance of the term stipulated for its payment in the treaty aforesaid; whenever they remove in compliance of the terms of this agreement.

In testimony whereof, the commissioner, James Gadsden, in behalf of the United States, and the undersigned chiefs and warriors have hereunto subscribed their names and affixed their seals.
Done at Tallahassee, in the territory of Florida, this eleventh day of October one thousand eight hundred and thirty-two, and of the Independence of the United States the fifty-seventh.

James Gadsden, commissioner, &c.
John Blunt, his x mark, O Saa-Hajo, or Davy, his x mark, Co-ha-thlock-co, or Cockrane, his x mark,

Witnesses: Wm. P. Duval, superintendent, Stephen Richards, interpreter, Robt. W. Williams, R. Lewis, Tho. Brown, James D. Westcott, jr.

TREATY WITH THE CHICKASAW {1832, Oct. 20}
Proclamation Mar. 1, 1833.

Articles of a treaty made and entered into between Genl. John Coffee, being
duly authorised thereto, by the President of the United States, and the whole
Chickasaw Nation, in General Council assembled, at the Council House, on
Pontitock Creek on the twentieth day of October, 1832.

The Chickasaw Nation find themselves oppressed in their present situation; by
being made subject to the laws of the States in which they reside. Being ignorant of the language and laws of the white man, they cannot understand or obey
them. Rather than submit to this great evil, they prefer to seek a home in the
west, where they may live and be governed by their own laws. And believing
that they can procure for themselves a home, in a country suited to their wants
and condition, provided they had the means to contract and pay for the same,
they have determined to sell their country and hunt a new home. The President
has heard the complaints of the Chickasaws, and like them believes they cannot
be happy, and prosper as a nation, in their present situation and condition, and
being desirous to relieve them from the great calamity that seems to await
them, if they remain as they areHe has sent his Commissioner Genl. John Coffee, who has met the whole Chickasaw nation in Council, and after mature deliberation, they have entered into the following articles, which shall be binding
on both parties, when the same shall be ratified by the President of the United
States by and with the advice and consent of the Senate.

ARTICLE 1. For the consideration hereinafter expressed, the Chickasaw nation do hereby cede, to the United States, all the land which they own on the
east side of the Mississippi river, including all the country where they at present
live and occupy.

ARTICLE 2. The United States agree to have the whole country thus ceded,
surveyed, as soon as it can be conveniently done, in the same manner that the
public lands of the United States are surveyed in the States of Mississippi and
Alabama, and as soon thereafter as may be practicable, to have the same prepared for sale. The President of the United States will then offer the land for
sale at public auction, in the same manner and on the same terms and conditions as the other public lands, and such of the land as may not sell at the public
sales shall be offered at private sale, in the same manner that other private sales
are made of the United States lands.

ARTICLE 3. As a full compensation to the Chickasaw nation, for the country
thus ceded, the United States agree to pay over to the Chickasaw nation, all the
money arising from the sale of the land which may be received from time to
time, after deducting therefrom the whole cost and expenses of surveying and
selling the land, including every expense attending the same.

ARTICLE 4. The President being determined that the Chickasaw people shall not deprive themselves of a comfortable home, in the country where they now are, until they shall have provided a country in the west to remove to, and settle on, with fair prospects of future comfort and happinessIt is therefore agreed to, by the Chickasaw nation, that they will endeavor as soon as it may be in their power, after the ratification of this treaty, to hunt out and procure a home for their people, west of the Mississippi river, suited to their wants and condition; and they will continue to do so during the progress of the survey of their present country, as is provided for in the second article of this treaty. But should they fail to procure such a country to remove to and settle on, previous to the first public sale of their country here then and in that event, they are to select out of the surveys, a comfortable settlement for every family in the Chickasaw nation, to include their present improvements, if the land is good for cultivation, and if not they may take it in any other place in the nation, which is unoccupied by any other person.
Such settlement must be taken by sections. And there shall be allotted to each family as follows (to wit): To a single man who is twenty-one years of age, one sectionto each family of five and under that number two sectionsto each family of six and not exceeding ten, three sections, and to each family over ten in number, four sectionsand to families who own slaves, there shall be allowed, one section to those who own ten or upwards and such as own under ten, there shall be allowed half a section.

If any person shall now occupy two places and wish to retain both, they may do so, by taking a part at one place, and a part at the other, and where two or more persons are now living on the same section, the oldest occupant will be entitled to remain, and the others must move off to some other place if so required by the oldest occupant. All of which tracts of land so selected and retained, shall be held, and occupied by the Chickasaw people, uninterrupted until they shall find and obtain a country suited to their wants and condition. And the United States will guaranty to the Chickasaw nation, the quiet possession and uninterrupted use of the said reserved tracts of land, so long as they may live on and occupy the same. And when they shall determine to remove from said tracts of land, the Chickasaw nation will notify the President of the United States of their determination to remove, and thereupon as soon as the Chickasaw people shall remove, the President will proclaim the said reserved tracts of land for sale at public auction and at private sale, on the same terms and conditions, as is provided for in the second article of this treaty, to sell the same, and the net proceeds thereof, to be paid to the Chickasaw nation, as is provided for in the third article of this treaty.

ARTICLE 5. If any of the Chickasaw families shall have made valuable improvements on the places where they lived and removed from, on the reservation tracts, the same shall be valued by some discreet person to be appointed by the President, who shall assess the real cash value of all such improvements, and also the real cash value of all the land within their improvements, which they may have cleared and actually cultivated, at least one year in good farming order and condition. And such valuation of the improvements and the value of the cultivated lands as before mentioned, shall be paid to the person who shall have made the same. To be paid out of the proceeds of the sales of the ceded lands. The person who shall value such land and improvements, shall give to the owner thereof, a certificate of the valuation, which shall be a good voucher for them to draw the money on, from the proper person, who shall be appointed to pay the same, and the money shall be paid, as soon as may be convenient, after the valuation, to enable the owner thereof to provide for their families on their journey to their new homes.

The provisions of this article are intended to encourage industry and to enable the Chickasaws to move comfortably. But least the good intended may be abused, by designing persons, by hiring hands and clearing more land, than they otherwise would do for the benefit of their families It is determined that no payment shall be made for improved lands, over and above one-eighth part of the tract allowed and reserved for such person to live on and occupy.

ARTICLE 6. The Chickasaw nation cannot receive any part of the payment for their land until it shall be surveyed and sold; therefore, m order to the greater facilitate, in surveying and preparing the land for sale, and for keeping the business of the nation separate and apart from the business and accounts of the United States, it is proposed by the Chickasaws, and agreed to, that a Surveyor General be appointed by the President, by and with the advice and consent of the Senate, to superintend alone the surveying of this ceded country or so much thereof as the President may direct, who shall appoint a sufficient number of deputy surveyors, as may be necessary to complete the survey, in as short a time as may be reasonable and expedient. That the said Surveyor General be allowed one good clerk, and one good draftsman to aid and assist him in the business of his office, in preparing the lands for sale. It is also agreed that one land office be established for the sale of the lands, to have one Register and one Receiver of monies, to be appointed by the President, by and with the advice and consent of the Senate, and each Register and Receiver to have one good clerk to aid and assist them in the duties of their office.

The Surveyor's office, and the office of the Register and Receiver of money, shall be kept somewhere central in the nation, at such place as the President of the United States may direct. As the before mentioned officers, and clerks, are to be employed entirely in business of the nation, appertaining to preparing and selling the land, they will of course be paid out of the proceeds of the sales of the ceded lands. That the Chickasaws, may now understand as near as may be, the expenses that will be incurred in the transacting of this business It is proposed and agreed to, that the salary of the Surveyor General be fifteen hundred dollars a year, and that the Register and Receiver of monies, be allowed twelve hundred dollars a year each, as a full compensation for their services, and all expenses, except stationary and postages on their official business, and that each of the clerks and draftsman be allowed seven hundred and fifty dollars a year, for their services and all expenses.

ARTICLE 7. It is expressly agreed that the United States shall not grant any right of preference, to any person, or right of occupancy in any manner whatsoever, but in all cases, of either public or private sale, they are to sell the land to the highest bidder, and also that none of the lands be sold in smaller tracts than quarter sections or fractional sections of the same size as near as may be, until the Chickasaw nation may require the President to sell in smaller tracts. The Chiefs of the nation have heard that at some of the sales of the United States lands, the people there present, entered into combinations, and united in purchasing much of the land, at reduced prices, for their own benefit, to the great prejudice of the Government, and they express fears, that attempts will be made to cheat them, in the same manner when their lands shall be offered at public auction. It is therefore agreed that the President will use his best endeavours to prevent such combinations, or any other plan or state of things which may tend to prevent the land selling for its full value.

ARTICLE 8. As the Chickasaws have determined to sell their country, it is desirable that the nation realize the greatest possible sum for their lands, which can be obtained. It is therefore proposed and agreed to that after the President shall have offered their lands for sale and shall have sold all that will sell for the Government price, then the price shall be reduced, so as to induce purchasers to buy, who would not take the land at the Government minimum price ;and it is believed, that five years from and after the date of the first sale, will dispose of all the lands, that will sell at the Government price. If then at the expiration of five years, as before mentioned, the Chickasaw nation may request the President to sell at such reduced price as the nation may then propose, it shall be the duty of the President to comply with their request, by first offering it at public and afterwards at private sale, as in all other cases of selling public lands.

ARTICLE 9. The Chickasaw nation express their ignorance, and incapacity to live, and be happy under the State laws, they cannot read and understand them, and therefore they will always need a friend to advise and direct them. And fearing at some day the Government of the United States may withdraw from them, the agent under whose instructions they have lived so long and happy-They therefore request that the agent may be continued with them, while here, and wherever they may remove to and settle. It is the earnest wish of the United States Government to see the Chickasaw nation prosper and be happy, and so far as is consistent they will contribute all in their power to render them sotherefore their request is granted. There shall be an agent kept with the

Chickasaws as heretofore, so long as they live within the jurisdiction of the United States as a nation, either within the limits of the States where they now reside, or at any other place. And whenever the office of agent shall be vacant, and an agent to be appointed, the President will pay due respect to the wishes of the nation in selecting a man in all respects qualified to discharge the responsible duties of that office.

ARTICLE 10. Whenever the Chickasaw nation shall determine to remove from, and leave their present country, they will give the President of the United States timely notice of such intention, and the President will furnish them, the necessary funds, and means for their transportation and journey, and for one years provisions, after they reach their new homes, in such quantity as the nation may require, and the full amount of such funds, transportation and provisions, is to be paid for, out of the proceeds of the sales of the ceded lands. And should the Chickasaw nation remove, from their present country, before they receive money, from the sale of the lands, hereby ceded; then and in that case, the United States shall furnish them any reasonable stun of money for national purposes, which may be deemed proper by the President of the United States, which sum shall also be refunded out of the sales of the ceded lands.

ARTICLE 11. The Chickasaw nation have determined to create a perpetual fund, for the use of the nation forever, out of the proceeds of the country now ceded away. And for that purpose they propose to invest a large proportion of the money arising from the sale of the land, in some safe and valuable stocks, which will bring them in an annual interest or dividend, to be used for all national purposes, leaving the principal untouched, intending to use the interest alone. It is therefore proposed by the Chickasaws, and agreed to, that the sum to be laid out in stocks as above mentioned, shall be left with the government of the United States, until it can be laid out under the direction of the President of the United States, by and with the advice and consent of the Senate, in such safe and valuable stock as he may approve [360] of, for the use and benefit of the Chickasaw nation.

The sum thus to be invested, shall be equal to, at least three-fourths of the whole net proceeds of the sales of the lands; and as much more, as the nation may determine, if there shall be a surplus after supplying all the national wants. But it is hereby provided, that if the reasonable wants of the nation shall require more than one fourth Of the proceeds of the sales of the land, then they may, by the consent of the President and Senate, draw from the government such sum as may be thought reasonable, for valuable national purposes, out of the three-fourths reserved to be laid out in stocks. But if any of the monies shall be thus drawn out of the sum first proposed, to be laid out on interest, the stall shall be replaced, out of the first monies of the nation, which may come into the possession of the United States government, from the sale of the ceded lands, over and above the reasonable wants of the nation.

At the expiration of fifty years from this date, if the Chickasaw nation shall have improved in education and civilization, and become so enlightened, as to be capable of managing so large a sum of money to advantage, and with safety, for the benefit of the nation, and the President of the United States, with the Senate, shall be satisfied thereof, at that time, and shall give their consent thereto, the Chickasaw nation may then withdraw the whole, or any part of the fund now set apart, to be laid out in stocks, or at interest, and dispose of the same, in any manner that they may think proper at that time, for the use and benefit of the whole nation; but no part of said fund shall ever be used for any other purpose, than the benefit of the whole Chickasaw nation. In order to facilitate the survey and sale of the lands now ceded, and to raise the money therefrom as soon as possible, for the foregoing purpose, the President of the United States is authorised to commence the survey of the land as soon as may be practicable, after the ratification of this treaty.

ARTICLE 12. The Chickasaws feel grateful to their old chiefs, for their long and faithful services, in attending to the business of the nation. They believe it a duty, to keep them from want in their old and declining agewith those feelings, they have looked upon their old and beloved chief Tish-o-mingo, who is now grown old, and is poor and not able to live, in that comfort, which his valuable life and great merit deserve. It is therefore determined to give him out of the national funds, one hundred dollars a year during the balance of his life, and the nation request him to receive it, as a token of their kind feelings for him, on account of his long and valuable services.

Our old and beloved Queen Pue-caunda, is now very old and very poor. Justice says the nation ought not to let her suffer in her old age; it is therefore determined to give her out of the national funds, fifty dollars a year during her life, the money to be put in the hands of the agent to be laid out for her support, under his direction, with the advice of the chiefs.

ARTICLE 13. The boundary line between the lands of the Chickasaws and Choctaws, has never been run, or properly defined, and as the Choctaws have sold their country to the United States, they now have no interest in the decision of that question. It is therefore agreed to call on the old Choctaw chiefs to determine the line to be run, between the Chickasaws and their former country. The Chickasaws, by a treaty made with the United States at Franklin in Tennessee, in Aug. 31, 1830, (a) declared their line to run as follows, to wit: Beginning at the mouth of Oak tibby-haw and running up said stream to a point, being a marked tree, on the old Natches road, one mile southwardly from Wall's old place.

Thence with the Choctaw boundary, and along it, westwardly through the Tunicha old fields, to a point on the Mississippi river, about twenty-eight miles by water, below where the St. Francis river enter said stream on the west side. It is now agreed, that the surveys of the Choctaw country which are now in progress, shall not cross the line until the true line shall be decided and determined; which shall be done as follows, the agent of the (Choctaws on the west side of the Mississippi shall call on the old and intelligent chiefs of that nation, and lay before them the line as claimed by the Chickasaws at the Franklin treaty, and if the Choctaws shall determine that line to be correct, then it shall be established and made the permanent line, but if the Choctaws say the line strikes the Mississippi river higher up said stream, then the best evidence which can be had from both nations, shall be taken by the agents of both nations, and submitted to the President of the United States for his decision, and on such evidence, the President will determine the true line on principles of strict justice.

ARTICLE 14. As soon as the surveys are made, it shall be the duty of the chiefs, with the advice and assistance of the agent to cause a correct list to be made out of all and every tract of land, which shall be reserved, for the use and benefit of the Chickasaw people, for their residence, as is provided for in the fourth article of this treaty, which list, will designate the sections of land, which are set apart for each family or individual in the nation, shewing the precise tracts which shall belong to each and every one of them, which list shall be returned to the register of the land office, and he shall make a record of the same, m his office, to prevent him from offering any of said tracts of land for sale, and also as evidence of each person's lands. All the residue of the lands will be offered by the President for sale.

ARTICLE 15. The Chickasaws request that no persons be permitted to move in and settle on their country before the land is sold. It is therefore agreed, that no person, whatsoever, who is not Chickasaw or connected with the Chickasaws by marriage, shall be permitted to come into the country and settle on any part of the ceded lands until they shall be offered for sale, and then there shall not be any person permitted to settle on any of the land, which has not been sold, at the time of such settlement, and in all cases of a person settling on any of the ceded lands contrary to this express understanding, they will be intruders, and must be treated as such, and put off of the lands of the nation.

In witness of all and every thing herein determined, between the United States and the whole Chickasaw nation in general council assembled, the parties have hereunto set their hands and seals, at the council-house, on Pontitock creek, in the Chickasaw nation, on the twentieth day of October, one thousand eight hundred and thirty-two.

John Coffee,
Ish-te-ho-to-pa, (king) his x mark, Tish-o-min-go, his x mark, Levi Colbert, his x mark, George Colbert, his x mark, William M'Gilvery, his x mark, Samuel

Sely, his x mark, To-pul-kah, his x mark, Isaac Albertson, his x mark, Em-ub-by, his x mark, Pis-tah-lah-tubbe, his x mark, Ish-tim-o-lut-ka, his x mark, James Brown, his x mark, Im-mah-hoo-lo-tubbe, his x mark, Ish-ta-ha-chah, his x mark, Lah-fin-hubbe, his x mark, Shop-pow-me, his x mark, Nin-uck-ah-umba, his x mark, lm-mah-hoo-la-tubbe, his x mark, Illup-pah-umba, his x mark, Pitman Colbert, Con-mush-ka-ish-kah, his x mark, James Wolfe, Bah-ha-kah-tubbe, his x mark, E. Bah-kah-tubbe, his x mark, Captain Thompson, his x mark, New-berry, his x mark, Bah-ma-hah-tubbe, his x mark,
John Lewis, his x mark, I-yah-hou-tubbe, his x mark, Tok-holth-la-chah, his x mark, Oke-lah-nah-nubbe, his x mark, Im-me-tubbe, his x mark, In-kah-yea, his x mark, Ah-sha-eubbe, his x mark, Im-mah-ho-bah, his x mark, Fit-ehah-pla, his x mark, Unte-mi-ah-tubbe, his x mark, Oke-lah-hin-lubbe, his x mark, John Glover, his x mark, Bah-me-hubbe, his x mark, Hush-tah-tah-ubbe, his x mark, Un-ti-ha-kah-tubbe, his x mark, Yum-mo-tubbe, his x mark, Oh-ha-cubbe, his x mark, Ah-fab-mah, his x mark, Ah-ta-kin-tubbe, his x mark, Ah-to-ko-wah, his x mark, Tah-ha-cubbe, his x mark, Kin-hoi-cha, his x mark, Ish-te-ah-tubbe, his x mark, Chick-ah-shah-nan-ubbe, his x mark, Che-wut-ta-ha, his x mark, Fo-lut-ta-chah, his x mark,
No-wo-ko, his x mark, Win-in-a-pa, his x mark, Oke-lah-shah-cubbe, his x mark, Ish-ta-ki-yu-ka-tubbe, his x mark, Mah-te-ko-shubbe, his x mark, Tom-chick-ah, his x mark, Ei-o-che-tubbe, his x mark, Nuck-sho-pubbe, his x mark, Fah-lah-mo-tubbe, his x mark, Co-chub-be, his x mark, Thomas Sely, his x mark, Oke-lah-sha-pi-a, his x mark,

Signed and sealed in the presence of: Ben. Reynolds, Indian agent, George Wightman, of Mississippi, John L. Allen, subagent, John Donley, Tennessee, Nath. Anderson, secretary to the commissoner, D.S. Parrish, Tennessee, S. Daggett, Mississippi, Benj. Love, United States interpreter, Wm. A. Clurm, Robert Gordon, Mississippi, G. Long.

TREATY WITH THE CHICKASAW {1832, Oct. 22}

Articles supplementary to, and explanatory of, a Treaty which was entered unto on the 20th instant, between General John Coffee on the part of the United States, and the whole Chickasaw nation in General Council assembled.

The fourth article of the treaty to which this is a supplement, provides that each Chickasaw family, shall have a tract of land, reserved for the use of the family, to live on and occupy, so long as the nation resides in the country where they now are. And the fifth article of the treaty provides that each family or individual shall be paid for their improvements, and the value of their cleared lands, when the nation shall determine to remove and leave the said reserved tracts of land. It is now proposed and agreed to, that no family or person of the Chickasaw nation, who shall or may have tracts of land, reserved for their residence

236

while here, shall ever be permitted to lease any of said land, to any person whatsoever, nor shall they be permitted to rent any of said land, to any person, either white, red, or black, or mixed blood of either. As the great object of the nation is to preserve the land, and timber, for the benefit of posterity, provided the nation shall continue to live here, and if they shall at any time determine to remove and sell the land, it will be more valuable, and will sell for more money, for the benefit of the nation, if the land and timber be preserved.

It is also expressly declared by the nation, that, whenever the nation shall determine to remove from their present country, that every tract of land so reserved in the nation, shall be given up and sold for the benefit of the nation. And no individual or family shall have any right to retain any of such reserved tracts of land, for their own use, any longer than the nation may remain in the country where they now are.
As the reserve tracts of land above alluded to, will be the first choice of land in the nation, it is determined that the minimum price of all the reserved tracts, shall be three dollars an acre, until the nation may determine to reduce the price, and then they will notify the President, of their wishes, and the price to which they desire to reduce it.

The Chiefs still express fears that combinations may be formed at the public sales, where their reserved tracts of land shall be offered for sale, and that they may not be sold so high as they might be sold, by judicious agents at private sale. They therefore suggest the propriety of the President determining on some judicious mode of selling the reserves at private sale.

It is therefore agreed that the suggestion be submitted to the President, and if he and the Chiefs can agree on a plan of a sale, different from the one proposed in the treaty, to which this is a supplement, and which shall be approved of by both parties, then they may enter into such agreement and the President shall then be governed by the same, in the sale of the reserved tracts of land, whenever they may be offered for sale.

In the provisions of the fourth article of the treaty to which this is a supplement, for reserves to young men who have no families, it expresses that each young man, who is twenty-one years of age, shall have a reserve. But as the Indians mature earlier than white men, and generally marry younger, it is determined to extend a reserve, to each young man who is seventeen years of age. And as there are some orphan girls in the nation or whose families do not provide for them, and also some widows in the same situation, it is determined to allow to each of them a reservation of one section, on the same terms and conditions in all respects, with the other reservations for the nation generally, and to be allowed to the same ages, as to young men.

Colbert Moore and family have always lived in the Chickasaw nation, and he requests the liberty to continue with the nation. The Chiefs and nation agree to his request, and they also agree to allow him and his family a reserve tract of land to live on and occupy in the same manner, and on the same terms and conditions as is provided for the Chickasaw families, in the nation generally, during his good behavior. The Chiefs of the nation represent that they in behalf of the nation gave a bond to James Colbert for a debt due to him, of eighteen hundred and eleven dollars, ninety-three and three fourth cents principal, that James Colbert transferred said note to Robert Gordon and that said note, and the interest thereon is yet due and unpaid, and the said Robert Gordon has proposed to take a section of land for said note, and interest up to this date. It is therefore agreed by the nation to grant him a section of land, to be taken any where in the nation, so as not to interfere with any reserve which has been provided as a residence for the Chickasaws, which shall be in full for said note and interest.

The Treaty, to which this is a supplement provides that there shall be offices kept some where central in the nation, at such place as the President shall determine, for transacting the business of the nation in selling their lands &c. It is now agreed to by the nation, that the President may select a section of land, or four quarter sections adjoining, at such place as he may determine agreeably to that provision of the Treaty, to establish the said offices on, and for all the necessary uses thereto attached, and he is permitted to improve the said tract of land in any manner, whatsoever, but when it shall cease to be used for the purposes, for which it is set apartfor offices &c.then the same shall be sold under the direction of the Presidentand the proceeds thereof shall be paid to the Chickasaw nation, after deducting therefrom the value of all the improvements on the land, which value shall be assessed by the President, and in no case shall it exceed one half the sale of the land.

The Chickasaw nation request the Government to grant them a cross mail route through the nation as follows, one to pass from Tuscumbia in Alabama, by the Agency, and by the place to be selected for the offices to be kept and to Rankin in Mississippi on horse back, once a week each way. The other to run from Memphis in Tennessee, by the offices and to the Cotton Gin in Mississippito pass once a week each [364] way. They conceive these mails would be useful to the nation, and indispensible to the carrying on the business of the nation when the offices are established, but they would respectfully solicit the mails to be started as soon as possible, to open the avenues of information into their country.

John Donkey has long been known in this nation as a mail carrier; he rode on the mails through our nation when a boy and for many years after he was grown; we think he understands that business as well, if not better than any other manand we should prefer him to carry our mails to any other personand if he is given the contract, the nation will set apart a section of land for his use while we remain here in this country, which section he may select with the advice of the Chiefs any where that suits him best, so as not to interfere with any of the reserves, and he may use it in any manner to live on, or make such improvements as may be necessary for keeping his horses, or to raise forage for them. But when the nation shall move away and leave this country this tract of land must be sold for the benefit of the nation, in the same manner that the reserve tracts are sold &c. and he is not to claim of the nation any pay for improving said tract of land.

In witness of all and every thing herein determined between the United States and the whole Chickasaw nation, in general council assembled, the parties have hereunto set their hands and seals at the council house, on Pontitock creek, in the Chickasaw nation, on this twenty-second day of October one thousand eight hundred and thirty-two.

Jno. Coffee,

Ish-te-ho-to-pa, his x mark, Tish-o-min-go, his x mark, Levi Colbert, his x mark, George Colbert, his x mark, William MeGlivery, his x mark, Samuel Sely, his x mark, To-pul-kah, his x mark, Isaac Albertson, his x mark, Im-mubbe, his x mark, Pis-ta-la-tubbe, his x mark, Ish-tim-o-lut-ka, his x mark, James Brown, his x mark, Im-ma-hoodo-tubbe, his x mark, Ish-ta-ha-eha, his x mark, Lah-fin-hubbe, his x mark, Shop-pow-we, his x mark, Nin-uck-ah-umba, his x mark, Im-mah-hoo-lo-tubbe, his x mark, Il-lup-pah-umba, his x mark,

Pitman Colbert, Con-nush-koish-kah, his x mark, James Wolf, Bah-ha-kah-tubbe, his x mark, E-bah-kah-tubbe, his x mark, Captain Thompson, his x mark, New-berry, his x mark, Bah-me-hah-tubbe, his x mark,
John Lewis, his x mark, I-yah-hou-tubbe, his mark, Tok-holth-la-chah, his x mark, Oke-lah-nah-nubbe, his x mark, Im-me-tubbe, his x mark, In-kah-yea, his x mark, Ah-shah-cubbe, his x mark,
Im-mah-ho-bah, his x mark, Fit-chah-ple, his x mark, Unte-mi-ah-tubbe, his x mark, Oke-lah-hin-lubbe, his x mark, John Glover, his x mark, Bah-me-hubbe, his x mark, Ah-to-ko-wah, his x mark, Hush-tah-tah-hubbe, his x mark, Un-ti-ha-kah-tubbe, his x mark, Yum-me-tubbe, his x mark, Oh-ha-eubbe, his x mark, Ah-fah-mah, his x mark, Ah-takc-in-tubbe, his x mark, Tah-ha-cubbe, his x mark, Kin-hoi-cha, his x mark, Ish-te-ah-tubbe, his x mark,
Chick-ah-shah-nan-ubbe, his x mark, Chee-wut-ta-ha, his x mark, Fo-lut-ta-ehah, his x mark, No-wo-ko, his x mark, Win-in-a-pa, his x mark, Oke-lah-shah-eubbe, his x mark, Ish-ta-ki-yu-ka-tubbe, his x mark, Mah-ta-ko-shubbe, his x mark, Tom-ah-chich-ah, his x mark, Ehi-o-ehe-tubbe, his x mark, Nuck-sho-pubbe, his x mark, Fah-lah-mo-tubbe, his x mark, Co-chub-be, his x mark, Thomas Sely, his x mark, Oke-lah-sha-pi-a, his x mark,

Signed and sealed in presence of: Ben. Reynolds, Indian agent, John Donley, John L. Allen, subagent, D.S. Parrish, Nath. Anderson, secretary to commissioner, S. Daggett, of Mississippi, Wm. A. Clurm, of Mississippi.

TREATY WITH THE SENECA AND SHAWNEE {1832, Dec. 29}
Proclamation, Mar. 22,1833.

Articles of agreement, made, and concluded at the Seneca agency, on the head waters of the Cowskin river, this 29th day of December, in the year of our Lord one thousand eight hundred and thirty-two, by and between Henry L. Ellsworth and John F. Schermerhorn, Commissioners, on behalf of the United States, and the Chiefs and Headmen of the "United Nation" of the Senecas and Shawnee Indians, on behalf of said Tribe or Nation.

WHEREAS certain articles of agreement and convention were concluded at Lewistown, Ohio, on the 20th day of July, A. D. 1831, by and between the United States and the Chiefs and Warriors of the mixed band of the Senecas and Shawnee Indians, residing at or near [384] Lewistown, in the State of Ohio: And whereas, by the and article of said agreement, the United States stipulated and agreed, with said Tribe, in the words following, to wit: "to grant by patent, in fee simple, to them, and their heirs forever, as long as they shall exist as a nation and remain on the same, a tract of land, to contain sixty thousand acres, to be located trader the direction of the President of the United States, contiguous to the lands granted to the Senecas of Sandusky, by the treaty made with them at the City of Washington, on the 28th of February 1831, and the Cherokee settlementsthe east line of said tract shall be within two miles of the west line of the lands granted to the Senecas of Sandusky.

The south line shall be within two miles of the north line of the lands held by the Cherokeesand said two miles between the aforesaid lines, shall serve as a common passway between the before-mentioned Tribes, to prevent them from intruding upon the lands of each other." And the treaty aforesaid was ratified and confirmed by the President and Senate of the United States, on the 6th day of April, A. D. 1832. And whereas, the said mixed Band of Senecas and Shawnees removed from their homes in Ohio to settle upon the lands assigned them west of the Mississippi, in pursuance of the provisions and stipulations of the treaty aforesaid: And whereas, the said Senecas from Sandusky, and the mixed Band of Senecas and Shawnees, have lately formed a confederacy, and have expressed their anxiety to unite as one Tribe or Nation, to be called the "United Nation of Senecas and Shawnees," to occupy their land as tenants in common and have the whole of the country provided for them by the United States located on the east side of Ne-o-sho or Grand river, which runs through and now divides the same: For the purpose of affording a more convenient and satisfactory location to said United Nation, the parties aforesaid do, therefore, hereby stipulate and agree its follows:

ARTICLE 1. The United Tribe of Senecas and Shawnee Indians do hereby cede, relinquish and forever quit claim to the United States, all the land granted to them on the west side of Ne-o-sho or Grand river, by treaties made respectively with the Senecas of Sandusky and the mixed Band of Senecas and Shawnees of Lewistown, Ohio, on the 20th day of July, 1831, and on the 28th day of February, 1831.

ARTICLE 2. In consideration of said lands, described and ceded as aforesaid, the United States will grant, by letters patent, to the Tribe or Nation of Indians aforesaid, in manner as hereinafter mentioned, the following tract of land lying on the east side of Ne-o-sho or Grand river, viz: bounded on the east by the west line of the State of Missouri; south by the present established line of the Cherokee Indians; west by Ne-o-sho or Grand river; and north by a line running parallel with said south line, and extending so far from the present north line of the Seneca Indians from Sandusky, as to contain sixty thousand acres, exclusive of the land now owned by said Seneca Indians, which said boundaries include, however, all the land heretofore granted said Senecas of Sandusky, on the east side of Grand river.

And the United States will grant said tract of land, by two letters patent; the north half, in quantity, to be granted to the mixed band of the Senecas and Shawnees of Ohio, and the south half to the Senecas from Sandusky, aforesaid: the whole to be occupied in common, so long as the said Tribes or Bands shall desire the same. The said patents shall be granted in fee simple; but the lands shall not be sold or ceded without the consent of the United States.

ARTICLE 3. The United States, at the request of said "United Nation," agree to erect immediately a grist mill, a saw mill and a blacksmith shop, and furnish the necessary tools and machinery in anticipation of a re-imbursement from sales of land, ceded to the United rates, by the treaties aforesaid, of 28th of February, 1831, and July 20th, 1831, and so far in fulfillment of the same.

ARTICLE 4. The United Nation of Seneca and Shawnees having presented a claim for money advanced by them for forage while removing to their new homes in the west, and for horses and other property lost on the journey, the United States, in order to a final settlement of such claim, agree to pay one thousand dollars, as follows, viz:six hundred dollars to the Seneca tribe of Indians from Sandusky; and the sum of four hundred dollars to the Senecas and Shawnees from Lewistown, Ohio, to be distributed by their respective tribes among the claimants, as they may deem just and equitable; and to be received by them in full payment and satisfaction of all the claims aforesaid.

ARTICLE 5. Nothing in these articles of agreement shall be construed to affect the respective rights of the Seneca tribe of Indians from Sandusky, and the Senecas and Shawnees from Lewistown, Ohio, as secured by existing treaties, except so far as said treaties are inconsistent with the provisions of the articles aforesaid.

ARTICLE 6. This agreement or treaty shall be binding and obligatory upon the contracting parties from and after its ratification by the President and Senate of the United States.

In testimony whereof, the said Henry L. Ellsworth and John F. Schermerhorn, commissioners, and the chiefs and head men of the United Nation of Seneca and Shawnee Indians, have hereunto signed their names and affixed their seals, on the day and year above written,

Henry L. Ellsworth, John F. Schermerhorn,
Seneca chiefs: Cornstick, (first chief Seneca nation) his x mark, Seneca Steel, his x mark, Small Cloud Spicer, his x mark, George Curly Hair, his x mark, Tall Chief, his x mark, Captain Good Hunter, his x mark, Hard Hickory, his x mark, Wiping Stick, his x mark, Seneca John, his x mark, John Johnson, his x mark, John Sky, his x mark, Isaac White, his x mark, Joseph Smith, his x mark, Captain Smith, his x mark,
Chiefs of mixed band: Me-tho-mea, or Civil John, (first chief Senecas and Shawnees) his x mark, Pe-wy-a-che, his x mark, Skilleway or Robbin, his x mark, John Jackson, his x mark, Quash-acaugh or Little Lewis, his x mark, To-ta-la or John Young, his x mark, Mingo Carpenter, his x mark, Jemmv McDaniel, his x mark, Civil John's son, his x mark, Yankee Bill, his x mark, Big Ash, his x mark, Civil John's young son, his x mark,

Signed, sealed, and delivered in the presence of us: S.C. Stambaugh, secretary to commissioners, St. John F. Sane, Indian agent, Augt. A. Chouteau, Wm. Young, George Herron, Seneca interpreter, Baptiste Peoria, Shawnee interpreter. Benjamin Love, United States interpreter, G.W. Long, Robt. Gordon, of Mississippi, W.D. King, George Wightman, John H. McKennie.

TREATY WITH THE WESTERN CHEROKEE {1833, Feb. 14}
Proclamation, Apt. 12, 1834.

Articles of agreement and convention made and concluded at Fort Gibson, on the Arkansas river on the fourteenth day of February one thousand eight hundred and thirty-three, by and between Montfort Stokes, Henry L. Ellsworth and John Y. Schermerhorn duly appointed Commissioners on the part of the United States and the undersigned Chiefs and Head-men of the Cherokee nation of Indians west of the Mississippi, they being duly authorized and empowered by their nation.

WHEREAS articles of Convention were concluded at the city of Washington, on the sixth day of May one thousand eight hundred and twenty-eight, between James Barbour Secretary of War, being specially authorized therefor by the President of the United States, and the [386] chiefs and head men of the Cherokee nation of Indians west of the Mississippi, which articles of convention were duly ratified. And whereas it was agreed by the second article of said convention as follows "That the United States agree to possess the Cherokees, and to guarantee it to them forever, and that guarantee is solemnly pledged, of seven millions of acres of land, said land to be bounded as follows; viz, commencing at a point on Arkansas river, where the eastern Choctaw boundary line strikes said river, and running thence with the western line of Arkansas Territory to the southwest corner of Missouri, and thence with the western boundary line of Missouri till it crosses the waters of Neasho, generally called Grand river, thence due west, to a point from which a due south course will strike the present northwest corner of Arkansas Territory, thence continuing due south on and with the present boundary line on the west of said Territory, to the main branch of Arkansas river, thence down said river to its junction with the Canadian, and thence up, and between said rivers Arkansas and Canadian to a point at which a line, running north and south, from river to river, will give the aforesaid seven millions of acres, thus provided for and bounded.

The United States further guarantee to the Cherokee nation a perpetual outlet west, and a free and unmolested use of all the country lying west of the western boundary of the above-described limits; and as far west, as the sovereignty of the United States and their right of soil extend. And whereas there was to said articles of convention and agreement, the following proviso viz: "Provided nevertheless, that said convention, shall not be so construed, as to extend the northern boundary of said perpetual outlet west, provided for and guarantied in the second article of said convention, north of the thirty-sixth degree of north latitude, or so as to interfere with the lands assigned, or to be assigned, west of the Mississippi river, to the Creek Indians who have emigrated, or may emigrate, from the States of Georgia and Alabama, under the provision of any treaty, or treaties, heretofore concluded, between the United States, and the Creek tribe of Indians and provided further, that nothing in said convention, shall be construed, to cede, or assign, to the Cherokees any lands heretofore ceded, or assigned, to any tribe, or tribes of Indians, by any treaty now existing and in force, with any such tribe or tribes."

And whereas, it appears from the Creek treaty, made with the United States, by the Creek nation, dated twenty-fourth day of January eighteen hundred and twenty-six, at the city of Washington; that they had the right to select, and did select, a part of the country described within the boundaries mentioned above in said Cherokee articles of agreements and whereas, both the Cherokee and Creek nations of Indians west of the Mississippi, anxious to have their boundaries settled in an amicable manner, have met each other in council, and, after full deliberation mutually agreed upon the boundary lines between them Now therefore, the United States on one part, and the chiefs and head-men of the Cherokee nation of Indians west of the Mississippi on the other part, agree as follows:

ARTICLE 1. The United States agree to possess the Cherokees, and to guarantee it to them forever, and that guarantee, is hereby pledged, of seven millions of acres of land, to be bounded as follows viz: Beginning at a point on the old western territorial line of Arkansas Territory, being twenty-five miles north from the point, where the Territorial line crosses Arkansas riverthence running from said north point, south, on the said Territorial line, to the place where said Territorial line crosses the Verdigris riverthence down said Verdigris river, to the Arkansas riverthence down said Arkansas to a point, where a stone is placed opposite to the east or lower bank of Grand river at its junction with the Arkansasthence running south, forty-four degrees west, one mile thence in a straight line to a point four miles northerly [387] from the month of the north fork of the Canadianthence along the said four miles line to the Canadianthence down the Canadian to the Arkansasthence, down the Arkansas, to that point on the Arkansas, where the eastern Choctaw boundary strikes, said river; and running thence with the western line of Arkansas Territory as now defined, to the southwest corner of Missourithence along the western Missouri line, to the land assigned the Senecas.

Thence, on the south line of the Senecas to Grand river; thence, up said Grand river, as far as the south line of the Osage reservation, extended if necessarythence up and between said south Osage line, extended west if necessary and a line drawn due west, from the point of beginning, to a certain distance west, at which, a line running north and south, from said Osage line, to said due west line, will make seven millions of acres within the whole described boundaries. In addition to the seven millions of acres of land, thus provided for, and bounded, the United States, further guarrantee to the Cherokee nation, a perpetual outlet west and a free and unmolested use of all the country lying west, of the western boundary of said seven millions of acres, as far west as the sovereignty of the United States and their right of soil extendProvided however, that if the saline, or salt plain, on the great western prairie, shall fall within said limits prescribed for said outlet, the right is reserved to the United States to permit other tribes of red men, to get salt on said plain in common with the Cheerokeesand letters patent shall be issued by the United States as soon as practicable for the land hereby guarranteed.

ARTICLE 2. The Cherokee nation hereby relinquish and quit claim to the United States all the right interest and title which the Cheerokees have, or claim to have in and to all the land ceded, or claimed to have been ceded to said Cheerokee nation by said treaty of sixth of May one thousand eight hundred and twenty-eight, and not embraced within the limits or boundaries fixed in this present supplementary treaty or articles of convention and agreement.

ARTICLE 3. The Cherokee nation, having particularly requested the United States to annul and cancel the sixth article of said treaty of sixth May, one thousand eight hundred and twenty-eight, the United States, agree to cancel the same, and the same is hereby annulled-Said sixth article referred to, is in the following words"It is moreover agreed by the United States, when the Cheerokees may desire it, to give them a plain set of laws, suited to their conditionalso when they may wish to lay off their lands and own them individually, a surveyor shall be sent to survey them at the expense of the United States.

ARTICLE 4. In consideration of the establishment of new boundaries in part, for the lands ceded to said Cheerokee nation, and in view of the improvement of said nation, the United States will cause to be erected, on land now guaranteed to the said nation, four blacksmith shops, one wagon maker shop, one wheelwright shop, and necessary tools and implements furnished for the same; together with one ton of iron, and two hundred and fifty pounds of steel, for each of said blacksmith shops, to be worked up, for the benefit of the poorer class of red men, belonging to the Cherokee nationAnd the United States, will employ four blacksmiths, one wagon-maker, and one wheelwright, to work in said shops respectively, for the benefit of said Cheerokee nation; and said materials shall be furnished annually and said services continued, so long as the President may deem properAnd said United States, will cause to be erected on said lands, for the benefit of said Cheerokees, eight patent railway corn mills, in lieu of the mills to be erected according_to the stipulation of the fourth article of said treaty, of sixth of May, one thousand eight hundred twenty-eight, from the avails of the sale of the old agency.

ARTICLE 5. These articles of agreement and convention are to be considered supplementary, to the treaty before mentioned between the United States, and the Cherokee nation west of the Mississippi dated sixth of May one thousand eight hundred and twenty-eight, and not to vary the rights of the parties to said treaty, any further, than said treaty is inconsistent with the provisions of this treaty, now concluded, or these articles of convention or agreement.

ARTICLE 6. It is further agreed by the Cherokee nation, that one mile square shall be reserved and set apart from the lands hereby guaranteed, for the accommodation of the Cheerokee agency; and the location of the same shall be designated by the Cherokee nation, in conjunction with the agent of the Government of the United States.

ARTICLE 7. This treaty, or articles of convention, after the same have been ratified, by the President and Senate shall be obligatory on the United States and said Cherokee nation.

In testimony whereof, the said Montfort Stokes, Henry L. Ells-worth, and John F. Schermerhorn, commissioners as aforesaid, and the chiefs and head men of the Cherokee nation aforesaid, have hereunto set their hands, at Fort Gibson on the Arkansas river, on the 14th day of February, one thousand eight hundred and thirty-three.

Montfort Stokes, Walter Weller, Henry L. Ellsworth,

Principal chiefs: J.F. Schermerhorn, John Rogers, president commissioners, John Jolly, his x mark

Glass, president council, Black Coat, his x mark.

Signed, sealed, and delivered in our presence: S.C. Stambaugh, secretary commissioners, M. Arbuckle, colonel Seventh Infantry, Geo. Vashon, agent Cherokees west, Jno. Campbell, agent Creeks. Alexander Brown, his x mark, Jno. Hambly, Interpreters, Wilson Nesbitt, Peter A. Carns, N. Young, major U. S. Army, W. Seawell, lieutenant Seventh Infantry, Wm. Thornton, clerk committee, Charles Webber, clerk council.

TREATY WITH THE CREEKS {1833, Feb. 14}
Proclamation, Apr. 12, 1834.

Articles of agreement and convention, made and concluded at Fort Gibson, between Montfort Stokes, Henry L. Ellsworth and John F. Schermerhorn, Commissioners on the part of the United States, and the undersigned Chiefs and Head-men of the Muskogee or Creek nation of Indians, this 14th day of February, A. D. 1833.

WHEREAS, certain articles of a treaty were concluded at the City of Washington, on the 24th day of January one thousand eight hundred and twenty-six, by and between James Barbour, Secretary of War, on be, half of the United States, and the Chiefs and head-men of the Creek nation of Indians; by which it is agreed that the said Indians shall remove to a country west of the Mississippi river: and whereas the sixth article of said treaty provides as follows:" that a deputation of five persons shall be sent by them, (the Creek nation) at the expense of the United States, immediately after the ratification of the treaty, to examine the country west of the Mississippi, not within the limits of the States or Territories, and not possessed by the Choctaws or Cherokees. And the United States agree to purchase for them, if the same can conveniently be done upon reasonable terms, wherever they may select, a country, whose extent shall in the opinion of the President, be proportioned to their numbers. And if such purchase can not be thus made, it is then agreed that the selection shall be made where the President may think proper, just reference being had to the wishes of the emigrating party.

And whereas, the Creek Indians aforesaid, send five persons as delegates, to explore the country pointed out to them by their treaty; which delegates selected a country west of the Territory of Arkansas, lying and being along and between the Verdigris, Arkansas, and Canadian rivers: and to the country thus selected, a party of the Creek Indians emigrated the following year. And whereas certain articles of treaty or convention, were concluded at the city of Washington on the 6th day of May, A. D. one thousand eight hundred and twenty-eight, by and between James Barbour Secretary of War, on behalf of the United States, and certain chiefs and head-men of the Cherokee nation of Indians; by the second article of which convention, a country was assigned to the Cherokee Indians aforesaid, including within its boundaries some of the lands previously selected and claimed by the Creek Indians, under their treaty aforesaid.

And whereas, the President and Senate of the United States, for the purpose of protecting the rights secured to the Creek Indians, by their treaty stipulations, and with a view to prevent collison and misunderstanding between the two nations, ratified and confirmed the Cherokee treaty, on the 28th day of May, 1828, with the following proviso: viz: "Provided, nevertheless, that the said convention shall not be so construed as to extend the northern boundary of the perpetual outlet west, provided for and guarranteed in the second article of said convention, north of the 36th deg. of north latitude, or so as to interfere with the lands assigned, or to be assigned, west of the Mississippi river to the Creek Indians, who have emigrated or may emigrate from the States of Georgia and Alabama, under the provisions of any treaty or treaties heretofore concluded between the United States and the Creek tribe of Indians.

And provided further, that nothing in the said convention shall be construed to cede or assign to the Cherokees any lands heretofore ceded or assigned to any tribe or tribes of Indians, by any treaty now existing and in force, with any such tribe or tribes." And whereas the said proviso and ratification of the Cherokee treaty, was accepted by the delegates of the nation, then at the City of Washington as satisfactory to them, as is shown in and by their certain instrument in writing, bearing date the 31st day of May 1828, appended to and published with their treaty aforesaid. But, afterwards, the Cherokees of Arkansas and many of those residing east of the Mississippi at the time that treaty was concluded, removed to the country described in the second article of their treaty and settled upon a certain portion of the land claimed by the Creek Indians under their treaty provisions and stipulations.

And whereas difficulties and dissentions thus arose between the Cherokees and Creek tribes about their boundary lines, which occasioned an appeal to the

President of the United States for his interposition, and final settlement of the question, which they were unable to settle between themselves. And whereas the commissioners of the United States, whose names are signed hereto, in pursuance of the power and authority vested in them by the President of the United States, met the chiefs and head-men of the Cherokee and Creek nations of Indians, in council, on the 29th ultimo; and after a full and patient hearing and careful examination of all the claims, set up and brought forward by both the contending parties, they have this day effected an adjustment of all their difficulties, and have succeeded in defining and establishing boundary lines to their country west of the Mississippi, which have been acknowledged, in open council, this day, to be mutually satisfactory to both nations.

Now, therefore, for the purpose of securing the great objects contemplated by an amicable settlement of the difficulties heretofore existing between the Cherokee and Muskogee or Creek Indians, or injurious to both parties; and in order to establish boundary lines which will secure a country and permanent home to the whole Creek [390] nation of Indians, including the Seminole nation who are anxious to join them, the undersigned commissioners, duly authorized to act on behalf of the United States, and the chiefs and head-men of the said Muskogee or Creek Indians, having full power and authority to act for their people west of the Mississippi, hereby agree to the following articles:

ARTICLE 1. The Muskogee or Creek nation of Indians, west of the Mississippi declare themselves to be the friends and allies of the United States, under whose parental care and protection they desire to continue: and that they are anxious to live in peace and friendship not only with their near neighbors and brothers, the Cherokees, but with all the surrounding tribes of Indians.

ARTICLE 2. The United States hereby agree, by and with the consent of the Creek and Cherokee delegates, this day obtained, that the Muskogee or Creek country west of the Mississippi, shall be embraced within the following boundaries, viz:Beginning at the mouth of the north fork of the Canadian river, and run northerly four milesthence running a straight line so as to meet a line drawn from the south bank of the Arkansas river opposite to the east or lower bank of Grand river, at its junction with the Arkansas, and which runs a course south, 44 deg. west, one mile, to a post placed in the groundthence along said line to the Arkansas, and up the same and the Verdigris river, to where the old territorial line crosses itthence along said line north to a point-twenty-five miles from the Arkansas river where the old territorial line crosses the samethence running a line at right angles with the territorial line aforesaid, or west to the Mexico linethence along the said line southerly to the Canadian river or to the boundary of the Choctaw countrythence down said river to the place of beginning.

The lines, hereby defining the country of the Muskogee Indians on the north and east, bound the country of the Cherokees along these courses, as settled by the treaty concluded this day between the United States and that tribe.

ARTICLE 3. The United States will grant a patent, in fee simple, to the Creek nation of Indians for the land assigned said nation by this treaty or convention, whenever the same shall have been ratified by the President and Senate of the United Statesand the right thus guaranteed by the United States shall be continued to said tribe of Indians, so long as they shall exist as a nation, and continue to occupy the country hereby assigned them.

ARTICLE 4. t is hereby mutually understood and agreed between the parties to this treaty, that the land assigned to the Muskogee Indians, by the second article thereof, shall be taken and considered the property of the whole Muskogee or Creek nation, as well of those now residing upon the land, as the great body of said nation who still remain on the east side of the Mississippi: and it is also understood and agreed that the Seminole Indians of Florida, whose removal to this country is provided for by their treaty with the U. S. dated May 9th, 1832, shall also have a permanent and comfortable home on the lands hereby set apart as the country of the Creek nation: and they (the Seminoles) will hereafter be considered a constituent part of said nation, but are to be located on some part of the Creek country by themselveswhich location will be selected for them by the commissioners who have signed these articles of agreement or convention.

ARTICLE 5. As an evidence of the kind feeling of the United States towards the Muskogee Indians, and as a testimonial of the (their) gratification with the present amicable and satisfactory adjustment of their difficulties with the Cherokees, experienced by the commissioners, they agree on behalf of the United States, to furnish to the Creek Indians west of the Mississippi, one blacksmith and one wheelwright or wagonmaker, as soon as they may be required by the nation, in addition to those already employedalso, to erect shops and furnish tools for the same, and supply the smith shops with one ton of iron and two hundred and fifty pounds of steel each; and allow the said Creek Indians, annually, for education purposes, the sum of one thousand dollars, to be expended under the direction of the President of the United Statesthe whole of the above grants to be continued so long as the President may consider them conducive to the interest and welfare of the Creek Indians: And the United States will also cause to be erected, as soon as conveniently can be done, four patent railway mills, for grinding corn; and will immediately purchase for them twenty-four cross-cut saws.

It being distinctly understood, however, that the grants thus made to the Creek Indians, by this article, are intended solely for the use and benefit of that portion of the Creek nation, who are now settled west of the Mississippi.

ARTICLE 6. The United States agree that the improvements which the Creek Indians may be required to leave, in consequence of the boundary lines this day settled between their people and the Cherokees, shall be valued with as little delay as possible, and a fair and reasonable price paid for the same by the United States.

ARTICLE 7. It is hereby agreed by the Creek nation, parties hereto, that if the saline or salt plains on the great western prairies, should come within the boundaries defined by this agreement, as the country of the Creek nation, then, and in that case the President of the United States, shall have the power to permit all other friendly Indian tribes to visit said salt plains and procure thereon and carry away salt sufficient for their subsistence, without hindrance or molestation from the said Creek Indians.

ARTICLE 8. It is agreed by the parties to this convention, that the country hereby provided for the Creek Indians, shall be taken in lieu of and considered to be the country provided or intended to be provided, by the treaty made between the United States and the Creek nation on the 24th day of January, 18'26, under which they removed to this country.

ARTICLE 9. This agreement shall be binding and obligatory upon the contracting parties, as soon as the same shall be ratified and confirmed by the President and Senate of the United States.

Done in open council, at fort Gibson, this 14th day of February, A. D. one thousand eight hundred and thirty-three.

Montfort Stokes, Henry L. Ellsworth, J. F. Schermerhorn, Roly McIntosh, his x mark, Fuss-hatchie Micoe, his x mark, Benj. Perryman, his x mark, Hospottock Harjoe, his x mark, Cowo-coogee, Maltha, his x mark, Holthimotty Tuston-nucky, his x mark, Toatkah Hanssic, his x mark., Istauchoggo Harjoe, his x mark, Chocoatie Tustonnucky, his x mark, Chiefs of Creek nation.

Signed, sealed, and delivered in our presence: S.C. Stambaugh, secretary to comms, M. Arbucklc, colonel Seventh Infantry, Jno. Campbell, agent Creeks, Geo. Vashon, agent Cherokee, west, N. Young, major U. S. Army, Wilson Nesbitt, W. Seawell, lieutenant Seventh Infantry, Peter A. Carns, Jno. Hambly, interpreter, Alex. Brown, his x mark, Cherokee interpreter.

TREATY WITH THE OTTAWA {1833, Feb. 18}
Proclamation, Mar. 22, 1833.

Articles of a treaty made at Maumee in the State of Ohio, on the eighteenth day of February in the year of our Lord one thousand eight hundred and thirty-three, between George B. Porter, Commissioner on the part of the United States, of the one part; and the undersigned Chiefs and Head men of the Band of Ottawa Indians, residing on the Indian Reserves, on the Miami of Lake Erie, and in the vicinity thereof, representing the whole of said band, of the other part:

WHEREAS, by the twentieth article of the treaty concluded at the foot of the Rapids of the Miami of Lake Erie, on the twenty-ninth day of September A. D. 1817, it is provided as follows: "The United States also agree to grant, by patent, to the Chiefs of the Ottawa tribe of Indians for the use of the said tribe, a tract of land, to contain thirty-four square miles, to be laid out as nearly in a square form as practicable, not interfering with the lines of the tracts reserved by the treaty of Greenville, on the south side of the Miami River of Lake Erie, and to include Tush-que-gan, or McCarty's village; which tracts, thus granted, shall be held by the said tribe, upon the usual conditions of Indian reservations, as though no patent were issued."

And whereas by the sixth article of the treaty concluded at Detroit, on the seventeenth day of November A. D. 1807, it is provided, for the accommodation of the Indians named in the treaty, that certain tracts of land, within the cession then made, should be reserved to the said Indian nations, among which is a reservation described as follows: "Four miles square on the Miami Bay, including the villages where Meskeman and Waugan now live," which reservation was expressly made for the Ottawa tribe.

By virtue of which stipulations and reservations the said Band of Ottawas are now in the occupancy and enjoyment of the two tracts of land therein described;and for the consideration hereinafter stated, have agreed to cede the same to the United States; and bind themselves to each and all of the articles, and conditions which follow:

ARTICLE 1. The said Ottawa Band cede to the United States all their land on each or either side of the Miami River of Lake Erie, or on the Miami Bay, being all the lands mentioned or intended to be included in the two reservations aforesaid, or to which they have any claim. No claims to be made for improvements.

ARTICLE 2. It is agreed that out of the lands hereby ceded, the following reservations shall be made: and that patents for each tract shall be granted by the United States to the individuals respectively and their heirs for the quantity hereby assigned to each, that is to say :A tract of fifteen hundred and twenty acres shall be laid off at the mouth of the River, on the south side thereof, and to be so surveyed as to accommodate the following persons, for whose use respectively, each tract hereinafter described is reserved, viz: three hundred and twenty acres for Au-to-kee, a Chief, at the mouth of the river, to include

Presque Isle :eight hundred acres for Jacques, Robert, Peter, Antoine, Francis and Alexis Navarre, to include their present Improvements:one hundred and sixty acres for Way-say-on, the son of Tush-qua-guan, to include his father's old cabin :the remaining two hundred and forty acres to be set off in the rear of these two sections:eighty acres hereof for Pe-tau, and if practicable to include her cabin and field: eighty acres more thereof for Che-no, a Chief, above, or higher up the little creek, and the other eighty acres thereof, for Joseph Le Cavalier Ranjard, in trust for himself, and the legal representatives of Albert Ranjard, deceased. Also, the following tracts on the north side of said river:one hundred and sixty acres for Wau-sa-on-o-quet, a Chief, to include the improvement where he now lives on Pike creek, and to front on the Bay :eighty acres for Leon Guoin and his children, adjoining the last and on the south side thereof :one hundred and sixty acres for Aush-cush and Ke-tuck-kee, Chiefs, to be laid off on the north side of Ottawa creek, fronting on the same, and above the place where the said Aush-cush now lives.

One hundred and sixty acres for Robert A. Forsyth of Maumee, to be laid off on each side of the turnpike road where half-way creek crosses the same: and one hundred and sixty acres, fronting on the Maumee River, to include the place where Ke-ne-wau-ba formerly resided:-one hundred and sixty acres for John E. Hunt, fronting on the said river, immediately above and adjoining the last; and also one hundred and sixty acres, to adjoin the former tract, on the turnpike road. The said tracts to be surveyed and set off, under the direction of the President of the United States.

The said Au-to-kee, Wa-say-on, Pe-tau-che-no, Wau-sa-on-o-quet, Aush-cush, and Ke-tuck-kee, being Indians, the lands hereby reserved for them, are not to be alienated without the approbation of the President of the United States.
The said Leon Guoin has resided, for a long time among these Indians ;has subsisted them when they would otherwise have suffered, and they are greatly attached to him. They request that the grant be to him and his present wife, during their joint lives, and the life of the survivor, and to their children in fee.

The said Jacques, Robert, Peter, Antoine, Francis and Alexis Navarre have long resided among these Indiansintermarried with them, and been valuable friends.
The said Albert Ranjard, deceased, had purchased land of them previous to the late war, upon which, before he died, he had paid them three hundred dollars, for which his family have never received any equivalent.
The reservations to the said Robert A. Forsyth and John E. Hant, being at the especial request of the said band, in consideration of their long residence among them, and the many acts of kindness they have extended to them.

ARTICLE 3. In consideration of which it is agreed that the United States shall pay to the said band of Indians the sum of twenty-nine thousand four hundred and forty dollars, to be, by direction of the said band, applied in extinguishment of their debts, in manner following: that is to say, to John Hollister and Company, seven thousand three hundred and sixty-five dollars, which includes other claims, directed by the said Indians to be by him paid, amounting to thirteen hundred and nine-five dollars, as per schedule A. herewith:To John E. Hunt, nine thousand nine hundred and twenty-nine dollars, which includes other claims, directed by the said Indians to be by him paid, amounting to two thousand six hundred and seventy-five dollars, and sixty-three cents, as per schedule B. herewith :To Robert A. Forsyth of Maumee, ten thousand eight hundred and ninety dollars, which includes other claims directed by the said Indians to be by him paid, amounting to four thousand four hundred and ten dollars, as per schedule C. herewith.To Louis Beaufit seven hundred dollars. To Pierre Menard four hundred dollars. To John King, one hundred dollars. To Louis King fifty-six dollars. (These schedules are not on file at Washington.)

Within six months after payment by the United States, of the said consideration money the said Indians agree to remove from all the lands herein ceded. And it is expressly understood that in the meantime no interruption shall be offered to the survey of the same by the United States.

And whereas the said Band have represented to the said Commissioner that under the treaty, as interpreted to them, entered into with John B. Gardiner, Commissioner on the part of the United States, on [394] the 30th day of August, 1831, for the cession of a part of their lands, there is due to them, jointly with that portion of the tribe that has emigrated, eighteen thousand dollars, and for which they have made claim: whenever this deficiency shall be paid, it is agreed that out of said fund there shall be paid to Joseph Leronger in full satisfaction of all his claim, four hundred dollars; and to Pierre Menard in like satisfaction, sixteen hundred dollars; to Gabriel Godfroy, junior, in like satisfaction, two hundred dollars, to Waubee's daughter Nau-quesh-kum-o-qua, fifty dollars; to Charles Leway or Nau-way-nes, fifty dollars; to Dr. Horatio Conant, two hundred dollars in full satisfaction of all his claim; to Joseph F. Marsac, fifty dollars.

This treaty, after the same shall have been ratified by the President and Senate of the United States, shall be binding on the contracting parties.
In testimony whereof, the said George B. Porter, and the undersigned chiefs and head men of the said band, have hereunto set their hands, at Maumee, the said day and year.

G. B. Porter,
Wau-see-on-o-quet, his x mark, An-to-kee, his x mark, She-no, his x mark, Wau-be-gaiokek, his x mark, Shaw-wa-no, his x mark, Kee-tuk-kee, his x mark, Aush-cush, his x mark, No-ten-o, his x mark, Way-say-on, his x mark, Sas-sain, his x mark; Nau-qua-gai-shik, his x mark, O-sage, his x mark, Me-sau-kee, his x mark, Kin-je-way-no, his x mark, An-he-qua-to, his x mark,

Meesh-quet, his x mark, Sa-see-go-wa, his x mark, Pe-ton-o-quet, his x mark, Saw-ga-nosh, his x mark, Enne-me-kee, his x mark, Aish-qua-bee, his x mark.

In presence of: J. A. Brush, secretary, Kintzing Pritchette, Henry Conner, Louis Beaufait, James Jackson, sub-agent, John E. Hunt, Chs. C. P. Hunt, G. B. Knaggs, John Hollister, James H. Forsyth, J. D. Beaugrand.

TREATY WITH THE SEMINOLE {1833, Mar. 28}
Proclamation, Apr. 12, 1834.

WHEREAS, the Seminole Indians of Florida, entered into certain articles of agreement, with James Gadson, (Gadsden) Commissioner on behalf of the United States, at Payne's landing, on the 9th day of May, 1832: the first article of which treaty or agreement provides, as follows: "The Seminoles Indians relinquish to the United States all claim to the land they at present occupy in the Territory of Florida, and agree to emigrate to the country assigned to the Creeks, west of the Mississippi river; it being understood that an additional extent of territory proportioned to their number will be added to the Creek country, and that the Seminoles will be received as a constituent part of the Creek nation, and be re-admitted to all the privileges as members of the same."

And whereas, the said agreement also stipulates and provides, that a delegation of Seminoles should be sent at the expense of the United States to examine the country to be allotted them among the Creeks, and should this delegation be satisfied with the character of the country and of the favorable disposition of the Creeks to unite with them as one people, then the aforementioned treaty would be considered binding and obligatory upon the parties. And whereas a treaty was made between the United States and the Creek Indians west of the Mississippi, at Fort Gibson, on the 14th day of February 1833, by which a country was provided for the Seminoles in pursuance of the existing arrangements between the United States and that tribe. And whereas, the special delegation, appointed by the Seminoles on the 9th day of May 1832, have since examined the land designated for them by the undersigned Commissioners, on behalf of the United States, and have expressed themselves satisfied with the same, in and by their letter dated, March 1833, addressed to the undersigned Commissioners.

Now, therefore, the Commissioners aforesaid, by virtue of the power and authority vested in them by the treaty made with Creek Indians on the 14th day of February 1833, as above stated, hereby designate and assign to the Seminole tribe of Indians, for their separate future residence, forever, a tract of country lying between the Canadian river and the north fork thereof, and extending west to where a line running north and south between the main Canadian and north branch, will strike the forks of Little river, provided said west line does not extend more than twenty-five miles west from the mouth of said Little river. And the undersigned Seminole chiefs, delegated as aforesaid, on behalf of their nation hereby declare themselves well satisfied with the location provided for them by the Commissioners, and agree that their nation shall commence the removal to their new home, as soon as the Government will make arrangements for their emigration, satisfactory to the Seminole nation.

And whereas, the said Seminoles have expressed high confidence in the friendship and ability of their present agent, Major Phagen, and desire that he may be permitted to remove them to their new homes west of the Mississippi; the Commissioners have considered their request, and cheerfully recommend Major Phagan as a suitable person to be employed to remove the Seminoles as aforesaid, and trust his appointment will be made, not only to gratify the wishes of the Indians but as conducive to the public welfare.

In testimony whereof, the commissioners on behalf of the United States, and the delegates of the Seminole nation, have hereunto signed their names, this 28th day of March, A. D. 1833, at fort Gibson.

Montfort Stokes, Henry L. Ellsworth, John F. Schermerhorn.
Seminole Delegates: John Hick, representing Sam Jones, his x mark, Holata Emartta, his x mark, Jumper, his x mark, Col Hadgo, his x mark, Charley Emartta, his x mark, Ya-ha-hadge, his x mark, Ne-ha-tho-clo, representing Fuch-a-lusti-hadgo, his x mark, On behalf of the Seminole nation.

TREATY WITH THE APPALACHICOLA BAND {1833, June 18}
Proclamation Apr., 12, 1834.

The undersigned Chiefs for and in behalf of themselves, and Warriors voluntarily relinquish all the privileges to Which they are entitled as parties to a treaty concluded at Camp Moultrie on the 18th of September 1823, and surrender to the United States all their right, title and interest to a reservation of land made for their benefit in the additional article of the said Treaty and which is described in the said article as commencing "on the Appalachicola, at a point to include Yellow Hare's improvements, thence up said river four miles; thence, west, one mile; thence southerly to a point one mile west of the beginning; and thence, east, to the beginning point."

ARTICLE 2. For, and in consideration of said cession the U. States agree to grant, and to convey in three (3) years by patent to Mulatto King or Vacapasacy; and to Tustenuggy Hajo, head Chief of Emat-lochees town, for the benefit of themselves, sub-Chiefs, and Warriors, a section and a half of land to each; or contiguous quarter and fractional sections containing a like quantity of acres; to be laid off hereafter under the direction of the President of the U.

States so as embrace the said Chiefs' fields and improvements, after the lands shall have been surveyed, and the boundaries to correspond with the public surveys; it being understood that the aforesaid Chiefs may with the consent and under the advisement of the Executive of the Territory of Florida, at any time previous to the expiration of the above three years, dispose of the said sections of land, and migrate to a country of their choice; but that should they remain on their lands, the U. States will so soon as Blunt's band and the Seminoles generally have migrated under the stipulations of the treaties concluded with them, withdraw the immediate protection hitherto extended to the aforesaid Chiefs and Warriors and that they thereafter become subject to the government and laws of the territory of Florida.

ARTICLE 3.   The U. States stipulate to continue to Mulato King and Tustenuggy Hadjo, their sub-Chiefs and Warriors their proportion of the annuity of (5000) five thousand dollars to which they are entitled under the treaty of Camp Moultrie, so long as the Seminoles remain in the Territory, and to advance their proportional amount of the said annuity for the balance of the term stipulated for its payment in the treaty aforesaid, whenever the Seminoles finally remove in compliance with the terms of the treaty concluded at Payne's Landing on 9th May 1832.

ARTICLE 4.   If at any time hereafter the Chiefs and Warriors, parties to this agreement, should feel disposed to migrate from the Territory to Florida to the country allotted to the Creeks and Seminoles in Arkansas, should they elect to sell their grants of land as provided for in the first article of this treaty, they must defray from the proceeds of the sales of said land, or from their private resources all the expenses of their migration, subsistence, &c.but if they prefer they may by surrendering to the U. States all the rights and privileges acquired under the provisions of this agreement, become parties to the obligations, provisions and stipulations of the treaty concluded at Payne's landing with the Seminoles on the 9th of May 1832, as a constituent part of said tribe, and reunite with said tribe in their new abode on the Arkansas. The U. States, in that event, agreeing to pay (3,000)three thousand dollars for the reservation relinquished in the first article of this treaty, in addition to the rights and immunities the parties may acquire under the aforesaid treaty at Payne's landing.

In testimony whereof, the commissioner, James Gadsden, in behalf of the United States, and the undersigned chiefs and warriors, have hereunto subscribed their names, and affixed their seals

Done at Pope's, Fayette county, in the territory of Florida, this eighteenth day of June, one thousand eight hundred and thirty-three, and of the independence of the United States, the fifty-eighth.. James Gadsden,

Mulatto King, or Vacapachacy, his x mark, Tustenuggy Hajo, his x mark, Yellow Hare, his x mark, John Walker, his x mark, Yeo-lo-hajo, his x mark, Cath-a-hajo, his x mark, Lath-la-yahola, his x mark, Pa-hosta Tustenuckey, his x mark, Tuse-caia-hajo, his x mark,

Witnesses: Wm. S. Pope, sub-agent, Robert Larance, Joe Miller, interpreter, his x mark, Jim Walker, interpreter, his x mark.

Relinquishment by certain chiefs, of land reserved by the treaty of 18th Sept. 1823.

TREATY WITH THE FLORIDA INDIANS
June 18, 1833.

The undersigned Chiefs for and in behalf of themselves, and Warriors voluntarily relinquish all the privileges to which they are entitled as parties to a treaty concluded at Camp Moultrie on the 18th of September 1823, and surrender to the United States all their right, title and interest to a reservation of land made for their benefit in the additional article of the said treaty and which is described in said article as "commencing on the Chattahoochie, one mile below Econchatimico's house; thence up said river four miles; thence one mile west; thence southerly to a point, one mile west of the beginning; thence east to the beginning point."

ARTICLE 2. For and in consideration of said cession the U. States agree to grant and to convey in three (3) years, by patent to Econchatimico for the benefit of himself, sub-Chiefs and Warriors three sections of land; (or contiguous quarter and fractional sections containing a like quantity of acres) to be laid off hereafter under the direction of the President of the U. States so as to embrace the said Chiefs fields, improvements, &c., after the lands shall have been surveyed, and the boundaries to correspond with the public surveys; it being understood that the aforesaid Chief may with the consent and under the advisement of the Executive of the Territory of Florida, at any time previous to the expiration of the above three years dispose of the said sections of land, and migrate to a country of their choice; but that, should they remain on their lands, the U. States will, so soon as Blunt's band and the Seminoles generally have migrated under the stipulations of the treaty concluded with them, withdraw the immediate protection hitherto extended to the aforesaid Chief, his sub-Chiefs and Warriors, and that they thereafter become subject to the government and laws of the Territory of Florida.

ARTICLE 3. The United States stipulate to continue to Econchati-mico, his sub-Chiefs and Warriors their proportion of the annuity of (5000) five thousand dollars to which they are entitled under the treaty of Camp Moultrie, so long as the Seminoles remain in the Territory, and to advance their proportional amount of said annuity for the balance of the term stipulated for its payment in the treaty aforesaid, whenever the Seminoles finally remove in compliance with the terms of the treaty concluded at Payne's landing on 9th May 1832.

ARTICLE 4. If at any time hereafter, the Chiefs and Warriors, parties to this agreement, should feel disposed to migrate from the Territory of Florida to the country allotted to the Creeks and Seminoles in Arkansas; should they elect to sell their grants of land as provided for in the first article of this treaty, they must defray from the proceeds of the sales of said laud, or from their private resources, all the expenses of their migration, subsistence, &c. But, if they prefer, they may, by surrendering to the U. States all the rights and privileges acquired under the provisions of this agreement, become parties to the obligations, provisions and stipulations of the treaty concluded at Payne's landing with the Seminoles on the 9th May 1832 as a constituent part of said tribe, and re-unite with said tribe in their new abode on the Arkansas, the United States, in that event agreeing to pay (3000) three thousand dollars for the reservation relinquished in the first article of this treaty; in addition to the rights and immunities the parties may acquire under the aforesaid treaty at Payne's landing.

In testimony whereof, the commissioner, James Gadsden, in behalf of the United States, and the undersigned chiefs and warriors, have hereunto subscribed their names and affixed their seals.
Done at Pope's Fayette county, in the territory of Florida, this eighteenth day of June, one thousand eight hundred and thirty-three, and of the independence of the United States, the fifty-eighth.

James Gadsden,
Econ-chati-mico, his x mark, Billy Humpkin, his x mark, Kaley Senehah, his x mark, Elapy Tustenuckey, his x mark, Vauxey Hajo, his x mark, Fose-e-mathla, his x mark, Lath-la-fi-cicio, his x mark,

Witnesses: Wm. S. Pope, sub-agent, Robert Larance, Joe Miller, his x mark, interpreter.
Jim Walker, his x mark, interpreter.

TREATY WITH THE CHICKASAW {1834, May 24}
Proclamation, July 1, 1834.

Articles of convention and agreement proposed by the Commissioners on the part of the United States, in pursuance of the request made, by the Delegation representing the Chickasaw nation of Indians, and which have been agreed to.

ARTICLE 1. It is agreed that perpetual amity, peace and friendship, shall exist between the United States, and the Chickasaw nation of Indians.

ARTICLE 2. The Chickasaws are about to abandon their homes, which they have long cherished and loved; and though hitherto unsuccessful, they still hope to find a country, adequate to the wants and support of their people, somewhere west of the Mississippi and within the territorial limits of the United States; should they do so, the Government of the United States, hereby consent to protect and defend them against the inroads of any other tribe of Indians, and from the whites; and agree to keep them without the limits of any State or Territory. The Chickasaws pledge themselves never to make war upon any Indian people, or upon the whites, unless they are so authorized by the United States. But if war be made upon them, they will be permitted to defend themselves, until assistance, be given to them by the United States, as shall be the case.

ARTICLE 3. The Chickasaws are not acquainted with the laws of the whites, which are extended over them; and the many intruders which break into their country, interrupting their rights and disturbing their repose, leave no alternative whereby restraint can be afforded, other than an appeal to the military force of the country, which they are unwilling to ask for, or see resorted to; and therefore they agree to forbear such a request, for prevention of this great evil.

It is with the understanding, which is admitted, that the agent of the United States, upon the application of the chiefs of the nation, will resort to every legal civil remedy, (at the expense of the United States) to prevent intrusions upon the ceded country; and to restrain and remove trespassers from any selected reservations, upon application of the owner of the same.

And it is also agreed, that the United States, will continue some discreet person as agent, such as they now have, to whom they can look for redress of wrongs and injuries which may be attempted against them; and it is consented, that if any of their property, be taken by persons of the United States, covertly or forcibly, the agent on satisfactory and just complaint being made, shall pursue all lawful civil means, which the laws of the State permit, in which the wrong is done, to regain the same, or to obtain a just remuneration; and on failure or inability to procure redress, for the offended, against the offending party; payment for the loss sustained, on production of the record, and certificate of the facts, by the agent, shall be made by the United States; but in all such cases, satisfactory proof, for the establishing of the claim, shall be offered.

ARTICLE 4. The Chickasaws desire to have within their own direction and control, the means of taking care of themselves. Many of their people are quite competent to manage their affairs, though some are not capable, and might be imposed upon by designing persons; it is therefore agreed that the reservations hereinafter admitted, shall not be permitted to be sold, leased, or disposed of unless it appear by the certificate of at least two of the following persons, to wit: Ish-ta-ho-ta-pa the King, Levi Colbert, George Colbert, Martin Colbert, Isaac Alberson Henry Love, and Benj Love, of which five have affixed their names to this treaty, that the party owning or claiming the same, is capable to manage, and to take care of his or her affairs; which fact, to the best of his knowledge and information, shall be certified by the agent; and furthermore that a fair consideration has been paid.

And thereupon, the deed of conveyance shall be valid provided the President of the United States, or such other person as he may designate shall approve of the same, and endorse it on the deed; which said deed and approval, shall be registered, at the place, and within the time, required by the laws of the State, in which the land may be situated; otherwise to be void. And where such certificate is not obtained; upon the recommendation of a majority of the Delegation, and the approval of the agent, at the discretion of the President of the United States, the same may be sold; but the consideration thereof, shall remain as part of the general Chickasaw fund in the hands of the Government, until such time as the chiefs in council shall think it advisable to pay it to the claimant or to those, who may rightfully claim under said claimant, and shall so recommend it.

And as the King, Levi Colbert, and the Delegation, who have signed this agreement, and to whom certain important and interesting duties purtaining to the nation, are assigned, may die, resign, or remove, so that their people may be without the benefit of their services, it is stipulated, that as often as any vacancy happens, by death, resignation, or otherwise, the chiefs shall select some discrete person of their nation to fill the occurring vacancy, who, upon a certificate of qualification, discretion and capability, by the agent, shall be appointed by the Secretary of War; whereupon, he shall possess all the authority granted to those who are here named, and the nation will make to the person so appointed, such reasonable compensation, as they with the assent of the agent and the Secretary of War, may think right, proper and reasonable to be allowed.

ARTICLE 5. It is agreed that the fourth article of the "Treaty of Pontitock," be so changed, that the following reservations be granted in fee:To heads of families, being Indians, or having Indian families, consisting of ten persons, and upwards, four sections of land are reserved. To those who have five and less than ten persons, three sections. Those who have less than five, two sections. Also those who own more than ten slaves, shall be entitled to one additional section; and those owning ten and less than ten to half a section. These reservations shall be confined, to the sections or fractional sections on which the party claiming lives, or to such as are contiguous or adjoining to the sections resided upon, subject to the following restrictions and conditions:.

Firstly. In cases where there are interferences arising, the oldest occupant or settler, shall have the preference, or, Secondly. Where the land is adjudged unfit for cultivation, by the Agent, and three of the seven persons, named in the fourth article above, the party entitled, shall be, and is, hereby authorized, to locate his claim upon other lands, which may be unappropriated, and not subject to any other claim; and where two or more persons, insist upon the entry of the same unappropriated section or fractional section, the priority of right shall be determined by lot; and where a fractional section is taken, leaving a balance greater or less than the surveyed subdivision of a section, then the deficiency shall be made up, by connecting all the deficiencies so arising: and the Register and Receiver thereupon, shall locate full or fractional sections, fit for cultivation, in the names respectively of the different persons claiming which shall be held by them as tenants in common, according to the respective interests [420] of those who are concerned; and the proceeds when sold by the parties claiming, shall be divided according to the interests, which each may have in said section or fractional section, so located, or the same may be divided agreeably to quality or quantity.

ARTICLE 6. Also reservations of a section to each, shall be granted to persons male and female, not being heads of families, who are of the age of twenty-one years, and upwards, a list of whom, within a reasonable time shall be made out by the seven persons herein before mentioned, and filed with the Agent, upon whose certificate of its believed accuracy, the Register and Receiver, shall cause said reservations to be located upon lands fit for cultivation, but not to interfere with the settlement rights of others. The persons thus entitled, are to be excluded from the estimated numbers contained in any family enumeration, as is provided for in the fifth article preceding: and as to the sale, lease, or disposition of their reserves, they are to be subject to the conditions and restrictions, set forth in the fourth article.

In these and in all other reserves where the party owning or entitled, shall die, the interest in the same shall belong to his wife, or the wife and children, or to the husband, or to the husband and children, if there be any; and in cases of death, where there is neither husband, wife, nor children left, the same shall be disposed of for the general benefit; and the proceeds go into the general Chickasaw fund. But where the estate as is prescribed in this article, comes to the children, and having so come, either of them die, the survivor or survivors of them, shall be entitled to the same. But this rule shall not endure longer than for five years, nor beyond the period when the Chickasaws may leave their present for a new home.

ARTICLE 7. Where any white man, before the date hereof has married an Indian woman, the reservation he may be entitled to under this treaty, she being alive, shall be in her name, and no right of alienation of the same shall purtain to the husband unless he divest her of the title, after the mode and manner that feme coverts, usually divest them selves of title to real estate, that is, by the acknowledgment of the wife which may be taken before the Agent, and certified by him, that she consents to the sale freely, and without compulsion from her husband, who shall at the same time certify that the head of such family is prudent, and competent to care of and manage his affairs; otherwise the proceeds of said sale shall be subject to the provisions and restrictions contained in the fourth article of this agreement. Rights to reservations as are herein, and in other articles of this agreement secured, will purtain to those who have heretofore intermarried with the Chickasaws and are residents of the nation.

ARTICLE 8. Males and females below the age of twenty-one years, whose father being dead, the mother again has married, or who have neither father nor mother, shall each be entitled to half a section of land, but shall not be computed as parts of families under the fifth article, the same to be located under the direction of the Agent, and under the supervision of the Secretary of War, so as not to interfere with any settlement right. These lands may be sold upon a recommendation of a majority of the seven persons, heretofore named in this agreement, setting forth that it will prove advantageous to the parties interested; subject however, to the approval of the President, or such other person as he shall designate. If sold, the funds arising shall be retained, in the possession of the Government, or if the President deem it advisable they shall be invested in stocks for the benefit of the parties interested, if there be a sufficient sum to be invested, (and it can be invested)until said persons marry or come of age, when the amount shall be paid over to those who are entitled to receive it, provided a majority of the seven persons, with the Agent, shall certify, that in their opinion, it will be to their interest and advantage, then, and in that case, the proceeds shall be paid over to the party or parties entitled to receive them.

ARTICLE 9. But, in running the sectional lines, in some cases it will happen, that the spring and the dwelling house, or the spring and the cleared land, or the cleared land and the dwelling house of settlers, may be separated by sectional lines, whereby manifest inconvenience and injury will be occasioned; it is agreed, that when any of these occurrences arise, the party shall be entitled as parts and portions of his reservations, to the adjoining section or fraction, as the case may be, unless there be some older occupant, claiming a preference; and in that event, the right of the party shall extend no farther than to give to the person, thus affected and injured, so much of his separated property, as will secure the spring; also, where a sectional line shall separate any improvement, dwelling house, kitchen or stable, so much of the section, which contains them, shall be added into the occupied section, as will secure them to their original owner; and then and in that case, the older occupant being deprived of preference, shall have his deficiency thus occasioned, made up to him by some fractional section, or after the mode pointed out in the latter part of the fifth article of this treaty.

ARTICLE 10. Reservations are admitted to the following persons, in addition to those which may be claimed under the fifth article of this Treaty to wit:Four sections to their beloved and faithful old Chief Levi Colbert; To George Colbert, Martin Colbert, Isaac Alberson, Henry Love and Benj. Love, in consideration of the trouble they have had in coming to Washington, and of the farther trouble hereafter to be encountered in taking care of the interests of their people, under the provisions of this treaty, one section of land to each. Also there is a fractional section, between the residence of George Colbert, and the Tennessee river, upon which he has a ferry, it is therefore consented that said George Colbert shall own and have so much of said fraction, as may be contained in the following lines, to wit.beginning near Smith's ferry at the point where the base meridian line and the Tennessee river come in contact,thence south so far as to pass the dwelling-house, (and sixty yards beyond it) within which is interred the body of his wife,thence east of the river and down the same to the point of begining. Also there shall be reserved to him an island, in said river, nearly opposite to this fraction, commonly called Colberts Island.
A reservation also of two sections is admitted to Ish-ta-ho-ta-pa the King of the Chickasaw nation. And to Min-ta-ho-yea the mother of Charles Colbert one section of land. Also one section, each, to the following persons :Im-mub-bee, Ish-tim-o-lut-ka, Ah-to-ho-woh, Pis-tah-lah-tubbe, Capt. Samuel Seley and William McGilvery. To Col. Benj. Reynolds their long tried and faithful Agent, who has guarded their interests and twice travelled with their people far west, beyond the Mississippi, to aid them in seeking and finding a home, there is granted two sections of land.

Jointly to William Cooper and John Davis, lawyers of Mississippi who have been faithful to the Indians, in giving them professional advice, and legal assistance, and who are to continue to do so, within the States of Tennessee, Alabama and Mississippi, while the Chickasaw people remain in said States, one section is granted. To Mrs. Margt. Allen wife of the subagent in her own right, half a section. These reservations to Benj. Reynolds, William Cooper, James Davis and Margt. Allen, are to be located so as not to interfere with the Indian reservations.

ARTICLE 11. After the reservations are taken and located, which shall be the case as speedily as may be after the surveys are completed, of which the Register and Receiver shall give notice, the residue of the Chickasaw country shall be sold, as public lands of the United States are sold, with this difference; The lands as surveyed shall be offered at public sale at a price not less than one dollar and a quarter per acre; and thereafter for one year those which are unsold, and which shall have been previously offered at public sale, shall be liable to private entry and sale at that price; Thereafter, and for one year longer they shall be subject to entry and private sale, at one dollar per acre; Thereafter and during the third year, they shall be subject to sale and entry, at fifty cents per acre; Thereafter, and during the fourth year, at twenty-five cents per acre; and afterwards at twelve and a half cents per acre. But as it may happen, in the fourth and after years, that the expenses may prove greater than the receipts, it is agreed, that at any time after the third year, the Chickasaws may declare the residue of their lands abandoned to the United States, and if so, they shall be thenceforth acquitted of all and every expense on account of the sale of the same.

And that they may be advised of these matters it is stipulated, that the Government of the United States, within six months after any public sale takes place, shall advise them of the receipts and expenditures, and of balances in their favor; and also at regular intervals of six months, after the first report is made, will afford them information of the proceeds of all entries and sales. The funds thence resulting, after the necessary expenses of surveying and selling, and other advances which may be made, are repaid to the United States, shall from time to time be invested in some secure stocks, redeemable within a period of not more than twenty years; and the United States will cause the interest arising therefrom, annually to be paid to the Chickasaws.

ARTICLE 12. When any portion of the country is fully surveyed, the President may order the same to be sold, but will allow six months, from the date of the first notice to the first sale; and three months' notice of any subsequent intended public sale, within which periods of time, those who can claim reservations, in the offered ranges of country, shall file their applications and entries with the Register and Receiver; that the name of the owner or claimant of the same, may be entered and marked on the general plat, at the office, whereby mistakes in the sales may be avoided, and injuries be prevented.

ARTICLE 13. f the Chickasaws shall be so fortunate as to procure a home, within the limits of the United States, it is agreed, that with the consent of the President and Senate so much of their invested stocks, as may be necessary to the purchase of a country for them to settle in, shall be permitted to them to be sold, or the United States will advance the necessary amount, upon a guarantee and pledge of an equal amount of their stocks; also, as much of them may be sold, with the consent of the President and Senate, as shall be adjudged necessary for establishing schools, mills, blacksmiths shops; and for the education of their children; and for any other needful purpose, which their situation and condition, may make, and by the President and Senate be considered, necessary; and on the happening of such a contingency, and information thereof being given of an intention of the whole or any portion of the nation to remove; the United States will furnish competent persons, safely to conduct them to their future destination, and also supplies necessary to the same, and for one year after their arrival at the west, provided the Indians shall desire supplies, to be furnished for so long a period; the supplies so afforded, to be chargeable to the general Chickasaw account, provided the funds of said nation shall be found adequate to the expenses which under this and other articles of this agreement may be required.

ARTICLE 14. It is understood and agreed, that articles twelve and thirteen of the "Treaty of Pontitock," of the twentieth day of October, one thousand, eight hundred and thirty-two, and which was concluded, with Genl. John Coffee shall be retained; all the other articles of said treaty, inconsistent in any respect with the provisions of this, are declared to be revoked. Also so much of the supplemental treaty as rebates to Colbert Moore; to the bond of James Colbert transferred to Robert Gordon; to the central position of the Land Office; to the establishment of mail routes through the Chickasaw country; and as it respects the privilege given to John Donely; be, and the same are declared to be in full force.

ARTICLE 15. By the sixth article of a treaty made with the Chickasaw nation, by Andrew Jackson and Isaac Shelby, on the nineteenth day of October, one thousand eight hundred and eighteen, it was provided that a Commissioner should be appointed, to mark the southern boundary of said cession; now it is agreed that the line which was run and marked by the Commissioner on the part of the United States, in pursuance of said treaty, shall be considered the true line to the extent that the rights and interests of the Chickasaws are concerned, and no farther.

ARTICLE 16. The United States agree that the appropriation made by Congress, in the year one thousand eight hundred and thirty-three, for carrying into effect "the treaty with the Chickasaws," shall be applicable to this; to be reimbursed by them; and their agent may receive and be charged with the same, from time to time, as in the opinion of the Secretary of War, any portion may be wanted for national purposes, by the Chickasaws; of which nature and character, shall be considered their present visit to Washington City.

Done at the city of Washington, on the 24th day of May, one thousand eight hundred and thirty-four.

Jn. H. Eaton, commissioner on the part of the United States.

George Colbert, his x mark, Isaac Albertson, his x mark, Martin Colbert, Henry Love, Benjamin Love,

Witnesses: Charles F. Little, secretary to commissioner, Ben. Reynolds, Indian agent, G. W. Long, James Startdefer, Thomas S. Smith, Saml. Swartwout, Wni. Gordon, F. W. Armstrong, C. agent, John M. Millard.

The undersigned, appointed by the Chickasaw nation of Indians in the two-fold capacity of a delegate and interpreter, hereby declares that in all that is set forth

in the above articles of convention and agreement, have been by him fully and accurately interpreted and explained, and that the same has been approved by the entire delegation.
May 24, 1834.

Benjamin Love, delegate and interpreter.
Charles F. Little, secretary to commissioner.
Ben. Reynolds, Indian agent.

May 24, 1834.

Articles supplementary to those concluded and signed, by the United States Commissioner, and the Chickasaw delegation on the 24th day of May, one thousand eight hundred and thirty-four which being agreed to by the President and Senate of the United States, are to stand as part of said treaty.

ARTICLE 1. It is represented that the old chiefs Levi Colbert and Isaac Alberson, who have rendered many and valuable services to their nation, desire on account of their health, to visit some watering place, during the present year, for recovery and restoration; it is agreed that there be paid to the agent for these purposes, and to discharge some debts which are due and owing from the nation, the sum of three thousand dollars, out of the appropriation of one thousand eight hundred and thirty-three, for carrying into effect the "treaty of Pontitock," which said sum so far as used is to be hereafter reimbursed to the nation, by said Levi Colbert and Isaac Alberson, and by the nation to the United States, as other advances are to be reimbursed, from the sale of their lands.

ARTICLE 2. The Chickasaw people express a desire that the Government shall at the expense of the United States, educate some of their children, and they urge the justice of their application, on the ground, that they have ever been faithful and friendly to the people of this country,that they have never raised the tomahawk, to-shed the blood of an American, and have given up heretofore to their white brothers, extensive and valuable portions of their country, at a price wholly inconsiderable and inadequate; and from which the United States have derived great wealth and important advantages; therefore, with the advice and consent of the President and Senate of the United States, it is consented, that three thousand dollars for fifteen years, be appropriated and applied under the direction of the Secretary of War, for the education and instruction within the United States, of such children male and female or either, as the seven persons named in the treaty to which this is a supplement, and their successors, with the approval of the agent, from time to time may select and recommend.

ARTICLE 3. The Chickasaw nation desire to close finally, all the business they have on the east side of the Mississippi, that their Great Father, may be no more troubled with their complaints, and to this end, they ask the Government to receive from them a tract of land, of four miles square, heretofore reserved under the 4th article of their "Treaty of 1818," and to pay them within three months, from the date of this arrangement, the Government price of one dollar and a quarter per acre, for said reserve; and accordingly the same is agreed to, provided a satisfactory relinquishment of title from the parties interested, be filed with the Secretary of War, previous to said payment being made.

ARTICLE 4. Benj. Reynolds, agent at the time of paying their last annuity, had stolen from him by a negro slave of the Chickasaws, a box containing one thousand dollars; the chiefs of the Chickasaw people satisfied of the fact, and hence unwilling to receive the lost amount from their agent, ask, and it is agreed, that the sum so stolen and lost, shall be passed to the credit of their nation by the United States, to be drawn on hereafter for their national purposes.

ARTICLE 5. The Chickasaw people are aware that one clerk is insufficient to the bringing of their lands early into market; and rather than encounter the delay which must ensue, they prefer the increased expense of an additional one. It is therefore stipulated that the President shall appoint another clerk, at the same annual compensation, agreed upon by the "Treaty of Pontitock;" who shall be paid after the manner prescribed therein. But whenever the President shall be of opinion that the services of any officer employed under this treaty, for the sale of lands can be dispensed with; he will in justice to the Chickasaws, and to save them from unnecessary expenses, discontinue the whole, or such as can be dispensed with.

Signed the 24th of May, 1834.

Jn. H. Eaton, commissioner on the part of the United States.
George Colbert, his x mark, Isaac Albertson, his x mark, Martin Colbert, Henry Love, Benjamin Love,

Witnesses:

Charles F. Little, secretary to commissioner, Ben. Reynolds, Indian agent, G. W. Long, James Standefer, Thomas S. Smith, Saml. Swartwout, Wm. Gordon, F. W. Armstrong, C. agent, John M. Millard.

TREATY WITH THE CHEROKEE {1835, Dec. 29}
Proclamation, May 23, 1836.

Articles of a treaty, concluded at New Echota in the State of Georgia on the 29th day of Decr. 1835 by General William Carroll and John F. Schemerhorn commissioners on the part of the United States and the Chiefs Head Men and People of the Cherokee tribe of Indians.

WHEREAS the Cherokees are anxious to make some arrangements with the Government of the United States whereby the difficulties they have experienced by a residence within the settled parts of the United States under the jurisdiction and laws of the State Governments may be terminated and adjusted; and with a view to reuniting their people in one body and securing a permanent home for themselves and their posterity in the country selected by their forefathers without the territorial limits of the State sovereignties, and where they can establish and enjoy a government of their choice and perpetuate such a state of society as may be most consonant with their views, habits and condition; and as may tend to their individual comfort and their advancement in civilization.

And whereas a delegation of the Cherokee nation composed of Messrs. John Ross Richard Taylor Danl. McCoy Samuel Gunter and William Rogers with full power and authority to conclude a treaty with the United States did on the 28th day of February 1835 stipulate and agree with the Government of the United States to submit to the Senate to fix the amount which should be allowed the Cherokees for their claims and for a cession of their lands east of the Mississippi river, and did agree to abide by the award of the Senate of the United States themselves and to recommend the same to their people for their final determination.

And whereas on such submission the Senate advised "that a sum not exceeding five millions of dollars be paid to the Cherokee Indians for all their lands and possessions east of the Mississippi river."

And whereas this delegation after said award of the Senate had been made, were called upon to submit propositions as to its disposition to be arranged in a treaty which they refused to do, but insisted that the same "should be referred to their nation and there in general council to deliberate and determine on the subject in order to ensure harmony and good feeling among themselves."

And whereas a certain other delegation composed of John Ridge Elias Boudinot Archilla Smith S. W. Bell John West Wm. A. Davis and Ezekiel West, who represented that portion of the nation in favor of emigration to the Cherokee country west of the Mississippi entered into propositions for a treaty with John F. Schermerhorn commissioner on the part of the United States which were to be submitted to their nation for their final action and determination:
And whereas the Cherokee people, at their last October council at Red Clay, fully authorized and empowered a delegation or committee of twenty persons of their nation to enter into and conclude a treaty with the United States commissioner then present, at that place or elsewhere and as the people had good reason to believe that a treaty would then and there be made or at a subsequent

council at New Echota which the commissioners it was well known and under-stood, were authorized and instructed to convene for said purpose; and since the said delegation have gone on to Washington city, with a view to close ne-gotiations there, as stated by them notwithstanding they were officially in-formed by the United States commissioner that they would not be received by the President of the United States; and that the Government would transact no business of this nature with them, and that if a treaty was made it must be done here in the nation, where the delegation at Washington last winter urged that it should be done for the purpose of promoting peace and harmony among the people

And since these facts have also been corroborated to us by a communication recently received by the commissioner from the Government of the United States and read and explained to the people in open council and therefore be-lieving said delegation can effect nothing and since our difficulties are daily increasing and our situation is rendered more and more precarious uncertain and insecure in consequence of the legislation of the States; and seeing no ef-fectual way of relief, but in accepting the liberal overtures of the United States.

And whereas Genl William Carroll and John F. Schermerhorn were appointed commissioners on the part of the United States, with full power and authority to conclude a treaty with the Cherokees east and were directed by the President to convene the people of the nation in general council at New Echota and to sub-mit said propositions to them with power and authority to vary the same so as to meet the views of the Cherokees in reference to its details, And whereas the said commissioners did appoint and notify a general council of the nation to convene at New Echota on the 21st day of December 1835; and informed them that the commissioners would be prepared to make a treaty with the Cherokee people who should assemble there and those who did not come they should conclude gave their assent and sanction to whatever should be transacted at this council and the people having met in council according to said notice.

Therefore the following articles of a treaty are agreed upon and concluded be-tween William Carroll and John F. Schermerhorn commissioners on the part of the United States and the chiefs and head men and people of the Cherokee na-tion in general council assembled this 29th day of Decr 1835.

ARTICLE 1. The Cherokee nation hereby cede relinquish and convey to the United States all the lands owned claimed or possessed by them east of the Mississippi river, and hereby release all their claims upon the United States for spoliations of every kind for and in consideration of the sum of five millions of dollars to be expended paid and invested in the manner stipulated and agreed upon in the following articles But as a question has arisen between the commis-sioners and the Cherokees whether the Senate in their resolution by which they advised "that a sum not exceeding five millions of dollars be paid to the Cherokee Indians for all their lands and possessions east of the Mississippi river" have included and made any allowance or consideration for claims for spoliations it is therefore agreed on the part of the United States that this question shall be again submitted to the Senate for their consideration and decision and if no allowance was made for spoliations that then an additional sum of three hundred thousand dollars be allowed for the same.

ARTICLE 2. Whereas by the treaty of May 6th 1828 and the supplementary treaty thereto of Feb. 14th 1833 with the Cherokees west of the Mississippi the United States guarantied and secured to be conveyed by patent, to the Cherokee nation of Indians the following tract of country "Beginning at a point on the old western territorial line of Arkansas Territory being twenty-five miles north from the point where the territorial line crosses Arkansas river, thence running from said north point south on the said territorial line where the said territorial line crosses Verdigris river; thence down said Verdigris river to the Arkansas river; thence down said Arkansas to a point where a stone is placed opposite the east or lower bank of Grand river at its junction with the Arkansas; thence running south forty-four degrees west one mile; thence in a straight line to a point four miles northerly, from the mouth of the north fork of the Canadian; thence along the said four mile line to the Canadian

Thence down the Canadian to the Arkansas; thence down the Arkansas to that point on the Arkansas where the eastern Choctaw boundary strikes said river and running thence with the western line of Arkansas Territory as now defined, to the southwest corner of Missouri; thence along the western Missouri line to the land assigned the Senecas; thence on the south line of the Senecas to Grand river; thence up said Grand river as far as the south line of the Osage reservation, extended if necessary; thence up and between said south Osage line extended west if necessary, and a line drawn due west from the point of beginning to a certain distance west, at which a line running north and south from said Osage line to said due west line will make seven millions of acres within the whole described boundaries. In addition to the seven millions of acres of land thus provided for and bounded, the United States further guaranty to the Cherokee nation a perpetual outlet west, and a free and unmolested use of all the country west of the western boundary of said seven millions of acres, as far west as the sovereignty of the United States and their right of soil extend:

Provided however That if the saline or salt plain on the western prairie shall fall within said limits prescribed for said outlet, the right is reserved to the United States to permit other tribes of red men to get salt on said plain in common with the Cherokees; And letters patent shall be issued by the United States as soon as practicable for the land hereby guarantied.

And whereas it is apprehended by the Cherokees that in the above cession there is not contained a sufficient quantity of land for the accommodation of the whole nation on their removal west of the Mississippi the United States in consideration of the sum of five hundred thousand dollars therefore hereby covenant and agree to convey to the said Indians, and their descendants by patent, in fee simple the following additional tract of land situated between the west line of the State of Missouri and the Osage reservation beginning at the southeast corner of the same and runs north along the east line of the Osage lands fifty miles to the northeast corner thereof; and thence east to the west line of the State of Missouri; thence with said line south fifty miles; thence west to the place of beginning; estimated to contain eight hundred thousand acres of land; but it is expressly understood that if any of the lands assigned the Quapaws shall fall within the aforesaid bounds the same shall be reserved and excepted out of the lands above granted and a pro rata reduction shall be made in the price to be allowed to the United States for the same by the Cherokees.

ARTICLE 3. The United States also agree that the lands above ceded by the treaty of Feb. 14 1833, including the outlet, and those ceded by this treaty shall all be included in one patent executed to the Cherokee nation of Indians by the President of the United States according to the provisions of the act of May 28 1830. It is, however, agreed that the military reservation at Fort Gibson shall be held by the United States. But should the United States abandon said post and have no further use for the same it shall revert to the Cherokee nation. The United States shall always have the right to make and establish such post and military roads dad forts in any part of the Cherokee country, as they may deem proper for the interest and protection of the same and the free use of as much land, timber, fuel and materials of all kinds for the construction and support of the same as may be necessary; provided that if the private rights of individuals are interfered with, a just compensation therefor shall be made.

ARTICLE 4. The United States also stipulate and agree to extinguish for the benefit of the Cherokees the titles to the reservations within their country made in the Osage treaty of 1825 to certain half-breeds and for this purpose they hereby agree to pay to the persons to whom the same belong or have been assigned or to their agents or guardians whenever they shall execute after the ratification of this treaty a satisfactory conveyance for the same, to the United States, the sum of fifteen thousand dollars according to a schedule accompanying this treaty of the relative value of the several reservations.

And whereas by the several treaties between the United States and the Osage Indians the Union and Harmony Missionary reservations which were established for their benefit are now situated within the country ceded by them to the United States; the former being situated in the Cherokee country and the latter In the State of Missouri. It is therefore agreed that the United States shall pay the American Board of Commissioners for Foreign Missions for the improvements on the same what they shall be appraised at by Capt. Geo. Vashon Cherokee sub-agent Abraham Redfield and A. P. Chouteau or such persons as the President of the United States shall appoint and the money allowed for the same shall be expended in schools among the Osages and improving their condition. It is understood that the United States are to pay the amount allowed for the reservations in this article and not the Cherokees.

ARTICLE 5. The United States hereby covenant and agree that the lands ceded to the Cherokee nation in the forgoing article shall, in no future time without their consent, be included within the territorial limits or jurisdiction of any State or Territory. But they shall secure to the Cherokee nation the right by their national councils to make and carry into effect all such laws as they may deem necessary for the government and protection of the persons and property within their own country belonging to their people or such persons as have connected themselves with them: provided always that they shall not be inconsistent with the constitution of the United States and such acts of Congress as have been or may be passed regulating trade and intercourse with the Indians; and also, that they shall not be considered as extending to such citizens and army of the United States as may travel or reside in the Indian country by permission according to the laws and regulations established by the Government of the same.

ARTICLE 6. Perpetual peace and friendship shall exist between the citizens of the United States and the Cherokee Indians. The United States agree to protect the Cherokee nation from domestic strife and foreign enemies and against intestine wars between the several tribes. The Cherokees shall endeavor to preserve and maintain the peace of the country and not make war upon their neighbors they shall also be protected against interruption and intrusion from citizens of the United States, who may attempt to settle in the country without their consent; and all such persons shall be removed from the same by order of the President of the United States. But this is not intended to prevent the residence among them of useful farmers mechanics and teachers for the instruction of Indians according to treaty stipulations.

ARTICLE 7. The Cherokee nation having already made great progress in civilization and deeming it important that every proper and laudable inducement should be offered to their people to improve their condition as well as to guard and secure in the most effectual manner the rights guarantied to them in this treaty, and with a view to illustrate the liberal and enlarged policy of the Government of the United States towards the Indians in their removal beyond the territorial limits of the States, it is stipulated that they shall be entitled to a delegate in the House of Representatives of the United States whenever Congress shall make provision for the same.

ARTICLE 7. The United States also agree and stipulate to remove the Cherokees to their new homes and to subsist them one year after their arrival there and that a sufficient number of steamboats and baggage-wagons shall be furnished to remove them comfortably, and so as not to endanger their health, and that a physician well supplied with medicines shall accompany each detachment of emigrants removed by the Government. Such persons and families as in the opinion of the emigrating agent are capable of subsisting and removing themselves shall be permitted to do so; and they shall be allowed in full for all claims for the same twenty dollars for each member of their family; and in lieu of their one year's rations they shall be paid the sum of thirty-three dollars and thirty-three cents if they prefer it.

Such Cherokees also as reside at present out of the nation and shall remove with them in two years west of the Mississippi shall be entitled to allowance for removal and subsistence as above provided.

ARTICLE 8. The United States agree to appoint suitable agents who shall make a just and fair valuation of all such improvements now in the possession of the Cherokees as add any value to the lands; and also of the ferries owned by them, according to their net income; and such improvements and ferries from which they have been dispossessed in a lawless manner or under any existing laws of the State where the same may be situated.

The just debts of the Indians shall be paid out of any monies due them for their improvements and claims; and they shall also be furnished at the discretion of the President of the United States with a sufficient sum to enable them to obtain the necessary means to remove themselves to their new homes, and the balance of their dues shall be paid them at the Cherokee agency west of the Mississippi. The missionary establishments shall also be valued and appraised in a like manner and the amount of them paid over by the United States to the treasurers of the respective missionary societies by whom they have been established and improved in order to enable them to erect such buildings and make such improvements among the Cherokees west of the Mississippi as they may deem necessary for their benefit. Such teachers at present among the Cherokees as this council shall select and designate shall be removed west of the Mississippi with the Cherokee nation and on the same terms allowed to them.

ARTICLE 9. The President of the United States shall invest in some safe and most productive public stocks of the country for the benefit of the whole Cherokee nation who have removed or shall remove to the lands assigned by this treaty to the Cherokee nation west of the Mississippi the following sums as a permanent fund for the purposes hereinafter specified and pay over the net income of the same annually to such person or persons as shall be authorized or appointed by the Cherokee nation to receive the same and their receipt shall be a full discharge for the amount paid to them viz: the sum of two hundred thousand dollars in addition to the present annuities of the nation to constitute a general fund the interest of which shall be applied annually by the council of the nation to such purposes as they may deem best for the general interest of their people. The sum of fifty thousand dollars to constitute an orphans' fund the annual income of which shall be expended towards the support and education of such orphan children as are destitute of the means of subsistence.

The sum of one hundred and fifty thousand dollars in addition to the present school fund of the nation shall constitute a permanent school fund, the interest of which shall be applied annually by the council of the nation for the support of common schools and such a literary institution of a higher order as may be established in the Indian country. And in order to secure as far as possible the true and beneficial application of the orphans' and school fund the council of the Cherokee nation when required by the President of the United States shall make a report of the application of those funds and he shall at all times have the right if the funds have been misapplied to correct any abuses of them and direct the manner of their application for the purposes for which they were intended.

The council of the nation may by giving two years' notice of their intention withdraw their funds by and with the consent of the President and Senate of the United States, and invest them in such manner as they may deem most proper for their interest. The United States also agree and stipulate to pay the just debts and claims against the Cherokee nation held by the citizens of the same and also the just claims of citizens of the United States for services rendered to the nation and the sum of sixty thousand dollars is appropriated for this purpose but no claims against individual persons of the nation shall be allowed and paid by the nation The sum of three hundred thousand dollars is hereby set apart to pay and liquidate the just claims of the Cherokees upon the United States for spoliations of every kind, that have not been already satisfied under former treaties.

ARTICLE 10. The Cherokee nation of Indians believing it will be for the interest of their people to have all their funds and annuities under their own direction and future disposition hereby agree to commute their permanent annuity of ten thousand dollars for the sum of two hundred and fourteen thousand dollars, the same to be invested by the President of the United States as a part of the general fund of the nation; and their present school fund amounting to about fifty thousand dollars shall constitute a part of the permanent school fund of the nation.

ARTICLE 11. Those individuals and families of the Cherokee nation that are averse to a removal to the Cherokee country west of the Mississippi and are desirous to become citizens of the States where they reside and such as are qualified to take care of themselves and their property shall be entitled to receive their due portion of all the personal benefits accruing under this treaty for their claims, improvements and per capita; as soon as an appropriation is made for this treaty.

Such heads of Cherokee families as are desirous to reside within the States of No. Carolina Tennessee and Alabama subject to the laws of the same; and who are qualified or calculated to become useful citizens shall be entitled, on the certificate of the commissioners to a preemption right to one hundred and sixty acres of land or one quarter section at the minimum Congress price; so as to include the present buildings or improvements of those who now reside there and such as do not live there at present shall be permitted to locate within two years any lands not already occupied by persons entitled to pre-emption privilege under this treaty and if two or more families live on the same quarter section and they desire to continue their residence in these states and are qualified as above specified they shall, on receiving their pre-emption certificate be entitled to the right of pre-emption to such lands as they may select not already taken by any person entitled to them under this treaty.

It is stipulated and agreed between the United States and the Cherokee people that John Ross James Starr George Hicks John Gunter George Chambers John Ridge Elias Boudinot George Sanders John Martin William Rogers Roman Nose Situwake and John Timpson shall be a committee on the part of the Cherokees to recommend such persons for the privilege of pre-emption rights as may be deemed entitled to the same under the above articles and to select the missionaries who shall be removed with the nation; and that they be hereby fully empowered and authorized to transact all business on the part of the Indians which may arise in carrying into effect the provisions of this treaty and settling the same with the United States. If any of the persons above mentioned should decline acting or be removed by death; the vacancies shall be filled by the committee themselves.

It is also understood and agreed that the sum of one hundred thousand dollars shall be expended by the commissioners in such manner as the committee deem best for the benefit of the poorer class of Cherokees as shall remove west or have removed west and are entitled to the benefits of this treaty. The same to be delivered at the Cherokee agency west as soon after the removal of the nation as possible.

ARTICLE 12. In order to make a final settlement of all the claims of the Cherokees for reservations granted under former treaties to any individuals belonging to the nation by the United States it is therefore hereby stipulated and agreed and expressly understood by the parties to this treatythat all the Cherokees and their heirs and descendants to whom any reservations have been made under any former treaties with the United States, and who have not sold or conveyed the same by deed or otherwise and who in the opinion of the commissioners have complied with the terms on which the reservations were granted as far as practicable in the several cases; and which reservations have since been sold by the United States shall constitute a just claim against the United States and the original reservee or their heirs or descendants shall be entitled to receive the present value thereof from the United States as unimproved lands. And all such reservations as have not been sold by the United States and where the terms on which the reservations were made in the opinion of the commissioners have been complied with as far as practicable, they or their heirs or descendants shall be entitled to the same.

They are hereby granted and confirmed to themand also all persons who were entitled to reservations under the treaty of 1817 and who as far as practicable in the opinion of the commissioners, have complied with the stipulations of said treaty, although by the treaty of 1819 such reservations were included in the unceded lands belonging to the Cherokee nation are hereby confirmed to them and they shall be entitled to receive a grant for the same. And all such reservees as were obliged by the laws of the States in which their reservations were situated, to abandon the same or purchase them from the States shall be deemed to have a just claim against the United States for the amount by them paid to the States with interest thereon for such reservations and if obliged to abandon the same, to the present value of such reservations as unimproved lands.

In all cases where the reservees have sold their reservations or any part thereof and conveyed the same by deed or otherwise and have been paid for the same, they their heirs or descendants or their assigns shall not be considered as having any claims upon the United States under this article of the treaty nor be entitled to receive any compensation for the lands thus disposed of. It is expressly understood by the parties to this treaty that the amount to be allowed for reservations under this article shall not be deducted out of the consideration money allowed to the Cherokees for their claims for spoliations and the cession of their lands; but the same is to be paid for independently by the United States as it is only a just fulfilment of former treaty stipulations.

ARTICLE 13. It is also agreed on the part of the United States that such warriors of the Cherokee nation as were engaged on the side of the United States in the late war with Great Britain and the southern tribes of Indians, and who were wounded in such service shall be entitled to such pensions as shall be allowed them by the Congress of the United States to commence from the period of their disability.

ARTICLE 14. It is expressly understood and agreed between the parties to this treaty that after deducting the amount which shall be actually expended for the payment for improvements, ferries, claims, for spoliations, removal subsistence and debts and claims upon the Cherokee nation and for the additional quantity of lands and goods for the poorer class of Cherokees and the several sums to be invested for the general national funds; provided for in the several articles of this treaty the balance whatever the same may be shall be equally divided between all the people belonging to the Cherokee nation east according to the census just completed; and such Cherokees as have removed west since June

1833 who are entitled by the terms of their enrolment and removal to all the benefits resulting from the final treaty between the United States and the Cherokees east they shall also be paid for their improvements according to their approved value before their removal where fraud has not already been shown in their valuation.

ARTICLE 15. It is hereby stipulated and agreed by the Cherokees that they shall remove to their new homes within two years from the ratification of this treaty and that during such time the United States shall protect and defend them in their possessions and property and free use and occupation of the same and such persons as have been dispossessed of their improvements and houses; and for which no grant has actually issued previously to the enactment of the law of the State of Georgia, of December 1835 to regulate Indian occupancy shall be again put in possession and placed in the same situation and condition, in reference to the laws of the State of Georgia, as the Indians that have not been dispossessed; and if this is not done, and the people are left unprotected, then the United States shall pay the several Cherokees for their losses and damages sustained by them in consequence thereof. And it is also stipulated and agreed that the public buildings and improvements on which they are situated at New Echota for which no grant has been actually made previous to the passage of the above recited act if not occupied by the Cherokee people shall be reserved for the public and free use of the United States and the Cherokee Indians for the purpose of settling and closing all the Indian business arising under this treaty between the commission-era of claims and the Indians.

The United States, and the several States interested in the Cherokee lands, shall immediately proceed to survey the lands, shall immediately proceed to survey the lands ceded by this treaty; but it is expressly agreed and understood between the parties that the agency buildings and that tract of land surveyed and laid off for the use of Colonel R. J. Meigs Indian agent or heretofore enjoyed and occupied by his successors in office shall continue subject to the use and occupancy of the United States, or such agent as may be engaged specially superintending the removal of the tribe.

ARTICLE 16. All the claims arising under or provided for in the several articles of this treaty shall be examined and adjudicated by such commissioners as shall be appointed by the President of the United States by and with the advice and consent of the Senate of the United States for that purpose and their decision shall be final and on their certificate of the amount due the several claimants they shall be paid by the United States. All stipulations in former treaties which have not been superseded or annulled by this shall continue in full force and virtue.

ARTICLE 17. Whereas in consequence of the unsettled affairs of the Cherokee people and the early frosts, their crops are insufficient to support their families and great distress is likely to ensue and whereas the nation will not, until after their removal be able advantageously to expend the income of the permanent funds of the nation it is therefore agreed that the annuities of the nation which may accrue under this treaty for two years, the time fixed for their removal shall be expended in provision and clothing for the benefit of the poorer class of the nation; and the United States hereby agree to advance the same for that purpose as soon after the ratification of this treaty as an appropriation for the same shall be made. It is however not intended in this article to interfere with that part of the annuities due the Cherokees west by the treaty of 1819.

ARTICLE 18. This treaty after the same shall be ratified by the President and Senate of the United States shall be obligatory on the contracting parties.

ARTICLE 19. (Supplemental article. Stricken out by Senate.) In testimony whereof, the commissioners and the chiefs, head men, and people whose names are hereunto annexed, being duly authorized by the people in general council assembled, have affixed their hands and seals for themselves, and in behalf of the Cherokee nation.

I have examined the foregoing treaty, and although not present when it was made, I approve its provisions generally, and therefore sign it.
Wm. Carroll, J. F. Schermerhom.
Major Ridge, his x mark, James Foster, his x mark, Tesa-ta-esky, his x mark, Charles Moore, his x mark, George Chambers, his x mark, Tah-yeske, his x mark, Archilia Smith, his x mark,
Signed and sealed in presence of: Western B. Thomas, secretary, C.M Hitch-cock, M.D., assistant surgeon, Ben. F. Currey, special agent. U.S.A, M.Wolfe Batruan, first lieutenant, sixth, G.W. Currey, U.S. Infantry, disbursing agent.

In compliance with instructions of the council at New Echota, we sign this treaty.

Stand Watie, John Ridge.
March 1,1836.

Witnesses: Elbert Herring, Wm. Y. Hansell, Alexander H. Everett, Samuel J. Pods,

Dec. 31,1835.

Whereas the western Cherokees have appointed a delegation to visit the eastern Cherokees to assure them of the friendly disposition of their people and their desire that the nation should again be united as one people and to urge upon them the expediency of accepting the overtures of the Government; and that, on their removal they may be assured of a hearty welcome and an equal participation with them in all the benefits and privileges of the Cherokee country west and the undersigned two of said delegation being the only delegates in the eastern nation from the west at the signing and sealing of the treaty lately concluded at New Echota between their eastern brethren and the United States; and having fully understood the provisions of the same they agree to it in behalf of the western Cherokees. But it is expressly understood that nothing in this treaty shall affect any claims of the western Cherokees on the United States.

In testimony whereof, we have, this 31st day of December, 1835, hereunto set our hands and seals.
James Rogers, John Smith. Delegates from the western Cherokees.
Test: Ben. F. Currey, special agent, M.W. Batman, first lieutenant, Sixth Infantry, Jno. L. Hooper, lieutenant, Fourth Infantry, Blias Boudinot.
Schedu/e and estimated value of the Osage ha{{breed reservations within ceded to the Cherokees west of the Miss issiflpi, (referred to in article 5 on the foregoing treaty) viz.

Augustus Clamont one section	$6,000
James	1,000
Paul	1,300
Henry	800
Anthony	1,800
Rosalie	1,800
Bmilia D, of Mihanga	1,000
Emilia D, of Shemianga	1,300
	$15,000

I hereby certify that the above schedule is the estimated value of the Osage reservations; as made out and agreed upon with C&. A. P. Choteau who represented himself as the agent or guardian of the above reservees.
J. F. Schermerhorn.
March 14, 1835.

March 1,1836.
Proclamation, May 23,1836.

Supplementary articles to a treaty concluded at New Echota, Georgia, December 29,]835, between the United States and Cherokee people.

WHEREAS the undersigned were authorized at the general meeting of the Cherokee people held at New Echota as above stated, to make and assent to such alterations in the preceding treaty as might be thought necessary, and whereas the President of the United States has expressed his determination not to allow any pre-emptions or reservations his desire being that the whole

Cherokee people should remove together and establish themselves in the country provided for them west of the Mississippi river.

ARTICLE 1. It is therefore agreed that all the pre-emption rights and reservations provided for in articles 12 and 13 shall be and are hereby relinquished and declared void.

ARTICLE 2. Whereas the Cherokee people have supposed that the sum of five millions of dollars fixed by the Senate in their resolution of day of March, *1835,* as the value of the Cherokee lands and possessions east of the Mississippi river was not intended to include the amount which may be required to remove them, nor the value of certain claims which many of their people had against citizens 6f the United States, which suggestion has been confirmed by the opinion expressed to the War Department by some of the Senators who voted upon the question and whereas the President is willing that this subject should be referred to the Senate for their consideration and if it was not intended by the Senate that the above-mentioned sum of five millions of dollars should include the objects herein specified that in that case such further provision should be made therefor as might appear to the Senate to be just.

ARTICLE 3. It is therefore agreed that the sum of six hundred thousand dollars shall be and the same is hereby allowed to the Cherokee people to include the expense of their removal, and all claims of every nature and description against the Government of the United States not herein otherwise expressly provided for, and to be in lieu of the said reservations and pre-eruptions and of the sum of three hundred thousand d&lars for spoliations described in the 1st article of the above-mentioned treaty. This sum of six hundred thousand dollars shall be applied and distributed agreeably to the provisions of the said treaty, and any surplus which may remain after removal and payment of the claims so ascertained shall be turned over and belong to the education fund. But it is expressly understood that the subject of this article is merely referred hereby to the consideration of the Senate and if they shall approve the same then this supplement shall remain part of the treaty.

ARTICLE 4. It is also understood that the provisions in article 16, for the agency reservation is not intended to interfere with the occupant right of any Cherokees should their improvement fafl within the same.

It is also understood and agreed, that the one hundred thousand dollars appropriated in article 12 for the poorer class of Cherokees and intended as a set-off to the pre-emption rights shall now be transferred from the funds of the nation and added to the general national fund of four hundred thousand dollars so as to make said fund equal to five hundred thousand dollars.

ARTICLE 5. The necessary expenses attending the negotiations of the afore-said treaty and supplement and also of such persons of the delegation as may sign the same shall be defrayed by the United States.

In testimony whereof, John F. Schermerhorn, commissioner on the part of the United States, and the undersigned delegation have hereunto set their hands and seals, this first day of March, in the year one thousand eight hundred and thirty-six.

J.F. Schermerhorn.
Major Ridge, his x mark, James Foster, his x mark, Jah-ye-ske, his x mark, Long Shell Turtle, his x mark, John Fields, his x mark, James Fields, his x mark, George Welch, his x mark, Andrew Ross, William Rogers, John Gunter, Witnesses: Elbert Herring, Thos. Glascock, Alexander H. Everett, Jno Garland, Major, U.S. Army, C.A. Harris, John Robb, Wm. Y Hansell

TREATY WITH THE OTTAWA, ETC. {1836, Mar. 28}
Proclamation, May 27, 1836.

Articles of a treaty made and concluded at the city of Washington in the District of Columbia, between Henry R. Schoolcraft, commissioner on the part of the United States, and the Ottawa and Chippewa nations of Indians, by their chiefs and delegates.

ARTICLE 1. The Ottawa and Chippewa nations of Indians cede to the United States all the tract of country within the following boundaries: Beginning at the mouth of Grand river of Lake Michigan on the north bank thereof, and following up the same to the line called for, in the first article of the treaty of Chicago of the 29th of August 1821, thence, in a direct line, to the head of Thunder-bay river, thence with the line established by the treaty of Saganaw of the 24th of September 1819, to the mouth of said river, thence northeast to the boundary line in Lake Huron between the United States and the British province of Upper Canada, thence northwestwardly, following the said line, as established by the commissioners acting under the treaty of Ghent, through the straits, and river St. Mary's, to a point in Lake Superior north of the mouth of Gitchy Seebing, or Chocolate river, thence south to the mouth of said river and up its channel to the source thereof, thence, in a direct line to the head of the Skonawba river of Green bay, thence down the south bank of said river to its mouth, thence, in a direct line, through the ship channel into Green bay, to the outer part thereof, thence south to a point in Lake Michigan west of the north cape, or entrance of Grand river, and thence east to the place of beginning, at the cape aforesaid, comprehending all the lands and islands, within these limits, not hereinafter reserved.

ARTICLE 2. From the cession aforesaid the tribes reserve for their own use, to be held in common the following tracts for the term of five years from the date of the ratification of this treaty; and no longer; unless the United States shall grant them permission to remain on said lands for a longer period, namely: One tract of fifty thousand acres to be located on Little Traverse bay: one tract of twenty thousand acres to be located on the north shore of Grand Traverse bay, one tract of seventy thousand acres to be located on, or, north of the Pierre Marquetta river, one tract of one thousand acres to be located by Chingassanoo,or the Big Sail, on the Cheboigan. One tract of one thousand acres, to be located by Mujeekewis, on Thunder-bay river.

ARTICLE 3. There shall also be reserved for the use of the Chippewas living north of the straits of Michilimackinac, the following tracts for the term of five years from the date of the ratification of this treaty, and no longer, unless the United States shall grant them permission to remain on said lands for a longer period, that is to say: Two tracts of three miles square each, on the north shores of the said straits, between Point-au-Barbe and Mille Coquin river, including the fishing grounds in front of such reservations, to be located by a council of the chiefs. The Beaver islands of Lake Michigan for the use of the Beaver-island Indians. Round island, opposite Michilimackinac, as a place of encampment for the Indians, to be under the charge of the Indian department.

The islands of the Chenos, with a part of the adjacent north coast of Lake Huron, corresponding in length, and one mile in depth. Sugar island, with its islets, in the river of St. Mary's. Six hundred and forty acres, at the mission of the Little Rapids. A tract commencing at the mouth of the Pississowinig river, south of Point Iroquois, thence running up said stream to its forks, thence westward, in a direct line to the Red water lakes, thence across the portage to the Tacquimenon river, and down the same to its mouth, including the small islands and fishing grounds, in front of this reservation. Six hundred and forty acres, on Grand island, and two thousand acres, on the main land south of it.

Two sections, on the northern extremity of Green bay, to be located by a council of the chiefs. All the locations, left indefinite by this, and the preceding articles, shall be made by the proper chiefs, under the direction of the President. It is understood that the reservation for a place of fishing and encampment, made under the treaty of St. Mary's of the 16th of June 1820, remains unaffected by this treaty.

ARTICLE 4. In consideration of the foregoing cessions, the United States engage to pay to the Ottawa and Chippewa nations, the following sums, namely. First. An annuity of thirty thousand dollars per annum, in specie, for twenty years; eighteen thousand dollars, to be paid to the Indians between Grand River and the Cheboigun; three thousand six hundred dollars, to the Indians on the Huron shore, between the Cheboigan and Thunder-bay river; and seven thousand four hundred dollars, to the Chippewas north of the straits, as far as the cession extends; the remaining one thousand dollars, to be invested in stock by the Treasury Department and to remain incapable of being sold, without the consent of the President and Senate, which may, however, be given, after the expiration of twenty-one years.

Second. Five thousand dollars per annum, for the purpose of education, teachera, school-houses, and books in their own language, to be continued twenty years, and as long thereafter as Congress may appropriate for the object.
Third. Three thousand dollars for missions, subject to the conditions mentioned in the second clause of this article.
Fourth. Ten thousand dollars for agricultural implements, cattle, mechanics' tools, and such other objects as the President may deem proper.

Fifth. Three hundred dollars per annum for vaccine matter, medicines, and the services of physicians, to be continued while the Indians remain on their reservations.

Sixth. Provisions to the amount of two thousand dollars; six thousand five hundred pounds of tobacco; one hundred barrels of salt, and five hundred fish barrels, annually, for twenty years.

Seventh. One hundred and fifty thousand dollars, in goods and provisions, on the ratification of this treaty, to be delivered at Michilimackinac, and also the sum of two hundred thousand dollars, in consideration of changing the permanent reservations in article two and three to reservations for five years only, to be paid whenever their reservations shall be surrendered, and until that time the interest on said two hundred thousand dollars shall be annually paid to the said Indians.

ARTICLE 5. The sum of three hundred thousand dollars shall be paid to said Indians to enable them, with the aid and assistance of their agent, to adjust and pay such debts as they may justly owe, and the overplus, if any, to apply to such other use as they may think proper.

ARTICLE 6. The said Indians being desirous of making provision for their half-breed relatives, and the President having determined, that individual reservations shall not be granted, it is agreed, hat in lieu thereof, the sum of one hundred and fifty thousand dollars shall be set apart as a fund for said half-breeds. No person shall be entitled to any part of said fund, unless he is of Indian descent and actually resident within the boundaries described in the first article of this treaty, nor shall any thing be allowed to any such person, who may have received any allowance at any previous Indian treaty. The following principles, shall regulate the distribution. A census shall be taken of all the men, women, and children, coming within this article. As the Indians hold in higher consideration, some of their half-breeds than others, and as there is much difference in their capacity to use and take care of property, and, consequently, in their power to aid their Indian connexions, which furnishes a strong ground for this claim

It is, therefore, agreed, that at the council to be held upon this subject, the commissioner shall call upon the Indian chiefs to designate, if they require it, three classes of these claimants, the first of which, shall receive one-half more than the second, and the second, double the third.

Each man woman and child shall be enumerated, and an equal share, in the respective classes, shall be allowed to each. If the father is living with the family, he shall receive the shares of himself, his wife and children. If the father is dead, or separated from the family, and the mother is living with the family, she shall have her own share, and that of the children. If the father and mother are neither living with the family, or if the children are orphans, their share shall be retained till they are twenty-one years of age; provided, that such portions of it as may be necessary may, under the direction of the President, be from time to time applied for their support. All other persons at the age of twenty-one years, shall receive their shares agreeably to the proper class. Out of the said fund of one hundred and fifty thousand dollars, the sum of five thousand dollars shall be reserved to be applied, under the direction of the President, to the support of such of the poor half breeds, as may require assistance, to be expended in annual instalments for the term of ten years, commencing with the second year. Such of the half-breeds, as may be judged incapable of making a proper use of the money, allowed them by the commissioner, shall receive the same in instalments, as the President may direct.

ARTICLE 7. In consideration of the cessions above made, and as a further earnest of the disposition felt to do full justice to the Indians, and to further their well being, the United States engage to keep two additional blacksmith-shops, one of which, shall be located on the reservation north of Grand river, and the other at the Sault Ste. Marie. A permanent interpreter will be provided at each of these locations. It is stipulated to renew the present dilapidated shop at Michilimackinac, and to maintain a gunsmith, in addition to the present smith's establishment, and to build a dormitory for the Indians visiting the post, and appoint a person to keep it, and supply it with fire-wood. It is also agreed, to support two farmers and assistants, and two mechanics, as the President may designate, to teach and aid the Indians, in agriculture, and in the mechanic arts. The farmers and mechanics, and the dormitory, will be continued for ten years, and as long thereafter, as the President may deem this arrangement useful and necessary; but the benefits of the other stipulations of this article, shall be continued beyond the expiration of the annuities, and it is understood that the whole of this article shall stand in force, and inure to the benefit of the Indians, as long after the expiration of the twenty years as Congress may appropriate for the objects.

ARTICLE 8. It is agreed, that as soon as the said Indians desire it, a deputation shall be sent to the southwest of the Missouri River, there to select a suitable place for the final settlement of said Indians, which country, so selected and of reasonable extent, the United States will forever guaranty and secure to said Indians. Such improvements as add value to the land, hereby ceded, shall be appraised, and the amount paid to the proper Indian. But such payment shall, in no case, be assigned to, or paid to, a white man. If the church on the Cheboigan, should fall within this cession, the value shall be paid to the band owning it. The net proceeds of the sale of the one hundred and sixty acres of land, upon the Grand River upon which the missionary society have erected their buildings, shall be paid to the said society, in lieu of the value of their said improvements. When the Indians wish it, the United States will remove them, at their expence, provide them a year's subsistence in the country to which they go, and furnish the same articles and equipments to each person as are stipulated to be given to the Pottowatomies in the final treaty of cession concluded at Chicago.

ARTICLE 9. Whereas the Ottawas and Chippewas, feeling a strong consideration for aid rendered by certain of their half-breeds on Grand river, and other parts of the country ceded, and wishing to testify their gratitude on the present occasion, have assigned such individuals certain locations of land, and united in a strong appeal for the allowance of the same in this treaty; and whereas no such reservations can be permitted in carrying out the special directions of the President on this subject, it is agreed, that, in addition to the general fund set apart for half-breed claims, in the sixth article, the sum of forty-eight thousand one hundred and forty-eight dollars shall be paid for the extinguishment of this class of claims, to be divided in the following manner: To Rix Robinson, in lieu of a section of land, granted to his Indian family, on the Grand river rapids, (estimated by good judges to be worth half a million) at the rate of thirty-six dollars an acre: To Leonard Slater, in trust for Chiminonoquat, for a section of land above said rapids, at the rate of ten dollars an acre: To John A. Drew, for a tract of one section and three quarters, to his Indian family, at Cheboigan rapids, at the rate of four dollars; to Edward Biddle, for one section to his Indian family at the fishing grounds, at the rate of three dollars.

To John Holiday, for five sections of land to five persons of his Indian family, at the rate of one dollar and twenty-five cents; to Eliza Cook, Sophia Biddie, and Mary Holiday, one section of land each, at two dollars and fifty cents: To Augustin Hamo-lin junr, being of Indian descent, two sections, at one dollar and twenty-five cents; to William Lasley, Joseph Daily, Joseph Trotier, Henry A. Levake, for two sections each, for their Indian families, at one dollar and twenty-five cents: To Luther Rice, Joseph Lafrombois, Charles Butterfield, being of Indian descent, and to George Moran, Louis Moran, G.D. Williams, for half-breed children under their care, and to Daniel Marsac, for his Indian child, one section each, at one dollar and twenty-five cents.

ARTICLE 10. The sum of thirty thousand dollars shall be paid to the chiefs, on the ratification of this treaty, to be divided agreeably to a schedule hereunto annexed.

ARTICLE 11. The Ottawas having consideration for one of their aged chiefs, who is reduced to poverty, and it being known that he was a firm friend of the American Government, in that quarter, during the late war, and suffered much in consequence of his sentiments, it is agreed, that an annuity of one hundred dollars per annum shall be paid to Ningweegon or the Wing, during his natural life, in money or goods, as he may choose. Another of the chiefs of said nation, who attended the treaty of Greenville in 1793, and is now, at a very advanced age, reduced to extreme want, together with his wife, and the Government being apprized that he has pleaded a promise of Gen. Wayne, in his behalf, it is agreed that Chusco of Michilimackinac shall receive an annuity of fifty dollars per annum during his natural life.

ARTICLE 12. All expenses attending the journeys of the Indians from, and to their homes, and their visit at the seat of Government, together with the expenses of the treaty, including a proper quantity of clothing to be given them, will be paid by the United States.

ARTICLE 13. The Indians stipulate for the right of hunting on the lands ceded, with the other usual privileges of occupancy, until the land is required for settlement.

In testimony whereof, the said Henry R. Schoolcraft, commissioner on the part of the United States, and the chiefs and delegates of the Ottawa and Chippewa nation of Indians, have hereunto set their hands, at Washington the seat of Government, this twenty-eighth day of March, in the year one thousand eight hundred and thirty-six.

Henry R. Schoolcraft.
John Hulbert, secretary.
Oroun Aishkum, of Maskigo, his x mark, Wassangaze, of Maskigo, his x mark, Osawya, of Maskigo, his x mark, Wabi Windego, of Grand river, his x mark, Megiss Ininee, of Grand river, his x mark, Nabun Ageezhig, of Grand river, his x mark, Winnimissagee, of Grand river, his x mark, Mukutaysee, of Grand river, his x mark, Wasaw Bequm, of Grand river, his x mark, Ainse, of Michilimackinac, his x mark, Chabowaywa, of Michilimackinac, his x mark, Jawba Wadiek, of Sault Ste. Marie, his x mark,
Waub Ogeeg, of Sault Ste. Marie, his x mark, Kawgayosh, of Sault Ste. Marie, his x mark, Apawkozigun, of L'Arbre Croche, his x mark, Keminitchagun, of

L'Arbre Croche, his x mark, Tawaganee, of L'Arbre Croche, his x mark, Ki-noshamaig, of L'Arbre Croche, his x mark, Naganigobowa, of L'Arbre Croche, his x mark, Onaisino, of L'Arbre Croche, his x mark, Mukuday Benais, of L'Arbre Croche, his x mark, Chingassamo, of L'Arbre Croche, his x mark, Aishquagonabee, of Grand Traverse, his x mark, Akosa, of Grand Traverse, his x mark, Oshawun Epenaysse, of Grand Traverse, his x mark. [455] Lucius Lyon, R. P. Parrott, captain, U. S. Army, W. P. Zantzinger, purser, U. S. Navy, Josiah F. Polk, John Holiday, John A. Drew, Rix Bobinson, Leonard Slater, Louis Moran, Augustin Hamelin, jr., Henry A. Lenake, William Lasley, George W. Woodward, C. O. Ermatinger.

Schedule referred to, in the tenth article.
1. The following chiefs constitute the first class, and are entitled to receive five hundred dollars each, namely: On Grand river, Muccutay Osha, Namatippy, Nawequa Geezhig or Noon Day, Nabun Egeezhig son of Kewayguabowequa, Wabi Windego or the White Giant, Cawpe-mossay or the Walker, Mukutay Oquot or Black Cloud, Megis Ininee or Wampum-man, Winnimissagee: on the Maskigo, Osawya, and Owun Aishcum; at L'Arbre Croche, Apawkozigun, or Smoking Weed, Niso-wakeout, Keminechawgun; at Grand Travers, Aishquagonabee, or the Feather of Honor, Chabwossun, Mikenok: on the Cheboigan, Chingas-samo, or the Big Sail; at Thunder-bay; Mujeekiwiss; on the Maniatic North, Mukons Ewyan; at Oak Point on the straits, Ains: at the Chenos, Chabowaywa: at Sault Ste. Marie, Iawba Wadick and Kewayzi Shawano; at Tac quimenon, Kawgayosh; at Grand Island, Oshawun Epenaysee, or the South Bird.

2. The following chiefs constitute the second class, and are entitled to receive two hundred dollars each, namely: On Grand river, Keesha-owash, Nugogikaybee, Kewaytowaby, Wapoos or the Rabbit, Wabitou-guaysay, Kewatondo, Zhaquinaw, Nawiqua Geezhig of Flat river, Ke-naytinunk, Weenonga, Pabawboco, Windecowiss, Muccutay Penay or Black Patridge, Kaynotin Aishcum, Boynashing, Shagwabeno son of White Giant, Tushetowun, Keway Gooshcum the former head chief, Pamossayga; at L'Arbre Croche, Sagitondowa, Ogiman Wininee, Me-gisawba, Mukuday Benais; at the Cross, Nishcajininee, Nawamushcota, Pabamitabi, Kimmewun, Gitchy Mocoman; at Grand Traverse, Akosa, Nebauquaum, Kabibonocca; at Little Traverse, Miscomamaingwa or Red Butterfly, Keezhigo Benais, Pamanikinong, Paimossega; on the Cheboigan, Chonees, or Little John, Shaweenossegay; on Thunder bay, Suganikwato; on Maskigo, Wassangazo; on Ossigomico or Platte river, Kaigwaidosay; at Maniatee, Keway Gooshcum: on river Pierre Markette, Saugima: at Saulte Ste. Marie, Neegaubayun, Mukuday-wacquot, Cheegud; at Carp river west of Grand island, Kaug Wya-nais: at Mille Cocquin on the straits, Aubunway: at Michilimackinac, Missutigo, Saganoah, Akkukogeesh, Chebyawboas.

3. The following persons constitute the third class, and are entitled to one hundred dollars each, namely: Kayshewa, Penasee or Gun lake, Kenisoway, Keenable of Grand river: Wasso, Mosaniko, Unwatin Oashcum, Nayogirna, Itawachkochi, Nanaw Ogomoo, Gitchy, Peen-dowan or Scabbard, Mukons, Kinochimaig, Tekamosimo, Pewaywitum, Mudji Keguabi, Kewayaum, Paushkizigun or Big Gun, Onaausino, Ashquabaywiss, Negaunigabowi, Petossegay, of L'Arbre Croche: Poiees or Dwarf and Pamossay of Cheboigan: Gitchv Ganocquot and Pamossegay of Thunder Bay: Tabusshy Geeshick and Mikenok, of Carp river south of Grand Traverse; Wapooso, Kaubinau, and Mudjeekee of river Pierre Markuette: Pubokway, Manitowaba, and Mis-hewatig, of White river: Shawun Epenaysee and Agausgce of Grand Traverse: Micqumisut, Chusco of Mackinac; Keeshkidjiwum, Waub Ojeeg, Aukudo, Winikis, Jaubeens, Maidosagee, Autya, Ishquag-unaby, Shaniwaygwunabi son of Kakakee, Nittum Egabowi, Magisan-ikway, Ketekewegauboway, of Sault Ste. Marie: Chegauzehe and Waubudo of Grand island: Ashegons, Kinuwais, Misquaonaby and [456] Mongons of Carp and Chocolate rivers; Gitchy Penaisson of Grosse Tete, and Waubissaig of Bay de Nocquet: Kainwaybekis and Pazhik-waywitum of Beaver islands: Neczhick Epenais of the Ance: Ahda-nima of Maniatic: Mukwyon, Wahzahkoon, Oshawun, Oneshannocquot of the north shore of Lake Michigan: Nagauniby and Keway Goosh-kum of the Chenos.

Henry R. Schoolcraft, Commissioner.

SUPPLEMENTAL ARTICLE. To guard against misconstruction in some of the foregoing provisions, and to secure, by further limitations, the just rights of the Indians, it is hereby agreed: that no claims under the fifth article shall be allowed for any debts contracted previous to the late war with Great Britain, or for goods supplied by foreigners to said Indians, or by citizens, who did not withdraw from the country, during its temporary occupancy by foreign troops, for any trade carried on by such persons during the said period. And it is also agreed: that no person receiving any commutation for a reservation, or any portion of the fund provided by the sixth article of this treaty, shall be entitled to the benefit of any part of the annuities herein stipulated. Nor shall any of the half-breeds, or blood relatives of the said tribes, commuted with, under the provisions of the ninth article, have any further claim on the general commutation fund, set apart to satisfy reservation claims, in the said sixth article. It is also understood, that the personal annuities, stipulated in the eleventh article, shall be paid in specie, in the same manner that other annuities are paid. Any excess of the funds set apart in the fifth and sixth articles, shall, in lieu of being paid to the Indians, be retained and vested by the Government in stock under the conditions mentioned in the fourth article of this treaty.

In testimony whereof, the parties above recited, have hereunto set their hands, at Washington the seat of Government, this thirty-first day of March, in the year one thousand eight hundred and thirty-six.

Henry R. Schoolcraft.
John Hulbert, Secretary.

Owun Aaishkum, of Maskigo, his x mark, Wassangazo, of Maskigo, his x
mark, Osawya, of Maskigo, his x mark, Wabi Widego, of Grand river, his x
mark, Megiss Ininee, of Grand river, his x mark, Nabun Ageezhig, of Grand
river, his x mark, Ainse, of Michilimackinac, his x mark, Chabowaywa, of Michilimackinac, his x mark, Jauba Wadic, of Sault Ste. Marie, his x mark, Waub
Ogeeg, of Sault Ste. Marie, his x mark, Kawgayosh, of Sault Ste. Marie, by
Maidosagee, his x mark,
Apawkozigun, of L'Arbre Croche, his x mark, Keminitchagun, of L'Arbre Cro-
che, his x mark, Tawagnee, of L'Arbre Croche, his x mark, Kinosheinaig, of
L'Arbre Croche, his x mark, Naganigabawi, of L'Arbre Croche, his x mark,
Oniasino, of L'Arbre Croche, his x mark, Mukaday Benais, of L'Arbre Croche,
his x mark, Chingassamoo, of Cheboigan, his x mark, Aishquagonabee, of
Grand Traverse, his x mark, Akosa, of Grand Traverse, his x mark, Oshawun
Epenaysee, of Grand Traverse, his x mark.

Robert Stewart, Wm. Mitchell, John A Drew, Augustin Hamelin, jr, Rix Robinson.

TREATY WITH THE WYANDOT {1836, Apr. 23}
Proclamation, May 16, 1836.

Articles of a treaty made and concluded between John A. Bryan, commissioner
on the part of the United States, and William Walker, John Barnett, and Peacock, chiefs and principal men of the Wyandot tribe of Indians in Ohio, acting
for and on behalf of the said tribe.

ARTICLE 1. The Wyandot tribe of Indians in Ohio cede to the United States a
strip of land five miles in extent, on the east end of their reservation in Crawford county in said Statealso, one section of land lying in Cranberry Swamp, on
Broken Sword creek, being the one mile square specified and set forth in the
treaty made with the said tribe on the twenty-ninth day of September in the year
of our Lord one thousand eight hundred and seventeenalso, one hundred and
sixty acres of land which is to be received in the place and stead of an equal
quantity set apart in a supplemental treaty made with the said Indians on the
seventeenth day of September in the following year, all situate and being in the
said county of Crawford.

ARTICLE 2. The said five mile tract, as also the additional quantities herein
set forth, are each to be surveyed as other public lands are surveyed by the Sur-

veyor General, and to be sold at such time and place, allowing sixty days' notice of the sale, as the President may direct.

ARTICLE 3. A Register and Receiver shall be appointed by the President and Senate, in accordance with the wishes of the delegation of chiefs, whose duties shall be similar to those of other Registers and Receivers.

They shall receive such compensation for services rendered, not exceeding five dollars per day for every day necessarily employed in the discharge of their duties, as the President may determine.

ARTICLE 4. All expenses incurred in the execution of this treaty, and in the sale of the lands included in it, shall be defrayed out of the funds raised therefrom, including such expenses and disbursements as may have been incurred by the delegation to Washingtonand such allowance to individuals who have assisted in the negotiation, as the chiefs in council, after a full and fair investigation, may adjudge to be reasonable and just, shall in all cases be made.

ARTICLE 5. Such portion of the monies not exceeding twenty thousand dollars, arising from the sales as the chiefs may deem necessary for the rebuilding of mills, repair and improvement of roads, establishing schools, and other laudable public objects for the improvement of their condition, shall be properly applied under their direction, and the remainder to be distributed among the individuals of said tribe as annuities are distributed.

ARTICLE 6. The monies raised by the sales of the lands for all the above mentioned objects, except the last, shall be paid by the receiver on the order of the chiefs;and such order, together with the receipt of the persons to whom payment shall be made, shall be the proper voucher for the final settlement of the accounts of the Receiver;but the funds for the tribe shall be distributed by the Register and Receiver to each person entitled thereto.

ARTICLE 7. By the 21st article of the treaty concluded at the foot of the rapids of the Miami of Lake Erie, dated the twenty-ninth day of September in the year one thousand eight hundred and seventeen, and the schedule thereunto attached, there was granted to Daonquot, or half King, Rontondee, or Warpole, Tayarrontoyea, or Between the Logs, Danwawtout, or John Hicks, Mononcue, or Thomas, Tayondot-tauseh, or George Punch, Hondaua-waugh, or Matthews, chiefs of the Wyandot nation, two sections of land each, within the Wyandot res-ervation-The aforesaid chiefs, their heirs or legal representatives, are entitled to, and allowed one section of land each, in the above designated tract of five miles, to be selected by them previous to sale, and [461] the same shall be sold as the other lands are sold, and they allowed to receive the respective sums arising from said sale.

ARTICLE 8. If during the progress of the sale, the Indians are not satisfied with the prices at which the lands sell, the Register and Receiver shall, on the written application of the chiefs, close the sale, and report the proceedings to the War Departmentand the President may appoint such other time for the sale as he may deem proper.

ARTICLE 9. The President shall give such directions he may judge necessary for the execution of this treaty, through the proper Departments of the Government.

Signed this twenty-third day of April, in the year of our Lord one thousand eight hundred and thirty-six.

John A. Bryan, Com'r. on the part of the United States, Wm. Walker, John Barnett, his x mark, Peacock, his x mark.

In presence of us: Jn. McClene, John McElvain, C. O. Ermatinger.

TREATY WITH THE CHOCTAW AND CHICKASAW {1837, Jan. 17}
Proclamation Mar. 24, 1837.

Articles of convention and agreement made on the seventeenth day of January, 1837, between the undersigned chiefs and commissioners duly appointed and empowered by the Choctaw tribe of red people, and John McLish, Pitman Colbert, James Brown, and James Perry, delegates of the Chickasaw tribe of Indians, duly authorized by the chiefs and head-men of said people for that purpose, at Doaksville, near Towson, in the Choctaw country.

ARTICLE 1. It is agreed by the Choctaws that the Chickasaws shall have the privilege of forming a district within the limits of their country, to be held on the same terms that the Choctaws now hold it, except the right of disposing of it, (which is held in common with the Choctaws and Chickasaws) to be called the Chickasaw district of the Choctaw Nation; to have an equal representation in their general council, and to be placed on an equal footing in every other respect with any of the other districts of said nation, except a voice in the management of the consideration which is given for these rights and privileges; and the Chickasaw people to be entitled to all the rights and privileges of Choctaws, with the exception of participating in the Choctaw annuities and the consideration to be paid for these rights and privileges, and to be subject to the same laws to which the Choctaws are; but the Chickasaws reserve to themselves the sole right and privilege of controlling and managing the residue of their funds as far as is consistent With the late treaty between the said people and the Government of the United States, and of making such regulations and electing such officers for that purpose as they may think proper.

ARTICLE 2. The Chickasaw district shall be bounded as follows, viz: beginning on the north bank of Red River, at the mouth of Island Bayou, about eight or ten miles below the mouth of False Wachitta; thence running north along the main channel of said bayou to its source; thence along the dividing ridge between the Wachitta and Low Blue Rivers to the road leading from Fort Gibson to Fort Wachitta; thence along said road to the line dividing Musha-la-tubbee and Push-meta-haw districts; thence eastwardly along said district line to the source of Brushy Creek; thence down said creek to where it flows into the Canadian River, ten or twelve miles above the mouth of the south fork of the Canadian; thence west along the main Canadian River to its source, if in the limits of the United States, or to those limits; and thence due south to Red River, and down Red River to the beginning.

ARTICLE 3. The Chickasaws agree to pay the Choctaws, as a consideration for these rights and privileges, the sum of five hundred and thirty thousand dollars thirty thousand of which shall be paid at the time and in the manner that the Choctaw annuity of 1837 is paid, and the remaining five hundred thousand dollars to be invested in some safe and secure stocks, under the direction of the Government of the United States, redeemable within a period of not less than twenty yearsand the Government of the United States shall cause the interest arising therefrom to be paid annually to the Choctaws in the following manner: twenty thousand dollars of which to be paid as the present Choctaw annuity is paid, for four years, and the residue to be subject to the control of the general council of the Choctaws; and after the expiration of the four years the whole of said interest to be subject to the entire control of the said council.

ARTICLE 4. To provide for the future adjustment of all complaints or dissatisfaction which may arise to interrupt the peace and harmony which have so long and so happily existed between the Choctaws and Chickasaws, it is hereby agreed by the parties that all questions relative to the construction of this agreement shall be referred to the Choctaw agent to be by him decided; reserving, however, to either party, should it feel itself aggrieved thereby, the rights of appealing to the President of the United States, whose decision shall be final and binding. But as considerable time might elapse before the decision of the President could be had, in the mean time the decision of the said agent shall be binding.

ARTICLE 5. It is hereby declared to be the intention of the parties hereto; that equal rights and privileges shah pertain to both Choctaws and Chickasaws to settle in whatever district they may think proper, and to be eligible to all the different offices of the Choctaw Nation, and to vote on the same terms in whatever district they may settle, except that the Choctaws are not to vote in anywise for officers in relation to the residue of the Chickasaw fund.

In testimony whereof, the parties hereto have hereunto subscribed their names and affixed their seals, at Doaksville, near fort Towson in the Choctaw country, on the day and year first above written.

In the presence of: Wm. Armstrong, Acting Superintendent Western Territory, Henry R. Carter, Conductor of the Chickasaw Delegation, Josiah S. Doak, Vincent B. Tims, Daniel McCurtain, United States Interpreter, P. J. Humphreys, J. T. Sprague, Lieutenant U. S. Marine Corps, Thomas Lafloor, his x mark, Chief of Oaklafalaya district, Nituchachue, his x mark, Chief of Pushmatahaw district, Joseph Kincaid, his x mark, Chief of Mushalatubbee district.

Commissioners of the Choctaw Nation: P. P. Pitchlynn, George W. Haskins, Israel Folsom, R. M. Jones, Silas D. Fisher, Samuel Wowster, John McKenney, his x mark, Eyachahofaa, his x mark, Nathaniel Folsom, his x mark, Lewis Breashears, his x mark, James Fletcher, his x mark, George Pusley, his x mark.

Captains: Oak-chi-a, his x mark, Thomas Hays, his x mark, Pis-tam-bee, his x mark, Ho-lah-ta-ho-ma, his x mark, E-yo-tah, his x mark, Isaac Perry, his x mark, No-wah-ham-bee, his x mark.
Chickasaw delegation: J. McLish, Pitman Colbert, James Brown, his x mark, James Perry, his x mark.

TREATY WITH THE NEW YORK INDIANS {1838, Jan. 15}
Proclamation, Apr. 4, 1840.

Articles of a treaty made and concluded at Buffalo Creek in the State of New York, the fifteenth day of January in the year of our Lord one thousand eight hundred and thirty-eight, by Ransom H. Gillet, a commissioner on the part of the United States, and the chiefs, head men and warriors of the several tribes of New York Indians assembled in council witnesseth:

WHEREAS, the six nations of New York Indians not long after the close of the war of the Revolution, became convinced from the rapid increase of the white settlements around, that the time was not far distant when their true interest must lead them to seek a new home among their red brethren in the West: And whereas this subject was agitated in a general council of the Six nations as early as 1810, and resulted in sending a memorial to the President of the United States, inquiring whether the Government would consent to their leaving their habitations and their removing into the neighborhood of their western brethren, and if they could procure a home there, by gift or purchase, whether the Government would acknowledge their title to the lands so obtained in the same manner it had acknowledged it in those from whom they might receive it; and further, whether the existing treaties would, in such a case remain in full force, and their annuities be paid as heretofore.

And whereas, with-the approbation of the President of the United States, purchases were made by the New York Indians from the Menomonie and Winnebago Indians of certain lands at Green Bay in the Territory of Wisconsin, which after much difficulty and contention with those Indians concerning the extent of that purchase, the whole subject was finally settled by a treaty between the United States and the Menomonie Indians, concluded in February, 1831, to which the New York Indians gave their assent on the seventeenth day of October 1832. And whereas, by the provisions of that treaty, five hundred thousand acres of land are secured to the New York Indians of the Six Nations and the St. Regis tribe, as a future home, on condition that they all remove to the same, within three years, or such reasonable time as the President should prescribe: And whereas, the President is satisfied that various considerations have prevented those still residing in New York from removing to Green Bay, and among other reasons, that many who were in favour of emigration, preferred to remove at once to the Indian territory, which they were fully persuaded was the only permanent and peaceful home for all the Indians.

And they therefore applied to the President to take their Green Bay lands, and provide them a new home among their brethren in the Indian territory. And whereas, the President being anxious to promote the peace, prosperity and happiness of his red children, and being determined to carry out the humane policy of the Government in removing the Indians from the east to the west of the Mississippi, within the Indian territory, by bringing them to see and feel, by his justice and liberality, that it is their true policy and for their interest to do so without delay.

Therefore, taking into consideration the foregoing premises, the following articles of a treaty are entered into between the United States of America and the several tribes of the New York Indians, the names of whose chiefs, head men and warriors are hereto subscribed, and those who may hereafter give their assent to this treaty in writing, within such time as the President shall appoint.

GENERAL PROVISIONS.

ARTICLE 1. The several tribes of 'New York Indians, the names of whose chiefs, head men, warriors and representatives are hereunto annexed, in consideration of the premises above recited, and the covenants hereinafter contained, to be performed on the part of the United States, hereby cede and relinquish to the United States all their right, title and interest to the lands secured to them at Green Bay by the Menomonie treaty of 1831, excepting the following tract, on which a part of the New York Indians now reside: beginning at the southwesterly corner of the French grants at Green Bay, and running thence southwardly to a point on a line to be run from the Little Cocaclin, parallel to a line of the French grants and six miles from Fox River; from thence on said parallel line, northwardly six miles; from thence eastwardly to a point on the northeast line of the Indian lands, and being at right angles to the same.

ARTICLE 2. In consideration of the above cession and relinquishment, on the part of the tribes of the New York Indians, and in order to manifest the deep interest of the United States in the future peace and prosperity of the New York Indians, the United States agree to set apart the following tract of country, situated directly west of the State of Missouri, as a permanent home for all the New York Indians, now residing in the State of New York, or in Wisconsin, or elsewhere in the United States, who have no permanent homes, which said country is described as follows, to wit: Beginning on the west line of the State of Missouri, at the northeast corner of the Cherokee tract, and running thence north along the west line of the State of Missouri twenty-seven miles to the southerly line of the Miami lands; thence west so far as shall be necessary, by running a line at right angles, and parallel to the west line aforesaid, to the Osage lands, and thence easterly along the Osage and Cherokee lands to the place of beginning to include one million eight hundred and twenty-four thousand acres of land, being three hundred and twenty acres for each soul of said Indians as their numbers are at present computed.

To have and to hold the same in fee simple to the said tribes or nations of Indians, by patent from the President of the United States, issued in conformity with the provisions of the third section of the act, entitled "An act to provide for an exchange of lands, with the Indians residing in any of the States or Territories, and for their removal west of the Mississippi," approved on the 28th day of May, 1830, with full power and authority in the said Indians to divide said lands among the different tribes, nations, or bands, in severalty, with the right to sell and convey to and from each other, under such laws and regulations as may be adopted by the respective tribes, acting by themselves, or by a general council of the said New York Indians, acting for all the tribes collectively. It is understood and agreed that the above described country is intended as a future home for the following tribes, to wit: The Senecas, Onondagas, Cayugas, Tuscaroras, Oneidas, St. Regis, Stockbridges, Munsees, and Brothertowns residing in the State of New York, and the same is to be divided equally among them, according to their respective numbers, as mentioned in a schedule hereunto annexed.

ARTICLE 3. It is further agreed that such of the tribes of the New York Indians as do not accept and agree to remove to the country set apart for their new homes within five years, or such other time as the President may, from time to time, appoint, shall forfeit all interest in the lands so set apart, to the United States.

ARTICLE 4. Perpetual peace and friendship shall exist between the United States and the New York Indians; and the United States hereby guaranty to protect and defend them in the peaceable possession and enjoyment of their new homes, and hereby secure to them, in said country, the right to establish their own form of government, appoint their own officers, and administer their own laws; subject, however, to the legislation of the Congress of the United States, regulating trade and intercourse with the Indians. The lands secured to them by patent under this treaty shall never be included in any State or Territory of this Union. The said Indians shall also be entitled, in all respects, to the same political and civil rights and privileges, that are granted and secured by the United States to any of the several tribes of emigrant Indians settled in the Indian Territory.

ARTICLE 5. The Oneidas are to have their lands in the Indian Territory, in the tract set apart for the New York Indians, adjoining the Osage tract, and that hereinafter set apart for the Senecas; and the same shall be so laid off as to secure them a sufficient quantity of timber for their use. Those tribes, whose lands are not specially designated in this treaty, are to have such as shall be set apart by the President.

ARTICLE 6. It is further agreed that the United States will pay to those who remove west, at their new homes, all such annuities, as shall properly belong to them. The schedules hereunto annexed shall be deemed and taken as a part of this treaty.

ARTICLE 7. It is expressly understood and agreed, that this treaty must be approved by the President and ratified and confirmed by the Senate of the United States before it shall be binding upon the parties to it. It is further expressly understood and agreed that the rejection, by the President and Senate, of the provisions thereof, applicable to one tribe, or distinct branch of a tribe, shall not be construed to invalidate as to others, but as to them it shall be binding, and remain in full force and effect.

ARTICLE 8. It is stipulated and agreed that the accounts of the Commissioner, and expenses incurred by him in holding a council with the New York Indians, and concluding treaties at Green Bay and Duck Creek, in Wisconsin, and in the State of New York, in 1836, and those for the exploring party of the New York Indians, in 1837, and also the expenses of the present treaty, shall be allowed and settled according to former precedents.

SPECIAL PROVISIONS FOR THE ST. REGIS.

ARTICLE 9. It is agreed with the American party of the St. Regis Indians, that the United States will pay to the said tribe, on their removal west, or at such time as the President shall appoint, the sum of five thousand dollars, as a remuneration for monies laid out by the said tribe, and for services rendered by their chiefs and agents in securing the title to the Green Bay lands, and in removal to the same, the same to be apportioned out to the several claimants by the chiefs of the said party and a United States' Commissioner, as may be deemed by them equitable and just. It is further agreed, that the following reservation of land shall be made to the Rev. Eleazor Williams, of said tribe, which he claims in his own right, and in that of his wife, which he is to hold in fee simple, by patent from the President, with full power and authority to sell and dispose of the same, to wit: beginning at a point in the west bank of Fox River thirteen chains above the old milldam at the rapids of the Little Kockalin; thence north fifty-two degrees and thirty minutes west, two hundred and forty chains; thence north thirty-seven degrees and thirty minutes east, two hundred chains, thence south fifty-two degrees and thirty minutes east, two hundred and forty chains to the bank of Fox river; thence up along the bank of Fox river to the place of beginning.

SPECIAL PROVISIONS FOR THE SENECAS.

ARTICLE 10. It is agreed with the Senecas that they shall have for themselves and their friends, the Cayugas and Onondagas, residing among them, the easterly part of the tract set apart for the New York Indians, and to extend so far west, as to include one half-section (three hundred and twenty acres) of land for each soul of the Senecas, Cayugas and Onandagas, residing among them; and if, on removing west, they find there is not sufficient timber on this tract for their use, then the President shall add thereto timber land sufficient for their accommodation, and they agree to remove; to remove from the State of New York to their new homes within five years, and to continue to reside there.

And whereas at the making of this treaty, Thomas L. Ogden and Joseph Fellows the assignees of the State of Massachusetts, have purchased of the Seneca nation of Indians, in the presence and with the approbation of the United States Commissioner, appointed [506] by the United States to hold said treaty, or convention, all the right, title, interest, and claim of the said Seneca nation, to certain lands, by a deed of conveyance a duplicate of which is hereunto annexed; and whereas the consideration money mentioned in said deed, amounting to two hundred and two thousand dollars, belongs to the Seneca nation, and the said nation agrees that the said sum of money shall be paid to the United States. The United States agree to receive the same, to be disposed of as follows: the sum of one hundred thousand dollars is to be invested by the President of the United States in safe stocks, for their use, the income of which is to be paid to them at their new homes, annually, and the balance, being the sum of one hundred and two thousand dollars, is to be paid to the owners of the improvements on the lands so deeded, according to an appraisement of said improvements and a distribution and award of said sum of money among the owners of said improvements, to be made by appraisers, hereafter to be appointed by the Seneca nation, in the presence of a United States Commissioner, hereafter to be appointed, to be paid by the United States to the individuals who are entitled to the same, according to said apprisal and award, on their severally relinquishing their respective possessions to the said Ogden and Fellows.

SPECIAL PROVISIONS FOR THE CAYUGAS.

ARTICLE 11. The United States will set apart for the Cayugas, on their removing to their new homes at the west, two thousand dollars, and will invest the same in some safe stocks, the income of which shall be paid them annually, at their new homes. The United States further agree to pay to the said nation, on their removal west, two thousand five hundred dollars, to be disposed as the chiefs shall deem just and equitable.

SPECIAL PROVISIONS FOR THE ONONDAGAS RESIDING ON THE SENECA RESERVATIONS.

ARTICLE 12. The United States agree to set apart for the Onondagas, residing on the Seneca reservations, two thousand five hundred dollars, on their removing west, and to invest the same in safe stocks, the income of which shall be paid to them annually at their new homes. And the United States further agree to pay to the said Onondagas, on their removal to their new homes in the west, two thousand dollars, to be disposed of as the chiefs shall deem equitable and just.

SPECIAL PROVISIONS FOR THE ONEIDAS RESIDING IN THE STATE OF NEW YORK.

ARTICLE 13. The United States will pay the sum of four thousand dollars, to be paid to Baptista Powlis, and the chiefs of the first Christian party residing at Oneida, and the sum of two thousand dollars shall be paid to William Day, and the chiefs of the Orchard party residing there, for expenses incurred and services rendered in securing the Green Bay country, and the settlement of a portion thereof; and they hereby agree to remove to their new homes in the Indian territory, as soon as they can make satisfactory arrangements with the Governor of the State of New York for the purchase of their lands at Oneida.

SPECIAL PROVISIONS FOR THE TUSCARORAS.

ARTICLE 14. The Tuscarora nation agree to accept the country set apart for them in the Indian territory, and to remove there within five years, and continue to reside there. It is further agreed that the Tuscaroras shall nave their lands in the Indian country, at the forks of the Neasha river, which shall be so laid off as to secure a sufficient quantity of timber for the accommodation of the nation. But if on examination they are not satisfied with this location, they are to have their lands at such place as the President of the United States shall designate. The United States will pay to the Tuscarora nation, on their settling at the West, three thousand dollars, to be disposed of as the chiefs shah deem most equitable and just. Whereas the said nation owns, in fee simple, five thousand acres of land, lying in Niagara county, in the State of New York which was conveyed to the said nation by Henry Dearborn and they wish to sell and convey the same before they remove West.

Now therefore, in order to have the same done in a legal and proper way, they hereby convey the same to the United States and to be held in trust for them, and they authorize the President to sell and convey the same, and the money which shall be received for the said lands, exclusive of the improvements, the President shall invest in safe stocks for their benefit, the income from which shall be paid to the nation, at their new homes, annually; and the money which shall be received for improvements on said lands shall be paid to the owners of the improvements When the lands are sold. The President shall cause the said lands to be surveyed, and the improvements shall be appraised by such persons as the nation shall appoint; and said lands shall also be appraised, and shall not be sold at a less price than the appraisal, without the consent of James Cusick, William Mountpleasant and William Chew, or the survivor, or survivors of them; and the expenses incurred by the United States in relation to this trust are to be deducted from the moneys received before investment.

And whereas, at the making of this treaty, Thomas L. Ogden and Joseph Fellows, the assignees of the State of Massachusetts, have purchased of the Tuscarora nation of Indians, in the presence and with the approbation of the commissioner appointed on the part of the United States to hold said treaty or convention, all the right, title, interest, and claim of the Tuscarora nation to certain lands, by a deed of conveyance, a duplicate of which is hereunto annexed: And whereas, the consideration money for said lands has been secured to the said nation to their satisfaction, by Thomas L. Ogden and Joseph Fellows; therefore the United States hereby assent to the said sale and conveyance and sanction the same.

ARTICLE 15. The United States hereby agree that they will appropriate the sum of four hundred thousand dollars, to be applied from time to time, under the direction of the President of the United States, in such proportions, as may be most for the interest of the said Indians, parties to this treaty, for the following purposes, to wit: To aid them in removing to their homes, and supporting themselves the first year after their removal; to encourage and assist them in education, and in being taught to cultivate their lands; in erecting mills and other necessary houses; in purchasing domestic animals, and farming utensils and acquiring a knowledge of the mechanic arts.

In testimony whereof, the commissioner and the chiefs, head men, and people, whose names are hereto annexed, being duly authorized, have hereunto set their hands, and affixed their respective seals, at the time and place above mentioned.

R. H. Gillet, Commissioner.

Senecas: Haw-naw-wah-es, or Levi Halftown, Dao-nepho-gah, or Little Johnson, Goat-hau-oh, or Billy Shanks, Da-ga-o-geas, or Daniel Twoguns, Hau-sa-nea-nes, or White Seneca, Gee-odow-neh, or Captain Pollard, Howah-do-goh-deh, or George Bennet, Joh-nes-ha-dih, or James Stevenson, Hays-tah-jih, or

Job Pierce, Hure-hau-stock, or Captain Strong, Sho-nan-do-wah, or John Gordon, So-ne-a-ge, or-Captain Snow, Noh-sok-dah, or Jim Jonas, Hau-neh-hoy's-oh, or Blue Eyes, Shaw-neh-dik, or William Johnson, Gaw-neh-do-au-ok, or Reuben Pierce,

Shaw-go-nes-goh-sha-oh, or Morris Half-town, Shaw-go-za-sot-hoh, or Jacob Jameson, Gua-wa-no-oh, or George Big Deer, Joh-que-ya-suse, or Samuel Gordon, Gua-ne-oh-doh, or Thompson S. Harris, Gau-geh-queh-doh, or George Jimeson, Hon-non-de-uh, or Nathaniel T. Strong, Nuh-joh-gau-eh, or Tall Peter, Sho-nauk-ga-nes, or Tommy Jimmy, So-joh-gwa-us, or John Tall Chief, Shau-gau-nes-es-tip, or George Fox, Go-na-daw-goyh, or Jabez Stevenson, Tit-ho-yuh, or William Jones, Juneah-dah-glence, or George White, by his agent White Seneca, Gau-nu-su-goh, or Walter Thompson, by his agent Daniel Twoguns,

Dau-ga-se, or Long John, Gua-sa-we-dah, or John Bark, Gau-ni-dough, or George Lindsay, Ho-ma-ga-was, or Jacob Bennet, On-di-heh-oh, or John Bennet, Nis-ha-nea-nent, or Seneca White, Ha-dya-no-doh, or Maria Pierce, Yoh-dih-doh, or David White, James Shongo, Ka-non-da-gyh, or William Cass, Nige-jos-a, or Samuel Wilson, Jo-on-da-goh, or John Seneca.

Tuscaroras: Ka-nat-soyh, or Nicholas Cusick, Sacharissa, or William Chew, Kaw-we-ah-ka, or William Mt. Pleasant, Kaw-re-a-roek-ka, or John Fox, Gee-me, or James Cusick, Ju-hu-ru-at-kak, or John Patterson, O-tah-guaw-naw-wa, or Samuel Jacobs, Ka-noh-sa-ta, or James Anthony, Gou-ro-quan, or Peter Elm, Tu-nak-she-a-han, or Daniel Peter.
Oneidas residing in the State of New-York, for themselves and their parties: Baptiste Powlish.
Oneidas at Green Bay: John Anthony, Honjoit Smith, Henry Jordan, Thomas King.
St. Regis: Eleazer Williams, chief and agent.
Oneidas residing on the Seneca Reservation: Hon-no-ne-ga-doh, or Silversmith, (For himself and in behalf of his nation.), Hoge-wayhtah, or William Jacket, Sah-hu-gae-ne, or Button George.

Principal Onondaga Warriors, in behalf of themselves and the Onondaga Warriors: Ka-noh-qua-sa, or William John, Dah-gu-o-a-dah, or Noah Silversmith.
Cayugas: Skok-no-eh, or King William, Geh-da-or-loh, or James Young, Gay-
on-wek, or Jack Wheelbarrow, D'yo-ya-tek, or Joseph Isaac, For themselves
and in behalf of the nation.
Warriors: Hah-oh-u, or John Crow, Ho-na-e-geh-dah, or Snow Darkness,
Gone-ah-ga-u-do, or Jacob G. Seneca, Di-i-en-use, or Ghastly Darkness, Hon-
ho-gah-dyok, or Thomas Crow, Wau-wah-wa-na-onk, or Peter Wilson, So;en-
dagh, or Jonathan White, Sago-gan-e-on-gwus, or Harvey Rowe, To-ga-ne-ah-
doh, or David Crow, Soh-win-dah-neh, or George Wheeler, Do-goh-no-do-nis;
or Simon Isaac, He-dai-ses, or Joseph Peter, Sa-go-di-get-ka, or Jacob Jackson.

Witnesses: James Stryker, Sub-agent, Six Nations, New York Indians, Na-
thaniel T. Strong, United States Interpreter, New York agency, H. B. Potter,
Orlando Allen, H. P. Wilcox, Charles H. Allen, Horatio Jones, Spencer H.
Cone, W. W. Jones, J. F. Schermerhorn, Josiah Trowbridge.

(To the Indian names are subjoined a mark and seal.)

SCHEDULE A.
CENSUS OF THE NEW YORK INDIANS AS TAKEN IN 1837.
Number Residing on the Seneca reservations.

Senecas   2, 309
Onondagas   194
Cayugas 130
          2, 633
Onondagas, at Onondaga   300
Tuscaroras   273
St. Regis, in New York   350
Oneidas, at Green Bay   600
Oneidas, in New York   620
Stockbridges   217
Munsees 132
Brothertowns   360
The above was made before the execution of the treaty.

R. H. Gillet, Commissioner.

SCHEDULE B.
The following is the disposition agreed to be made of the sum of three thousand dollars provided in this treaty for the Tuscaroras, by the chiefs, and assented to by the commissioner, and is to form a part of the treaty:
To Jonathan Printess, ninety-three dollars.

To William Chew, one hundred and fifteen dollars. To John Patterson, forty-six dollars.
To William Mountpleasant, one hundred and seventy-one dollars. To James Cusick, one hundred and twenty-five dollars. To David Peter, fifty dollars.
The rest and residue thereof is to be paid to the nation. The above was agreed to before the execution of the treaty.

R. H. Gillet, Commissioner.

SCHEDULE C.
Schedule applicable to the Onondagas and Cayugas residing on the Seneca reservations. It is agreed that the following disposition shall be made of the amount set apart to be divided by the chiefs of those nations, in the preceding parts of this treaty, any thing therein to the contrary notwithstanding.

To William King, one thousand five hundred dollars. Joseph Isaacs, seven hundred dollars. Jack Wheelbarrow, three hundred dollars. Silversmith, one thousand dollars. William Jacket, five hundred dollars. Buton George, five hundred dollars.

The above was agreed to before the treaty was finally executed.

R. H. Gillet, Commissioner.
Jan. 15, 1838.

At a treaty held under the authority of the United States of America, at Buffalo Creek in the county of Erie, and State of New York, between the chiefs and head men of the Seneca nation of Indians, duly assembled in council, and representing and acting for the said nation, on the one part, and Thomas Ludlow Ogden of the city of New York and Joseph Fellows of Geneva, in the county of Ontario, on the other part, concerning the purchase of the right and claim of the said Indians m and to the lands within the State of New York remaining in their occupation: Ransom H. Gillet, Esquire, a commissioner appointed by the President of the United States to attend and hold the said treaty, and also Josiah Trowbridge, Esquire, the superintendent on behalf of the Commonwealth of Massachusetts, being severally present at the said treaty, the said chiefs and head men, on behalf of the Seneca nation did agree to sell and release to the said Thomas Ludlow Ogden and Joseph Fellows, and they the said Thomas Ludlow Ogden and Joseph Fellows did agree to purchase all the right, title and claim of the said Seneca nation of, in and to the several tracts, pieces, or parcels of land mentioned, and described in the instrument of writing next hereinafter set forth, and at the price or sum therein specified, as the consideration, or purchase money for such sale and release; which instrument being read and explained to the said parties and mutually agreed to, was signed and sealed by the said contracting parties, and is in the words following:

This indenture, made this fifteenth day of January in the year of our Lord one thousand eight hundred and thirty-eight, between the chiefs and head men of the Seneca nation of Indians, duly assembled in council, and acting for and on behalf of the said Seneca nation, of the first part, and Thomas Ludlow Ogden, of the city of New York, and Joseph Fellows of Geneva, in the county of Ontario, of the second part witnesseth: That the said chiefs and head men of the Seneca nation of Indians, in consideration of the sum of two hundred and two thousand dollars to them in hand paid by the said Thomas Ludlow Ogden and Joseph Fellows, the receipt whereof is hereby acknowledged, have granted, bargained, sold, released and confirmed, and by these presents do grant, bargain, sell, release and confirm unto the said Thomas Ludlow Ogden and Joseph Fellows, and to their heirs and assigns, all that certain tract, or parcel of land situate, lying and being in the county of Erie and State of New York Commonly called and known by the name of Buffalo Creek reservation, containing, by estimation forty-nine thousand nine hundred and twenty acres be the contents thereof more or less.

Also, all that certain other tract, or parcel of land, situate, lying and being in the counties of Erie, Chatauque, and Cattaraugus in said State commonly called and known by the name of Cattaraugus reservation, containing by estimation twenty-one thousand six hundred and eighty acres, be the contents thereof more or less. Also, all that certain other tract, or parcel of land, situate, lying and being in the said county of Cattaraugus, in said State, commonly called and known by the name of the Allegany reservation, containing by estimation thirty thousand four hundred and sixty-nine acres, be the contents more or less. And also, all that certain other tract or parcel of land, situate, lying and being partly in said county of Erie and partly in the county of Genesee, in said State, commonly called and known by the name of the Tonawando reservation, and containing by estimation twelve thousand, eight hundred acres, be the same more or less; as the said several tracts of land have been heretofore reserved and are held and occupied by the said Seneca nation of Indians, or by individuals thereof, together with all and singular the rights, privileges, hereditaments and appurtenances to each and every of the said tracts or parcels of land belonging or appertaining; and all the estate, right, title, interest, claim, and demand of the said party of the first part, and of the said Seneca nation of Indians, of, in, and to the same, and to each and every part and parcel thereof: to have and to hold all and singular the above described and released premises unto the said Thomas Ludlow Ogden and Joseph Fellows, their heirs and assigns, to their proper use and behoof for ever, as joint tenants, and not as tenants in common.

In witness whereof, the parties to these presents have hereunto and to three other instruments of the same tenor and date one to remain with the United States, one to remain with the State of Massachusetts, one to remain with the Seneca nation of Indians, and one to remain with the said Thomas Ludlow

Ogden and Joseph Fellows, interchangeably set their hands and seals the day and year first above written.

Little Johnson, Daniel Two Guns, Captain Pollard, James Stevenson, Captain Strong, Captain Snow, Blue Eyes, Levi Halftown, Billy Shanks, White Seneca, George Bennet, John Pierce, John Gordon, Jim Jonas, William Johnson, Reuben Pierce, Morris Halftown, Jacob Jimeson, Samuel Gordon, Thompson S. Harris, George Jemison, Nathaniel T. Strong, Tall Peter, Tommy Jimmy, John Tall Chief, George Fox, Jabez Stevenson, William Jones.

I have attended a treaty of the Seneca Nation of Indians, held at Buffalo Creek, in the county of Erie, in the State of New York, on the fifteenth day of January in the year of our Lord one thousand eight hundred and thirty-eight, when the within instument was duly executed, in my presence, by the chiefs of the Seneca Nation, being fairly and properly understood by them. I do, therefore, certify and approve the same.

R. H. Gillet, Commissioner.

Jan.15,1838.

At a treaty held under and by the authority of the United States of America, at Buffalo Creek, in the county of Erie, and State of New York, between the sachems, chiefs and warriors of the Tuscarora nation of Indians, duly assembled in council and representing and acting for the said nation, on the one part and Thomas Ludlow Ogden of the city of New York and Joseph Fellows of Geneva in the county of Ontario, on the other part, concerning the purchase of the right and claim of the said nation of Indians in and to the lands within the State of New York, remaining in their occupation: Ransom H. Gillet, Esquire, a commissioner appointed by the President of the United States to attend and hold the said treaty, and also Josiah Trowbridge, Esquire, the superintendent on behalf of the Commonwealth of Massachusetts, being severally present at the said treaty, the said sachems, chiefs and warriors, on behalf of the said Tuscarora nation, did agree to sell and release to the said Thomas Ludlow Ogden and Joseph Fellows, and they, the said Thomas Ludlow Ogden and Joseph Fellows did agree to purchase all the right, title and claim of the said Tuscarora nation of, in and to the tract, piece, or parcel of land mentioned and described in the instrument of writing next hereinafter set forth, and at the price, or sum therein specified, as the consideration or purchase money for such sale and release; which instrument being read and explained to the said parties, and mutually agreed to, was signed and sealed by the said contracting parties, and is in the words following:

This indenture, made this fifteenth day of January in the year of our Lord one thousand eight hundred and thirty-eight, between the sachems, chiefs, and warriors of the Tuscarora nation of Indians, duly assembled in council, and acting for and on behalf of the said Tuscarora nation of the first part, and Thomas Ludlow Ogden of the city of New York, and Joseph Fellows of Geneva, in the county of Ontario, of the second part witnesseth: That the said sachems, chiefs and warriors of the Tuscarora nation,, in consideration of the sum of nine thousand six hundred dollars, to them in hand paid by the said Thomas Ludlow Ogden and Joseph Fellows, the receipt whereof is hereby acknowledged, have granted, bargained, sold released, and confmned, and by these presents do grant, bargain, sell, release and confirm to the said Thomas Ludlow Ogden and Joseph Fellows, and to their heirs and assigns, all that tract or parcel of land situate, lying and being in the county of Niagara and State of New York, commonly called and known by the name of the Tuscarora reservation or Seneca grant, containing nineteen hundred and twenty acres, be the same more, or less, being the lands in their occupancy, and not included in the land conveyed to them by Henry Dearborn, together with all and singular, the rights, privileges, heraditaments, and appurtenances to the said tract or parcel of land belonging, or appertaining, and all the estate, right, title, interest,, claim and demand of the said party of the first part, and of the said Tuscarora nation of Indians of, in and to the same, and to every part and parcel thereof. To have and to hold all and singular the above described and released premises unto the said Thomas Ludlow Ogden and Joseph Fellows, and their heirs and assigns, to their proper use and behoof for ever, as joint tenants and not as tenants in common.

In witness whereof, the parties to these presents have hereunto and to three other instnunents of the same tenor and date, one to remain 15121 with the United States, one to remain with the State of Massachusetts, one to remain with the Tuscarora nation of Indians and one to remain with the said Thomas Ludlow Ogden and Joseph Fellows, interchangeably set their hands and seals, the day and year first above written.

Nicholas Cusick, John Patterson, William Chew, Samuel Jacobs, William Mountpleasant, James Anthony, John Fox, Peter Elm, James Cusick, Daniel Peter.

Sealed and delivered in presence of James Stryker. R. H. Gillet. Charles H. Allen. J. F. Schermerhom. Nathaniel T. Strong, U. S. interpreter. H. B. Potter. Orlando Allen.

(To the Indian names are subjoined a mark and seal.)

At the abovementioned treaty, held in my presence, as superintendent on the part of the Commonwealth of Massachusetts, and this day concluded, the foregoing instrument was agreed to by the contracting parties therein named, and was in my presence executed by them; and being approved by me, i do hereby certify and declare such my approbation thereof.

Woodlands Indian Treaties

Witness my hand and seal, at Buffalo Creek, this 15th day of January, in the year 1838.

J. Trowbridge, Superintendent.

I have attended a treaty of the Tuscarora nation of Indians, held at Buffalo Creek,, in the county of Erie in the State of New York, on the fifteenth day of January in the year of our Lord one thousand eight hundred and thirty-eight, when the within instrument was duly executed in my presence, by the sachems, chiefs, and warriors of the said nation, being fairly and property understood and transacted by all the parties of Indians concerned and declared to be done to their full satisfaction. I do therefore certify and approve the same.

Supplemental article to the treaty concluded at Buffalo Creek, in the State of New York, on the]5th ofjanuary 1338, concluded between Ransom H. Gillet, commissioner on the part of the United States, and chiefs and head men of the St. Regis. Indians, concluded on the]3th day offebruary 1838.

Supplemental article to the treaty concluded at Buffalo Creek in the State of New York, dated January 15 1838.

The undersigned chiefs and head men of the St. Regis Indians residing in the State of New York having heard a copy of said treaty read by Ransom H. Gillet, the commissioner who concluded that treaty on the part of the United States, and he having fully and publicly explained the same, and believing the provisions of the said treaty to be very liberal on the part of the United States and calculated to be highly beneficial to the New York Indians, including the St. Regis, who are embraced in its provisions do hereby assent to every part of the said treaty and approve the same. And it is finther agreed, that any of the St. Regis Indians who wish to do so, shall be at liberty to remove to the said country at any time hereafter within the time specified in this treaty, but under it the Government shall not Compel [513] them to remove. The United States will, within one year after the ratification of this treaty, pay over to the American party of said Indians one thousand dollars, part of the sum of five thousand dollars mentioned in the special provisions for the St. Regis Indians, any thing in the article contained to the contrary notwithstanding.

Done at the council house at St. Regis, this thirteenth day of February in the year of our Lord one thousand eight hundred and thirty-eight. Witness our hands and seals.

R. H. Gillet, Commissioner.

Lover-taie-enve, Louis-taio-rorio-te, Michael Gavcault, Lose-sori-sosane, Louis-tioonsate, Jok-ta-nen-shi-sa, Ermoise-gana-saien-to, Tomos-tataste, Tierte-gonotas-en, Tier-sokoia-ni-saks, Sa-satis-otsi-tsia-ta-gen, Tier-sgane-korhapse-e, Ennios-anas-ota-ka, Louis-te-ganota-to-ro, Wise-afla-taronne, Tomasouta-gosa, Sose-te-gaomsshke, Louis-orisake-wha, Sosatis-atis-tsiaks, Tier-anasaken-rat, Louis-tar-oria-keshon, Jasen-karato-on.

The foregoing was executed in our presence

A. K. Williams, Agent on the part of New York for St. Regis Indians. W. L. Gray, Interpreter:

> Owen C. Donnelly., Say Saree.

(To the Indian names are subjoined a mark and seal.)

We the undersigned chiefs of the Seneca tribe of New York Indians, residing in the State of New York, do hereby give our free and voluntary assent to the foregoing treaty as amended by the resolution of the Senate of the United States on the eleventh day of June 1838, and to our contract therewith, the swne having been submitted to us by Ransom H. Gillet, a Commissioner on the part of the United States, and fully and fairly explained by him, to our said tribe, in council assembled.

Dated Buffalo Creek September 28 1838.

Captain Pollard, Captain Strong, White Seneca, Blue Eyes, George Bennett, Job Pierce, Tommy Jimmy, William Johnson, Reuben Pierce, Morris Halftown, Levi Halftown, George Big Deer, Jim Jonas, George Jimeson, Thomas Jimeson, George Fox, N.T. Strong, Thompson S. Harris, Samuel Gordon, Jacob Jimeson, John Gordon, Tall Peter, Billy Shanks, James Stevenson, Walter Thompson, John Bennett, John Seneca, John General, Major Jack Berry, John Tall Chief, Jabez Stevenson.

(To the Indian names are subjoined marks.)

The above signatures were freely and voluntarily given after the treaty and amendments had been fully and fairly explained in open council

R. H. Gillet, Commissioner.

Witness:

XH. A. S. Dearborn, Superintendent of Massachusetts. James Stryker, U. S. Agent.

Little Johnson, Samuel Wilson, John Buck, William Cass, Long John, Sky Carrier, Charles Greybeard, John Hutchinson, Charles F. Pierce, John Snow.

(To the Indian names are subjoined marks.) [5141

These ten chiefs signed in my presence except the last John Snow.

H. A. S. Dearborn, Superintendent of Massachusetts.

Signed in presence of

Nathl. T. Strong, U. S. Interpreter. James Stryker, U. S. Agent. R. H. Gillet, James Stryker.

These ten chiefs signed in my presence except the last John Snow.

H. A. S. Dearborn, Superintendent of Massachusetts.

Signed in presence of

Nathl. T. Strong, U. S. Interpreter. James Stryker, U. S. Agent. George Kenququide, by his attorneys. N. T. Strong. White Seneca.R., H. Gillet, James Stryker.

The signature of George Kenququide was added by his attorneys in our presence.

R. H. Gillet James Stryker

18th January 1839.

We the undersigned chiefs of the Oneida tribe of New York Indians do hereby give our free and voluntary assent to the foregoing treaty as amended by the resolution of the Senate of the United States on the eleventh day of June 1838, the same having been submitted to us by Ransom H. Gillet, a commissioner on the part of the United States and fully and fairly explained by him to our said tribe in council assembled. Dated August 9th 1838 at the Oneida Council House.

Executed in the presence of Timothy Jenkins.

First Christian Party:

Baptista Powlis, Anthony Big Knife, Peter Williams, Jacob]Powlis, Anthony Anthony, Peter Martin, Cornelius Summer, Isaac Wheelock, Thomas Doxtater, William Hill, Baptiste Denny.

Orchard Party: Jonathan Jotdon, Thomas Scanado, Henry Jordon, William Day.

Second Christian Party: Abraham Denny, Adam Thompson, Peter Elm, Lewis Denny, Martin Denny.

(To the Indian names are subjoined marks.)

The above assent was voluntarily freely and fairly given in my presence, after being fully and fairly explained by me.

R. H. Gillet, Commissioner, &c.

We the undersigned sachems chiefs and head men of the Tuscarora nation of Indians residing in the State of New York, do hereby give our free and voluntary assent to the foregoing treaty as amended by the resolution of the Senate of the United States on the eleventh day of June 1838, and to our contract connected therewith, the same having been submitted to us by Ransom H. Gillet, a commissioner on the part of the United States, and fully and fairly explained by him to our said tribe in council assembled.

Dated August 14th, 1838.

Nicholas Cusick, William Chew, William Mountpleasant, John Patterson, Matthew Jack, George L. Printup, James Cusick, Jonathan Printup, Mark Jack, Samuel JacobS.

Executed in presence of J. S. Buckingham, D. Judson, Leceister S. Buckingham, Orlando Allen.

(To the Indian names are subjoined marks.)

The above assent was freely and voluntarily given after being fully and fairly explained by me.

R.H. Gillet, Comissioner

We the undersigned chiefs and head men of the tribe of Cayuga Indians residing in the State of New York do hereby give our free and voluntary assent to the foregoing treaty as amended by the resolution of the Senate of the United States on the eleventh day of June 1838, the same having been submitted to us by Ransom H. Gillet, a commissioner on the part of the United States, and fully and fairly explained by him to our said tribe in council assembled.

Dated August 30th 1838.

Thomas Crow, Ghastly Darkness, John Crow, Jacob G. Seneca.

Executed in presence of James Young.

(To the Indian names are subjoined marks.)

The above four signatures were freely given in our presence.

R. H. Gillet, Commissioner. H. A. S. Dearborn, Superintendent of Massachusetts.

We the undersigned sachems, chiefs and head men of the American party of the St. Regis Indians residing in the State of New York, do hereby give our free and voluntary assent to the foregoing treaty as amended by the Senate of the United States on the eleventh day of June 1838, the same having been submitted to us by Ransom H. Gillet a commissioner on the part of the United States, and fully and fairly explained by him to our said tribe in council assembled. The St. Regis Indians shall not be compelled to remove under the treaty or amendments.

Dated October 9th, 1838.

Lorenn-taie-enne, Sase-sori-bogane, Louis-taw-roniate, Thomas-talsete, Saro-ako-ba-gi-tha, Louis-te-ka-nota-tiron, Michael Gareault, W. L. Gray, Int. Louis-tio-on-sate, Tier-ana-sa-ker-rat, Tomas-ska-en-to-gane, Tier-sa-ko-eni-saks, Saro-tsio-her-is-en, Sak-tho-te-ras-en, Saro-saion-gese, Louis-onia-rak-ete, Louis-aion-gahes, Sak-tha-nen-ris-hon, Sa-ga-tis-ania-ta-ri-co, Louis-sa-ka-na-tie, Sa-ga-tis-asi-kgar-a-tha, Simon-sa-he-rese, Resis-tsis-kako, Ennias-kar-igiio, Sak-tsior-ak-gisen, Tier-kaien-take-ron, Kor-ari-hata-ko, To mas-te-gaki-gasen, Saro-thar-on-ka-tha, Ennias-anas-ota-ko, Wishe-te-ka-nia-tasoken, Tomas-tio-nata-kgente, W is he-aten-en-rah es, Tomas-ioha-hiio, En nias-kana-gai en-ton, Louis-taro-nia-ke-thon, Louis-ari-ga-ke-wha, Sak-tsio-ri-te-ha, Louis-te-ga-ti-rhon, Tier-atsi-non-gis-aks.

The foregoing assent was signed in our presence. R. H. Gillet, Commissioner.

Witnesses:

James B. Spencer. Heman W. Tucker.

A. K. Williams, Agent St. Regis Indians. Frs. Marcoux Dictre.

(To the Indian names are subjoined marks.) [5161

We, the undersigned, chiefs, head men and warriors of the Onondaga tribe of Indians residing on the Seneca reservations in the State of New-York, do hereby give our free and voluntary assent to the foregoing treaty as amended by the Senate of the United States on the eleventh day of June, 1838, the same having been submitted to us, by Ransom H. Gillet, a commissioner on the part of the United States and fully and fairly explained by him to our said tribe on council assembled.

Dated August 31st, 1838.

Silversmith, Noah Silversmith, William Jacket

(To the Indian names are subjoined marks.)

The above signatures were freely given in our presence.

R.H. Gillet, Commissioner.

H.A.S. Dearborn, Superintendent of Massachussetts.

TREATY WITH THE WYANDOT {1842, Mar. 1}
Proclamation Oct. 5, 1842.

John Tyler, President of the United States of America, by John Johnston, formerly agent for Indian affairs, now a citizen of the State of Ohio, commissioner duly authorized and appointed to treat with the Wyandott Nation of Indians for a cession of all their lands lying and being in the States of Ohio and Michigan; and the duly constituted chiefs, counsellors, and head-men, of the said Wyandott Nation, in full council assembled, on the other part, have entered into the following articles and conditions, viz:

ARTICLE 1. The Wyandott Nation of Indians do hereby cede to the United States all that tract of land situate, lying, and being in the county of Crawford and State of Ohio, commonly known as the residue of the large reserve, being all of their remaining lands within the State of Ohio, and containing one hundred and nine thousand one hundred and forty-four acres, more or less. The said nation also hereby cedes to the United States all their right and title to the Wyandotte Reserve, on both sides of the river Huron, in the State of Michigan, containing four thousand nine hundred and ninety-six acres, be the same more or less, being all the remaining lands claimed or set apart for the use of the Wyandotts within the State of Michigan; and the United States hereby promises to pay the sum of five hundred dollars towards the expenses of removing the Indians of the river Huron to Upper Sandusky, but before the latter clause of this article is binding on the contracting parties, the consent of the head-men of the river Huron Wyandotts is to be had in writing.

ARTICLE 5. In consideration of the foregoing cession, the United States hereby grant to the aforesaid Wyandott Nation a tract of land west of the Mississippi River, to contain one hundred and forty-eight thousand acres, and to be located upon any lands owned by the United States, now set apart, or may in future be set apart for Indian use, and not already assigned to any other tribe or nation.

ARTICLE 3. The United States agree to pay the Wyandott Nation a perpetual annuity of seventeen thousand five hundred dollars in specie, the first payment to be made within the present year, 1842, to enable the nation the more speedily to remove to their new home in the West; this includes all former annuities.

ARTICLE 4. The United States agree to make a permanent provision of five hundred dollars per annum, for the support of a school, to be under the direction of the chiefs, and for no other purpose whatever, the first payment to be made three years hence, and afterwards at the payment of the annuity in each succeeding year.

ARTICLE 5. The United States agree to pay the Wyandotts the full value of their improvements in the country hereby ceded by them in Ohio and Michigan, which valuation shall be made by two persons to be appointed by the President of the United States, who shall be sworn faithfully to do justice to the parties, the amount of such valuation to be paid at any time after the 1st day of April, 1843, as shall be acceptable to the Wyandott chiefs, to meet their arrangements for emigrating.

ARTICLE 6. The United States hereby agree to pay the debts due by members of the Wyandott Nation to citizens of the United States, amounting to twenty-three thousand eight hundred and sixty dollars, in conformity to a schedule hereto annexed.

ARTICLE 7. The Wyandotts shall be allowed the use and occupancy of their improvements until the 1st of April, 1844, on the condition that they nor any persons claiming or occupying under them by lease or otherwise shall not commit waste or damage on the premises hereby ceded, but this is not to prevent the United States from surveying and selling the land at any time previous to the said 1st day of April, 1844.

ARTICLE 8. The United States engage to provide and support a blacksmith and an assistant blacksmith for the Wyandott Nation, and to furnish annually a sufficient quantity of iron, steel, coal, files, tools, and all other things necessary and proper in such on establishment, and to erect a suitable shop and house or houses for the residence of the blacksmith and his assistant.

ARTICLE 9. The United States engage to maintain and support a sub-agent and interpreter to reside among the Wyandotts to aid them in the protection of their persons and property, and to manage their intercourse with the Government and citizens of the United States.

ARTICLE 10. The buildings and farm occupied by the mission of the Methodist Episcopal Church shall remain in possession of the present incumbents until the 1st day of April, 1844, and permission is hereby given to harvest and remove the crop of fall-grain which may be then sown.

ARTICLE 11. All persons identified as members of the Wyandott Nation, and their heirs, and who may emigrate to the west, shall participate equally in the benefits of the annuity, and all other national privileges, and it is expressly understood that those who do not emigrate, and any that may hereafter cease to remain with the nation, will not be entitled to the benefits and privileges aforesaid,

ARTICLE 12. Whereas by the 8th article of the treaty of Miami Rapids of September 29th, 1817, (proclaimed January 4, 1819) there was granted unto Horonu, or Cherokee Boy, a Wyandott chief, one section of land, to contain six hundred and forty acres; and whereas the said Horonu did during his life-time sell and convey to James Whitaker one quarter-section of said land, containing 160 acres, which sale was confirmed by the President of the United States. The said Horonu died in the month of March, 1826, having by his last will bequeathed the remaining three quarter-sections, containing 480 acres, to Squeendehtee and Sooharress, or Isaac Williams, they being the nearest of kin to the deceased, now to the intent that the purposes of [536] the testator may be fully complied with, it is hereby agreed the 480 acres of land, as aforesaid, shall be immediately sold under the directions of the President of the United States, and the net proceeds, after deducting all expenses, be paid over to the heirs aforesaid.

ARTICLE 13. The chiefs of the Wyandott Nation hereby agree to remove their whole people to the west of the Mississippi River with out any other cost to the United States than the sum of ten thousand dollars; five thousand dollars of which is to be paid the said chiefs when the first detachment of their people sets out on their journey to the west, and the remaining five thousand dollars on the arrival of the whole nation at the place of their destination in the west.

ARTICLE 14. The United States agree to grant by patent in fee-simple to each of the following-named persons, and their heirs all of whom are Wyandotts by blood or adoption, one section of land of six hundred and forty acres each, out of any lands west of the Missouri River set apart for Indian use, not already claimed or occupied by any person or tribe, viz: Silas Armstrong, John M. Armstrong, Matthew R. Walker, William Walker, Joel Walker, Charles B. Garrett, George Garrett, George J. Clark, Irwin P. Long, Ethan A. Long, Joseph L. Tennery, Robert Robertaile, Jared S. Dawson, Joseph Newell, John T. Walker, Peter D. Clark, James Rankin, Samuel McCulloch, Elliot, McCulloch, Isaiah Walker, William M. Tennery, Henry Clay Walker, Ebenezer Z. Reed, and Joel Walker Garrett, and to the following chiefs and councillors one section each: Francis A. Hicks, James Washington, Squeendehtee, Henry Jaques, Tauroonce, Doctor Grey Eyes, George Armstrong, Warpole, John Hicks, Peacock, and George Punch. The lands hereby granted to be selected by the grantees, Surveyed and patented at the expense of the United States, but never to be conveyed by them or their heirs without the permission of the President of the United States.

ARTICLE 15. The United States agree to pay to William Walker and Joel Walker, each, the sum of two hundred and fifty dollars, and to John M. Armstrong the sum of one hundred and fifty dollars, for services rendered as interpreters in the progress of the negotiation; and to Warpole, a former chief of the Wyandott Nation, one hundred and fifty dollars, money expended by him as one of the party who accompanied Joseph McCutchen, a former commissioner of the United States, to the city of Washington in September, 1839.

ARTICLE 16. In the year 1812 the houses, barns, stables, fences, horses, cattle, and hogs, with farming utensils and household furniture, to a large amount, the property of the late William Walker, of Brownstown, in the Territory of Michigan, was destroyed by the enemy while in the occupancy of the United States forces; and by reason of his attachment to the cause of his country, being a native citizen, taken prisoner in early life by the Wyandott Indians, intermarried, and ever afterward living among them, the evidence of all which is ample and conclusive. There is therefore granted unto Catharine Walker, widow of the said William Walker, and to his heirs, the sum of three thousand dollars, in full satisfaction of their claim, to be paid by the United States to her or them after the ratification of this treaty.

ARTICLE 17. There shall be reserved from sale, and forever devoted to public use, two acres of ground as near as can be in a square form, to include the stone meeting-house and burying-ground near to and north of Upper Sandusky, one acre to include the burying-ground on the bank near the council-house at Upper Sandusky, and one-half acre to include the burying-ground on the farm of Silas Armstrong, which several lots of ground shall forever remain open and free to all persons for the purpose of interment and houses of worship, and for no other purposes whatever.

ARTICLE 18. This treaty shall take effect and be obligatory on the contracting parties as soon as the same shall be ratified by the President of the United States, by and with the advice and consent of the Senate thereof.
In testimony whereof the said John Johnston, commissioner as aforesaid, and the chiefs and councillors and headmen of the Wyandott nation in open council, at the council-house at Upper Sandusky in the county of Crawford, and the State of Ohio, on the seventeenth day of March, in the year of our Lord one thousand eight hundred and forty-two, have set their names.

John Johnston.
Fran. A. Hicks, Principal Chief, James Washington (x), Squeendehtee (x), Henry Jaquis (x),
Tauroone (x), George Armstrong (x), Doctor Grey Eyes (x)

Signed in the presence of: John W. Bear, Sub. Indian Agent, James Rankin, U. S. Interpreter, G. C. Worth, John Gary, Samuel Newell, Stephen Fowler, Charles Graham, John Walker, Chester Wells, I. Duddleson, Andrew Gardner, jur, John Justus.

We, the undersigned, chiefs and counsellors of the Wyandott nation of Indians, residing in the State of Ohio, and representing also the Wyandotts of the River Huron, in Michigan, do hereby give our free and voluntary assent to the amendments made by the Senate of the United States on the 17th day of August; one thousand eight hundred and forty-two, to the treaty concluded by us with the United States on the 17th day of March, 1842, the same having been submitted and fully explained to us by John Johnston, commissioner on the part of the United States for that purpose, in full council assembled.

In testimony whereof, we have hereunto set our hands and affixed our seals, respectively, at Upper Sandusky, Ohio, the sixteenth day of September, one thousand eight hundred and forty-two, 1842.

Henry Jacques, Principal Chief this year, his x mark, Tauroomee, his x mark, James Washington, his x mark, Doctor Grey Eyes, his x mark, Geroge Punch, sen., his x mark, James Big Tree, his x mark, Francis A. Hicks,

In the presence of: John Johnston, U. S. Commissioner, James Rankin, U. S. Interpreter Wyandotts., John , ary, Joseph Chaffee, James Wheeler, Missionary to the Methodist Episcopal Church, William M. Buell, Chas. Graham, H. J. Starr.

TREATY WITH THE SENECA {1842, May 20}
Proclamation, Aug. 26, 1842.

Articles of a treaty made and concluded at Buffalo Creek, in the State of New York, on the twentieth day of May in the year one thousand eight hundred and forty-two, between the United States of America, acting herein by Ambrose Spencer their Commissioner, thereto duly authorized, on the one part, and the chiefs, headmen and warriors of the Seneca nation of Indians, duly assembled in council, on the other part.

WHEREAS a treaty was heretofore concluded, and made between the said United States, and the chiefs, headmen, and warriors of the several tribes of New York Indians, dated the fifteenth day of January in the year one thousand eight hundred and thirty-eight, which treaty having been afterwards amended, was proclaimed by the President of the United States, on the fourth of April one thousand eight hundred and forty, to have been duly ratified.
And whereas on the day of making this treaty, and bearing even date herewith, a certain indenture was made executed and concluded by and between the said Seneca nation of Indians and Thomas L. Ogden, and Joseph Fellows, assignees under the State of Massachusetts, in the presence, and with the approbation of a Commissioner appointed by the United States, and in the presence and with the approbation of Samuel Hoare, a superintendent on the part of the common-wealth of Massachusetts, which indenture is in the words and figures following to wit:

"THIS INDENTURE made and concluded between Thomas Ludlow Ogden of the city of New York, and Joseph Fellows of Geneva, in the county of Ontario of the one part, and the chiefs and headmen of the Seneca nation of Indians, on the other part at a council duly assembled and held at Buffalo Creek in the State of New York on the twentieth day of May in the year one thousand eight hundred and forty-two in the presence of Samuel Hoare, the superintendent thereto

315

authorized and appointed by and on the part of the commonwealth of Massachusets, an of Ambrose Spencer a Commissioner thereto duly appointed and authorized on the part of the United States.

"Whereas at a council held at Buffalo Creek on the fifteenth day of January in the year one thousand eight hundred and thirty eight, an indenture of that date was made and executed by and between the parties to this agreement, whereby the chiefs and headmen of the Seneca nation of Indians for the consideration of two hundred and two thousand dollars did grant, bargain, release and confirm unto the said Thomas Ludlow Ogden and Joseph Fellows, all those four several tracts of land, situate within the State of New York, then and yet occupied by the said nation, or the people thereof, severally described in the said indenture, as the Buffalo Creek Reservation, containing by estimation forty-nine thousand nine hundred and twenty acres of land, the Cattaraugus Reservation containing by estimation twenty-one thousand six hundred and eighty acres of land, the Allegany Reservation, containing by estimation thirty thousand four hundred and sixty-nine acres of land, and the Tonnewanda Reservation containing by estimation twelve thousand eight hundred acres of land; a duplicate of which indenture was annexed to a treaty of the same date made between the United States of America and the chiefs, headmen, and warriors of the several tribes of New York Indians assembled in council; which treaty was amended and proclaimed by the President of the United States on the fourth of April one thousand eight hundred and forty, as having been duly ratified; as by the said indenture, treaty and proclamation more fully appear.

"And whereas divers questions and differences having arisen between the chiefs and headmen of the Seneca nation of Indians or some of them, and the said Thomas Ludlow Ogden and Joseph Fellows in relation to the said indenture, and the rights of the parties thereto, and the provisions contained in the said indenture being still unexecuted, the said parties have mutually agreed to settle, compromise and finally terminate all such questions and differences on the terms and conditions hereinafter specified.

"Now therefore it is hereby mutually declared, and agreed, by and between the said parties as follows.

"ARTICLE 1. The said Thomas Ludlow Ogden, and Joseph Fellows in consideration of the release and agreements hereinafter contained, on the part of the said Seneca nation do on their part consent, covenant and agree that they the said nation (the said indenture notwithstanding) shall and may continue in the occupation and enjoyment of the whole of the said two several tracts of land, called the Cattaraugus [539] Reservation, and the Allegany Reservation with the same right and title in all things, as they had and possessed therein immediately before the date of the said indenture, saving and reserving to the said Thomas Ludlow Ogden, and Joseph Fellows the right of pre-emption, and all other the right and title which they then had or held in or to the said tracts of land.

"ARTICLE 2. The chiefs and headmen of the Seneca nation of Indians in consideration of the foregoing, and of the agreement next hereinafter contained, do on their part grant, release and confirm unto the said Thomas Ludlow Ogden, and Joseph Fellows, and to their heirs and assigns, in joint tenancy, the whole of the said two tracts of land severally called the Buffalo Creek Reservation, and the Tonnewanda Reservation, and all the right and interest therein of the said nation.

"ARTICLE 3. It is mutually agreed, between the parties hereto that in lieu of the sum expressed in the said indenture, as the consideration of the sale, and release of the said four tracts of land, there shall be paid to the said nation a just consideration sum, for the release of the two tracts, hereby confirmed to the said Ogden and Fellows, to be estimated and ascertained as follows.
"The present value of the Indian title to the whole of the said four tracts of land including the improvements thereon, shall for all the purposes of this present compact, be deemed and taken to be two hundred and two thousand dollars, of which sum one hundred thousand dollars shall be deemed to be the value of such title in and to all the lands within the said four tracts exclusive of the improvements thereon, and one hundred and two thousand dollars to be the value of all the improvements within the said four tracts, and of the said sum of one hundred thousand dollars the said Ogden and Fellows shall pay to the Seneca nation such proportion as the value of all the lands within the said two tracts called the Buffalo Creek, and Tonnewanda Reservations shall bear to the value of all the lands within all the said four tractsand of the said sum of one hundred and two thousand dollars, the said Ogden and Fellows shall pay such proportion as the value of the improvements on the same two tracts, shall bear to the value of the improvements on all the said four tracts.

"ARTICLE 4. The amount of the consideration monies to be paid in pursuance of the last preceding article, shall be determined by the judgment and award of arbitrators, one of whom shall be named by the Secretary of the War Department of the United States, and one by the said Ogden and Fellows, which arbitrators in order to such judgment and award, and to the performance of the other duties hereby imposed on them, may employ suitable surveyors to explore examine and report on the value of the said lands and improvements, and also to ascertain the contents of each of the said four tracts, which contents shall govern the arbitrators as to quantity in determining the amount of the said consideration money.

"The same arbitrators shall also award and determine the amount to be paid to each individual Indian out of the sum which on the principles above stated, they shall ascertain and award to be the proportion.-ate value of the improvements on the said two tracts called the Buffalo Creek Reservation and the Tonnewanda Reservation, and in case the said arbitrators shall disagree as to any of the matters hereby submitted to them, they may choose an umpire whose decision thereon shall be final and conclusive, and the said arbitrators shall make a report in writing of their proceedings in duplicate, such reports to be acknowledged or proved according to the laws of the State of New York, in order to their being recorded, one of such reports to be filed in the office of the Secretary of the Department of War, and the other thereof to be delivered to the said Thomas L. Ogden and Joseph Fellows.

"ARTICLE 5. It is agreed, that the possession of the two parts hereby confirmed, to the said Ogden and Fellows, shall be surrendered and delivered up to them, as follows, viz: The forest or unimproved lands on the said tracts, within one month after the report of the said arbitrators shall be filed, in the office of the Department of War, and the improved lands within two years after the said report shall have been so filed; Provided always that the amount to be so ascertained and awarded, as the proportionate value of the said improvements, shall on the surrender thereof be paid to the President of the United States, to be distributed among the owners of the said improvements, according to the determination and award of the said arbitrators, in this behalf, and provided further that the consideration for the release and conveyance of the said lands shall at the time of the surrender thereof be paid or secured to the satisfaction of the said Secretary of the War Department, the income of which is to be paid to the said Seneca Indians annually.

But any Indian having improvements may surrender the same, and the land occupied by him and his family at any time prior to the expiration of the said two years, upon the amount awarded to him for such improvements being paid to the President of the United States, or any agent designated by him for that purpose by the said Ogden and Fellows, which amount shall be paid over to the Indian entitled to the same, under the direction of the War Department.

ARTICLE 6. It is hereby agreed and declared to be the understanding and intent of the parties hereto, that such of the said Seneca nation, as shall remove from the State of New York, under the provisions of any treaty, made or to be made, between the United States and the said Indians, shall be entitled in proportion to their relative numbers to the funds of the Seneca nation, and that the interest and income of such their share and proportion of the said funds, including the consideration money to be paid to the said nation in pursuance of this Indenture, and of all annuities belonging to the said Nation shall be paid to the said Indians so removing at their new homes, and whenever the said tracts called the Allegheny and the Cattaraugus Reservations, or any part thereof shall be sold and conveyed by the Indians remaining in the State of New York, the Indians so removing shall be entitled to share in the proceeds of said sales in the like proportion.

And it is further agreed and declared, that such Indians owning improvements in the Cattaraugus and Alleghany tracts as may so remove from the State of New York, shall be entitled on such removal, and on surrendering their improvements to the Seneca nation, for the benefit of the nation to receive the like compensation for the same, according to their relative values, as in the third and fourth articles of this treaty are stipulated to be paid, to the owners of improvements in the Buffalo Creek and Tonnewanda Tracts, on surrendering their improvements; which compensations may be advanced by the President of the United States, out of any funds in the hands of the Government of the United States, belonging to the Seneca nation, and the value of these improvements shall be ascertained and reported by the Arbitrators, to be appointed in pursuance of the fourth article.

ARTICLE 7. This Indenture is to be deemed to be in lieu of, and as a substitute for the above recited Indenture made and dated the fifteenth day of January, one thousand eight hundred and thirty eight, so far as the provisions of the two instruments may be inconsistent, or contradictory, and the said Indenture so far as the same may be inconsistent with the provisions of this compact, is to be regarded and is hereby declared to be rescinded and released.

ARTICLE 8. All the expenses attending the execution of this Indenture and compact including those of the arbitration and surveys hereinbefore referred to and also those of holding the treaty now in negotiation between the United States and the said Seneca Nation, except so far as may be provided for by the United States, shall be advanced and paid by the said Ogden and Yellows.

ARTICLE 9. The parties to this compact mutually agree to solicit the influence of the Government of the United States to protect such of the lands of the Seneca Indians, within the State of New York, as may from time to time remain in their possession from all taxes, and assessments for roads, highways, or any other purpose until such lands shall be sold and conveyed by the said Indians, and the possession thereof shall have been relinquished by them.

In witness whereof, the parties to these presents have hereunto, and to three other instruments of the same tenor and date, one to remain with the United States, one to remain with the State of Massachusetts, one to remain with the Seneca Nation of Indians, and one to remain with the said Thomas Ludlow Ogden and Joseph Yellows, interchangeably set their hands and seals the day and year first above written."

THEREFORE taking into consideration the premises it is agreed and stipulated by and between the United States of America and the Seneca nation of Indians, as follows, to wit:

First, The United States of America consent to the several articles and stipulations contained in the last recited Indenture between the said nation, and the said Thomas Ludlow Ogden and Joseph Fellows, above set forth.
Second, The United States further consent and agree that any number of the said nation, who shall remove from the State of New York, under the provisions of the above mentioned Treaty proclaimed as aforesaid, on the fourth day of April one thousand eight hundred and forty, shall be entitled in proportion to their relative numbers to all the benefits of the said Treaty.

Third, The United States of America further consent and agree, that the tenth article of said Treaty proclaimed as aforesaid on the fourth day of April one thousand eight hundred and forty, be deemed, and considered as modified, in conformity with the provisions of the Indenture hereinabove set forth, so far as that the United States will receive and pay the sum stipulated to be paid as the consideration money of the improvements therein specified, and will receive hold and apply the sum to be paid, or the securities to be given for the lands therein mentioned, as provided for in such Indenture.

In testimony whereof the undersigned Ambrose Spencer Commissioner on the part of the United States of America, and the undersigned chiefs and headmen of the Seneca nation of Indians, have to two parts of this treaty, one thereof to remain with the United States, and the other thereof with the Seneca nation of Indians, set their hands and affixed their seals the day and year first above mentioned.

Ambrose Spencer.

Saul Lagure,

N. T. Strong, Jabez Stevenson, William Krouse, Thompson S. Harris, Tit-ho-yah, or William Jones, Gau-gch-gruh-doh, or George Jimison, Hau-neh-hoys-soh, or Blue Eyes, Samuel Wilson, or Ni-ge-jos-a, Sah-go-en-toh, or Morris Halftown, Ten-wan-ne-us, or Governor Black Snake, Doa-ne-pho-gah, or Little Johnson, Joh-nesh-ha-dih, or James Stevenson, Ho-wah-tan-eh-goh, or John Pierce, Da-gon-on-de, or William Patterson, Samuel Goudon, Tunis Halftown, Hau-sa-nea-nes, or White Seneca,
Gah-nang-ga-eot, or Young Chief,

Thomas Jimeson, Moses Stevenson, Jonah Armstrong, Joseph Silverheels, Da-o-as-sah-au, or Jo. Hunlock, George Fox, Yaw-sau-ge, or Peter Johnson, Noh-sok-dah, or Jim Jonas, Dih-no-se-du, or Jacob Shongo, John Seneca, or Jo-on-da-goh, Ho-no-yea-os, or Jocob Bennett, George Turkey, Daniel Fau Guns, Goat-hau-oh, or Billy Shanks, James Pierce, Gi-eut-twa-geh, or Robert Watt,

Seneca White, Gesh-u-aw, or James Shongo, Jarvis Spraing, Ti-at-tah-co, or Adam Dextador, Moris B. Pierce, So-gooh-quas, or John Tallchief, Isaac Half-town, David Snow, John Bark, George Killbuck, George Dennis, John Kennedy, sen., Abram John, Job Pierce, Saw-da-ne, or George Deer, Ga-na-waw, or John Cook, Jaw-ne-es, or John Dickey, George Big Deer, Nah-joh-gau-eh, or Tall Peter, John Kennedy, jr.

Signed sealed and delivered in the presence of : A. Dixon, Commissioner on the part of New York, Benj. Ferris, Orlando Allen, Asher Wright, O.H. Marshall, Elam R. Sewett, Cortland B. Stebbins, Joseph S. Wasson.

(To the Indian names are subjoined a mark and seal.)

AGREEMENT WITH THE DELAWARES AND WYANDOT
{1843, Dec. 14}

Ratified July 25,. 1848, with the proviso: "That the Wyandot Indian Nation shall take no better right or interest in and to said lands than is now vested in the Delaware Nation of Indians.

Agreement between the Delaware and Wyandot nations of Indians, concluded on the 14th day of December, 1843.

Whereas from a long and intimate acquaintance, and the ardent friendship which has for a great many years existed between the Delawares and Wyandots and from a mutual desire that the same feeling shall continue and be more strengthened by becoming near neighbors to each other; therefore the said parties, the Delawares on one side, and the Wyandots on the other, in full council assembled, have agreed, and do agree, to the following stipulations, to Wit:-

ARTICLE 1. The Delaware nation of Indians, residing between the Missouri and Kansas rivers, being very anxious to have their uncles, the Wyandots, to settle and reside near them, do hereby donate, grant and quitclaim forever, to the Wyandot nation, three sections of land, containing six hundred and forty acres each, lying and being situated at the point of the junction of the Missouri and Kansas Rivers.

ARTICLE 2. The Delaware chiefs, for themselves, and by the unanimous consent of their people; do hereby cede, grant, quitclaim to the Wyandot nation and their heirs forever, thirty-six sections of land, each containing six hundred and forty acres, situated between the aforesaid Missouri and Kansas rivers, and adjoining on the west the aforesaid three donated sections, making in all thirty-nine sections of land, bounded as follows, viz:: Commencing at the point at the junction of the aforesaid Missouri and Kansas rivers, running west along the

Kansas river sufficiently far to include the aforesaid thirty-nine sections: thence running north to the Missouri river; thence down the said river with its meanders to the place of beginning; to be surveyed in as near a square form as the rivers and territory ceded will admit of.

ARTICLE 3. In consideration of the foregoing donation and cession of land, the Wyandot chiefs bind themselves, successors in office, and their people to pay to the Delaware nation of Indians, forty-six thousand and eighty dollars, as follows, viz: six thousand and eighty dollars to be paid the year eighteen hundred and forty-four, and four thousand dollars annually thereafter for ten years.

ARTICLE 4. It is hereby distinctly understood, between the contracting parties, that the aforesaid agreement shall not be binding or obligatory until the President of the United States shall have approved the same and caused it to be recorded in the War Department.

In testimony whereof, we, the chiefs and headmen of the Delaware nation, and the chiefs and headmen of the Wyandott nation, have, this fourteenth day of December, eighteen hundred and forty-three, set our signatures.

Delaware chiefs: Nah-koo-mer, his x mark, Captain Ketchum, his x mark, Captain Suavec, his x mark, Jackenduthen, his x mark, San-kock-sa, his x mark, Cock-i-to-wa, his x mark, Sa-sar-sit-tona, his x mark, Pemp-scah, his x mark, Nah-que-non, his x mark,
Wyandotts: Henry Jacquis, his x mark, James Washington, his x mark
Matthew Peacock, his x mark, James Bigtree, his x mark, George Armstrong, his x mark, Tan-roo-mie, his x mark, T. A. Hicks.

Signed in open council in presence of: Jonathan Phillips, Sub-agent for the Wyandotts, Richard W. Cummins, Indian Agent, James M. Simpson, Charles Graham, Joel Walker, Secretary of the Wyandott Council, Henry Tiblow, Indian interpreter, Delaware."

TREATY WITH THE CREEKS AND SEMINOLE {1845, Jan. 4}
Proclamation, July 18, 1845.

Articles of a treaty made by William Armstrong, P.M. Butler, Logan, and Thomas L. Judith, commissioners in behalf of the United States, of the first part; the Creek tribe of Indians, of the second; and the Seminole tribe of Indians, of the third part.

WHEREAS it was stipulated, in the fourth article of the Creek treaty of 1833, that the Seminoles should thenceforward be considered a constituent part of the Creek nation, and that a permanent and comfortable home should be secured for them on the lands set apart in said treaty as the country of the Creeks; and whereas many of the Seminoles have settled and are now living in the Creek country, while others, constituting a large portion of the tribe, have refused to make their homes in any part thereof, assigning as a reason that they are unwilling to submit to Creek laws and government, and that they are apprehensive of being deprived, by the Creek authorities, of their property; and whereas repeated complaints have been made to the United States government, that those of the Seminoles who refused to go into the Creek country have, without authority or right, settled upon lands secured to other tribes, and that they have committed numerous and extensive depredations upon the property of those upon whose lands they have intruded:

Now, therefore, in order to reconcile all difficulties respecting location and jurisdiction, to settle all disputed questions which have arisen, or may hereafter arise, in regard to rights of property, and especially to preserve the peace of the frontier, seriously endangered by the restless and warlike spirit of the intruding Seminoles, the parties to this treaty have agreed to the following stipulations:

ARTICLE 1. The Creeks agree that the Seminoles shall be entitled to settle in a body or separately, as they please, in any part of the Creek country; that they shall make their own town regulations, subject, however, to the general control of the Creek council, in which they shall be represented; and, in short, that no distinctions shall be made between the two tribes in any respect, except in the management of their pecuniary affairs, in which neither shall interfere with the other.

ARTICLE 2. The Seminoles agree that those of their tribe who have not done so before the ratification of this treaty, shall, immediately thereafter, remove to and permanently settle in the Creek country.

ARTICLE 3. It is mutually agreed by the Creeks and Seminoles, that all contested cases between the two tribes, concerning the right of property, growing out of sales or transactions that may have occurred previous to the ratification of this treaty, shall be subject to the decision of the President of the United States.

ARTICLE 4. The Creeks being greatly dissatisfied with the manner in which their boundaries were adjusted by the treaty of 1833, which they say they did not understand until after its execution, and it appearing that in said treaty no addition was made to their country for the use of the Seminoles, but that, on the contrary, they were deprived, without adequate compensation, of a considerable extent of valuable territory: And, moreover, the Seminoles, since the Creeks first agreed to receive them, having been engaged in a protracted and bloody contest, which has naturally engendered feelings and habits calculated to make them troublesome neighbors: The United States in consideration of these circumstances, agree that an additional annuity of three thousand dollars for purposes of education shall be allowed for the term of twenty years; that the annuity of three thousand dollars provided in the treaty of 1832 for like purposes shall be continued until the determination of the additional annuity above mentioned. It is further agreed that all the education funds of the Creeks, including the annuities above named, the annual allowance of one thousand dollars, provided in the treaty of 1833, and also all balances of appropriations for education annuities that may be due from the United States, shall be expended under the direction of President of the United States, for the purpose of education aforesaid.

ARTICLE 5. The Seminoles having expressed a desire to settle in a body on Little River, some distance westward of the present residence of the greater portion of them, it is agreed that rations shall be issued to such as may remove while on their way to their new homes; and that, after their emigration is completed, the whole tribe shall be subsisted for six months, due notice to be given that those who do not come into the Creek country before the issues commence shall be excluded. And it is distinctly understood that all those Seminoles who refuse to remove to, and settle in, the Creek Country, within six months after this treaty is ratified, shall not participate in any of the benefits it provides: Except those now in Florida, who shall be allowed twelve months from the date of the ratification of this treaty for their removal.

ARTICLE 6. The sum of fifteen thousand four hundred dollars, provided in the second article of the treaty of Payne's Landing, shall be paid in the manner therein pointed out, immediately after the emigration of those Seminoles who may remove to the Creek country is completed; also, as soon after such emigration as practicable, the annuity of three thousand dollars for fifteen years, provided in the fourth article of said treaty, and, in addition thereto, for the same period, two thousand dollars per annum in goods suited to their wants, to be equally divided among all the members of the tribe.

ARTICLE 7. To avoid all danger of encroachment, on the part of either Creeks or Seminoles, upon the territory of other nations, the northern and western boundary lines of the Creek country shall be plainly and distinctly marked.

In full satisfaction and discharge of all claims for property left or abandoned in Florida at the request of the officers of the United States, under promise of remuneration, one thousand dollars per annum, in agricultural implements, shall be furnished the Seminoles for five years.

In witness whereof, the said Commissioners and the undersigned Chiefs and Head Men of the Creek and Seminole tribes, have hereunto set their hands, at the Creek Agency, this fourth day of January, 1845.

Wm. Armstrong, Acting Superintendent Western Territory, P.M. Butler, Cherokee Agent, James Logan,, reek Agent, Thomas L. Judge, Seminole Sub-Agent.
Creeks: Roly McIntosh, To-marth-le Micco, Eu-faula Harjo, O-poeth-le Yoholo, Yargee, Samuel Miller, Cot-char Tustunnuggee, *K. Lewis, Tuskunar Harjo, Tinthlanis Harjo, To-cose Fixico, *Samuel C. Brown, Ho-tul-gar Harjo, Oak-chun Harjo, Art-tis Fixico, Joseph Carr, Ar-ar-te Harjo, Samuel Perryman, O-switchee Emarthlar, Talloaf Harjo, David Barnett, Jim Boy, *B. Marshall, Tinthlanis H arjo, Co-ah-coo-che Emarthlar, Thlathlo Harjo, E-cho Harjo,

Co-ah-thlocco, Ke-sar-che Harjo, No cose Harjo, Yar-dick-ah Harjo, Yo-ho-lo Chop-ko, Phil Grayson, Chu-ille, E-cho Emarthla, Pol-1ot-ke, Kot-che Harjo, To-cose Micco, Henry Marshall, Matthew Marshall, Che-was-tiah Fixleo, Tom Cart.
Seminoles: Miccanope, Coah-coo-che,or Wild Cat, Alligator, Nocose Yoholo, Halleck Tustunnuggee, Emah-thloo-chee, Octi-ar-chee, Tus-se-kiah, Pos-coffar, E-con-chat-te-micco, Black Dirt, Itch-hos-se Yo-ho-lo, Kap-pe-chum-e-coo-che, O-tul-ga Harjo, Yo-ho-lo Harjo, O-switchee Emarthla, Kub-bit-che, An-lo-ne, Yah-hah Fixleo, Fus-hat-chee, Micco, O-chee-see Micco, Tus-tun-nug-goo-chee.

In the presence of: J. B. Luce, secretary to commissioners, Samuel C. Brown, U. S. interpreter.
B. Marshall, Creek Nation interpreter, Abraham, U. S. interpreter for Semi noles, J. P. Davis, captain U. S., rmy, A. Cady, captain Sixth Infantry, J.B.S. Todd, captain Sixth Infantry, George W. Clarke, Jno. Dillard, J.L. Alexander, J.H. Heard.

TREATY WITH THE CHEROKEE {1846, Aug. 6}
Ratified Aug. 8,1846.
Proclaimed Aug. 17, 1846.

Articles of a treaty made and concluded at Washington, in the District of Columbia, between the United States of America, by three commissioners, Edmund Burke, William, Armstrong, and Albion K. Parris; and John Rose, principal chief of the Cherokee Nation; David Vann, William S. Goody, Richard Taylor, T. H. Walker, Clement V. McNair, Stephen Foreman, John Drew, and Richard Field, delegates duly appointed by the regularly constituted authorities of the Cherokee Nation; George W. Adair, John A. Bell, Stand Watie, Joseph M. Lynch, John Huss, and Brice Martin, a delegation appointed by, and representing that portion of the Cherokee tribe of Indians known and recognized as the "Treaty Party;" John Brown, Captain Dutch, John L. McCoy, Richard Drew, and Ellis Phillips, delegates appointed by, and representing, that portion of the Cherokee Tribe of Indians known and recognized as "Western Cherokees," or " Old Settlers."

WHEREAS serious difficulties have, for a considerable time past, existed between the different portions of the people constituting and recognized as the Cherokee Nation of Indians, which it is desirable should be speedily settled, so that peace and harmony may be restored among them; and whereas certain claims exist on the part of the Cherokee Nation, and portions of the Cherokee people, against the United States; Therefore, with a view to the final and amicable settlement of the difficulties and claims before mentioned, it is mutually agreed by the several parties to this convention as follows, viz:

ARTICLE 1. That the lands now occupied by the Cherokee Nation shall be secured to the whole Cherokee people for their common use and benefit; and a patent shall be issued for the same, including the eight hundred thousand acres purchased, together with the outlet west, promised by the United States, in conformity with the provisions relating thereto, contained in the third article of the treaty of 1835, and in the third section of the act of Congress, approved May twenty-eighth, 1830, which authorizes the President of the United States, in making exchanges of lands with the Indian tribes, "to assure the tribe or nation with which the exchange is made, that the United States will forever secure and guarantee to them, and their heirs or successors, the country so exchanged with them; and if they prefer it, that the United States will cause a patent or grant to be made and executed to them for the same: Provided, always, That such lands shall revert to the United States if the Indians become extinct or abandon the same."

ARTICLE 2. All difficulties and differences heretofore existing between the several parties of the Cherokee Nation are hereby settled and adjusted, and shall, as far as possible, be forgotten and forever buried in oblivion. All party distinctions shall cease, except so far as they may be necessary to carry out this convention or treaty. A general amnesty is hereby declared. All offences and crimes committed by a citizen or citizens of the Cherokee Nation against the nation, or against an individual or individuals, are hereby pardoned. All Cherokees who are now out of the nation are invited and earnestly requested to return to their homes, where they may live in peace, assured that they shall not be prosecuted for any offence heretofore committed against the Cherokee Nation, or any individual thereof. And this pardon and amnesty shall extend to all who may now be out of the nation, and who shall return thereto on or before 1st day of December next. The several parties agree to unite in enforcing the laws against all future offenders. Laws shall be passed for equal protection, and for the security of life, liberty, and property; and full authority shall be given by law, to all or any portion of the Cherokee people, peaceably to assemble and petition their own government, or the Government of the United States, for the redress of grievances, and to discuss their rights. All armed police, light horse, and other military organization, shall be abolished, and the laws enforced by the civil authority alone.

No one shall be punished for any crime or misdemeanor except on conviction by a jury of his country, and the sentence of a court duly authorized by law to take cognizance of the offence. And it is further agreed, all fugitives from justice, except those included in the general amnesty herein stipulated, seeking refuge in the territory of the United States, shall be delivered up by the authorities of the United States to the Cherokee Nation for trial and punishment.

ARTICLE 3. Whereas certain claims have been allowed by the several boards of commissioners heretofore appointed under the treaty of 1835, for rents, under the name of improvements and spoliations, and for property of which the Indians were dispossessed, provided for under the 16th article of the treaty of 1835; and whereas the said claims have been paid out of the $5,000,000 fund; and whereas said claims were not justly chargeable to that fund, but were to be paid by the United States, the said United States agree to re-imburse the said fund the amount thus charged to said fund, and the same shall form a part of the aggregate amount to be distributed to the Cherokee people, as provided in the 9th article of this treaty; and whereas a further amount has been allowed for reservations under the provisions of the 13th article of the treaty of 1835, by said commissioners, and has been paid out of the said fund, and which said sums were properly chargeable to, and should have been paid by, the United States, the said United States further agree to re-imburse the amounts thus paid for reservations to said fund; and whereas the expenses of making the treaty of New Echoto were also paid out of said fund, when they should have been borne by the United States, the United States agree to re-imburse the same, and also to re-imburse all other sums paid to any agent of the government, and improperly charged to said fund; and the same also shall form a part of the aggregate amount to be distributed to the Cherokee people, as provided in the 9th article of this treaty.

ARTICLE 4. And whereas it has been decided by the board of commissioners recently appointed by the President of the United States to examine and adjust the claims and difficulties existing against and between the Cherokee people and the United States, as well as between the Cherokees themselves, that under the provisions of the treaty of 1828, as well as in conformity with the general policy of the United States in relation to the Indian tribes, and the Cherokee Nation in particular, that that portion of the Cherokee people known as the "Old Settlers," or "Western Cherokees," had no exclusive title to the territory ceded in that treaty, but that the same was intended for the use of, and to be the home for, the whole nation, including as well that portion then east as that portion then west of the Mississippi; and whereas the said board of commissioners further decided that, inasmuch as the territory before mentioned became the common property of the whole Cherokee Nation by the operation of the treaty of 1828, the Cherokees then west of the Mississippi, by the equitable operation of the same treaty, acquired a common interest in the lands occupied by the Cherokees east of the Mississippi river, as well as in those occupied by themselves west of that river, which interest should have been provided for in the treaty of 1835, but which was not, except in so far as they, as a constituent portion of the nation, retained, in proportion to their numbers, a common interest in the country west of the Mississippi, and in the general funds of the nation; and therefore they have an equitable claim upon the United States for the value of [563] that interest, whatever it may be.

Now, in order to ascertain the value of that interest, it is agreed that the following principle shall be adopted, viz: All the investments and expenditures which are properly chargeable upon the sums granted in the treaty of 1835, amounting in the whole to five millions six hundred thousand dollars, (which investments and expenditures are particularly enumerated in the 15th article of the treaty of 1835)to be first deducted from said aggregate sum, thus ascertaining the residuum or amount which would, under such marshalling of accounts, be left for per capita distribution among the Cherokees emigrating under the treaty of 1835, excluding all extravagant and improper expenditures, and then allow to the Old Settlers (or Western Cherokees) a sum equal to one third part of said residuum-, to be distributed per capita to each individual of said party of "Old Settlers," or "Western Cherokees."

It is further agreed that, so far as the Western Cherokees are concerned, in estimating the expense of removal and subsistence of an Eastern Cherokee, to be charged to the aggregate fund of five million six hundred thousand dollars above mentioned, the sums for removal and subsistence stipulated in the 8th article of the treaty of 1835, as commutation money in those cases in which the parties entitled to it removed themselves, shall be adopted. And as it affects the settlement with the Western Cherokees, there shall be no deduction from the fund before mentioned in consideration of any payments which may hereafter be made out of said fund; and it is hereby further understood and agreed, that the principle above defined shall embrace all those Cherokees west of the Mississippi, who emigrated prior to the treaty of 1835.

In the consideration of the foregoing stipulation on the part of the United States, the "Western Cherokees," or "Old Settlers," hereby release and quitclaim to the United States all right, title, interest, or claim they may have to a common property in the Cherokee lands east of the Mississippi River, and to exclusive ownership to the lands ceded to them by the treaty of 1833 west of the Mississippi, including the outlet west, consenting and agreeing that the said lands, together with the eight hundred thousand acres ceded to the Cherokees by the treaty of 1835, shall be and remain the common property of the whole Cherokee people, themselves included.

ARTICLE 5. It is mutually agreed that the per capita allowance to be given to the "Western Cherokees," or "Old Settlers," upon the principle above stated, shall be held in trust by the Government of the United States, and paid out to each individual belonging to that party or head of family, or his legal representatives. And it is further agreed that the per capita allowance to be paid as aforesaid shall not be assignable, but shall be paid directly to the persons entitled to it, or to his heirs or legal representatives, by the agent of the United States, authorized to make such payments.

And it is further agreed that a committee of five persons shall be appointed by the President of the United States, from the party of "Old Settlers," whose duty it shall be, in conjunction with an agent of the United States, to ascertain what persons are entitled to the per capita allowance provided for in this and the preceding article.

ARTICLE 6. And whereas many of that portion of the Cherokee people known and designated as the "Treaty Party" have suffered losses and incurred expenses in consequence of the treaty of 1835 therefore, to indemnify the treaty party, the United States agree to pay to the said treaty party the sum of one hundred and fifteen thousand dollars, of which-the sum of five thousand dollars shall be paid by the United States to the heirs or legal representatives of Major Ridge, the sum of five thousand dollars to the heirs or legal representatives of John Ridge, and the sum of five thousand dollars to the heirs or legal representatives of Elias Boudinot, and the balance, being the sum of one hundred thousand dollars, which shall be paid by the United States, in such amounts and to such persons as may be certified by a committee to be appointed by the treaty party, and which committee shall consist of not exceeding five persons, and approved by an agent of the United States, to be entitled to receive the same for losses and damages sustained by them, or by those of whom they are the heirs or legal representatives

Provided, That out of the said balance of one hundred thousand dollars, the present delegation of the treaty party may receive the sum of twenty-five thousand dollars, to be by them applied to the payment of claims and other expenses. And it is further provided that, if the said sum of one hundred thousand dollars should not be sufficient to pay all the claims allowed for losses and damages, that then the same shall be paid to the said claimants pro rata, and which payments shall be in full of all claims and losses of the said treaty party.

ARTICLE 7. The value of all salines which were the private property of individuals of the Western Cherokees, and of which they were dispossessed, provided there be any such, shall be ascertained by the United States agent, and a commissioner to be appointed by the Cherokee authorities; and, should they be unable to agree, they shall select an umpire, whose decision shall be final; and the several amounts found due shall be paid by the Cherokee Nation, or the sa-lines returned to their respective owners.

ARTICLE 8. The United States agree to pay to the Cherokee Nation the sum of two thousand dollars for a printing-press, materials, and other property de-stroyed at that time; the sum of five thousand dollars to be equally divided among all those whose arms were taken from them previous to their removal West by order of an officer of the United States; and the further sum of twenty thousand dollars, in lieu of all claims of the Cherokee Nation, as a nation, prior to the treaty of 1835, except all lands reserved, by treaties heretofore made, for school funds.

ARTICLE 9. The United States agree to make a fair and just settlement of all moneys due to the Cherokees, and subject to the per capita division under the treaty of 29th December, 1835, which said settlement shall exhibit all money properly expended under said treaty, and shall embrace all sums paid for im-provements, ferries, spoliations, removal, and subsistence, and commutation therefor, debts and claims upon the Cherokee Nation of Indians, for the addi-tional quantity of land ceded to said nation; and the several sums provided in the several articles of the treaty, to be invested as the general funds of the na-tion; and also all sums which may be hereafter properly allowed and paid under the provisions of the treaty of 1835. The aggregate of which said several sums shall be deducted from the sum of six millions six hundred and forty-seven thousand and sixty-seven dollars, and the balance thus found to be due shall be paid over, per capita, in equal amounts, to all those individuals, heads of fami-lies, or their legal representatives, entitled to receive the same under the treaty of 1835, and the supplement of 1836, being all those Cherokees residing east at the date of said treaty and the supplement thereto.

ARTICLE 10. It is expressly agreed that nothing in the foregoing treaty con-tained shall be so construed as in any manner to take away or abridge any rights or claims which the Cherokees now residing in States east of the Mississippi River had, or may have, under the treaty of 1835 and the supplement thereto.

ARTICLE 11. Whereas the Cherokee delegations contend that the amount ex-pended for the one year's subsistence, after their arrival in the west, of the East-ern Cherokees, is not properly chargeable to the treaty fund: it is hereby agreed that that question shall be submitted to the Senate of the United States for its decision, which shall decide [565] whether the subsistence shall be borne by the United States or the Cherokee funds, and if by the Cherokees, then to say, whether the subsistence shall be charged at a greater rate than thirty-three, 33/100 dollars per head; and also the question, whether the Cherokee Nation shall be allowed interest on whatever sum may be found to be due the nation, and from what date and at what rate per annum.

ARTICLE 12. (Stricken out.)

ARTICLE 13. This treaty, after the same shall be ratified by the President and Senate of the United States, shall be obligatory on the contracting parties.
In testimony whereof, the said Edmund Burke, William Armstrong, and Albion K. Parris, Commissioners as aforesaid, and the several delegations aforesaid, and the Cherokee nation and people, have hereunto set their hands and seals, at Washington aforesaid, this sixth day of August, in the year of our Lord one thousand eight hundred and forty-six.

Edmund Burke, Wm. Armstrong, Albion K. Parris.
Delegation of the Government Party: Jno. Ross, W. S. Coody, R. Taylor, C. V. McNair, Stephen Foreman, John Drew, Richard Fields.
Delegation of the Treaty Party: Geo. W. Adair, J. A. Bell, S. Watie, Joseph M. Lynch, John Huss, Brice Martin (by J. M. Lynch, his attorney).
Delegation of the Old Settlers: Jno. Brown, Wm. Dutch, John L. McCoy, Richard Drew, Ellis F. Phillips.
(To each of the names of the Indians a seal is affixed.)

In presence of: Joseph Bryan, of Alabama, Geo. W. Paschal, John P. Wolf, (Secretary of Board.) W. S. Adair, Jno. F. Wheeler.

TREATY WITH THE WYANDOT {1850, Apr. 1}
Ratified Sept. 24, 1850.
Proclaimed Sept. 30, 1850.

Articles of a convention concluded in the city of Washington, this first day of April, one thousand eight hundred and fifty, by and between Ardavan S. Loughery, commissioner especially appointed by the President of the United States, and the undersigned head chief and deputies of the Wyandot tribe of Indians, duly authorized and empowered to act for their tribe.

WHEREAS, By the treaty of March 17, 1842, between the United States and the Wyandot nation of Indians, then chiefly residing within the limits of the State of Ohio, the said nation of Indians agreed to sell and transfer, and did thereby sell and transfer, to the United States their reservations of land, one hundred and nine thousand acres of which was in the State of Ohio, and Six thousand acres were in the State of Michigan, and to remove to the west of the Mississippi River: And whereas, among other stipulations it was agreed that the United States should convey to said Indians a tract of country for their permanent settlement in the Indian territory west of the Mississippi River, to contain one hundred an (and) forty-eight thousand acres of land: And whereas, The said Indians never did receive the said one hundred and forty-eight thousand acres of land from the United States, but were forced to purchase lands from the Delaware nation of Indians, which purchase was agreed to and ratified by the United States: Now, in order to settle the claim of the Wyandot tribe of Indians to said land, the United States having appointed A. S. Loughery a commissioner on their part, who, with the undersigned delegates from the Wyandot nation, have agreed to the following treaty:

ARTICLE 1. The United States, in consideration that the Wyandot nation of Indians shall and do hereby release, relinquish, and give up all claim to the said one hundred and forty-eight thousand acres of land agreed to be assigned and given to them by the treaty of March 17, 1842, hereby stipulate and agree to pay to the said Wyandot tribe of Indians the sum of one hundred and eighty-five thousand dollars, being at and after the rate of one dollar and twenty-five cents per acre, in the manner and form following, to wit: One hundred thousand dollars to be invested in United States Stocks, bearing five per cent interest per annum, which interest shall be paid to them at the time and in the manner in which their present annuities are paidand for the purpose of enabling the Wyandot Indians to pay and extinguish all their just debts, as well what is now due to the Delawares for the purchase of their lands as to others, the balance of said sum, being the sum of eighty-five thousand dollars, shall be paid to the Wyandot nation, or on their drafts, specifically describing for what the drafts are given.

ARTICLE 2. All the reasonable expenses attending the negotiation of this treaty, including a reasonable allowance for the expenses of the delegation, signers hereto, in coming to Washington, whilst here on the business connected herewith, and m returning to their nation, shall be defrayed by the United States.
In testimony whereof, the said commissioners on the part of the United States, and the said head chief and deputies, delegates on the part of the Wyandot tribe or nation of Indians, have hereunto set their hands, at the city of Washington, D.C., this first day of April, in the year of our Lord eighteen hundred and fifty.

Ardavan S. Loughery, United States Commissioner.
F. A. Hick, Geo. J. Clark, Joel Walker, William B. Waugh, Secretary.

In presence of: R. W. Johnson, James X. MacLanahan Geo. F. Wood, James Myer, A. M. Mitchell, Jno. G. Camp, Richard Fields, S.C. Stambaugh, Sam. J. Potts.

TREATY WITH THE DELAWARES {1854, May 6}
Ratified July 11, 1854.
Proclaimed July 17, 1854.

Articles of agreement and convention made and concluded at the city of Washington this sixth day of May, one thousand eight hundred and fifty-four, by George W. Manypenny, as commissioner on the part of the United States, and the following-named delegates of the Delaware tribe of Indians, viz: Sarcoxey; Ne-con-he-cond; Kock-ha-to-wha; Qua-cor-now-ha, or James Segondyne; Ne-sha-pa-na-cumin, or Charles Journeycake; Que-sha-to-wha, or John Ketchem; Pandoxy, or George Bullet; Kock-kock-quas, or James Ketchem; Ah-lah-a-chick, or James Conner, they being thereto duly authorized by said tribe.

ARTICLE 1. The Delaware tribe of Indians hereby cede, relinquish, and quitclaim to the United States all their right, title, and interest in and to their country lying west of the State of Missouri, and situate in the fork of the Missouri and Kansas Rivers, which is described in the article supplementary to the treaty of October third, one thousand eight hundred and eighteen, concluded, in part, on the twenty-fourth September, one thousand eight hundred and twenty-nine, at Council Camp, on James' Fork of White River, in the State of Missouri; and finally concluded at Council Camp, in the fork of the Kansas and Missouri Rivers, on the nineteenth October, one thousand eight hundred and twenty-nine; and also their right, title, and interest in and to the "outlet" mentioned and described in said supplementary article, excepting that portion of said country sold to the Wyandot tribe of Indians, by instrument sanctioned by act of Congress approved July twenty-fifth, one thousand eight hundred and forty-eight, and also excepting that part of said country lying east and south of a line beginning at a point on the line between the land of the Delawares and the half-breed Kanzas, forty miles, in a direct line, west of the boundary between the Delawares and Wyandots, thence north ten miles, thence in an easterly course to a point on the south bank of Big Island Creek, which shall also be on the bank of the Missouri River where the usual high-water line of said creek intersects the high-water line of said river.

ARTICLE 2. The United States hereby agree to have the ceded country (excepting the said "outlet") surveyed, as soon as it can be conveniently done, in the same manner that the public lands are surveyed -- such survey to be commenced and prosecuted as the President of the United States may deem best. And the President will, so soon as the whole or any portion of said lands are surveyed, proceed to offer such surveyed lands for sale, at public auction, in such quantities as he may deem proper, being governed in all respects, in conducting such sales, by the laws of the United States respecting the sales of the public lands; and such of the lands as may not he sold at the public sales, shall thereafter be subject to private entry, in the same manner that private entries are made of United States lands; and any, or all, of such lands as remain unsold, after being three years subject to private entry, at the minimum Government price, may, by act of Congress, be graduated and reduced in price, until all said lands are sold; regard being had in said graduation and reduction to the interests of the Delawares, and also to the speedy settlement of the country.

ARTICLE 3. The United States agree to pay to the Delaware tribe of Indians the sum of ten thousand dollars; and, in consideration thereof, the; Delaware tribe of Indians hereby cede, release, and quit-claim to the United States, the said tract of country hereinbefore described as the "outlet." And as a further and full compensation for the cession made by the first article, the United States agree to pay to said tribe all the moneys received from the sales of the lands provided to be surveyed in the preceding article, after deducting therefrom the cost of surveying, managing, and selling the same.

ARTICLE 4. The Delaware Indians have now, by treaty stipulation, the following permanent annuities, to wit: One thousand dollars per fourth article of the treaty of third August, one thousand seven hundred and ninety-five. Five hundred dollars, per third article of the treaty of thirtieth of September, one thousand eight hundred and nine. Four thousand dollars per fifth article of the treaty of the third October, one thousand eight hundred and eighteen. One thousand dollars per supplemental treaty of twenty-fourth September, one thousand eight hundred and twenty-nine. One hundred dollars for salt annuity, per third article of the treaty of June seventh, one thousand eight hundred and three.
 Nine hundred and forty dollars, for blacksmith annuity, per sixth article of the treaty of third October, one thousand eight hundred and eighteen. All which several permanent annuities they hereby relinquish and forever absolve the United States from the further payment thereof; in consideration whereof the United States agree to pay to them, under the direction of the President, the sum of one hundred and forty-eight thousand dollars, as follows: seventy-four thousand dollars in the month of October, one thousand eight hundred and fifty-four, and seventy-four thousand dollars in the month of October, one thousand eight hundred and fifty-five. The object of converting the permanent annuities into these two payments being to aid the Delawares in making improvments on their present farms, and opening new ones on the land reserved, building houses, buying necessary household furniture, stock, and farming-utensils, and such other articles as may be necessary to their comfort.

ARTICLE 5. It is agreed that the sum of forty-six thousand and eighty dollars, being the value of the thirty-six sections of land set apart for school purposes by the supplemental treaty of one thousand eight hundred and twenty-nine, remain for the present at five per cent. interest, as stipulated by the resolution of the Senate of the nineteenth January, one thousand eight hundred and thirty-eight.

ARTICLE 6. The Delawares feel now, as heretofore, grateful to their old chiefs for their long and faithful services. In former treaties, when their means were scanty, they provided, by small life-annuities, for the wants of these chiefs, some of whom are now receiving them. These chiefs are poor, and the Delawares believe it their duty to keep them from want in their old and declining age. It is the wish of the Delawares, and hereby stipulated and agreed, that the sum of ten thousand dollars, the amount provided in the third article as a consideration for the "outlet," shall be paid to their five chiefs, to wit: Captain Ketchem, Sarkoxey, Segondyne, Neconhecond, and Kock-ka-to-wha, in equal shares of two thousand dollars each, to be paid as follows: to each of said chiefs, annually, the sum of two hundred and fifty dollars, until the whole sum is paid: Provided, That if any one or more of said chiefs die before the whole or any part of the sum is paid, the annual payments remaining to his share shall be paid to his male children, and, in default of male heirs, then to the legal representatives of such deceased chief or chiefs; and it is understood that the small life-annuities stipulated for by former treaties, shall be paid as directed by said treaties.

ARTICLE 7. It is expected that the amount of moneys arising from the sales herein provided for will be greater than the Delawares will need to meet their current wants; and as it is their duty, and their desire also, to create a permanent fund for the benefit of the Delaware people, it is agreed that all the money not necessary for the reasonable wants Of the people, shall from time to time be invested by the President of the United States, in safe and profitable stocks, the principal to remain unimpaired, and the interest to be applied annually for the civilization, education, and religious culture of the Delaware people, and such other objects of a beneficial character, as in his judgment, are proper and necessary.

ARTICLE 8. As the annual receipts from the sales of the lands cannot now be determined, it is agreed that the whole subject be referred to the judgment of the President, who may, from time to time, prescribe how much of the net proceeds of said sales shall be paid out to the Delaware people, and the mode and manner of such payment, also how much shall be invested, and in distributing the funds to the people, due regard and encouragement shall be given to that portion of the Delawares who are competent to manage their own affairs, and who know and appreciate the value of money; but Congress may, at any time, and from time to time, by law, make such rules and regulations in relation to the funds arising from the sale of said lands, and the application thereof for the benefit and improvement of the Delaware people, as may in the wisdom of that body, seem just and proper.

ARTICLE 9. The debts of Indians, contracted in their private dealings as individuals, whether to traders or otherwise, shall not be paid from the general fund.

ARTICLE 10. The Delawares promise to renew their efforts to suppress the introduction and the use of ardent spirits in their country and among their people, and to encourage industry, integrity, and virtue, so that every one may become civilized, and, as many now are, competent to manage their business af-

335

fairs; but should some of them [617] unfortunately continue to refuse to labor, and remain or become dissipated and worthless, it shall be discretionary with the President to give such direction to the portion of funds, from time to time, due to such persons, as will prevent them from squandering the same, and secure the benefit thereof to their families.

ARTICLE 11. At any time hereafter, when the Delawares desire it, and at their request and expense, the President may cause the country reserved for their permanent home to be surveyed in the same manner as the ceded country is surveyed, and may assign such portion to each person or family as shall be designated by the principal men of the tribe: Provided, Such assignment shall be uniform.

ARTICLE 12. In the settlement of the country adjacent to the Delaware reservation, roads and highways will become necessary, and it is agreed that all roads and highways laid out by authority of law, shall have a right of way through the reserved lands, on the same terms that the law provides for their location through the lands of citizens of the United States; and railroad companies, when the lines of their roads necessarily pass through the said reservation, shall have the right of way, on payment of a just compensation therefor in money.

ARTICLE 13. The Christian Indians live in the country herein ceded, and have some improvements. They desire to remain where they are, and the Delawares are willing, provided the Christian Indians can pay them for the land. It is therefore agreed that there shall be confirmed by patent to the said Christian Indians, subject to such restrictions as Congress may provide, a quantity of land equal to four sections, to be selected in a body from the surveyed lands, and to include their present improvements: Provided, The said Christian Indians, or the United States for them, pay to the Secretary of the Interior for the use of the Delaware Indians, within one year from the date of the ratification of this treaty, the sum of two dollars and fifty cents per acre therefor: And provided further, That the provisions of article twelve, in relation to roads, highways, and railroads, shall be applicable to the land thus granted to the Christian Indians.

ARTICLE 14. The Delawares acknowledge their dependence on the Government of the United States, and invoke its protection and care, They desire to be protected from depredations and injuries of every kind, and to live at peace with all the Indian tribes; and they promise to abstain from war, and to commit no depredations on either citizens or Indians; and if, unhappily, any difficulty should arise, they will at all times, as far as they are able, comply with the law in such cases made and provided, as they will expect to be protected and their rights vindicated by it, when they are injured.

ARTICLE 15. A primary object of this instrument being to advance the interests and welfare of the Delaware people, it is agreed, that if it prove insufficient to effect these ends, from causes which cannot now be foreseen, Congress may hereafter make such further provision, by law, not inconsistent herewith, as experience may prove to be necessary to promote the interests, peace, and happiness of the Delaware people.

ARTICLE 16. It is agreed by the parties hereto, that the provisions of the act of Congress, approved third of March, one thousand eight hundred and seven, in relation to lands ceded to the United States, shall, so far as applicable, be extended to the lands herein ceded.

ARTICLE 17. It is further stipulated, that should the Senate of the United States reject the thirteenth article hereof, such rejection shall in no wise affect the validity of the other articles.

ARTICLE 18. This instrument shall be obligatory on the contracting parties as soon as the same shall be ratified by the President, and the Senate, of the United States.
In testimony whereof the said George W. Manypenny, commissioner as aforesaid, and the said delegates of the Delaware tribe of Indians, have hereunto set their hands and seals, at the place and on the day and year hereinbefore written.

George W. Manypenny, Commissioner.

Sarcoxey, his x mark, Ne-con-he-cond, his x mark, Kock-ka-to-wha, his x mark, Qua-cot-now-ha, or James Segondyne, his x mark, Ne-sha-pa-na-cumin, or Charles Journeycake, Que-sha-to-wha, or John Ketchera, his x mark, Pondoxy, or George Bullet, his x mark, Kock-kock-quas, or James Ketchera, Ah-lah-a-chick, or James Conner, his x mark.

Executed in the presence of: Thos. Johnson, Charles Calvert, Douglas H. Cooper, Wm. B. Waugh, Henry Beard, B. F. Robinson, Indian agent, Henry Tiblow, United States interpreter.

TREATY WITH THE CREEKS {1854, June 13}
Ratified July 21, 1854.

Supplementary article to the treaty with the Creek tribe of Indians made and concluded at Fort Gibson on the twenty-third day of November, in the year eighteen hundred and thirty-eight.

Whereas the third article of said treaty provided for the investment by the United States of the sum of three hundred and fifty thousand dollars for the benefit of certain individuals of the Creek nation, but which sum remains uninvested; and the fourth article of the same treaty further provides that at the expiration of twenty-five years from the date thereof, the said sum of three hundred and fifty thousand dollars shall be appropriated for the common benefit of the Creek nation; which provision has caused great dissatisfaction, the individuals to whom the fund rightfully belongs never having authorized or assented to such a future disposition thereof.

And whereas the chiefs and people of the Creek nation recognize and consider the said fund as the exclusive property of said individuals, and are opposed to their hereafter being deprived thereof; and whereas the annual interest thereon is of no advantage to the great body of the persons to whom it is payable, and the distribution of the principal of the fund would be far more beneficial for them and prevent probable contest and difficulty hereafter; and such distribution has been requested by the chiefs representing both the nation and the individual claimants of said fund.

The following supplementary article to the aforesaid treaty of 1838, has this day been agreed to and entered into, by and between William H. Garrett, United States agent for the Creeks and Tuckabatche Micco, Hopoithle Yoholo, Benjamin Marshall, and George W. Stid-ham, chiefs and delegates of the Creek nation duly empowered to represent and act for the same and the individuals thereof to wit:

ARTICLE. It is hereby agreed and stipulated by and between the aforementioned parties, that the third and fourth articles of the treaty with the Creek nation of November 23, 1838, shall be and the same are hereby annulled; and the fund of three hundred and fifty thousand dollars therein mentioned and referred to shall be divided and paid out to the individuals of said nation for whose benefit the same was originally set apart, according to their respective and proportionate interests therein, as exemplified and shown by the schedule mentioned in the second article of said treaty; the said division and payment to be made by the United States so soon as the necessary appropriation for that purpose can be obtained from Congress.

In testimony whereof the said parties have hereunto set their hands and seals on this thirteenth day of June in the year of our Lord one thousand eight hundred and fifty-four.

W. H. Garrett, United States agent for the Creeks.
Tuckabatche Micco, his x mark, Hopothlegoholo, his x mark, B. Marshall, G. W. Stidham,

Signed and sealed in the presence of: James Abercrombie, Sen. Andrew R. Ports, Robert A. Allen, Philip H. Raiford.

TREATY WITH THE CHOCTAW AND CHICKASAW {1854, Nov. 4}
Ratified Feb. 28, 1855.
Proclaimed Apr. 10, 1855.

Whereas a convention and agreement was made and entered into by the Choctaw and Chickasaw Indians, at Doaksville, near Fort Towson, in the Choctaw
country, on the seventeenth day of January, A. D. one thousand eight hundred
and thirty-seven; and, whereas, difficulties have arisen between said tribes in
regard to the line of boundary, between the Chickasaw district and other districts of the Choctaw nation, described in article second of said convention and
agreement; and, whereas, it is the desire of the said tribes, that there shall no
longer exist any dispute in regard to the boundary of the Chickasaw district, the
undersigned, Thomas J. Pitchlynn, Edmund McKenny, R. M. Jones, Daniel
Folsom, and Samuel Garland, commissioners duly appointed and empowered
by the Choctaw tribe of red people; and Edmund Pickens, Benjamin S. Love,
James T. Gaines, Sampson Folsom, and Edmund Perry, commissioners duly
appointed and empowered by the Chickasaw tribe of Indians, to settle all matters in dispute between their respective tribes, which require new articles of
agreement between them, have solemnly made the following articles of convention and agreement, on the fourth day of November, A. D. one thousand
eight hundred and fifty-four, at Doaksville, near Fort Tow-son, in the Choctaw
country, subject to the approval of the President and the Senate of the United
States.

ARTICLE 1. It is agreed by the Choctaw and Chickasaw tribes of Indians, in
lieu of the boundaries established under article second of the convention and
agreement entered into between said tribes, January 17th, A. D. 1837, the
Chickasaw district of the Choctaw nation shall be bounded as follows, viz: Beginning on the north bank of the Red River, at the mouth of island Bayou,
where it empties into the Red River, about twenty-six miles on a straight, line,
below the mouth of False Wachitta, thence running a northwesterly course,
along the main channel of said bayou to the junction of three prongs of said
bayou nearest the dividing ridge between Wachitta and Low Blue rivers, as laid
down upon Capt. R. L. Hunter's map; thence, northerly along the eastern prong
of Island Bayou to its source; thence, due north to the Canadian River, thence
west, along the main Canadian, to one hundred degrees of west longitude;
thence south to Red River, and down Red River to the beginning: Provided,
however, if the line running due north from the eastern source of Island Bayou
to the main Canadian shall not include Allen's or Wa-pa-nacka academy within
the Chickasaw district, then an offset shall be made from said line so as to leave
said academy two miles within the Chickasaw district, north, west, and south
from the lines of boundary.

ARTICLE 2. It is agreed by the Choctaws, that the Chickasaws employ a surveyor or engineer to run out and mark the eastern line of the Chickasaw district, and by the Chickasaws that they will pay all expenses incurred in running out and marking said line; and it is mutually agreed that the chiefs of each district of the Choctaw nation shall appoint one commissioner to attend and supervise the running and marking of said line; the chief of the Chickasaw district giving them at least thirty days' notice of the time when the surveyor or engineer will proceed to run out and mark the line agreed upon; which shall be plainly marked upon trees, where there is timber, and by permanent monuments of stone, at every mile, where there is not sufficient timber upon which the line can be marked in a permanent manner, before the first day of August, A. D. one thousand eight hundred and fifty-five.

In testimony whereof, the parties to this convention and agreement have hereunto subscribed their names and affixed their seals.
Done in triplicate at Doaksville, near Fort Towson, Choctaw Nation, the day and year first above written.

Thos. J. Pitchlynn, Edmund McKenny, R. M. Jones, Daniel Folsom, Samuel Garland, Commissioners on the part of Choctaws, Edmund Pickens, Benjamin S. Love, James T. Gaines, Sampson Folsom, Edmund Perry, Commissioners on the part of the Chickasaws.

In presence of: Geo. W. Harkins, Peter Folsom, Nicholas Cochnaner, Jackson Frazier, Chiefs of the Choctaw Nation, Douglas H. Cooper, United States Indian agent, William K. McKean.

TREATY WITH THE CHOCTAW AND CHICKASAW {1855, June 22}
Ratified Feb. 2 1, 1856.
Proclaimed Mar. 4, 1856.

Articles of agreement and convention between the United States and the Choctaw and Chickasaw tribes of Indians, made and concluded at the city of Washington, the twenty-second day of June, A.D. one thousand eight hundred and fifty-five, by George W. Manypenny, commissioner on the part of the United States, Peter P. Pitchlynn, Israel Folsom, Samuel Garland, and Dixon W. Lewis, commissioners on the part of the Choctaws; and Edmund Pickens and Sampson Folsom, commissioners on the part of the Chickasaws:

Whereas, the political connection heretofore existing between the Choctaw and the Chickasaw tribes of Indians, has given rise to unhappy and injurious dissensions and controversies among them, which render necessary a re-adjustment of their relations to each other and to the United States: and

Whereas the United States desire that the Choctaw Indians shall relinquish all claim to any territory west of the one hundredth degree of west longitude, and also to make provision for the permanent settlement within the Choctaw country, of the Wichita and certain other tribes or bands of Indians, for which purpose the Choctaws and Chickasaws are willing to lease, on reasonable terms, to the United States, that portion of their common territory which is west of the ninety-eighth degree of west longitude: and

Whereas, the Choctaws contend, that, by a just and fair construction of the treaty of September 27, 1830, they are, of right, entitled to the net proceeds of the lands ceded by them to the United States, under said treaty, and have proposed that the question of their right to the same, together with the whole subject-matter of their unsettled claims, whether national or individual, against the United States, arising under the various provisions of said treaty, shall be referred to the Senate of the United States for final adjudication and adjustment, and whereas, it is necessary for the simplification and better understanding of the relations between the United States and the Choctaw Indians, that all their subsisting treaty stipulations be embodied in one comprehensive instrument:

Now, therefore, the United States of America, by their commissioner, George W. Manypenny, the Choctaws, by their commissioners, Peter P. Pitchlynn, Israel Folsom, Samuel Garland, and Dickson W. Lewis, and the Chickasaws, by their commissioners, Edmund Pickens and Sampson Folsom do hereby agree and stipulate as follows, viz:

ARTICLE 1. The following shall constitute and remain the boundaries of the Choctaw and Chickasaw country, viz: Beginning at a point on the Arkansas River, one hundred paces east of old Fort Smith, where the western boundary-line of the State of Arkansas crosses the said river, and running thence due south to Red River; thence up Red River to the point where the meridian of one hundred degrees west longitude crosses the same; thence north along said meridian to the main Canadian River; thence down said river to its junction with the Arkansas River; thence down said river to the place of beginning.

And pursuant to an act of Congress approved May 28, 1830, the United States do hereby forever secure and guarantee the lands embraced within the said limits, to the members of the Choctaw and Chickasaw tribes, their heirs and successors, to be held in common; so that each and every member of either tribe shall have an equal, undivided interest in the whole: Provided, however, No part thereof shall ever be sold without the consent of both tribes, and that said land shall revert to the United States if said Indians and their heirs become extinct or abandon the same.

ARTICLE 2. A district for the Chickasaws is hereby established, bounded as follows, to wit: Beginning on the north bank of Red River, at the mouth of Island Bayou, where it empties into Red River, about twenty-six miles in a straight line, below the mouth of False Wachitta; thence running a northwesterly course, along the main channel of said bayou, to the junction of the three prongs of said bayou, nearest the dividing ridge between Wachitta and Low Blue Rivers, as laid down on Capt. R. L. Hunter's map; thence northerly along the eastern prong of Island Bayou to its source; thence due north to the Canadian River; thence west along the main Canadian to the ninety-eighth degree of west longitude; thence south to Red River; and thence down Red River to the beginning: Provided, however, If the line running due north, from the eastern source of Island Bayou, to the main Canadian shall not include Allen's or Wapa-nacka Academy, within the Chickasaw District, then, an offset shall be made from said line, so as to leave said academy two miles within the Chickasaw district, north, west and south from the lines of boundary.

ARTICLE 3. The remainder of the country held in common by the Choctaws and Chickasaws, shall constitute the Choctaw district, and their officers and people shall at all times have the right of safe conduct and free passage through the Chickasaw district.

ARTICLE 4. The government and laws now in operation and not incompatible with this instrument, shall be and remain in full force and effect within the limits of the Chickasaw district, until the Chickasaws shall adopt a constitution, and enact laws, superseding, abrogating, or changing the same. And all judicial proceedings within said district, commenced prior to the adoption of a constitution and laws by the Chickasaws, shall be conducted and determined according to existing laws.

ARTICLE 5. The members of either the Choctaw or the Chickasaw tribe, shall have the right, freely, to settle within the jurisdiction of the other, and shall thereupon be entitled to all the rights, privileges, and immunities of citizens thereof; but no member of either tribe [708] shall be entitled to participate in the funds belonging to the other tribe. Citizens of both tribes shall have the right to institute and prosecute suits in the courts of either, under such regulations as may, from time to time, be prescribed by their respective legislatures.

ARTICLE 6. Any person duly charged with a criminal offence against the laws of either the Choctaw or the Chickasaw tribe, and escaping into the jurisdiction of the other, shall be promptly surrendered, upon the demand of the proper authorities of the tribe, within whose jurisdiction the offence shah be alleged to have been committed.

ARTICLE 7. So far as may be compatible with the Constitution of the United States and the laws made in pursuance thereof, regulating trade and intercourse with the Indian tribes, the Choctaws and Chickasaws shall be secured in the unrestricted right of self-government, and full jurisdiction, over persons and property, within their respective limits; excepting, however, all persons, with their property, who are not by birth, adoption, or otherwise citizens or members of either the Choctaw or Chickasaw tribe, and all persons not being citizens or members of either tribe, found within their limits, shall be considered intruders, and be removed from, and kept out of the same, by the United States agent, assisted if necessary by the military, with the following exceptions, viz: Such individuals as are now, or may be in the employment of the Government, and their families; those peacefully travelling, or temporarily sojourning in the country or trading therein, under license from the proper authority of the United States, and such as may be permitted by the Choctaws or Chickasaws, with the assent of the United States agent, to reside within their limits, without becoming citizens or members of either of said tribes.

ARTICLE 8. In consideration of the foregoing stipulations, and immediately upon the ratification of this convention, there shall be paid to the Choctaws, in such manner as their national council shall direct, out of the national fund of the Chickasaws held in trust by the United States, the sum of one hundred and fifty thousand dollars.

ARTICLE 9. The Choctaw Indians do hereby absolutely and forever quit-claim and relinquish to the United States all their right, title, and interest in, and to any and all lands, west of the one hundredth degree of west longitude; and the Choctaws and Chickasaws do hereby lease to the United States all that portion Of their common territory west of the ninety-eighth degree of west longitude, for the permanent settlement of the Wichita and such other tribes or bands of Indians as the Government may desire to locate therein; excluding, however, all the Indians of New Mexico, and also those whose usual ranges at present are north of the Arkansas River, and whose permanent locations are north of the Canadian River, but including those bands whose permanent ranges are south of the Canadian, or between it and the Arkansas; which

Indians shall be subject to the exclusive control of the United States, under such rules and regulations, not inconsistent with the rights and interests of the Choctaws and Chickasaws, as may from time to time be prescribed by the President for their government: Provided, however, The territory so leased shall remain open to settlement by Choctaws and Chickasaws as heretofore.

ARTICLE 10. In consideration of the foregoing relinquishment and lease, and as soon as practicable after the ratification of this convention, the United States will pay to the Choctaws the sum of six hundred thousand dollars, and to the Chickasaws the sum of two hundred thousand dollars, in such manner as their general councils shall respectively direct.

ARTICLE 11. The Government of the United States, not being prepared to assent to the claim set up under the treaty of September the twenty-seventh, eighteen hundred and thirty and so earnestly contended [709] for by the Choctaws as a rule of settlement, but justly appreciating the sacrifices, faithful services, and general good conduct of the Choctaw people, and being desirous that their rights and claims against the United States shall receive a just, fair, and liberal consideration, it is therefore stipulated that the following questions be submitted for adjudication to the Senate of the United States.

First. Whether the Choctaws are entitled to, or shall be allowed, the proceeds of the sale of the lands ceded by them to the United States, by the treaty of September the twenty-seventh, eighteen hundred and thirty, deducting therefrom the cost of their survey and sale, and all just and proper expenditures and payments under the provisions of said treaty; and if so, what price per acre shall be allowed to the Choctaws for the lands remaining unsold, in order that a final settlement with them may be promptly effected. Or,
Second. Whether the Choctaws shall be allowed a gross sum in further and full satisfaction of all their claims national and individual against the United States; and, if so, how much.

ARTICLE 12. In case the Senate shall award to the Choctaws the net proceeds of the lands, ceded as aforesaid, the same shall be received by them in full satisfaction of all their claims against the United States, whether national or individual, arising under any former treaty; and the Choctaws shall thereupon become liable and bound to pay all such individual claims as may be adjudged by the proper authorities of the tribe to be equitable and justthe settlement and payment to be made with the advice and under the direction of the United States agent for the tribe; and so much of the fund, awarded by the Senate to the Choctaws, as the proper authorities thereof shall ascertain and determine to be necessary for the payment of the just liabilities of the tribe, shall on their requisition be paid over to them by the United States. But should the Senate allow a gross sum, in further and full satisfaction of all their claims, whether national or individual, against the United States, the same shall be accepted by the Choctaws, and they shall thereupon become liable for, and bound to pay, all the individual claims as aforesaid; it being expressly understood that the adjudication and decision of the Senate shall be final.

ARTICLE 13. The amounts secured by existing treaty stipulationsviz: permanent annuity of three thousand dollars, under the second article of the treaty of eighteen hundred and five; six hundred dollars per annum for the support of light-horse men under the thirteenth article of the treaty of eighteen hundred and twenty; permanent annuity of six thousand dollars for education; under the second article of the treaty of eighteen hundred and twenty-five; six hundred dollars per annum permanent provision for the support of a blacksmith, under the sixth article of the treaty of eighteen hundred and twenty; and three hundred and twenty dollars permanent provision for iron and steel, under the ninth article of the treaty of eighteen hundred and twenty-fiveshall continue to be paid to, or expended for the benefit of, the Choctaws as heretofore; or the same may be applied to such objects of general utility as may, from time to time, be designated by the general council of the tribe, with the approbation of the Government of the United States. And the funds now held in trust by the United States for the benefit of the Choctaws under former treaties, or otherwise, shall continue to be so held; together with the sum of five hundred thousand dollars out of the amount payable to them under articles eighth and tenth of this agreement, and also whatever balance shall remain, if any, of the amount that shall be allowed the Choctaws, by the Senate, under the twelfth article hereof, after satisfying the just liabilities of the tribe.

The sums so to be held in trust shall constitute a general Choctaw fund, yielding an annual interest of not less than five per centum; no part of which shall be paid out as annuity, but shall be regularly and judiciously applied, under the direction of the general council of the Choctaws, to the support of their government for purposes of education, and such other objects as may be best calculated to promote and advance the improvement, welfare, and happiness of the Choctaw people and their descendants.

ARTICLE 14. The United States shall protect the Choctaws and Chickasaws from domestic strife, from hostile invasion, and from aggression by other Indians and white persons not subject to their jurisdiction and laws; and for all injuries resulting from such invasion or aggression, full indemnity is hereby guaranteed to the party or parties injured, out of the Treasury of the United States, upon the same principle and according to the same rules upon which white persons are entitled to indemnity for injuries or aggressions upon them, committed by Indians.

ARTICLE 15. The Choctaws and Chickasaws shall promptly apprehend and deliver up all persons accused of any crime or offence against the laws of the United States, or of any State thereof, who may be found within their limits, on demand of any proper officer of a State, or of the United States.

ARTICLE 16. All persons licensed by the United States to trade with the Choctaws or Chickasaws shall be required to pay to the respective tribes a moderate annual compensation for the land and timber used by them; the amount of such compensation, in each case, to be assessed by the proper authorities of said tribe, subject to the approval of the United States agent.

ARTICLE 17. The United States shall have the right to establish and maintain such military posts, post-roads, and Indian agencies, as may be deemed necessary within the Choctaw and Chickasaw country, but no greater quantity of land or timber shall be used for said purposes, than shall be actually requisite; and if, in the establishment or maintenance of such posts, post-roads, and agencies, the property of any Choctaw or Chickasaw shall be taken, injured, or destroyed, just and adequate compensation shall be made by the United States.

Only such persons as are, or may be in the employment of the United States, or subject to the jurisdiction and laws of the Choctaws, or Chickasaws, shall be permitted to farm or raise stock within the limits of any of said military posts or Indian agencies. And no offender against the laws of either of said tribes, shall be permitted to take refuge therein.

ARTICLE 18. The United States, or any incorporated company, shall have the right of way for railroads, or lines of telegraphs, through the Choctaw and Chickasaw country; but for any property taken or destroyed in the construction thereof, full compensation shall be made to the party or parties injured, to be ascertained and determined in such manner as the president of the United States shall direct.

ARTICLE 19. The United States shall, as soon as practicable, cause the eastern and western boundary lines of the tract of country described in the 1st article of this convention, and the western boundary of the Chickasaw district, as herein defined, to be run and permanently marked.

ARTICLE 20. That this convention may conduce as far as possible to the restoration and preservation of kind and friendly feeling among the Choctaws and Chickasaws, a general amnesty of all past offences, committed within their country, is hereby declared.
And in order that their relations to each other and to the United States may hereafter be conducted in a harmonious and satisfactory manner, there shall be but one agent for the two tribes.

ARTICLE 21. This convention shall supersede and take the place of all former treaties between the United States and the Choctaws, and also, of all treaty stipulations between the United States and the Chickasaws, and between the Choctaws and Chickasaws, inconsistent with this agreement, and shall take effect and be obligatory upon the contracting parties, from the date hereof, whenever the same shall be ratified by the respective councils of the Choctaw and Chickasaw tribes, and by the President and Senate of the United States.

ARTICLE 22. It is understood and agreed that the expenses of the respective commissioners of the two tribes, signing these articles of agreement and convention, in coming to, and returning from this city, and while here, shall be paid by the United States.
In testimony whereof, the said George W. Manypenny, commissioner on the part of the United States, and the said commissioners on the part of the Choctaws and of the Chickasaws, have hereunto set their hands and seals.

Done in triplicate at the city of Washington, on this twenty-second day of June, in the year of our Lord one thousand eight hundred and fifty-five.

George W. Manypenny, United States, Commissioner.
P. P. Pitchlynn, Israel Folsom, Sam'l Garland, Dickson W. Lewis, Choctaw Commissioners.
Edmund Pickens, his x mark, Sampson Folsom, Chickasaw Commissioners.

Executed in presence of: A. O. P. Nicholson, James G. Berret, Douglas H. Cooper, United States Indian agent.

And whereas the said treaty having been submitted to the general council of the Chickasaw tribe, the general council did, on the third day of October, A. D. one thousand eight hundred and fifty-five, assent to, ratify, and confirm the same, with the following amendment: "Add to the 19th article, By commissioners to be appointed by the contracting parties hereto" by an instrument in writing, in the words and figures following, to wit:

Whereas articles of agreement and convention were made and concluded on the twenty-second day of June, A. D. one thousand eight hundred and fifty-five, by and between George W. Manypenny, commissioner on the part of the United States; Peter P. Pitchlynn, Israel Folsom, Samuel Garland, and Dickson W. Lewis, commissioners on the part of the Choctaws; and Edmund Pickens, and Sampson Folsom, commissioners on the part of the Chickasaws, at the city of Washington, in the District of Columbia, the preamble whereof is in the words and figures following, "to wit:" Whereas, the political connection heretofore existing between the Choctaw and Chickasaw tribes of Indians, has given rise to unhappy and injurious dissensions and controversies among them, which render necessary a readjustment of their relations to each other and to the United States; and whereas, the United States desire that the Choctaw Indians shall relinquish all claim to any territory west of the one hundredth degree of west longitude

And also to make provision for the permanent settlement within the Choctaw country of the Wichita and certain other tribes or bands of Indians, for which purpose the Choctaws and Chickasaws are willing to lease, on reasonable terms, to the United States, that portion of their common territory which is west of the ninety-eighth degree of west longitude; and whereas the Choctaws contend that, by a just and fair construction of the treaty of September 27, 1830, they are of right entitled to the net proceeds of the lands ceded by them to the United States, under said treaty, and have proposed that the question of their right to the same, together with the whole subject-matter of their unsettled claims, whether national or individual, against the United States, arising under the various provisions of said treaty, shall be referred to the Senate of the United States for final adjudication and adjustment; and whereas it is necessary, for the simplification and better understanding of the relations between the United States and the Choctaw Indians, that all their subsisting treaty stipulations be embodied in one comprehensive instrument; and whereas, in the twenty-first article thereof, it is, among other things, recited that said agreement "shall take effect and be obligatory upon the contracting parties from the date hereof, whenever the same shall be ratified by the respective councils of the Choctaw and Chickasaw tribes of Indians and by the President and Senate of the United States."

Now, therefore, be it known, that the Chickasaws, in general council assembled, having duly considered said articles of agreement and convention, and each and every clause thereof, and being satisfied therewith, do, upon their part, hereby assent to, ratify, and confirm the same, as stipulated and required, with the following amendment: "Add to the nineteenth article, "By commissioners to be appointed by the contracting parties hereto."

Done and approved at Tishomingo, in the Chickasaw district of the Choctaw nation, this third day of October, in the year of our Lord, one thousand eight hundred and fifty-five.

Joel Kemp, President.
D. Colbert, F. C.
Passed the council Attest, Cyrus Harris, clerk of the council.

And whereas the Chickasaws, in general council assembled, did, on the 13th day of December, A. D. 1855, recede from and rescind the said amendment, and did ratify and confirm the said treaty, and every part thereof, by an instrument in writing, in the words and figures following, to wit:

Whereas the Chickasaws, in general council assembled, after having duly considered the stipulations contained in a certain convention and agreement, made and entered into at the city of Washington, on the 22d day of June, A. D. 1855, between George W. Manypenny, commissioner on the part of the United States; Peter P. Pitchlynn, Israel Folsom, Samuel Garland, and Dickson W. Lewis, commissioners on the part of the Choctaws; Edmund Pickens and Sampson Folsom, commissioners on the part of the Chickasaws, did, on the third day of October, A. D. 1855, at Tisho-mingo, in the Chickasaw district, Choctaw nation, assent to, ratify, and confirm each and every part of said convention and agreement, with the following amendment, viz: "

Add to the 19th article, By commissioners to be appointed by the contracting parties hereto.'" And whereas, said amendment was not duly considered and concurred in by the Choctaws in general council assembled; but said agreement and convention, and every part thereof, was assented to, ratified, and confirmed by said council without amendment. Now, therefore, be it known, that the Chickasaws, in general council assembled, having reconsidered said proposed amendment, do hereby recede from, and rescind the same, hereby assenting to, ratifying, and confirming said agreement and convention, and every part thereof.

Done and approved at the council-house at Tisho-mingo, Chickasaw district, Choctaw nation, this 13th day of December, A. D. 1855.
Approved December 13, 1855.

J. McCoy, President of the Council.
Dougherty Colbert, F. C.

Attest: Cyrus Harris, Secretary.

Signed in presence of: Jackson Frazier, Chief Chickasaw district, Choctaw nation, Douglas H. Cooper, United States Indian agent.

And whereas the said treaty having been submitted to the general council of the Choctaw tribe, the said general council did, on the 16th day of November, A. D. one thousand eight hundred and fifty-five, consent to and ratify the same by an instrument in the words and figures following, to wit:

Whereas articles of agreement and convention were made and concluded on the twenty-second day of June, A. D. one thousand eight hundred and fifty-five, by and between George W. Manypenny, commissioner on the part of the United States; Peter P. Pitchlynn, Israel Folsom, Samuel Garland, and Dickson W. Lewis, commissioners on the part of the Choctaws; and Edmund Pickens and Sampson Folsom, commissioners on the part of the Chickasaws, at the city of Washington, in the District of Columbia, the preamble whereof is in the words and figures following, viz: "Whereas the political connection heretofore existing between the Choctaw and the Chickasaw tribes of Indians, has given rise to unhappy and injurious dissensions and controversies among them, which render necessary a readjustment of their relations to each other and to the United States

And whereas the United States desire that the Choctaw Indians shall relinquish all claim to any territory west of the one hundredth degree of west longitude, and also to make provision for the permanent settlement within the Choctaw country, of the Wichita and certain other tribes or bands of Indians, for which purpose the Choctaws and Chickasaws are willing to lease, on reasonable terms, to the United States, that portion of their common territory which is west of the ninety-eighth degree of west longitude; and whereas, the Choctaws contend that, by a just and fair construction of the treaty of September 27, 1830, they are, of right, entitled to the net proceeds of the lands ceded by them to the United States, under said treaty, and have proposed that the question of their right to the same, together with the whole subject-matter of their unsettled claims, whether national or individual, against the United States arising under the various provisions of said treaty, shall be referred to the Senate of the United States, for final adjudication and adjustment; and whereas it is necessary, for the simplification and better understanding of the relations between the United States and the Choctaw Indians, that all their subsisting treaty stipulations be embodied in one comprehensive instrument;" and whereas, in the twenty-first article thereof, it is, among other things, recited that said agreement "shall take effect and be obligatory upon the contracting (parties) from the date hereof, whenever the same shall be ratified by the respective councils of the Choctaw and Chickasaw tribes and by the President and Senate of the United States."

Now, therefore, be it known, that the Choctaws, in general council assembled, having duly considered said articles of agreement and convention, and each and every clause thereof, and being satisfied therewith, do, upon their part, hereby assent to, ratify, and confirm the same as stipulated and required. [714]

Done and approved at the council-house, at Fort Towson, in the Choctaw nation, this sixteenth day of November, in the year of our Lord one thousand eight hundred and fifty-five.

Tandy Walker, President of the Senate.
Kenned, M. Curtain, Speaker of the House of Representatives.

Approved:
Geo. W. Harkins, Chief of Ahpuck District.
N. Cochnaner, Chief of Pushematahn District.
Adam Christy, Speaker, and Acting Chief of Moosholatubbee District.

Signed in presence of: Douglas H. Cooper, U. S. Indian Agent for Choctaw Tribe.

TREATY WITH THE OTTAWA AND CHIPPEWA {1855, July 31}
Ratified April 15, 1856.
Proclaimed Sept. 10, 1856.

Articles of agreement and convention made and concluded at the city of Detroit, in the State of Michigan, this the thirty-first day of July, one thousand eight hundred and fifty-five, between George W. Many-penny and Henry C. Gilbert, commissioners on the part of the United States, and the Ottawa and Chippewa Indians of Michigan, parties to the treaty of March 28, 1836.

In view of the existing condition of the Ottowas and Chippewas, and of their legal and equitable claims against the United States, it is agreed between the contracting parties as follows:

ARTICLE 1. The United States will withdraw from sale for the benefit of said Indians as hereinafter provided, all the unsold public lands [726] within the State of Michigan embraced in the following descriptions, to wit:

First. For the use of the six bands residing at and near Saulte Ste. Marie, sections 13, 14, 23, 24, 25, 26, 27, and 28, in township 47 north, range 5 west; sections 18, 19, and 30, in township 47 north, range 4 west; sections 11, 12, 13, 14, 15, 22, 23, 25, and 26, in township 47 north, range 3 west, and section 29 in township 47 north, range 2 west; sections 2, 3, 4, 11, 14, and 15 in township 47 north, range 2 east, and section 34 in township 48 north, range 2 east; sections 6, 7, 18, 19, 20, 28, 29, and 33 in township 45 north, range 2 east; sections 1, 12, and 13, in township 45 north, range 1 east, and section 4 in township 44 north, range 2 east.

Second. For the use of the bands who wish to reside north of the Straits of Macinac townships 42 north, ranges 1 and 2 west; township 43 north, range 1 west, and township 44 north, range 12 west.

Third. For the Beaver Island BandHigh Island, and Garden Island, in Lake Michigan, being fractional townships 38 and 39 north, range 11 west40 north, range 10 west, and in part 39 north, range 9 and 10 west.

Fourth. For the Cross Village, Middle Village, L'Arbrechroehe and Bear Creek bands, and of such Bay du Noc and Beaver Island Indians as may prefer to live with them, townships 34 to 39, inclusive, north, range 5 westtownships 34 to 38, inclusive, north, range 6 westtown-ships 34, 36, and 37 north, range 7 west, and all that part of township 34 north, range 8 west, lying north of Pine River.

Fifth. For the bands who usually assemble for payment at Grand Traverse, townships 29, 30, and 31 north, range 11 west, and townships 29, 30, and 31 north, range 12 west, and the east half of township 29 north, range 9 west.

Sixth. For the Grand River bands, township 12 north, range 15 west, and townships 15, 16, 17 and 18 north, range 16 west.

Seventh. For the Cheboygan band, townships 35 and 36 north, range 3 west.

Eighth. For the Thunder Bay band, section 25 and 36 in township 30 north, range 7 east, and section 22 in township 30 north, range 8 east.

Should either of the bands residing near Sault Ste. Marie determine to locate near the lands owned by the missionary society of the Methodist Episcopal Church at Iroquois Point, in addition to those who now reside there, it is agreed that the United States will purchase as much of said lands for the use of the Indians as the society may be willing to sell at the usual Government price.

The United States will give to each Ottowa and Chippewa Indian being the head of a family, 80 acres of land, and to each single person over twenty-one years of age, 40 acres of land, and to each family of orphan children under twenty-one years of age containing two or more persons, 80 acres of land, and to each single orphan child under twenty-one years of age, 40 acres of land to be selected and located within the several tracts of land hereinbefore described, under the following rules and regulations:

Each Indian entitled to land under this article may make his own selection of any land within the tract reserved herein for the band to which he may belong-Provided, That in case of two or more Indians claiming the same lot or tract of land, the matter shall be referred to the Indian agent, who shall examine the case and decide between the parties.

For the purpose of determining who may be entitled to land under the provisions of this article, lists shall be prepared by the Indian agent, which lists shall contain the names of all persons entitled, designating them in four classes. Class 1st, shall contain the names of heads of families; class 2d, the names of single persons over twenty-one years of age; class 3d, the names of orphan children under twenty-one years of age, comprising families of two or more persons, and class 4th, the names of single orphan children under twenty-one years of age, and no person shall be entered in more than one class. Such lists shall be made and closed by the first day of July, 1856, and thereafter no applications for the benefits of this article will be allowed.

At any time within five years after the completion of the lists, selections of lands may be made by the persons entitled thereto, and a notice thereof, with a description of the land selected, filed in the office of the Indian agent in Detroit, to be by him transmitted to the Office of Indian Affairs at Washington City.
All sections of land under this article must be made according to the usual subdivisions; and fractional lots, if containing less than 60 acres, may be regarded as forty-acre lots, if over sixty and less than one hundred and twenty acres, as eighty-acre lots. Selections for orphan children may be made by themselves or their friends, subject to the approval of the agent.

After selections are made, as herein provided, the persons entitled to the land may take immediate possession thereof, and the United States will thenceforth and until the issuing of patents as hereinafter provided, hold the same in trust for such persons, and certificates shall be issued, in a suitable form, guaranteeing and securing to the holders their possession and an ultimate title to the land. But such certificates shall not be assignable and shall contain a clause expressly prohibiting the sale or transfer by the holder of the land described therein.

After the expiration of ten years, such restriction on the power of sale shall be withdrawn, and a patent shall be issued in the usual form to each original holder of a certificate for the land described therein, Provided That such restriction shall cease only upon the actual issuing of the patent; And provided further That the President may in his discretion at any time in individual cases on the recommendation of the Indian agent when it shall appear prudent and for the welfare of any holder of a certificate, direct a patent to be issued. And provided also, That after the expiration of ten years, if individual cases shall be reported to the President by the Indian agent, of persons who may then be incapable of managing their own affairs from any reason whatever, he may direct the patents in such cases to be withheld, and the restrictions provided by the certificate, continued so long as he may deem necessary and proper.

Should any of the heads of families die before the issuing of the certificates or patents herein provided for, the same shall issue to the heirs of such deceased persons.

The benefits of this article will be extended only to those Indians who are at this time actual residents of the State of Michigan, and entitled to participate in the annuities provided by the treaty of March 28, 1836; but this provision shall not be construed to exclude any Indian now belonging to the Garden River band of Sault Ste. Marie.

All the land embraced within the tracts hereinbefore described, that shall not have been appropriated or selected within five years shall remain the property of the United States, and the same shall thereafter, for the further term of five years, be subject to entry in the usual man-her and at the same rate per acre, as other adjacent public lands are then held, by Indians only; and all lands, so purchased by Indians, shall be sold without restriction, and certificates and patents shall be issued for the same in the usual form as in ordinary cases; and all lands remaining unappropriated by or unsold to the Indians after the expiration of the last-mentioned term, may be sold or disposed of by the United States as in the case of all other public lands.

Nothing contained herein shall be so construed as to prevent the appropriation, by sale, gift, or otherwise, by the United States, of any tract or tracts of land within the aforesaid reservations for the location of churches, school-houses, or for other educational purposes, and for such purposes purchases of land may likewise be made from the Indians, the consent of the President of the United States, having, in every instance, first been obtained therefor.

It is also agreed that any lands within the aforesaid tracts now occupied by actual settlers, or by persons entitled to pre-emption thereon, shall be exempt from the provisions of this article; provided, that such pre-emption claims shall be proved, as prescribed by law, before the 1st day of October next.
Any Indian who may have heretofore purchased land for actual settlement, under the act of Congress known as the Graduation Act, may sell and dispose of

the same; and, in such case, no actual occupancy or residence by such Indians on lands so purchased shall be necessary to enable him to secure a title thereto.

In consideration of the benefits derived to the Indians on Grand Traverse Bay by the school and mission established in 1838, and still continued by the Board of Foreign Missions of the Presbyterian Church, it is agreed that the title to three separate pieces of land, being parts of tracts Nos. 3 and 4, of the west fractional half of section 35, township 30 north, range 10 west, on which are the mission and school buildings and improvements, not exceeding in all sixty-three acres, one hundred and twenty-four perches, shall be vested in the said board on payment of $1.25 per acre; and the President of the United States shall issue a patent for the same to such person as the said board shall appoint.

The United States will also pay the further sum of forty thousand dollars, or so much thereof as may be necessary, to be applied in liquidation of the present just indebtedness of the said Ottawa and Chippewa Indians; provided, that all claims presented shall be investigated under the direction of the Secretary of the Interior, who shall prescribe such rules and regulations for conducting such investigation, and for testing the validity and justness of the claims, as he shall deem suitable and proper; and no claim shall be paid except upon the certificate of the said Secretary that, in his opinion, the same is justly and equitably due; and all claimants, who shall not present their claims within such time as may be limited by said Secretary within six months from the ratification of the treaty, or whose claims, having been presented, shall be disallowed by him, shall be forever precluded from collecting the same, or maintaining an action thereon in any court whatever; and provided, also, that no portion of the money due said Indians for annuities, as herein provided, shall ever be appropriated to pay their debts under any pretence whatever; provided, that the balance of the amount herein allowed, as a just increase of the amount due for the cessions and relinquishments aforesaid, after satisfaction of the awards of the Secretary of the Interior, shall be paid to the said Chippewas or expended for their benefit, in such manner as the Secretary shall prescribe, in aid of any of the objects specified in the second article of this treaty.

ARTICLE 2. The United States will also pay to the said Indians the sum of five hundred and thirty-eight thousand and four hundred dollars, in manner following, to wit:

First. Eighty thousand dollars for educational purposes to be paid in ten equal annual instalments of eight thousand dollars each, which sum shall be expended under the direction of the President of the United States; and in the expenditure of the same, and the appointment of teachers and management of schools, the Indians shall be consulted, and their views and wishes adopted so far as they may be just and reasonable.

Second. Seventy-five thousand dollars to be paid in five equal annual instalments of fifteen thousand dollars each in agricultural implements and carpenters' tools, household furniture and building materials, cattle, labor, and all such articles as may be necessary and useful for them in removing to the homes herein provided and getting permanently settled thereon.
Third. Forty-two thousand and four hundred dollars for the support of four blacksmith-shops for ten years.

Fourth. The sum of three hundred and six thousand dollars in coin, as follows: ten thousand dollars of the principal, and the interest on the whole of said last-mentioned sum remaining unpaid at the rate of five per cent annually for ten years, to be distributed per capita in the usual manner for paying annuities. And the sum of two hundred and six thousand dollars remaining unpaid at the expiration of ten years, shall be then due and payable, and if the Indians then require the payment of said sum in coin the same shall be distributed per capita in the same manner as annuities are paid, and in not less than four equal annual instalments.

Fifth. The sum of thirty-five thousand dollars in ten annual instalments of three thousand and five hundred dollars each, to be paid only to the Grand River Ottawas, which is in lieu of all permanent annuities to which they may be entitled by former treaty stipulations, and which sum shall be distributed in the usual manner per capita.

ARTICLE 3. The Ottawa and Chippewa Indians hereby release and discharge the United States from all liability on account of former treaty stipulations, it being distinctly understood and agreed that the grants and payments hereinbefore provided for are in lieu and satisfaction of all claims, legal and equitable on the part of said Indians jointly and severally against the United States, for land, money or other thing guaranteed to said tribes or either of them by the stipulations of any former treaty or treaties; excepting, however, the right of fishing and encampment secured to the Chippewas of Sault Ste. Marie by the treaty of June 16, 1820.

ARTICLE 4. The interpreters at Sault Ste. Marie, Mackinac, and for the Grand River Indians, shall be continued, and another provided at Grand Traverse, for the term of five years, and as much longer as the President may deem necessary.

ARTICLE 5. The tribal organization of said Ottawa and Chippewa Indians, except so far as may be necessary for the purpose of carrying into effect the provisions of this agreement, is hereby dissolved; and if at any time hereafter, further negotiations with the United States, in reference to any matters contained herein, should become necessary, no general convention of the Indians shall be called; but such as reside in the vicinity of any usual place of payment, or those only who are immediately interested in the questions involved, may arrange all matters between themselves and the United States, without the concurrence of other portions of their people, and as fully and conclusively, and with the same effect in every respect, as if all were represented.

ARTICLE 6. This agreement shall be obligatory and binding on the contracting parties as soon as the same shall be ratified by the President and Senate of the United States.

In testimony whereof the said George W. Manypenny and the said Henry C. Gilbert, commissioners as aforesaid, and the undersigned chiefs and headmen of the Ottawas and Chippewas, have hereto set their hands and seals, at the city of Detroit the day and year first above written.

Geo. W. Manypenny, Henry C. Gilbert, Commissioners on the part of the United States

J. Logan Chipman, Rich'd M. Smith, Secretaries.

Sault Ste. Marie Bands: O-shaw-waw-no-ke-wain-ze, chief, his x mark, Waw-bo-jieg, chief, his x mark, Kay-bay-no-din, chief, his x mark, O-maw-no-maw-he, chief, his x mark, Shaw-wan, chief, his x mark, Pi-aw-be-daw-sung, chief, his x mark, Waw-we-gun,headman, his x mark, Pa-ne-gwon, headman, his x mark, Bwan, headman, his x mark, Taw-meece, headman, his x mark, Naw-o-ge-zhick, headman, his xmark, Saw-gaw-giew, headman, his x mark.
Grand River Bands: Ne-baw-nay-ge-zhick, chief, his x mark, Shaw-gwaw-baw-no, chief, his x mark, Aish-ke-baw-gosh, 2d chief, his x mark, Nay-waw-goo, chief, his x mark, Ne-be-ne-seh, chief, his x mark, Waw-be-gay-kake, chief, his x mark, Ke-ne-we-ge-zhick, chief, his x mark, Men-daw-waw-be,chief, his x mark, Maish-ke-aw-she,chief, his x mark, Pay-shaw-se-gay, chief, his x mark, Pay-baw-me, headman, his x mark, Pe-go, chief, his x mark, Ching-gwosh, chief, his x mark, Shaw-be-quo-ung,chief, his x mark, Andrew J. Blackbird, headman, his x mark, Ke-sis-swaw-bay, headman, his x mark, Naw-te-naish-cum, headman, his x mark.
Grand Traverse Bands: Aish-quay-go-nay-be, chief, his x mark, Ah-ko-say, chief, his x mark, Kay-quay-to-say, chief, his x mark, O-naw-maw-nince,chief, his x mark, Shaw-bwaw-sung,chief, his x mark, Louis Mick-saw-bay, headman, his x mark, May-dway-aw-she, headman, his x mark, Me-tay-o-meig, chief, his x mark, Me-naw-quot, headman, his x mark.
Little Traverse Bands: Waw-so, chief, his x mark, Mwaw-ke-we-naw, chief, his x mark, Pe-taw-se-gay, headman, his x mark, Ke-ne-me-chaw-gun, chief, his x mark, May-tway-on-daw-gaw-she, headman, his x mark, Me-ge-se-mong, headman, his x mark, Pi-a-zhick-way-we-dong. headman, his x mark, Key-way-ken-do, headman, his x mark.

Mackinac Bands: O-saw-waw-ne-me-ke, chief, his x mark, Ke-no-zhay, headman, his x mark, Peter Hanse, headman, his x mark, Shaw-be-co-shing, chief, his x mark, Shaw-bway-way, chief, his x mark, Pe-ane, headman, his x mark, Saw-gaw-naw-quaw-do, headman, his x mark, Nay-o-ge-maw, chief, (Little Traverse) his x mark.

Executed in the presence of: Jno. M.D. Johnston, John F. Godfroy, Gbt. Johnston, Aug. Hamlin, Interpreters, L. Campau, Joseph F. Mursul, G. D. Williams, P. B. Barbeau, A. M. Fitch, W. H. Godfroy.

We, the undersigned chiefs and headmen of the Chippewa Indians living near Sault Ste. Marie, Mich., having had the amendments adopted by the Senate of the United States to the treaty concluded at Detroit on the 31st day of July, 1855, fully explained to us and being satisfied therewith, do hereby assent to and ratify the same.

In witness whereof we have hereunto set our hands this 27th day of June, A. D. 1856.

Pi-aw-be-daw-sung, his x mark, Te-gose, his x mark, Saw-gaw-jew, his x mark, Shaw-ano, his x mark, Waw-bo-jick, his x mark, Ray-bay-no-din, his x mark, Shaw-wan, his x mark, O-me-no-rnee-ne, his x mark, Pay-ne-gown, his x mark, Waw-we-gown, his x mark, Ma-ne-do-scung, his x mark, Naw-we-ge-zhick, his x mark, Yaw-mence, his x mark, Bawn, his x mark.

Signed in presence: Ebenzr Warner, Jno. M. Johnston, United States Indian Interpreter, Placidus Ord.

We, the undersigned chiefs and headmen of the Ottowa and Chippewa nation, having heard the foregoing amendments read and explained to us by our agent, do hereby assent to and ratify the same.
In witness whereof we have hereto affixed our signatures this 2d day of July, A. D. 1856, at Little Traverse, Mich.

Waw-so, his x mark, Pe-taw-se-gay, his x mark, Mwaw-ke-we-naw, his x mark, Ke-ne-me-chaw-gun, his x mark, Ne-saw-waw-quot, his x mark, May-tway-on-day-gaw-she, his x mark, Aw-se-go, his x mark, Me-ge-se-mong, his x mark, Ke-zhe-go-ne, his x mark, Key-way-ken-do, his x mark, Kain-waw-be-kiss-se, his x mark, Nay-o-ge-maw, his x mark, Pe-aine, his x mark.

In the presence of: Henry C. Gilbert, Indian Agent, Aug. Hamlin, Interpreter, John F. Godfroy, Interpreter, G. T. Wendell, A. J. Blackbird.

We, the chiefs and headmen of the Ottowa and Chippewa Indians residing near Grand Traverse Bay, having heard the foregoing amendments adopted by the

Senate of the United States to the treaty of July 31, 1855, read, and the same having been fully explained to us by our agent, do hereby assent to and ratify the same.

Done at Northport on Grand Traverse Bay, Mich., this 5th day of July, A. D. 1856.

Aish-quay-go-nay-be, his x mark, Ah-ko-say, his x mark, O-naw-mo-neece, his x mark, Kay-qua-to-say, his x mark, Peter-waw-ka-zoo, his x mark, Shaw-bwaw-sung, his x mark, Louis-mick-saw-bay, his x mark.

In presence of: H. C. Gilbert, Indian agent, J. F. Godfroy, interpreter, Geo. N. Smith, Peter Dougherty, Normon Barnes.

We, the undersigned, chiefs and headmen of the Grand River bands of the Ottowa and Chippewa Indians of Michigan having heard the amendments of the Senate to the treaty of the 31st of July, 1855, read, and the same having been fully explained to us, do hereby assent to and ratify the same.
Done at Grand Rapids in the State of Michigan this 31st day of July, A. D. 1856.

Caw-ba-mo-say, his x mark, Gaw-ga-gaw-bwa, his x mark, Shaw-gwaw-baw-no, his x mark, Note-eno-kay, his x mark, Aish-ke-baw-gosh, his x mark, Ne-baw-nay-ge-zhick, his x mark, Waw-be-gay-kake, his x mark, Pay-baw-me, his x mark, Ne-ba-ne-seh, his x mark, Shaw-be-quo-ung, his x mark, Ching-gwosh, his x mark, Men-daw-waw-be, his x mark, Mash-caw, his x mark.

In presence of: John F. Godfroy, United States interpreter, Wm. Cobmosy, F. N. Gonfry.

TREATY WITH THE CREEKS, ETC. {1856, Aug. 7}
Ratified Aug. 16, 1856.
Proclaimed Aug. 28, 1856.

Articles of agreement and convention between the United States and the Creek and Seminole Tribes of Indians, made and concluded at the city of Washington the seventh day of August, one thousand eight hundred and fifty-six, by George W. Manypenny, commissioner on the part of the United States, Tuck-a-batchee-Micco, Echo-Harjo, Chilly McIntosh, Benjamin Marshall, George W. Stidham, and Daniel N. McIntosh, commissioners on the part of the Creeks; and John Jumper, Tuste-nuc-o-chee, Pars-co-fer, and James Factor, commissioners on the part of the Seminoles:

Whereas the convention heretofore existing between the Creek and Seminole tribes of Indians west of the Mississippi River, has given rise to unhappy and injurious dissensions and controversies among them, which render necessary a readjustment of their relations to each Other and to the United States; and Whereas the United States desire, by providing the Seminoles remaining in Florida with a comfortable home west of the Mississippi River, and by making a liberal and generous provision for their welfare, to induce them to emigrate and become one people with their brethren already west, and also to afford to all the Seminoles the means of education and civilization, and the blessings of a regular civil government; and Whereas the Creek Nation and individuals thereof, have, by their delegation, brought forward and persistently urged various claims against the United States, which it is desirable shall be finally adjusted and settled; and

Whereas it is necessary for the simplification and better understanding of the relations between the United States and said Creek and Seminole tribes of Indians, that all their subsisting treaty stipulations shall, as far as practicable, be embodied in one comprehensive instrument;

Now, therefore, the United States, by their commissioner, George W. Manypenny, the Creek tribe of Indians, by their commissioners, Tuck-a-batchee-Micco, Echo-Harjo, Chilly McIntosh, Benjamin Marshall, George W. Stidham, and Daniel N. McIntosh; and the Seminole tribe of Indians, by their commissioners, John Jumper, Tuste-nuc-o-chee, Pars-co-fer, and James Factor, do hereby agree and stipulate as follows, viz:

ARTICLE 1. The Creek Nation doth hereby grant, cede, and convey to the Seminole Indians, the tract of country included within the following boundaries, viz: beginning on the Canadian River, a few miles east of the ninety-seventh parallel of west longitude, where Ock-hi-appo, or Pond Creek, empties into the same; thence, due north to the north fork of the Canadian; thence up said north fork of the Canadian to the southern line of the Cherokee country; thence, with that line, west, to the one hundredth parallel of west longitude; thence, south along said parallel of longitude to the Canadian River, and thence down and with that river to the place of beginning.

ARTICLE 2. The following shall constitute and remain the boundaries of the Creek country, viz: beginning at the mouth of the north fork of the Canadian River, and running northerly four miles; thence running a straight line so as to meet a line drawn from the south bank of the Arkansas River, opposite to the east or lower bank of Grand River, at its junction with the Arkansas, and which runs a course, south, forty-four degrees, west, one mile, to a post placed in the ground; thence along said line to the Arkansas and up the same and the Verdigris River, to where the old territorial line crosses it; thence along said line, north, to a point twenty-five miles from the-Arkansas River, where the old territorial line crosses the same; thence running west with the southern line of the Cherokee country, to the north fork of the Canadian River, where the boundary of the session to the Seminoles defined in the preceding article, first strikes said Cherokee line; thence down said north fork, to where the eastern boundary-line of the said cession to the Seminoles strikes the same; thence, with that line, due south to the Canadian River, at the mouth of the Ock-hi-appo, or Pond Creek; and thence down said Canadian River to the place of beginning.

ARTICLE 3. The United States do hereby solemnly guarantee to the Seminole Indians the tract of country ceded to them by the first article of this convention; and to the Creek Indians, the lands included within the boundaries defined in the second article hereof; and likewise that the same shall respectively be secured to and held by said Indians by the same title and tenure by which they were guaranteed and secured to the Creek Nation by the fourteenth article of the treaty of March twenty-fourth, eighteen hundred and thirty-two, the third article of the treaty of February fourteenth, eighteen hundred and thirty-three, and by the letters-patent issued to the said Creek Nation, on the eleventh day of August, eighteen hundred and fifty-two, and recorded in volume four of records of Indian deeds in the Office of Indian Affairs, pages 446 and 447. Provided however, That no part of the tract of country so ceded to the Seminole Indians, shall ever be sold, or otherwise disposed of without the consent of both tribes legally given.

ARTICLE 4. The United States do hereby, solemnly agree and bind themselves, that no State or Territory shall ever pass laws for the government of the Creek or Seminole tribes of Indians, and that no portion of either of the tracts of country defined in the first and second articles of this agreement shall ever be embraced or included within, or annexed to, any Territory or State, nor shall either, or any part of either, ever be erected into a Territory without the full and free consent of the legislative authority of the tribe owning the same.

ARTICLE 5. The Creek Indians do hereby absolutely and forever quit-claim and relinquish to the United States all their right, title, and interest in and to any lands heretofore owned or claimed by them, whether east or west of the Mississippi River, and any and all claim for or on account of any such lands, except those embraced within the boundaries described in the second article of this agreement; and it doth also, in like manner, release and fully discharge the United States from all other claims and demands whatsoever, which the Creek Nation or any individual thereof may now have against the United States, excepting only such as are particularly or in terms provided for and secured to them by the provisions of existing treaties and laws; and which are as follows, viz: permanent annuities in money amounting to twenty-four thousand five hundred dollars, secured to them by the fourth article of the treaty of seventh August, seventeen hundred and ninety, the second article of the treaty of June sixteenth, eighteen hundred and two, and the fourth article of the treaty of

January twenty-fourth, eighteen hundred and twenty-six; permanent provision for a wheelwright, for a blacksmith and assistant; blacksmith-shop and tools, and for iron and steel under the eighth article of the last-mentioned treaty; and costing annually one thousand seven hundred and ten dollars; two thousand dollars per annum, during the pleasure of the President, for assistance in agricultural operations under the same treaty and article

Six thousand dollars per annum for education for seven years, in addition to the estimate for present fiscal year, under the fourth article of the treaty of January fourth, eighteen hundred and forty-five; one thousand dollars per annum during the pleasure of the President, for the same object, under the fifth article of the treaty of February fourteenth, eighteen hundred and thirty-three; services of a wagon-maker, blacksmith and assistant, shop and tools, iron and steel, during the pleasure of the President, under the same treaty and article, and costing one thousand seven hundred and ten dollars annually; the last instalment of two thousand two hundred and twenty dollars for two blacksmiths and assistants, shops and tools, and iron and steel, under the thirteenth article of the treaty of March twenty-fourth, eighteen hundred and thirty-two, and which last it is hereby stipulated shall be continued for seven additional years.

The following shall also be excepted from the foregoing quit-claim, relinquishment, release, and discharge, viz: the fund created and held in trust for Creek orphans under the second article of the treaty of March twenty-fourth, eighteen hundred and thirty-two; the right of such individuals among the Creeks as have not received it, to the compensation in money provided for by the act of Congress of March third, eighteen hundred and thirty-seven, in lieu of reservations of land to which they were entitled, but which were [759] not secured to them, under the said treaty of eighteen hundred and thirty-two; the right of the reservees under the same treaty, who did not dispose of their reservations to the amounts for which they have been or may be sold by the United States; and the right of such members of the tribe to military-bounty lands, as are entitled thereto under existing laws of the United States. The right and interest of the Creek Nation and people in and to the matters and things so excepted, shall continue and remain the same as though this convention had never been entered into.

ARTICLE 6. In consideration of the foregoing quit-claim, relinquishment, release, and discharge, and of the cession of a country for the Seminole Indians contained in the first article of this agreement, the United States do hereby agree and stipulate to allow and pay the Creek Nation the sum of one million of dollars, which shall be invested and paid as follows, viz: two hundred thousand dollars to be invested in some safe stocks, paying an interest of at least five per cent. per annum; which interest shall be regularly and faithfully applied to purposes of education among the Creeks; four hundred thousand dollars to be paid per capita, under the direction of the general council of the Creek Nation to the individuals and members of said nation, except such portion as they shall, by order of said national council, direct to be paid to the treasurer of said nation for any specified national object not exceeding ($100, 000) one hundred thousand dollars, as soon as practicable after the ratification of this agreement; and two hundred thousand dollars shall be set apart to be appropriated and paid as follows, viz: ten thousand dollars to be equally distributed and paid to those individuals and their heirs, who, under act of Congress of March third, eighteen hundred and thirty-seven, have received money in lieu of reservations of land to which they were entitled, but which were not secured to them under the treaty of March twenty-fourth, eighteen hundred and thirty-two; one hundred and twenty thousand dollars to be equally and justly distributed and paid, under the direction of the general council, to those Creeks, or their descendants, who emigrated west of the Mississippi River prior to said treaty of eighteen hundred and thirty two, and to be in lieu of and in full compensation for the claims of such Creeks

To an allowance equivalent to the reservations granted to the eastern Creeks by that treaty, and seventy thousand dollars for the adjustment and final settlement of such other claims of individual Creek Indians, as may be found to be equitable and just by the general council of the nation: Provided, however, That no part of the three last-mentioned sums shall be allowed or paid to any other person or persons, whatsoever, than those who are actual and bona-fide members of the Creek Nation and belonging respectively to the three classes of claimants designated; said sums to be remitted and paid as soon as practicable after the general council shall have ascertained and designated the persons entitled to share therein. And provided further, That any balance of the said sum of seventy thousand dollars, which may be found not to be actually necessary for the adjustment and settlement of the claims for which it is set apart, shall belong to the nation, and be applied to such object or objects of utility or necessity as the general council shall direct.

The remaining sum of two hundred thousand dollars shall be retained by the United States, until the removal of the Seminole Indians, now in Florida, to the country west of the Mississippi River herein provided for their tribe; whereupon the same, with interest thereon, at five per cent, from the date of the ratification of this agreement, shall be paid over to, or invested for the benefit of the Creek Nation, as may then be requested by the proper authorities thereof. Provided however, That if so paid over, it shall be equally divided and paid per capita to all the individuals and members of the Creek Nation, or be used and applied only for [760] such objects or purposes of a strictly national or beneficial character as the interests and welfare of the Creek people shall actually require.

ARTICLE 7. it being the desire of the Creeks to employ their own teachers, mechanics, and farmers, all of the funds secured to the nation for educational, mechanical, and agricultural purposes, shall as the same become annually due, be paid over by the United States to the treasurer of the Creek Nation. And the annuities in money due the nation under former treaties, shall also be paid to the same officer, whenever the general council shall so direct.

ARTICLE 8. The Seminoles hereby release and discharge the United States from all claims and demands which their delegation have set up against them, and obligate themselves to remove to and settle in the new country herein provided for them as soon as practicable. In consideration of such release, discharge, and obligation, and as the Indians must abandon their present improvements, and incur considerable expense in re-establishing themselves, and as the Government desires to secure their assistance in inducing their brethren yet in. Florida to emigrate and settle with them west of the Mississippi River, and is willing to offer liberal inducements to the latter peaceably so to do, the United States do therefore agree and stipulate as follows, viz: To pay to the Seminoles now in the west the sum of ninety thousand dollars, which shall be in lieu of their present improvements, and in full for the expenses of their removal and establishing themselves in their new country; to provide annually for ten years the sum of three thousand dollars for the support of schools; two thousand dollars for agricultural assistance.

And two thousand two hundred dollars for the support of smiths and smithshops among them, said sums to be applied to these objects in such manner as the President shall direct. Also to invest for them the sum of two hundred and fifty thousand dollars, at five per cent. per annum, the interest to be regularly paid over to them per capita as annuity; the further sum of two hundred and fifty thousand dollars shall be invested in like manner whenever the Seminoles now remaining in Florida shall have emigrated and joined their brethren in the west, whereupon the two sums so invested, shall constitute a fund belonging to the united tribe of Seminoles, and the interest on which, at the rate aforesaid, shall be annually paid over to them per capita as an annuity; but no portion of the principal thus invested, or the interest thereon annually due and payable, shall ever be taken to pay claims or demands against said Indians, except such as may hereafter arise under the intercourse laws.

ARTICLE 9. The United States agree to remove comfortably to their new country west, all those Seminoles now in Florida who can be induced to emigrate thereto; and to furnish them with sufficient rations of wholesome subsistence during their removal and for twelve months after their arrival at their new homes; also, to provide each warrior of eighteen years of age and upwards, who shall so remove, with one rifle-gun, if he shall not already possess one; with two blankets, a supply of powder and lead, a hunting-shirt, one pair of shoes, one and a half yards of strouding, and ten pounds of good tobacco; and each woman, youth, and child with a blanket, pair of shoes, and other necessary articles of comfortable clothing, and to expend for them in improvements, after they shall all remove, the sum of twenty thousand dollars. And to encourage the Seminoles to devote themselves to the cultivation of the soil, and become a sober, settled, industrious, and independent people, the United States do further agree to expend three thousand dollars in the purchase of ploughs and other agricultural implements, axes, seeds, looms, cards, and wheels; the same to be proportionately distributed among those now west, and those who shall emigrate from Florida.

ARTICLE 10. The Seminoles west do hereby agree and bind themselves to furnish, at such time or times as the President may appoint, a delegation of such member's of their tribe as shall be selected for the purpose, to proceed to Florida, under the direction of an agent of the Government, to render such peaceful services as may be required of them, and otherwise to do all in their power to induce their brethren remaining in that State to emigrate and join them in the west; the United States agreeing to pay them and such members of the Creek tribe as may voluntarily offer to join them and be accepted for the same service, a reasonable compensation for their time and services, as well as their travelling and other actual and necessary expenses.

ARTICLE 11. It is further hereby agreed that the United States shall pay Foc-te-lus-te-harjo, his heirs or assigns, the sum of four hundred dollars, in consideration of the unpaid services of said Foc-te-luc-te-harjoe, or Black Dirt, rendered by him as chief of the friendly band of Seminole warriors who fought for the United States during the Florida war.

ARTICLE 12. So soon as the Seminoles west shall have removed to the new country herein provided for them, the United States will then select a site and erect the necessary buildings for an agency, including a council-house for the Seminoles.

ARTICLE 13. The officers and people of each of the tribes of Creeks and Seminoles shall, at all times, have the right of safe conduct and free passage through the lands and territory of the other. The members of each shall have the right freely to settle within the country of the other, and shall thereupon be entitled to all the rights, privileges, and immunities of members thereof, except that no member of either tribe shall be entitled to participate in any funds belonging to the other tribe. Members of each tribe shall have the right to Institute and prosecute suits in the courts of the other, under such regulations as may, from time to time, be prescribed by their respective legislatures.

ARTICLE 14. Any person duly charged with a criminal offense against the laws of either the Creek or Seminole tribe, and escaping into the jurisdiction of the other, shall be promptly surrendered upon the demand of the proper authority of the tribe within whose jurisdiction the offense shall be alleged to have been committed.

ARTICLE 15. So far as may be compatible with the Constitution of the United States, and the laws made in pursuance thereof, regulating trade and intercourse with the Indian tribes, the Creeks and Seminoles shall be secured in the unrestricted right of self-government, and full jurisdiction over persons and property, within their respective limits; excepting, however, all white persons, with their property, who are not, by adoption or otherwise, members of either the Creek or Seminole tribe; and all persons not being members of either tribe, found within their limits, shall be considered intruders, and be removed from and kept out of the same by the United States agents for said tribes, respectively; (assisted, if necessary, by the military ;) with the following exceptions, viz: such individuals with their families as may be in the employment of the Government of the United States; all persons peaceably travelling, or temporarily sojourning in the country, or trading therein under license from the proper authority of the United States; and such persons as may be permitted by the Creeks or Seminoles, with the assent of the proper authorities of the United States, to reside within their respective limits without becoming members of either of said tribes.

ARTICLE 16. The Creeks and Seminoles shall promptly apprehend and deliver up all persons accused of any crime against the laws of the United States, or of any State thereof, who may be found within their limits, on demand of any proper officer of a State or of the United States.

ARTICLE 17. All persons licensed by the United States to trade with the Creeks or Seminoles shall be required to pay to the tribe within whose country they trade, a moderate annual compensation for the land and timber used by them, the amount of such compensation, in each ease, to be assessed by the proper authorities of said tribe, subject to the approval of the United States agent therefor.

ARTICLE 18. The United States shall protect the Creeks and Semi-holes from domestic strife, from hostile invasion, and from aggression by other Indians and white persons, not subject to their jurisdiction and laws; and for all injuries resulting from such invasion or aggression, full indemnity is hereby guaranteed to the party or parties injured out of the Treasury of the United States, upon the same principle and according to the same rules upon which white persons are entitled to indemnity for injuries or aggressions upon them, committed by Indians.

ARTICLE 19. The United States shall have the right to establish and maintain such military posts, military and post-roads and Indian agencies as may be deemed necessary within the Creek and Seminole country, but no greater quantity of land or timber shall be used for said purposes than shall be actually requisite; and if, in the establishment or maintenance of such posts, roads, or agencies, the property of any Creek or Seminole be taken, destroyed, or injured, or any property of either nation, other than land and timber, just and adequate compensation shall be made by the United States. Such persons only as are or may be in the employment of the United States, in any capacity, civil or military, or subject to the jurisdiction and laws of the Creeks and Seminoles, shall be permitted to farm or raise stock within the limits of any of said military posts or Indian agencies. And no offender against the laws of either of said tribes shall be permitted to take refuge therein.

ARTICLE 20. The United States, or any incorporated company, shall have the right of way for railroads, or lines of telegraphs, through the Creek and Seminole countries; but in the case of any incorporated company, it shall have such right of way only upon such terms, and payment of such amount to the Creeks and Seminoles, as the case may be, as may be agreed upon between it and the national council thereof: or, in case of disagreement by making full compensation, not only to individual parties injured, but also to the tribe for the right of way, all damage and injury done to be ascertained and determined in such manner as the President of the United States shall direct. And the right of way granted by either of said tribes for any railroad shall be perpetual or for such shorter term as the same may be granted, in the same manner as if there were no reversion of their lands to the United States provided for, in case of abandonment by them, or of extinction of their tribe.

ARTICLE 21. The United "States will cause such portions of the boundaries of the Creek and Seminole countries, as do not consist of well-defined natural boundaries, to be surveyed and permanently marked and established. The Creek and Seminole general councils may each appoint a commissioner from their own people to attend the running of their respective boundaries, whose expenses and a reasonable allowance for their time and services, while engaged in such duty, shall be paid by the United States.

ARTICLE 22. That this convention may conduce, as far as possible, to the restoration and preservation of kind and friendly feelings among the Creeks and Seminoles; a general amnesty of all past offences committed within their country, either west or east of the Mississippi, is hereby declared.

ARTICLE 23. A liberal allowance shall be made to each of the delegations signing this convention; including, with the Seminole delegation, George W. Brinton, the interpreter, as a compensation for their travelling and other expenses in coming to and remaining in this city and returning home.

ARTICLE 24. Should the Seminoles in Florida desire to have a portion of the country described in the first article of this agreement, set apart for their residence, it is agreed that the Seminoles west may make such arrangement, not inconsistent with this instrument, as may be satisfactory to their brethren in Florida.

ARTICLE 25. The Creek laws shall be in force and continue to operate in the country herein assigned to the Seminoles, until the latter remove thereto; when they shall cease and be of no effect.

ARTICLE 26. This convention shall supersede and take the place of all former treaties, between the United States and the Creeks, between the United States and the Florida Indians and Seminoles, and between the Creeks and Seminoles, inconsistent herewith; and shall take effect and be obligatory on the contracting parties from the date hereof, whenever it shall be ratified by the Senate and President of the United States.

ARTICLE 27. And it is further agreed, that nothing herein contained shall be so construed as to release the United States from any liability other than those in favor of said nations or individuals thereof.

In testimony whereof, the said George W. Manypenny, commissioner on the part of the United States, and the said commissioners on the part of the Creeks and Seminoles, have hereunto set their hands and seals.
Done in triplicate at the city of Washington, on the day and year first above written.

Geo. W. Manypenny, United States Commissioner.

Tuck-a-batchee-micco, his x mark, Echo-harjo, his x mark, Chilly McIntosh, Benjamin Marshall, George W. Stidham, Daniel N. McIntosh, Creek Commissioners, John Jumper, his x mark, Tus-te-nuc-o-chee, his x mark, Pars-co-fer, his x mark, James Factor, his x mark, Seminole Commissioners.

Executed in presence of: John W. Allen, Edward Hanrick, W. H. Garrett, Creek agent, J. W. Washbourne, Seminole agent, G. W. Stidham, United States interpreter, Geo. W. Brinton, interpreter, James R. Roche, Chs. O. Joline.

TREATY WITH THE SENECA, TONAWANDA BAND {1857, Nov. 5}
Ratified June 4,1858.
Proclaimed Mar. 31, 1859.

Articles of agreement and convention made this fifth day of November, in the year one thousand eight hundred and fifty seven, at the meeting house on the Tonawanda reservation, in the county of Genesee, and State of New York, between Charles E. Mix, commissioner on behalf of the United States, and the following persons, duly authorized thereunto by the Tonawanda band of Seneca

Indians, viz: Jabez Ground, Jesse Spring, Isaac Shanks, George Sky, and Ely S. Parker.

Whereas a certain treaty was heretofore made between the Six Nations of New York Indians and the United States on the 15th day of January, 1838, and another between the Seneca Nation of Indians and the United States on the 20th day of May, 1842, by which, among other things, the Seneca Nation of Indians granted and conveyed to Thomas Ludlow Ogden and Joseph Fellows the two certain Indian reservations in the State of New York known as the Buffalo Creek and the Tonawanda reservations, to be surrendered to the said Ogden and Fellows, on the performance of certain conditions-precedent defined i n said treaties; and

Whereas in and by the said treaties there were surrendered and relinquished to the United States 500,000 acres of land in the then Territory of Wisconsin; and Whereas the United States, in and by said treaties, agreed to set apart for said Indians certain lands in the Indian Territory immediately west of the Missouri, and to grant the same to them, to be held and enjoyed in fee-simple, the quantity of said lands being computed to afford 320 acres to each soul of said Indians, and did agree that any individual, or any number of said Indians, might remove to said Territory, and thereupon be entitled to hold and enjoy said lands, and all the benefits of said treaties, according to numbers, respectively; and

Whereas the United States did further agree to pay the sum of $400,000 for the removal of the Indians of New York to the said Territory, and for their support and assistance during the first year of their residence in said Territory; and Whereas the said Ogden and Fellows did agree to pay to the said Seneca Nation of Indians, as the consideration of the surrender and relinquishment of the said two reservations, known as the Buffalo Creek and Tonawanda reservations, certain sums of money, one part of which was to be paid to the individual Indians residing upon said reservations, for the improvements held and owned by them in severalty, the amount of which "improvement money" heretofore apportioned to those residing upon the Tonawanda reservation, being $15,018 36/100, which money has been paid into, and still remains in the Treasury of the United States; and

Whereas, for divers reasons and differences, the said treaties remain unexecuted as to the said Tonawanda reservation, and the band of Senecas residing thereon; and

Whereas it is ascertained, at the date of these articles, that the Seneca Indians, composing the Tonawanda band and residing upon the Tonawanda reservation, amount to 650 souls in number; and

Whereas the United States are willing to exercise the liberal policy which has heretofore been exercised in regard to the Senecas, and for the purpose of relieving the Tonawandas of the difficulties and troubles trader which they labor, These articles are entered into:

ARTICLE 1. The said persons, authorized as in the caption hereof stated, hereby surrender and relinquish to the United States all claims severally and in common as a band of Indians, and as a part of the Seneca Nation, to the lands west of the State of Missouri, and all right and claim to be removed thither, and for support and assistance after such removal, and all other claims against the United States under the aforesaid treaties of 1838 and 1842, except, however; such moneys as they may be entitled to under said treaties, paid or payable by the said Ogden and Fellows.

ARTICLE 2. In consideration of which aforesaid surrender and relinquishment, the United States agree to pay and invest, in the manner hereinafter specified, the sum of $256,000 for the said Tonawanda band of Indians.

ARTICLE 3. It is hereby agreed that the Tonawanda band may purchase of the said Ogden and Fellows, of the survivor of them, or of their heirs or assigns, the entire Tonawanda reservation, or such portions thereof as they may be willing to sell and said band may be willing to purchase; and the United States undertake and agree to pay for the same out of the said sum of $256,000, upon the express condition that the rate of purchase shall not exceed, on an average, $20 per acre.

The land so purchased shall be taken by deed of conveyance to the Secretary of the Interior of the United States, and his successors in office, in fee, to be held by him in trust for the said Tonawanda band of Indians and their exclusive use, occupation, and enjoyment, until the legislature of the State of New York shall pass an act designating some persons, or public officer of that State, to take and hold said land upon a similar trust for said Indians; whereupon they shall be granted by the said Secretary to such persons or public officer.

ARTICLE 4. And the said Tonawanda band of Indians hereby agree to surrender, relinquish, and give up to the said Ogden and Fellows, the survivor of them, or their assignsprovided the whole reservation shall not be purchasedthe unimproved lands which they shall not purchase, as aforesaid, within thirty days after this treaty shall be proclaimed by the President of the United States, and the improved lands which they shall not purchase, as aforesaid, on the 1st day of June, 1859.

ARTICLE 5. For the purpose of contracting for and making purchase of the lands contemplated herein, a majority of the chiefs and head-men of said Tonawanda band, in council assembled, may appoint one or more attorneys with adequate powers, which appointment must be approved by the Secretary of the Interior before such attorney or attorneys can have power to act in the premises.

ARTICLE 6. Whenever a quantity of said lands, amounting to 6,500 acres, at the least, upon the terms hereinbefore provided, may be purchased, written notice, executed by the chiefs and head-men in council, and acknowledged before a justice of the supreme court of New York, or judge of the superior court of the city of Buffalo, shall be given to the Secretary of the Interior, whereupon the portion of said sum of $256,000, not expended in the purchase of lands, as aforesaid, shall be invested by the said Secretary of the Interior in stocks of the United States, or in stocks of some of the States, at his discretion; and the increase arising from such investment shall be paid to the said Tonawanda Indians, at the time and in the manner that the annuities are paid which said Indians are now entitled to receive from the United States.

ARTICLE 7. It is hereby agreed that the sum of $15,018 36/100 "improvement money," heretofore apportioned to the Indians upon the Tonawanda reservation, shall be again apportioned by an agent, to be appointed by the chiefs and head-men in council assembled, to be approved by the Secretary of the Interior, which agent shall make a report of such apportionment to the said Secretary of the Interior, and if he contour therein, the shares so ascertained shall be paid to the individual Indians entitled thereto, who shall surrender and relinquish to the said Ogden and Fellows, or the survivor of them, or their assigns, their improvements, and any balance remaining shall be paid to the chiefs and head-men of the band, to be disbursed by them in payment of the debts or for the use of the band. The services of the agent to be thus appointed, and all other expenses attending the execution of these articles, are to be paid by the United States out of any moneys coming to the Tonawandas.

In Testimony whereof the said Charles E. Mix, commissioner, as aforesaid, and the undersigned persons, representing the Tonawanda band of Seneca Indians, have hereunto set their hands and seals the day and year first above written.

Charles E. Mix, commissioner.
Isaac x Shanks, George x Sky, Jabez x Ground, Jesse x Spring, Ely S. Parker.

The foregoing instrument was, on the day of the date thereof, executed in our presence, and we have hereunto at the same time affixed our names as subscribing witnesses.

John H. Martindale, Frederick Follett, William G. Bryan, C. B. Rich, Leander Mix, Henry Bittinger, Nicholson H. Parker, United States interpreter.

Also, the following chiefs and headmen heartily concur in the foregoing articles in behalf of themselves and their people: Jesse x Spring, Wm. x Parker, Jabez x Ground, John x Wilson, John x Bigfire, Thomson x Blinkey, James x Mitten, John x Joshua, James x Williams,

Headmen: John x Smith, Small x Peter, John x Beaver, John x Farmer, Tommy x White, John x Griffin, Geo. x Moses, Henry x Moses, Saml. x Blue Sky, James x Scroggs, Monroe x Jonas, Wm. x Johnson, Jackson x Ground, Harrison x Scrogg, George x Sky, Snow x Cooper, Isaac x Doctor, Isaac x Shanks, William x Moses, David x Printup, Benj. x Jonas, Addison x Charles, John x Hatch, Wm. x Alick, Wm. x Stewart, Andrew x Blackchief, John x Infant, Wm. x Taylor, James x Billy, Danl. x Peter, John x Hill, John x Jones, John x Shanks, Levi x Parker, John x Jemison, Chauncey x Abram.

Signed in open council, in presence of: Frederick Follett, Nicholson H. Parker, United States interpreter.

Supplemental articles of agreement and convention, made this fifth day of November, in the year one thousand eight hundred and fifty-seven, at the meeting-house on the Tonawanda reservation, in the county of Genesee, State of New York, between, Charles E. Mix, commissioner on behalf of the United States, of the first part, and the following person, duly authorized thereunto by the Tonawanda band of Seneca Indians, viz: Jabez Ground, Jesse Spring, Isaac Shanks, George Sky, and Ely S. Parker, of the second part.

Whereas, at the date hereof and concurrent with the execution of this instrument, articles of agreement and convention have been entered into between the parties aforesaid, in and by which articles it is provided that the said Tonawanda band of Seneca Indians may purchase portions of the Tonawanda reservation, "upon the express condition that the rate of purchase shall not exceed $20 per acre on an average."

And whereas the President of the United States may deem it discreet and expedient that certain portions of said reservations, held in severalty by the assigns of said Ogden and Fellows, should be purchased by said Indians if it shall be necessary so to do, at a rate exceeding $20 per acre on an average.

Now therefore, the said parties of the second part agree, that portions of said reservation may be purchased by the authorized agents of said Indians for them, and paid for out of said sum of $256,000, at a rate exceeding $20 per acre on an average, provided the contract or contracts therefor shall be first submitted to and approved by the President, or some public officer to be designated by him. And the said parties of the second part solicit the President to accept and adopt this supplement as a part of the said articles of agreement and convention entered into concurrent with the execution of this agreement.

In testimony whereof the said Charles E. Mix, commissioner as aforesaid, and the undersigned persons representing the Tonawanda band of Seneca Indians, have hereunto set their hands and seals the day and year first above written.

Charles E. Mix, Commissioner.

Isaac x Shanks, George x Sky, Jabez x Ground, Jesse x Spring, Ely S. Parker.

The foregoing instrument was, on the day of the date thereof, executed in our presence, and we have hereunto, at the same time, affixed our names as subscribing witnesses: John H. Martindale, Frederick Follett, William G. Bryan, C. B. Rich, Leander Mix, Henry Bittinger, Nicholson H. Parker, Urnted States interpreter.

Also, the following chiefs and headmen heartily concur in the foregoing supplemental articles in behalf of themselves and their people:

Lewis x Poodry, Jesse x Spring, Wm. x Parker, Jabez x Ground, John x Wilson, Isaac x Shanks, Snow x Cooper, Isaac x Doctor, John x Bigfire, William x Moses, Thomson x Blinkey, James x Mitten, John x Joshua, James x Williams, Samuel x Parker, George x Sky, David x Printup, Benj. x Jonas, Addison x Charles, John x Hatch.

Headmen: John x Smith, Small x Peter, John x Beaver, John x Farmer, Tommy x White, John x Griffin, George x Moses, Henry x Moses, John x Hill, John x Jones, Monroe x Jonas, Wm. x Johnson, Jackson x Ground, Harrison x Scrogg, Wm. x Alick, Wm. x Stewart, Andrew x Blackchief, John x Infant, Wm. x Taylor, James x Billy, Danl. x Peter, Saml. x Blue Sky, James x Scrogg, John x Shanks, Levi x Parker, John x Jemison, Chauncey x Abram

Signed in open council, in presence of: Frederick Follett, Nicholson H. Parker, United States interpreter.

TREATY WITH THE DELAWARES {1861, July 2}
Ratified, Aug. 6, 1861.
Proclaimed, Oct. 4, 1861.

Whereas a treaty or agreement was made and concluded at Leavenworth City Kansas, on the second day of July, one thousand eight hundred and sixty-one, between the United States of America and the Delaware tribe of Indians, relative to certain lands of that tribe conveyed to the Leavenworth, Pawnee, and Western Railroad Company, and to bonds executed to the United States by the said company for the payment of the said Indians, which treaty or agreement, with the preliminary and incidental papers necessary to the full understanding of the same, is in the following words, to wit:

Whereas, by the treaty of May 30, 1860, between the United States and the Delaware tribe of Indians, it is provided that the surplus lands of said Delawares, not included in their "home reserve," should be surveyed and appraised under direction of the Secretary of the Interior: and that in order to aid in the construction of a railroad near and through their said "home reserve," the Leavenworth, Pawnee, and Western Railroad Company of Kansas, duly organized and incorporated under the laws of said Territory, should have the right t9 purchase such surplus lands at such appraised value on condition, however, that after paying for said lands, said company should only receive title to one-half of them on completing and equipping, within a reasonable time, twenty-five (25) miles of said railroad from Leavenworth City westward; and should only receive title to the remaining half of said lands on completing and equipping said road, within a reasonable time, to the western boundary of the "Delaware Reserve;" and that in case said company should fail to pay for said lands, or having paid, should forfeit the same, or any part thereof, before receiving title, by failing to construct either the first or the second section of said road within such reasonable time, then the lands so forfeited, or not paid for, should be sold in quantities not exceeding one hundred and sixty (160) acres, at not less than such appraised value; the proceeds of such sale, subject to a certain contingent deduction, to be invested by the President of the United States in "safe and profitable stocks," for the benefit of said Delaware Indians: and

Whereas said surplus lands, to the amount of 223,966 78/100 acres, have been duly surveyed and appraised at an aggregate valuation of two hundred and eighty-six thousand seven hundred and forty-two and 15/100 ($286,742 15/100) dollars: and

Whereas the said Leavenworth, Pawnee, and Western Railroad Company has executed, under their corporate seal, and by the hand of Thomas Ewing, jr., their agent, their twenty-nine (29) several bonds, all of even date herewith, and numbered from one to twenty-nine, inclusive, for sums amounting in the aggregate to $286,742 15/100, being the amount of the valuation of said surplus lands as above stated, twenty eight (28) of which said bonds are for the sum of ten thousand ($10,000) dollars each; and one is for the sum of six thousand and seven hundred and forty-two and 15/100 ($6,742 15/100) dollars, and payable in ten (10) years after their date, at the office of the assistant treasurer of the United States, in the city of New York, to the Commissioner of Indian Affairs of the United States or bearer, with interest at the rate of six per cent. per annum, payable annually at the same place on interest-warrants attached to said bonds, which said bonds have been delivered by said company to Archibald Williams, judge of the United States court for the district of Kansas, and have been by him received and receipted for as agent of the United States for that purpose specially appointed, in accordance with the instructions of the President of the United States of June 10, 1861, hereto attached and made part hereof, and for the consideration and use in said instructions set forth:

Now, therefore, to secure the payment of said bonds and every part thereof, and of all interest to become due thereon, according to the terms thereof, the Leavenworth, Pawnee, and Western Railroad Company by its agent hereto specially authorized by resolution of the board of directors of said company of April 11, 1861, a certified copy of which said resolution is hereto attached, hereby agrees with the United States, as trustee for said Delaware tribe of Indians, that in case said company shall at any time hereafter neglect or fail to pay the whole or any part of the interest on all or any one of said bonds, or shall neglect or fail to pay the whole or any part of the principal of all or any one of said bonds, when any such payment, either of principal or of interest, shall become due and payable, then the said railroad company shall be deemed and held to have forfeited all right and title of any kind whatever to the one hundred thousand (100,000) acres of land herein described, to wit:

Description	Section	Township	Range	Meridian P.M.
Southeast quarter	2	10	17 E.	6th
Section	12	10	17 E.	6th
West half	13	10	17 E.	6th
East half	14	10	17 E.	6th
Section	24	10	17 E.	6th
West half	25	10	17 E.	6th
Section	36	10	17 E.	6th
South half	3	10	18 E.	6th
South half	4	10	18 E.	6th
Section	9	10	18 E.	6th
South half	25	10	19 E.	6th
Section	26	10	19 E.	6th
Section	28	10	19 E.	6th
West half	30	10	19 E.	6th
Section	32	10	19 E.	6th
Section	34	10	19 E.	6th
Section	36	10	19 E.	6th
South half	2	10	20 E.	6th
South half	4	10	20 E.	6th
S. W. quarter	5	10	20 E.	6th
East half	19	10	18 E.	6th
East half	24	10	18 E.	6th
North half	25	10	18 E.	6th
East half	26	10	18 E.	6th
West half	28	10	18 E.	6th
East half	30	10	18 E.	6th

West half	32	10	18 E.	6th
Section	35	10	18 E.	6th
South half	1	10	19 E.	6th
South half	3	10	19 E.	6th
South half	5	10	19 E.	6th
East half	7	10	19 E.	6th
Section	9	10	19 E.	6th
Section	11	10	19 E.	6th
Section	13	10	19 E.	6th
Section	15	10	19 E.	6th
Section	17	10	19 E.	6th
East half	19	10	19 E.	6th
West half	20	10	19 E.	6th
Section	22	10	19 E.	6th
East half	23	10	19 E.	6th
Section	24	10	19 E.	6th
S. E. quarter	6	10	20 E.	6th
Section	8	10	20 E.	6th
Section	10	10	20 E.	6th
Section	12	10	20 E.	6th
Section	14	10	20 E.	6th
West half	15	10	20 E.	6th
Section	17	10	20 E.	6th
East half	19	10	20 E.	6th
East half	20	10	20 E.	6th
West half	21	10	20 E.	6th
Section	22	10	20 E.	6th
Section	94	10	20 E.	6th
Section	26	10	20 E.	6th
Section	28	10	20 E.	6th
Section	30	10	20 E.	6th
Section	32	10	20 E.	6th
Section	34	10	20 E.	6th
Section	36	10	20 E.	6th
Section	8	10	21 E.	6th
Section	10	10	91 E.	6th
Section	12	10	21 E.	6th
Section	13	10	21 E.	6th
Section	15	10	21 E.	6th
Section	17	10	21 E.	6th
Section	19	10	21 E.	6th
Section	1	10	21 E.	6th
Section	3	10	21 E.	6th
Section	5	10	21 E.	6th
Section	7	10	21 E.	6th

Section	9	10	21 E.	6th
Section	1	10	21 E.	6th
Section	3	10	21 E.	6th
Section	5	10	21 E.	6th
Section	10	22 E.	6th	
Section	10	29 E.	6th	
Section	1	10	22 E.	6th
Section	3	10	22 E.	6th
Section	5	10	22 E.	6th
Section	7	10	29 E.	6th
Section	9	10	22 E.	6th
Section	1	10	22 E.	6th
Section	23	10	22 E.	6th
Section	25	10	22 E.	6th.
Section	27	10	21 E.	6th
Section	29	10	22 E.	6th
Section	31	10	22 E.	6th
Section	33	10	22 E.	6th
Section	35	10	22 E.	6th
Section	7	10	23 E.	6th
Section	9	10	23 E.	6th
Section	11	10	23 E.	6th
Scction	19	10	23 E.	6th
South half	1	11	17 E.	6th
South half	12	11	17 E.	6th
North half	13	11	17 E.	6th
South half	24	11	17 E.	6th
South half	2	11	18 E.	6th
South half	4	11	18 E.	6th
East half	6	11	18 E.	6th
East half	7	11	18 E.	6th
Section	8	11	18 E.	6th
Section	10	11	18 E.	6th
Section	12	11	18 E.	6th
Section	14	11	18 E.	6th
West half	15	11	18 E.	6th
East half	17	11	18 E.	6th
East half	18	11	18 E.	6th
West half	20	11	18 E.	6th
East half	22	11	18 E.	6th
West half	23	11	18 E.	6th
West half	24	11	18 E.	6th
East half	25	11	18 E.	6th
South half	1	11	19 E.	6th
South half	3	11	19 E.	6th

South half	5	11	19 E.	6th
East half	7	11	19 E.	6th
Section	9	11	19 E.	6th
Section	11	11	19 E.	6th
Section	13	11	19 E.	6th
Section	15	11	19 E.	6th
Section	17	11	19 E.	6th
East half	18	11	19 E.	6th
East half	19	11	19 E.	6th
Section	21	11	19 E.	6th
Section	23	11	19 E.	6th
Section	25	11	19 E.	6th
East half	24	11	19 E.	6th
Section	27	11	19 E.	6th
Section	29	11	19 E.	6th
East half	30	11	19 E.	6th
East half	33	11	19 E.	6th
West half	34	11	19 E.	6th
North half	35	11	19 E.	6th
Section	36	11	19 E.	6th
South half	1	11	20 E.	6th
South half	2	11	20 E.	6th
South half	3	11	20 E.	6th
South half	4	11	20 E.	6th
East half	7	11	20 E.	6th
South half	8	11	20 E.	6th
South half	9	11	20 E.	6th
N. W. quarter	13	11	20 E.	6th
S. W. quarter	15	11	20 E.	6th
North half	17	11	20 E.	6th
East half	18	11	20 E.	6th
East half	19	11	20 E.	6th
North half	20	11	20 E.	6th
West half	21	11	20 E.	6th
East half	22	11	20 E.	6th
South half	23	11	20 E.	6th
South half	24	11	20 E.	6th
Section	25	11	20 E.	6th
South half	26	11	20 E.	6th
East half	27	11	20 E.	6th
East half	33	11	20 E.	6th
Section	34	11	20 E.	6th
Section	36	11	20 E.	6th
South half	1	11	21 E.	6th
South half	3	11	21 E.	6th

South half	5	11	21 E.	6th
East half	7	11	21 E.	6th
Section	8	11	21 E.	6th
Section	10	11	21 E.	6th
Section	12	11	21 E.	6th
South half	13	11	21 E.	6th
Section	14	11	21 E.	6th
West half	15	11	21 E.	6th
Section	17	11	21 E.	6th
East half	18	11	21 E.	6th
East half	19	11	21 E.	6th
East h~lf	20	11	21 E.	6th
West half	21	11	21 E.	6th
Section	22	11	21 E.	6th
South half	27	11	21 E.	6th
Section	28	11	21 E.	6th
West half	29	11	21 E.	6th
East half	30	11	21 E.	6th
East half	31	11	21 E.	6th
Section	32	11	21 E.	6th
Section	34	11	21 E.	6th
Section	3	11	22 E.	6th
Section	5	11	22 E.	6th
East half	7	11	22 E.	6th
West half	8	11	22 E.	6th
Section	9	11	22 E.	6th
Section	15	11	22 E.	6th
Section	17	11	23 E.	6th
East half	18	11	23 E.	6th
Section	1	12	19 E.	6th
East half	2	13	19 E.	6th
South half	12	13	19 E.	6th
N. E. quarter	13	12	19 E.	6th
Section	1	13	20 E.	6th
Section	3	12	30 E.	6th
Section	5	12	30 E.	6th
East half	6	12	20 E.	6th
East half	7	12	20 E.	6th
Section	9	12	20 E.	6th
Section	11	12	20 E.	6th
Section	12	12	20 E.	6th
Section	14	12	20 E.	6th
East half	5	12	20 E.	6th
East half	18	12	20 E.	6th
East half	19	12	20 E.	6th

Section	21	12	20 E.	6th
North half	29	12	20 E.	6th
S. E. quarter	21	12	20 E.	6th
Section	16	12	20 E.	6th

156¼ sections, or 100,000 acres.

And immediately on such failure, the United States may take possession of and sell said lands for the exclusive benefit of said Delaware Indians.

And in case said company shall forfeit the one hundred thousand (100,000) acres above described, it shall thereupon also forfeit all its right and title to all the lands purchased by it from said Indians, not earned and patented at the date of such forfeiture.

And said company further agree that, on the completion of the first section of said road, it shall only be entitled to a patent for one-half of the lands not pledged for the payment of said bonds; and on the completion of said second section it shall have a patent for only the remaining half; and that no patent shall issue to it for any of the lands so pledged, until after said bonds and the interest warrants attached shall all and every part of them have been fully and promptly paid and cancelled.

In witness whereof, the said Leavenworth, Pawnee, and Western Railroad Company, by Thomas Ewing, jr., their agent aforesaid, have executed this instrument and attached thereto the seal of said company, this 2d day of July, 1861.

The Leavenworth, Pawnee, and Western Railroad Company, by their agent, Thomas Ewing. Jr.

State of Kansas, Leavenworth County, On this second day of July, A. D. 1861, before me, the undersigned authority, a notary public in and for the county aforesaid, in the State aforesaid, personally came Thomas Ewing, jr., agent of the Leavenworth, Pawnee, and Western Railroad Company, to me personally known to be the identical person who signed the foregoing instrument of writing, and whose name is thereto affixed as grantor, and he acknowledged the same to be his own voluntary act and deed.

Witness my hand and notarial seal, this 2d day of July, A. D. 1861.

S. Van Doren, Notary Public, Leavenworth County, Kansas.

At a called meeting of the board of directors of the Leavenworth, Pawnee, and Western Railway Company, on Monday, July 1st, 1861, at the office of A. J.

Isacks, in Leavenworth City, Kansas, was present Jas. C. Stone, Amos Rees, Thomas Ewing, jr., and Thomas S. Gladding.

Resolved: That Thomas Ewing, jr., be authorized and directed, as agent of the company, to make, execute, and deliver to Archibald Williams, as agent of the United States, the bonds and interest-war-rants of the company for $286,742 15/100, payable in ten years from their date, with 6 per cent interest, payable annually, payable to the Commissioner of Indian Affairs, or bearer, at the office of the assistant treasurer of the United States in the city of New York; and also to make and execute to the United States, and cause to be recorded and delivered to said Williams, as such agent, a mortgage of the company on the one hundred thousand acres of Delaware Indian lands, described in the letter of the Commissioner of Indian Affairs to the Secretary of the Interior, on May 29th, 1861; such mortgage to contain all the conditions prescribed in the paper signed by the President of the United States, of June 10th, 1861, the terms of which are hereby accepted by the company.

I hereby certify that at a meeting of the board of directors of the Leavenworth, Pawnee, and Western Railroad Company, held at the office of A. J. Isacks, in the city of Leavenworth, in the State of Kansas, on the 1st day of July, 1861, the foregoing proceedings were had and recorded on the journal of the company; and that the same is a true and correct transcript of the same from the journal of said company.

In testimony whereof I hereunto sign my name and affix the official seal of the company.

Thos. S. Gladding, Secretary L. P. & W. R. R. Co.

Whereas, by the treaty of Sarcoxieville, amended by the United States Senate, and finally ratified by the President of the United States on the 22d day of August, 1860, a principal object of both parties was the construction of a certain contemplated railroad therein named; and to that end the Leavenworth, Pawnee, and Western Railroad Company were to pay into the United States Treasury, in gold or silver coin, a sum of money, afterwards ascertained to be $286,742.15, as the appraised value of certain lands in Kansas belonging to the Delaware tribe of Indians; which sum of money, after expending a sufficient part of it to enable the Indians to commence agricultural pursuits under favorable circumstances, was to be, by the President, for said Indians, invested in safe and profitable stocks; and

Whereas the said railroad company is not able to pay said sum of money within time, according to said treaty; and

Whereas the President is of opinion that it is not for the interest of either party that said object of the treaty shall fail, but not knowing what would be the desire of said Indians on this point, not knowing whether any part of said sum would be needed to enable the Indians to commence agricultural pursuits under favorable circumstances, but supposing it probable that no part of it would be so needed, as said Indians now have over fifty thousand dollars lying idle in the United States Treasury; Therefore It is directed by the President that said Railroad Company may execute their bonds, with interest-warrants or coupons attached, according to the forms hereto annexed, the principal of which bonds shah amount to the aggregate sum of $286,742.15, and deposit the same with Archibald Williams, of Kansas, hereby appointed to receive and receipt for the same, to be by him transmitted to the Commissioner of Indian Affairs for the use of said Indians; and also shall, in due and proper form, execute a mortgage upon one hundred thousand acres of the land contemplated in and by said treaty to aid in the construction of said railroad, the said one hundred thousand acres to be the lands designated in the letter of the Commissioner of Indian Affairs to the Secretary of the Interior, dated May 29, 1861

Said mortgage to be conditioned for the full payment of said bonds, both as to interest and principal, and that on any failure to pay either when due all right and interest of said railroad company in and to said mortgaged land, and also to all such of said land not mortgaged as shall not at that time be earned and patented according to said treaty, shall be forfeited, and said land again become the absolute property of the United States [821] in trust for said Indians; and said mortgaged lands to be in no event patented to said until said bonds, principal and interest, shall be fully paid. And upon said bonds being so made and deposited, and said mortgage being so executed and duly recorded in Leavenworth County, Kansas, all matters, so far as not necessarily varied by this arrangement, shall proceed in conformity to said treaty, as if the money had been paid by said railroad company and had been invested by the President in said railroad bonds.

Provided always, That this arrangement shall be of no effect until Archibald Williams, judge of the United States court for the district of Kansas, shall have endorsed a certificate upon this paper that he has carefully examined the same, and also the bonds and mortgage offered in compliance with its provisions, and has found that bonds and mortgage do in fact comply with and fulfil said provisions; and also that he has had before him the chiefs and headmen named in said treaty, as John Connor, Sar-cox-ie, Ne-con-he-con, and Rock-a-to-wha, and has fully explained to them the nature and effect of this departure from the terms of said treaty, and that they freely assented to the same.

Abraham Lincoln.
JUNE 10, 1861.

Form of Bond.
$10,000; No. 1.

Know all men by these presents: That the Leavenworth, Pawnee, and Western Railroad Company is held and bound to the United States, as trustee for the Delaware tribe of Indians, in the sum of ten thousand dollars, to be paid to the Commissioner of Indian Affairs, or bearer, at the office of the assistant treasurer of the United States, in the city of New York, in ten years from the date hereof, on the surrender of this bond, with interest on said sum from the same date, at six per cent. per annum, payable annually at the same office, on the surrender, as they severally fall due, of the annexed interest-warrants. This bond being one of twenty-nine bonds for sums amounting in the aggregate to $290,560, the payment of which, with the interest-warrants attached, is secured by mortgage of even date herewith on one hundred thousand acres of the land acquired by said company, under the conditions and provisions of the treaty between the United States and the Delaware tribe of Indians of May 30, 1860.

In witness whereof the Leavenworth, Pawnee, and Western Railroad Company, by Thomas Ewing, jr., their agent, have signed this obligation, and have attached thereto their corporate seal this 14th day of May, 1861.
The Leavenworth, Pawnee, and Western Railroad Company by
Thomas Ewing, Jr., Their Agent.

Form of Warrant
The Leavenworth, Pawnee, and Western Railroad Company promises to pay to the Commissioner of Indian Affairs of the United States or bearer, on the 14th day of May, 1862, at the office of the assistant treasurer of the United States, in the city of New York, six hundred dollars, interest due that day on their bond No. 1.
The Leavenworth, Pawnee, and Western Railroad Company, by

Thomas Ewing Jr., Their Agent.

OFFICE OF REGISTER OF DEEDS, County of Leavenworth, State of Kansas, ss:
I, W. S. Van Doren, register of deeds within and for the county aforesaid, do hereby certify that the within and foregoing instruments of writing were received by me for record this second day of July. A. D. 1861, at 3 1/2 o'clock p. m., and that the same are duly recorded in Book P, for recording mortgages, at page 230, &c.

In testimony whereof I have hereunto set my hand and official seal of office, the day and year aforesaid.

W.S. Van Doren, Register of Deeds.

I, Archibald Williams, judge of the United States court for the district of Kansas, do hereby certify that I have carefully examined the within paper signed by the President of the United (States) and have also examined and approved the bonds and mortgage offered by the Leavenworth, Pawnee, and Western Railroad Company in compliance with its provisions, and have accepted said bonds and mortgage, and receipted to said company for the same, as agent of the United States, and caused said mortgage to be duly recorded in the office of the recorder of deeds for Leavenworth County, Kansas.

And I do further certify, that I have had before me the chiefs and head-men therein named, as John Connor, Sar-cox-ie, and Ne-con-he-con, and also James Connor, who was the delegate at large of said tribe, in making the treaty of 1860, and read to them the said paper signed by the President, and fully explained to them the nature and effect of the proposition set forth in said paper; and that, after they had fully discussed the proposition, John Connor, in English, and James Connor, Sar-cox-ie, and Ne-con-he-con, through the said John Connor and other interpreters, declared that they understood it thoroughly, and each freely assented to the same; and that evidence has been presented to me by John Connor and other chiefs of said tribe, by which I am satisfied that Rock-a-to-wha died several months ago, and that no chief has been appointed in his place.

Given under my hand at Leavenworth city, Kansas, this 2d day of July, 1861.
Archibald Williams.

And whereas the said treaty or agreement having been submitted to the Senate of the United States for its constitutional action thereon, the Senate did, on the sixth of August, one thousand eight hundred and sixty-one, advise and consent to the ratification of the same by a resolution, and with amendments, in the words and figures following, to wit:

"IN EXECUTIVE SESSION, "Senate of the United States, August 6, 1861. Resolved, (two-thirds of the Senators present concurring) That the Senate advise and consent to the ratification of the treaty or agreement between the United States of America and the Delaware tribe of Indians relative to certain lands of that tribe conveyed to the Leavenworth, Pawnee, and Western Railroad Company, and to bonds executed to the United States by the said company for the payment of the said Indians, done the second day of July, eighteen hundred and sixty-one:

"Provided, That the provisions of this treaty shall not be held to apply to any lands not heretofore surveyed and appraised and not included within the limits of said reserve, nor any lands included in any fort or reservation for military purposes:

"Provided further, That if twenty-five miles of said railroad, from Leavenworth city westwardly, is not completed and equipped within [823] five years from the ratification hereof, said company shall thereupon forfeit all right, title, and interest, legal and equitable, in and to all and every part of said lands; and if the remaining section to the western boundary of the said reserve be not completed and equipped within three years from the date fixed for the completion of said first section, said company shall thereupon forfeit all right, title, and inter-eat, legal and equitable, in and to all of said lands not theretofore earned and patented.

"Provided further, That in the event of a failure of the said Railroad Company to pay the annual interest accruing upon the bonds, secured as above, within thirty days after the same falls due at the end of any year, then and in such case the contract included in this treaty shall be rescinded and shall be of no binding efficacy upon either party thereto.

"Provided further, That no part of said lands shall be patented to said Railroad Company until the money price for such part shall have been fully paid therefor.

"And provided, That this treaty shall not go into operation and be binding on them until accepted by the Indians thus amended.

"Attest:
J.W. Forney, Secretary.

And whereas William P. Dole, commissioner of Indian affairs, was designated by the Executive to present the treaty, as above amended, to the Indians, through their chiefs and headmen, for their acceptance, and to take such acceptance, if freely given, with the signatures of said Indian chiefs and headmen, and to certify his proceedings therein to the Executive; and the foregoing amendments having been fully interpreted and explained to the chiefs and headmen of the Delaware tribe aforesaid, they did thereunto, on the second day of September, one thousand eight hundred and sixty-one, give their free and voluntary assent in the words and figures following, to wit:

We, the undersigned, chiefs, councillors, and headmen of the Delaware tribe of Indians, acting for and on behalf of said tribe, this day in full council assembled, having had read and carefully explained and interpreted to us the within and foregoing treaty or agreement between the United States of America and the Delaware tribe of Indians, concluded on (the) 2d day of July, 1861, together with the within and foregoing amendments thereto, made by the Senate of the United States on the 6th day of August, 1861, do hereby accept and consent to said treaty as so amended.

In witness whereof, we have hereunto set our hands and affixed our seals this 2d day of September, 1861.

John Connor, head chief, his x mark, Ne-con-he-con, chief of the Wolf Band, his x mark, Sar-cox-ie, chief of the Turtle Band, his x mark, James Connor, delegate, his x mark, Charles Journeycake.

Signed and sealed in presence of: Isaac Golmarke, United States interpreter, F. Johnson, H. B. Branch, W. G. Coffin, (As to Sar-cox-ie.)

I hereby certify that the foregoing treaty or agreement between the United States and the Delaware tribe of Indians, concluded on the 2d day of July, 1861, together with the foregoing amendments thereto, made by the Senate of the United States on the 6th day of August, 1861, were read and fully explained by me to said Indians, except Sar-cox-ie, through Isaac Journeycake, the United States interpreter, and to Sar-cox-ie through Charles Journeycake; and that the delegate, chiefs, councillors, and headmen above named, on behalf of said tribe, [824] this day, in council assembled, did freely accept and consent to said treaty, together with said amendments, and subscribed their names and affixed their seals thereto in my presence.

Given under my hand this 2d September, 1861.
Wnl. P. Dole, Commissioner Indian Affairs.

Now, therefore, be it known that I, Abraham Lincoln, President of the United States of America, do, in pursuance of the advice and consent of the Senate, as expressed in their resolution of the sixth of August, one thousand eight hundred and sixty-one, accept, ratify, and confirm said treaty, with the amendments, as aforesaid.

In testimony whereof, I have caused the seal of the United States to be hereto affixed, having signed the same with my hand. Done at the city of Washington, this fourth day of October, in the year of our Lord one thousand eight hundred and sixty-one, and of the Independence of the United States the eighty-sixth.

Abraham Lincoln.
By the President:
William II. Seward, Secretary of State.

TREATY WITH THE OTTAWA OF BLANCHARD'S FORK AND ROCHE DE BOEUF {1862, June 24}
Ratified July 16, 1862.
Proclaimed July 28, 1862.

Articles of agreement and convention, made and concluded at Washington City, on the twenty-fourth day of June, eighteen hundred and sixty-two, by and between William P. Dole, commissioner, on the part of the United States, and the following-named chief and councilmen of the Ottawa Indians of the united bands of Blanchard's Fork and of Roche de Boeuf, now in Franklin County, Kansas, viz: Pem-ach-wung, chief; John T. Jones William Hurr, and James Wind, councilmen, they being thereto duly authorized by said tribe.

ARTICLE 1. The Ottawa Indians of the united bands of Blanchard's Fork and of Roche de Boeuf, having become sufficiently advanced in civilization, and being desirous of becoming citizens of the United States, it is hereby agreed and stipulated that their organization, and their relations with the United States as an Indian tribe, shall be dissolved [831] and terminated at the expiration of five years from the ratification of this treaty; and from and after that time the said Ottawas, and each and every one of them, shall be deemed and declared to be citizens of the United States, to all intents and purposes, and shall be entitled to all the rights, privileges, and immunities of such citizens, and shall, in all respects, be subject to the laws of the United States, and of the State or States thereof in which they may reside.

ARTICLE 2. It is hereby made the duty of the Secretary of the Interior to cause a survey of the reservation of the said Ottawas to be made as soon as practicable after the ratification of this treaty, dividing it into eighty-acre tracts, with marked stones set at each corner; and said Ottawas having already caused their reservation to be surveyed, and quarter-section stones set, it is hereby stipulated that such survey shall be adopted, in so far as it shall be found correct.

ARTICLE 3. It being the wish of said tribe of Ottawas to remunerate several of the chiefs, councilmen, and head-men of the tribe, for their services to them many years without pay, it is hereby stipulated that five sections of land is (are) reserved and set apart for that purpose, to be apportioned among the said chiefs, councilmen, and head-men as the members of the tribes shall in full council determine; and it shall be the duty of the Secretary of the Interior to issue patents, in fee-simple, of said lands, when located and apportioned, to said Indians. In addition thereto, said last-named persons, and each and every head of a family in said tribe, shall receive 160 acres of land, which shall include his or her house and all improvements, so far as practicable; and all other members of the tribe shall receive 80 acres of land each, and all the locations for the heads of families, made in accordance with this treaty, shall be made adjoining, and in as regular and compact form as possible, and with due regard to the rights of each individual and of the whole tribe.

ARTICLE 4. To enable said tribe to establish themselves more fully in agriculture, and gradually to increase their preparations for assuming the responsibilities and duties of citizenship, it is stipulated that, subject to the limitations hereinafter mentioned, the sum of eighteen thousand ($18,000) dollars shall be paid to said tribe in the manner of annuities, out of their-moneys now in the hands of the United States, in September, 1862, and subject to the limitations of this treaty. There shall be paid to them in four equal annual payments thereafter, as near as may be, all the moneys which the United States hold, or may hold, in any wise for them, with accruing interest on all moneys remaining with the United States.

ARTICLE 5. It being the desire of the tribe to pay all lawful and just debts against them contracted since they were removed to Kansas, it is agreed that such demands as the council of the tribe and the agent shall approve, when confirmed by the Secretary of the Interior, may be received in payment for the lands hereinafter provided to be sold, or otherwise such debts shall be paid out of the funds of said Ottawas, but in no case shall more than $15,000 be allowed and paid for such debts.

ARTICLE 6. The Ottawas deeming this a favorable opportunity to provide for the education of their posterity, and feeling that they are able to do so by the co-operation of the United States, now, in pursuance of this desire of the Ottawas, after the selections and allotments herein provided have been made, there shall be set apart, under the direction of the Secretary of the Interior, twenty thousand acres of average lands for the purpose of endowing a school for the benefit of said Ottawas; also one section of land, upon which said school shall be located, which section of land shall be inalienable, and upon which, and all the appurtenances and property for school purposes thereon, no tax shall ever be laid by any authority whatever.

Five thousand acres of said land may be sold by the trustees hereinafter named, the proceeds of which may be devoted to the erection of proper buildings and improvements upon said section for reception of the pupils; and the residue of the school-lands may, in like manner, be sold from time to time, as full prices can be obtained for the same. The money received therefor shall be loaned upon good real estate security, to be improved farms in the county of the reservation, the same not to be a security for more than half the appraised value of the land as returned by the county assessor, and no land to be taken as security for such loan or loans which shall be encumbered in any man-her, or the title to which shall have been derived from or held by any judicial, administrator, or executor's sale, or by the sale of any person acting in a fiduciary capacity. The security shall never be avoided on account of any rate of interest reserved, and the interest only shall be applied to the support of the school, so that the principal sum shall never be diminished.

And to the end that the Ottawas may derive the greatest advantage from said school, the pupils shall be instructed and practiced in industrial pursuits suitable to their age and sex, as well as in such branches of learning as the means of the institution and the capacity of the pupils will permit.

The lands hereby set apart shall not be subject to taxation until they are sold. They may be sold upon such credit as the trustees may think most for the interest of the enterprise. Security for the payment shall be taken with interest, the interest to be paid annually, but no title shall be made until the purchase money is all paid.

John T. Jones, James Wind, William Hurt, Joseph King, who are Ottawas, and John G. Pratt, and two other citizens of Kansas, who shall be elected by the said Ottawa Indians, are, by the parties agreed, to be trustees to manage the funds and property by this article set apart. They and their successors shall have the control and management of the school, and the funds arising from the sales of lands set apart therefor, and also the reserved section whereon the school is situated. Upon the death, resignation, or refusal to act, by either of them, the vacancy shall be filled by the survivors, provided that the board of trustees shall always have three white citizens members of said board.

A majority of the trustees shall form a quorum to transact business, but there shall be two of the white trustees present at the transaction of business. All acts of the trustees shall be recorded in a book or books to be by them kept for that purpose, and the proceedings of each meeting shall be signed by the president, to be by them elected out of their number. They shall also elect a treasurer and secretary from their number. All contracts of the trustees shall be in the name of their treasurer, who shall be competent to sue and be sued in all matters affecting the trust; he shall give bond conditioned for the faithful discharge of his duty, and the proper accounting for all money or property of the trust coming to his hands, with at least two good freehold sureties, in the penalty of ten thousand dollars, to be approved by a judge of a court of record in Kansas.

And the secretary and treasurer may be allowed, from time to time, such sum, from the proceeds of the trust, as the trustees in their judgment shall think just. Upon a sale of any of the lands by the trustees, upon their request, the same shall be conveyed by the United States, by patent, to the purchaser.
And it is hereby expressly provided and agreed that the children of the Ottawas and their descendants, no matter where they may emigrate, shall have the right to enter said school and enjoy all the privileges thereof, the same as though they had remained upon the lands by this treaty allotted.

ARTICLE 7. There shall be set apart ten acres of land for the benefit of the Ottawa Baptist church, and said land shall include the church buildings, mission-house, and graveyard, and the title to said property shall be vested in a board of five trustees, to be appointed by said church, in accordance with the laws of the State of Kansas.

And in respect for the memory of Rev. J. Meeker, deceased, who labored with unselfish zeal for nearly twenty years among said Ottawas, greatly to their spiritual and temporal welfare, it is stipulated that 80 acres of good land shall be, and hereby is, given, in fee-simple, to each of the two children of said Meeker, viz, Emmeline and Eliza; their lands to be selected and located as the other allotments herein provided are to be selected and located, which lands shall be inalienable to the same as the lands allotted to the Ottawas.

And all the above-mentioned selections of lands shall be made by the agent of the tribe, under the direction of the Secretary of the Interior. And plats and records of all the selections and locations shall be made, and upon their completion and approval proper patents by the United States shall be issued to each individual member of the tribe and person entitled for the lands selected and allotted to them, in which it shall be stipulated that no Indian, except as herein provided, to whom the same may be issued, shall alienate or encumber the land allotted to him or her in any manner, until they shall, by the terms of this treaty, become a citizen of the United States; and any conveyance or encumbrance of said lands, done or suffered, except as aforesaid, by any Ottawa Indian, of the lands allotted to him or her, made before they shall become a citizen, shall be null and void.

And forty acres, including the houses and improvements of the allottee, shall be inalienable during the natural lifetime of the party receiving the title: Provided, That such of said Indians as are not under legal disabilities by the local laws may sell to each other such portions of their lands as are subject to sale, with the consent of the Secretary of the Interior, at any time.

ARTICLE 8. That upon the ratification of this treaty a census of all the Ottawas entitled to land or money under the treaty shall be taken under the direction of the Secretary of the Interior. The principal to be paid to the minors shall be paid to their parents, unless the council of the tribe shall object because of the incompetency of the parent, growing out of ignorance, profligacy, or any other good cause; the council may also object to the payment of the money to any such incompetent which may be coming to himself or herself; and in all such cases the principal sum shall be withheld, and only the annuity paid, until such minor comes of age, or the disability is removed by the action of the council: Provided further, That the money of minors may, in all cases, be paid to guardians appointed by the local laws.

ARTICLE 9. It being the desire of the said Ottawas, in making this treaty, to insure, as far as possible, the settlement of their reservation by industrious whites, whose example shall be of benefit to the tribe at large, it is stipulated that after all the above-mentioned locations, assignments, and sales are made, the remainder of the land shall be sold to actual settlers at not less than $1.25 per acre, in the following manner: Any white person desiring to obtain any un-sold, unlocated tract of the land, may file his proposition, in writing, with the agent of the Ottawas, for the purchase of the tract, stating the price which he proposes to pay for said tract, not less than $1.25 per acre, a copy of which proposition, as well as all others herein contemplated, shall be posted for thirty days, dating from the first posting at the agency, in some conspicuous place; and if no person will propose a better price therefor within thirty days next after the first posting, in which further proposition the first person may join, he, or such other person as shall have offered the best price, shall upon the payment of one-quarter of the price offered, be taken and deemed the purchaser of said tract, and shall be entitled to a patent therefor from the United States at the end of one year, if he shall pay the remainder of the price offered, have occupied the land, and placed lasting and valuable improvements upon said tract to the extent and value of two hundred dollars to each quarter section entered: Pro-vided, That if said Ottawas, by their council, shall, at any time before any per-son shall become the purchaser of any tract of land, file their protest in writing against such purchaser, he shall not be permitted to enter upon said lands or become the purchaser thereof, and white persons not purchasers shall not be permitted to settle upon said lands, it being the duty of the agent to prevent such settlement, or their occupancy by the whites who are not purchasers, and only to the extent of their purchase.

And provided, further, That if any purchaser shall fail to pay for the land by him purchased under this treaty at the time stipulated, it shall be the duty of the agent to dispossess him as an intruder upon the lands, and his advances, pay-ments, and all his improvements, shall enure to the benefit of the Ottawas, and the land shall be sold for their benefit, as herein provided. But no person under this article shall be entitled to enter more than 320 acres. And all the lands which are not thus entered with the agent within two years from the ratification of this treaty may, upon the request of the council, be offered for sale at not less than $1.25 per acre, upon a credit of one year, under the direction of the Secre-tary of the Interior; and if any lands thereafter remain unsold, they may be sold upon such terms as the council of said tribe and the Secretary of the Interior shall mutually agree upon. And all the moneys derived from the sales of the above-described lands shall be paid at the time and place where the Secretary of the Interior may direct.

ARTICLE 10. And it is stipulated that the United States shall pay to the said Ottawas the claims for stolen ponies, cattle, and timber, already reported and approved by the Secretary of the Interior, amounting to $13,005 95/100. And also other claims for damages within two years, or since the taking of testimony for the above-mentioned damages, upon the presentation of sufficient proof: Provided, Such last-mentioned claims shall not exceed $3,500.

ARTICLE 11. It is hereby made the duty of the Indian Department to appoint an interpreter for said tribe, in the customary manner, to be continued during the pleasure of the Secretary of the Interior. And it is expressly understood that all expenses incurred by the stipulations of this treaty shall be paid out of the funds of the aforementioned tribe of Ottawas, and their annuities shall be paid semi-annually.

In testimony whereof, the said Wm. P. Dole, commissioner, as aforesaid, and the undersigned chief and councilman of the United Bands of Blanchard's Fork and of Roche de Boeuf, in Franklin county, Kansas, have hereunto set their hands and seals at the place and on the day and year hereinbefore written.
Wm. P. Dole, commissioner.
Pem-ach-wung, his x mark, John T. Jones, William Hurr, James Wind.

Interpreted by John T. Jones and signed by the respective parties in presence of Clinton C. Hutchinson, Indian agent, Charles E. Mix, Antoine Gokey, his x mark, United States interpreter.

AGREEMENT WITH THE CHEROKEE
AND OTHER TRIBES IN THE INDIAN TERRITORY {1865, Sept. 13}
Unratified.
FORT SMITH, ARKANSAS, September 13, 1865.

Articles of agreement entered into this thirteenth day of September, 1865, between the commissioners designated by the President of the United States and the persons here present representing or connected with the following named nations and tribes of Indians located within the Indian country, viz: Cherokees, Creeks, Choctaws, Chickasaws, Osages, Seminoles, Senecas, Senecas and Shawnees, and Quapaws.

Whereas the aforesaid nations and tribes, or bands of Indians, or portions thereof, were induced by the machinations of the emissaries of the so-called Confederate States to throw off their allegiance to the government of the United States, and to enter into treaty stipulations with said so-called Confederate States, whereby they have made themselves liable to a forfeiture of all rights of every kind, character, and description which had been promised and guaranteed to them by the United States; and whereas the government of the United States has maintained its supremacy and authority within its limits; and whereas it is the desire of the government to act with magnanimity with all parties deserving its clemency, and to re-establish order and legitimate authority among the Indian tribes; and whereas the undersigned representatives or parties connected with said nations or tribes of Indians have become satisfied that it is for the general good of the people to reunite with and be restored to the relations which

391

formerly existed between them and the United States, and as indicative of our personal feelings in the premises, and of our several nations and tribes, so far as we are authorized and empowered to speak for them; and whereas questions have arisen as to the status of the nations, tribes, and bands that have made treaties with the enemies of the United States, which are now being discussed, and our relations settled by treaty with the United States commissioners now at Fort Smith for that purpose:

The undersigned do hereby acknowledge themselves to be under the protection of the United States of America, and covenant and agree, that hereafter they will in all things recognize the government of the United States as exercising exclusive jurisdiction over them, and will not enter into any allegiance or conventional arrangement with any state, nation, power or sovereign whatsoever; that any treaty of alliance for cession of land, or any act heretofore done by them, or any of their people, by which they renounce their allegiance to the United States, is hereby revoked, cancelled, and repudiated.

In consideration of the foregoing stipulations, made by the members of the respective nations and tribes of Indians present, the United states, through its commissioners, promises that it will re-establish peace and friendship with all the nations and tribes of Indians within the limits of the so-called Indian country; that it will afford ample protection for the security of the persons and property of the respective nations or tribes, and declares its willingness to enter into treaties to arrange and settle all questions relating to and growing out of former treaties with said nations, as affected by any treaty made by said nations with the so-called Confederate States, at this council now convened for that purpose, or at such time in the future as may be appointed. *

In testimony whereof, the said commissioners on the part of the United States, and the said Indians of the several nations and tribes, as respectively hereafter enumerated, have hereunto subscribed their names, and affixed their seals, on the day and year first above written.

(Note. This treaty is presumed to have been signed, as indicated by the report of the proceedings at Fort Smith, by the commissioners of the United States and the delegations of Indians represented in the Council. Their names follow:)

Hon. D. N. Cooley, president, Hon. Elijah Sells, Thomas Wistar, Brig. Gen. W. S. Harney, U. S. Army, Col. Ely S. Parker, Commissioners, Charles E. Mix, George L. Cook, W. R. Irwin, John B. Garrett, Secretaries.
Creeks: Ock-tar-sars-ha-jo, head chief, Mik-ko-hut-kee, little white chief, Cow-we-ta-mik-ko, Cah-cho, he, Thlo-cos-ya-lo, Loch-er-ha-jo, Co-me-ha-jo, Tul-wah-mik-ko-che, Tul-wah-mik-ko, David Grayson, David, ield, Tuka-basha-ha-jo, Captain Johnneh, Cap-tah-ka-na, Passa, Sa-to-wee, Co-lo-ma-ha-

jo, Tul-me-mek-ko, Jacob Conal, David Berryhill, Sanford Berryman, Co-nip Fix-i-co, and others.

Wm. F. Brown, clerk.

Harry Island, interpreter for Creeks.

John Marshal, interpreter for Euchees.

Delegates for the black population living among the Creeks and Euchees: Ketch Barnett, John McIntosh, Scipio Barnett, Jack Brown, Cow Tom, Osages, White Hair, principal chief, Po-ne-no-pah-she, second, hief, ig Hill band, Wah-dah-ne-gah, counsellor, Me-lo-tah-mo-ne, "Twelve o'clock., Ko-she-ce-gla, Ge-ne, -ne-gla, (brave.) "Catch Alive., Mah-ha-ah-ba-so, (brave) "Sky-reaching man, "Shar-ba-no-sha, (brave), Done brown."

Interpreters: Alexander Bayette, Augustus Captain.

Senecas and Shawnees: Lewis Davis, chief, A. McDonald, Goodhunt, Jas. Tallchief, Lewis Denny Interpreter, Lewis Davis.

Cherokees: Kah-sah-nie, Smith Christie, Ah-yes-takie, Thomas Pegg, Oo-nee-na-kah-ah-nah-ee, White, atcher, Cha-loo-kie, Fox Flute, Da-wee-oo-sal-chut-tee, David Rowe, A h-tah-lah-ka-no-skee-skee, Nathan, ish, Koo-nah-vah, W. B. Downing, Ta-la-la, Oo-too-lah, ta-neh, Charles Conrad, Ooda-what-tee, Samuel, mith, Tah-skee-kee-tee-hee, Jesse Baldridge, Suu-kee, Mink Downing, Chee-chee, Tee-coa-le-to-ske, H. D, Reese, Colonel Lewis Downing, acting and assistant principal chief.

Seminoles: , ohn Shup-col Pascofa, Fo-hut-she, Fos-har-go, Chut-cote-har-go.

Interpreters: Robert Johnson, Cesar Bruner.

Shawnees: Charles Blue Jacket, first chief, Graham Rogers, second chief, Moses Silverheels, Solomon, Madden, Eli Blackhoof.

Interpreter, Matthew King.

Wyandotts: Silas Armstrong, first chief, Matthew Mud-eater, second chief.

Quapaws: George Wa-te-sha, Ca-ha-she-ka, Wa-she-hon-ca, S. G. Valier, in-terpreter.

Chickasaws: Et Tor Lutkee, Louis Johnson, Esh Ma Tubba, A. G. Griffith, Maharda Colbert, headmen.

Frazier McCrean, Benjamin Colbert, Ed Colbert, Jackson, Jim Doctor, Simp-son Killcrease, A. B. Johnson, Corman, George Jonson, Wolburn.

Choctaws: William S. Patton, Robert B. Patton, A. J. Stanton, Jeremiah Ward, Indian agents: Major G. C., now, for Osages, George A. Reynolds, for Semi-noles, Isaac Coleman, for Choctaws and Chickasaws, Justin Harlan, for Chero-kees, J. W. Dunn, for Creeks, Milo Gookins, for Wichitas, J. B. Abbott, for Shawnees.

(*) This document is claimed by the Indian Office not to be a treaty, but simply an agreement which formed the bases for the treaty with the Seminole of May 21, 1866, (ante p. 910) and of the treaty with the Creeks of June 14, 1866, (ante p. 931). It is not on file in the Indian Office and is found only in the Report of the Commissioner of Indian Affairs for 1865.

In the Seminole and Creek treaties mention is made of the treaty of peace and amity at Fort Smith September 10, 1865. This date is evidently erroneous, as no treaty was made at Fort Smith on that date. The agreement of September 13, 1865, must have been the one referred to.

As to the signatories of the agreement the Commissioner of Indian Affairs, in his annual report for 1865, page 35, says:
"All of the delegates representing the following tribes and sections of tribes, in the order given, had signed treaties, (some of them holding out for several days until they could agree among themselves:) Senecas, Senecas and Shawnees, Quapaws, loyal Seminoles, loyal Chickasaws, loyal Creeks, Kansas, Shawnees (uncalled for, but asking to be permitted again to testify their allegiance) loyal Osages, tribes of the Wichita agency, loyal Cherokees, disloyal Seminoles, disloyal Creeks, disloyal Cherokees, disloyal Osages, Comanches, disloyal Choctaws, and Chickasaws.

"Friendly relations were established between the members of the various tribes hitherto at variance, except in the case of the Cherokees. The ancient feuds among this people are remembered still."
For the full proceedings at Fort Smith see Annual Report of the Commissioner of Indian Affairs for 1865, pp. 312-353.

TREATY WITH THE SEMINOLE {1866, Mar. 21}
Ratified, July 19, 1866.
Proclaimed, Aug. 16, 1866.

Articles of a treaty made and concluded at Washington, D.C., March 21, A. D., 1866, between the United States Government, by its commissioners, D. N. Cooley, Commissioner of Indian Affairs, Elijah Sells, superintendent of Indian affairs, and Ely S. Parker, and the Seminole Indians, by their chiefs, John Chup-co, or Long John, Cho-cote-harjo, Fos-ha(r)-jo, John F. Brown.

Whereas existing treaties between the United States and the Seminole Nation are insufficient to meet their mutual necessities; and
Whereas the Seminole Nation made a treaty with the so-called Confederate States, August 1st, 1861, whereby they threw off their allegiance to the United States, and unsettled their treaty relations with the United States, and thereby incurred the liability of forfeiture of all lands and other property held by grant or gift of the United States; and whereas a treaty of peace and amity was entered into between the United States and the Seminole and other tribes at Fort Smith, September 13 (10,) 1865, {(a) A copy of this agreement, which has never been ratified, is found in an Appendix to the Report of the Commissioner of Indian Affairs for 1865, with the report of the negotiating commissioners, which copy has been reproduced in the Appendix to this compilation, post, p.

1050} whereby the Seminoles revoked, cancelled, and repudiated the said treaty with the so-called Confederate States; and whereas the United States, through its commissioners, in said treaty of peace promised to enter into treaty with the Seminole Nation to arrange and settle all questions relating to and growing out of said treaty with the so-called Confederate States; and whereas the United States, in view of said treaty of the Seminole Nation with the enemies of the Government of the United States, and the consequent liabilities of said Seminole Nation, and in view of its urgent necessities for more lands in the Indian Territory, requires a cession by said Seminole Nation of part of its present reservation, and is willing to pay therefor a reasonable price, while at the same time providing new and adequate lands for them:

Now, therefore, the United States, by its commissioners aforesaid, and the above-named delegates of the Seminole Nation, the day and year above written, mutually stipulate and agree, on behalf of the respective parties, as follows, to wit:

ARTICLE 1. There shall be perpetual peace between the United States and the Seminole Nation, and the Seminoles agree to be and remain firm allies of the United States, and always faithfully aid the Government thereof to suppress insurrection and put down its enemies.

The Seminoles also agree to remain at peace with all other. Indian tribes and with themselves. In return for these pledges of peace and friendship, the United States guarantee them quiet possession of their country, and protection against hostilities on the part of other tribes; and, in the event of such hostilities, that the tribe commencing and prosecuting the same shall make just reparation therefor. Therefore the Seminoles agree to a military occupation of their country at the option and expense of the United States.

A general amnesty of all past offences against the laws of the United States, committed by any member of the Seminole Nation, is hereby declared; and the Seminoles, anxious for the restoration of kind and friendly feelings among themselves, do hereby declare an amnesty for all past offenses against their government, and no Indian or Indians shall be proscribed or any act of forfeiture or confiscation passed against those who have remained friendly to or taken up arms against the United States, but they shall enjoy equal privileges with other members of said tribe, and all laws heretofore passed inconsistent herewith are hereby declared inoperative.

ARTICLE 2. The Seminole Nation covenant that henceforth in said nation slavery shall not exist, nor involuntary servitude, except for and in punishment of crime, whereof the offending party shall first have been duly convicted in accordance with law, applicable to all the members of said nation. And inasmuch as there are among the Seminoles many persons of African descent and blood, who have no interest or property in the soil, and no recognized civil rights, it is stipulated that hereafter these persons and their descendants, and such other of the same race as shall be permitted by said nation to settle there, shall have and enjoy all the rights of native citizens, and the laws of said nation shall be equally binding upon all persons of whatever race or color, who may be adopted as citizens or members of said tribe.

ARTICLE 3. In compliance with the desire of the United States to locate other Indians and freedmen thereon, the Seminoles cede and convey to the United States their entire domain, being the tract of land ceded to the Seminole Indians by the Creek Nation under the provisions of article first, (1st) treaty of the United States with the Creeks and Seminoles, made and concluded at Washington, D.C., August 7, 1856, in consideration of said grant and cession of their lands, estimated at two million one hundred and sixty-nine thousand and eighty (2,169,080) acres, the United States agree to pay said Seminole Nation the sum of three hundred and twenty-five thousand three hundred and sixty-two ($325,362) dollars, said purchase being at the rate of fifteen cents per acre.
The United States having obtained by grant of the Creek Nation the westerly half of their lands, hereby grant to the Seminole Nation the portion thereof hereafter described, which shall constitute the national domain of the Seminole Indians. Said lands so granted by the United States to the Seminole Nation are bounded and described as follows, to wit: Beginning on the Canadian River where the line dividing the Creek lands according to the terms of their sale to the United States by their treaty of February 6 1866.

(a) This refers to the Creek treaty of June 14, 1866, post, p. 931. See Annual Report of Commissioner of Indian Affairs, 1866, p. 10} following said line due north to where said line crosses the north fork of the Canadian River; thence up said north fork of the Canadian River a distance sufficient to make two hundred thousand acres by running due south to the Canadian River; thence down said Canadian River to the place of beginning. In consideration of said cession of two hundred thousand acres of land described above, the Seminole Nation agrees to pay therefor the price of fifty cents per acre, amounting to the sum of one hundred thousand dollars, which amount shall be deducted from the sum paid by the United States for Seminole lands under the stipulations above written. The balance due the Seminole Nation after making said deduction, amounting to one hundred thousand dollars.

The United States agree to pay in the following manner, to wit: Thirty thousand dollars shall be paid to enable the Seminoles to occupy, restore, and improve their farms, and to make their nation independent and self-sustaining, and shall be distributed for that purpose under the direction of the Secretary of the Interior; twenty thousand dollars shall be paid in like manner for the purpose of purchasing agricultural implements, seeds, cows, and other stock; fifteen thousand dollars shall be paid for the erection of a mill suitable to accommodate said nation of Indians; seventy thousand dollars to remain in the United States Treasury, upon which the United States shall pay an annual interest of five per cent.; fifty thousand of said sum of seventy thousand dollars shall be a permanent school-fund, the interest of which shall be paid annually and appropriated to the support of schools

The remainder of the seventy thousand dollars, being twenty thousand dollars, shall remain a permanent fund, the interest of which shall be paid annually for the support of the Seminole government; forty thousand three hundred and sixty-two dollars shall be appropriated and expended for subsisting said Indians, discriminating in favor of the destitute; all of which amounts, excepting the seventy thousand dollars, to remain in the Treasury as a permanent fund, shall be paid upon the ratification of said treaty, and disbursed in such manner as the Secretary of the interior may direct. The balance, fifty thousand dollars, or so much thereof as may be necessary to pay the losses ascertained and awarded as hereinafter provided, shall be paid when said awards shall have been duly made and approved by the Secretary of the Interior.

And in case said fifty thousand dollars shall be insufficient to pay all said awards, it shall be distributed pro rata to those whose claims are so allowed; and until said awards shall be thus paid, the United States agree to pay to said Indians, in such manner and for such purposes as the Secretary of the Interior may direct, interest at the rate of five per cent. per annum from the date of the ratification of this treaty.

ARTICLE 4. To reimburse such members of the Seminole Nation as shall be duly adjudged to have remained loyal and faithful to their treaty relations to the United States, during the recent rebellion of the so-called Confederate States for the losses actually sustained by them thereby, after the ratification of this treaty, or so soon thereafter as the Secretary of the Interior shall direct, he shall appoint a board of commissioners, not to exceed three in number, who shall proceed to the Seminole country and investigate and determine said losses. Previous to said investigation the agent of the Seminole Nation shall prepare a census or enumeration of said tribe, and make a roll of all Seminoles who did in no manner aid or abet the enemies of the Government, but remained loyal during said rebellion; and no award shall be made by said commissioners for such losses unless the name of the claimant appear on said roll, and no compensation shall be allowed any person for such losses whose name does not appear on said roll, unless said claimant, within six months from the date of the completion of said roll, furnishes proof satisfactory to said board, or to the Commissioner of Indian Affairs, that he has at all times remained loyal to the United States, according to his treaty obligations.

All evidence touching said claims shall be taken by said commissioners, or any of them, under oath, and their awards made, together with the evidence, shall be transmitted to the Commissioner of Indian Affairs, for his approval, and that of the Secretary of the Interior. Said commissioners shall be paid by the United States such compensation as the Secretary of the Interior may direct. The provisions of this article shall extend to and embrace the claims for losses sustained by loyal members of said tribe, irrespective of race or color, whether at the time of said losses the claimants shall have been in servitude or not; provided said claimants are made members of said tribe by the stipulations of this treaty.

ARTICLE 5. The Seminole Nation hereby grant a right of way through their lands to any company which shall be duly authorized by Congress, and shall, with the express consent and approbation of the Secretary of the Interior, undertake to construct a railroad from any point on their eastern to their western or southern boundary; but said railroad company, together with all its agents and employes, shall be subject to the laws of the United States relating to the intercourse with Indian tribes, and also to such rules and regulations as may be prescribed by the Secretary of the Interior for that purpose. And the Seminoles agree to sell to the United States, or any company duly authorized as aforesaid, such lands, not legally owned or occupied by a member or members of the Seminole Nation lying along the line of said contemplated railroad, not exceeding on each side thereof a belt or strip of land three miles in width, at such price per acre as may be eventually agreed upon between said Seminole Nation and the party or parties building said roadsubject to the approval of the President of the United States: Provided, however, That said land thus sold shall not be reconveyed, leased, or rented to, or be occupied by, any one not a citizen of the Seminole Nation, according to its laws and recognized usages.

Provided also, That officers, servants, and employes of said railroad necessary to its construction and management shall not be excluded from such necessary occupancy, they being subject to the provisions of the Indian-intercourse laws, and such rules and regulations as may be established by the Secretary of the Interior: nor shall any conveyance of said lands be made to the party building and managing said road, until its completion as a first-class railroad and its acceptance as such by the Secretary of the Interior.

ARTICLE 6. Inasmuch as there are no agency buildings upon the new Seminole reservation, it is therefore further agreed that the United States shall cause to be constructed, at an expense not exceeding ten thousand (10,000) dollars, suitable agency buildings, the site whereof shall be selected by the agent of said tribe, under the direction of the superintendent of Indian affairs; in consideration whereof, the Seminole Nation hereby relinquish and cede forever to the United States one section of their lands upon which said agency buildings shall be directed, (erected,) which land shall revert to said nation when no longer used by the United States, upon said nation paying a fair value for said buildings at the time vacated.

ARTICLE 7. The Seminole Nation agrees to such legislation as Congress and the President may deem necessary for the better administration of the rights of person and property within the Indian Territory: Provided, however, (that) said legislation shall not in any manner interfere with or annul their present tribal organization, rights, laws, privileges, and customs.

The Seminole Nation also agree that a general council, consisting of delegates elected by each nation, a tribe lawfully resident within the Indian Territory, may be annually convened in said Territory, which council shall be organized in such manner and possess such powers as are hereinafter described:

First. After the ratification of this treaty, and as soon as may be deemed practicable by the Secretary of the Interior, and prior to the first session of said council, a census or enumeration of each tribe lawfully resident in said Territory shall be taken, under the direction of the superintendent of Indian affairs, who, for that purpose, is hereby authorized to designate and appoint competent persons, whose compensation shall be fixed by the Secretary of the Interior and paid by the United States.

Second. The first general council shall consist of one member from each tribe, and an additional member for each one thousand Indians, or each fraction of a thousand greater than five hundred, being members of any tribe lawfully resident in said Territory, and shall be elected by said tribes, respectively, who may assent to the establishment of said general council; and if none should be thus formally selected by any nation or tribe, the said nation or tribe shall be represented in said general council by the chiefs and head-men of said tribes, to be taken in the order of their rank, in the same number and proportion as above indicated. After the said census shall have been taken and completed, the superintendent of Indian affairs shall publish and declare to each tribe the number of members of said council to which they shall be entitled under the provisions of this article; and the persons so entitled to represent said tribe shall meet at such time and place as he shall appoint; but thereafter the time and place of the sessions of said council shall be determined by its action: Provided, That no session in any one year shall exceed the term of thirty days, And provided That special sessions of said council may be called by said superintendent whenever, in his judgment, or that of the Secretary of the Interior, the interest of said tribes shall require.

Third. Said general council shall have power to legislate upon all rightful subjects and matters pertaining to the intercourse and relations of the Indian tribes and nations resident in said Territory; the arrest and extradition of criminals and offenders escaping from one tribe to another; the administration of justice between members of the several tribes of said Territory, and persons other than Indians and members of said tribes or nations; the construction of works of internal improvement and the common defence and safety of the nation of said

Territory. All laws enacted by said council shall take effect at such time as may therein be provided, unless suspended by direction of the Secretary of the Interior or the President of the United States. No law shall be enacted inconsistent with the Constitution of the United States, or the laws of Congress, or existing treaty stipulations with the United States; nor shall said council legislate upon matters pertaining to the organization, laws, or customs of the several tribes, except as herein provided for.

Fourth. Said council shall be presided over by the superintendent of Indian affairs, or, in case of his absence for any cause, the duties of said superintendent enumerated in this article shall be performed by such person as the Secretary of the Interior may direct.

Fifth. The Secretary of the Interior shall appoint a secretary of said council whose duty it shall be to keep an accurate record of all the proceedings of said council, and who shall transmit a true copy of all such proceedings, duly certified by the superintendent of Indian affairs, to the Secretary of the Interior immediately after the session of said council. He shall be paid out of the Treasury of the United States an annual salary of five hundred dollars.

Sixth. The members of said council shall be paid by the United States the sum of four dollars per diem during the time actually in attendance upon the sessions of said council, and at the rate of four dollars for every twenty miles necessarily travelled by them in going to said council and returning to their homes, respectively, to be certified by the secretary of the said council and the sup(erintenden)t of Indian affairs.

Seventh. The Seminoles also agree that a court or courts may be established in said Territory, with such jurisdiction and organized in such manner as Congress may by law provide.

ARTICLE 8. The stipulations of this treaty are to be a full settlement of all claims of said Seminole Nation for damages and losses of every kind growing out of the late rebellion, and all expenditures by the United States of annuities in clothing and feeding refugee and destitute Indians since the diversion of annuities for that purpose, consequent upon the late war with the so-called Confederate States. And the Seminoles hereby ratify and confirm all such diversions of annuities heretofore made from the funds of the Seminole Nation by the United States. And the United States agree that no annuities shall be diverted from the object for which they were originally devoted by treaty stipulations, with the Seminoles, to the use of refugee and destitute Indians, other than the Seminoles or members of the Seminole Nation, after the close of the present fiscal year, June thirtieth, eighteen hundred and sixty-six.

ARTICLE 9. The United States re-affirms and reassumes all obligations of treaty stipulations entered into before the treaty of said Seminole Nation with the so-called Confederate States, August first, eighteen hundred and sixty-one, not inconsistent herewith; and further agree to renew all payments of annuities accruing by force of said treaty stipulations, from and after the close of the present fiscal year, June thirtieth, in the year of our Lord-one thousand eight hundred and sixty-six, except as is provided in article eight.

ARTICLE 10. A quantity of land not exceeding six hundred and forty acres, to be selected according to legal subdivisions, in one body and which shall include their improvements, is hereby granted to every religious society or denomination which has erected, or which, with the consent of the Indians. May hereafter erect, buildings within the Seminole country for missionary or educational purposes; but no land thus granted, nor the buildings which have been or may be erected thereon, shall ever be sold or otherwise disposed of except with the consent and approval of the Secretary of the Interior. And whenever any such land or buildings shall be so sold or disposed of, the proceeds thereof shall be applied, under the direction of the Secretary of the Interior, to the support and maintenance of other similar establishments for the benefit of the Seminoles and such other persons as may be, or may hereafter become, members of the tribe according to its laws, customs, and usages.

ARTICLE 11. It is further agreed that all treaties heretofore entered into between the United States and the Seminole Nation which are inconsistent with any of the articles or provisions of this treaty shall be, and are hereby, rescinded and annulled.

In testimony whereof, the said Dennis N. Cooley, Commissioner of Indian affairs, Elijah Sells, superintendent of Indian affairs, and Col. Ely S. Parker, as aforesaid, and the undersigned, persons representing the Seminole nation, have hereunto set their hands and seals the day and year first above written.

Dennis N. Cooley, Commissioner of Indian Affairs.
Elijah Sells, Superintendent Indian Affairs.
Col. Ely S. Parker, Special commissioner.

John Chup-co, his x mark, King or head chief.
Cho-cotc-harjo, his x mark, Counsellor.
Fos-harjo, his x mark, chief.
John F. Brown, Special delegate for Southern Semiholes.

In presence of: Robert Johnson, his x mark, United States interpreter for Seminole Indians.

Geo. A. Reynolds, United States Indian agent for Semiholes.

Ok-tus-sus-har-jo, his x mark, or Sands, Cow-e-to-me-ko, his x mark, Che-chu-chee, his x mark.

Harry Island, his x mark, United States interpreter for Creek Indians, W. Dnnn, United States Indian agent for the Creek Nation, Perry Fuller.

Signed by John F. Brown, special delegate for the Southern Seminoles, in presence of, this June thirtieth, eighteen hundred and sixty-six
W. R. Irwin, J. M. Tebbetts, Geo. A. Reynolds, United States Indian agent, Robert Johnson, his x mark, United States interpreter.

TREATY WITH THE CHOCTAW AND CHICKASAW {1866, April 2}
Ratified June 28, 1866.
Proclaimed July 10, 1866.

Articles of agreement and convention between the United States and the Choctaw and Chickasaw Nations of Indians, made and concluded at the City of Washington the twenty-eighth day of April, in the year eighteen hundred and sixty-six, by Dennis N. Cooley, Elijah Sells, and E S. Parker, special commissioners on the part of the United States, and Alfred Wade, Allen Wright, James Riley, and John Page, commissioners on the part of the Choctaws, and Winchester Colbert, Edmund Pickens, Holmes Colbert, Colbert Garter, and Robert H. Love, commissioners on the part of the Chickasaws.

ARTICLE 1. Permanent peace and friendship are hereby established between the United States and said nations; and the Choctaws and Chickasaws do hereby bind themselves respectively to use their influence and to make every exertion to induce Indians of the plains to maintain peaceful relations with each other, with other Indians, and with the United States.

ARTICLE 2. The Choctaws and Chickasaws hereby covenant and agree that henceforth neither slavery nor involuntary servitude, otherwise than in punishment of crime whereof the parties shall have been duly convicted, in accordance with laws applicable to all members of the particular nation, shall ever exist in said nations.

ARTICLE 3. The Choctaws and Chickasaws, in consideration of the sum of three hundred thousand dollars, hereby cede to the United States the territory west of the 98 deg. west longitude, known as the leased district, provided that the said sum shall be invested and held by the United States, at an interest not less than five per cent, in trust for the said nations, until the legislatures of the Choctaw and Chickasaw Nations respectively shall have made such laws, rules, and regulations as may be necessary to give all persons of African descent, resident in the said nation at the date of the treaty of Fort Smith, and their descendants, heretofore held in slavery among said nations, all the rights, privileges, and immunities, including the right of suffrage, of citizens of said nations, except in the annuities, moneys, and public domain claimed by, or belonging to, said nations respectively; and also to give to such persons who were residents as aforesaid, and their descendants, forty acres each of the land of said nations on the same terms as the Choctaws and Chickasaws, to be selected on the survey of said land, after the Choctaws and Chickasaws and Kansas Indians have made their selections as herein provided; and immediately on the enactment of such laws, rules, and regulations, the said sum, of three hundred thousand dollars shall be paid to the said Choctaw and Chickasaw Nations in the proportion of three-fourths to the former and one-fourth to the latter,-less such sum, at the rate of one hundred dollars per capita, as shall be sufficient to pay such persons of African descent before referred to as within ninety days after the passage of such laws, rules, and regulations shall elect to remove and actually remove from the said nations respectively.

And should the said laws, rules, and regulations not be made by the legislatures of the said nations respectively, within two years from the ratification of this treaty, then the said sum of three hundred thousand dollars shall cease to be held in trust for the said Choctaw and Chickasaw Nations, and be held for the use and benefit of such of said persons of African descent as the United States shall remove from the said Territory in such manner as the United States shall deem proper,the United States agreeing, within ninety days from the expiration of the said two years, to remove from said nations all such persons of African descent as may be willing to remove; those remaining or returning after having been removed from said nations to have no benefit of said sum of three hundred thousand dollars, or any part thereof, but shall be upon the same footing as other citizens of the United States in the said nations.

ARTICLE 4. The said nations further agree that all negroes, not otherwise disqualified or disabled, shall be competent witnesses in all civil and criminal suits and proceedings in the Choctaw and Chickasaw courts, any law to the contrary notwithstanding; and they fully recognize the right of the freedmen to a fair remuneration-on reasonable and equitable contracts for their labor, which the law should aid them to enforce. And they agree, on the part of their respective nations, that all laws shall be equal in their operation upon Choctaws, Chickasaws, and negroes, and that no distinction affecting the latter shall at any time be made, and that they shall be treated with kindness and be protected against injury; and they further agree, that while the said freedmen, now in the Choctaw and Chickasaw Nations, remain in said nations, respectively, they shall be entitled to as much land as they may cultivate for the support of themselves and families, in cases where they do not support themselves and families by hiring, not interfering with existing improvements without the consent of the occupant, it being understood that in the event of the making of the laws, rules, and regulations aforesaid, the forty acres aforesaid shall stand in place of the land culti- vated as last aforesaid.

ARTICLE 5. A general amnesty of all past offences against the laws of the United States, committed before the signing of this treaty by any member of the Choctaw or Chickasaw Nations, is hereby declared; and the United States will especially request the States of Missouri. Kansas, Arkansas, and Texas to grant the like amnesty as to all offences committed by any member of the Choctaw or Chickasaw Nation. And the Choctaws and Chickasaws, anxious for the restora- tion of kind and friendly feelings among themselves, do hereby declare an am- nesty for all past offences against their respective governments, and no Indian or Indians shall be proscribed, or any act of forfeiture or confiscation passed against those who may have remained friendly to the United States, but they shall enjoy equal privileges with other members of said tribes, and all laws heretofore passed inconsistent herewith are hereby declared inoperative. The people of the Choctaw and Chickasaw Nations stipulate and agree to deliver up to any duly authorized agent of the United States all public property in their possession which belong to the late "so-called Confederate States of America," or the United States, without any reservation whatever; particularly ordnance, ordnance-stores, and arms of all kinds.

ARTICLE 6. The Choctaws and Chickasaws hereby grant a right of way through their lands to any company or companies which shall be duly author- ized by Congress, or by the legislatures of said nations, respectively, and which shall, with the express consent and approbation of the Secretary of the Interior, undertake to construct a railroad through the Choctaw and Chickasaw Nations from the north to the south thereof, and from the east to the west side thereof, in accordance with the provisions of the 1Sth article of the treaty of June twenty- second, one thousand eight hundred and fifty-five, which provides that for any property taken or destroyed in the construction thereof full compensation shall be made to the party or parties injured, to be ascertained and determined in such manner as the President of the United States shall direct.

But such railroad company or companies, with all its or their agents and em- ployes shall be subject to the laws of the United States relating to intercourse with Indian tribes, and also to such rules and regulations as may be prescribed by the Secretary of the Interior for that purpose. And it is also stipulated and agreed that the nation through which the road or roads aforesaid shall pass may subscribe to the stock of the particular company or companies such amount or amounts as they may be able to pay for in alter-hate sections of unoccupied lands for a space of six miles on each side of said road or roads, at a price per acre to be agreed upon between said Choctaw and Chickasaw Nations and the said company or companies, subject to the approval of the President of the United States: Provided, however, That said land, thus subscribed, shall not be sold, or demised, or occupied by any one not a citizen of the Choctaw or Chickasaw Nations; according to their laws and recognized usages:

Provided, That the officers, servants, and employes of such companies necessary to the construction and management of said road or roads shall not be excluded from such occupancy as their respective functions may require, they being subject to the provisions of the Indian intercourse law and such rules and regulations as may be established by the Secretary of the Interior: And provided also, That the stock thus subscribed by either of said nations shall have the force and effect of a first-mortgage bond on all that part of said road, appurtenances, and equipments situated and used within said nations respectively, and shall be a perpetual lien on the same, and the said nations shall have the right, from year to year, to elect to receive their equitable proportion of declared dividends of profits on their said stock, or interest on the par value at the rate of six per cent. per annum.

Second. And it is further declared, in this connection, that as fast as sections of twenty miles in length are completed, with the rails laid ready for use, with all water and other stations necessary to the use thereof, as a first-class road, the said company or companies shall become entitled to patents for the alternate sections aforesaid, and may proceed to dispose thereof in the manner herein provided for, subject to the approval of the Secretary of the Interior.

Third. And it is further declared, also, in case of one or more of said alternate sections being occupied by any member or members of said nations respectively, so that the same cannot be transferred to the said company or companies, that the said nation or nations, respectively, may select any unoccupied section or sections, as near as circumstances will permit, to the said width of six miles on each side of said road or roads, and convey the same as an equivalent for the section or sections so occupied as aforesaid.

ARTICLE 7. The Choctaws and Chickasaws agree to such legislation as Congress and the President of the United States may deem necessary for the better administration of justice and the protection of the rights of person and property within the Indian Territory: Provided, however, Such legislation shall not in anywise interfere with or annul their present tribal organization, or their respective legislatures or judiciaries, or the rights, laws, privileges, or customs of the Choctaw and Chickasaw Nations respectively.

ARTICLE 8. The Choctaws and Chickasaws also agree that a council, consisting of delegates elected by each nation or tribe lawfully resident within the Indian Territory, may be annually convened in said Territory, to be organized as follows:

First. After the ratification of this treaty, and as soon as may be deemed practicable by the Secretary of the Interior, and prior to the first session of said assembly, a census of each tribe, lawfully resident in said Territory, shall be taken, under the direction of the Superintendent of Indian Affairs, by competent persons, to be appointed by him, whose compensation shall be fixed by the Secretary of the Interior and paid by the United States.

Second. The council shall consist of one member from each tribe or nation whose population shall exceed five hundred, and an additional member for each one thousand Indians, native or adopted, or each fraction of a thousand greater than five hundred being members of any tribe lawfully resident hi said Territory, and shall be selected by the tribes or nations respectively who may assent to the establishment of said general assembly; and if none should be thus formally selected by any nation or tribe, it shall be represented in said general assembly by the chief or chiefs and head-men of said tribes, to be taken in the order of their rank as recognized ill tribal usage in the number and proportions above indicated.

Third. After the said census shall have been taken and completed, the superintendent of Indian affairs shall publish and declare to each tribe the number of members of said council to which they shall be entitled under the provisions of this article; and the persons so to represent the said tribes shall meet at such time and place as he shall designate, but thereafter the time and place of the sessions of the general assembly shall be determined by itself: Provided, That no session in any one year shall exceed the term of thirty days, and provided that the special sessions may be called whenever, in the judgment of the Secretary of the Interior, the interests of said tribes shall require it.

Fourth. The general assembly shall have power to legislate upon all subjects and matters pertaining to the intercourse and relations of the Indian tribes and nations resident in the said Territory, the arrest and extradition of criminals escaping from one tribe to another, the administration of justice between members of the several tribes of the said Territory, and persons other than Indians and members of said tribes or nations, the construction of works of internal improvement, and the common defence and safety of the nations of the said Territory. All laws enacted by said council shall take effect at the times therein provided, unless suspended by the Secretary of the Interior or the President of the United States. No law shall be enacted inconsistent with the Constitution of the United States or the laws of Congress, or existing treaty stipulations with the United States; nor shall said council legislate upon matters pertaining to the legislative, judicial, or other organization, laws, or customs of the several tribes or nations, except as herein provided for.

Fifth. Said council shall be presided over by the superintendent of Indian affairs, or, in case of his absence from any cause, the duties of the superintendent enumerated in this article shall be performed by such person as the Secretary of the Interior shall indicate.

Sixth. The Secretary of the Interior shall appoint a secretary of said council, whose duty it shall be to keep an accurate record of all the proceedings of said council, and to transmit a true copy thereof, duly certified by the superintendent of Indian affairs, to the Secretary of the Interior immediately after the sessions of said council shall terminate. He shall be paid five hundred dollars, as an annual salary, by the United States.

Seventh. The members of the said council shall be paid by the United States four dollars per diem while in actual attendance thereon, and four dollars mileage for every twenty miles going and returning therefrom by the most direct route, to be certified by the secretary of said council and the presiding officer.
Eighth. The Choctaws and Chickasaws also agree that a court or courts may be established in said Territory with such jurisdiction and organization as Congress may prescribe: Provided, That the same shall not interfere with the local judiciary of either of said nations.

Ninth. Whenever Congress shall authorize the appointment of a Delegate from said Territory, it shall be the province of said council to elect one from among the nations represented in said council.

Tenth. And it is further agreed that, the superintendent of Indian affairs shall be the executive of the said Territory, with the title of "governor of the Territory of Oklahoma," and that there shall be a secretary of the said Territory, to be appointed by the said superintendent; that the duty of the said governor, in addition to those already imposed on the superintendent of Indian affairs, shall be such as properly belong to an executive officer charged with the execution of the laws, which the said council is authorized to enact under the provisions of this treaty; and that for this purpose he shall have authority to appoint a marshal of said Territory and an interpreter; the said marshal to appoint such deputies, to be paid by fees, as may be required to aid him in the execution of his proper functions, and be the marshal of the principal court of said Territory that may be established under the provisions of this treaty.

Eleventh. And the said marshal and the said secretary shall each be entitled to a salary of five hundred dollars per annum, to be paid by the United States, and such fees in addition thereto as shall be established by said governor, with the approbation of the Secretary of the Interior, it being understood that the said fee-lists may at any time be corrected and altered by the Secretary of the Interior, as the experience of the system proposed herein to be established shall show to be necessary, and shall in no case exceed the fees paid to marshals of the United States for similar services.

The salary of the interpreter shall be five hundred dollars, to be paid in like manner by the United States.

Twelfth. And the United States agree that in the appointment of marshals and deputies, preference, qualifications being equal, shall be given to competent members of the said nations, the object being to create a laudable ambition to acquire the experience necessary for political offices of importance in the respective nations.

Thirteenth. And whereas it is desired by the said Choctaw and Chickasaw Nations that the said council should consist of an upper and lower house, it is hereby agreed that whenever a majority of the tribes or nations represented in said council shall desire the same, or the Congress of the United States shall so prescribe, there shall be, in addition to the council now provided for, and which shall then constitute the lower house, an upper house, consisting of one member from each tribe entitled to representation in the council now provided forthe relations of the two houses to each other being such as prevail in the States of the United States; each house being authorized to choose its presiding officer and clerk to perform the duties appropriate to such offices: and it being the duty, in addition, of the clerks of each house to make out and transmit to the territorial secretary fair copies of the proceedings of the respective houses immediately after their respective sessions, which copies shall be dealt with by said secretary as is now provided in the case of copies of the proceedings of the council mentioned in this act, and the said clerks shall each be entitled to the same per diem as members of the respective houses, and the presiding officers to double that sum.

ARTICLE 9. Such sums of money as have, by virtue of treaties existing in the year eighteen hundred and sixty-one, been invested for the purposes of education, shall remain so invested, and the interest thereof shall be applied for the same purposes, in such manner as shall be designated by the legislative authorities of the Choctaw and Chickasaw Nations, respectively.

ARTICLE 10. The United States re-affirms all obligations arising out of treaty stipulations or acts of legislation with regard to the Choctaw and Chickasaw Nations, entered into prior to the late rebellion, and in force at that time, not inconsistent herewith; and further agrees to renew the payment of all annuities and other moneys accruing under such treaty stipulations and acts of legislation, from and after the close of the fiscal year ending on the thirtieth of June, in the year eighteen hundred and sixty-six.

ARTICLE 11. Whereas the land occupied by the Choctaw and Chickasaw Nations, and described in the treaty between the United States and said nations, of June twenty-second, eighteen hundred and fifty-five, is now held by the members of said nations in common, under the provisions of the said treaty; and whereas it is believed that the holding of said land in severalty will promote the general civilization of said nations, and tend to advance their permanent welfare and the best interests of their individual members, it is hereby agreed that, should the Choctaw and the Chickasaw people, through their respective legislative councils, agree to the survey and dividing their land on the system of the United States, the land aforesaid east of the ninety-eighth degree of west longitude shall be, in view of the arrangements hereinafter mentioned, surveyed and laid off in ranges, townships, sections, and parts of sections; and that for the purpose of facilitating such surveys and for the settlement and distribution of said land as hereinafter provided, there shall be established at Boggy Depot, in the Choctaw Territory, a land-office; and that, in making the said surveys and conducting the business of the said office, including the appointment of all necessary agents and surveyors, the same system shall be pursued which has heretofore governed in respect to the public lands of the United States, it being understood that the said surveys shall be made at the cost of the United States and by their agents and surveyors, as in the case of their own public lands, and that the officers and employes shall receive the same compensation as is paid to officers and employes in the land-offices of the United States in Kansas.

ARTICLE 12. The maps of said surveys shall exhibit, as far as practicable, the outlines of the actual occupancy of members of the said nations, respectively; and when they are completed, shall be returned to the said land-office at Boggy Depot for inspection by all parties interested, when notice for ninety days shall be given of such return, in such manner as the legislative authorities of the said nations, respectively, shall prescribe, or, in the event of said authorities failing to give such notice in a reasonable time, in such manner as the register of said land-office shall prescribe, calling upon all parties interested to examine said maps to the end that errors, if any, in the location of such occupancies, may be corrected.

ARTICLE 13. The notice required in the above article shall be given, not only in the Choctaw and Chickasaw Nations, but by publication in newspapers printed in the States of Mississippi and Tennessee, Louisiana, Texas, Arkansas, and Alabama, to the end that such Choctaws and Chickasaws as yet remain outside of the Choctaw and Chickasaw Nations, may be informed and have opportunity to exercise the rights hereby given to resident Choctaws and Chickasaws: Provided, That before any such absent Choctaw or Chickasaw shall be permitted to select for him or herself, or others, as hereinafter provided, he or she shall satisfy the register of the land-office of his or her intention, or the intention of the party for whom the selection is to be made, to become bona-fide resident in the said nation within five years from the time of selection; and should the said absentee fail to remove into said nation, and occupy and commence an improvement on the land selected within the time aforesaid, the said selection shall be cancelled, and the land shall thereafter be discharged from all claim on account thereof.

ARTICLE 14. At the expiration of the ninety days aforesaid the legislative authorities of the said nations, respectively, shall have the right to select one quarter-section of land in each of the counties of said nations respectively, in trust for the establishment of seats of justice therein, and also as many quarter-sections as the said legislative councils may deem proper for the permanent endowment of schools, seminaries, and colleges in said nation, provided such selection shall not embrace or interfere with any improvement in the actual occupation of any member of the particular nation without his consent; and provided the proceeds of sale of the quarter-sections selected for seats of justice shall be appropriated for the erection or improvement of public buildings in the county in which it is located.

ARTICLE 15. At the expiration of the ninety days' notice aforesaid, the selection which is to change the tenure of the land in the Choctaw and Chickasaw Nations from a holding in common to a holding in severalty shall take place, when every Choctaw and Chickasaw shall have the right to one quarter-section of land, whether male or female, adult or minor, and if in actual possession or occupancy of land improved or cultivated by him or her, shall have a prior right to the quarter-section in which his or her improvement lies; and every infant shall have selected for him or her a quarter-section of land in such location as the father of such infant, if there be a father living, and if no father living, then the mother or guardian, and should there be neither father, mother, nor guardian, then as the probate judge of the county, acting for the best interest of such infant, shall select.

ARTICLE 16. Should an actual occupant of land desire, at any time prior to the commencement of the surveys aforesaid, to abandon his improvement, and select and improve other land, so as to obtain the prior right of selection thereof, he or she shall be at liberty to do so; in which event the improvement so abandoned shall be open to selection by other parties: Provided, That nothing herein contained shall authorize the multiplication of improvements so as to increase the quantity of land beyond what a party would be entitled to at the date of this treaty.

ARTICLE 17. No selection to be made under this treaty shall be permitted to deprive or interfere with the continued occupation, by the missionaries established in the respective nations, of their several missionary establishments; it being the wish of the parties hereto to promote and foster an influence so largely conducive to civilization and refinement. Should any missionary who has been engaged in missionary labor for five consecutive years before the date of this treaty in the said nations, or either of them, or three consecutive years prior to the late rebellion, and who, if absent from the said nations, may desire to return, wish to select a quarter-section of land with a view to a permanent home for himself and family, he shall have the privilege of doing so, provided no selection shall include any public buildings, schools or seminary; and a quantity of land not exceeding six hundred and forty acres, to be selected according to legal subdivisions in one body, and to include their improvements, is hereby granted to every religious society or denomination which has erected, or which, with the consent of the Indians, may hereafter erect buildings within the Choctaw and Chickasaw country for missionary or educational purposes.

But no land thus granted, nor the buildings which have been or may be erected thereon, shall ever be sold or otherwise disposed of, except with the consent of the legislatures of said nations respectively and approval of the Secretary of the Interior; and whenever such lands or buildings shall be sold or disposed of, the proceeds thereof shall be applied, under the direction of the Secretary of the Interior, to the support and maintenance of other similar establishments for the benefit of the Choctaws and Chickasaws, and such other persons as may hereafter become members of their nations, according to their laws, customs, and usages.

ARTICLE 18. In making a selection for children the parent shall have a prior right to select land adjacent to his own improvements or selection, provided such selection shall be made within thirty days from the time at which selections under this treaty commence.

ARTICLE 19. The manner of selecting as aforesaid shall be by an entry with the register of the land-office, and all selections shall be made to conform to the legal subdivisions of the said lands as shown by the surveys aforesaid on the maps aforesaid; it being understood that nothing herein contained is to be construed to confine a party selecting to one section but he may take contiguous parts of sections by legal subdivisions in different sections, not exceeding together a quarter-section.

ARTICLE 20. Prior to any entries being made under the foregoing provisions, proof of improvements, or actual cultivation, as well as the number of persons for whom a parent or guardian, or probate judge of the county proposes to select, and of their right to select, and of his or her authority to select, for them, shall be made to the register and receiver of the land-office, under regulations to be prescribed by the Secretary of the Interior.

ARTICLE 21. In every township the sections of land numbered sixteen and thirty-six shall be reserved for the support of schools in said township: Provided, That if the same has been already occupied by a party or parties having the right to select it, or it shall be so sterile as [926] to be unavailable, the legislative authorities of the particular nations shall have the right to select such other unoccupied sections as they may think proper.

ARTICLE 22. The right of selection hereby given shall not authorize the selection of any land required by the United States as a military post, or Indian agency, not exceeding one mile square, which, when abandoned, shall revert to the nation in which the land lies.

ARTICLE 23. The register of the land-office shall inscribe in a suitable book or books, in alphabetical order, the name of every individual for whom a selection shall be made, his or her age, and a description of the land selected.

ARTICLE 24. Whereas it may be difficult to give to each occupant of an improvement a quarter-section of land, or even a smaller subdivision, which shall include such improvement, in consequence of such improvements lying in towns, villages, or hamlets, the legislative authorities of the respective nations shall have power, where,, in their discretion, they think it expedient, to lay off into town lots any section or part of a section so occupied, to which lots the actual occupants, being citizens of the respective nations, shall have pre-emptive right, and, upon paying into the treasury of the particular nation the price of the land, as fixed by the respective legislatures, exclusive of the value of said improvement, shall receive a conveyance thereof. Such occupant shall not be prejudiced thereby in his right to his selection elsewhere.

The town lots which may be unoccupied shall be disposed of for the benefit of the particular nation, as the legislative authorities may direct from time to time. When the number of occupants of the same quarter-section shall not be such as to authorize the legislative authorities to lay out the same, or any part thereof, into town lots, they may make such regulations for the disposition thereof as they may deem proper, either by subdivision of the same, so as to accommodate the actual occupants, or by giving the right of prior choice to the first occupant in point of time, upon paying the others for their improvements, to be valued in such way as the legislative authorities shall prescribe, or otherwise. All occupants retaining their lots under this section,, and desiring, in addition, to make a selection, must pay for the lots so retained, as in the case of town Jots. And any Choctaw or Chickasaw who may desire to select a sectional division other than that on which his homestead is, without abandoning the latter,, shall have the right to purchase the homestead sectional division at such price as the respective legislatures may prescribe.

ARTICLE 25. During ninety days from the expiration of the ninety days'notice aforesaid, the Choctaws and Chickasaws shall have the exclusive right to make selections, as aforesaid, and at the end of that time the several parties shall be entitled to patents for their respective selections, to be issued by the President of the United States, and countersigned by the chief executive officer of the nation in which the land lies, and recorded in the records of the executive office of the particular nation; and copies of the said patents, under seal, shall be evidence in any court of law or equity.

ARTICLE 26. The right here given to the Choctaws and Chickasaws, respectively, shall extend to all persons who have become citizens by adoption or intermarriage of either of said nations, or who may hereafter become such.

ARTICLE 27. In the event of disputes arising in regard to the rights of parties to select particular quarter-sections or other divisions of said land, or in regard to the adjustment of boundaries, so as to make them conform to legal divisions and subdivisions such disputes shall be set-t, led by the register of the land-office and the chief executive officer of the nation in which the land lies, in a summary way, after hearing the parties; and if said register and chief officer cannot agree, the two to call in a third party, who shall constitute a third referee, the decision of any two of whom shall be final without appeal.

ARTICLE 28. Nothing contained in any law of either of the said nations shall prevent parties entitled to make selections contiguous to each other; and the Choctaw and Chickasaw Nations hereby agree to repeal all laws inconsistent with this provision.

ARTICLE 29. Selections made under this treaty shall, to the extent of one quarter-section, including the homestead or dwelling, be inalienable for the period of twenty-one years from the date of such selection,, and upon the death of the party in possession shall descend according to the laws of the nation where the land lies; and in the event of his or her death without heirs,, the said quarter-section shall escheat to and become the property of the nation.

ARTICLE 30. The Choctaw and Chickasaw Nations will receive into their respective districts east of the ninety-eighth degree of west longitude, in the proportion of one-fourth in the Chickasaw and three-fourths in the Choctaw Nation,, civilized Indians from the tribes known by the general name of the Kansas Indians, being Indians to the north of the Indian Territory, not exceeding ten thousand in number, who shall have in the Choctaw and Chickasaw Nations, respectively, the same rights as the Choctaws and Chickasaws, of whom they shall be the fellow-citizens, governed by the same laws, and enjoying the same privileges, with the exception of the right to participate in the Choctaw and Chickasaw annuities and other moneys, and in the public domain,, should the same, or the proceeds thereof, be divided per capita among the Choctaws and Chickasaws, and among others the right to select land as herein provided for Choctaws and Chickasaws, after the expiration of the ninety days during which the selections of land are to be made, as aforesaid, by said Choctaws and Chickasaws; and the Choctaw and Chickasaw Nations pledge themselves to treat the said Kansas Indians in all respects with kindness and forbearance, aiding them in good faith to establish themselves in their new homes, and to respect all their customs and usages not inconsistent with the constitution and laws of the Choctaw and Chickasaw Nations respectively.

In making selections after the advent of the Indians and the actual occupancy of land in said nation, such occupancy shall have the same effect in their behalf as the occupancies of Choctaws and Chickasaws; and after the said Choctaws and Chickasaws have made their selections as aforesaid, the said persons of African descent mentioned in the third article of the treaty, shall make their selections as therein provided, in the event of the making of the laws, rules, and regulations aforesaid, after the expiration of ninety days from the date at which the Kansas Indians are to make their selections as therein provided, and the actual occupancy of such persons of African descent shall have the same effect in their behalf as the occupancies of the Choctaws and Chickasaws.

ARTICLE 31. And whereas some time must necessarily elapse before the surveys, maps, and selections herein provided for can be completed so as to permit the said Kansas Indians to make their selections in their order,, during which time the United States may desire to remove the said Indians from their present abiding places, it is hereby agreed that the said Indians may at once come into the Choctaw and Chickasaw Nations, settling themselves temporarily as citizens of the said nations, respectively, upon such land as suits them and is not already occupied.

ARTICLE 32. At the expiration of two years, or sooner, if the President of the United States shall so direct, from the completion of the Choctaw surveys and maps aforesaid, the officers of the land-offices aforesaid [9281 shall deliver to the executive departments of the Choctaw and Chickasaw Nations, respectively, all such documents as may be necessary to elucidate the land-title as settled according to this treaty, and forward copies thereof, with the field-notes, records, and other papers pertaining to said titles, to the Commissioner of the General Land Office; and thereafter grants of land and patents therefor shall be issued in such manner as the legislative authorities of said nations may provide for A the unselected portions of the Choctaw and Chickasaw districts as defined by the treaty of June twenty-second, eighteen hundred and fifty-five.

ARTICLE 33. All lands selected as herein provided shall thereafter be held in severalty by the respective parties, and the unselected land shall be the common property of the Choctaw and Chickasaw Nations, in their corporate capacities, subject to the joint control of their legislative authorities.

ARTICLE 34. Should any Choctaw or Chickasaw be prevented from selecting for him or herself during the ninety days aforesaid, the failure to do so shall not authorize another to select the quarter-section containing his improvement, but he may at any time make his selection thereof, subject to having his boundaries made to conform to legal divisions as aforesaid.

ARTICLE 35. Should the selections aforesaid not be made before the transfer of the land records to the executive authorities of said nations,, respectively, they shall be made according to such regulations as the legislative authorities of the two nations, respectively, may prescribe, to the end that full justice and equity may be done to the citizens of the respective territories.

ARTICLE 36. Should any land that has been selected under the provisions of this treaty be abandoned and left uncultivated for the space of seven years by the party selecting the same, or his heirs,, except in the case of infants under the age of twenty-one years, or married women, or persons non compos mentis, the legislative authorities of the nation where such land lies may either rent the same for the benefit of those interested, or dispose of the same otherwise for their benefit,, and may pass all laws necessary to give effect to this provision.

ARTICLE 37. In consideration of the right of selection hereinbefore accorded to certain Indians other than the Choctaws and Chickasaws, the United States agree to pay to the Choctaw and Chickasaw Nations, out of the funds of Indians removing into said nations respectively, under the provisions of this treaty, such sum as may be fixed by the legislatures of said nations, not exceeding one dollar per acre, to be divided between the said nations in the proportion of one-fourth to the Chickasaw Nation and three-fourths to the Choctaw Nation, with the understanding that at the expiration of twelve months the actual number of said immigrating Indians shall be ascertained, and the amount paid that may be actually due at the rate aforesaid; and should still further immigrations take place from among said Kansas Indians, still further payments shall be made accordingly from time to time.

ARTICLE 38. Every white person who, having married a Choctaw or Chickasaw, resides in the said Choctaw or Chickasaw Nation, or who has been adopted by the legislative authorities, is to be deemed a member of said nation, and shall be subject to the laws of the Choctaw and Chickasaw Nations according to his domicile, and to prosecution and trial before their tribunals, and to punishment according to their laws in all respects as though he was a native Choctaw or Chickasaw.

ARTICLE 39. No person shall expose goods or other articles for sale as a trader without a permit of the legislative authorities of the nation he may propose to trade in; but no license shall be required to authorize any member of the Choctaw or Chickasaw Nations to trade in the [9291 Choctaw or Chickasaw country who is authorized by the proper authority of the nation, nor to authorize Choctaws or Chickasaws to sell flour, meal, meat, fruit, and other provisions, stock, wagons, agricultural implements, or tools brought from the United States into the said country.

ARTICLE 40. All restrictions contained in any treaty heretofore made, or in any regulation of the United States upon the sale or other disposition of personal chattel property by Choctaws or Chickasaws are hereby removed.

ARTICLE 41. All persons who are members of the Choctaw or Chickasaw Nations, and are not otherwise disqualified or disabled, shall hereafter be competent witnesses in all civil and criminal suits and proceedings in any courts of the United States, any law to the contrary notwithstanding.

ARTICLE 42. The Choctaw and Chickasaw Nations shall deliver up persons accused of crimes against the United States who may be found within their respective limits on the requisition of the governor of any State for a crime committed against the laws of said State, and upon the requisition of the judge of the district court of the United States for the district within which the crime was committed.

ARTICLE 43. The United States promise and agree that no white person, except officers, agents, and employees of the Government, and of any internal improvement company, or persons travelling through, or temporarily sojourning in, the said nations, or either of them, shall be permitted to go into said Territory, unless formally incorporated and naturalized by the joint action of the authorities of both nations into one of the said nations of Choctaws and Chickasaws, according to their laws, customs, or usages; but this article is not to be construed to affect parties heretofore adopted, or to prevent the employment temporarily of white persons who are teachers, mechanics, or skilled in agriculture, or to prevent the legislative authorities of the respective nations from authorizing such works of internal improvement as they may deem essential to the welfare and prosperity of the community, or be taken to interfere with or invalidate any action which has heretofore been had in this connection by either of the said nations.

ARTICLE 44. Post-offices shall be established and maintained by the United States at convenient places in the Choctaw and Chickasaw Nations, to and from which the mails shall be carried at reasonable intervals, at the rates of postage prevailing in the United States.

ARTICLE 45. All the rights, privileges, and immunities heretofore possessed by said nations or individuals thereof, or to which they were entitled under the treaties and legislation heretofore made and had in connection with them, shall be, and are hereby declared to be, in full force, so far as they are consistent with the provisions of this treaty.

ARTICLE 46. Of the moneys stipulated to be paid to the Choctaws and Chickasaws under this treaty for the cession of the leased district, and the admission of the Kansas Indians among them, the sum of one hundred and fifty thousand dollars shall be advanced and paid to the Choctaws, and fifty thousand dollars to the Chickasaws, through their respective treasurers, as soon as practicable after the ratification of this treaty, to be repaid out of said moneys or any other moneys of said nations in the hands of the United States; the residue, not affected by any provisions of this treaty, to remain in the Treasury of the United States at an annual interest of five per cent, no part of which shall be paid out as annuity, but shall be annually paid to the treasurer of said nations, respectively, to be regularly and judiciously applied, under the direction of their respective legislative councils, to the support of their government, the purposes of education, and such other objects as may be best calculated to promote and advance the welfare and happiness of said nations and their people respectively.

ARTICLE 47. As soon as practicable after the lands shall have been surveyed and assigned to the Choctaws and Chickasaws in severalty as herein provided, upon application of their respective legislative councils, and with the assent of the President of the United States, all the annuities and funds invested and held in trust by the United States for the benefit of said nations respectively shall be capitalized or converted into money, as the case may be; and the aggregate amounts thereof belonging to each nation shall be equally divided and paid per capita to the individuals thereof respectively, to aid and assist them in improving their homesteads and increasing or acquiring flocks and herds, and thus encourage them to make proper efforts to maintain successfully the new relations which the holding of their lands in severalty will involve: Provided, nevertheless, That there shall be retained by the United States such sum as the President shall deem sufficient of the said moneys to be invested, that the interest thereon may be sufficient to defray the expenses of the government of said nations respectively, together with a judicious system of education, until these objects can be provided for by a proper system of taxation; and whenever this shah be done to the satisfaction of the President of the United States, the moneys so retained shall be divided in the manner and for the purpose above mentioned.

ARTICLE 48. Immediately after the ratification of this treaty there shall be paid, out of the funds of the Choctaws and Chickasaws in the hands of the United States, twenty-five thousand dollars to the Choctaw and twenty-five thousand dollars to the Chickasaw commissioners, to enable them to discharge obligations incurred by them for various incidental and other expenses to which they have been subjected, and for which they are now indebted.

ARTICLE 49. And it is further agreed that a commission, to consist of a person or persons to be appointed by the President of the United States, not exceeding three, shall be appointed immediately on the ratification of this treaty, who shall take into consideration and determine the claim of such Choctaws and Chicka-saws as allege that they have been driven during the late rebellion from their homes in the Choctaw (and Chickasaw) Nations on account of their adhesion to the United States, for damages, with power to make such award as may be con-sistent with equity and good conscience, taking into view all circumstances, whose report, when ratified by the Secretary of the Interior, shall be final, and authorize the payment of the amount from any moneys of said nations in the hands of the United States as the said commission may award.

ARTICLE 50. Whereas Joseph G. Heald and Reuben Wright, of Massachusetts, were licensed traders in the Choctaw country at the commencement of the rebel-lion, and claim to have sustained large losses on account of said rebellion,, by the use of their property by said nation, and that large sums of money are due them for goods and property taken, or sold to the members of said nation,, and money advanced to said nation; and whereas other loyal citizens of the United States may have just claims of the same character: It is hereby agreed and stipulated that the commission provided for in the preceding article shall investigate said claims, and fully examine the same; and such sum or sums of money as shall by the report of said commission, approved by the Secretary of the Interior, be found due to such persons, not exceeding ninety thousand dollars, shall be paid by the United States to the persons entitled thereto, out of any money belonging to said nation in the possession of the United States: Provided. That no claim for goods or property of any kind shall be allowed or paid, in whole or part, which shall have been used by said nation or any member thereof in aid of the rebellion, with the consent of said claimants: Provided also, That if the aggregate of said claims thus allowed and approved shall exceed said sum of ninety thousand dollars, then that sum shall be applied pro rata in payment of the claims so allowed.

ARTICLE 51. It is further agreed that all treaties and parts of treaties inconsistent herewith be, and the same are hereby, declared null and void. In testimony whereof, the said Dennis N. Cooley, Elijah Sells, and E. S. Parker, commission-ers in behalf of the United States, and the said commissioners on behalf of the Choctaw and Chickasaw nations, have hereunto set their hands and seals the day and year first above written.

D. N. Cooley, Commissioner of Indian Affairs, Elijah Sells, superintendent of Indian affairs, E. S. Parker, special commissioner, Commissioners for United States.

Alfred Wade, Allen Wright, James Riley, John Page, Choctaw commissioners. Winchester Colbert, Edmund, his x mark, Pickens, Holmes Colbert, Colbert Garter, Robert H. Love, Chickasaw commissioners. Campbell Leftore, Secretary of Choctaw delegation. E. S. Mitchell. Secretary of Chickasaw delegation.

In presence of:
Jno. H. B. Latrobe, P. P. Pitchlynn, Principal chief Choctaws. Douglas H. Cooper. J. Harlan. Charles E. Mix.

TREATY WITH THE CREEKS {1866, June 14}
Ratified July 1866.
Proclaimed Aug. 11. 1866

Treaty of cession, and indemnity concluded at the city of Washington on the fourteenth day of June, in the year of our Lord one thousand eight hundred and sixty-six, by and between the United States, represented by Dennis N. Cooley, Commissioner of Indian Affairs, Elija Sells, superintendent of Indian affairs for the southern superintendency, and Col. Ely S. Parker, special commissioner, and the Creek Nation of Indians, represented by Ok-tars-sars-harjo, or Sands; Cow-e-to-me-co and Che-chu-chee, delegates at large, and D. N. McIntosh and James Smith, special delegates of the Southern Creeks.

Whereas existing treaties between the United States and the Creek Nation have become insufficient to meet their mutual necessities; and whereas the Creeks made a treaty with the so-called Confederate States, on the tenth of July, one thousand eight hundred and sixty-one, whereby they ignored their allegiance to the United States, and unsettled the treaty relations existing between the Creeks and the United States, and did so render themselves liable to forfeit to the [932] United States all benefits and advantages enjoyed by them in lands, annuities, protection, and immunities, including their lands and other property held by grant or gift from the United States; and whereas m view of said liabilities the United States require of the Creeks a portion of their land whereon to settle other Indians; and whereas a treaty of peace and amity was entered into between the United States and the Creeks and other tribes at Fort Smith, September thirteenth (tenth) eighteen hundred and sixty-five.

(a) This agreement, a copy of which has been obtained from the report of the negotiating commissioners, found accompanying the Report of the Commissioner of Indian Affairs for 1865, is set forth in the Appendix to this Compilation, post, p. 1050) whereby the Creeks revoked, cancelled, and repudiated the aforesaid treaty made with the so-called Confederate States; and whereas the United States, through its commissioners, in said treaty of peace and amity, promised to enter into treaty with the Creeks to arrange and settle all questions relating to and growing out of said treaty with the so-called Confederate States: Now, therefore, the United States, by its commissioners, and the above-named delegates of the Creek Nation, the day and year above mentioned, mutually stipulate and agree, on behalf of the respective parties, as follows, to wit:

ARTICLE 1. There shall be perpetual peace and friendship between the parties to this treaty, and the Creeks bind themselves to remain firm allies and friends of the United States, and never to take up arms against the United States, but always faithfully to aid in putting down its enemies. They also agree to remain at peace with all other Indian tribes; and, in return, the United States guarantees them quiet possession of their country, and protection against hostilities on the part of other tribes. In the event of hostilities, the United States agree that the tribe commencing and prosecuting the same shall, as far as may be practicable, make just reparation therefor. To insure this protection, the Creeks agree to a military occupation of their country, at any time, by the United States, and the United States agree to station and continue in said country from time to time, at its own expense, such force as may be necessary for that purpose. A general amnesty of all past offenses against the laws of the United States, committed by any member of the Creek Nation, is hereby declared. And the Creeks, anxious for the restoration of kind and friendly feelings among themselves, do hereby declare an amnesty for all past offenses against their government, and no Indian or Indians shall be proscribed, or any act of forfeiture or confiscation passed against those who have remained friendly to, or taken up arms against, the United States, but they shall enjoy equal privileges with other members of said tribe, and all laws heretofore passed inconsistent herewith are hereby declared inoperative.

ARTICLE 2. The Creeks hereby covenant and agree that henceforth neither slavery nor involuntary servitude, otherwise than in the punishment of crimes, whereof the parties shall have been duly convicted in accordance with laws applicable to all members of said tribe, shall ever exist in said nation; and inasmuch as there are among the Creeks many persons of African descent, who have no interest in the soil, it is stipulated that hereafter these persons lawfully residing in said Creek country under their laws and usages, or who have been thus residing in said country, and may return within one year from the ratification of this treaty, and their descendants and such others of the same race as may be permitted by the laws of the said nation to settle within the limits of the jurisdiction of the Creek Nation as citizens (thereof,) shall have and enjoy all the rights and privileges of native citizens, including an equal interest in the soil and national funds, and the laws of the said nation shall be equally binding upon and give equal protection to all such persons, and all others, of whatsoever race or color, who may be adopted as citizens or members of said tribe.

ARTICLE 3. In compliance with the desire of the United States to locate other Indians and freedmen thereon, the Creeks hereby cede and convey to the United States, to be sold to and used as homes for such other civilized Indians as the United States may choose to settle thereon, the west half of their entire domain, to be divided by a line running north and south; the eastern half of said Creek lands, being retained by them, shall, except as herein otherwise stipulated, be forever set apart as a home for said Creek Nation; and in consideration of said cession of the west half of their lands, estimated to contain three millions two hundred and fifty thousand five hundred and sixty acres, the United States agree to pay the sum of thirty (30) cents per acre, amounting to nine hundred and seventy-five thousand one hundred and sixty-eight dollars, in the manner hereinafter provided, to wit: two hundred thousand dollars shall be paid per capita in money, unless otherwise directed by the President of the United States, upon the ratification of this treaty, to enable the Creeks to occupy, restore, and improve their farms, and to make their nation independent and self-sustaining, and to pay the damages sustained by the mission schools on the North Fork and the Arkansas Rivers, not to exceed two thousand dollars, and to pay the delegates such per diem as the agent and Creek council may agree upon, as a just and fair compensation, all of which shall be distributed for that purpose by the agent, with the advice of the Creek council, under the direction of the Secretary of the Interior.

One hundred thousand dollars shall be paid in money and divided to soldiers that enlisted in the Federal Army and the loyal refugee Indians and freedmen who were driven from their homes by the rebel forces, to reimburse them in proportion to their respective losses; four hundred thousand dollars be paid in money and divided per capita to said Creek Nation, unless otherwise directed by the President of the United States, under the direction of the Secretary of the Interior, as the same may accrue from the sale of land to other Indians. The United States agree to pay to said Indians, in such manner and for such purposes as the Secretary of the Interior may direct, interest at the rate of five per cent. per annum from the date of the ratification of this treaty, on the amount hereinbefore agreed upon for said ceded lands, after deducting the said two hundred thousand dollars; the residue, two hundred and seventy-five thousand one hundred and sixty-eight dollars, shall remain in the Treasury of the United States, and the interest thereon, at the rate of five per centum per annum, be annually paid to said Creeks as above stipulated.

ARTICLE 4. Immediately after the ratification of this treaty the United States agree to ascertain the amount due the respective soldiers who enlisted in the Federal Army, loyal refugee Indians and freedmen, in proportion to their several losses, and to pay the amount awarded each, in the following manner, to wit: A census of the Creeks shall be taken by the agent of the United States for said nation, under the direction of the Secretary of the Interior, and a roll of the names of all soldiers that enlisted in the Federal Army, loyal refugee Indians, and freedmen, be made by him. The superintendent of Indian affairs for the Southern superintendency and the agent of the United States for the Creek Nation shall proceed to investigate and determine from said roll the amounts due the respective refugee Indians, and shall transmit to the Commissioner of Indian affairs for his approval, and that of the Secretary of the Interior, their awards, together with the reasons therefor. In case the awards so made shall be duly approved, said awards shall be paid from the proceeds of the sale of said lands within one year from the ratification of this treaty, or so soon as said [934] amount of one hundred thousand ($100,000)dollars can be raised from the sale of said land to other Indians.

ARTICLE 5. The Creek Nation hereby grant a right of way through their lands, to the Choctaw and Chickasaw country, to any company which shall be duly authorized by Congress, and shall, with the express consent and approbation of the Secretary of the Interior, undertake to construct a railroad from any point north of to any point in or south of the Creek country, and likewise from any point on their eastern or southern boundary, but said railroad company, together with all its agents and employes, shall be subject to the laws of the United States relating to intercourse with Indian tribes, and also to such rules and regulations as may be prescribed by the Secretary of the Interior for that purpose, and the Creeks agree to sell to the United States, or any company duly authorized as aforesaid, such lands not legally owned or occupied by a member or members of the Creek Nation, lying along the line of said contemplated railroad, not exceeding on each side thereof a belt or strip of land three miles in width, at such price per acre as may be eventually agreed upon between said Creek Nation and the party or parties building said road, subject to the approval of the President of the United States.

Said land thus sold shall not be reconveyed, leased, or rented to, or be occupied by any one not a citizen of the Creek Nation, according to its laws and recognized usages: Provided, also, That officers, servants, and employes of said railroad necessary to its construction and management, shall not be excluded from such necessary occupancy, they being subject to the provisions of the Indian intercourse law and such rules and regulations as may be established by the Secretary of the Interior, nor shall any conveyance of any of said lands be made to the party building and managing said road until its completion as a first-class railroad, and its acceptance as such by the Secretary of the Interior.

ARTICLE 6. (Stricken out.)

ARTICLE 7. The Creeks hereby agree that the Seminole tribe of Indians may sell and convey to the United States all or any portion of the Seminole lands, upon such terms as may be mutually agreed upon by and between the Seminoles and the United States.

ARTICLE 8. It is agreed that the Secretary of the Interior forthwith cause the line dividing the Creek country, as provided for by the terms of the sale of Creek lands to the United States in article third of this treaty, to be accurately surveyed under the direction of the Commissioner of Indian Affairs, the expenses of which survey shall be paid by the United States.

ARTICLE 9. Inasmuch as the agency buildings of the Creek tribe have been destroyed during the late war, it is further agreed that the United States shall at their own expense, not exceeding ten thousand dollars, cause to be erected suitable agency buildings, the sites whereof shall be selected by the agent of said tribe, in the reduced Creek reservation, under the direction of the superintendent of Indian affairs.

In consideration whereof, the Creeks hereby cede and relinquish to the United States one section of their lands, to be designated and selected by their agent, under the direction of the superintendent of Indian affairs upon which said agency buildings shall be erected, which section of land shall revert to the Creek nation when said agency buildings are no longer used by the United States, upon said nation paying a fair and reasonable value for said buildings at the time vacated.

ARTICLE 10. The Creeks agree to such legislation as Congress and the President of the United States may deem necessary for the better administration of justice and the protection of the rights of person and property within the Indian territory: Provided, however, (That) said [935] legislation shall not in any manner interfere with or annul their present tribal organization, rights, laws, privileges, and customs. The Creeks also agree that a general council, consisting of delegates elected by each nation or tribe lawfully resident within the Indian territory, may be annually convened in said territory, which council shall be organized in such manner and possess such powers as are hereinafter described.
First. After the ratification of this treaty, and as soon as may be deemed practicable by the Secretary of the Interior, and prior to the first session of said council, a census, or enumeration of each tribe lawfully resident in said territory, shall be taken under the direction of the superintendent of Indian affairs, who for that purpose is hereby authorized to designate and appoint competent persons, whose compensation shall be fixed by the Secretary of the Interior, and paid by the United States.

Second. The first general council shall consist of one member from each tribe, and an additional member from each one thousand Indians, or each fraction of a thousand greater than five hundred, being members of any tribe lawfully resident in said territory, and shall be selected by said tribes respectively, who may assent to the establishment of said general council, and if none should be thus formerly selected by any nation or tribe, the said nation or tribe shall be represented in said general council by the chief or chiefs and head men of said tribe, to be taken in the order of their rank as recognized in tribal usage, in the same number and proportion as above indicated. After the said census shall have been taken and completed, the superintendent of Indian affairs shall publish and declare to each tribe the number of members of said council to which they shall be entitled under the provisions of this article, and the persons entitled to so represent said tribes shall meet at such time and place as he shall appoint, but thereafter the time and place of the sessions of said council shall be determined by its action: Provided, That no session in any one year shall exceed the term of thirty days, and provided that special sessions of said council may be called whenever, in the judgment of the Secretary of the Interior, the interest of said tribe shall require.

Third. Said general council shall have power to legislate upon all rightful subjects and matters pertaining to the intercourse and relations of the Indian tribes and nations resident in said territory, the arrest and extradition of criminals and offenders escaping from one tribe to another, the administration of justice between members of the several tribes of said territory, and persons other than Indians and members of said tribes or nations, the construction of works of internal improvement, and the common defence and safety of the nations of said territory. All laws enacted by said general council shall take effect at such time as may therein be provided, unless suspended by direction of the Secretary of the Interior or the President of the United States. No law shall be enacted inconsistent with the Constitution of the United States, or the laws of Congress, or existing treaty stipulations with the United States, nor shah said council legislate upon matters pertaining to the organization, laws, or customs of the several tribes, except as herein provided for.

Fourth. Said council shall be presided over by the superintendent of Indian affairs, or, in case of his absence from any cause, the duties of said superintendent enumerated in this article shall be performed by such person as the Secretary of the Interior may direct.

Fifth. The Secretary of the Interior shall appoint a secretary of said council, whose duty it shall be to keep an accurate record of all the proceedings of said council, and who shall transmit a true copy of all such proceedings, duly certified by the superintendent of Indian affairs, to the Secretary of the Interior immediately after the sessions of said [936] council shall terminate. He shall be paid out of the Treasury of the United States an annually salary of five hundred dollars.

Sixth. The members of said council shall be paid by the United States the sum of four dollars per diem during the time actually in attendance on the sessions of said council, and at the rate of four dollars for every twenty miles necessar(il)ly traveled by them in going to and returning to their homes respectively, from said council, to be certified by the secretary of said council and the superintendent of Indian affairs.

Seventh. The Creeks also agree that a court or courts may be established in said territory, with such jurisdiction and organized in such manner as Congress may by law provide.

ARTICLE 11. The stipulations of this treaty are to be a full settlement of all claims of said Creek Nation for damages and losses of every kind growing out of the late rebellion and all expenditures by the United States of annuities in clothing and feeding refugee and destitute Indians since the diversion of annuities for that purpose consequent upon the late war with the so-called Confederate States; and the Creeks hereby ratify and confirm all such diversions of annuities heretofore made from the funds of the Creek Nation by the United States, and the United States agree that no annuities shall be diverted from the objects for which they were originally devoted by treaty stipulations with the Creeks, to the use of refugee and destitute Indians other than the Creeks or members of the Creek Nation after the close of the present fiscal year, June thirtieth, eighteen hundred and sixty-six.

ARTICLE 12. The United States re-affirms and re-assumes all obligations of treaty stipulations with the Creek Nation entered into before the treaty of said Creek Nation with the so-called Confederate States, July tenth, eighteen hundred and sixty-one, not inconsistent herewith: and further agrees to renew all payments accruing by force of said treaty stipulations from and after the close of the present fiscal year, June thirtieth, eighteen hundred and sixty-six, except as is provided in article eleventh.

ARTICLE 13. A quantity of land not exceeding one hundred and sixty acres, to be selected according to legal subdivision, in one body, and to include their improvements, is hereby granted to every religious society or denomination, which has erected, or which, with the consent of the Indians, may hereafter erect, buildings within the Creek country for missionary or educational purposes; but no land thus granted, nor the buildings which have been or may be erected thereon, shall ever be sold or otherwise disposed of, except with the consent and approval of the Secretary of the Interior; and whenever any such lands or buildings shall be so sold or disposed of, the proceeds thereof shall be applied, under the direction of the Secretary of the Interior, to the support and maintenance of other similar establishments for the benefit of the Creeks and such other persons as may be or may hereafter become members of the tribe according to its laws, customs, and usages; and if at any time said improvements shall be abandoned for one year for missionary or educational purposes, all the rights herein granted for missionary and educational purposes shall revert to the said Creek Nation.

ARTICLE 14. It is further agreed that all treaties heretofore entered into between the United States and the Creek Nation which are inconsistent with any of the articles or provisions of this treaty shall be, and are hereby, rescinded and annulled; and it is further agreed that ten thousand dollars shall be paid by the United States, or so much thereof as may be necessary, to pay the expenses incurred in negotiating the foregoing treaty.

In testimony whereof, we, the commissioners representing the United States and the delegates representing the Creek nation, have [937] hereunto set our hands and seals at the place and on the day and year above written.

D. N. Cooley, Commissioner Indian Affairs, Elijah Sells, Superintendent Indian Affairs Ok-ta-has Harjo, his x mark, Cow Mikko, his x mark, Cotch-cho-chee, his x mark, D. N. McIntosh, James M. C. Smith.

In the presence of: J. W. Dunn, United States Indian agent, J. Harlan, United States Indian agent, Charles E. Mix. J. M. Tebbetts, Geo. A. Reynolds, United States Indian agent, John B. Sanborn, John F. Brown, Seminole delegate, John Chupco, his x mark, Fos-har-jo, his x mark, Cho-cotc-huga, his x mark, R. Fields, Cherokee delegate, Douglas H. Cooper, Wm. Penn Adair, Harry Island, his x mark, United States interpreter, Creek Nation, Suludin Watie.

TREATY WITH THE DELAWARES {1866, July 4}
Ratified July 26, 1866.
Proclaimed Aug. 10, 1866.

Articles of agreement between the United States and the chiefs and councillors of the Delaware Indians, on behalf of said tribe, made at the Delaware Agency, Kansas, on the fourth day of July, eighteen hundred and sixty-six.

Whereas Congress has by law made it the duty of the President of the United States to provide by treaty for the removal of the Indian tribes from the State of Kansas; and whereas the Delaware Indians have expressed a wish to remove from their present reservation in said State to the Indian country, located between the States of Kansas and Texas; and whereas the United States have, by treaties negotiated with the Choctaws and Chickasaws, with the Creeks, and with the Seminoles, Indian tribes residing in said Indian country, acquired the right to locate other Indian tribes within the limits of the same; and whereas the Missouri River Railroad Company, a corporation existing in the State of Kansas by the laws thereof,and which company has built a railroad connecting with the Pacific Railroad, from near the mouth of the Kaw River to Leavenworth, in aid of which road the Delawares, by treaty in eighteen hundred and sixty-four, agreed to dispose of their lands,has expressed a desire to purchase the present

Delaware Indian reservation in the said State, in a body, at a fair price:It is hereby agreed between Thomas Murphy, superintendent of Indian affairs, John G. Pratt, agent for the Delawares, and William H. Watson, special commissioner, who are duly appointed to act for the United States; and Captain John Connor, Captain Sarcoxie, and Charles Journeycake, chiefs, and James Ketchum, James Connor, Andrew Miller, and John Sarcoxie, councillors, duly appointed and authorized by said Delaware Indians to act for them and in their behalf, viz:

ARTICLE 1. That the United States shall secure and cause to be paid to said Indians the full value of all that part of their reservation, with the improvements then existing on the same, heretofore sold to the Leavenworth, Pawnee, and Western Railroad Company, according to the terms of a treaty ratified August twenty-second, eighteen hundred and sixty, and supplemental treaties, and in accordance with the conditions, restrictions, and limitations thereof.

ARTICLE 2. That the Secretary of the Interior shall be, and he is, authorized to sell to said Missouri River Railroad Company, or to other responsible party or parties, in a body, all the remaining part of said reservation, being the lands conveyed to said Delaware Indians in pursuance of the provisions of the supplemental treaty of September twenty-fourth, eighteen hundred and twenty-nine, and all other lands owned by the said tribe in the State of Kansas not previously disposed of, except as hereinafter provided, for a price not less than two dollars and fifty cents per acre, exclusive of improvements.

ARTICLE 3. It shall be the duty of the Secretary of the Interior to give each of all the adult Delaware Indians who have received their proportion of land in severalty an opportunity, free from all restraint, to elect whether they will dissolve their relations with their tribe and become citizens of the United States: and the lands of all such Indians as may elect so to become citizens, together with those of their minor children, held by them in severalty, shall be reserved from the sale hereinbefore provided for. And the Secretary of the Interior shall cause any and all improvements made on any of the said lands, the sale of which is provided for, whether held in common or in severalty, to be appraised.

And the value thereof added to the price of said lands, to be paid for when payment is made for the lands upon which said improvements exist; and the money received for the improvements on the land of each Indian held in severalty shall be paid to him at any time after its payment to the Secretary of the Interior, when the Department shall be notified that said Indian is ready to remove to the Indian country, to provide for his removal to, and to enable him to make improvements on his new home therein: Provided, That whenever it shall be ascertained under the registry above provided for what lands will be vacated, there shall be set apart from the lands held in common, for each child of Delaware blood, born since the allotment of land to said tribe in severalty was made under previous treaties, a quantity of land equal to the amount to which they would have been entitled had they been born before said allotment, provided that selections for children belonging to families whose head may elect to remain may be made from lands which are to be vacated by those who elect to remove: And provided further, That in case there shall be improvements upon any heretofore allotted lands, so selected for children of the Delawares, payment shall be made for such improvements, at their appraised value, by the parents or guardians of said children, at the same time as if the said lands had been sold to the railroad company or other parties.

ARTICLE 4. The U-aired States agree to sell to the said Delaware Indians a tract of land ceded to the Government by the Choctaws and Chickasaws, the Creeks, or the Seminoles, or which may be ceded by the Cherokees in the Indian country, to be selected by the Delawares in one body in as compact a form as practicable, so as to contain timber, water, and agricultural lands, to contain in the aggregate, if the said Delaware Indians shall so desire, a quantity equal to one hundred and sixty (160) acres for each man, woman, and child who shall remove to said country, at the price per acre paid by the United States for the said lands, to be paid for by the Delawares out of the [939] proceeds of sales of lands in Kansas, heretofore provided for. The said tract of country shall be set off with clearly and permanently marked boundaries by the United States; and also surveyed as public lands are surveyed, when the Delaware council shall so request, when the same may, in whole or in part, be allotted by said council to each member of said tribe residing in said country, said allotment being subject to the approval of the Secretary of the Interior.

ARTICLE 5. The United States guarantee to the said Delawares peaceable possession of their new home herein provided to be selected for them in the Indian country, and protection from hostile Indians and internal strife and civil war, and a full and just participation in any general council or territorial government that may be established for the nations and tribes residing in said Indian country.

ARTICLE 6. It is agreed that the proceeds of the sale of the Delaware lands herein provided for shah be paid to said Indians in the manner following, to wit: Whenever the Department of the Interior shall be notified by the council, through the agent, that any of the Delawares who hold land in severalty are ready to remove, at the same time describing their allotments, there shall be paid to each such person the value of his allotment, and that of his family, to enable him to remove to and improve his new home, provided the money for the said allotment shall have been paid to the Secretary of the Interior; and while said money, or any part thereof, shall remain in the Treasury of the United States, the Delawares shall be entitled to receive interest on the amount so retained, at the rate of five (5) per cent. per annum. And the residue of the proceeds of the sale of the Delaware lands, being those which have not been allotted, or which have once been allotted, but have been abandoned by the allottees, shall be added to the general fund of the Delawares, interest thereon to be paid to the Indians in the same manner as is now provided in regard to that fund.

Within 30 days of the ratification of this treaty, it shall be the duty of the Secretary of the Interior to give the said Missouri River Railroad Company notice that he is authorized to contract with them or other responsible party or parties for the sale of said lands on the terms specified in this treaty, indicating the approximate quantity thereof; and within twenty days after receiving said notice at their usual place of doing business in the State of Kansas it shall be competent for said company to elect to make the purchase, by filing with the said secretary their bond, with approved security, in double the amount proposed to be paid by them for the whole of said lands, guaranteeing that they will purchase all of the lands to be sold under the provisions of this treaty, and that they will pay for them in accordance with the terms thereof. And upon the filing of a satisfactory bond as above provided by said company, the contract for such purchase shall be concluded by the said secretary with said Missouri River Railroad Company, at not less than two dollars and fifty cents per acre for the whole of the lands herein provided to be sold: Provided, however, That if said railroad company shall not within the twenty days above limited file its bond for the purchase as herein prescribed, the Secretary of the Interior may at the expiration of that time accept any offer for the whole of said lands in one body, at not less than two dollars and fifty cents per acre, from any other responsible parties; but no offer shall be considered from other parties than said Missouri River Railroad Company, unless accompanied by a certificate of deposit in the First National Bank of the city of Washington, D.C., to the credit of the said secretary, for an amount equal to ten per cent. of the aggregate value of the land at the price proposed, to be forfeited for the use of the Delawares if the sale should be awarded to said person or corporation so proposing to purchase the lands, and said party should fail to make payment as hereinafter provided.

ARTICLE 8. That within sixty days after the sale of said land shall have been effected, the purchaser shall pay to the said Secretary, in trust for the Delawares, the stipulated price of said unallotted lands, with the appraised value of improvements thereon, excepting therefrom the mill reservation and the quarter sections upon which the council-house and blacksmith-shops are built, the use of which shall be retained until the final removal of the Delawares, and for which payment shall not be required from the purchaser until possession is delivered; and from time to time thereafter, as often as the Secretary of the Interior shall notify the said purchaser that ten thousand acres or more of said lands have been vacated by said Indians within three months thereafter, said purchaser shall pay to the Secretary of the Interior, in trust for the said Indians, the stipulated price for said lands, with the appraised value of the improvements; and so on until all are paid for, according to the true intent and meaning hereof; and as said lands shall be paid for, patents therefor, conveying the same in fee-simple, shall be from time to time issued to said purchaser, or to his or its assigns, by the President of the United States.

ARTICLE 9. It is also stipulated that the Secretary of the Interior shall cause a registry to be made of the names of all of said Delawares who have elected to dissolve their tribal relations and to become citizens of the United States, as provided in this treaty, with the names, ages, and sex of the members of the family of each of said Delawares, and present a certified copy of the same to the judge of the district court of the United States for the district of Kansas, and cause a copy to be filed in the office of the Commissioner of Indian Affairs, after which any of said Delawares, being adults, may appear before the said judge in open court, and make the same proof and take the same oath of allegiance as is provided by law for the naturalization of aliens, and also make proof, to the satisfaction of said court, that he is sufficiently intelligent and prudent to control his own affairs and interests, that he has adopted the habits of civilized life, and has been able to support, for at least five years, himself and family; when he shall receive a certificate of the same under the seal of the said court; and on the filing of the said certificate in the office of the Commissioner of Indian Affairs, the said Delaware Indian shall be constituted a citizen of the United States, and be entitled to receive a patent, in fee-simple, with power of alienation, for the land-heretofore allotted him, and his just proportion, in cash or in bonds, of the cash value of the credits of said tribe, principal and interest, then held in trust by the United States; and also, as the same may be received, his proportion of the proceeds of the sale of lands under the provisions of this treaty, when he shall cease to be a member of said tribe.

Whereupon all of the minor children of those who have become citizens shall be construed to have elected to sever their connection with said tribe for the time being, and be entitled to their just proportion of the annuities of the tribe, to be paid to the head of the family to be expended for their support and education until they shall attain the age of twenty-one years, after which each shall elect to remove to his tribe or to become a citizen of the United States, as hereinbefore provided, and if thus admitted to citizenship, shall be entitled to all the privileges and interests herein provided for the head of the family. Should any minor as aforesaid, arriving at the age of twenty-one years, and electing to become a citizen of the United States, or any adult Indian having so elected, fail to be admitted, he shall not be compelled to remove, but the Secretary of the Interior shall provide proper guardianship for the protection of his rights and interests and those of his family. There shall be granted to each of the Delawares-who have thus become citizens, a patent, in fee-simple, for the lands heretofore allotted to them, and, if they do not remove with the nation, their pro rata share of all annuities and trust-property held by the United States for them, the division to be made under the direction of the President of the United States, after which such persons shall cease to be members of the Delaware tribe, and shall not further participate in their councils, nor share in their property or annuities.

ARTICLE 10. It is further agreed that the funds of the Delawares shall never be applied by the Government to the payment of the debt or debts of any individual member or members of the nation; nor shall any person be licensed to trade with the Delawares without the consent of the chiefs and council; and the salaries of the chiefs shall henceforward be four hundred dollars per annum.

ARTICLE 11. The Delawares acknowledge their dependence upon the United States, and again renew their pledges of devotion to the Government thereof, and ask its protection; and the United States agree to protect, preserve, and defend them in all their just rights.

ARTICLE 12. It is also agreed that if the said Secretary should not be able to sell the said lands as hereinbefore provided, he may cause the same to be appraised, in separate tracts, at their fair cash value, no tract to be valued at less than two dollars and fifty cents per acre, and the same when appraised may be sold at not less than the appraised value, and for as much more as the same will bring, and the money arising from the sale to be applied and distributed as hereinbefore provided.

ARTICLE 13. It is agreed by the Delawares that railroad companies engaged in building roads whose routes shall lie through their new reservation in the Indian country shall have a right of way through and over said lands, not exceeding two hundred feet in width for any such road, and also the right to enter on all lands and take and use such gravel, stone, and other material except timber as may be necessary for the construction of such roads, compensation to be made for any damages done in obtaining such material, and for any damages arising from the location or running of such roads to improvements which shall have been made before such road shall have been located, such damages to be ascertained under regulations to be prescribed by the Secretary of the Interior.

ARTICLE 14. The United States further agree that, in accordance with the general provisions of the sixth article of the Delaware treaty of May thirty, eighteen hundred and sixty, which have not yet been fulfilled, there shall be credited to the Delawares, in the purchase of their new reservation in the Indian country, the sum of thirty thousand dollars, which credit by the United States shall be received by the Delawares as a full settlement of all claims against the Government for depredations upon timber to the date of the signing of this treaty; and the Delawares shall receive, without cost, from the United States, land included within their new reservation to the amount of twenty-three sections, in place of the twenty-three sections of half-breed Kaw lands referred to in said sixth section of the treaty of eighteen hundred and sixty; and inasmuch as the Delawares claim that a large amount of stock has been stolen from them by whites since the treaty of eighteen hundred and fifty-four, the United States agree to have a careful examination of such claims made under the direction of the Secretary of the Interior, and when the value of such stolen stock shall have

431

been ascertained, the same shall be reported to Congress with a recommendation for an appropriation to pay for the same; and all moneys appropriated for such purpose shall be paid to the owners of said stock.

ARTICLE 15. It is also agreed by the contracting parties that nothing contained in this treaty shall be so construed as to require the Delawares to remove from their present homes, until after they shall have selected and received title to lands for new homes elsewhere.

In testimony whereof, the said superintendent, agent, and special commissioner, on behalf of the United States, and the said chiefs and councillors on behalf of the Delawares, have hereunto set their hands and seals this fourth day of July, one thousand eight hundred and sixty-six.

Thos. Murphy, Superintendent, John G. Pratt, Agent. W. H. Watson, Special Commissioner, John Connor, his x mark, Head Chief, Captain Sarcoxie, his x mark, Assistant Chief, Charles Journeycake, Assistant Chief. James Ketch(u)m, James Connor, his x mark, Andrew Miller, his x mark, John Sarcoxie, his x mark, Councillors. Isaac Johnycake, United States interpreter.
In presence of: Henry S. Bulkley, Edward S. Menager, Louis A. Menager.

TREATY WITH THE CHEROKEE {1866, July 19}
Ratified July 27, 1866.
Proclaimed Aug. 11, 1866.

Articles of agreement and convention at the city of Washington on the nineteenth day of July, in the year of our Lord one thousand eight hundred and sixty-six, between the United States, represented by Dennis N. Cooley, Commissioner of Indian Affairs, (and) Elijah Sells, superintendent of Indian affairs for the southern superintendency, and the Cherokee Nation of Indians, represented by its delegates, James McDaniel, Smith Christie, White Catcher, S. H. Benge, J.B. Jones, and Daniel H. RossJohn Ross, principal chief of the Cherokees, being too unwell to join in these negotiations.
Whereas existing treaties between the United States and the Cherokee Nation are deemed to be insufficient, the said contracting parties agree as follows, viz:

ARTICLE 1. The pretended treaty made with the so-called Confederate States by the Cherokee Nation on the seventh day of October, eighteen hundred and sixty-one, and repudiated by the national council of the Cherokee Nation on the eighteenth day of February, eighteen hundred and sixty-three, is hereby declared to be void.

ARTICLE 2. Amnesty is hereby declared by the United States and the Cherokee Nation for all crimes and misdemeanors committed by one Cherokee on the person or property of another Cherokee, or of a citizen of the United States, prior to the fourth day of July, eighteen hundred and sixty-six; and no right of action arising out of wrongs committed in aid or in the suppression of the rebellion shall be prosecuted or maintained in the courts of the United States or in the courts of the Cherokee Nation. [943] But the Cherokee Nation stipulate and agree to deliver up to the United States, or their duly authorized agent, any or all public property, particularly ordnance, ordnance stores, arms of all kinds, and quartermaster's stores, in their possession or control, which belonged to the United States or the so-called Confederate States, without any reservation.

ARTICLE 3. The confiscation laws of the Cherokee Nation shall be repealed, and the same, and all sales of farms, and improvements on real estate, made or pretended to be made in pursuance thereof, are hereby agreed and declared to be null and void, and the former owners of such property so sold, their heirs or assigns, shall have the right peaceably to re-occupy their homes, and the purchaser under the confiscation laws, or his heirs or assigns, shall be repaid by the treasurer of the Cherokee Nation from the national funds, the money paid for said property and the cost of permanent improvements on such real estate, made thereon since the confiscation sale; the cost of such improvements to be fixed by a commission, to be composed of one person designated by the Secretary of the Interior and one by the principal chief of the nation, which two may appoint a third in cases of disagreement, which cost so fixed shall be refunded to the national treasurer by the returning Cherokees within three years from the ratification hereof.

ARTICLE 4. All the Cherokees and freed persons who were formerly slaves to any Cherokee, and all free negroes not having been such slaves, who resided in the Cherokee Nation prior to June first, eighteen hundred and sixty-one, who may within two years elect not to reside northeast of the Arkansas River and southeast of Grand River, shall have the right to settle in and occupy the Canadian district southwest of the Arkansas River, and also all that tract of country lying northwest of Grand River, and bounded on the southeast by Grand River and west by the Creek reservation to the northeast corner thereof; from thence west on the north line of the Creek reservation to the ninety-sixth degree of west longitude; and thence north on said line of longitude so far that a line due east to Grand River will include a quality of land equal to one hundred and sixty acres for each person who may so elect to reside in the territory above-described in this article: Provided, That that part of said district north of the Arkansas River shall not be set apart until it shall be found that the Canadian district is not sufficiently large to allow one hundred and sixty acres to each person desiring to obtain settlement under the provisions of this article.

ARTICLE 5. The inhabitants electing to reside in the district described in the preceding article shall have the right to elect all their local officers and judges, and the number of delegates to which by their numbers they may be entitled in any general council to be established in the Indian Territory under the provisions of this treaty, as stated in Article 12, and to control all their local affairs, and to establish all necessary police regulations and rules for the administration of justice in said district, not inconsistent with the constitution of the Cherokee Nation or the laws of the United States; Provided, The Cherokees residing in said district shall enjoy all the rights and privileges of other Cherokees who may elect to settle in said district as hereinbefore provided, and shall hold the same rights and privileges and be subject to the same liabilities as those who elect to settle in said district under the provisions of this treaty; Provided also, That if any such police regulations or rules be adopted which, in the opinion of the President, bear oppressively on any citizen of the nation, he may suspend the same. And all rules or regulations in said district, or in any other district of the nation, discriminating against the citizens of other districts, are prohibited, and shall be void.

ARTICLE 6. The inhabitants of the said district hereinbefore described shall be entitled to representation according to numbers in the national council, and all laws of the Cherokee Nation shall be uniform throughout said nation. And should any such law, either in its provisions or in the manner of its enforcement, in the opinion of the President of the United States, operate unjustly or injuriously in said district, he is hereby authorized and empowered to correct such evil, and to adopt the means necessary to secure the impartial administration of justice, as well as a fair and equitable application and expenditure of the national funds as between the people of this and of every other district in said nation.

ARTICLE 7. The United States court to be created in the Indian Territory; and until such court is created therein, the United States district court, the nearest to the Cherokee Nation, shall have exclusive original jurisdiction of all causes, civil and criminal, wherein an inhabitant of the district hereinbefore described shall be a party, and where an inhabitant outside of said district, in the Cherokee Nation, shall be the other party, as plaintiff or defendant in a civil cause, or shall be defendant or prosecutor in a criminal case, and all process issued in said district by any officer of the Cherokee Nation, to be executed on an inhabitant residing outside of said district, and all process issued by any officer of the Cherokee Nation outside of said district, to be executed on an inhabitant residing in said district, shall be to all intents and purposes null and void, unless indorsed by the district judge for the district where such process is to be served, and said person, so arrested, shall be held in custody by the officer so arresting him, until he shall be delivered over to the United States marshal, or consent to be tried by the Cherokee court: Provided, That any or all the provisions of this treaty, which make any distinction in rights and remedies between the citizens of any district and the citizens of the rest of the nation, shall be abrogated whenever the President shall have ascertained, by an election duly ordered by him, that a majority of the voters of-such district desire them to be abrogated, and he shall have declared such abrogation.

And provided further, That no law or regulation, to be hereafter enacted within said Cherokee Nation or any district thereof, prescribing a penalty for its violation, shall take effect or be enforced until after ninety days from the date of its promulgation, either by publication in one or more newspapers of general circulation in said Cherokee Nation, or by posting up copies thereof in the Cherokee and English languages in each district where the same is to take effect, at the usual place of holding district courts.

ARTICLE 8. No license to trade in goods, wares, or merchandise shall be granted by the United States to trade in the Cherokee Nation, unless approved by the Cherokee national council, except in the Canadian district, and such other district north of Arkansas River and west of Grand River occupied by the so-called southern Cherokees, as provided in Article 4 of this treaty.

ARTICLE 9. The Cherokee Nation having, voluntarily, in February, eighteen hundred and sixty-three, by an act of the national council, forever abolished slavery, hereby covenant and agree that never hereafter shall either slavery or involuntary servitude exist in their nation otherwise than in the punishment of crime, whereof the party shall have been duly convicted, in accordance with laws applicable to all the members of said tribe alike. They further agree that all freedmen who have been liberated by voluntary act of their former owners or by law, as well as all free colored persons who were in the country at the commencement of the rebellion, and are now residents therein, or who may return within six months, and their descendants, shall have all the rights of native Cherokees: Provided, That owners of slaves so emancipated in the Cherokee Nation shall never receive any compensation or pay for the slaves so emancipated.

ARTICLE 10. Every Cherokee and freed person resident in the Cherokee Nation shall have the right to sell any products of his farm, including his or her live stock, or any merchandise or manufactured products, and to ship and drive the same to market without restraint, paying any tax thereon which is now or may be levied by the United States on the quantity sold outside of the Indian Territory.

ARTICLE 11. The Cherokee Nation hereby grant a right of way not exceeding two hundred feet wide, except at stations, switches, water-stations, or crossing of rivers, where more may be indispensable to the full enjoyment of the franchise herein granted, and then only two hundred additional feet shall be taken, and only for such length as may be absolutely necessary, through all their lands, to any company or corporation which shall be duly authorized by Congress to construct a railroad from any point north to any point south, and from any point east to any point west of, and which may pass through, the Cherokee Nation. Said company or corporation, and their employes and laborers, while constructing and repairing the same, and in operating said road or roads, including all necessary agents on the line, at stations, switches, water tanks, and all others necessary to the successful operation of a railroad, shall be protected in the discharge of their duties, and at all times subject to the Indian intercourse laws, now or which may hereafter be enacted and be in force in the Cherokee Nation.

ARTICLE 12. The Cherokees agree that a general council, consisting of delegates elected by each nation or tribe lawfully residing within the Indian Territory, may be annually convened in said Territory, which council shall be organized in such manner and possess such powers as hereinafter prescribed.
First. After the ratification of this treaty, and as soon as may be deemed practicable by the Secretary of the Interior, and prior to the first session of said council, a census or enumeration of each tribe lawfully resident in said Territory shall be taken under the direction of the Commissioner of Indian Affairs, who for that purpose is hereby authorized to designate and appoint competent persons, whose compensation shall be fixed by the Secretary of the Interior, and paid by the United States.

Second. The first general council shall consist of one member from each tribe, and an additional member for each one thousand Indians, or each fraction of a thousand greater than five hundred, being members of any tribe lawfully resident in said Territory, and shall be selected by said tribes respectively, who may assent to the establishment of said general council; and if none should be thus formally selected by any nation or tribe so assenting, the said nation or tribe shall be represented in said general council by the chief or chiefs and headmen of said tribes, to be taken in the order of their rank as recognized in tribal usage, in the same number and proportion as above indicated. After the said census shall have been taken and completed, the superintendent of Indian affairs shall publish and declare to each tribe assenting to the establishment of such council the number of members of such council to which they shall be entitled under the provisions of this article, and the persons entitled to represent said tribes shall meet at such time and place as he shall approve; but thereafter the time and place of the sessions of said council shall be determined by its action: Provided, That no session in any one year shall exceed the term of thirty days: And provided, That special sessions of said council may be called by the Secretary of the Interior whenever in his judgment the interest of said tribes shall require such special session.

Third. Said general council shall have power to legislate upon matters pertaining to the intercourse and relations of the Indian tribes and nations and colonies of freedmen resident in said Territory; the arrest and extradition of criminals and offenders escaping from one tribe to another, or into any community of freedmen; the administration of [946] justice between members of different tribes of said Territory and persons other than Indians and members of said tribes or nations; and the common defence and safety of the nations of said Territory. All laws enacted by such council shall take effect at such time as may therein be provided, unless suspended by direction of the President of the United States. No law shall be enacted inconsistent with the Constitution of the United States, or laws of Congress, or existing treaty stipulations with the United States. Nor shall said council legislate upon matters other than those above indicated: Provided, however, That the legislative power of such general council may be enlarged by the consent of the national council of each nation or tribe assenting to its establishment, with the approval of the President of the United States.

Fourth. Said council shall be presided over by such person as may be designated by the Secretary of the Interior.

Fifth. The council shall elect a secretary, whose duty it shall be to keep an accurate record of all the proceedings of said council, and who shall transmit a true copy of all such proceedings, duly certified by the presiding officer of such council, to the Secretary of the Interior, and to each tribe or nation represented in said council, immediately after the sessions of said council shall terminate. He shall be paid out of the Treasury of the United States an annual salary of five hundred dollars.

Sixth. The members of said council shall be paid by the United States the sum of four dollars per diem during the term actually in attendance on the sessions of said council, and at the rate of four dollars for every twenty miles necessarily traveled by them in going from and returning to their homes, respectively, from said council, to be certified by the secretary and president of the said council.

ARTICLE 13. The Cherokees also agree that a court or courts may be established by the United States in said Territory, with such jurisdiction and organized in such manner as may be prescribed by law: Provided. That the judicial tribunals of the nation shall be allowed to retain exclusive jurisdiction in all civil and criminal cases arising within their country in which members of the nation, by nativity or adoption, shall be the only parties, or where the cause of action shall arise in the Cherokee Nation, except as otherwise provided in this treaty.

ARTICLE 14. The right to the use and occupancy of a quantity of land not exceeding one hundred and sixty acres, to be selected according to legal subdivisions in one body, and to include their improvements, and not including the improvements of any member of the Cherokee Nation, is hereby granted to every society or denomination which has erected, or which with the consent of the national council may hereafter erect, buildings within the Cherokee country for missionary or educational purposes. But no land thus granted, nor buildings which have been or may be erected thereon, shall ever be sold or (o)therwise disposed of except with the consent and approval of the Cherokee national council and the Secretary of the Interior. And whenever any such-lands or buildings shall be sold or disposed of, the proceeds thereof shall be applied by said society or societies for like purposes within said nation, subject to the approval of the Secretary of the Interior.

ARTICLE 15. The United States may settle any civilized Indians, friendly with the Cherokees and adjacent tribes, within the Cherokee country, on unoccupied lands east of 96o, on such terms as may be agreed upon by any such tribe and the Cherokees, subject to the approval of the President of the United States, which shall be consistent with the following provisions, viz: Should any such tribe or band of Indians settling in said country abandon their tribal organization, there being first paid into the Cherokee national fund a sum of money which shah sustain the same proportion to the then existing national fund that the number of Indians sustain to the whole number of Cherokees then residing in the Cherokee country, they shall be incorporated into and ever after remain a part of the Cherokee Nation, on equal terms in every respect with native citizens. And should any such tribe, thus settling in said country, decide to preserve their tribal organizations, and to maintain their tribal laws, customs, and usages, not inconsistent with the constitution and laws of the Cherokee Nation, they shall have a district of country set off for their use by metes and bounds equal to one hundred and sixty acres, if they should so decide, for each man, woman, and child of said tribe, and shall pay for the same into the national fund such price as may be agreed on by them and the Cherokee Nation, subject to the approval of the President of the United States, and in cases of disagreement the price to be fixed by the President.

And the said tribe thus settled shall also pay into the national fund a sum of money, to be agreed on by the respective parties, not greater in proportion to the whole existing national fund and the probable proceeds of the lands herein ceded or authorized to be ceded or sold than their numbers bear to the whole number of Cherokees then residing in said country, and thence afterwards they shall enjoy all the rights of native Cherokees. But no Indians who have no tribal organizations, or who shall determine to abandon their tribal organizations, shall be permitted to settle east of the 96o of longitude without the consent of the Cherokee national council, or of a delegation duly appointed by it, being first obtained. And no Indians who have and determine to preserve the tribal organizations shall be permitted to settle, as herein provided, east of the 96o of longitude without such consent being first obtained, unless the President of the United States, after a full hearing of the objections offered by said council or delegation to such settlement, shall determine that the objections are insufficient, in which case he may authorize the settlement of such tribe east of the 96o of longitude.

ARTICLE 16. The United States may settle friendly Indians in any part of the Cherokee country west of 96 o, to be taken in a compact form in quantity not exceeding one hundred and sixty acres for each member of each of said tribes thus to be settled; the boundaries of each of said districts to be distinctly marked, and the land conveyed in fee-simple to each of said tribes to be held in common or by their members in severalty as the United States may decide.

Said lands thus disposed of to be paid for to the Cherokee Nation at such price as may be agreed on between the said parties in interest, subject to the approval of the President; and if they should not agree, then the price to be fixed by the President.

The Cherokee Nation to retain the right of possession of and jurisdiction over all of said country west of 96o of longitude until thus sold and occupied, after which their jurisdiction and right of possession to terminate forever as to each of said districts thus sold and occupied.

ARTICLE 17. The Cherokee Nation hereby cedes, in trust to the United States, the tract of land in the State of Kansas which was sold to the Cherokees by the United States, under the provisions of the second article of the treaty of 1835; and also that strip of the land ceded to the nation by the fourth article of said treaty which is included in the State of Kansas, and the Cherokees consent that said lands may be included in the limits and jurisdiction of the said State.

The lands herein ceded shall be surveyed as the public lands of the United States are surveyed, under the direction of the Commissioner of the General Land-Office, and shall be appraised by two disinterested persons, one to be designated by the Cherokee national council and one by the Secretary of the Interior, and, in case of disagreement [948] by a third person, to be mutually selected by the aforesaid appraisers. The appraisement to be not less than an average of one dollar and a quarter per acre, exclusive of improvements.

And the Secretary of the Interior shall, from time to time, as such surveys and appraisments are approved by him, after due advertisements for sealed bids, sell such lands to the highest bidders for cash, in parcels not exceeding one hundred and sixty acres, and at not less than the appraised value: Provided, That whenever there are improvements of the value of fifty dollars made on the lands not being mineral, and owned and personally occupied by any person for agricultural purposes at the date of the signing hereof, such person so owning, and in person residing on such improvements, shall, after due proof, ,made under such regulations as the Secretary of the Interior may prescribe, be entitled to buy, at the appraised value, the smallest quantity of land in legal subdivisions which will include his improvements, not exceeding in the aggregate one hundred and sixty acres; the expenses of survey and appraisement to be paid by the Secretary out of the proceeds of sale of said land: Provided, That nothing in this article shall prevent the Secretary of the Interior from selling the whole of said lands not occupied by actual settlers at the date of the ratification of this treaty, not exceeding one hundred and sixty acres to each person entitled to preemption under the pre-emption laws of the United States, in a body, to any responsible party, for cash, for a sum not less than one dollar per acre.

ARTICLE 18. That any lands owned by the Cherokees in the State of Arkansas and in States east of the Mississippi may be sold by the Cherokee Nation in such manner as their national council may prescribe, all such sales being first approved by the Secretary of the Interior.

ARTICLE 19. All Cherokees being heads of families residing at the date of the ratification of this treaty on any of the lands herein ceded, or authorized to be sold, and desiring to remove to the reserved country, shall be paid by the purchasers of said lands the value of such improvements, to be ascertained and appraised by the commissioners who appraise the lands, subject to the approval of the Secretary of the Interior; and if he shall elect to remain on the land now occupied by him, shall be entitled to receive a patent from the United States in fee-simple for three hundred and twenty acres of land to include his improvements, and thereupon he and his family shall cease to be members of the nation. And the Secretary of the interior shall also be authorized to pay the reasonable costs and expenses of the delegates of the southern Cherokees. The moneys to be paid under this article shall be paid out of the proceeds of the sales of the national lands in Kansas.

ARTICLE 20. Whenever the Cherokee national council shall request it, the Secretary of the Interior shall cause the country reserved for the Cherokees to be surveyed and allotted among them, at the expense of the United States.

ARTICLE 21. It being difficult to learn the precise boundary line between the Cherokee country and the States of Arkansas, Missouri, and Kansas, it is agreed that the United States shall, at its own expense, cause the same to be run as far west as the Arkansas, and marked by permanent and conspicuous monuments, by two commissioners, one of whom shall be designated by the Cherokee national council.

ARTICLE 22. The Cherokee national council, or any duly appointed delegation-thereof, shall have the privilege to appoint an agent to examine the accounts of the nation with the Government of the United States at such time as they may see proper, and to continue or discharge [949] such agent, and to appoint another, as may be thought best by such council or delegation; and such agent shall have free access to all accounts and books in the executive departments relating to the business of said Cherokee Nation, and an opportunity to examine the same in the presence of the of officer having such books and papers in charge.

ARTICLE 23. All funds now due the nation, or that may hereafter accrue from the sale of their lands by the United States, as hereinbefore provided for, shall be invested in the United States registered stocks at their current value, and the interest on all said funds shall be paid semi-annually on the order of the Cherokee Nation, and shall be applied to the following purposes, to wit: Thirty-five per cent. shall be applied for the support of the common-schools of the nation and educational purposes; fifteen per cent, for the orphan fund, and fifty per cent, for general purposes, including reasonable salaries of district officers; and the Secretary of the Interior, with the approval of the President of the United States, may pay out of the funds due the nation, on the order of the national council or a delegation duly authorized by it, such amount as he may deem necessary to meet outstanding obligations of the Cherokee Nation, caused by the suspension of the payment of their annuities, not to exceed the sum of one hundred and fifty thousand dollars.

ARTICLE 24. As a slight testimony for the useful and arduous services of the Rev. Evan Jones, for forty years a missionary in the Cherokee Nation, now a cripple, old and poor, it is agreed that the sum of three thousand dollars be paid to him, under the direction of the Secretary of the Interior, out of any Cherokee fund in or to come into his hands not otherwise appropriated.

ARTICLE 25. A large number of the Cherokees who served in the Army of the United States having died, leaving no heirs entitled to receive bounties and arrears of pay on account of such service, it is agreed that all bounties and arrears for service in the regiments of Indian United States volunteers which shall remain unclaimed by any person legally entitled to receive the same for two years from the ratification of this treaty, shall be paid as the national council may direct, to be applied to the foundation and support of an asylum for the education of orphan children, which asylum shall be under the control of the national council, or of such benevolent society as said council may designate, subject to the approval of the Secretary of the Interior.

ARTICLE 26. The United States guarantee to the people of the Cherokee Nation the quiet and peaceable possession of their country and protection against domestic feuds and insurrections, and against hostilities of other tribes. They shall also be protected against inter(r)uptions or intrusion from all unauthorized citizens of the United States who may attempt to settle on their lands or reside in their territory. In case of hostilities among the Indian tribes, the United States agree that the party or parties commencing the same shall, so far as practicable, make reparation for the damages done.

ARTICLE 27. The United States shall have the right to establish one or more military posts or stations in the Cherokee Nation, as may be deemed necessary for the proper protection of the citizens of the United States lawfully residing therein and the Cherokee and other citizens of the Indian country. But no sutler or other person connected therewith, either in or out of the military organization, shall be permitted to introduce any spirit(u)ous, vinous, or malt liquors into the Cherokee Nation, except the medical department proper, and by them only for strictly medical purposes. And all persons not in the military service of the United States, not citizens of the Cherokee Nation, are to be prohibited from coming into the Cherokee Nation, or remaining in the same, except as herein otherwise provided; and it is the duty of the United States Indian agent for the Cherokees to have such persons, not lawfully residing or sojourning therein, removed from the nation, as they now are, or hereafter may be, required by the Indian intercourse laws of the United States.

ARTICLE 28. The United States hereby agree to pay for provisions and clothing furnished the army under Appotholehala in the winter of 1861 and 1862, not to exceed the sum of ten thousand dollars, the accounts to be ascertained and settled by the Secretary of the Interior.

ARTICLE 29. The sum of ten thousand dollars or so much thereof as may be necessary to pay the expenses of the delegates and representatives of the Cherokees invited by the Government to visit Washington for the purposes of making this treaty, shall be paid by the United States on the ratification of this treaty.

ARTICLE 30. The United States agree to pay to the proper claimants all losses of property by missionaries or missionary societies, resulting from their being ordered or driven from the country by United States agents, and from their property being taken and occupied or destroyed by United States troops, not exceeding in the aggregate twenty thousand dollars, to be ascertained by the Secretary of the Interior.

ARTICLE 31. All provisions of treaties heretofore ratified and in force, and not inconsistent with the provisions of this treaty, are hereby re-affirmed and declared to be in full force; and nothing herein shall be construed as an acknowledgment by the United States, or as a relinquishment by the Cherokee Nation of any claims or demands under the guarantees of former treaties, except as herein expressly provided.

In testimony whereof, the said commissioners on the part of the United States, and the said delegation on the part of the Cherokee Nation, have hereunto set their hands and seals at the city of Washington, this ninth. (nineteenth) day of July, A. D. one thousand eight hundred and sixty-six.

D. N. Cooley, Commissioner of Indian Affairs, Elijah Sells, Superintendent of Indian Affairs, Smith Christie, White, atcher, James McDaniel, S. H. Benge, Danl. H. Ross, J. B. Jones.

Delegates of the Cherokee Nation, appointed by Resolution of the National Council.

In presence of: W. H. Watson, J. W. Wright.
Signatures witnessed by the following-named persons, the following inter-lineations being made before signing: On page 1st the word "the" interlined, on page 11 the word "the" struck out, and to said page 11 sheet attached requiring publication of laws; and on page 34th the word "ceded" struck out and the words "neutral lands" inserted. Page 47½ added relating to expenses of treaty.
Thomas Ewing, jr, Wm. A. Phillips, J. W. Wright.

TREATY WITH THE SENECA, MIXED SENECA
AND SHAWNEE, QUAPAW, ETC. {1867, Feb. 23}
Ratified June 18, 1868.
Proclaimed Oct. 14, 1868.

Articles of agreement, concluded at Washington, D.C., the twenty-third day of February, one thousand eight hundred and sixty-seven, between the United States, represented by Lewis E Bogy, Commissioner of Indian Affairs, W. H. Watson, special commissioner, Thomas Murphy, superintendent of Indian Af-fairs, George C. Snow, and G. A. Colton, U. S. Indian agents, duly authorized, and the Senecas, represented by George Spicer and John Mush; the Mixed Se-necas and Shawnees, by John Whitetree, John Young, and Lewis Davis; the Quapaws, by S. G. Vallier and Ka-zhe-cah; the Confederated Peorias, Kas-kaskias, Weas, and Piankeshaws, by Baptiste Peoria, John Mitchell, and Ed-ward Black; the Miamies, by Thomas Metosenyah and Thomas Richardville, and the Ottawas of Blanchard's Fork and Roche de Boeuf, by John White and J. T. Jones, and including certain Wyandott(e)s, represented by Tauromee, or John Hat, and John Karaho.

Whereas it is desirable that arrangements should be made by which portions of certain tribes, parties hereto, now residing in Kansas, should be enabled to re-move to other lands in the Indian country south of that State, while other por-tions of said tribes desire to dissolve their tribal relations, and become citizens; and whereas it is necessary to provide certain tribes, parties hereto, now resid-ing in the Indian country, with means of rebuilding their houses, re-opening their farms, and supporting their families, they having been driven from their reservations early in the late war, and suffered greatly for several years, and being willing to sell a portion of their lands to procure such relief; and whereas a portion of the Wyandottes, parties to the treaty of one thousand eight hundred and fifty-five, although taking lands in severalty, have sold said lands, and are still poor, and have not been compelled to become citizens, but have remained without clearly recognized organization, while others who did become citizens are unfitted for the responsibilities of citizenship; and whereas the Wyandottes,

443

treated with in eighteen hundred and fifty-five, have just claims against the Government, which will enable the portion of their people herein referred to begin anew a tribal existence: Therefore it is agreed:

ARTICLE 1. The Senecas cede to the United States a strip of land on the north side of their present reservation in the Indian country; the land so ceded to be bounded on the east by the State of Missouri, on the north by the north line of the reservation, on the west by the Neosho River, and running south for the necessary distance, to contain twenty thousand acres; for which the Government is to pay twenty thousand dollars upon the ratification of this treaty; the south line of said tract to be ascertained by survey, at the cost of the United States.

ARTICLE 2. The Senecas now confederated with the Shawnees, and owning an undivided half of a reservation in the Indian country immediately north of the Seneca reservation mentioned in the preceding article, cede to the United States one-half of said Seneca and Shawnee reserve, which it is mutually agreed shall be the north half, bounded on the east by the State of Missouri, north by the Quapaw reserve, west by the Neosho River, and south by an east and west line bisecting the present Seneca and Shawnee reserve into equal parts, the said line to be determined by survey, at the expense of the United States; for which tract of land, estimated to contain about thirty thousand acres, the United States will pay the sum of twenty-four thousand dollars.

ARTICLE 3. The Shawnees, heretofore confederated with the Senecas, cede to the United States that portion of their remaining lands, bounded as follows, beginning at a point where Spring River crosses the south line of the tract in the second article ceded to the United States, thence down said river to the south line of the Shawnee reserve, thence west to the Neosho River, thence up said river to the south line of the tract ceded in the second article, and thence east to the place of beginning; supposed to contain about twelve thousand acres, the area to be ascertained by survey, at the expense of the United States; the United States to pay for the same at the rate of one dollar per acre, as soon as the area shall be ascertained.

ARTICLE 4. The Quapaws cede to the United States that portion of their land lying in the State of Kansas, being a strip of land on the north line of their reservation, about one half mile in width, and containing about twelve sections in all, excepting therefrom one half section to be patented to Samuel G. Vallier, including his improvements. Also the further tract within their present reserve, bounded as follows: Beginning at a point in the Neosho River where the south line of the Quapaw reserve strikes that stream, thence east three miles, thence north to the Kansas boundary-line, thence west on said line to the Neosho River, thence down said river to the place of beginning; and the United States will pay to the Quapaws for the half-mile strip lying in Kansas at the rate of one dollar and twenty-five cents per acre, whenever the area of the same shall be ascertained; and for the other tract described in this article at the rate of one dollar and fifteen cents per acre, whenever the area of the same shall be ascertained by survey, said survey to be made at the cost of the tribe to which said tract is herein provided to be sold under the pre-emption laws of the United States; but all such pre-emption shah be paid in the money of the United States, at the proper land-office, within one year from the date of entry and settlement.

PROVISIONS RELATING TO THE SENECAS.

ARTICLE 5. The Senecas now confederated with the Shawnees, the said Shawnees thereto consenting, agree to dissolve their connection with the said Shawnees, and to unite with the Senecas, parties to the treaty of February twenty-eighth, one thousand eight hundred and thirty-one, upon their reservation described in article second of said treaty; and the several bands of Senecas will unite their funds into one common fund for the benefit of the whole tribe; and an equitable division shall be made of all funds or annuities now held in common by the Senecas and Shawnees.

ARTICLE 6. Of the sum of twenty-four thousand dollars to be paid to the Senecas, as provided in the second article, the stun of four thousand dollars shall be paid to them immediately after the ratification of this treaty, to enable them to re-establish their homes and provide themselves with agricultural implements, seed, and provisions for themselves and their families; and the balance of the said first-mentioned sum, being twenty thousand dollars, shall be consolidated with the twenty thousand dollars in the first article provided to be paid, and invested for the tribe of Senecas, as constituted by this treaty, at five per cent. interest, to be paid per capita semi-annually; and their annuity of five hundred dollars in specie, provided by article four of the treaty of September twenty-ninth, one thousand eight hundred and seventeen, shall likewise become the property of the tribe.

ARTICLE 7. The amount annually due the Senecas under the provisions of article four of the treaty of February twenty-eight, one thousand eight hundred and thirty-one, for blacksmith, after their separation from the Shawnees, shall be annually paid to them as a [962] national fund, to enable them to purchase such articles for their wants and improvements in agriculture as the chiefs, with the consent of their agent, may designate; and this provision shall apply also to the fund for support of a miller belonging to the Senecas heretofore occupying the southernmost reserve referred to in this treaty; and there shall be added to the said fund whatever amount belonging to either band of the Senecas shah be found due and unpaid upon an examination of their accounts with the Government, and particularly the amount of bonds and stocks invested in their name; and the interest thereon shall be annually paid to the said Senecas for the purposes mentioned in this article.

PROVISIONS RELATING TO THE SHAWNEES.

ARTICLE 8. Of the amount in the third article provided to be paid to the Shawnees by the United States for the lands therein ceded, the sum of two thousand dollars shall be advanced to them to be used in establishing their homes, and the balance of the said amount shall be invested for the said tribe, under the name of Eastern Shawnees, and five per cent be paid semi-annually thereon; and the amount due and unpaid upon the bonds or stocks invested in their name shall be paid to them, as well as the interest thereon hereafter to become due, to be used under the direction of the chiefs, with the consent of the agent, for the purchase of agricultural implements or other articles necessary for the general welfare of the people; and the one-half of the blacksmith fund remaining after the division to be made with the Senecas provided for in article five shall remain devoted to the same purpose, and the Government will add thereto the sum of five hundred dollars annually for five years.

PROVISIONS RELATING TO THE QUAPAWS.

ARTICLE 9. Of the amount to be paid to the Quapaws for the lands ceded by them in the fourth article of this treaty, the sum of five thousand dollars shall be paid to them upon the ratification of this treaty, to assist them in re-establishing themselves at their homes upon their remaining reservation; and the balance of said amount shall be invested as a permanent fund at five per cent. interest, payable per capita, semi-annually.

ARTICLE 10. If the Osage mission school should be closed, so that the school fund of the Quapaws cannot be used for them to advantage at that institution, the said fund shall remain in the Treasury of the United States until such time as it can, under the direction of the Secretary of the Interior, with the consent of the chiefs, be used to advantage in establishing a school upon their reservation.

ARTICLE 11. The amount now due and unpaid for a farmer, under the provisions of the third article of their treaty of May thirteen one thousand eight hundred and thirty-eight (three), may be used by the chiefs and council for the purchase of provisions, farming-implements, seed, and otherwise for the purpose of assisting the people in agriculture; and their annual income now paid for farmer shall hereafter be set apart for the purposes of assistance and improvement in agriculture.

CLAIMS FOR LOSSES BY THE WAR.

ARTICLE 12. Whereas the aforesaid Senecas, Mixed Senecas and Shawnees, and Quapaws were driven from their homes during the late war, and their property destroyed, it is agreed that a commission of not to exceed two persons shall be appointed by the Secretary of the Interior, who shall proceed to their country and make careful investigation of their claims for losses, and make full report of the same to the Department; and the Secretary of the Interior shall report the same to Congress.

PROVISIONS IN RELATION TO THE WYANDOTTES.

ARTICLE 13. The United States will set apart for the Wyandottes for their future home the land ceded by the Senecas in the first article hereof, and described in said article, to be owned by the said Wyandottes in common; and the Secretary of the Interior is hereby authorized and required to appoint three persons whose duty it shall be to ascertain and report to the Department the amount of money, if any, due by the United States to the Wyandott(e) Indians under existing treaty stipulations, and the items mentioned in Schedule A, appended to this treaty, and the report of the persons so appointed, with the evidence taken, shall be submitted to Congress for action at its next session. A register of the whole people, resident in Kansas and elsewhere, shall be taken by the agent of the Delawares, under the direction of the Secretary of the Interior, on or before the first of July, one thousand eight hundred and sixty-seven, which shall show the names of all who declare their desire to be and remain Indians, and in a tribal condition, together with incompetents and orphans, as described in the treaty of one thousand eight hundred and fifty-five; and all such persons, and those only, shall hereafter constitute the tribe: Provided, That no one who has heretofore consented to become a citizen, nor the wife or children of any such person, shall be allowed to become members of the tribe, except by the free consent of the tribe after its new organization, and unless the agent shall certify that such party is, through poverty or incapacity, unfit to continue in the exercise of the responsibilities of citizenship of the United States, and likely to become a public charge.

ARTICLE 14. Whenever the register in the next preceding article shall have been completed and returned to the Commissioner of Indian Affairs, the amount of money in said article acknowledged to be due to the Wyandott(e)s shall be divided, and that portion equitably due to the citizens of said people shall be paid to them or their heirs, under the direction of the Secretary of the Interior; and the balance, after deducting the cost of the land purchased from the Senecas by the first article hereof, and the sum of five thousand dollars to enable the Wyandott(e)s to establish themselves in their new homes, shall be paid to the Wyandott(e) tribe per capita.

ARTICLE 15. All restrictions upon the sale of lands assigned and patented to "incompetent" Wyandott(e)s under the fourth article of the treaty of one thousand eight hundred and fifty-five, shall be removed after the ratification of this treaty, but no sale of lands heretofore assigned to orphans or incompetents shall be made, under decree of any court, or otherwise, for or on account of any claim, judgment, execution, or order, or for taxes, until voluntarily sold by the patentee or his or her heirs, with the approval of the Secretary of the Interior; and whereas many sales of land belonging to this class have heretofore been made, contrary to the spirit and intent of the treaty of one thousand eight hundred and fifty-five, it is agreed that a thorough examination and report shall be made, under direction of the Secretary of the Interior, in order to ascertain the facts relating to all such cases, and, upon a full examination of such report, and hearings of the parties interested, the said Secretary may confirm the said sales, or require an additional amount to be paid, or declare such sales entirely void, as the very right of the several cases may require.

PROVISIONS RELATING TO THE OTTAWAS.

ARTICLE 16. The west part of the Shawnee reservation, ceded to the United States by the third article, is hereby sold to the Ottawas, at one dollar per acre; and for the purpose of paying for said reservation the United States shall take the necessary amount, whenever [964] the area of such land shall be found by actual survey, front the funds in the hands of the Government arising from the sale of the Ottawa trust-lands, as provided in the ninth article of the treaty of one thousand eight hundred and sixty-two, and the balance of said fund, after the payment of accounts provided for in article five of the treaty of one thousand eight hundred and sixty-two, shall be paid to the tribe per capita.

ARTICLE 17. The provisions of the Ottawa treaty of one thousand eight hundred and sixty-two, under which all the tribe were to become citizens upon the sixteenth of July, one thousand eight hundred and sixty-seven, are hereby extended for two years, or until July sixteenth, one thousand eight hundred and sixty-nine; but any time previous to that date any member of the tribe may appear before the United States district court for Kansas, and declare His intention to become a citizen, when he shall receive a certificate of citizenship, which shall include his family, and thereafter be disconnected with the tribe, and shall be entitled to his proportion of the tribal fund; and all who shall not have made such declaration previous to the last-mentioned date shall still be considered members of the tribe. In order to enable the tribe to dispose of their property in Kansas, and remove to their new homes and establish themselves thereon, patents in fee-simple shall be given to the heads of families and to all who have come of age among the allottees under the treaties of one thousand eight hundred and sixty-two, so that they may sell their lands without restriction; but the said lands shall remain exempt from taxation so long as they may be retained by members of the tribe down to the said sixteenth of July, one thousand eight hundred and sixty-nine; and the chiefs and council of the said tribe shall decide in the case of disputed heirship to real estate, taking as a rule the laws of inheritance of the State of Kansas.

ARTICLE 18. The United States agree to pay the claim of J. T. Jones, for which a bill of appropriation has passed one of the branches of Congress, but which has been withdrawn from before Congress, being for destruction by tire of his dwelling and other property by whites in one thousand eight hundred and fifty-six, shall be allowed and paid to him, amounting to six thousand seven hundred dollars.

ARTICLE 19. The sixth article of the treaty of one thousand eight hundred and sixty-two shall remain unchanged, except as provided in this article. The children of the tribe between the ages of six and eighteen (6 and 18) shall be entitled to be received at said institution, and to be subsisted, clothed, educated, and attended in sickness, where the sickness is of such a nature that the patient promises a return to study within a reasonable period; the children to be taught and practised in industrial pursuits, suitable to their age and sex, and both sexes in such branches of learning, and to receive such advantages as the means of the institution will permit; these rights and privileges to continue so long as any children of the tribe shall present themselves for their exercise. And the Secretary of the Interior and the senior corresponding secretary of the American Baptist Home Mission Society shall be members ex officio of the board of trustees, with power to vote in person or by proxy, it being the special intention of this provision to furnish additional supervision of the institution, so that the provisions of this article may be carried into effect in their full spirit and intent.

ARTICLE 20. it is further agreed that the remaining unsold portion of trustlands of the Ottawas, amounting to seven thousand two hundred and twenty-one and twenty one-hundredths acres, shall be sold to the trustees of Ottawa University, to be disposed of for the benefit of said institution at the appraised value thereof, and that the said [965] trustees shall have until July sixteenth, one thousand eight hundred and sixty-nine, to dispose of the same and pay to the Government the value of said lands: Provided, That the said trustees shall furnish, within thirty days after the ratification of this treaty, to the Secretary of the Interior, a satisfactory bond for the fulfilment of their obligations.

PROVISIONS RELATING TO THE PEORIAS, KASKASKIAS, WEAS, AND PIANKESHAWS.

ARTICLE 21. Whereas certain arrangements have been made by the chiefs of the confederated tribes of Peorias, Kaskaskias, Weas, and Piankeshaws, for the sale to actual settlers of the lands held by them in common, being nine and one-half sections, for a reasonable consideration, according to the terms of a certain petition of the said tribe, with schedule annexed, (which schedule is annexed to this treaty, and marked "B,") dated December twenty-sixth, one thousand eight hundred and sixty-six, filed in the office of the Commissioner of Indian Affairs, it is agreed that the said arrangements shall be carried into full effect, and the purchasers thereunder shall receive patents from the United States for the lands so purchased, upon making full payment for the same to the Secretary of the Interior, and the amount already paid by said purchasers, as appears from said schedule, and in the hands of the chiefs, shall be paid to the Secretary of the Interior, and the whole amount of the purchase-money shall also be paid to the said Secretary on or before the first day of June, one thousand eight hundred and sixty-seven, and shall be held by him for the benefit of the tribe, subject to the provisions of this treaty.

ARTICLE 22. The land in the second and fourth articles of this treaty pro-posed to be purchased from the Senecas and Quapaws, and lying south of Kan-sas, is hereby granted and sold to the Peorias, &c., and shall be paid for, at the rate paid for the same by the Government, out of the proceeds of the nine and a half sections referred to in the last preceding article, adding thereto whatever may be necessary out of other moneys in the hands of the United States be-longing to said Peorias, &c.

ARTICLE 23. The said Indians agree to dispose of their allotments in Kansas and remove to their new homes in the Indian country within two years from the ratification of this treaty; and to that end the Secretary of the Interior is author-ized to remove altogether the restrictions upon the sales of their lands, provided under authority of the third article of the treaty of May thirtieth, one thousand eight hundred and fifty-four, in such manner that adult Indians may sell their own lands, and that the lands of minors and incompetents may be sold by the chiefs, with the consent of the agent, certified to the Secretary of the Interior and approved by him. And if there should be any allotments for which no owner or heir thereof survives, the chiefs may convey the same by deed, the purchase-money thereof to be applied, under the direction of the Secretary, to the benefit of the tribe; and the guardianship of orphan children shall remain in the hands of the chiefs of the tribe, and the said chiefs shall have the exclusive right to determine who are members of the tribe and entitled to be placed upon the pay-rolls.

ARTICLE 24. An examination shall be made of the books of the Indian Office, and an account-current prepared, stating the condition of their funds, and the representations of the Indians for overcharges for sales of their lands in one thousand eight hundred and fifty-seven and one thousand eight hundred and fifty-eight shall be examined and reported to Congress; and in order further to assist them in preparing for removal and in paying their debts, the further amount of twenty-five thousand dollars shall be at the same time paid to them per capita from the sum of one hundred and sixty-nine thousand six hundred and eighty-six dollars and seventy-five cents, invested for said Indians tinder act of Congress of July twelfth, one thousand eight hundred and sixty-two; and the balance of said sum of one hundred and sixty-nine thousand six hundred and eighty-six dollars and seventy-five cents, together with the sum of ninety-eight thousand dollars now invested on behalf of the said Indians in State stocks of Southern States, and the sum of three thousand seven hundred dollars, being the balance of interest, at five per cent. per annum, on thirty-nine thousand nine hundred-and fifty dollars held by the United States, from July; one thousand eight hundred and fifty-seven, till vested in Kansas bonds in December, one thousand eight hundred and sixty-one, after crediting five thousand dollars thereon heretofore receipted for by the chiefs of said Indians, shall be and remain as the permanent fund of the said tribe, and five per cent be paid semi-annually thereon, per capita, to the tribe

The interest due upon the sum of twenty-eight thousand five hundred dollars in Kansas bonds, and upon sixteen thousand two hundred dollars in United States stocks, now held for their benefit, shall be paid to the tribe semi-annually in two equal payments, as a permanent school-fund income: Provided, That there shall be taken from the said invested fund and paid to the said tribe, per capita, on the first of July, one thousand eight hundred and sixty-eight, the sum of thirty thousand dollars, to assist them in establishing themselves upon their new homes; and at any time thereafter, when the chiefs shall represent to the satisfaction of the Secretary of the Interior that an additional sum is necessary, such sum may be taken from their invested fund: And provided also, That the said invested fund shall be subject to such division and diminution as may be found necessary in order to pay those who may become citizens their share of the funds of the tribe.

ARTICLE 25. Whereas taxes have been levied by the authority of the State of Kansas upon lands allotted to members of the tribe, the right and justice of which taxation is not acknowledged by the Indians, and on which account they have suffered great vexation and expense, and which is now a matter in question in the Supreme Court of the United States, it is agreed that, in case that court shall decide such taxes unlawful the Government will take measures to secure the refunding of said taxes to such of the Indians as have paid them.

ARTICLE 26. The Peorias, Kaskaskias, Wens, and Piankeshaws agree that the Miamies may be confederated with them upon their new reservation, and own an undivided right in said reservation in proportion to the sum paid, upon the payment by the said Miamies of an amount which, in proportion to the number of the Miamies who shall join them, will be equal to their share of the purchase-money in this treaty provided to be paid for the land, and also upon the payment into the common fund of such amount as shall make them equal in annuities to the said Peorias, &c., the said privilege to remain open to the Miamies two years from the ratification of this treaty.

ARTICLE 27. The United States agree to pay the said Indians the sum of one thousand five hundred dollars per year for six years for their blacksmith, and for necessary iron and steel and tools; in consideration of which payment the said tribe hereby relinquish all claims for damages and losses during the late

451

war, and, at the end of the said six years, any tools or materials remaining shall be the property of the tribe.

ARTICLE 28. Inasmuch as there may be those among them who may desire to remain in Kansas and become citizens of the United States, it is hereby provided that, within six months after the ratification of this treaty, a register shall be taken by the agent, which shall show the names separately of all who voluntarily desire to remove, and all who desire to remain and become citizens; and those who shall elect to remain may appear before the judge of the United States district court for Kansas and make declaration of their intention to become citizens, and take the oath to support the Constitution of the United States; and upon filing of a certificate of such declaration and oath in the office of the Commissioner of Indian Affairs they shall be entitled to receive the proportionate share of themselves and their children in the invested funds and other common property of the tribe.

Therefrom they and their children shall become citizens, and have no further rights in the tribe; and all the females who are heads of families, and single women of full age shall have the right to make such declaration and become disconnected from the tribe.

ARTICLES 29 to 39, inclusive. (Stricken out.)

ARTICLE 40. If any amendments shall be made to this treaty by the Senate, it shall only be necessary to submit the same for the assent of the particular tribe or tribes interested; and should any such amendments be made, and the assent of the tribe or tribes interested not be obtained, the remainder of the treaty not affected by such amendment shall nevertheless take effect and be in force.

ARTICLE 41. (Stricken out.)

In testimony whereof, the before-named commissioners on behalf of the United States, and the before-named delegates on behalf of the Senecas, mixed Senecas and Shawnees, Quapaws, confederated Peorias, Kaskaskias, Weas, and Piankeshaws, Miamies, Ottawas, and Wyandottes have hereunto set our hands and seals the day and year first above written.

Lewis V. Bogy, Commissioner of Indian Affairs, W. H. Watson, Special Commissioner, Thos. Murphy, Superintendent, of Indian Affairs, G. C. Snow, United States Indian Agent, Neosho Agency.

G. A. Colton, United States Indian Agent for Miamis, Peorias, &c, George Spicer, his x mark, John Mush, his x mark. Senecas: John Whitetree, his x mark, John Young, his x mark, Lewis Davis, his x mark.

Senecas and Shawnees: S. G. Valier, Ka-she-cah, his x mark.
Quapaws: Baptiste Peoria, his x mark, John Mitchell, his x mark, Edward Black.

Peorias, &c: Thomas Metosenyah, his x mark, Thos. F. Richardville.
Miamies: John Wilson, his x mark, J. T. Jones.
Ottawas: Tauromee, his x mark, John Karaho, his x mark.

In presence of:Frank Valle, his x mark, United States Interpreter for Osage River Agency, John B. Roubideau, his x mark, United States Interpreter for Miamis, Wm. Hurr,

Interpreter for Ottawas, Geo. Wright, interpreter for, yandottes, Abelard Guthrie, George B. Jonas, Thos. E. McGraw, Lewis S. Hayden, Charles Sims, R. McBratney.

Witnesses to signature of Lewis Davis: G. L. Young. G. C. Snow, United States Indian Agent.

TREATY WITH THE CHEROKEE {1868, Apr. 27}
Ratified June 6, 1868.
Proclaimed June 10, 1868.

Supplemental article to a treaty concluded at Washington City, July 19th, A. D. 1866; ratified with amendments, July 27th, A. D. 1866; amendments accepted, July 31st, A. D. 1866; and the whole proclaimed, August 11th, A. D. 1866, between the United States of America and the Cherokee Nation of Indians.

Whereas under the provisions of the seventeenth article of a treaty and amendments thereto made between the United States and the Cherokee Nation of Indians, and proclaimed August 11th, A. D. 1866, a contract was made and entered into by James Harlan, Secretary of the Interior, on behalf of the United States, of the one part, and by the American Emigrant Company, a corporation chartered and existing under the laws of the State of Connecticut, of the other part, dated August 30th, A. D. 1866, for the sale of the so-called "Cherokee neutral lands," in the State of Kansas, containing eight hundred thousand acres, more or less, with the limitations and restrictions set forth in the said seventeenth article of said treaty as amended, on the terms and conditions therein mentioned, which contract is now on file in the Department of the Interior; and

Whereas Orville H. Browning, Secretary of the Interior, regarding said sale as illegal and not in conformity with said treaty and amendments thereto, did, on the ninth day of October, A. D. 1867, for and in behalf of the United States, enter into a contract with James F. Joy, of the city of Detroit, Michigan, for the

453

sale of the aforesaid lands on the terms and conditions in said contract set forth, and which is on file in the Department of the Interior; and

Whereas, for the purpose of enabling the Secretary of the Interior, as trustee for the Cherokee Nation of Indians, to collect the proceeds of sales of said lands and invest the same for the benefit of said Indians, and for the purpose of preventing litigation and of harmonizing the conflicting interests of the said American Emigrant Company and of the said James F. Joy, it is the desire of all the parties in interest that the said American Emigrant Company shall assign their said contract and all their right, title, claim, and interest in and to the said "Cherokee neutral lands" to the said James F. Joy, and that the said Joy shall assume and conform to all the obligations of said company under their said contract, as hereinafter modified:

It is, therefore, agreed, by and between Nathaniel G. Taylor, commissioner on the part of the United States of America, and Lewis Downing, H. D. Reese, Wm. P. Adair, Elias C. Boudinot, J. A. Scales, Archie Scraper, J. Porum Davis, and Samuel Smith, commissioners on the part of the Cherokee Nation of Indians, that an assignment of the contract made and entered into on the 30th day of August, A. D. 1866, by and between James Harlan, Secretary of the Interior, for and in behalf of the United States of America, of the one part, and the American Emigrant Company, a corporation chartered and existing under the laws of the State of Connecticut, of the other part, and now on file in the Department of the Interior, to James F. Joy, of the city of Detroit, Michigan, shall be made; and that said contract, as hereinafter modified, be and the same is hereby, with the consent of all parties, re-affirmed and declared valid; and that the contract entered into by and between Orville H. Browning, for and in behalf of the United States, of the one part, and James F. Joy, of the city of Detroit, Michigan, of the other part.

On the 9th day of October, A. D. 1867, and now on file in the Department of the Interior, shall be relinquished and cancelled by the said James F. Joy, or his duly authorized agent or attorney; and the said first contract as hereinafter modified, and the assignment of the first contract, and the relinquishment of the second contract, are hereby ratified and confirmed, whenever said assignment of the first contract and the relinquishment of the second shall be entered of record in the Department of the Interior, and when the said James F. Joy shall have accepted said assignment and shall have entered into a contract with the Secretary of the Interior to assume and perform all obligations of the said American Emigrant Company under said first-named contract, as hereinafter modified.

The modifications hereinbefore mentioned of said contract are hereby declared to be:

1. That within ten days from the ratification of this supplemental article the sum of seventy-five thousand dollars shall be paid to the Secretary of the Interior as trustee for the Cherokee Nation of Indians.

2. That the other deferred payments specified in said contract shall be paid when they respectively fall due, with interest only front the date of the ratification hereof.

It is further agreed and distinctly understood that, under the conveyance of the "Cherokee neutral lands" to the said American Emigrant Company, "with all beneficial interests therein," as set forth in said contract, the said company and their assignees shall take only the residue of said lands after securing to "actual settlers" the lands to which they are entitled under the provisions of the seventeenth article and amendments thereto of the said Cherokee treaty of August 11th, 1866; and that the proceeds of the sales of said lands, so occupied at the date of said treaty by "actual settlers," shall enure to the sole benefit of, and be retained by, the Secretary of the Interior as trustee for the said Cherokee Nation of Indians.

In testimony whereof, the said commissioners on the part of the United States, and on the part of the Cherokee nation of Indians, have hereunto set their hands and seals, at the city of Washington, this 27th day of April, A. D. 1868.

N. G. Taylor, Commissioner in behalf of the United States.
Delegates of the Cherokee Nation: Lewis Downing, Chief of Cherokees, H. D. Reese, Chairman of Delegation, Samuel Smith, Wm. P. Adair, J. P. Davis, Elias C. Boudinot, J. A. Scales, Arch. Scraper, Cherokee Delegates.

In presence of: H. M. Watterson, Charles E. Mix.